LIBERTY IN PERIL

1850–1920

LIBERTY IN AMERICA
1600 TO THE PRESENT

VOLUME THREE

Liberty in Peril
1850-1920

Oscar and Lilian Handlin

Cornelia & Michael Bessie Books
An Imprint of HarperCollins*Publishers*

In the preparation of this volume we enjoyed the assistance of the Lucius N. Littauer Foundation and of Kathleen Marotta.

HarperCollins books may be purchased for educational, business, or sales promotional use. For information, please call or write: Special Markets Department, HarperCollins Publishers, Inc., 10 East 53rd Street, New York, NY 10022. Telephone: (212) 207-7528; Fax: (212) 207-7222.

FIRST EDITION

Designed by Sidney Feinberg

Library of Congress Cataloging-in-Publication Data
(Revised for vol. 3)

Handlin, Oscar, 1915–
   Liberty in America, 1600 to the present.
   "A Cornelia & Michael Bessie book"—V. 1, t.p.
   Vol. 3 published by Cornelia & Michael Bessie Books.
   Includes bibliographical references and index.
   Contents: v. 1. Liberty and power,
1600–1760—v. 2. Liberty in expansion, 1760–1850.—v. 3. Liberty in peril, 1850–1920.
   1. United States–Politics and government. 2. United
States—History. I. Handlin, Lilian. II. Title.
E183.H32 1986   973   85-45997
ISBN 0-06-039059-X (v. 1)
ISBN 0-06-039092-1 (v. 2)
ISBN 0-06-039143-X (v. 3)

92 93 94 95 96 CC/HC 10 9 8 7 6 5 4 3 2 1

For
Jonathan and Laura Manley

CONTENTS

PREFACE

In 1923, when Benedetto Croce outlined his history of Europe in the nineteenth century, he found a consistent theme ready to hand—the steady unfolding of human liberty to its culmination in his own days. Firm believers in progress saw no flaws in that beneficent formula. Taking a long view of the ascent, Croce discerned in the past only occasional dips, preparatory to new rises; at most, tactical retreats preparing for ever greater leaps forward.[1]

Certainly the view of the United States as it was in 1850 justified optimism. In 544 pages of blank verse, a Philadelphian sang the nation's past and future:

> The wondrous story of our pilgrim sires
> Whose toils for Freedom have a triumph gained,
> Till nations all in the glad paean join
> And Earth no King reveres but Him of heaven.

The struggle for liberty had then proven victorious on several fronts, if not in Europe or in the rest of the world, then at least in the United States. The experience of 150 years of settlement after Jamestown, dominated by the struggle for bread and sheer survival, had succeeded. Having moved beyond the palisades where they had long huddled in fear, the colonists acquired the ability to act, to exercise the will, although the ways of organizing power brought from Europe proved inappropriate to the new setting. In a land of immense spaces, power depended on consent. Without forethought, by trial and error, the fledgling societies developed rules and rule-making bodies that permitted some to command and induced others to obey. New kinds of communities developed. Held together by voluntary acquiescence rather than compulsion, they housed in the eigh-

ix

teenth century a distinctive personality type, as changing forms of worship and modifications in family relations produced a recognizable American character—rude, assertive, prone to risky innovation, trusting calculation above habit. Enterprising men and women in 1760 confronted a growing economy based on abundant resources. Slowly clarifying the meanings of liberty, they discovered that the freedom of each depended on the enjoyment of rights that did not emanate from ancient documents but that developed as aspects of a way of life. Americans implemented liberty, the capacity to act, by participation in the exercise of power.[2]

Between 1760 and 1850, independence and expansion provided a basis for republican government, for an increasingly democratic society, and for affirmation of the rights of individuals to life, liberty, and the pursuit of happiness. Efforts to use government aid, after the European fashion, failed in the face of insistence upon equality of opportunity. As a result, people fell back upon their own resources and developed habits of self-reliance along with distinctive patterns of cooperation in voluntary associations. The strains of achievement, combined with modes of existence unaided by established habits of stable communities, created new men and women, autonomous, largely rational individuals, venturesome risk takers, uninhibited in pursuit of the opportunities expansion created. Their situation affected the terms on which husbands dealt with wives, parents with children, and masters with servants, and shaped the patterns of their lives in the larger context of a rapidly enlarging economy, continuing demographic growth, and a new spacial and time framework.[3]

At midcentury, shadows—notably slavery—remained prominently in the background but failed to undermine the prevailing faith in progress. Few Americans measured, as Ecclesiastes did, the compulsive force of circumstance. They believed themselves free to choose their course. Their bold New World for a time indulged in the dream of freedom.

Improvement, however, did not follow. The years between 1850 and 1920 witnessed a retreat from liberty, a contraction of the ability of many people to act; and that despite the growth in national strength and wealth. The great wars that open and close the period traversed in this volume called forth unparalleled displays of state power to repress dissent, and did so with widespread popular support, unjustified by the actual gravity of any danger to the Republic. A muzzled puppy who growled a little and had to make his bed in such a dusty, dirty mess, warned: Now, puppies, do as you are bid . . . be gentle dogs or quit.[4]

Liberty in Peril thus examines the low point in the history of liberty in America. The United States then degenerated into a period of brutal repression after 250 years of slowly but steadily enlarging people's capacity to act and ensuring recognition of popular rights. The volume analyzes the nature of the restraints in a democratic society still expanding territorially and economically, yet narrowing the limits set on tolerance of individual behavior and expression, a process that culminated in the rejection of freedom after 1917.

The boundaries of tolerance narrowed when controls by a powerful political system, operating through organized parties, steadily expanded the scope of government action: national, state, and local. At the same time, the governed communities, having lost unity and coherence, could act through voluntary organizations only in a fragmented and disjointed fashion. What had functioned well in the past, proved inadequate after 1850. Moreover, mounting prejudice, increasingly racist in character, excluded large parts of the population from active participation, while many other Americans, dislodged, drifted in isolation. American society, a visitor wrote, doomed the spirit to superficiality. Self-deluded humans felt themselves freer than ever before, but "in modern, highly developed society . . . intellectual life [could not] escape the degradation, the leveling and the mechanization . . . indissolubly bound up with . . . commercialization." The penetration of the world of the mind by business methods and economic forms of reckoning, the reduction of free-wheeling sports to rules, forms, uniforms, and organized combats, all smacked of mechanization, which made men and women helpless slaves of the perfected means of material and social technology.[5]

Demands for increased government action also followed upon efforts at social reform, whether religious in derivation or springing from progressive dreams of scientific improvement by applying knowledge to correct ills. Both reform impulses aimed to control individuals *for their own good* by compulsion rather than by allowing them to make their own decisions. The sanctions of law reinforced subtle cultural pressures to conform.

> 'tis a whited sepulchre you raise,
> Whereon shall this stern epitaph be read:
> "Here, at the silent parting of the ways,
> Fell Liberty, betrayed, beguiled, misled.
> Pray for her, stranger, that in happier days
> She may be resurrected from the dead."

The two great wars that bracketed the period proved expensive, not only in lives and treasure wasted, but also in the narrowing human spirit that cast long shadows over the prospect for future recovery.[6]

*

Repression no doubt bore some relationship to the turbulent growth of an industrial economy, to the spread of new forms of agriculture into vast, theretofore unfamiliar regions, and to the appearance of great cities of unprecedented size and complexity. Inventions intended to release mental energy and unlock natural resources made possible mechanisms over which the person no longer had complete control. Guidance and regulation, distributed over a multitude, became enforced obedience, especially with the development of political agencies armed with massive power.

Their heads stuffed with the rhetoric of liberty, many Americans embraced repression. Although they still cherished their ability to act as autonomous individuals, they also reached out for aid to confront life's many crises. But the little groupings earlier relied upon disappeared, or had lost familiar form, either swallowed up in great impersonal associations or transformed by strange qualities in the novel context. Ever more often people then turned to the state for help, and not just for justice and law but also for guidance toward goodness and improvement and for the instruments by which to move forward. In doing so, Americans learned to accept the loss of will, and external control made necessary by the unfamiliar demands of a shattered view of human nature and of the unsettling challenge of obtrusive technology and science. They also devised a new vocabulary to express unparalleled developments and unprecedented needs, for which the language of individualism proved sadly inadequate.[7]

Only in a view of development unobstructed by theories of inevitability do these forces become comprehensible. It did not have to happen as it did. Certainly what occurred after 1850 was the product of antecedents in the preceding centuries, but not their inevitable outcome. The potential for decline existed, as did the potential for progress; the promise for expanding liberty but also the threat of its contraction. Americans enjoyed all the options into the second half of the nineteenth century, with neither course predetermined.

To understand the repression that actually unfolded after 1850 requires the acknowledgment that it did not have to be so, a perspective that leaves open also the possibility that the future after 1920 remained uncommitted either to a widening or contraction of freedom.

This volume traverses more familiar terrain than did its predecessors, not only for its chronological proximity to our own time span, but also for the wealth of monographic treatments of relevant subjects. Although it has profited from that work, this narrative employs its own vocabulary. It does not allow the terms *expansion, modernization, industrialization, urbanization,* to become catchwords that abstract the experiences of men and women in a time of great achievement, attained at a bitter price. The true story remains theirs, in all its concreteness.

I

REPRESSION

THE SHIP CAST OFF and moved down the harbor, taking eastward a cargo of failed dreams—its passengers, undesirables deported as threats to the Republic (1919). The *Buford*, a "sea roller" used as an army transport in the Spanish-American War, now carried 249 aliens back to Russia, the land of their birth—"blasphemous creatures who not only rejected America's hospitality and assailed her institutions but also sought by a campaign of assassination and terrorism to ruin her as a nation of free men."

Among its more flamboyant travelers, the Red Ark took Emma Goldman (born 1869) to retrace a route she had traveled westward three decades earlier, her hopes for the future now displaced to a new promised land—ironically the old one she had once fled. Then she had been a girl of seventeen, by no means beautiful but passionate and self-willed. Czarist Russia had afforded her no breathing space, and she had escaped along with millions of others to the New World where she hoped freedom awaited her. Her compatriot Mary Antin, who later made the same journey, did indeed find her own promised land in America. But Emma, ever restless, refused to compromise, would accept nothing less than perfect realization of her dream of liberation in a just society. She took a lover—more than one—enlisted in the cause of labor, and mounted the lecture platform, from which she preached the doctrines of anarchism and direct action, titillating audiences with talk of violence, birth control, and pacifism, all the glittering abstractions of her day.[1]

Total commitment and absolute certainty about the correctness of her ideas befogged the real outlines of the world in which she lived, and persuaded her that the end always justified the means. Infuriated with the brutality of the Homestead strike, she agreed when her lover Alexander Berkman undertook to assassinate Henry C. Frick, whom they held

1

responsible—nothing personal, they insisted. However, in Pittsburgh Berkman encountered two obstacles—lack of a weapon and of the means to acquire one. The penniless Emma undertook to do her part by raising the necessary sum; frantic, desperate to help, she determined to resort to the one means she believed always available to poor girls. Yes, she knew from Dostoyevski's *Crime and Punishment* how exploited young women turned to the streets for money. She would do whatever the occasion required. On Union Square, at the corner of Fourteenth Street and Fourth Avenue, a knowledgeable man took her in hand only to dismiss her with ten dollars when he discovered her lack of skill. An obliging sister provided the rest. Never mind: Berkman got the needed money, bungled the task, and wound up in prison. Several prominent Pittsburgh attorneys offered to defend him, but ever the true anarchist, he declined thus to recognize the state's legitimacy.[2]

In 1917 Emma Goldman would have nothing to do with Wilson's war; obstruction of the draft and defiance of the sedition laws earned her a place on the Ark. She regretted nothing—as yet. For the star of freedom had risen in the east; and at the age of fifty she gladly renewed her commitment to the struggle, now in the Soviet Union—which she left after two years, disillusioned, more perceptive than Lincoln Steffens, who had fatuously proclaimed, "I have been over into the future and it works."

Her disappointment with, and deportation from, the United States measured the slackening of American devotion to freedom. Citizens who for centuries had explored the widening meanings of liberty by 1919 no longer tolerated dissent, but had slipped into habits of repression, both of deviant acts and of unconventional opinions. In 1920 the attorney general announced that his card file contained detailed information about more than two hundred thousand undesirables, gathered by a small army hot on the trail of subversion; and a study by Professor Richard C. Cabot revealed the extensive use of espionage by employers and by labor unions.[3]

At about the same time, reversal of other historic policies also marked the end of an era. Open borders, free to immigrants from almost every part of the world, had fueled the expansion of settlement. But in the closing decades of the nineteenth century, doubts about the continued utility of that course began to nag at some Americans. A few New England intellectuals, worried about the future, whined about their culture, damaged by alien, therefore inferior, peoples. Regarding with dismay the profound social alterations connected with the spread of great factories and the growth of cities, they and others blamed the disorders on the newcomers. New racial theories cast doubt upon the prospects for assimilation and reinforced the objections to unlimited immigration. And the organized labor movement, which feared the competition for jobs, in time joined the call for change.[4]

The earliest restrictive steps applied to unwelcome individuals—the insane, paupers likely to become public charges, and criminals. Exclusion of whole non-European groups then met slight resistance—Africans, Chinese, and Japanese. In time hostility spread to eastern and southern Europeans, and attempts to impose qualitative restrictions on them culminated in the literacy test—vetoed by Presidents Cleveland, Taft, and Wilson, then finally enacted by override in 1917. When that measure failed to stop the flow, demands mounted for a more effective barrier. The nationalist fervor stirred up by war heightened fears of the foreigners and in 1921 gained support for a law that not only limited the number of new entries but also set quotas in racial terms in order to preserve the existing character of the American population.[5]

Americans did not turn abruptly to repression and to a restrictive immigration policy. From 1850 onward, a long course of development had pointed in the direction of the later shifts.

Few Americans in 1920 recalled the events of the 1850s that had culminated in civil war. Back then, anguished frustration over the future of slavery that would, in time, divide the nation turned impatient people away from touchy political controversy. The freedom to speak and to print had everywhere suffered. The South required no censorship by law to repress adverse comment on its peculiar institution. It proceeded to do so informally but effectively. The citizens of Mobile forcefully expelled William Strickland, a bookseller who ventured to stock works critical of bondage (1858). Well before then, the region had driven out the abolitionists, had closed the mails to their papers, and had made their petitions unwelcome in Congress. An Arkansas representative, infuriated by a statement in Horace Greeley's *Tribune,* had attacked the editor in Washington, evidence, to Northerners, that the cotton lordlings, "fresh from beating women slaves," imported their plantation airs to the federal city (1856). That year Congressman Preston Brooks assaulted Senator Charles Sumner on the floor of the upper chamber, and spectators could observe in the capitol "fifty middle-aged and elderly gentlemen pitching into each other like so many Tipperary savages . . . most of them incapable, from want of wind and muscle, of doing each other any serious harm."[6]

In defending institutions of coercion, some Southerners rejected free society in favor of a community of interests that permitted the full realization of civil power, wisdom, and goodness. George Fitzhugh's *Sociology for the South* (1854) argued that man could develop his proper nature only in a slave society, while socialism, perfectionism, and Mormonism, all mistaken Northern quests for community, revealed individualism's shortcomings. Henry Hughes, too, assumed that Northern political liberty concealed a system of economic license rather than order. Liberty was not the capacity to act, but freedom within a necessary order, to be attained by systematic association, adaptation, and regulation, essential and methodic, by superiors and inferiors, the warrantors and the warrantees. Free speech had no place in that order.[7]

Many Northern communities also proved inhospitable to inflammatory rhetoric and publications. Respectable types in Boston made trouble for William Lloyd Garrison; and the "most bestial of the Irish population armed with guns" drove away an antislavery speaker in Springfield, Illinois.

But abolitionists and Free-Soilers themselves ignored legality when it sheltered injustice, as in the fugitive slave cases. Determined resistance greeted efforts to enforce the new law incorporated in the Compromise of 1850. "I will not obey it, by God," exclaimed Ralph Waldo Emerson (secure in Concord). But in Boston, a respectable mob succeeded in rescuing the Crafts; another furious assembly led by free blacks delivered the slave Shadrach out of the hands of his captors, and juries refused to convict the rioters. Judge Edward G. Loring lost his position as a result of his effort to enforce the letter of the law. The city mourned when force failed to free Thomas Sims, captured and dragged back into bondage, although his master found little satisfaction in a success that cost twenty thousand dollars, more than the market value of the human property. Nor could the authorities secure a conviction in Christiana, Pennsylvania (1851), of those who murdered a slave catcher pursuing his legitimate business. In Indianapolis, John Freeman, a respectable black, suffered sixty-eight days of incarceration until he proved he was not a runaway. A month later, therefore, the Friends of Freedom in Racine, Wisconsin, including the city's first men for character, honesty, and integrity, liberated a fugitive by a writ of *vox populi* that superseded the statutes (1854). In vain a sheriff explained (1854) that he took neither side of the controversy but only wished to retain custody of any person committed to him; a higher law animated those who rejected civil legality. The appeal to divine authority against the letter of the ordinances became commonplace; silent acquiescence inflicted wounds upon freedom and justified popular resistance though all the tyrannical courts in the land perished. In some states, personal liberty acts deliberately contravened the federal law Chief Justice Taney declared supreme. Such rulings could not bind an aroused populace.[8]

Kansas bled in 1856 not only from bodily wounds inflicted on men and women, but also from damage to the cherished idea of government by consent of the governed, as rival gangs armed to defend rival constitutions. Without agreement on the fundamental law, no one exercised legitimate power. So much for popular sovereignty. Injunctions to passive obedience or passive disobedience became alike irrelevant in the face of an invasion by barbarian hordes, undeserving even of the protection of free speech. In desperation, John Brown, infuriated by damage suffered and inflicted in the territory, launched an armed attack against the federal arsenal in Harpers Ferry; and many abolitionists, until then pacifists, sympathized with, even supported, his mad cause. Some of them continued to threaten liberation/insurrection well after his trial, conviction, and execution. The impulse to violence deepened and imperceptibly approached the climax at secession in 1861.[9]

The fabric, once rent, came apart in place after place. In Baltimore, juries would not convict the murderer of a United States marshall, with the maximum sentence but one year in jail. In Memphis, Tennessee, a lynch mob took after the murdering gambler John Able. In Chicago, a riot followed when Germans convicted of selling liquor without a license, on their own, ruled the law unconstitutional. Respect for constituted authority in that city faded when the aldermen voted themselves gold-headed canes as emblems of their dignity. The Great American Traveler, announcing his candidacy for the presidency in 1856, proclaimed himself the equal of Webster and the superior of Clay, and promised to make the poor rich and the rich richer. And nativism and patriotism served as cloaks for swindlers as they did for the brash woman who collected seven thousand dollars for a nonexistent American Female Orphan Asylum—no foreigners admitted.[10]

For more than a century Americans had recognized that individuals as human beings enjoyed rights immune from interference by others and even by governments; and formal constitutional statements, in federal and state bills of rights, had protected the inalienable freedom to enjoy life, liberty, and the pursuit of happiness. But all those terms, imprecise and vague, carried weight only when supported by the force of popular consensus, which also established the boundaries of permissible dissent. In the sparsely populated early nineteenth-century towns, the arguers who addressed people very much like themselves said what they wished, used whatever language they chose. The village atheist, the crackerbox orator, the local visionary, could challenge popular opinion because firm institutions and beliefs soaked up dissent without endangering others.

But in time the context changed. The nation swarmed with theorists who wished to "reconstruct society outright and govern it afterward by mass meetings in continuous session," thus encouraging "the discontent and indolence of the men who believe they ought to be paid high wages for very light work." In urban centers, large, undifferentiated audiences transformed the context of speech; no one knew who spoke or wrote, who heard or read, what phrases stirred the emotions. Emma Goldman listened to a sixteen-year-old anarchist, just arrived, address in Italian an audience which did not know the language: "Maria's strange beauty and the music of her speech aroused the whole assembly to the tensest enthusiasm." When feelings took over, reasonable discourse ceased to count. Leagues, unions, federations, associations, orders, and rings formed themselves among the restless, unstable elements as easily as clouds. Any boldly ignorant inventor of a new economical theory or a new political doctrine or a new cornerstone for the fabric of society could set on foot a movement from Maine to California; and that invested popular ignorance with terror (1894). With villages no longer isolated, an action in one place reverberated in another. Informal local limitations of the damage from dissent, effective where citizens knew the troublemaker's reputation, elsewhere faded out. Throughout the country, pressure from outsiders disturbed communal consensus and created problems by discord. For many, the capitalist took the place of the slave as a being with rights no one respected, while his relationship with workers—a state of war—unloosed the destructive instincts of the multitudes, which only adequate force and repression could counteract.[11]

Old conflicts between divergent views of the nature of law raised the tensions. As in the past, few Americans after 1850 accepted as binding a fixed body of inherited rules or the dictates of a remote legislature; whatever the courts held, citizens insisted that legitimacy derived from the common sense applied by the community to maintain order and administer justice. Once it had been easy to boast that as long as natives of the soil, Germans, Scandinavians, Scotchmen, Frenchmen, and a goodly number of Irishmen, rallied around the banner of liberty, nothing could endanger the system that made the protection of individual rights a matter of common interest. That unity began to disintegrate in the 1850s. Twenty years later, observers complained that the government did not govern, that an inefficient Congress deprived the executive of its necessary strength, and that state legislatures ceased to concentrate public sentiment, having become clearinghouses for the adjustment of claims, as communal sentiments of shared enterprise gave way to rivalries of interests and needs.[12]

Northerners, at first unaware of the seriousness of the secession crisis, in 1861 regarded rebellion with a "feeling one-half of contempt, and the other half composed of anger and incredulity." In anticipation of possible hostilities, the town of Pawlet, Vermont, in 1860 formed three baseball clubs in order "to harden the muscles and invigorate the physical functions." "Our little domestic strife," wrote the nation's leading historian in September 1860, would soon subside. In mid-April 1861, however, the excitement in Philadelphia reached a fever pitch and with it intolerance and repression. Crowds gathered in the streets and forced official institutions to display the flag. Merchants suspected of Southern sympathies had to do the same. In New York, *The Daily News,* known for pro-Southern views, attracted a mob that demanded to see the Union flag. Elsewhere shopkeepers had to join "spontaneous boycotts" of shipments to the South. Then as the flames spread and costs mounted up and sank in, determined bitterness infused the ranks at home and on the battlefields. The poet uttered "a shrill song of curses on him who would dissever the Union." Ralph Waldo Emerson felt enormous relief when fighting broke out, for he saw in it the force that would translate self-reliant beings into a cohesive community, substituting a religion of love for mean egoism. But neither he nor his fellow intellectuals foresaw the price of that sense of community.[13]

The war dragging on for four years counted liberty among its victims.

Despite his commitment to a new birth of freedom, President Lincoln brushed aside any obstacles to victory and in the process shook off inconvenient constitutional restraints. By executive proclamation he declared the seceded states in a condition of insurrection and assumed the power to suppress them, enjoying congressional support in these matters (the Southerners having withdrawn). He closed down the *Freemen's Journal* and other uncooperative newspapers despite First Amendment guarantees. Copperheads, friends of the South, pacifists, and principled opponents of the war suffered. Passports limited the right to travel. A test oath (July 1862) aimed to filter the hesitant out of Congress; the treatment of suspected Tories during the Revolution provided a precedent for the use of such loyalty declarations against any dissenters. Few considered the effects on consent of the governed, some thereby deprived of representation.[14]

Woebetide those in the 1860s who aided or even sympathized with the enemy. Pacifists received short shrift of it. While sons, husbands, and brothers risked their lives on distant battlefields, their parents, wives, and sisters spared no compassion for the disloyal or the lukewarm. When the political opposition grew bolder after Democratic victories in the congressional elections of 1862, and when strong-willed Republicans in Congress and the Cabinet made trouble, the president acted abruptly against those he thought impeded the war effort. Already in 1861 he had suspended the privilege of the writ of habeas corpus, and he disregarded the Supreme Court's ruling (in *ex parte Merryman*) which denied his power to do so. Chief Justice Roger B. Taney there held that only Congress could limit access to habeas corpus, even in wartime; but in due course the necessary legislation empowered the president to act. Shortly after the war *ex parte Milligan* (1866) narrowed executive discretion when it held that military commissions could not try civilians in districts where the civil courts functioned. Though the decision left liberated blacks unprotected, the crisis had passed. However, until the peace, the president clapped into military prisons recalcitrant public officials, critical newspaper editors, and others suspected of disloyalty or espionage. A conscription law (March 3, 1863) introduced a compulsory draft, and riots against it generated swift repression. The faint-hearted rushed to file exemption claims or else planned flight abroad. Men clamoring for certificates of alienage swamped the passport bureau and foreign consulates. Those who dashed for the borders or seaports without papers found themselves under arrest without benefits of habeas corpus. In Chicago the *Tribune* noted the "disgraceful spectacle of full grown able bodied men slinking off to Canada." In areas occupied by the army, military rule suspended all civilian liberties until 1866. In the frantic hours after Lincoln's assassination, people faced arrest in the streets for saying, "Pity it had not been done before." When the funeral procession passed through New York City, houses not draped in mourning were tarred.

In the wartime Confederacy a harsh conscription law created inequities and stimulated desertions, and Quakers suffered more than they did in the North. There, too, men rushed into occupations that would spare them army duty, and thousands declared themselves foreigners and aliens, while others wandered away, for no one could be conscripted outside the state of which he was a citizen. To counteract the evil effects of speculation and hoarding, judges encouraged vigorous and often extralegal measures; people needed no urging to take the law into their own hands as bread riots spread. Hungry army officers confiscated whatever they needed, and ownership became moot. Dissenting opinions met no toleration; those who held them could only flee or go underground. Pearson, chief justice of the Supreme Court of North Carolina, for a time spoke up against unconstitutional measures, then conformed when his colleagues held against him.

Later (1866) Justice Jeremiah Black noted that legal rights, in no danger during peacetime, only survived to the extent that the Constitution remained unbroken when the wave of power lashed itself into violence and surged against the barriers made to confine it. The fears, uncertainties, and forebodings that followed Southern defeat, stoked the violence. Legality and constitutions seemed flimsy barriers to anarchy at a time when many expected a vengeful North to obliterate the Southern way of life, turning the whole region into a fiefdom of the victorious lords of the loom.[15]

Repressive government action surprised no American aware of the narrow margin of tolerance in the society. Force already ruled in many places, and would do so in the future. After 1850, as earlier, individuals and self-constituted groups casually resorted to violence. Congressman Daniel E. Sickles cold-bloodedly murdered his wife's lover—an act in accord with the code of the times. Congressman Herbert went unpunished after he killed the waiter in Willard's Hotel who refused to serve him breakfast after eleven A.M.; menials, though white, had to accept the liabilities of their position, he asserted (1856). In the same establishment Major Heiss severely whipped the editor of the *Star*. California Senator Broderick was not alone to lose his life in a duel.[16]

All along, mobs as well as governments mounted threats to freedom; citizens continued to take the law into their own hands in the North as well as in the South, in the East as in the West. Like the masked Wild Hordes of the Middle Ages, they attacked persons transgressing village rules. Lynching, a Kentuckian explained to a foreign visitor, provided a "quicker and more effective" remedy than courtroom comedies (1857), a judgment confirmed when John Crawson, a brutal murderer, escaped from the jail at Freeport, Illinois. Better let vigilance committees or Regulators take care of killers with dispatch, as on the riverboat *Ohio Belle* or in Cumberland County (1856), and in Jackson County, Iowa (1857), and Noble County, Indiana (1858). The San Francisco Committee of Vigilance earned national attention; and doubts about its legality did not moderate the zeal of later imitators in Montana, Oregon, and Idaho. The drunken child molester deserved summary treatment—swift and certain. In the treatment of criminals, blacks and whites suffered alike. Guardians of local morality did not hesitate to take the ax to saloons and the torch to indecent publications. Few people condemned the Michigan ladies who tarred, feathered, and rode out of town Jehiel Robbins, keeper of a house of ill fame. Reinforcements dispersed the crowd intent upon lynching A. J. Nash, but not before the terrified murderer committed suicide (Carlinsville, 1854). Though incipient violence, bursting frequently forth, imperiled the security of persons and property and nullified the constitutionally guaranteed right to a jury trial, it had the virtues of certainty, simplicity, and economy. "No *expense* to the County"—explanation enough. In San Francisco through much of the 1850s, vigilantes administered what law existed.[17]

Baltimore long bore the distinction of "mob town." One election disturbance (1856) left eight dead and 150 wounded. Other places, however, challenged its primacy. Louisville's Mechanics and Hope fire companies repeatedly fought each other. In New Orleans, a vigilance committee deposed the mayor and seized virtual control of the city; and at one point the Plug Uglies, a gang, came down to the District of Columbia and took temporary possession of the national capitol.[18]

The war's unhappy side effects stoked outrageous behavior. Protests against the inequities of the draft added heat to the riots of 1863 in New York City, but so did cries of "down with the rich," panic at the clanging firebells, wild rumors, the readiness to use artillery against civilians, the desire for plunder, personal enmities, and old hostilities between the blacks and the Irish. Then, in a "mixed surf of muffled sound," rose the atheist roar of riot: in red arson's baleful glare, the town fell to its rats and man rebounded whole aeons back in nature—a grimy slur on the Republic's faith which held humans naturally good.[19]

Reconstruction further undermined respect for legality and exacerbated violence. Having been told through the course of the war that they were forever a part of a whole, indissoluble Union, the secessionist states wondered why restoration to the Union occasioned such difficulties after the peace. When the victorious armies overturned electoral results, many Southerners pondered whether Northern politicians had any right to oust the people's chosen representatives because of Confederate pasts. Southern states could not ratify the Fourteenth Amendment, which they did not share in drafting. Military Reconstruction showed that the rule of law no longer prevailed; an unprecedented level of angry violence followed, along with a temporary denial of such symbols of American liberty as the Fourth of July, which had in the past bound the two sections together. A pool of demobilized and resourceless veterans who had once solved difficulties through firepower still had the weapons to continue to do so, along with ordinary criminals who profited by the loosening of normal standards.

The passion long persisted. The Loyal Legion, the Grand Army of the Republic, and the Union League fanned the embers of sectional hatred. With the end of efforts at reconstruction and the withdrawal of federal troops from the South, the Ku Klux Klan in many areas ruled without legal formality, and force replaced the established procedures of law. Fear of lynchings became the normal tactic by which communities kept black freedmen under control; and the number of assaults grew steadily in the century's closing decade. Race riots erupted without warning, as in Atlanta (1906), in Springfield (1908), in East St. Louis (1917), and in Chicago (1919).[20]

The former slaves had the company of other victims. The Chinese in California, the Italians and Greeks in Omaha, also suffered. In New Orleans, rivalry over the privilege of unloading banana boats led ultimately to the lynching of eleven Italians; and in Georgia, the tragic fate of Leo Frank revealed the dangers some Jews faced. A German Turn-verein picnic celebration in Hoboken, New Jersey (1851), degenerated into a wild melee that left one person killed and dozens wounded. The Germans in Louisville, who responded to the Know-Nothings by organizing their own Sag Nichts, fought their opponents at the polls, and in 1855 confronted hostile police in gunfights. Nor were unpopular ethnic groups the only targets of brutality; several governors and three United States presidents fell to assassins, and the Hatfields and the McCoys blazed away at each other without regard to race, creed, or previous condition of servitude. Other great family feuds lasted for years. In southern Indiana, whippings by White Caps compelled lazy, shiftless whites to behave (1887). In the Ozarks, Bald Knobbers and Slickers skirmished for years in an area long ravished by Bushwackers and horse thieves (1884). Violence in the Phillipines later desensitized Americans to cruelty. In Kentucky, tobacco planters joined the Night Riders to maintain production quotas by force (1907).[21]

Mobs, and sometimes also government officials, showed scant respect for civil liberties. Newspapermen faced the dangers of libel suits, political pressure, and also of physical attack. A congressman assailed the journalists, "demented fragments of humanity," who hung about the halls to gather up bits of gossip. So much for the free press! Some libraries banned *Huckleberry Finn:* indecent. Those "moral icebergs" would double his sales, Mark Twain believed. The assistant librarian of the Boston Public Library advocated the exclusion of Rabelais, *The Decameron,* Fielding and Richardson; and the director removed from circulation a dirty book a person from San Francisco wished to read (1885).[22]

As for religion, a blasphemous depiction of the Crucifixion on the stage by the Keller Troupe aroused widespread indignation but no overt action. An uproar did rise after the reference to the United States as a Christian nation (1858). Conspiracy theories threw the gullible into a panic; New Yorkers charged that a secret Catholic society led by the bishop and a Wall Street banker secured the exclusion of the Bible from the public schools (1858). The American Protective Association in the 1880s and 1890s drew upon antipapist sentiments as deep as those of the 1850s. Hostility to the Church of the Latter-Day Saints also persisted. Missourians in 1858 welcomed the prospect of a war against Mormonism, seen as a disgusting compound of sensuality, despotism, and ferociousness (1858). The Edwards Act (1882) disqualified polygamists from serving in Congress and opened the way to a crackdown on Utah Territory. Then and later, calls for organic and spiritual unity of the people often implied curtailment of liberty.[23]

Meanwhile vagrancy laws curtailed freedom of movement, as Jack London discovered when a fee-hunting constable imprisoned him for thirty days without even the right to plead, for having no fixed abode and no visible means of support. Fear of the placeless effaced old ideas of freedom. Confronting an endless number of hoboes, an ominous mass of misfits, and parasites who lived by begging and stealing, Americans considered any measure of defense justified. A vast army marched around the land, refusing all work and receiving far more food and money than necessary, making country roads unsafe for women while cities swarmed with threatening, stalwart beggars (1880). Confine them all in a separate area in every county and grant relief in return for labor. In Elizabeth, New Jersey, officials kept an open boxcar on a siding, then each evening rounded up the tramps trapped inside. Protesting her arrest in Providence, Rhode Island, Emma Goldman received a short but pithy answer from the sergeant in the police station: "Anarchists have no rights in this community, see."[24]

Radicals who espoused opinions different from those of the majority did so at considerable and increasing risk, as abolitionists and other agitators who threatened order had earlier discovered. After 1850 the level of tolerance sank perceptibly and continued to do so into the twentieth century. Any individual, whether accused of heinous crimes or outlandish in appearance or suspected of expounding strange opinions, became vulnerable to mob violence, if not to governmental repression.

The anarchists and the Industrial Workers of the World (IWW) repeatedly encountered and made trouble, but so did pure and simple unions in the effort to organize. Labor difficulties ever more often sprang not from the protests of local carpenters or cordwainers as in the past, but from the emissaries of national or international organizations—outsiders, foreign to the community, insensitive to its fundamental institutions. Johann Most's glorification of dynamite and propaganda by deed made anarchism, violence, and unionism synonymous and elicited brutal responses. In Everett, Washington (1916), seven men died in a clash between Wobblies and the police. Tulsa, Oklahoma, tarred, feathered, and shipped out seventeen Wobblies (1918). A socialist parade in Cleveland ended in riot and bloodshed (1919) while the anti-IWW outburst in Centralia (1919) led to lynchings. Strangers, even though nonviolent, raised questions about the extent to which old guarantees applied under the new conditions.

Much depended upon the setting. In isolated mining towns and on the railroads remote from the organized forces of law and order, violence resolved disputes as often as negotiation or arbitration. In small cities with large laboring populations, efforts at improvement gained communal approval. The shopkeepers in Homestead, Pennsylvania, sympathized with the steel workers on whose business they depended. The textile strike in Lawrence, Massachusetts (1912), evoked enough sympathy to earn the employees a wage increase, not from the cadre of IWW people who led it but from the encouragement of involved ethnic and civic associations. In large cities, fury, generally bottled up, erupted in massive outbreaks, difficult to contain in the maze of streets where honest laborers and their families mingled with strangers intent on pillage, as in Chicago (1859) or Tompkins Square in New York (1874) or Pittsburgh (1877). The Haymarket bomb in Chicago (1886) killed seven people; of the innocent anarchists accused, four went to the gallows, one committed suicide, and three served in prison until pardoned by Governor Altgeld years later. Under these circumstances, passions boiled over. In the heat of the Pullman strike (1894), an uninvolved judge concluded that the military would have to kill some of the mob before the trouble ended; the six already dead he considered "hardly enough to make an impression."[25]

The situation deteriorated after 1900, when tough guys moved in— hired killers on both sides. Big Bill Haywood of the Western Federation of Miners and Albert E. Horsley (Harry Orchard) brandished dynamite and shotguns in open warfare that culminated when the McNamara brothers blew up the building of the *Los Angeles Times,* killing twenty (1910). The notorious black hole in Ludlow, Colorado (1914), took a toll of women and children as well as of the front-line warriors. The bomb flung at the San Francisco Preparedness Parade two years later retaliated—an eye for an eye.[26]

Throughout, the courts remained largely silent, with the Haymarket Trial a travesty of justice. On neither the state nor the federal level did they prove protectors of the individual's ability to act. Freedom of the press did not spare Johann Most a year's imprisonment for reprinting in *Die Freiheit* an article defending the assassination of kings that appeared shortly after the murder of President McKinley. Censorship fever was evident in 1917 when the Wisconsin State Library Commission declared neutrality disloyal, and called for removing unpatriotic books from the shelves; Hamlin Garland, among the authors affected, had criticized his father for leaving the family to fight in the Civil War "in an overflow of sentimentality over a striped silken rag." The library war service then helped the War Department compile an army index of about a hundred books alleged to be harmful, anti-British or pro-German, but also pacifist and socialist. The list included Ambrose Bierce, Norman Thomas, and Frederic C. Howe, commissioner of immigration, who had dedicated his *Why War* (1916) to Woodrow Wilson. President Nicholas Murray Butler's commencement address (1917) explained that tolerance persisted as long as the debate over national policies continued, but conditions changed once the nation spoke. "What had been wrong headedness was now sedition. What had been folly was now treason."

Often events passed too swiftly for review; but time did not help, and repressive legislation that provided the color of law for violence escaped judicial scrutiny. Many jurists showed more concern about the relation of property than of human rights to government action. The restraints of the federal Bill of Rights applied only to the Congress before 1920 and did not impede such measures as New York's Anarchy Act of 1902 and similar restrictive statutes in New Jersey, Massachusetts, and Washington (1909). Learned judges explained (1897) that the Bill of Rights did not apply in practice with absolute literalness but yielded when necessary to exceptions. Free speech did "not mean license, nor counseling disobedience to the law," but orderly expression, the court held in Emma Goldman's trial. The common law did not help, for as Judge Thomas Cooley observed, it neither protected nor defined free speech beyond the right to publish truth, with good motives, for justifiable ends. That judgment echoed earlier formulations by which speech that did not contribute to social betterment or that disrupted order deserved no legal protection. Furthermore, the bias in American constitutional law that glossed over abstract questions of justice and right also filled the

minds of legislators and judges with narrow thoughts of specific legal-
isms.[27]

American involvement in the First World War had therefore led
almost as a matter of course to repressive measures against dissenters and
outsiders. Long before he entered the White House, Woodrow Wilson
had described the Federalist Alien and Sedition Acts as fatal blunders
impinging upon freedom of speech and of the press and depriving foreigners of rights without accusation, without jury trial, and without
defense or counsel. On July 4, 1914, he explained the inadequacy of mere
declarations of the rights of man and insisted on the need to translate those
statements into definite actions. After 1917, his own administration repeated the Federalist error. The humorist who rejected the very idea of
a just war bitterly predicted that furious hordes before long would stone
speakers from the platform and strangle free speech. The whole nation—
pulpit and all—would take up the war cry and shout itself hoarse and
mob any honest man who opened his mouth. And everyone would
welcome those conscience-smoothing falsities that blamed the enemy.[28]

In time, the repressions hastened the development of a modern concept of freedom of the press and speech which made individual expression
about matters of public importance an end of itself, a public good worthy
of judicial protection. As the Supreme Court began to resolve the issues
raised by the prosecution of anarchists, socialists, and pacifists during the
war, it started to develop a concept of freedom based on the inherent
value of individual expression in a democracy. But that came after 1920.

Before the Civil War, expressions of patriotism had recalled the
founding fathers and had, as in Fourth of July celebrations, stressed the
universal import of Americanism—the cause of all mankind. Increasingly, as the nineteenth century drew to a close, emphasis shifted; as if
to help heal the wounds of battle and secession, Decoration Day com-
memorated all the sacred dead, reminded participants of the shared sufferings, North and South, while subtly excluding the uncomprehending and
the newly arrived. Edward Everett Hale's *Man without a Country* (1863)
persuaded thousands of readers that only those whose souls were dead
lacked attachment to a native land. Veterans' groups took form—the
Loyal Legion composed of Union officers, the Grand Army of the
Republic, along with societies like the Union League clubs and associations based on descent from venerated ancestors, for example, the Daugh-

ters of the American Republic and the First Families of Virginia. The fervor swept along the Red Cross and the YMCA.[29]

Patriotic zeal embittered the wartime treatment of dissent. Before 1917, only the strictly defined law of treason restricted the acts of individuals, although anticonspiracy provisions applied to people who associated for ends hostile to the government. Furthermore, limitations on search and seizure and on self-incrimination shielded the accused. The Espionage and Sedition Acts of 1917 and 1918, however, broadened the scope of criminal acts to advocacy, including false statements damaging the war effort, causing insubordination in the armed forces, or obstructing enlistment. An amendment in May 1918 forbade expressions of opinion against liberty bonds, the Constitution, the flag, and the uniform. Severe penalties thereafter punished not simply overt actions but also the articulation of unpopular views. The courts, for decades occupied with protecting property rights from excessive state interference, saw no need for similar defense of personal rights. Some 2,000 prosecutions resulted in the conviction of 877 persons, not simply for attacking the war but also for criticizing the Red Cross or the YMCA and for urging taxes rather than loans to finance the conflict or for refusing to subscribe to liberty bonds.

The fine distinctions drawn in earlier discussions of freedom of the press blurred in the heat of war. Blackstone's previous restraint, Cooley's free discussion of public events, liberty as against license, use as against abuse—all such differentiations lost relevance. No one, the courts held, could do, say, or write anything that detracted from the war effort or postponed "for a single moment the early coming of the day when the success of our arms shall be a fact."

Under the Espionage Acts, Postmaster General Burleson excluded from the mail journals critical of the government, among them two leading socialist papers, *The Masses* and *The Milwaukee Leader*. In *The Masses* case, the Supreme Court, reversing Learned Hand's sensible contrary opinion, enunciated the doctrine of remote bad tendency and punished the mere intention to cause acts that might injure the state, whether those acts indeed occurred or not. In *The United States* v. *The Spirit of '76,* the judges held that a motion picture unfavorably depicting British behavior during the Revolution violated the Espionage Act. They also regarded as objectionable any criticism of English policy in Ireland or India or any sympathy with the Russian Revolution.[30]

Repression emanating from Washington conformed to popular sentiment expressed locally and in state ordinances and may, indeed, have forestalled a wave of lynchings sparked by rumors of German submarine landings, spies, and sneaky Bolsheviks. Vigilantes hunted down slackers;

and some states enacted their own espionage acts, broad enough in Washington to punish a newspaper article defaming George Washington. Under Montana law, insults to the flag earned a twenty-year jail term. Some thirty-three states punished subversive advocacy through criminal syndicalism laws. Under the Minnesota statute, a man went to jail for telling women knitting for the servicemen, "no soldier ever sees these socks." Without legal formality, Germans suffered severe constraints; even citizens or indeed those native-born feared censorship of the mail and subservience to John Bull. Hence the German-American Bank became the Liberty Bank. Hysteria made English the official language of Iowa; and that state, along with Delaware and Montana, forbade the teaching of German in the schools. Freedom of speech and of religion, Governor W. L. Harding explained, did not sanction the use of other languages in churches, telephone conversations, trains, or indeed any public places. People who did not like the constraint could worship at home. Such restrictions interfered not only with the ability of foreigners to express themselves, but also with the rights of citizens to hear their views. Montana established councils of defense that became cloaks for vigilante activity; and the American Protective Association furnished a national organization to unify regional efforts. Meanwhile colleges cracked down on dissent.

The zeal for rooting out disagreement impinged upon the right to self-government. The House of Representatives denied Congressman Victor Berger of Wisconsin, a socialist, the seat to which election entitled him. The government denied him, Morris Hillquit, and Algernon Lee, delegates to the socialist peace conference at Stockholm, passports, on the spurious grounds that they might negotiate for the United States. When Max Eastman questioned the power to use the post office to destroy socialist journals, the president replied that "a time of war must be regarded as wholly exceptional"; things innocent in ordinary circumstances then became very dangerous to the public welfare. Rose Pastor Stokes, also a Socialist, received a ten-year sentence for saying, "I am for the people and the government is for the profiteers." A *New York Times* editorial rejoiced at the intolerance toward such "anti-Americanism." The Socialist party suffered for publishing Scott Nearing's book, although the author was acquitted in his trial for publicly opposing the war, which began over two months after the peace. But Eugene V. Debs, jailed for a speech in June 1918, remained in prison until President Harding pardoned him in 1921.[31]

Juries readily returned guilty verdicts and the judges made no efforts to hold back the tide of public opinion, deferring in these cases to the clear expression of majority will. "The provisions of the Constitution," one of them explained, were "not mathematical formulas having their essence in their form," but "organic living institutions" and therefore adaptable to circumstances. Postmaster General Burleson explained to a journalist that "the instant you print anything calculated to dishearten the boys in the army or to make them think this is not a just or righteous war—that instant you will be suppressed and no amount of influence will save you." In the *Schenck* case, Oliver W. Holmes for the majority held that distribution of leaflets to draftees went beyond the right of free speech and involved a clear and present danger to the Republic. "The most stringent protection of free speech would not protect the man in falsely shouting *fire* in a theatre and causing a panic." In 1921 the Supreme Court upheld the postmaster general's power to declare matter nonmailable although that amounted to deprivation of property and the abridgement of freedom of speech.

But in *Abrams* v. *U.S.* (250 U.S., 624) (1919), Holmes, along with Louis D. Brandeis, dissented. In this case, he considered it absurd to think that two silly leaflets defending the Russian Revolution would seriously interfere with the war effort or present a "clear and imminent danger" to the nation. He held the issue of intent irrelevant. The government had a right to punish speech that produced substantive evil, a power greater in time of war than in time of peace, but within the limits of principle. The best test of truth remained the "power of the thought to get itself accepted in the competition of the market." "Only the present danger of immediate evil, or an intent to bring it about," warranted congressional limitations on the expression of opinion. The majority rejected his position.[32]

Moreover, the federal government undertook to control ideas directly through its Committee on Public Information, which managed the news and emitted a flow of propaganda designed to boost morale. Private groups hastened to participate. Hermann Hagedorn, along with four hundred other writers, labored to correct pro-German influences. The Fourth of July, 1918, turned into a demonstration of Americanism, as more than thirty-three nationality groups participated in parades, pageants, and mass meetings. George Creel conceived the idea of organizing a pilgrimage to Mount Vernon, by representatives of the various nationalities of the American population, headed by Woodrow Wilson, and including Mayflower descendents, Albanians, Finns, Syrians, and Ukrainians. A piano tucked away behind a clump of cedars accompanied the singer belting out the Battle Hymn of the Republic, as each of the thirty-three representatives laid a wreath upon Washington's tomb. A

Belgian-born American citizen delivered the message in the name of all. Woodrow Wilson then defined the essence of the struggle as the battle for "the reign of law, based upon the consent of the governed and sustained by the organized opinion of mankind."

To further that end, the National Research Council enlisted its associates for war service and 25 percent of the members of the American Psychological Association also served in some fashion. Universities made life uncomfortable for inadequately patriotic professors, as when Wellesley College dismissed Emily Balch for her outspoken pacifism.[33]

The armistice did not end but indeed intensified the repression. The collapse of some European monarchies and the Bolshevik Revolution in Russia generated a wave of fear lest all society plunge into disorder. A visiting English journalist detected "the feverish condition of the public mind . . . hagridden by the spectre of Bolshevism . . . and the horrid name 'Radical' covered the most innocent departure from conventional thought." America seemed the land of liberty—liberty to keep in step. Bombs mailed to judges and labor violence hinted at the approach of a cataclysm. The *Chicago Tribune* flaunted daily the motto "our country, right or wrong." Roger Baldwin, founder of the American Civil Liberties Union, erred in the belief that wholesale prosecutions would not deal with the radical organizations in America. Neither the Socialist party nor the IWW regained its prewar strength. A. Mitchel Palmer, the fighting Quaker, goaded on by the Senate, as attorney general launched the deportations and actively stimulated the red scare, exacerbated by the wave of strikes in 1919 attributed to subversives, in which four million workers participated. The *Washington Post* (December 24, 1919) explained that the radical, "a wildfire, voluntary dastardly coward and traitor," deserved death. Membership in labor unions began to decline, in part out of fear. Heavy casualties followed one American Legion attack on an IWW hall in Centralia, Washington, that met gunfire from the lumber workers within. Public anger at the massacre undermined the weak Wobbly organization. The great steel strike that year, led by William Z. Foster, formerly prominent in the IWW, and later a Communist, stoppages by textile, shipyard, garment, and harbor workers, and by telephone operators, produced a crisis atmosphere. People walked to work when the transit employees went out and stayed home when the actors closed the theaters. Seattle experienced a general strike, and a police job action in Boston touched off a wave of looting until the National Guard took over. Collapse seemed imminent. To combat "the insidious dangers" of bolshevism and lower-class radicalism, Charles W. Eliot, former president of Harvard College, proposed a pageant to celebrate the

Plymouth tercentenary. And the distinguished legal scholar John Henry Wigmore, in response to Holmes's dissent, insisted that "the moral right of the majority to enter upon the war" implied "the moral right to secure success by suppressing public agitation against completion of the struggle." Roger Baldwin discovered the true nature of American society in prison—its state servant of the business class, its Constitution a weak reed in crisis, and its working class trodden under foot.

Insecure Americans, sensitive to the importance of safeguarding control, insisted on silencing such critics and their champions. State criminal syndicalism and "red flag" laws attacked the symbols of communism and anarchism, and forbade "advocating, teaching or aiding and abetting the commission of crime, sabotage . . . or unlawful acts of force or violence or . . . terrorism as a means" of effecting any industrial or political change (California). The New York legislature refused to seat five Socialists, thus disfranchising thousands of voters and provoking even Charles Evans Hughes, Republican party leader, who denounced the action as absolutely opposed to the fundamental principles of American government. The quick evaporation of hostilities toward the "Hun" left a residue of antagonisms directed against newer dangers, a residual dislike of aliens and radicals.

The climax came in the deportation delirium of 1920, which counted Emma Goldman among its victims. In January 1920 alone, a roundup brought in four thousand suspected aliens—let them go back where they came from! Immigration inspectors decided in secret proceedings, with the secretary of labor's judgment final, subject to no appeal, since deportation was not a criminal procedure. Emma Goldman's case was not unique. John Meehan, arrested in Everett, Washington, for violating a billboard law, after eighteen months' incarceration found himself shipped to England, which he had left twenty-four years earlier and where he landed penniless with no kith or kin. As if by way of culmination, the Sacco and Vanzetti case erupted in 1920.[34]

Victory in the war and the triumphant peace that followed did not quiet fears of those other Hairy Ones, the Bolsheviks. Intolerance of radicals extended into the next decade, with even display of the red flag or the espousal of anarchism a crime. The New York State legislature in March 1919 charged the Lusk committee with the duty of exploring the extent of subversion. Uncertainty about whether to rely on the consent of the governed, the foundation of a free democracy, drained away faith in liberty; and dramatic increases in the mechanisms of state power extended control. The ability to manage opinion by force or by subtle manipulation now threatened individual autonomy—and atop it all, came Prohibition.

> Thy vices reft from thee,
> Sweet New Democracy,
> Of them I sing.
>
> . . . . . .
>
> Only the memories
> Of thy lost liberties
> May with us stay.
> No more the ponies prance;
> Closed are thy games of chance;
> No more the passing glance
> Makes bright the day.[35]

Uncertainty ignited fright of the aliens. In the nineteenth century, hostility to the foreign-born sometimes went beyond words. A Tennessee Know-Nothing had foreseen the need "to rise in arms and massacre the foreigners or make them our slaves in order to preserve the free institutions of our country," and natives who considered it intolerable to allow the subjects of a foreign potentate to vote, occasionally precipitated street brawls and riots against Catholics. But generally, verbal threats had done little damage. Cartoons showed immigrants from Europe entering the United States' ark of refuge to escape taxes, kings, military training, and dungeons.[36]

Color made yellow people the first general targets of prejudice. True, in 1857 a Charleston newspaper had urged the importation of coolies, cheaper to sustain than black slaves; but nothing came of that suggestion. Californians even then did not share the sentiment and instead demanded the exclusion of the immoral, thievish, and filthy Orientals. Senator Charles Sumner's proposal in 1870 to permit the naturalization of Chinese came to nothing, as hostility to them deepened. The virulence of the hatred erupted in the Rock Springs Massacre (1885) of laborers in the Colorado coal mines.

A California law of 1903 banned racial intermarriage between Chinese and whites; and Senator George L. Perkins of California expressed the sentiments of his constituency in 1906: "Bringing with them slavery, concubinage, prostitution, the opium vice, the disease of leprosy, the offensive and defensive organization of class and guilds, the lowest standard of living known, and a detestation of the people with whom they live and with whom they will not even leave their bones when dead, they form a community within a community within a community and there live the Chinese life." In the 1880s, United States policy effectively barred them.[37]

Race hatred spread from Orientals to some Europeans. Of course, all Americans had themselves once been foreign-born or descendants of the foreign-born. Now a drawing in *The World*—"Over There, Over Here!"—showed the enemy at home; as Uncle Sam watched the fighting overseas, an alien prepared to knife him in the back.

> Stood shivering on the Door-mat of Columbia
> Two cunning little Bolsheviks
> From far Fakeovia,
> Young Ivan Cutyourthroatavich,
> His little sister Alix Thengohangyourself
> And pleading, sad eyed, sought
> Admission to the hospitable door.

But Uncle Sam stood up in his big boots and refused to let those imps of Satan in. The courts had long upheld the government's right to exclude undesirables, a category that now expanded to include radicals. In his first message to Congress after the McKinley assassination, President Theodore Roosevelt called for the exclusion and deportation of alien anarchists; and Congress complied in 1903 with a law subsequently strengthened in 1907, 1917, and 1918.

Earlier Mr. Dooley had mocked the restrictionists who raised their voices against invasion by the paupers and anarchists of effete Europe. " 'Tis time we put our back again' th'open dure, an keep out th' savage horde" who did not assimilate with the country, said his friend. Asked what he would do with the offscourings of Europe, "I'd score them some," he answered. "There's one sure way to keep them out. What's that? Teach them all about our institutions before they come." If they knew the problems, they would stay home. Little did some Americans understand their institutions by then.[38]

Few laughed when the Dillingham commission's report recommended drastic restriction (1911), and when the literacy test passed in 1917 over President Wilson's veto. Those departures from long-standing American policy revealed the effects of racism that classified some peoples as genetically inferior to others. Unabashedly, William Earl Dodge Stokes, uncle by marriage of Rose Pastor Stokes, in *The Right to Be Well Born, or Horse Breeding in Its Relation to Eugenics* (1917), invoked the inalienable right of every child to come into the world free from disease, from hereditary ailments, and from mental and physical defects. A predetermined world fixed each individual's destiny—"a shoemaker to his last and each to his calling"—eliminating weaklings and defectives and nurturing only the fittest and the best. What nature once accomplished, man now had to do on his own. The harsh New England climate and its rocky soil had once killed off the weak and unproductive, producing a pure and vigorous breed, now in danger of crossing with "the rotten, foreign, diseased blood" which the immigration laws allowed to flow in. For the sake of American babies he demanded an end to "this inflow of diseased blood"—America for Americans, and not for the imported scum of the earth.[39]

The heat of war raised the issue to the boiling point. Fear of sedition festered wherever large numbers of enemy aliens clustered. Even before American entry into the conflict, the interventionists bitterly attacked German and Irish Americans who advocated neutrality. Jewish and Polish Americans also became suspect because antagonism to czarist tyranny had turned their sympathies toward the central powers. Theodore Roosevelt proclaimed divided loyalty the equivalent of moral treason. The country, he feared, was becoming "merely a huge polyglot boarding-house and countinghouse in which dollar-hunters of twenty different nationalities" scrambled for gain while each really paid his soul's allegiance to some foreign power. The United States ambassador to London, Walter Hines Page, in 1917 furiously wrote of his desire to "hang our Irish agitators and shoot our hyphenates and bring up our children with reverence for English history and in awe of English literature." Stokes advocated courses in patriotism, hygiene, and heredity to replace ancient languages, music, or dancing, lest the rabble—outcasts of other nations—pervert American views of life. By 1917 six western states had sterilization laws and twelve regulated the marriages of the handicapped.[40]

In this atmosphere, the Quota Act of 1921 limited the number of aliens admitted from any country to 3 percent of the total of that nationality resident in the United States in 1910, a clear expression of preference for the old Nordic as against the new Slavic and Latin immigrants. A social psychologist who defined human beauty by North European standards argued that humanitarianism and modern medicine, by permitting the excessive propagation of the unfit, had retarded the progress of civilization. Such assumptions encouraged demands for a national Social Disease Act to register all syphilitic or diseased persons and to forbid marriages between races or between those who suffered from hereditary ailments (including deafness, insanity, and blindness). The federal government would issue all marriage certificates based on ancestral history and health. Only propertied white Americans would enjoy the right to vote. As proof of the scientific basis for eugenics, supporters cited the Jews, bred for centuries for money getting—and all because of Terah, who sired Abraham at the age of 130 and died himself when 205 years old. If the federal government could pass laws to ensure that only pure-blooded dogs entered the country, it could do no less against all "the human curs of Europe, the Orient and the rest of the world," polluting and diseasing "the standardized blood of the Plymouth Rock colony."

And it was no laughing matter at all when the Ku Klux Klan, revived in 1915, prepared to battle Catholics and Jews as well as blacks in the next decade. Its antecedents lay not only in the old hooded order of Reconstruction days but in generations of regulators, vigilantes, white caps, and purity leagues who hunted down road agents, horse thieves, Indians, brothel keepers, drunks, and child abusers, and found their targets, at night or in broad daylight, not only for order and moral purity, nor even for money or out of hatred, but sometimes just for fun and luck.[41]

It was not implausible in 1920 to raise the question, as some observers did, whether repression rolled on as the trend of the future, with liberty in retreat in the United States as well as in Europe. In the face of attack, Max Eastman, Roger Baldwin, and handfuls of socialists, pacifists, and liberals formed the American Civil Liberties Union. Their concern would have risen had they understood that the Russian Revolution produced not another free democratic society but a harshly repressive regime; and that ominous tendencies in Italy and Germany already pointed to the developments of the 1920s and 1930s. Indeed, even Britain and France heard serious expressions of anxiety about the future. The brief era of liberty in the West appeared to approach an end.

Within the United States the reversal had complex sources—in alterations of the democratic polity, in the increase of all governmental power, in abrupt changes in community structure, and in the inability to attain the equality demanded by complex patterns of the population's diversity. Paradoxically, some improvements increased the state's repressive power.

These changes came in a period when large sectors of the population lost confidence in accepted ideas and institutions, increasing the difficulty of defending inherited ideas of religion, family, property rights, monogamous marriage, diet, and drink. By the twentieth century, even moderate criticism provoked resistance because it touched matters about which individuals and community no longer felt as certain and secure as they once had. The increasing size and complexity of the country heightened the sense of insecurity and evoked resistance to challenges to once accepted opinions. Imperial connections, worldwide responsibilities, and a complex economy no one fully comprehended, heightened tensions. Old solutions did not apply to novel problems, augmenting the sense of disarray. And constitutional misconceptions created inflexibilities among people and governments that made adjustment harder. The process that resulted tested the validity and meaning of constitutional guarantees and explored the boundaries of efforts at repression, in a reciprocal interplay between the law recognized by the courts and popular opinion.

The unstable social environment sprang from the inadequacy of existing communities to compensate for the isolation of individuals and the difficulty of adjusting to the conditions of an economy developing in a totally novel fashion. The expansive impulses present from the seventeenth century onward now meshed with the massive mechanization of many aspects of life, and by the twentieth century put a premium on conformity and made a uniform of some sort the plausible garb for all men and women. And bracketing the whole period, two great wars raised serious questions about what was normal.

These circumstances made it appropriate to ask, What then happened to the ability to act, that is, to liberty?

I I

POWER IN A DEMOCRATIC POLITY

REPRESSION SPRANG FROM FEARS generated by complex changes in American society after 1850. Expansion, long familiar, then assumed an ominous cast; and the economy developed novel forms, altering work rhythms and further undermining already-unstable communities. Moreover, weapons of control, although ever more powerful, proved incapable of establishing social order. The Civil War immediately magnified the role of the federal government; and Reconstruction, industrial growth, and reform movements further inflated the importance of decisions made in Washington. However, those tendencies did not weaken the states or localities, which also gained steadily in power. Indeed, the roles of all political agencies swelled, with the accumulation of ever more responsibilities despite widespread discontent with their performances. Somehow all seemed inadequate to bear the burdens placed upon them.[1]

Hence the popular fear of exposure to uncontained blasts from out of the unknown, and hence too the search for defenses against the unpredictable. People no longer certain of their own ability to act sought safety in restraints upon the threatening others.

The United States moved into the nineteenth century's second half with its governmental structures firmly in place, and firmly resistant to change. In political organization, much seemed the same in 1920 as seventy years earlier—written constitutions, separation of powers, executive, legislative, and judicial branches.

But grave problems had affected the ways in which the mechanism functioned: federalism, slavery, wars, Reconstruction. Citizens still voted, as in Jackson's day; but a new situation altered democracy's meaning, casting new light on what they voted for and what their government did, that is, on the effect upon their liberties.

26

The American, strong for any revolution "that ain't goin' to happen" in his day, knew that nothing happened anyhow. He could see great changes taking place every day, but no change at all in fifty years. The country "pretinds to want to thry new experiments, but a sudden change gives it a chill," said Mr. Dooley. The formal allocation of authority among federal, state, and local agencies, as within each, among executives, legislatures, and courts, remained much as it had been in 1790, although conventions, notably in Massachusetts and New York (1915, 1916), seriously considered constitutional revisions. But despite the persistence of the familiar framework, operations changed drastically, not least through the tremendous increase of new administrative boards and commissions. Massachusetts, which in 1837 had only one, by the turn of the century had more than two hundred such units. New York, which in 1850 had only twenty, by 1914 had one hundred sixty-nine.[2]

Irony: the inflation of federal power came initially at the hands of a president who called eloquently for a new birth of freedom so that government of the people, by the people, for the people would not perish from the earth (November 19, 1863). He did not have a burgeoning bureaucracy in view.

Gloomy forebodings of assassination had shadowed Abraham Lincoln's trip to his inaugural, for early in life he had learned the force of necessity, by which he meant a power beyond personal control. Having moved with his family from the Kentucky backwoods, first to Indiana and then to Illinois, he had gone to school by littles, but had educated himself. Brief service in the state legislature and one term in Congress led to a nice legal practice. Drawn actively into politics by the Kansas-Nebraska Act, Lincoln had failed in his bid for the Illinois senatorship but had gained nationwide fame through debates with Stephen A. Douglas (1858) that attracted enormous crowds and widespread coverage. Although those who knew him valued his acute intellect—not learned in a bookish sense but master of fundamental principles—his nomination and election in 1860 surprised many. He took office with little executive experience, but he brought to the White House more valuable attributes—shrewd judgment, an ingrained respect for orderly procedures, and above all, a sense of the strengths and weaknesses of the American people. In the prolonged crisis of war he understood his task as leader: to remain close enough to his followers to share their emotions, and to explain the purpose for which they fought. Proceeding cautiously without losing sight of the ultimate goal, he drew strength for superb statements of policy not only from mastery of language but also from intimacy with the audience.[3]

Moved by almost mystical feelings about preservation of the Union—the last, best hope on earth for human aspiration to use power toward improvement—he regarded secession, its central idea the essence of anarchy, as a test of democracy and of legality, with worldwide consequences. The Union to him connoted the totality of orderly procedures that made the Republic viable, without which rival groups would check one another in an endless succession of stalemates. Only the ever-changing majority, restrained by the Constitution, the true sovereign of a free people, he believed, could prevent despotism.

Physically speaking, Lincoln insisted, the North and South could not separate, for that would leave each section worse off than before. Two separate countries could hardly resolve the old troublesome questions. The future of the territories and the return of fugitive slaves would generate endless conflicts. The new boundary line would cause other irritations. An alien power would hold the mouth of the Mississippi, which linked the great valley to the outer world; and Southern cotton would pass through the foreign port of New York. The truth was, Lincoln's Inaugural explained (March 1961), the nation could not divide peacefully. Though passion strained them, bonds of affection held North and South not enemies, but friends. The mystic chords of memory, stretching from every patriot grave to every living heart and hearthstone, would, Lincoln hoped, yet swell the chorus of the Union, when again touched by their better angels.

Vain hope!

To hold the border states, the Union abstained from positive action as long as possible. Kentucky, Missouri, and Maryland teetered on the edge, loyal yet committed to slavery. Moreover the Republican party, new to national power, suffered from internal divisions and from organizational uncertainties that left it vulnerable to factionalism.

The stalemate could not endure. The federal government, pretending that the seceded states remained within the Union, retained possession of Fort Sumter near Charleston. That affronted the Confederacy, which acted as an independent nation. Swayed not by reasonable estimates of the situation but by fury at the humiliating loss of the election of 1860, an implicit judgment of the wrongness and guilt of their social system, the fire-eaters moved along the course of madness, folly, and wickedness. "Believe me," wrote Mrs. Robert E. Lee of Virginia in February 1861, "those who have been foremost in this revolution will deserve the reprobation of the world, having destroyed the most glorious confederacy that ever existed." Soon her husband would cast his lot with them. An expedition to relieve Fort Sumter in April 1861 therefore released the militancy romantic warriors' fantasies had long nurtured in South Carolina. On April 12, 1861, the knights, clad in brilliant uniforms, opened fire on the fort. Few among the ladies who watched foresaw that the burst of shells across the harbor, forming a perfect palmetto, would reduce their own society to ashes. But James L. Petigru knew that the torch then set to "the temple of constitutional liberty" would leave them "no more peace forever."[4]

The nation thereupon passed over the precipice. Some churches had already divided along sectional lines, as had the faculty of the University of Mississippi. But few Americans realized in 1861 that war would follow secession. Inclined to inaction, like President Buchanan they had drifted for years, hoping that nature would somehow, sometime, extinguish slavery, denying the right to withdraw from the Union but denying also the power of the federal government to coerce a state. Like the spiritualist *Banner of Light,* moderate Northerners had suspected that the South exploited the disunion humbug to extort the largest possible concessions in a future compromise, as in 1850. *The Chicago Tribune* first hoped for reconciliation, then called for a bloodless separation. Strong antislavery people, among them Horace Greeley, the influential editor of *The New York Tribune,* wanted to let the wayward sisters depart in peace. The Union would improve without them. However, the maneuver of excessive demands moderated by compromise did not succeed in 1861, when Southerners wanted a mortgage on the future, a permanent ineradicable commitment to slavery, where it already existed and in any territories thereafter acquired.

The wish for assurance that the institution would spread on into the indefinite future, binding generations without end, differed from demands that led to earlier compromises. However willing to compromise on specifics, Lincoln could not yield without jeopardizing all prospects for republican government by making slavery the one unchangeable basis of the Constitution.

Abstract speculations got nowhere: Could a state commit treason, strictly defined as that was? Did the power to make war extend to civil war? Could a constitutional convention resolve outstanding issues? Those illusions vanished in April 1861 as all compromise mechanisms failed. The conflict, long irrepressible, became a full-scale war.

Four years of costly fighting followed. Slavery, the utter denial to some of the ability to act which had always belied the promise of freedom, had dissolved some of the common objectives Americans once shared. Southerners who believed that their peculiar institution would endure and spread had diverged from their fellow citizens in the understanding of the Republic's ultimate purpose and had thereby tested the national commitment to liberty for all.

Lincoln justified repressive measures by the danger dissenters posed to the war's noble purposes—Union and liberty. All along, some people urged an early peaceful settlement, while abolitionists sought more vigorous action. The Wade-Davis Manifesto in the summer of 1864 asserted the claim of the Congress to set Reconstruction policy and reflected the prevailing distrust of the president. Lincoln, playing one group off against the other, then won reelection against his more moderate opponent, General George McClellan. The president dealt abruptly with those he thought impeded the military effort, never losing sight of the new birth of freedom that he hoped would emerge from the sacrifices of battle. His assassination in 1865 enshrined him in the hearts of Americans as a martyr to liberty.[5]

Lincoln did not, however, restore the prestige and influence of the presidency that had waned since Jackson's day. Nor did the postwar chief executives do so. As individuals, they varied in effectiveness. Selected often as compromise dark horses or for their military reputations, they usually served but a single term, like Chester A. Arthur, "a non entity with side whiskers." William Walter Phelps lost the vice-presidential place in 1888 "largely because of ridicule that he parted his hair in the middle and combed it over his forehead bang style." His replacement, Levi Morton, fortunately boasted a head as bald as a billiard ball. Few possessed leadership qualities. Johnson quarreled bitterly with the Congress, and though he escaped conviction, impeachment drained away his authority. His successors, Grant, Hayes, Garfield, and Harrison, added no luster to the office. Garfield in 1880 campaigned from the front porch of his farm in Mentor, Ohio; and Harrison judged prospective cabinet members by whether they were Presbyterians or not. McKinley brought more experience to the White House and succeeded in the bid for reelection, as Taft did not. But only Cleveland, Theodore Roosevelt, and Woodrow Wilson proved more forceful national figures. Most of them exerted but slight influence on Americans' ability to act, more usually affected by events away from the nation's capital.[6]

Not all chief executives proved unworthy of the office, and the presidency offered the exceptional a platform for self-expression—a "bully pulpit," one of them put it. Furthermore, the president controlled substantial patronage on which Harrison spent four to six hours a day. He also became the central player in the national political process, which focused increasingly on the dramatic struggle for his nomination and election. Campaigns grew more intense; their military rhetoric underscoring the warlike attributes of political "battles" and the regular repetition every four years of the struggle for place kept the names of favorite sons in citizens' consciousness far in advance of the vote. The long process of nomination, the balloting at conventions—extended among the Democrats by the two-thirds rule—the partisan popular newspapers, the torchlight processions, and the florid campaign oratory, stirred up attention throughout the country. Rarely did ideology or abstract issues play a part. The ideal candidate, said Mr. Dooley, "must be in favor of sound money but not too sound, an anti-imperialist but f'r holding' onto what we've got, an inimy iv thrusts but a frind iv organized capital, a sympathizer with th' crushed an' diwnthrodden people but not be anny means hostile to vested inthrests; must advocate sthrikes, gover'mint by injunction, free silver, sound money, greenbacks, a single tax, a tariff f'r rivinoo, th' constitootion to follow th' flag as far as it can an' no further, civil service rayform iv th' laads in office an' all th' great an' glorious principles iv our great an' glorious party or any great and gloryous parts thereof. He must be akelly at home in Wall Sthreet an' th' stock yards, in th' parlors iv th' rich an' th' kitchens iv th' poor." No mortal fitted that bill; and the conflicting perceptions of national leadership reflected underlying confusions about the definition of liberty in an ever more fragmented society.[7]

The president's role gained some strength from the growing stability and coherence of the two dominant political parties, one of which he served as nominal chieftain. These organizations before 1860 had amounted to coalitions tightened every four years for campaign purposes, with the nominee often the only effective element of unity, and if successful the custodian of the cement of patronage. The limited tasks of the federal government then made it a minor partner in expanding the freedoms exercised by American citizens. Expansions in the ability to act emanated from below, generated by local movements and communal organizations. Nationwide political forces had only a tenuous impact on individual liberties.

The feeble antebellum parties collapsed in the 1850s. Desertions from both mounted after the Kansas-Nebraska Act (1854) repealed the Missouri Compromise of 1820 and ended the era of wishful thinking. Old "union-saving" orators like Edward Everett and Thomas H. Benton went unheeded. Northerners confronted the reality: slavery aggressively sought room for expansion. Americans would either have to live with the institution permanently or take steps to limit its spread. A house divided could not stand; the nation would become all slave or all free, and fidelity to the purposes of the Republic required aim at ultimate freedom. Yet when the Dred Scott decision (1858) incorporated bondage into the Constitution, killing the concept of squatter sovereignty, it left citizens helpless to keep a territory free by law. The lack of cohesive national political organizations capable of mustering widespread support complicated the approaching crisis. No party could unite the nation. The ensuing battle resulted from the inability of the political system to adjust peacefully to the slavery issue.[8]

Neither the North nor the South would accept the status quo of 1858. Expansionist slaveholders eyed Cuba and some demanded repeal of the law forbidding slave imports, for the rising price of field hands stimulated smuggling. A commercial convention in Vicksburg pointed out that it made no sense to bar additions to the stock from Africa and the West Indies in view of the legality of the domestic commerce in bondsmen and bondswomen. The Northern conception of liberty superimposed upon an unwilling South tended to obliterate its own definition of the term. Meanwhile Hinton R. Helper expressed the poor whites' hostility to blacks while calling for elimination of the plantation system.[9]

Northerners, too, refused to compromise since a growing consensus on the meanings of liberty excluded human bondage of any sort. New definitions of civility, human nature, political status, and society enlarged the meaning of the term and applied it to ever wider segments of the population. In some states personal liberty laws obstructed the return of fugitive slaves. Abolitionist activity mounted and audiences became more receptive as widened values theretofore private crept into the public realm. Women, ever more vocal in charitable and semipolitical organizations, gave broader social overtones to such notions as personal justice, fairness, and tolerance, previously articulated at home. Their willingness to act, by extralegal means if necessary, inhibited efforts at compromise.

On October 16, 1859, John Brown crossed the line to open violence. The old man, maddened by warfare with the slaveholders in Kansas, heard a call to lead an uprising. Some respectable abolitionists encouraged him in the scheme to seize the federal arsenal at Harpers Ferry, Virginia. The plot aroused concern in the border South, but led only to the gallows.

> Weird John Brown
> Hanging from the beam,
> The anguish hidden in the cap.
>
> So the future veiled its face.

> But in the streaming beard
> Is shown the portent.
> The meteor of war.

Some observers then concluded armed struggle was inevitable.[10]

The Democrats, holding national power, survived at least in name, but Whig organizations disintegrated, while less stable groupings briefly took form, none capable of coping with such new issues as temperance and public education. Puzzled Americans, dismayed by the threats to union, made scapegoats of the foreigners and particularly of militant Catholics. Secret national associations appeared. Father Gavazzi, an apostate Barnabite monk, and other antipopery preachers harangued street-corner crowds, and the arrival (1854) of the papal nuncio Gaetano Bedini touched off insults, mobs, assassination threats. In Cincinnati, a parade of two thousand, carrying transparencies inscribed "No priests, no kings, no popery, down with Bedini," ended in a fight with the police. The Order of the Star-Spangled Banner, known as the Know-Nothings, demanded a longer naturalization period and limits on the voting rights of the foreign-born who insolently aspired to devise plans to improve American liberty "into the likeness of the bloody and drunken dream of French and German liberty." Their heritage of civil discord disturbed the sedate and moderate conduct of American politics. The attractiveness of undercover agitation showed a turn of the political system against inclusiveness, replaced by underhandedness and secrecy. Not all were born to govern. To salvage republican liberty, the Know-Nothings vociferously sought to restrict it. The American party, an arm of the movement, in 1854 acquired substantial representation in Congress. To counter criticism that it possessed "about as many elements of persistence as an anti-cholera or anti-potato rot party would have," its leaders defined its position as "anti-Romanism, anti-Bedinism, anti-Papistalism, anti-Nunnerism, anti-Winking Virginianism, anti-Jesuitism," but also for "light, liberty, education, and absolute freedom of conscience, with a strong dash of devotion to one's native soil." The brief Know-Nothing prominence reflected the realignment process that would stretch through the war to 1868.[11]

Private, purely voluntary associations, unrecognized by law, extraconstitutional and responsible only to their own members, the parties struggled to develop coherent and consistent positions. In the short-lived American party, nativism papered over opposing views, balancing "the fanatics of freedom and the fanatics of slavery, disorganizers and disunionists both," defending a political system no longer responsive to popular demands or faithful to its traditions. New England abolitionists and reformers joined the Know-Nothing ranks in reaction to the region's most numerous immigrants, the Irish proslavery Democrats. In the South, by contrast, the movement attracted elements disturbed by the abolitionist sympathies of the German immigrants. In the middle states, the party drew people tired of agitation and eager for neutrality on divisive issues. Everywhere its supporters argued that small men, mousing politicians, had crept into power while election "degenerated from an open inquest for the opinion of the people to the simple question of who shall have the offices." In 1855, when sectional representatives assembled for the first time in national convention, discrepancies in ultimate objectives splintered, then destroyed the organization, which survived in the South and in some middle states only as a rallying point for unionism. Like hyenas, the Know-Nothings went forth in quest of dead bodies upon which to prey. The old party system had simply expired.[12]

New groupings emerged in the 1850s but developed fully after the Civil War against a background of sharp divisions about the future of the old Confederacy. By secession, the South had asserted its separate identity and its own definition of liberty. It had vainly attempted to develop its own nationality, with slavery its cornerstone; its intellectuals rejected the traditional Northern symbols of the hickory pole and the log cabin, seeking to defend the most fundamental beliefs of society in a nation where "none but an Arch demagogue could exercise power for even a limited time." Emancipation and defeat did not efface Southern distinctiveness. Indeed, sectional fissures deepened and profoundly affected political alignments, while liberty as the ability to act remained bound to skin color.[13]

The modern parties—Democratic and Republican—were neither homogeneous nor descended directly from those of the 1840s. The old Democrats had held the advantage of command of office in the 1850s and of Southern dominance, while the opposition had defined itself at most by a cautious commitment to free soil. But after 1861 war gave the Grand Old Party coherence and membership loyalty against opponents who favored reconciliation with the seceded states, while the Democrats, who had entered the war splintered, emerged after 1865 in better shape than before. The intense and stable partisanship, reflected in rising popular involvement, gained strength in the Northern states from religious and ethnic affiliations, in the South from race. In pace with population growth, voter turnout rose steadily until the mid-1890s, reflecting the newly created political dimensions of liberty.[14]

Hostile observers who commented on American political failings misunderstood the changes after 1850. Henry Adams, the grandson and great-grandson of presidents, concluded his novel *Democracy* (published anonymously in 1880) with resignation; past hopes had proven illusory, and moral regression paralleled material progress. Foreigners, no longer impressed with local institutions as de Tocqueville had been, noted more deficiencies than virtues. Local radicals like Victoria Woodhull found no mitigating circumstances in a rigid system that kept Democrats always Democrats. "Like the hard shell Baptists, you always know where to find them"—while the hard-core Republicans would always carry "the loaves and eat the fishes." A thoughtful young American professor in 1885 expressed a decided preference for the British parliamentary system, apparently more representative and more efficient than the government of his own country. In 1920, a prominent public man asked, "Is America Worth Saving?"[15]

Such critics focused on the recurring cycle of presidential elections— rituals that seemed to settle nothing and that failed to restrain widespread corruption, administrative failures, weak government, unregulated economic growth, greed and rapacity. But however valid these judgments, they obscured the parties' more important function—that of representing their members, serving as channels of communication between the governed and the government, and expressing politically the complex meanings of liberty. Party responsibility compelled officeholders at every level to take account of popular needs. Conceding that new congressmen lacked the intellect and scholarship of Edward Everett and Robert C. Winthrop, the editorialist insisted (1856) that Henry Wilson and Nathaniel P. Banks possessed qualities far better for the practical statesman in a day of progress in a less hierarchical society. Hearts that beat in unison with popular sympathies and responded to the calls of liberty and humanity offset any tendency to rigidity in class alignments.[16]

The postwar settlement hardened the two-party alignment. The military urgency that justified extreme measures in violation of liberty ended at Appomattox; but troops continued to occupy some Southern states until 1876, raising questions about the rights of residents, whether as citizens or as humans. Newly revealed tensions then called for redefinition of the ability to act. And traces of federal power persisted thereafter, making the central government a crucial participant in the struggle. The Thirteenth Amendment prohibited slavery or involuntary servitude except as punishment for a crime. The Fourteenth made all persons born or naturalized in the United States citizens of the United States and of the states in which they resided. No state could abridge their privileges or immunities or deprive any of life, liberty, or property without due process of law. No one could assume the debts of the Confederate states, and no rebel could hold office unless Congress by a two-thirds vote in each house removed the disability. The Fifteenth Amendment forbade denial of the right to vote on account of race, color, or previous condition of servitude.

These ringing assertions of principle aimed forever to safeguard the new meanings of liberty. But the import remained unclear, and not only for blacks. The Fifteenth Amendment, for instance, implied to a few radical souls, like Victoria Woodhull, that women as citizens already possessed the suffrage and needed only congressional guarantees for its exercise. For the time being, however, the effect of the amendments remained potential rather than actual, staying in abeyance for significant portions of the population.

Meanwhile, although the structure of government in place did not change for a half century, its operations depended ever more on the two-party system. Politics, said one of its foremost practitioners, was mostly pill-taking, by which he meant that loyalty often required swallows of the unsavory for higher ends. In that context, the party system became one of the crucial mechanisms of freedom, fixing the bounds between law and liberty so that the citizens would respect the rules while retaining the ability to act.[17]

After 1868, some presidents gained strength from their positions as nominal party leaders. Although Cleveland, Roosevelt, and Wilson did not come up from the ranks and occasionally expressed hostility to the machines, they, like other chief executives, used patronage to make their wills felt, unaffected by fledgling attempts at civil service reform. Garfield's appointment list read like the forty-second Regiment's muster roll or a Hiram class reunion, while Chester Arthur filled almost all vacancies with Stalwarts. Benjamin Harrison as senator helped his father-in-law, the Reverend John W. Scott, become a clerk in the mail division of the Pension Office, which paid more than his professional position as pastor, professor, or college president and which he resigned on Harrison's move to the White House. The number of positions at the victor's disposal grew steadily and provided channels for influence on the Congress, occasionally also for enlisting people who would otherwise have remained in private life.[18]

Though in time the parties developed traditions and myths, their ideologies remained flexible. Neither past nor future issues evoked commitment. The trauma of Reconstruction demonstrated to most people the futility of radical reform efforts; and while expansion continued, government remained largely passive, expecting private enterprise and free market mechanisms to lead. Moreover, the intrusion of racist and imperialist thought toward the end of the century raised other questions about citizenship and about the efficacy of political action. The parties became instruments not of decision but of compromise, their leaders, as in the past, intermediaries for softening sectional and group differences. "The crowding and complications of modern life" enormously increased the interdependence that required parties to adjust interests and needs.[19]

Party strength expanded with the growing influence of partisan newspapers and committed editors—among them Samuel Bowles of *The Springfield Republican,* Murat Halstead of *The Cincinnati Commercial,* Henry "Marse" Watterson of *The Louisville Courier-Journal,* Horace White of *The Chicago Tribune, The Quadrilateral* (supporters all of Liberal Republicans), and Horace Greeley of *The New York Tribune,* most often supporter of himself. In addition Edwin L. Godkin, civil service reformer and later advocate of "little America," founder of *The Nation,* commented vigorously. Then, too, individual journalists eagerly sought the prominence of political roles, an effort that produced tensions at *Harper's Weekly* between the cartoonist Thomas Nast and George William Curtis, its editor. So, too, William S. Bowen of the New York *World* launched an attack on Pennsylvania's Boss Quay in 1890. And in the same year that Greeley ran for office (1872), Victoria Woodhull, founder and coeditor of the *Woodhull and Claflin's Weekly,* became the first woman officially to seek the presidency (as well as the publisher of the first American translation of the *Communist Manifesto*). Scandal of any sort increased circulations; Joseph Pulitzer's *New York World* gained attention for a sensational headline, "How Babies Are Baked," above an article about 392 children who died during a heat wave. But though many publishers believed with James Gordon Bennett that "the newspaper's function is not to instruct but to startle," few could match the sexual innuendo of the *Police Gazette:*

SNARED BY A SCOUNDREL

AN INNOCENT COUNTRY BEAUTY, ON HER
TRAVELS, ENCOUNTERS HER FATE
IN AN ADVENTURER

OF THE WORST TYPE

HIS EASY CONQUEST OF THE UNSOPHISTI-
CATED GIRL THROUGH A GRAND BUT
DIAPHANOUS YARN,

AND HER SUBSEQUENT SAD FATE.

Politics provided a means almost as efficient as scandal for diffusing the massive editions modern printing technology churned out. No one quite matched William Randolph Hearst, who suggested the purchase of a big English steamer; sunk in the Suez Canal it could prevent the Spanish from sending fleet reinforcements to the Philippines. Thus practical patriotism combined with advertising. Domestic politics offered journalists juicy material in plenty. "Ivribody is inthrested in what ivrybody else is doin' that's wrong, that's what makes th' newspapers," said Mr. Dooley.[20]

Improved communications and rising literacy enabled national leaders to offset local influences and cement party loyalties even before the Civil War, and more so thereafter. Early concern about the impact of news wire services grew with the spread of the Associated Press network. The rival United Press founded in 1882 reflected dissatisfaction with an agency widely regarded as under eastern domination. Neither had a reputation for accuracy. Nor, in general, did the press, which seemed to visitors to subsist on invented stories, prying reporters, and an overtime libel department. Upton Sinclair complained in *The Brass Check* (1920) that American newspapers served as tools of plutocracy and of government oppressors bent on suppressing dissent and on depriving citizens of rightful information. E. L. Godkin believed by contrast that the newspapers, in alliance with the politicians, made war on the rational businessmen, in response to demands from an immense ignorant democracy eager to use its enormous power in brutal fashion without knowing how to do it (1895). The radical and the mandarin both erred—out of touch with the country, they presumed they knew. Neither appreciated the inner strength of the political system they derided, or the cohesive forces that tied society together. Voters, often unpersuaded by the printed word, relied on trusted leaders to help distinguish camouflaged propaganda from truth; or else, in fits of fury and bursts of indignation and rage at the appearance of invisible government, threw all the rascals out.[21]

Unwilling to alienate any sizeable bloc, politicians shied away from bold ideological positions and from espousal of particular causes, even in 1896 when the outcome depended "on whether most iv th' voters [were] . . . tired out or on'y a little tired." In every election, therefore, Democrats and Republicans shared the ballot with independent candidates who expounded specific reform ideas or voiced the complaints of the aggrieved. Occasionally such insurgents gained local, state, and even congressional offices. But their organizations lacked continuity and rested on a basis too narrow to attain national power. They drew attention to divisive issues but did not affect two-party control. Writing from experience, in 1914, Theodore Roosevelt noted the partisan loyalty of the average American, who voted with the opposition when angry with his own side but joined a third party only for temporary and local reasons. The good old, grand old, organization never died. "I've gone to sleep nights wondhrin where I'd throw away me vote," Mr. Dooley reported, but in the end "that crazy headed ol' loon iv a party with its hair sthreamin' in its eyes an' an axe in its hand, chasin raypublicans into th' tall grass" always came back. 'Twas never so good as when respectable people spoke of it in whispers and when it had only "one principal, to go in an' take it away fr'm th' other fellows."[22]

The rivalry of natives and of the foreign-born in 1854 briefly sustained the American, or Know-Nothing, party; the Labor Reform party (1872) called for a national circulating medium issued not by banks but by the government; the California Workingmen's party, led by Denis Kearney (1877), denounced the outrages of capitalism and favored Chinese exclusion, the abolition of contract labor in prisons, assessments on wealth, regulation of railroad and telegraph companies, an eight-hour day for labor employed by or for the government, and other "immortal issues, now dead." Greenback, nativist, and Prohibitionist candidates, along with a secret anti-Catholic, antiforeign "Order of the American Alliance," complicated the election of 1876; and later Populists, Socialists, and Progressives edged close to significant voting strength, rarely decisively. Once they split with Daniel De Leon's ideologists, the Socialists eventually gained control of thirty-three cities and towns, occasionally elected a member of Congress from New York or Wisconsin, but they functioned best when articulating a reformist program that aimed at immediate betterment of people's lives. The need to attract middle-of-the-road votes pulled the party toward the center. In 1856, 1860, and 1912, over a fifth of the electorate abandoned the two major parties, thereby broadening the ability to act by registering disgust with existing alternatives and opting for novel programs. In an extreme case, revulsion from the prevailing system led California Progressives to the idea of abolishing it through nonpartisan elections. The result temporarily weakened but never uprooted the state's two-party structure. Representing limited constituencies, insurgent groups lacked staying power and never even held the balance of power.[23]

Politics hardly absorbed the total attention of the populace. Portentous though the outcome of the election of 1860 would be, excitement about the Heenan and Sayers fight, between the respective pugilistic champions of the United States and England, eclipsed interest in the convention that chose the Democratic nominee, just as the visit of the Prince of Wales overshadowed earlier debates. But in time, when fully developed, parties mobilized and informed the electorate by offering it a choice of alternative candidates, rituals, slogans, and mythologies. Altogether apart from the issues, the drama of the contest sustained interest. The preliminary, tentative efforts of favorite sons elaborated in the press led to the excitement of the nominating convention, which soon acquired its own ritual. Candidates' appearances counted heavily—James A. Garfield's imposing stature and full beard lent authority to his emotional statements and inspired the confidence of religious people, particularly of those who did not know him personally. Youthful poverty, log cabin background, military record, effaced any hints of scandal. Pamphlets with titles like *From the Log Cabin to the White House* and *From the Tow Path to the White House,* and Horatio Alger's *From Canal Boy to President,* deluged the public in support of Garfield's presidential ambitions in 1880. Gone was the standard of other days, that the office should seek the modest, diffident man. Extended campaigns included Southern barbecues and New England clambakes, flag raisings, and monster rallies, gaslight parades, brass bands, tub-thumping oratory, and candidates flitting about by railroad. Impassioned Republicans waved the bloody shirt after the manner of Robert G. Ingersoll, whose plumed knight marched down the halls of the Congress and threw his shining lance full and fair against the brazen foreheads of the defamers of his country. In time, Democrats echoed the heart-rending phrases of the "Cross of Gold" after the manner of William J. Bryan. Voters swept up in the excitement of appeals for the Grand Old Party or the Lost Cause went to the polls in growing numbers, giving fresh meaning to the concept of consent.[24]

Contending for office, Democrats and Republicans cast the widest possible nets in quest of support from among the sectional and ethnic groupings in the electorate. Already in 1858, Chicago Scandinavian Republicans met in caucus; and in 1860 a "foreign department" in the Republican party's national committee sought to mobilize German-American voters and encouraged the political assimilation of newcomers. Those efforts never abated.[25]

The campaigns generated excitement quite disproportionate to their importance, since the contests almost everywhere became largely formal. Eighteen states in presidential elections always voted Republican and fourteen always Democratic. A Republican campaigning in Texas, Mr. Dooley suggested, better be an active sprinter. South Carolina, Florida, and Louisiana deviated only in 1876 while Reconstruction regimes held power; thereafter they remained safely Democratic. On election day, said Mr. Dooley, "th' people iv this grreat counthry gather at th' varyous temples iv liberty in barber shops an' livery stables an' indicate their choice iv evils. A grreat hush falls on the land as th' public pours out iv the side dure iv the saloons an' reverently gathers at th' newspaper offices to await with bated breath th' thrillin' news . . . an thin again we heard the old but niver tiresome story 'Texas give a Dimmycrat majority iv five hundred thousan' but will reopen th' polls if more is nicessry: the Dimmycrats hope, if th' prisint ratio is maintained, th' Raypublican victory in pinnsylvania will not be unanimous." Only in five states—Connecticut, New York, Indiana, Nevada, and California—were the rival parties so evenly matched that their electoral vote might swing to one side or the other. Shrewd operators like Matt Quay of Pennsylvania understood that the outcome of every contest turned on minor shifts in a very few places. Hence the importance of the national committees to coordinate organizational and financial efforts and to fry the fat by levying on contractors and on civil servants until the Pendleton Act (1883) halted the practice.[26]

Regional and ethnic differences as well as divergent economic interests and intellectual convictions cemented party loyalties. By and large, white Southerners' Democratic allegiance practically eliminated the opposition, once the freedmen lost the suffrage. Confederate precedents, memories of the Lost Cause, recollections of the nightmare of Reconstruction, relief that it had not been worse, and fears of uncontrollable blacks kept the region monolithic and loyal to its own definition of liberty. Irish Americans and German Catholics, North and South, voted Democratic also, partly because of prewar loyalties, partly out of mistrust of Republican impulses to control behavior, derived from Free-Soil antecedents, and from the powerful Yankee constituency that dragged the GOP toward temperance, Sabbath legislation, antipopery, and hostility to parochial schools. Where blacks could vote, they tended to choose the party of Lincoln, as did Protestants who sought temperance laws, protection of the Sabbath, and support of secular public education. The emotions such issues stirred developed cohesive behavior.[27]

National parties in the United States, never monolithic as in some European democracies like Britain, represented no single class interest and espoused no uniform ideology. Instead, the leaders acted by reconciling divergent groupings for support. Garfield thus sought the cooperation of Indiana Greenbackers whom he privately regarded as dangerous anarchists. Politicians edged gingerly toward change, but by persuasion. And from back in 1860 the "wire pulling gentry" cautiously manipulated primary meetings and caucuses that swayed large blocs of votes.[28]

Nevertheless, through the party network, the president could make and execute decisions, sometimes overriding or circumventing constitutional restraints. Cooperation with the Senate, which confirmed appointments and shared the patronage, and with the House of Representatives, called for compromises with, or conciliation of, potential opponents, with local congressional perspectives balancing the national view from the White House in policy as well as in patronage. The party became the mediating instrument. Some observers considered the cabinet "an asylum for aged and indigent politicians," a gathering of fossils "rarely found this side of the tombs of Egypt" (1857). But time made its utility clear after Presidents Johnson and Grant learned the danger of offending congressional oligarchs. Cabinet members then served not so much as administrators of departments, but as influential expeditors, arrangement agents, in collaboration with a few senators or representatives, sometimes through promises of patronage, sometimes through the exchange of favors, sometimes through corruption—if not pure, then simple.[29]

Already in the 1850s rumors of bribery floated through Washington; the government's wealth threw "a halo of fascination" about legislation that would gleam ever more brightly in the gilded age. Funds for river and harbor improvements and land grants to railroads, along with construction contracts, replenished the pork in the barrels and lubricated legislative wheels. Virtuous republicanism ebbed away. Public corruption spread through the overpowering influence of lobbies, the increase of public debt and taxes, crime, judicial delays, abuse of gubernatorial pardoning powers, defective juries, and the insecurity of life and property. At a time when "Scientific ideals, speculations, Parisian fraternity, socialism, Fourierism" and similar schemes assaulted the nation, some citizens hoped for salvation at the hands of women, who, though excluded from direct participation, wielded the social balance of power. Corruption, "the disgrace and wickedness of the times," a by-product of the war, but unchecked by peace, placed bargains and intrigues above the country's welfare (1869). The impure atmosphere of his calling emanated from Ratcliffe, a people's politician; the "coarse and animal expression" about his mouth reflected the "code of bad manners and worse morals" of the Senate in which he operated. The House had ceased to be a fit place for a gentleman during the long reign of slavery, when Southerners showed more confidence in the bowie knife and the bludgeon than in argument. A small army of lobbyists stood by, ready to act. Already in 1857 observers noted particularly the strong-minded female birds of passage who worked Willard's, Browns, and the National hotels. The ambivalence toward politics and politicians persisted, influenced by the degree to which complex issues required action—the more complex, the less the ability to resolve them swiftly, the greater the disgust of the public and its contempt for politics.

> ANXIOUS FATHER: If you continue your present course of cowardice and cruelty you will be fit for nothing but a member of Congress.
>
> MOTHER: O don't say that father, you will humiliate the boy.

Periodic bursts of housecleaning made a great deal of noise but evoked general complacency about the dust in the air. "We don't sweep things undher th' sofa," said Mr. Dooley.[30]

Congress retained the powers the Constitution granted it, but neither of its chambers remained the body envisioned in 1787. Membership in both reflected national growth. The ninety-six senators of 1920 could not comport themselves as had the twenty-six of 1791, but operated by increasingly formal and elaborate rules. Set orations, less common than formerly, rarely attracted national attention, and government by speaking declined while ever more power fell to committees. Inexperienced members who lacked the guidance of administrative departments discovered that electability differed from the ability to make informed decisions on complex, highly technical tariff schedules. Not unreasonably, seniority determined assignments to positions of prestige and authority; continuity of service mattered, and until 1916 that depended on solid relationships with the state legislatures which decided who would serve. On the other hand, a six-year term and influence over federal patronage gave the senator some freedom of maneuver and considerable power. Direct popular elections later made little difference in that respect. As before 1850, men of wealth most often served in the Senate, which acquired a convivial, clublike atmosphere, its decisions "governed by narrow political considerations" (1867) and often shaped by widespread apathy and a caucus with informal connections to the White House. The arrangement, explained Elihu Root, preserved liberty—not the liberty under which each grasped all he could, not the liberty of constant rebellion, "but the liberty of order and law, the liberty of individual opportunity and regulated power."[31]

The more volatile House of Representatives also grew in size, reflecting the country's expansion. That body, too, operated through committees; but short terms and popular elections made seniority less important than in the Senate. Already before the Civil War, power drifted toward the Speaker, who knew the members, controlled assignments, and managed the smooth flow of business, applying when needed the lash of caustic tongue and the salve of personal charm and favors. Periodic rebellions challenged the authority of such czars as Thomas B. Reed, Joseph Gurney, Joseph G. Cannon, and Champ Clark of Missouri. But each one displaced simply made room for a successor, very much the same.[32]

In both houses, itchy young newcomers and representatives of aggrieved constituents sometimes banded together in insurgencies, grabbing the headlines back home, troublesome for leaders impatient with vote-seeking chores at endless picnics, fairs, and church suppers. But protests rarely proved effective in the long run. Too cumbersome for informal operations—much of its work dull and politically unrewarding—the Congress depended on party discipline for order. A caucus of the faithful adjusted campaign platforms to reality, defined positions on important issues, and provided a means of communicating between one house and the other and between the legislature and the chief executive. Informal persuasion, the mutuality of one favor for another, and patronage and the pork barrel, generally kept the members in line.[33]

Andrew Johnson's defeat solidified congressional dominance. Honest and devoted to his duties, he insisted on going it alone and revived old fears of the imperial presidency. His limited view of Reconstruction and his poor-white bias blinded him to arguments for black suffrage; and he all too readily forgave his former enemies, the planters. His obstinacy evoked mounting opposition in Congress, cut away the grounds of the middle position, and made radicalism the only alternative to the status quo. Having failed to attach himself to a party, he could not stave off congressional "efforts to invade and destroy the executive department of the Government" through the Command of the Army and Tenure of Office acts. Though the effort to oust him failed, the House impeachment managers took his acquittal with poor grace and sniffed about for hints of bribery to account for the Senate's failure to convict. The prerogatives the Congress then asserted expanded its powers as against the president to an extent that would have troubled the founders, fearful of legislative tyranny. From the Committee on the Conduct of the War to the Pujo and Dillingham committees, congressional investigations became instruments for shaping policy. Unhampered by the limitations that bound the judiciary, disregarding the Bill of Rights, and wielding the weapon of exposure to sway public opinion, these legislative bodies exerted a widespread influence that explained Woodrow Wilson's complaints about congressional government. However, he exaggerated. Often the party in control of one house did not control the other; and by judicious manipulation, the president could sustain and even expand the influence of his office.[34]

Consent of the governed had come to mean popular participation in the electoral contest, by which the victors controlled the machinery to rule the country—within limits. But unlike in Europe, where an electoral victory gave a majority total power, in the United States success remained conditional upon a continuing process of approval and adaptation. The checks and balances on the exercise of absolute power usually prevented the government from absolutely suppressing any dissent on the pretext of defending the citizen's capacity to act. The ability to extend the benefits of freedom hinged upon the system's incapacity to deny it to anyone except during the ugly interlude of war. Speaker Joseph G. Cannon considered this arrangement the fulfillment of the teachings of Jesus, "the greatest political teacher the world has ever known." "It is the voice of the people at the fireside that rules. It is the people who rule themselves and govern the nation."[35]

The federal judiciary, though constitutionally independent, did not remain outside the political process, particularly after the Supreme Court's loss of authority as a result of the Dred Scott decision, which affected liberty in a fashion opposite to that the chief justice intended.

The case, litigated for ten years, could have been adjudicated in 1856 without a broad consideration of the meaning of slavery. Instead, the court sought to resolve the nation's political dilemma by examining the right of Congress to exclude bondage from the territories. President Buchanan's inaugural address (March 4, 1857) had optimistically noted that a ruling would shortly take the issue out of politics. The verdict delivered two days later roused passions North and South to new heights.

Chief Justice Roger B. Taney spoke for the majority in declaring Dred Scott forever a slave, holding Scott ineligible to sue because blacks were not citizens of the United States and therefore lacked the rights attached to that status—procedural grounds sufficient to dismiss the case. But the chief justice did not leave the matter there, and addressed the conjectural question: had Scott had a right to sue, what would have been the effect of his residence in territory from which Congress had excluded bondage? The opinion, an *obiter dictum* that exceeded the case at hand, held unconstitutional the Missouri Compromise and therefore any other law to limit the spread of slavery, for Congress had no right to deprive a citizen of any type of property without the due process of law guaranteed by the Fifth Amendment. Taney's tortuous course in arriving at this conclusion began with an assertion beyond dispute. Any measure that arbitrarily freed a slave, unconstitutionally deprived the master of his property, as would an act involving a horse or any other chattel. But in prohibiting bondage within territory under its jurisdiction by a general law, Congress professed to act not arbitrarily but by that due process to which the Constitution referred. Taney held such legislation unconstitutional, though not capricious; *due process* in his view referred not merely to procedures but also to substance, invalidating any measure, arbitrary or not, that diminished a master's right to enjoy his property.

Far from placing slavery beyond political contention, the decision ignited further controversy. The Northern press and pulpit condemned the "barbarous and unchristian" ruling in favor of the slave oligarchy; some states pointedly disregarded it; and Lincoln's First Inaugural denied that such rulings formed precedents for other cases or irrevocably fixed the answers to questions affecting the whole people.[36]

The case diminished the Supreme Court's authority. The Fourteenth Amendment overrode Taney's view of citizenship. More generally, the decision discredited use of judicial power to decide political matters. Judges played no part in the constitutional crisis of secession and thereafter attempted to stay clear of politics, reminded of the limits to their authority by repeated efforts to provide for popular review of judicial decisions.[37]

The *Dred Scott* case had also asserted the Court's right to declare acts of Congress unconstitutional, but judges after the Civil War claimed that power only cautiously. The Supreme Court under Justice Melville W. Fuller more frequently overturned state laws enlarging police power. More troubling, Taney's doctrine of due process became an important weapon for the assertion of substantive as well as procedural property rights, a trend that sustained the sanctity of private contracts and limited the government's regulatory and tax powers. The small but influential corps of lawyers with a particular stake in business issues approved. The Court did not, however, extend the concept of due process to other liberties—of speech, the press, and religion, for instance.

The federal judiciary attained a privileged position somewhat apart from politics and quite distinct from the state and local tribunals in which citizens usually encountered the law. Ever less often did United States judges come up through playing the party game. Remote, unobtrusive, insulated by the dignified austerity of their proceedings, they escaped contact with the voters, who did not yet regard them as bulwarks of liberty.[38]

*

The parties—voluntary associations unrecognized by law—only imperfectly coordinated the acts of the executive, legislative, and judicial branches. Federal power therefore expanded spasmodically, unpredictably, and uncertainly under the impact of Civil War and Reconstruction. Before 1861, the national government had shied away from measures not explicitly enumerated in the Constitution. Just as it had refrained from implementing President John Quincy Adams's ambitious plans, so it long refused even to establish a uniform time system, leaving the task to the Harvard College Observatory. So, too, an aversion to subsidies involving value judgments frustrated the effort to reward William T. G. Morton, the inventor of ether. On the other hand, it had supported scientific exploratory expeditions and had sponsored western military and post roads.

Combat compelled the Union to act affirmatively despite the Constitutional silence on such issues as the war powers, insurrection, confiscation of rebel property, and personal liberty. The evil of secession had followed from excessive states' rights and called for strengthened national government in the future. "The policy of this country," declared the chairman of the Senate Finance Committee, "ought to be to make everything national as far as possible."

Disregarding Revolutionary experience with the continentals, the Union issued greenbacks (1862), paper money declared legal tender; and the Confederacy depended even more on the printing press. Both currencies depreciated rapidly in value. The subsequent inflation raised prices, generating hardship when incomes lagged behind costs. Meanwhile the protectionist Tariff Act of 1861 established a basic policy that endured with brief interruptions for more than a half century. Other positive measures followed, whether directly related to the war or not. The land grant for the construction of the Illinois Central Railroad became a precedent for similar benefactions to the transcontinentals after 1862. Generally, in return for undertaking to complete their roads in ten or twelve years, the corporations received a specified number of sections along their rights of way. The Homestead Act of 1862 aimed to stimulate western settlement by giving any citizen a hundred and sixty acres without charge if he cultivated it for five years. The Morrill Act the same year granted substantial tracts to help state agricultural and mechanical colleges. The Banking Laws of 1863 and 1865 taxed the notes of state institutions out of existence and created a national system. These and other expanded federal powers proved permanent, though they did not amount to the centralization Joel Parker and Lord Bryce thought they perceived.

Nor did they give the central government a directing social or economic role.[39]

The military urgency that justified extreme measures ended at Appomattox; but troops occupied some Southern states until 1876 and federal power did not fade away at once. For more than a decade, Reconstruction policy widened Washington's scope of action. The Republican radicals, driven by humanitarian "striving to establish universal equality and individual liberty, without conventional rules, and regardless of constitutional freedom and constitutional restraints and limitation," did not scruple to trample on the rights secured by the organic law (1867). In the name of liberty, Democrats tended to resist. The issue therefore enabled the two parties to seek votes by formulating positions to guide the conduct of government. Their attitudes in the postwar era colored their long-range approaches to individual security and the citizens' ability to act. Southern resistance to Northern dictates and state efforts to hinder commands emanating from Washington, by shaping Republican and Democratic visions of the future, affected everyone but especially blacks.

Even moderate Northerners considered the South a conquered province and sought a thoroughgoing reconstruction of its society, by governmental authority inconceivable within the former parameters of state and national constitutions. Emancipation alone would not liberate the slaves. Without federal assistance, the freed men and women would relapse into dependence. Reconstruction demanded not a return to the status quo of 1860 but a program of rebuilding through education and welfare. That objective required the victorious Union to *"remain the absolute Dictator of the Republic until the spirit of the North"* became the spirit of the whole country (1865).[40]

Other Republicans thought of Reconstruction in purely political terms. Their party would not have even a toehold in the South should the rebel states return unrepentant. Moreover, that region would enjoy increased congressional representation, since, in apportionment according to population, the freed slaves would count as full rather than as three-fifths persons. Without a guarantee of black suffrage, the augmented block of Democrats would dominate the whole nation. The freedmen deserved the ballot, as others did, and their gratitude to the Republican Party would counterbalance Democratic influence. Only two-party rivalry could guarantee the spread southward of Northern definitions of liberty to offset Southern perceptions, which survived the demise of slavery and which gained strength from the problems of absorbing the blacks in a new status.

Passion infused these positions. The war, enormously expensive in dollars, in the toll of dead and wounded, in wrecked lives, must have had some purpose! People who had grown up in the optimistic midcentury decades, who believed in progress and in human perfectibility, could not accept the brutality of conflict without faith that some good would result in the form of redemption of the society from which the evil had sprung. The North defined that good as the stability of a free society. The South had yet to articulate its position once its organic and hierarchical social vision, based on enslaved labor and color lines, blurred.

The Democrats and other opponents of radical policies feared the effects of centralization upon personal liberty and upon regional and cultural diversity. However much good the Yankee schoolmarm might do, the twang of her accent and her straitlaced morality found no more welcome in Kentucky than in Alabama. The failure of efforts to remake the South narrowed federal power, which operated after 1876 by compromise rather than by principled policy. It also assured unreconstructed Southerners of their ability to salvage features of their older vision.[41]

Revelations of widespread corruption during the great barbecue diminished zeal for expanding the scope of the national government. Benevolent agencies like the Indian Bureau proved as exposed to graft as railroad construction companies. Better not expand—and besides, What for? The nation no longer pursued goals of its own. As the sense of communal purpose faded, the federal government gave up efforts to chart a consistent direction and contented itself with mediating among rival groups, interceding only to regulate the contest fought out in adversary proceedings by rival lawyers. Happily, a tiny military establishment kept the tax rate low, financed largely from the proceeds of the protective tariff, Washington's finest contribution to the public welfare. The political parties had armed government with the ability to act but had not supplied it an agenda, which would only emerge toward the end of the century through the pressure of outsiders.

Reformers who clung to the faith that law and administrative control could produce human improvement actively sought to enlarge political power. Using old slogans of benevolence and progress, they looked for new types of legislation to broaden authority and multiply functions. Undaunted by Reconstruction failures, they ignored its painful reminders of the limitations of force in efforts to transmute deeply ingrained values and forms of behavior. Increasingly, Henry George, Edward Bellamy, Lester Ward, and the social gospel movement advocated government action to strengthen the social order. "The publicists tell us we are governed too much, but the people are demanding more government, and, in obedience to this demand, law making bodies are rapidly extending the scope of the law." In response, an array of regulatory agencies and new departments appeared, each with its bureaucracy. A vast potential for federal action once demonstrated in war remained in abeyance until 1917, when it surfaced again. Soon Mr. Dooley looked nostalgically back to the days when "the on'y pollytics" that interested an American citizen was "wh's goin' to be ilicted asissor an' how much an' whin."[42]

The growth of federal power did not diminish the scope of action of the state and local governments. On the contrary, those jurisdictions also gained vigor. The old states' rights theories did fade away, their last monument two ponderous tomes by Alexander H. Stephens, Confederate vice president, who urged his countrymen to avoid the centralization of Asian empires and cling to the loose federation of the Greek democracies to preserve constitutional liberty, "the birthright of every American." Stephens had opposed the annexation of Mexican territories, conscription, martial law, the suspension of habeas corpus, and impressment. Americans did not heed his advice. So, too, Calhoun's claim that the South formed a distinct political entity with a character and interest different from those of other parts of the nation died on the field of battle. But the outcome did not create a homogeneous country with a unitary government. The states retained and, indeed, sometimes actually increased their power.[43]

The constitutional question raised by Reconstruction—how the seceded states could reenter the Union—concealed a deeper theoretical problem, since usually adequate population formed the only test of eligibility. Rebellion created difficulties. The Northern position of 1861 had denied any right to revolution or secession; since the rebel states had never left the Union, they could at once resume their places, and their leaders could return to positions of authority. On the other hand, by the Southern logic, the states had the power to break away; conquered, they lay in 1865 at the victors' disposal.[44]

Events proved the logic of 1861 irrelevant. Developing realities shaped the actual settlement. The Constitution had made no provision for this contingency, and Lincoln considered speculation in legal terms a pernicious abstraction. In December 1863, he proposed a plan to restore civil government in places already held by the Union. Except for high Confederate officials, rebels who took an oath of loyalty would receive an amnesty. When their number reached ten percent of the voters of 1860, they could form legitimate state governments. However, when Louisiana and Arkansas did so, the Congress rejected their representatives, arguing that the conquered areas formed territories subject like any others to legislative control. In July 1864, Lincoln vetoed a bill asserting this proposition, hoping thus to win over the Southern masses and sap their will to resist. The people themselves would determine the as yet unpredictable status of the blacks.[45]

Harsh congressional Reconstruction measures exacerbated sectional bitterness. But except for West Virginia, the old Confederate states retained their boundaries and characters. Northern radicals made no effort, as had their counterparts in France, Germany, or Italy, to redraw provincial lines in the interest of a stronger central government.

The American system remained federal in a distinctive sense, never as centralized as France or England, which made all important decisions in a single capital, Paris or London, but yet not feudal, with authority completely devolved to the localities. Washington's power grew within limits set by more particular jurisdictions, except to the extent that all responded to party discipline. Power thus fragmented did not readily impinge on individual liberties; yet popular majorities could act as Democrats, Republicans, or Populists, to regulate railroads or rum by mobilizing support across state, federal, and bicameral lines.[46]

Evolving political theories only partially reflected changing realities. No longer could a text assure its readers that a renovating efficacy in the bosoms of the people would remedy any damage to the Constitution (1835). After 1865 emphasis shifted from popular virtue to reverence for authority. Government, not regarded as a necessary evil, deserved respect, obedience, and love.

Societal needs therefore ranked higher than private needs. Few went as far as Charles Nordhoff, whose *Politics for Young Americans* (1876) presented a republican version of Christian teachings. Jesus condemned "self-seeking, covetousness, hypocrisy, class distinctions, envy, malice, undue and ignoble ambition," and he inculcated "self-restraint, repression of the lower and meaner passions, love to the neighbor, contentment, gentleness, regard for the rights and happiness of others and respect for law." Nordhoff therefore wished politics in a free state to deal "in the largest sense with the liberty and the prosperity of the people" and warned against legislative bodies' overstepping the limits of their power, also against an electorate tired of its duties. He viewed government not as an instrument for the control of human conduct, but as a positive force for good. The founding fathers had erred in mistrusting men and in instituting checks and balances, which had the effect of tying the hands of public servants.[47]

No other enlightened nation, critics complained, failed so lamentably to define and protect the rights of citizens in matters relating to person and property. By 1900 the divided sovereignty of the states and the national government scattered political power, caused internal strife, and demonstrated shortcomings by the numerous dishonest and incompetent officeholders. William R. Harper, president of the University of Chicago (1899), foresaw the need for radical modifications, while foreign scholars like the German Von Holst castigated Americans for their idolatry of the Constitution, thought American political theory vastly less mature than Europeans', considered their officials half-educated mediocrities, and detested the pharisaical self-righteousness which defined politics as a despised trade. Governor Peter H. Burnett of California urged conversion of the states into provinces, the prolongation of the presidential term to twenty years, that of senators for life, a plan echoing that of Moncure D. Conway (1872). John A. Wright defined the American government as "a loathsome disease." Gustave Le Bon analyzed the Pullman strike as a struggle which arrayed intelligence, capacity, and capital on one side, and the terrible army of the unfit on the other. Like others, he assumed that without change, the United States would splinter into rival republics or fall into another gigantic civil war.[48]

Theory could not account for American federalism. The states retained a kind of sovereignty, and indeed their power mounted in the face of social changes untreatable on a country-wide scale. In education, race relations, and the regulation of industry, experience demonstrated the limitations of national solutions. Such matters seemed better left to the states, able to take account of local distinctiveness.[49]

Furthermore, the traumas of Reconstruction left long-remembered wounds. The Southern dream of separate nationhood vanished after the war; but a sense of cultural, social, regional distinctiveness lingered. People elsewhere also cherished their uniqueness. Yankees, midwesterners, mountain folk, and residents of the Pacific coast, lacking "a high public feeling, a large national soul," turned to the states in pursuit of special goals. In a wide, complex country, smaller units proved more effective than larger ones in dealing with complex social and economic problems. Gustave Le Bon noted the "profound divergencies, diverse interests and conflicting tendencies" in a nation without unity or homogeneity. Not until the end of the nineteenth century did impulses from Washington begin to pervade the whole nation. Until then, pressure from conflicting and overlapping sectional, ethnic, and social loyalties, and from clashing ideologies and economic interests, made the political parties instruments for adjustment and compromise.

In addition, bitter popular hostility to privilege immobilized the federal government, which generally avoided positive action in domestic

affairs. Scandal often marked efforts to do more. The divisive consequences of the Kansas-Nebraska Act early showed the danger. Sectional
differences—South against North, West against East, the peripheries
against the core areas—and splits within individual states originated in
localism. Differences in relations to the world economy also played a role;
and ethnic divisions grew in importance after the expansion of the 1850s:
Yankees against Yorkers; in Ohio and Illinois, people from New England
against those from Kentucky. Californians divided over vigilante activities; and the impact of European immigration molded Germans and Irish
into political blocs with configurations that differed from place to place.
The cultural and economic implications of party loyalties militated
against coherent application of state or federal power. In the face of
continuing expansion, therefore, governments simply cleared the way for
individual action.[50]

Rival ideologies, less traceable because long buried in practical issues,
reflected clashes between the impulses to growth on the one hand and
privilege and order on the other. The collapse of the prewar parties
generated new alliances grounded in the problems of slavery and later of
freedmen's rights, eventually forming the Republican party. By contrast,
hostility to temperance and school laws attached many German, Scandinavian, and Irish citizens to the Democratic party. Voters and officeholders alike found all such issues less amenable on the federal level than
in the states closer to the consent of the governed, who preferred to fight
for liberty on home grounds.[51]

States acted often to further development. Maine and Texas used their
domains to aid railroad construction; others lent their credit for the same
purpose. But more generally they aimed to police their citizens' behavior
in response to exposures in the press, pressure from organized groups, and
political agitation for reform. Action of any sort depended, however, on
cooperation among executives, legislatures, and judges set apart by the
conventional separation of powers.

In the state capitals, as in Washington, the governors' ability to do
anything depended upon their roles as party leaders. Few disposed of
much patronage; the good posts required legislative confirmation, and in
some places independent boards of trustees appointed administrators of
state institutions. John Peter Altgeld of Illinois may have exaggerated
when he asked, in 1891, whether any of the nation's forty governors had,
"for ten years, done anything of an enduring character for their country
or for the progress of civilization"; but his own efforts foundered on the
lack of legislative cooperation. The chief executive, not content to act
the ceremonial dispenser of patronage, had to attract public attention

without "a particle of snobbery" in order to keep the legislature in line. The governors could put to some use their power to grant pardons; and the party organization gave them some leverage to transcend the separation of powers.

Having acquired office by election, they could also claim to act as popular spokesmen. Campaign rhetoric encouraged invective to establish ties to the populace; a hyena, a devil, and a coward were among the moderate terms that buttressed gubernatorial party leadership. Under Governor Johnson's prodding, Tennessee first committed state tax revenues to education. But even Benjamin F. Butler of Massachusetts, lawyer, businessman, general, congressman, and presidential aspirant, darling of reformers like Wendell Phillips and Susan B. Anthony, could not translate personal popularity into political clout and failed to get his agenda across in the face of hostile majorities in the state legislature. A disappointed reformer noted the difficulty of changes that clashed with "conventional prejudice or sentiment," under a system of "republican superstitions" that rested upon the authority of the past, the "powerful sanction of immemorial custom," and the timidity, ignorance, or mental indolence of those who submitted to it.[52]

State legislatures controlled the law-making process and the budgets, and disposed of privileges and franchises, all ample sources of corruption. Every year Ohio's "Cornstalk Brigade" descended on Columbus prepared to soak the cities, in the "base struggle for place and plunder." Everyone knew of the line to the Nebraska lawmakers from the hotel room of John M. Therston, Union Pacific attorney. In the "House of Mirth" (Albany, 1908) insurance companies paid off cooperative solons. Away from home and from the oversight of constituents, where the votes did not affect the folks back in the county, they went along with the party leaders' instructions or the suggestions of generous lobbyists. A centennial ode celebrated the "high officials sitting half in sight / To share the plunder and fix things right."[53]

The return to office depended, however, on the local machines. Parties retained their coherence more effectively on the state than on the national level; often old networks of influence persisted for generations, and local big men and big families continued to sway alliances in legislatures and to dominate gubernatorial elections. In Massachusetts, one generation of Quincys after another held office. In New York, the wealthy Arnot brothers gave David Bennett Hill the push that made him governor; and Thomas C. Platt stood behind Frank S. Black both before and after his entry to the executive mansion. Senators Nelson W. Aldrich and H. B. Anthony long ruled Rhode Island through Charles Brayton and other henchmen in Providence. It made no difference, said Elihu Root (1913), what name it bore, whether Fenton or Conkling or Cornell or Arthur or Platt; someone gave the orders, more likely from Broadway than from the capitol in Albany.[54]

In the last analysis, where it counted most, power still depended upon local control. Although demographic and economic changes sometimes upset familiar arrangements, in stable agricultural counties the old neighborhood big men retained their positions, if only out of inertia, and often competently absorbed newcomers who worked in or managed the mills or the mines. Informal pressures supplemented the formal instruments of government. In education or law enforcement, the combination of private and public controls enabled communities to cope with necessities. The sheriff remained in charge; but if things got out of hand, his posse or a group of vigilantes implemented the popular will despite legal technicalities. People could disregard pleadings they did not understand or accept, and could operate by their own standards in pursuit of their own interests. In May 1895, the judge pleaded with the lynching mob to disperse, assuring it that the jury was sure to convict two men charged with rape; but the crowd, fearing that "anarchist governor" John Peter Altgeld would turn the accused loose, stormed the jail and executed its own justice.[55]

At the hub of affairs in hundreds of rural counties stood an intimate circle composed of men in whom their neighbors had confidence—the banker, lawyer, newspaper editor, or enterprising farmer with time for public business. Personal connections counted; Tom Platt, from the corner drugstore in Owego, became the key figure first in Tioga County and then in New York State through the number of people he knew and the tight machine he controlled. Matt Quay from Beaver, Pennsylvania, played a similar role. A context that identified everyone made the purchase of votes unnecessary and usually left little margin for doubt in the award of places or contracts. Corruption generally intruded with reference to outsiders—no harm in mulcting the circus that sought a license. But control was fully as tight as in the great city.[56]

The machines, town and rural, mediated between the people and politics. Fragile links to Washington, the state capital, or city hall provided no substitute for the nearby ward or county boss, who deserved support in return for intercession when needed. The loyal vote betokened the citizen's political influence. Faith that the system opened avenues of approach to power to all, so that anyone could attain high office, softened criticism; politicians did not attack the Senate or the White House, which they might some day enter. The sullen acquiescence of the losers covered hopes of a better day to come.[57]

Localism and federalism sustained the two-party system, which gained strength also when the reformers' Australian ballot permitted a vote for the straight party ticket. No one, however, captured such total control as to eliminate the opposition totally. Grass roots organizations long remained intact even in defeat. The party in the minority, in a national or state election, always retained enough strength to fight another day. Only the South approached a virtual monopoly by one party. In newer areas like Kansas, Nebraska, or Montana, or even in California, recently established lines of authority remained tenuous. In Colorado, for instance, where the importance of federal patronage, aid to railroads, and mining laws kept citizens loyal to the Republicans in the White House, fierce political battles erupted within the party. Such local conflicts frequently broke out at points of social, ethnic, or religious change. The opening of a coal mine in a rural area created a new set of relationships that challenged the existing balance of forces. When the mine owner was the outsider, community pressure allied itself with the laborers. When the workers were immigrants, communal barriers excluded them. Mining activity or the establishment of a factory in the countryside disordered a sector of the population and threatened its welfare. Price fluctuations and economic changes tended to weaken agencies of control, sapping their effectiveness in containing outbreaks.

Local justice differed from that administered in the federal judiciary. Increasingly complex inferior tribunals reached down through various state courts of appeals to trial jurisdictions and to the police courts, which could not keep up with the growing volume of business before them and perforce gave heavy weight to practical and political factors. Among poorly paid county and municipal judges, learning in the law counted for less than ability to garner votes; and among attorneys at the bar, subtleties yielded to histrionics that could persuade a jury. In one case (San Francisco), William B. Ide served as justice of the peace, trial judge, defense council, and prosecutor—with no one else available. Of the Indiana chief justice, a newspaper commented (1858), "let Perkins shake his head to the right, shake it to the left, shake it up, shake it down or shake it any way . . . he would shake nothing out of it, for there was nothing in it." A resident of the Dakota Territory complained that instead of an upright territorial judiciary of "good men and good lawyers . . . we get to constitute our Supreme Court an ass, a knave and a drunkard." And it took a skillful practitioner to manipulate a jury composed of strangers. As a result, to the mass of the people a lawsuit, embedded in hieroglyphs called *Assumpsit, Trover, Replevin,* or some other barbarous name, amounted to a solemn unintelligible enigma with outcome conjectural but costs certain.[58]

At the frontier, at best, unreliable, entrepreneurial j.p.'s grabbed power and dispensed law. The Pikes Peakers in Colorado elected a legislature to enact their civil and criminal statutes, but informal miners' courts sprang up in the camps (1859). Professional code writers moved from place to place, helping the locals write up popular sovereignty in clear language. Elsewhere judges adapted traditional statutes to novel conditions, as did Chief Justice Moses Hallett of Colorado, who narrowed the jurisdiction of English common law and modified the doctrine of riparian rights, as they applied to mining. Roy Bean, less learned, came from Kentucky, set up as an officer and tavern-keeper on the Rio Grande and called himself "judge." Lacking a jail, he tied his prisoners to a tree, and expanded his powers and fees by granting divorces. He adored the popular English actress Lily Langtry, whose picture he had seen in the *Police Gazette,* and had the town named after her. Not until federal courts appeared did the situation improve. But the Las Vegas police force helped out the band of robbers who terrorized the town in the 1890s; and New Mexico long remained unstable.

Tribunals swamped by masses of petty civil litigation—debt, trespass, contracts—and by misdemeanors, disorderly conduct, burglary, paid scant regard to civil rights; and only rare cases inched themselves up to public notice through the appeals process. Few states allowed the courts to review the constitutionality of their statutes.[59]

Cities operated within more complex patterns.

In the great metropolitan centers, political adjustments lagged behind rapid population growth. New York City in 1920 had swollen to eight million, and Chicago to more than two million, barely able to control such multitudes despite the annexation of contiguous areas. Change in government remained slow and difficult. New York's sheriff still held his no longer relevant old prerogatives. New places insisted on adopting familiar, obsolete forms, although the encumbrance of old institutions impeded all services. By contrast, Europeans treated their towns as agencies of the state, controlled at the center as administrative entities by the ministry of the interior or its equivalent, except for a few German relics of the free-city tradition.

American local government could not keep pace with expanding communal needs in education, the care of dependents, and the wide range of activities encompassed in the term *police.* Besides, ambition moved cities to further economic development and civic improvements; persuaded that they could thus touch off a boom, many made donations or loans or, more usually, subscribed to railroad securities. Uncertainty about the boundary between the responsibilities of the municipalities and those of private associations confused matters. The complexities of administration repeatedly generated calls for elections based not on party spirit but on individual merit and technical competence (1853, 1856). Few attained that goal for any length of time; partisanship repeatedly asserted itself. In New York, for instance, the dominant machines in place before 1850 easily weathered occasional voter rebellions. Politicians absorbed new ethnic groups and nicely straddled social and economic issues, employing moderate corruption as well as crowd-pleasing tactics.[60]

Sustained popular interest increased the number of participants; in local contests the outcome mattered. In the struggle for the mayoralty of New York in 1886, for instance, Theodore Roosevelt, Abram S. Hewitt, and Henry George offered the electorate a genuine choice among differing approaches to municipal government. "What do I care who is President," said Iz Durham of Philadelphia, "so long as I carry my ward." At this level, politics also became important to a large part of the population. The citizens felt only remotely the effects of complex issues settled in Washington—the tariff, the currency, trusts, Indian policy, and relationships with Britain. Water supply, public baths, transit systems, and factory laws—issues settled in city hall or the state capital—had an immediate impact.[61]

At the local level also the political party mobilized and organized popular support. Independents, like the Mugwumps, who deserted the Republican party to support the Democrat Grover Cleveland, refused a total commitment and preferred to judge candidates and platforms without reference to labels. Occasionally they entered municipal elections on a nonpartisan ticket. But such incohesive and undisciplined efforts rarely succeeded. National issues occasionally intruded, as slavery did in the 1850s when Kansas ruffianism affected the Chicago elections. And consciousness of governors and legislatures empowered to alter charters and boundaries often fenced municipalities in. Nevertheless the local urban organizations gained steadily in strength.[62]

In this respect as well, the developing parties supplied the mechanism easing potential conflicts and coordinating and articulating the use of power. They enabled voters dimly to conceive of politics as a means to their own ends, expanding their sense of control. Few newcomers to the city had any previous direct involvement in government. The machines gave them a sense of participation, made politics a means of advancement.[63]

Respectable voters wished for municipal decisions independent of party or other corrupting influences. Concerned with honest and efficient government and with low taxes, they preferred to strengthen the mayor as against the council which represented the wards, hoping thus to create a responsible, businesslike executive, to pattern politics after the success of captains of industry. Such citizens drifted toward reform movements and toward positions hostile to immigrants and Catholics. Building a new jail in Brooklyn in 1886 "was a game which the politicians played, called money, money, who has got the money?" Suddenly an arraignment in court revealed charges against twenty-five New York aldermen, nineteen of them saloonkeepers. In the Chicago elections of 1856 and 1857, the Democratic city convention split among the Corkonians, the Connaught men, the Fardowners and Southdowners, as well as the Tipperary b'ys and a few Americans, while John Wentworth, the nominee for mayor who had theretofore campaigned as anti-Nebraska and anti-Know-Nothing, for the first time acknowledged that he belonged to the Republican party. References by Protestant ministers to the profligacy and flagrant misrule of the Irish Democracy—ignorant, credulous, brutalized by oppression, according to E. L. Godkin—only increased the solidarity of the group attacked, as did the impatience of temperance reformers who wished to apply force when persuasion failed. A prominent Brooklyn divine furiously attacked John Morrissey, who aspired to the state senate. Indicted for burglary, assault and battery with intent to kill, and (eighteen times) for maintaining gambling places, the candidate represented "a determined effort of the slums of New York to get representation in the State Government." Worse yet, in 1877 Patrick Shannon, owner of two gin mills, controlled the highest local offices—those of collector, police commissioner, fire commissioner, treasurer, and City Works commissioner. The "law breaker became law maker" in part because he also succeeded in bamboozling the better sort—Hamilton Fish, Peter Cooper, the Fifth Avenue equipage, and Murray Hill. *The New York Times* spoke for newcomers from upstate and from New England, Yankees with a sense of order and propriety, whose hostility allied groups otherwise divided. Even slum-dwellers had to consent to be governed. Riot and lawlessness occasionally enlivened elections, but day-to-day organizational loyalties counted more.[64]

Local alignments acquired permanent form. Organizations to mobilize voters reached down to the ward and neighborhood through gangs, clubs, and individuals able to gather a following. On New York's East

Side, the Buffaloes ran errands in the hope of gaining favor with the influential men—like Tom Foley, who began as a blacksmith, then acquired a saloon and ran a precinct in Big Tim Sullivan's district; or even better, like Silent Charlie Murphy, once catcher on a baseball team, then car-line driver, who became a Tammany power from his base as owner of four saloons. Often political control hinged on such personalities, saloonkeepers or grocers, undertakers or contractors capable of swaying neighbors and linked to counterparts in other districts. Sure they could find spots on the city payroll:

> Fifteen thousand Irishmen from Erin came across,
> Tammany put those Irish Indians on the police force.
> I asked one cop, if he wanted three platoons or four,
> He said: "keep your old platoons, I've got a cuspidor."

Favors held the machines together—jobs, licenses, and opportunities, if not from the municipality itself, then from contractors or from gas and traction companies that depended upon government good will—every street lamp lit by hand, every car at least one driver. James McManus of Philadelphia, trustee of the gas works, in 1879 disposed of more than five thousand places. Gangs from rival districts fought bitterly for supremacy, as did the Dead Rabbits from the Five Points and the Bowery Boys in New York's Sixth Ward in 1857; the Eleventh Ward that year also saw lively skirmishing; and across the river, two Brooklyn fire companies rioted, while Germans and Irishmen did battle in Williamsburgh, as in Chicago. Scores of dead and wounded then littered the streets. The bosses, aware that sporadic warfare did no one any good, in time developed unity. Under Mayor Fernando Wood, Tammany Hall thus gained control of the wards and assembly districts that later enabled Boss Tweed and his successors to rule the New York County Democratic party. Even in sparsely populated Wyoming, Democrats referred to their Republican opponents as "the Cheyenne Ring," implying that the cattlemen possessed political influence comparable to that of better-established Northern machines.[65]

Laxity at the ballot box was the common instrument of machine control. Vote early and often! Already in the 1850s in Chicago, many unnaturalized men swore in their votes; grasping the Bible, they kissed their thumbs instead of the Holy Book to ease their consciences. Force often ruled, though few attained the fame of John Morrissey, the American heavyweight champion (1853–1858), a well-known shoulder-hitter who intimidated voters in doubt and subsequently became a state senator, United States congressman, and the leading gambler in Saratoga Springs.

Verbal and physical abuse from such as he discouraged election judges
who might venture to challenge the eligibility of flophouse derelicts and
street bums. Boardinghouse keepers dutifully herded their lodgers to the
polls as time rendered scruples irrelevant and ballot stuffers and shoulder-
hitters reigned. One division in New York's Sixth Ward with a population of 850 cast 934 votes—more than its sum of men, women, children,
aliens, and dogs. In this game, anything went in the interest of victory
(1905):

> Hiawatha was an Indian, so was Navajo.
> Paleface organ grinders killed them many moons ago.
> But there is a band of Indians that will never die.
> When they're at the Indian club, this is their battle cry:
> Tammany, Tammany, big chief sits in his teepee
> Cheering braves to victory.
> Tammany, Tammany, swamp 'em, swamp 'em, get the wampum.
>   Tammany.
> Chris Colombo sailed from Spain, across the deep blue sea,
> Brought along the Dago vote to beat out Tammany.
> Tammany found Colombo's crew were livin' on a boat,
> Big chief said: "They're floaters," and he would not let them vote.
> Then to the tribe he wrote:
> Tammany, Tammany
> Get those Dagoes jobs at once. They can vote in twelve more months.
> Tammany, Tammany,
> Make those floaters Tammany voters, Tammany.

Fun, but more than a game.[66]

The political parties managed authority and linked federal, state, and
local, as well as private agencies, increasing the ability of some to act. San
Francisco's Irish David C. Broderick, Brooklyn's Hugh McLaughlin,
Chicago's King Mike McDonald and his successors Hinky Dink Kenna
and Bathhouse John Coughlin, Jersey City's Frank Hague, and Boston's
Martin Lomasney, "Mahatma of the West End," among others, controlled the localities in the interest of their followers, although some
dabbled also in liquor and gambling. The blind boss, Christopher Buck-
ley, who ran a private establishment in Sacramento, supplied the state
legislature enough whiskey to float an ordinary battleship, then found it
had an abnormal appetite for boodle. On the other hand, the chieftains
made use of respectable mouthpieces like Bourke Cochran, Irish-born
orator and lawyer who could charm the stiff shirt off any audience.[67]

The machine secured the acquiescence of loyal members and followers and also won elections and managed legislative and executive power. The parties maintained close if not cordial relationships with the press, ever in search of corruption for a sensational scoop. No hard feelings. Respectable reformers attacked the boss "as the deadly foe of popular government." The more sensible poet deplored the fashion among fops and dilettantes of decrying the dirty game of politics. Their ideal great statesman, said Mr. Dooley, was "a grocer with elastic bands on his shirt sleeves, ladlin' public policies out iv a bar'l with a wooden scoop. How much better wud Wash'nton and Lincoln have been if the'd known enough to inthrajooce business methods into pollyticks?" The shady minister whose trail of adulteries stretched from Massachusetts to California, when elected mayor of San Francisco, explained that the people expected officials to steal; and if they got rich by helping the poor, the recipients, whether city dwellers or western railroad men and cattlemen, never forgot the help. And for the time being at least, the cities thrived despite the elected failures and blatherers, despite the antics of parties and their half-brained nominees. The effective management of the apparatus of power, with consent, counted more than boodle and bribery.[68]

Solid business types generally neglected public affairs and often did not bother to vote; they held utterly opposing opinions, Charles F. Murphy implied. Full of cant and hypocrisy, they quickly tired of reformist zeal and preferred muddle and disorganization. Already in 1858 a plaintive complaint set forth the trials, tribulations, and expenses of a failed candidate—no home, no friends, no wife, no money. The desire of such people to stand aside eased machine control. His pleasant and well-educated hosts spoke to Rudyard Kipling with bitter scorn of such duties of citizenship as voting and taking an interest in offices; they "would as soon concern themselves with the public affairs of the city or state as rake muck." Now and then, a freewheeling rich man took it into his head to take a hand in the game. John Wanamaker of Pennsylvania and Theodore Roosevelt of New York, among others, misinterpreted their own desire for self-assertion as a call to service. William Randolph Hearst, loaded with cash and armed with a popular newspaper, decided in 1909 to clean up New York City by running for mayor. His successful Tammany opponent ridiculed the California adventurer, who advertised himself like a patent medicine. Ignorant of the rules or insistent on devising their own, independents made trouble unless shuffled off to harmless places of distinction in the United States Senate or in the diplomatic corps. W. F. Havemeyer bewailed the tendency of corrupt men to stamp out liberty. The form of a democratic government hardly remained. He could not understand "the listlessness and apathy of the people." Other reformers perceived no valid reason why party politics should influence municipal affairs. For Robert B. Roosevelt, the machine had pulled away the very keystone of the arch of liberty.[69]

In the face of deep social divisions, citizens backed away from political decisions that would leave one side dominant and one side weak, preferring to bypass problems and to mediate among clashing interests. Except when a dramatic breakdown in services or order threatened security, or when a deterioration of sanitary conditions endangered health, urban residents minded their own business and left municipal management to others. "Who ever heard of a father counselling his son to adopt Government service as a career?" (1909). James Bryce, however, recognized that the representative system and the lack of an ideology gave the party and the machine a vital role in American politics, replacing the aristocracy or the patricians in European cities.[70]

Hence the persistent revisions of municipal government, in the vague hope that somehow detachment from politics would raise efficiency. The general decline of competence evoked an increasing desire to entrust these functions to agencies not subject to direct popular consent. Ironically, the arguments for the change emphasized the desire for "genuine popular control of the machinery of government." Ultimately, however, machine rule proved a conservative force, turning masses of immigrants into citizens but rarely using power for social change. The bosses remained content to define the ability to act by the extent to which they met basic needs, making few efforts either to redefine the public good or to alter the social fabric. In Plunkitt's vision, civil service reform did more for anarchism than any other cause, for every anarchist was a man made to hate his country by failing the civil service examination.

Reforms bore no evident results. The commission plan replaced "boss-controlled partisan politics," the saloonkeepers, and the traction magnates. Direct primaries aimed to mobilize popular support behind the right people. The reform effort applied the seemingly successful methods of private enterprise, with business the source of ideas to replace the old political makeshifts. An end to politics in that sense would mean greater and not less democracy. Thereafter "only the public" was to blame if it elected officials who proved disappointing. The people alas did not acquiesce. Perhaps power would compel them to, *for their own good.*[71]

When it came to local government, the question of means proved more important than that of ends. The purpose of politics did not prove as troublesome as on the federal and state levels. Police and adherence to communal rules formed the basic tasks.

Laws, however, did not enforce themselves, and compulsion depended on the quite conditional ability to deploy force. When the sovereign turned mob intent upon lynching, the government's formal sanctions vanished. The legislature could legislate; the consequences required the power to exact obedience. Should orderly procedures fail, explained the New York City reformers, another method would be found. "You will hear it in the yells of an infuriated mob, in the fire and rapine and slaughter, in the noise of musketry and of cannon." Then, "some despot will put his iron heel upon a people, too sordid, too corrupt, too craven for liberty." The whims of juries long qualified all judicial procedures, as when artful colleagues deceived James Crutcher into voting to free a murderer in Kentucky (1854) or when twelve good men and true in Sacramento arrived at a verdict by drawing lots (1856). In some places service became a racket among loungers with nothing better to do than pocket the fees. Writs did not of themselves bear results. When the order-loving denizens of Skagway, Alaska, discovered the United States marshal and the federal attorney both in cahoots with the Soapy Smith gang (1898), they acted. "Soapy is dead," proclaimed the local paper, "shot through the heart, his cold body lies on a slab at People's Undertaking Parlors and the confidence men and bunco steerers which have had their headquarters here for some time, have suddenly taken their departure." "Don't ask for rights," said Mr. Dooley. "Take them. An' don't let any wan give thim to ye; a right that is handed to ye f'r nawthin has somethin the matther with it."[72]

Hence the growing importance of police. After 1850, old fears that professionals would endanger popular liberties yielded to necessity. One place after another followed London, New York, and Boston in employing a paramilitary corps, uniformed, disciplined, and prepared to apply force on command. Wanted: the ideal policeman—strong as Hercules, enough knowledge of English to make intelligible written reports, well enough versed in law to avoid mistakes, a "hero in peace as a soldier is a hero in war." Alas, the problems of order only took new forms. In the early decades, communities grudgingly set wages according to those paid mechanics, then complained of shortages of qualified manpower. Recruited from among the laboring population and largely Irish, the officers for a time refused to wear uniforms or even badges that might expose them to attack. Often their slight grasp of legality made the relation to the political parties and municipal machine more compelling than to the letter of the law, except when a crusading reformer like Theodore Roosevelt took charge. Low pay and lack of discipline tied the police to politics; a new administration could replace the entire force with its own people, so that the guardians of the law became pawns of the local machine.

Usually, prudence dictated restraint; policemen mediated between strict enforcement and adaptation to local habits. Better not to look at the saloon's back door. Touch a drunk and suffer a beating. Forget it. Reminded of their status as servants of the people from whom authority emanated, policemen in Galveston, Texas, had to be polite to strangers and assist the aged across the streets. Wichita made laziness and intoxication grounds for suspension. To this list Des Moines added cowardice, nonpayment of debts, and sitting down while on patrol. Everywhere, entering a saloon and immoral conduct called for disciplinary measures, lest (1859) "the most disgusting and diabolical offenses" destroy confidence in the law and give a corrupt mayor free reign. A little band of constables and night watchmen could after all get up a city ticket and seize power. From time to time, state experiments vested authority in the mayor, the city council, boards of commissioners, or officials appointed by the governor. The difference remained marginal.[73]

Furthermore, the municipal police held no monopoly on the use of force. In some places the county sheriff, his deputies, and his posse still functioned. States, unwilling to depend on the ability to mobilize citizens' militias in exceptional situations, created permanent police with a chain of command leading to the governor. The troopers proved crucial in rural regions or in mining and industrial towns which lacked any other dependable force. Federal authorities also developed means of compulsion. Marshals, long available to execute documents and serve the needs of the courts, acquired a broad range of law enforcement roles in territories not yet states and governed directly from Washington. Charged with enforcing federal law, often in the midst of violent racial and ethnic conflicts and local feuds, they occasionally suppressed radical dissent and political agitation in a setting where adaptability to local circumstances mattered more than fulfilling directives from the United States capital.

At one time, however, fear of federal police compelled the president to hire private guards when needed. The secret service for his protection appeared later. But the Treasury Department, with jurisdiction over customs and other federal taxes, took responsibility for the Coast Guard and related armed services. And Theodore Roosevelt, defying congressional opinion and concerned about internal security, authorized formation of a bureau of investigation within the Treasury Department, out of which the FBI developed. Only later would the implications for liberty emerge.[74]

Moreover, private persons and organizations long arranged their own protection. No one as yet challenged the constitutional right of individuals to bear arms and defend their lives and property. The railroads, whose lines ran through many jurisdictions, thus enlisted their own forces. The Pinkerton Agency provided detectives to businesses, sometimes in substantial numbers as during the Homestead strike. In Pennsylvania the Coal and Iron Police operated on the margin—legitimized by the state, yet serving the mine owners. Horse-thief detective associations spread through the Midwest; the one in Missouri had thirty-five thousand members in 1910. Other expedients, particularly in labor disputes, explored the area between public and private constabulary. A cordage company in Brooklyn thus organized a hundred armed men to guard its plant and dock in the face of a strike threat. In Des Moines, the commissioner of public safety assumed active charge of the police because of a threatened street railway strike.[75]

Private forces also operated more generally. While plainclothes municipal detectives seemed suspect, private sleuths flourished. The firm of C. P. Bradley and Company of Chicago recovered the large sum stolen by domestics from a merchant's home; but the mayor complained that such operators undermined public confidence in the city's police and themselves occasionally committed burglaries. Besides, they skimmed off the reward-rich robbery business while leaving lawmen the thankless tasks of searching for murderers and enforcing unpopular laws, tasks rendered more onerous after 1900 when pistols became more available and the motorcar increased the mobility of criminals. Before then, the Portland, Oregon, elected Board of Police Commissioners complained (1891) of the lack of arrests for gambling and operating saloons without a license, and wondered if the police were "the protectors or the sharers in the spoils." The Atlanta police force changed dramatically in the twentieth century. In 1895 it had dealt with five unhaltered mules running at large, with reckless driving of bicycles, and with fruit-selling on the Sabbath. Then a telephone system, a rudimentary training school, and an eight-man bicycle squad appeared, along with installation of the first flush toilets in the city jail, while a new chief mounted a campaign to prevent cruelty to animals. But some things did not change. In the bloody race riot of 1906, the police stood by and let the white mobs vent their rage on hapless blacks. A few theorists who challenged the concept of consent of the governed and defined liberty as the permission the state accorded to the individual to act on his own volition insisted that people obeyed very much as persons taken into custody agreed to go quietly to jail, much against their will but aware that resistance would only lead to the disagreeable use of force. Power, all there was to it, hardly proved adequate.[76]

Uncertainty also marked explorations of other dimensions of police power, which had once extended to everything affecting communal safety, health, and welfare—order, morality, philanthropy, cleanliness, sanitation, and fire. Specialization, already manifest in 1850, increased as particular functions devolved to bureaucratic agencies, local, state, and federal, each claiming technical expertise—commissions for fish, banking, and insurance, boards of forestry and charity, and bureaus for dairies and mining. Post office scandals often demonstrated government's ineffi- ciency—"no private business could be managed like this without going into bankruptcy," Boston's postmaster declared. But that did not check the local tendency to enlarge rather than contract the functions, a ten- dency validated by new theories that regarded society as an organism, something more than individuals and possessing rights paramount to theirs. That view affected definitions of liberty and also the extent to which local municipalities applied collective power.

In rural areas, limited methods sufficed. But in the growing cities, entirely novel conditions required novel approaches. The old volunteer fire associations had attracted men drawn by excitement and danger, by "the good fellowship of the engine houses and the chances for a row and a rumpus" (1857). One of them went to the penitentiary for six years, convicted of arson "committed only from the desire to give his hose cart or engine a chance to be first at the scene of destruction." A jubilant poem:

> O the fireman's joys!
> I hear the alarm at dead of night,
> I hear bells—shouts!—I pass the crowd—run!
> The sight of the flames maddens me with pleasure.

Changing attitudes after 1850 turned fire companies into departments of the city government to stop looting. Disciplined, paid professional forces more readily coped with conflagrations like Boston's and Chicago's than could volunteers, and also prevented pilfering. But the great conflagration that consumed Chicago in 1871 spread despite improved equipment such as a telegraphic fire alarm and horse-drawn water engines. It did not matter whether the fault lay with Mrs. O'Leary's cow that ignited the straw, or the Irish, the communists, or burglars, or the hand of God in judgment upon a modern Sodom; the loss amounted to $196 million and some four hundred dead.[77]

Since the eighteenth century, epidemics—smallpox, yellow fever, and later cholera—moving through the alleys and carrying off victims indiscriminately, had threatened whole populations. Crowding and poverty made matters worse in the nineteenth century, especially among collections of native and foreign-born immigrants from the rural countryside. The first line of defense, in pesthouses or quarantine, failed to prevent the spread of disease; and increased knowledge demanded broader controls. Migration of Southern blacks into Northern cities further raised sensitivity to the problem. Municipalities then moved from the fear of vaccination to requiring it of children, often using the schools as a means of enforcement. However, fears lest such measures "lessen too much the freedom of personal action" (1871) generated persistent organized resistance.[78]

The falling crude death rate (in New York City from thirty-five per thousand in 1870 to twenty-one in 1900 and to thirteen in 1920) did not quiet concern. Medical science meanwhile revealed the broader implications of good health. In the long run, tuberculosis, diarrheal diseases among infants, bacillary dysentery, typhoid and scarlet fever, diphtheria and pneumonia carried off more people than the dramatic epidemics: prevention could help if no cure yet existed, and regulatory action could lower the toll. Hypocrisy made matters worse. Venereal disease, not even acknowledged until the turn of the century, went untreated because respectable physicians feared reputations as "clap doctors," and hospitals closed their doors to victims who turned, in the absence of communal aid, to fraud and quackery, with disastrous results. Americans continued to believe that resistance to disease depended upon moral and salubrious living and upon an adequate sewerage system and a pure water supply, the importance of which the needs of fire control had already revealed. Lemuel Shattuck's Report of the Massachusetts Sanitary Commission (1850) outlined a comprehensive program; and the New York City campaign led by Stephen Smith and Peter Cooper resulted in a law (1866) giving wide powers to the Department of Health. New appliances for indoor plumbing later increased demands for water and sewers.[79]

Aesthetic grounds had long spurred action against noxious trades and polluting industries, if for no other reason, for offenses to the sense of smell. Municipalities early on banished to the outskirts slaughterhouses, bone and offal rendering establishments, and tanneries, just as they ceased to depend upon roving pigs for garbage disposal. The cities could act because the courts refused to extend the guarantees of state or federal bills of rights to violations of sanitary ordinances. With time, the wider implications justified more strenuous if not more efficient policing, in line with Benjamin Franklin's supposed dictum that public health was public wealth. The abstract proposition seemed clear: municipal government, proclaimed a Chicago meeting (1860), existed "for the protection and happiness of each and every citizen," so that it was "inexcusable to neglect the cleaning of streets and alleys." Such ideas from the big cities resounded in the distant corners of the land, carried by "the newspapers, the books, the traveling lecturers and teachers, the wandering merchants and artisans, the representatives of every conceivable organization." The word spread: appropriate action could prevent 40 percent of deaths (1909). The questions remained: by whom, how, at whose expense?[80]

The answers varied. Threats to health excited intense general concern, for disease respected no boundaries. The breakdown of New York City's municipal government after 1850 produced a tragic deterioration of services and a corresponding increase in the crude death rate. The alarmed Association for Improving the Condition of the Poor and the New York Academy of Medicine demanded a municipal agency to do something. The state legislature, however, relaxed until July 1863, when the draft riot turned into a mass attack upon property, alerting citizens to the bitter frustrations of the poor. Then the threat of Asiatic cholera enabled reformers to push through the bill creating the Metropolitan Board of Health. The desire for "regulation and coercion more prompt and summary" than available through the courts (1868) kept the agency alive despite corruption, organizational changes, and conflicts with the police and other departments. Fear sustained the level of concern when yellow fever in the South (1878) claimed twenty thousand lives. However, municipalities did not enjoy a monopoly of health-related activities. Some states intervened directly, as did Indiana to prevent diseased sheep from running at large and to prohibit the import of cattle infected with Texas fever. And in 1879 the federal government edged in when Congress created a National Board of Health to aid in enforcing quarantine orders.[81]

Sewers, water systems, and the disposal of garbage and rubbish, although initially the responsibility of each household, or supplied by private contractors, became municipal concerns. "The only good fly is a dead fly, the best fly is the fly that never was born," the Kansas Board of Health informed citizens, arguing that sickness was useless and disease preventable. The huge sums involved in construction and operation of facilities attracted venal politicians and greedy contractors as well as consulting engineers, so that neither the communities which depended on municipal ownership nor those which franchised private enterprises altogether satisfied consumers. Five million dollars went to waste when the District of Columbia miscalculated the grade level of its sewers. Cairo,

Illinois, never dealt with flooding and seepage. A weak and unstable city government and the lack of groups with a long-term vision of their future in the community prevented concerted action. Better do nothing, especially since many citizens agreed when a New Orleans physician (1880) argued that the state could not assume the duty of protecting health without infringing upon the law of equal freedom and "without retarding man's adaptation to the conditions imposed by nature on his existence."[82]

For citizens, as users and taxpayers, the gradations blurred between the essential and the desirable, between the necessary and the discretionary, between support from general taxes and from fees, whether supplied by franchised corporations or municipal departments, regulated, inspected—and by whom? Pure water? Vital. But milk? No, though closely linked to infant health. And if yes, how, when supplies originated outside and often across state lines? Bread, lest riots follow as in Paris, and no Louis Napoleon to set the price. Flour, grain, other food? Of course. Ancient practices required the regulation of markets to ensure a reliable supply and to prevent forestalling. But wranglings over rules and over the allocation of stalls persuaded some citizens that free trade in all goods was just as much a republican principle as the ballot. Markets, embracing inherited, customary practices, the particular interests of consumers and suppliers, and public concerns with sanitation and cleanliness, eluded rational administration and depended for organization upon numerous practical compromises. Appointed director of New York's Bureau of Food and Drugs, Lucius Polk Brown, earlier pure food and drug inspector in Tennessee, confronted strange foodstuffs and unknown produce, like dried oysters and sea ears. How was he to regulate squash leaves and stems—familiar to Italian consumers, but not to Southerners? Shelter? Housing remained a private concern, although building codes guaranteed jobs for little armies of inspectors and running arguments over the sidewalk space occupied by supplies. On the other hand, bathhouses ultimately yes, in some municipalities. Improvisations without consistency determined all the answers. "The right view of life is one of personal responsibility," intoned a popular health manual (1912), which wanted personal responsibility preached from every pulpit. "We must not look to others to do everything for us. Government nowadays is working incredible harm, by doing for people what the people ought to be doing for themselves."[83]

Such suggestions met fierce resistance from organized medicine, which capitalized on patriotism and sexual fears to declare war, in alliance with the government, on "the enemies of America's civilization," venereal diseases, which killed more people than fell during the battles in France. Although quacks and the unnecessarily prudish gave comfort to the enemy, there would "be no peace conference with the plenipotentiaries of disease." American public opinion mobilized against syphilis and gonorrhea. Physicians, the newspapers (which would spread correct information while denying access to quack advertisements), motion pictures, educators in the schools, law enforcement officials, and encouragers of physical recreation as a substitute for sexual energy, all joined the righteous fight. The campaign, however, fell short of its goal.

Nor did consistency mark the spread of hospitals or cemeteries, some private, others operated by the state, by the county, by the municipality, by eleemosynary, religious, or profit-making corporations, with the preferred arrangement private ownership and operation, though with oversight by inspection and regulation either through the state or the municipalities. The presumption of public use and maintenance for roads and streets did not prevent persons who wished to do so from constructing private ways and even exclusive neighborhoods. Gas and electric lighting and traction usually remained private, with only a few experiments in municipal ownership and operation. However, jurisdictional conflicts sometimes enlivened matters, as in Cairo, Illinois, where the city council favored the Southern Illinois Interurban against the Cairo Terminal Traction chartered under the state railroad law.[84]

Issues, apparently petty because particular and personal, kept testing the meaning of liberty. The police power asserted the public ability to act to shape the conditions of the common life, thus expanding the government's regulatory function to drastic direct intervention in order to prevent harm to others—what food to eat, what liquor to consume, how to deal with illness, even incarceration without conviction for a crime. Six cases of typhoid turned up in a household where Mary Mallon had served as cook for three weeks. Then the New York Department of Health traced seven more outbreaks to her. Hospitalized by force, against her will, Mary proved "a living culture tube in which the germs of typhoid multiplied." Released after three years on the promise never to handle food again, Mary disappeared, then left a trail of other cases. Re-arrested, she spent the twenty-three years until her death locked up, unprotected by the Bill of Rights, despite vain pleas to the courts for release.

Jacobson v. *Massachusetts* (1905) upheld a Cambridge ordinance requiring compulsory vaccination; the court asserted that "real liberty for all could not exist under the operation of a principle which recognizes the right of each individual person to use his own, whether in respect of his person or his property, regardless of the injury that may be done to others." Many citizens, including Christian Scientists, remained unpersuaded, the issue of liberty in the face of power unresolved.[85]

Whatever course taken by the political system, oversight required bureaucratic control to either operate or supervise services. The number of federal officeholders increased from 26,274 in 1851 to 100,020 in 1881 and to 1,655,000 in 1920, with state and local growth proportionate. And the swelling bureaucracy determined its own standards, removed from the consent of the governed.[86]

Another irony: the more citizens asked the government to act on their behalf, the more power slipped out of their own hands. The early civil service reformers sought no more than to replace corrupt patronage with appointment by merit. But to the extent that they succeeded, they detached officials from any democratic process, encouraged the development of an enclosed esprit de corps, and transferred control from elected to appointed officials. The powerless clerks of the past increasingly acquired quasi-police ability to act by their own rules. Street commissioners and collectors of assessments handling very large sums did not always withstand temptation. More important, they tended to regard the public as victims rather than as masters. A distinguished political scientist concluded (1903) that civil service reform had brought little improvement, but had exacerbated all the maladies it presumed to cure.[87]

When it came to health, it seemed almost self-evident that power ought to rest in the hands of physicians, that is, of a professional elite trained according to a prescribed course and independent of the majority will or preference. The proposition spread to other areas of competence as well: an academic economist, John R. Commons, led the Wisconsin Industrial Commission (1911), which received broad powers to oversee employment conditions. Engineers and practical scientists gained prominence, promising efficiency. Having declared the experiment of popular institutions in the management of large cities a failure, they sought to take over the metropolitan centers, neglecting the poet's early warning that corruption, bribery, falsehood, and maladministration saturated American bureaucracies—national, state, and municipal.[88]

Education early tested the ability to manage bureaucracies. The family, once the primary educator, ever more frequently delegated childhood training to a prescribed course of study administered by formal schools and teachers. The government then assumed the obligation of universal instruction, including the offspring of parents judged incompetent either because of foreign birth or because of poverty. The state also recognized teaching as a profession that required appropriate training. The one-room school disappeared, replaced by large, graded institutions operated by rigid rules along strictly structured lines. The change expanded and reinforced a bureaucracy with a will of its own, only slightly responsible to elected public officials or to the citizens served—except insofar as budgets depended on the allocation of municipal or state funds.

Financial stringency, especially when it came to education, remained the norm. A Vermont town—by no means the poorest—shortly before the Civil War annually expended some $956 on its schools, of which only $387 came from taxes. Ratcheting the amount upward was hard work, for schools competed for public funding with health, police, and fire and other services. The same situation obtained elsewhere. Cairo, Illinois, a small city, in 1905 stretched $28,000 in revenue to cover $60,000 in expenses with borrowed funds, despite the prevailing pay-as-you-go rule. However strong the local temperance movement, such places could not forgo the income from saloon licenses. To complicate matters further, a long tradition encouraged private institutions also to seek government support. The Tweed ring in New York in three years thus paid over two million dollars to such organizations, of which amount $1.4 million went to Catholic charities.

Outside the smallest towns, where mutual surveillance encouraged honesty, tax evasion was commonplace. In Massachusetts, under the most stringent laws, more than half the personal property escaped its lawful tax burden. And the insurance books of Lawrence, Kansas, showed more personal property insured within the city limits than found its way onto the tax rolls for the entire county. The assessor in Cairo, Illinois, in 1905 believed that perhaps eighty percent of the town's property never got onto his books. Not many places equaled that record, although New York City already suffered noteworthy delinquencies in 1857, and Chicago two years later.

The perennial shortage of funds sprang from the failure of assessments and returns to rise enough to keep pace with the demand, although the potential tax base expanded. Cairo's taxable property listed as $1,400,048 in 1880, had increased only to $1,940,433 twenty-eight years later, despite the great rise in the city's wealth.[89]

Persistent demands nevertheless expanded services to health, welfare, and safety, as the political system—federal, state, and local—satisfied needs otherwise neglected. Municipalities confronted demands to improve the navigation of their rivers, to prevent epidemics, and to tear down dangerous dwellings. Other appeals urged the states to support education and internal improvements. And still others turned to Washington for aid, regulation, and inspection, all expensive.

Development offered the one way out: raise population, wealth, real estate values, and incomes, expand the output of agriculture and industry, multiply jobs and elevate wages, and thereby make more available for taxes—painlessly. On that agenda, the labor unions and merchants' leagues, the civic associations and chambers of commerce, all agreed. The result would permit government to do more, while keeping everyone content. Hence numerous little places dreamed of becoming great railroad centers, and large ones dreamed of becoming larger. Alas, grandiose plans often floundered in the face of apathy, timidity, and lethargy. When no businessmen turned up at a meeting to establish a Cairo tobacco market (1869), the editor of the *Evening Bulletin* took it as a sign that the town would never amount to much.[90]

Where hope persisted, the scope of government action steadily broadened, and burst forth after 1917 in wartime activities. By then, the state touched every aspect of social experience and mobilized the power for repression, the price Americans paid for the fact that few objectives other than expansion held them together.

Humanity viewed in the lump puzzled the merely educated class of the nineteenth century, when taste, intelligence and culture (so called) viewed the masses with suspicion. By contrast to the dynastic world of lords and courts, so well dressed and so handsome, the people seemed ungrammatical and untidy and their sins gaunt and ill bred. But popular democracy had justified itself in battle in 1861—perhaps would again. The people, tried long by hopelessness, mismanagement, and defeat, then of their own choice sprang to arms, to the astonishment of the philosopher (Emerson) and the historian (Bancroft). The poet observed them in the Civil War, crouching behind breastworks or tramping in deep mud or amid pouring rain or thick-falling snow—vast, suffering swarms, divisions, corps, every single man grimed with sweat and dust, clothes all dirty, stained and torn, with sour accumulated sweat for perfume, with many a comrade staggering out, dying by the roadside of exhaustion— yet the great bulk bearing steadily on with unconquerable resolution. Proved by yet more fearful hospital tests—the wound, the amputation, the shattered face or limb, the slow, hot fever, the long impatient anchorage in bed—the boys preserved decorum, fortitude, and sweet affection, supplying the last needed proof of democracy, proof undeniable of perfect beauty, tenderness, and pluck that never feudal lord, nor Greek, nor Roman breed yet rivaled.

Meanwhile humanity, always full of perverse maleficence, revealed clearly enough the crude, defective streaks in all the strata of the common people—the vast collections of the ignorant, the credulous, the unfit and uncouth, the incapable, and the very low and poor. True! But the object of government reached beyond mere repression of disorder, to developing, to opening up to cultivation, to encouraging the possibilities for independence, pride, and self-respect latent in all; to train communities to rule themselves. For each single individual possessed something so transcendent that it placed all on a common level utterly regardless of distinctions of intellect, virtue, or station; so that the nation, as an aggregate of living identities, each a separate and complete subject for freedom, worldly thrift, and happiness, must grant each the vote, rendering democracy, of no account in itself, the fit trainer for immortal souls. To be a voter and to stand with the rest was to commence the grand experiment of forming a full-grown man or woman. Not that the people were essentially good or sensible, but that good or bad, rights or no rights, the democratic formula was the only safe one for modern times, endowing the masses with the suffrage not for their own but for the community's sake.[91]

III

COMMUNITIES UNDER PRESSURE

POLITICS, THAT IS, THE APPLICATION of force by consent according to accepted rules, changed drastically after 1850. Government expansion at all levels depended upon the strength of political parties that served as media of compromise and accommodation, eliciting obedience from citizens' identification with them. Yet, symptomatically, these vital organizations remained private, voluntary associations, constituted by no law.

The political system therefore operated in close relationship with the loosely jointed communities it served. The absence of any cement to hold groups together other than the will of their members explained the prevailing impression of inadequacy in the face of unremitting pressures from a changing environment. An American flag flying from the gilded dome of an East Side synagogue in New York astounded a suspicious critic. Nineteenth-century residents and sympathetic visitors to the New World commonly judged the United States unprepared for the tasks of social, economic, and cultural adjustment after Appomattox. Instability and the danger of outbreaks of domestic violence derived, they believed, from politicians prone to corruption and "actuated mainly by a desire . . . to acquire wealth by the exercise of power." But appraisals patterned after the criteria of centralized hierarchical communities failed to note quite different signs of strength, not those of a rigid framework but of a loosely articulated structure. The view of society as "an organic association . . . for mutual aid," based on common ideals of right and wrong, which sought to achieve common objects through cooperation, remained a goal persistently sought, never attained.[1]

Hence the paradox of repression in a democratic polity that valued freedom. Many functions once exercised informally filtered gradually into the realm of government; the same tasks continued to concern the civil communities, for political authority did not expand at their expense any more than increased federal power diminished that of the states or municipalities. All gained strength, local as well as national, communal as well as governmental, with the various realms supportive, not exclusive. Once mobilized, they could operate in an oppressive as well as in a constructive mode, although the absence of visible ligatures left an impression of chaos. The unwillingness to regard private activities as "constituents of a large collective process" troubled a sympathetic English observer. Americans saw the world in fragments, "all individuality . . . and all . . . unfused."[2]

American communities seemed chaotic because they did not consist of systematic, formally aligned subdivisions, identifiable by a table or plan of organization. Rather, each contained a congeries of unrelated, self-constituted, voluntary associations, capable of coercing only their own members within vaguely marked limits. Generally the law clothed such bodies with formidable defenses against external intrusion. The distinction between them and public agencies extended from churches and eleemosynary institutions to educational and business corporations, all strengthened by constitutional protections of property and of contractual obligations that extended to shares and memberships. The Fourteenth Amendment further inhibited state action by the additional restraint of substantive due process and added to the safeguards. Within wide, indefinable boundaries, voluntary associations acted as their members wished them to.

Citizens assumed that order would evolve not by imposition from some superior authority, but from competition, from the play of mutual antagonisms rather than from embrace in some overarching plan. Anyone could form an association, secure a charter, or act without one, while general laws and the balance of open rivalry protected the interests of outsiders and of the whole society. That looseness created the appearance, and sometimes the actuality, of disorder. Yet the "group consciousness of common ideals and common needs" satisfied in other countries by corporate or institutional means remained out of reach.[3]

The insecure at every social level preferred greater order—especially the possessors of new wealth who feared anarchy and lusted for the deference they considered appropriate to their eminence. Such people repeatedly tried to replicate the fixed European class structure. The Beacon Hill Brahmins, "between a Mayflower descendant and a Declaration Signer's great grandson," believed that when the Lord made that breed He was through, and that the rest just happened. In a land of contrasts, of "refinement and crudeness, luxury and misery, high virtue and profound immorality," the citizens were not a people without prejudices. "The most inveterate aristocrats at home," wrote a young Swedish visitor, did not talk more about family, good and old, about *societé comme il faut* than republican Americans. They hired fashionable architects to build chateaux, Norman castles, or Doric country houses, or plant Italian loggias on their town houses or lavish ornamental plaster on interiors. John Singer Sargent did their portraits in the English style. But without the institutional and legal supports of the Old World, such attempts invariably failed. Pathetic, desperate efforts to establish an aristocracy in the Eastern cities ran up against the persistent fluidity of life.[4]

Until the Civil War, Americans had recognized a rough equivalence among wealth, virtue, and status. They conceded leadership to the great planters of the South and the great merchants of the North, whose estates and public service earned the respect even of artisans or yeomen with divergent economic interests. In the 1850s, the Virginia and South Carolina Cavaliers, the Boston Brahmins, and the New York Knickerbockers, well-established families rich for several generations, took first place in their communities not only by virtue of their money but also by the polished, masterly qualities of long lineage, polite manners, and education. They took for granted positions at the pinnacle of society; and they held the attention of the whole country, setting the styles for other people who avidly followed their activities in the press. Marion Sims, a newcomer from the South, got nowhere in the effort to establish a hospital for women in New York City until a fortunate introduction to a distinguished lady brought him success. Reluctantly, the poet later conceded the "courage and generosity," the business powers and the "sharp almost demoniac intellect" of Boston, "with its circles of social mummies, swathed in cerements harder than brass—its bloodless religion (Unitarianism,) its complacent vanity of scientism and literature, lots of grammatical correctness, mere knowledge, (always wearisome, in itself)—its zealous abstractions, ghosts of reforms."[5]

Tendencies toward stratification lacked coherence. Local bankers and merchants in small communities maneuvered for position, and lawyers and doctors tried to strengthen the dignity, power, and wealth of their professions. Such people thought of society as ranged on ascending steps, with each person protecting his space against the climbers from below and at the same time trying to get a foothold in the rank above. Houses before the Civil War bespoke less the wealth than the character, respectability, and stability of their owners. Rufus Griswold's *Republican Court* (1854) described the Willing mansion of Philadelphia as typical of old elegance, simpler and nobler than the style of his own time. His second edition (1867) noted that the offices of the Pennsylvania Railroad Company had replaced the mansion, torn down in 1856.[6]

Upstarts of the post–Civil War decades far outdistanced the old families in wealth, although their dollars lacked respectability, tainted by recent speculation or by grimy factories, unlike the riches accumulated generations back from ships or plantations. (Few recalled the slaves and opium carried in that traffic.) The new millionaire appeared to have assembled his fortune as an end in itself, or like Silas Lapham knew not what to make of it. Such circles contained "as many elements of misery as the world" could produce. "No need to go into alleys to hunt up wretchedness." It spread in "perfection among the rich and fashionable." The masters of old wealth, sneering at *nouveaux arrivés* who thrived on gambling as John Law had before his downfall, often withdrew from brutal economic and political contests with plutocrats and immigrants, and got by bitterly on pessimism and contempt or else sought refuge in orientalism and medievalism. For the first time money took the field as an organized power in politics, raising the question, whether "educated and patriotic freemen, or the feudal serfs of corporate capital" would rule. Only a few struggled from protected social enclaves to transmit inherited cultural values to the engulfing aliens. Others fortified themselves against unwelcome contacts, in imitations of Renaissance palaces or French chateaux. Between them and the tenements of the poor sprouted homes of the middling sort, property but also seats of values, of citizenship, a defense against outside evils and a fortress against radicalism.[7]

No respectable American espoused monarchist sentiments, although Rufus Griswold sadly noted that the nation's leaders failed "to carry into public life the morals and the sentiments" that gave grace to private character. But guests at the regal Saratoga hotels and sponsors of the balls that greeted the Prince of Wales's visit in 1860 often wistfully contemplated the possibility that nobility would add a dash of elegance to the plebeian crudeness of their own society, whence the charge of Arkansas Governor Conway that the tour concealed a contrived English plan to break up the Union. And toward the end of the century the heiresses who married European titles took practical steps toward defining rank on their own, in the absence of a properly organized society.[8]

Hence the status endowed certain household objects unrelated to their actual use. The piano, once associated with aristocratic pretensions to cultivation, became common among the middle classes, its price "within the reach of the refined not rich," and more often used in the cottages of the less affluent than in the mansions of the ostentatious parvenues where it rarely emitted a sound. Perfected by Jonas Chickering, who produced fifteen hundred of them a year, these instruments became an antidote to the pernicious tendency to honor public men while denigrating the importance of those who labored in private. Chickering and his creation proved, contemporaries thought, the value of the heroes of the apron, the craftsmen, who by a life of conscientious toil placed a new source of happiness, or of force, within the reach of their fellow citizens. Pianos became focal points of family life, even more so than the dining table, "in the back room of a little store or in the carpeted sitting room of a farm house. . . . The future of the nation depended" upon such cultivation in "these humble abodes of refined intelligence."[9]

Ward McAllister fussed along through life—his mission to develop an aristocracy that would rescue his countrymen from "settling down into a humdrum rut and becoming merely a money-making and money-saving people!" And foster the arts! Extensive European travel and observation of authentic nobility prepared him for the task. Arranging a ball in San Francisco before street lighting appeared, he hired brawny stevedores, dressed them in classic robes, and placed them at intervals along the approach, each holding a flaming pitch pine torch. He brought to New York the necessary attributes—good family, elegant manners imported from the South, and money for a substantial estate near Newport, Rhode Island, the preeminent resort for people of distinction. By 1890, when he wrote his book *Society As I Have Found It,* McAllister played arbiter of the world of high society. One of his inventions, the Patriarchs, a select group, sponsored the city's most exclusive balls. His career approached its climax a few years later when Mrs. William Astor, who reminded observers of a walking chandelier when she entered a ballroom, dripping diamonds, asked him to identify the four hundred families worth knowing. Ultimately, published social registers made known who belonged and who did not.[10]

Who cared? Only the few who valued inclusion. Others, like Al Smith, condemned the snobs whose ancestors came over on the *Cauliflower.* Incessant change and the fluidity of life in the old and new cities frustrated such efforts, attached neither to economic nor to political power. Hundreds of etiquette books testified to the confusion about manners, behavior, social decorum, hierarchy, and expectations, while the widespread assumption that culture could somehow become a political tool to convert the underclasses into thinking citizens revealed the despair of those worried about the shaky foundations of their own status.

Genteel virtue therefore did not triumph in the second half of the nineteenth century. The fluid structure of government prevented big men from asserting control as they once had. Mrs. E. F. Ellet, in an effort to generate an imperial quality Washington sadly lacked (1869), described the elite, bedecked and bejeweled. Problems created "by the accession to society of many families suddenly grown rich and . . . anxious to become leaders" forced some Washingtonians to attend as many as six parties a day. Four supper receptions marked the marriage of the widow of Stephen Douglas to General Robert Williams. More serious, for a time few cared what the government did, a Washington newspaperman sadly noted. The New York press rarely carried more than half a column of Washington news.[11]

The Autocrat of the Breakfast Table who valued old silver, appropriate surroundings, and a coat of arms preferred the man with the gallery of family portraits over the one with the twenty-five-cent daguerreotype. Francis Parkman (1878) called on the great middle classes to beat off the "ignorant proletariat" and the "half-taught plutocracy." *Liberty* was the watchword. But in their hearts, the masses wanted equality more, made the self-made men their ideals, and remained ill-fitted to profit from civilization.

An exchange of gifts in Tennessee in 1854 reflected the elevated status of the aproned artisans and explained the autocrats' despair. Judge William Pepper of the circuit court sent Governor Andrew Johnson a fire shovel and in return received a handmade coat. The former had been a blacksmith before mounting the bench, the latter a tailor before entering the executive mansion. The fact that a farmer or mechanic stepped out of the field or shop into an office of distinction and profit offended the "upstart, swell headed, iron heeled, aristocracy" too lazy and proud to work, too timid to steal, incapable of defending inherited position. Yet perversely, new fortunes completely dwarfed those of the old established families, a crucial matter in the bidding for scarce servants. In that environment society followed the law of fluids—it became shallower the more it spread out. New York showed what happened when the newly rich, suddenly elevated to the top, set the tone—that exhibition of vulgar wealth, that extravagance in dress and entertainment.[12]

The failure to recognize an apex revealed the general incoherence of American society; the absence of a single peak resulted from the lack of any unifying structure. America's rich, said H. G. Wells, did not swell up into a sense of power, developed no sense of public duties. They did not form that upper social structure of leisure and state responsibility, which in Europe gave significance to the whole. Higher, richer, more powerful people differed from lower, poorer, weaker ones; but all the particles drifted about in unrelated orbits. "The rules of the game," explained a self-made merchant to his son, were "you have got to be a descendant to belong, and the farther you descend the harder you belong. The only difference is that in Europe the ancestor who made money enough so that his family could descend, has been dead so long that they have forgotten his shop; in New York, he is so recent that they can only pretend to have forgotten it, but in Chicago they can't lose it because the ancestor is hustling on the Board of Trade or out at the Stock Yards. . . . People who think that they are all the choice cuts off the critter, and that the rest of them are only fit for sausages are usually chuck steak when you get them under the knife."

Most Americans adhered to little clusters held together in various places at various levels by social, ethnic, religious, economic, or regional ties. And some clusters formed larger groupings with their own leaders and communal organizations. But the porous lines among them kept the bits from staying in place, and the fragments did not form a coherent whole except in a sense so general as to lack meaning.[13]

The physical setting, regional differences, and cultural diversities influenced the emerging communities, rural and urban. As in the past, internal migration and immigration contributed to fragmentation. Improved communications by rail and steamboats speeded up movement and eased some of the old hardships of travel by wooden sailing ships and emigrant wagons. But larger numbers, greater distances traversed, and the cultural gap between the old homes and the new created other difficulties. "Undisciplined," the word the English visitor used, described the scrambling, ill-mannered, undignified, unintelligent exploitation of resources. New York became an open trench, "the dumping ground of the cosmos." Chicago sounded one hoarse cry for discipline, the reek and scandal of the stockyards only a gigantic form of that same quality that made the sidewalks filthy, on a par with the elevated railroads of Boston and New York. Chaos left each man for himself, without order, foresight, or common plan. The imposing facades of railroad stations, department stores, and courthouses denoted wealth but often hid the emptiness beyond. Chicago's splendid restaurants, great hotels, and gleaming diamonds in jewelers' windows backed up upon small wooden houses in streets with wooden sidewalks and roadways of prairie black. Topsy-turvydom dismayed hostile observers—unreality "as greedily craved by the mob as alcohol by the dipsomaniac"; indeed New York's Luna Park manifested for its patrons "the jumbled nightmares of a morphine eater."[14]

Lest they go astray, recent arrivals clung together and formed sub-communities of their own. But internal migration and distinctions already in place by 1850 augmented the sense of ethnic difference. The pioneers of Wisconsin (1856) assembled the old-timers who had resided in the territory for twenty years. New Englanders in New York, Illinois, or California long retained their identity; from Eli Thayer to Josiah Strong, their spokesmen explained that the hard-working and God-fearing Yankee race would prove the social and political regenerators of the continent. A deep cultural and social line kept Yankees apart, and not only in Kansas, where the differences took explosive form. That they formed their own societies in New York and Brooklyn, in New Jersey and Pennsylvania, even in Toronto, St. Louis, Indianapolis, Cincinnati, and California, hardly surprised their neighbors. But they wished to preserve their identity also in Charleston, South Carolina. Those "scions of a softer age" memorialized the "rough nurse of a hero-brood." Though they wandered away, in their sad, fond dreams they kept alive the kindred loves of heaven and of home. The same romantic reveries contributed to the continued popularity of Scott's novels and later irritated George Horace Lorimer, who regarded them as endangering the United States, a nation unformed, a country of unassimilated regions and nationalities, its Americanism unarticulated. Lorimer used his *Saturday Evening Post* to cross barriers of space and literacy, reaching audiences not normally attracted by magazines. Its advertisements also fostered standardization and national distribution. But that uniformity spread slowly and late.[15]

An enormously complex pattern emerged from a national experience that encompassed diverse populations expected to coexist in places as far apart as Maine and California, as North Dakota and Florida; and if an English cowboy in Wyoming resembled his German, Spanish, or black counterparts, the British ranchers, German merchants, Scandinavian farmers, East European miners, and Basque shepherds formed clustered groupings wherever they were. The outcome transformed the concepts of community and the controls that regulated the relationship of the individual to society.[16]

Those changes reshaped the ideas of liberty inherited from the Revolution. Through the nineteenth century Americans clung to old norms of a simple life in which yeomen farmers lived independently, encountering neighbors only occasionally at the county seat. To some, nature acquired mystical powers, akin to primeval purity before the advent of man. Humans made the city, after all, while God made the countryside; and John Muir urged people to "come to the purest of terrestrial fountains. Come and receive baptism and absolution from civilized sins." The

Homestead Law, proposed in 1852 and enacted a decade later, embodied that aspiration. Already an anachronism then, the ideal nevertheless attracted people nostalgically loyal to a condition they may never actually have experienced but to which they longed to return. In 1864 an act of Congress signed by Lincoln granted to the state of California the tract of land including Yosemite Valley and the Mariposa Big Trees, "upon the express conditions that the premises shall be held for public use, resort and recreation and shall be held inalienable for all times," a novel feature of the management of the public domain. In the abstract the concept remained vital in 1920 to an industrial population totally detached from the soil. Henry Ford, one of the architects of a different reality, aimed to restore his employees to an ideal rural yeoman life in garden communities. Frederick Law Olmstead, the landscaping, environmental, and conservation movements, the rural cemeteries, and the city beautification projects expressed similar concerns. George Pullman's planned community sought to mold a superior type of American worker by engendering "habits of respectability," including propriety and good manners, self-improvement, education, cleanliness, and industriousness. To attain these goals, his town provided a setting of green lawns, flower beds, and lake vistas. Even Chicago's incredibly fast growth could improve upon nature by giving it a "finished appearance," "as if some enlightened nobleman had turned democrat, torn down his park walls and invited his neighbors to come in and build upon his rounded knolls and wave-like ridges."[17]

Attachment to the ideal covered over society's pervasive lack of any common interest other than the greed that kept even the rich working. Farmers, laborers, merchants, and manufacturers, by clinging to the yeoman concept, pretended they were not actually tearing at each other's throats, but cooperating to reach the same goal—at least abstractly.

No more than formerly did experiments in communal or cooperative living succeed. Complaints against oppression by merchants and factory owners from time to time conjured up visionary schemes for improving workingmen's conditions, as when in 1851 William M. Shinn established the Evergreen Hamlet Association just outside Pittsburgh. Only a half-dozen families joined his cooperative community, and the venture collapsed. The little bands of anarchists and socialists who valiantly tried later did no better. Such failures led mechanics instead to seek redress in politics, without much greater success. Nevertheless, the temptation to locate such experiments in the open American spaces persisted, and European newcomers as well as native-born Americans repeatedly responded. Only settlements held together by distinctive religious and communal bonds like those at Oneida and Amana endured and grew. Even the

Mormons fell back upon economic cooperation by individuals in the United Order after their communal efforts failed.[18]

Americans who employed figures of speech like the *melting pot* or *assimilation* to describe their society assumed that, sooner or later, national development would somehow yield a homogeneous population as an end product. Those expressions long endured, although after 1900 some observers thought of a more complex mosaic in which each element retained its own character though blending into a colorful whole. Mary Antin's *The Promised Land* appealed for sympathy for the impoverished and victimized European peasants who sought refuge in the slums; America's freedoms in the end would make them fine citizens. Although immigrants like the urban blacks for the time being retained their separate communal identities, all would merge into a national whole, as Booker T. Washington's popular autobiography, *Up from Slavery* (1901), foretold. "A Nation announcing itself, (many in one,)" rejected none, accepted all, forming the amplest poem: "Here is not merely a nation, but a teeming nation of nations." Never a good prophet, Emerson saw with joy the Irish landing at Boston and New York (1866). "There they go—to school," he said, not foreseeing how complex his own world would become. Two of his successors, Henry Adams and Henry James, bemoaned twentieth-century multiplicity, so unlike contemporary Britain or thirteenth-century Europe.[19]

Faith in an ultimate blend required total disregard for the bustling life that animated a country even more strikingly heterogeneous in 1920 than in 1850. An observer in Ellis Island in 1906 noted thousands "of crude Americans from Ireland and Poland and Italy and Syria and Finland and Albania, men, women, children, dirt and bags together." Revisiting his native land in the same year, Henry James shuddered at what New York City had become; and he saw only a fragment of its turbulent life. *Society* then referred not to Ward McAllister's rosters but to Dakota wheat farmers and miners, to Alabama croppers and steel workers, to the denizens of the Bowery and Chinatown and of Washington and Louisburg Squares, to laborers in the iron and cotton mills, to the clerks counting and measuring in stores and offices, to mothers cooking, scrubbing, sewing, as well as to their sisters at the machines, all of them forming communities unlike any ever elsewhere thrown together. A day's ride took the traveler to a region that revered what he laughed at and loathed what he adored. At nine A.M. at Lincoln's tomb he saw pilgrims with uncovered heads, while by noon he met people who held everything Lincoln represented in contempt. The endless variety of persons did not disappear beneath the appellation *Americans.* They remained different though becoming citizens; and their communities accommodated both the elements that set each apart and the identity that held them together.[20]

Frederick Jackson Turner accepted the kaleidoscopic society in the Portage, Wisconsin, of his youth—"a mixture of raftsmen from the pineries, of Irishmen (in the bloody first ward), of Pomeranian Immigrants . . . in old country garbs, of Scotch with Caledonia nearby; of Welsh with Cambria adjacent; of Germans some of them university trained (the beer hall of Carl Haertle was the town clubhouse); of Yankees from Vermont and Maine and Connecticut, chiefly of New York-Yankees, of Southerners (a few relatively); a few Negroes; many Norwegians and Swiss, some Englishmen, one or two Italians, who all got on together in this forming society."[21]

Gypsy bands also moved through the countryside, having learned by centuries of experience the knack of living as outsiders, and tolerated in the New World as in the old for the skills other rural people lacked. Southerners considered less menacing the Yankees

> Who worship in old Fan'il Hall,
> Old Fan'il Hall, that glorious spot,
> Where saints so oft blow cold and hot,
> And launch abroad their wordy thunder
> To fill th'astonished world with wonder.[22]

Nowhere did migration sprinkle settlers in a random pattern. Those intent upon agriculture knew something of their destinations, whether they departed from an older state or from across an ocean. Whether they moved as individuals or as members of land associations or colonies, they shaped their choices by the prospect of joining folk like themselves, for cooperation, mutual aid, religious worship, and for sharing the loneliness and the perils of existence in the strangeness. Those who did not understand the words found it a hard penance to be silent—and particularly in the intimacies of life. They sought the familiar accents of familiar phrases and wished their children also to know the old tongues. By 1898, seven western states permitted bilingual public education, an issue that stimulated ongoing ethnic political activity. Soon observers noted Polish farm communities on Long Island and in the Connecticut Valley. Then, too, little connections helped the ambitious in town or country; "the wee drop of Scotch bluid atween us" at critical moments eased Andrew Carnegie's ascent.[23]

Men thrown together in construction gangs, sharing the intimacy of bunkhouses and of the cheating commissary, sought at least the bonds of

common language. So, too, in the mines—Welsh anthracite, Scots bituminous, Cornishmen copper and lead, Englishmen iron. Every trade
developed its own lingo that in effect excluded outsiders.[24]

The urban setting persistently reminded Americans of their diversity.
Some despised Chicago, "this flat smear, this endless drawl of streets and
shanties, large and small, this ocean of smoke." In time (1915), however,
a poet would hail "the hog-butcher for the world, tool maker, stacker
of wheat, player with railroads and the nation's freight handler; stormy,
brawling city of the big shoulders." And even earlier the spectacle of
peoples mingling on ferries or on crowded streets in "mast-hemm'd
Manhattan" conveyed a sense of wonder—laborers, clerks, shopkeepers,
merchants, passing all unknown to one another, their human qualities
"comforting even heroic." Yet the same spectacle left many uneasy,
fearful of the potential disorder. The well-to-do shrank from the dangerous classes, but the poor also preferred social order out of fear of abandon-
ment in misfortune. Although the great places like New York, Chicago,
Philadelphia, and Boston differed from the middling ones like Pittsburgh,
Buffalo, Cleveland, and Detroit, they posed common problems to their
residents.[25]

Prudence dictated withdrawal to safer areas. Swiftly the suburbs
spread outward for those who could afford to commute; and rapid transit
networks steadily enlarged the numbers. Already in 1857 advertisements
appealed to Chicago ladies to interest their husbands in Hyde Park lots
refreshed by the lake breezes. Eastern cities began the dispersal even
sooner.[26]

However, strangers preferred to be with their own, whether at the
center or on the periphery. People from the same village or province, who
shared language, religious rituals, festivals, and food, and who adhered
to a common code of personal and family behavior, gravitated together.
In the Big Flat Tenement on Mott Street, New York, Kate Claghorn
found 478 residents, including 368 Jews, 31 Italians, 31 Irish, 30 Germans,
and 4 American-born. Usually, the requirements of the job tossed workers
about to factories, markets, piers, and construction sites in remote parts
of the city. But those who left in the morning returned at night to homes
in familiar neighborhoods that defined their places in a community.

Clusters of the foreign-born formed the most visible neighborhoods—districts known as Over the Rhine or Little Italy, as the East Side
or Chinatown, as Polish Greenpoint or South Brooklyn. Blacks who
entered the industrial cities after 1870 fell into similar patterns, as did
Yankees who moved from rural New England to Boston, New York,
or Buffalo, and Kentuckians who came over to Cincinnati or Chicago.
The lines separating these areas did not quite fit the municipal boundaries

of wards or of election districts, or for that matter of parishes, but developed informally out of personal preferences that excluded outsiders by making them uncomfortable. Already before the Civil War, "house brokers" in some cities influenced the choices of renters and buyers, but mostly to raise prices. Ethnic neighborhoods took form largely without such intervention and left an imprint on the outer districts to which the most fortunate residents moved—East Side Jews to Harlem and Williamsburgh, for instance.[27]

Fastidious strangers put off by pungent odors, by noise and dirt, condemned these areas as slums. Edith Elmer Wood explained (1919), "Our sons paid with their blood on the soil of France for the dark rooms of the Lower East Side," from which Leon Trotsky derived his distrust of the United States, and out of which, she believed, sprang the Bolshevik peace with Germany.

But refugees from dismal Old World villages accepted the new residences as home, despite overcrowding. The scrape of wheels and hooves on asphalt, the spray of snow from winter sleighs, the cries of the hokey pokey and the oyster and the popcorn and chestnut men, the sounds of the organ grinder and the knife grinder, of the fish and the vegetable and rag dealers, created a comforting context for daily life. Over in the First Ward, near Murphy's row of houses—"there's the Phalens and the Whalens . . . they are sitting on the railings with their children on their knees, all gossiping and talking"—sang Harrigan and Hart (1879).[28]

The array of services that defined a neighborhood included churches, funeral parlors, saloons, food shops, bars, and cafés, and also the quarters of local associations or of affiliates of national ones, operating person-to-person, with credit as much as cash passing across the counter, advice and information readily thrown in. Less formal occasions brought women together—those of a certain age or mothers or girls. They talked about common problems—the New World's meats and clothing, gossip, the family, the marriage brokers, the priests; shared experience lightened burdens. So, too, the men and young men and boys, all arranged by age. As in the smaller societies of the countryside and in Old World villages, gangs formed; the youngsters pitched pennies or played street games; and informal older groupings (sometimes descended from old fire companies) shared the latest information, looked to a trusted chief for counsel, lent a hand when possible, and provided defense against intrusive outsiders. Hanging around a favorite corner, smoking, spitting, not quite drunk and not quite sober, they passed on tips and odds and chummed with the police. Already before the Civil War in Baltimore the Plug Uglies, the Rip Raps and the Black Snakes proved more than a match for the officers.

The Greenpoint Savages in New York, and their counterparts in other cities on into the twentieth century, made their own law, terrifying Henry George with the prospect of total chaos. Not desert and forest but city slums nursed the barbarians who would do for the New World what huns and vandals did to the old.[29]

In the urban neighborhoods, gangs provided a means by which to reach for political power, as the Tammany braves had, by contrast to Europe, where municipal government remained beyond popular control. In rural county seats the old families still reigned. In those towns, people never said a good word of one another, believing everyone unscrupulous, ridiculous, weak, worthless. Forming no deep friendships, "they all hated each other in secret, there being much quiet satisfaction when one of them failed." Opinions in politics and business they derived second-hand.[30] But in Boston, New York, Chicago, or San Francisco, street gangs became clubs and the clubs parts of machines. With neighborly help if needed, naturalization made members voters and enlisted them in the party. Experience defined the head of the gang, the club, and the machine—the boss—just as other neighborhood organizations developed their own leaders. A fragmented society followed not a single but multiple elites.[31]

The incomplete oversight of once-dominant elements freed dissidents to pursue their own devices unless overtly threatening to others. With all affiliations voluntary, those who chose to go it alone or in the company of self-selected new groups did so without penalty. The shield of anonymity characteristic of the great cities nurtured tolerance. Little Bohemian districts like Greenwich Village sheltered artists and rebels as well as Italians. The failure to define and establish a genteel tradition in literature, art, and music, meant that while opinionated cultural custodians controlled prestigious magazines, the opera, and museums, those institutions established no one's dominance. Excluded groups generated their own popular literature, music, and stage, just as Louisa May Alcott gratified her passion for the theater in little Walpole, New Hampshire, or Al Smith at St. James's in New York, for neighborhood audiences. Some people attended the Hippodrome, others the Metropolitan; those not admitted to the cotillion at Mrs. Astor's could waltz with Casey and his strawberry blonde, or try the polka at Pulaski's. Luna Park, which claimed five million paid admissions in a single season, catered to everyone, forcing none into a coherent whole. Amusement parks aimed to please rather than instruct, appealed to the heart rather than the mind, and created an attractive aura of unreality. The critical freedom of association set American culture and society apart from those of France and England, which denigrated spontaneous group activities, suspected of conspiracy, while encouraging those privileged by appropriate patronage.[32]

Profound differences in tastes, habits, and traditions, made government irrelevant, worse an inappropriate use of compulsion to favor some as against others. The general reluctance to use such power expanded the areas reserved to voluntary associations, which left choices to individuals unencumbered by centralized decisions. The law treated all societies alike—educational, philanthropic, religious, ethnic, and business, all private, whatever the impact on their members or on the public they served. The *Dartmouth College* case had granted them the protection of the contract clause against government interference; and the Fourteenth Amendment's provision on due process strengthened that safeguard.[33]

Diversity prevailed, in part at least because migration remained the characteristic American experience—east to west, north to south, and south to north, as well as from across the oceans. Each move added to the cultural patchwork.

The foreign-born, most visible—"the copious humanity streaming from every direction toward America"—arrived in three distinct waves. The influx from Ireland, Britain, and Germany already under way in 1850 peaked in 1854 and then subsided. Northern Europe then felt the effects of social changes that had already transformed the West, unloosing a second movement out of Norway, Sweden, Denmark, and Finland; added to the older types, these newcomers amounted to about eight million. A third, even greater wave toward the end of the nineteenth century brought migration to a climax between 1890 and 1914, when more than twenty million newcomers swelled the population of the United States. By then the disturbing changes had spread to eastern and southern Europe, beginning with the German-Polish areas of Pomerania and Posen, then extending to the Austrian empire's aggrieved subject people like the Czechs, Slovaks, Hungarians, Slovenians, Serbs, and Poles. From Russia came other "Congress Poles," as well as Ukrainians and Ruthenians. About two million eastern European Jews joined co-religionists who had earlier arrived from England, Holland, and Germany. Some four million peasants fled Italy; and a sizable group came from Portugal. In addition, elements from Asia arrived, as did uncounted numbers who crossed the borders from Canada and Mexico. A bemused visitor (1883) came upon a village of Filipino fishers and alligator hunters in Manila, Louisiana. Steam that eased travel permitted some newcomers to return, but the overwhelming majority remained.[34]

Place of origin did not in itself determine group identity after arrival in the United States, for those who came off the ships differed among themselves socially, culturally, and in their motives for migration. Thousands of liberty-seeking people fled to America to escape political, racial, and religious persecution, among them the Polish revolutionaries of 1863, the victims of Russian and Romanian pogroms between 1880 and 1910, and Armenians and Greeks who escaped massacres in the first decade of the twentieth century.

Men and women dislocated by economic disturbances far outnumbered such refugees. The factories of Manchester and Milan and Warsaw robbed of customers the traditional skilled handloom-weavers and cobblers and tailors, who moved away to avoid a degrading fall into the ranks of the proletariat. America became their destination. At the same time, the spread of large commercial farms across Ireland, Scandinavia, Germany, Italy, and eastern Europe deprived millions of their small holdings; left landless and helpless, they too fled, hastened on by disastrous famines or plagues. Meanwhile, a constantly rising population sustained the state of crisis.

Nostalgia and sentiment occasionally linked the businessmen Andrew Carnegie and Spyros Skouras, the musicians Victor Herbert and Jascha Heifetz, the scientists Joseph Goldberger and Michael Pupin, the journalists Pulitzer and Scripps, with the lands of their births, just as J. P. Morgan presided over a New England Society dinner (1890). But such individuals stood apart from the great masses of peasants and laborers whose muscles and wills developed the economy. Unskilled lads from Cork and Kerry and coolies from Canton, wrestling with the clumsy rails and ties, laid the railroads across the mountains. Bakers and carpenters from the Rhineland helped feed and house the population of rapidly growing cities. Former ghetto residents sat at tenement sewing machines and supplied the nation's clothing. Peasants who had once tilled the fields of Poland and Hungary stood at steel mill furnaces and worked at the endlessly moving assembly lines that developed American power. By the end of the nineteenth century, the series of of essays Walter Hines Page commissioned for the *Atlantic Monthly* (1896–99) inadequately recognized the patchwork nature of American culture—inadequately, because they took as given the fixed lines of nationality. Yet the great majority of newcomers had not so identified themselves in the old homes, where they made themselves known by the name of the village or simply as *einheimische,* "local people." They discovered the larger identity by contrast with others and by the wish to establish distance around them.

Among the German speakers, the Anabaptist sects—some from Russia—stood apart from the northern Lutherans and Bavarian Catholics, to say nothing of the Wends, the Swiss, and sometimes the Jews.

Sneaky Bohemians and Prussians tried under false pretenses to obtain relief from the Chicago German Immigrant Aid Society (1858). Even the English established distinct Manx and Cornish organizations, and new-comers from Macclesfield and Ashton followed their own customs. The Jews, already divided into Sephardic and German, now faced complex new additions. Among the Yiddish speakers, often referred to as East Europeans, bitter acrimony and mutual contempt marked the encounters of Latvians and Galicians, with the Ukrainians and Breslauer species apart. Persians, Bulgarians, Ladino speakers, Greek speakers, and Arabic speakers also set themselves off from other Jews. Polish peasants distinguished among the *Prusak, Rosjanin, Galicjak,* the natives of the various partitions, as well as the quite different *Kasub* and the Jews, although they sometimes joined up with Lithuanians, themselves uncertain who they were. And the South Slavs, Greeks, Macedonians, and Portuguese recognized distinc-tions not perceptible to outsiders. No coherent social structure could encompass them all, even had the will to create it existed. Instead, each group formed its own little order to meet its own needs. A confused observer doubted that America would ever make "intelligently coopera-tive citizens of these people," who would remain forever "a very low lower class . . . [of] largely illiterate industrialized peasants." The country lacked the "organized means or effectual influences for raising these huge masses of humanity to the requirements of an ideal modern civilization." Frustrated reformers could not teach political morality under such cir-cumstances except through ethnic clubs that explained corrupt politicians did not rob the rich to give to the poor, but robbed the rich and in return gave them power to rob the poor.[35]

Mutual assistance, free loans to the deserving, philanthropy, decent burial for the dead, fraternity, religion, and recollections of common culture, as well as the desire for self-defense, sparked the appearance of many a German Saengerbund and Schutzenverein, as well as of various ethnic associations side by side with those already in existence. Or just "the pensive aching to be together—you know not why, and I know not why." Jacob Lanzit, an Austrian, in 1858 found New York altogether too big. The noise, the tumult, the rattling traffic, drove him out of his mind. In Chicago, however, he ran into a German hotel proprietor. "Oh, how my blood stopped in my veins, not having spoken a word to anyone during the whole journey."[36]

Much depended upon the numbers involved. The first handfuls at-tached themselves to any available grouping despite internal divisions, however significant in the Old World and however outlandish some accents. But growing numbers sparked contradictory impulses—on the one hand subdivision by region or village, as well as by social status; on the other hand, formation of inclusive nationwide organizations. Few ethnic groups attained a state of equilibrium or stability. Growth tempted them to expand, to take in ever more members in the interest of fiscal or political strength. Yet no one had to join; and local promoters found enough recruits for persistent fragmentation. Hundreds of little *landsmannshaften* and synagogues, each autonomous, divided the allegiance of eastern European Jews. Lines clear enough in the neighborhood blurred on the national scale, revealing underlying fissures. Increasing numbers produced divisions along religious as well as regional lines.[37]

Class and race distinctions also remained. Cultural, linguistic, and religious ties held together the relatively small group of Portuguese most heavily concentrated in New England, but the prevailing negative attitude toward color erected a barrier between white mainland or Azorean immigrants and the black Bravas from the Cape Verde islands. Portuguese ancestry burdened one family which changed its name to Wood; one of its members, William Madison Wood, became president of the American Woolen Company. A similar move effaced the Jewish antecedents of August Belmont and many others.[38]

Often, economic interest formed a bond as potent as cultural heritage. As a matter of course, like-minded people joined little groups to pursue common goals. In Cairo, Illinois, by no means a large city, businessmen formed a Merchants' League as well as a Board of Trade and then, to boost the place, a Greater Cairo movement, which appointed a Committee of Twenty to further development in excited anticipation of projected Panama Canal opportunities.

Many more people became involved in workingmen's associations and in the labor movement. These efforts long floundered upon uncertainty of objectives—whether to aim at improvements for their own members, or to pursue some more general social goal. The old craft unions, which reached back to a much earlier era, had a clear view of their purposes, as when the Cincinnati seamstresses organized for mutual relief and adequate prices. The mechanics and laborers of the Chicago, Alton, and St. Louis Railroad disregarded the company's threats to import foreign workers and went out without regard to nationality (1856). So, too, in Chicago the masons (1858) and the German and Irish bricklayers struck against a wage cut (1859), as did the printers and the journeymen in the city's "mechanical bakery" (1860). The mariners that year needed no direct action to set their monthly wages and conditions of employment. Ethnic attachments then reinforced the ties of craft.[39]

Unions of working people under such circumstances generated communal action. The pathos of a lost cause long evoked sympathetic responses. "Hear the poor orphans tell their sad story, 'Father was killed by the Pinkerton men.' "

> The freedom of the city in Scotland far away
> 'Tis presented to the millionaire suave
> But here in Free America

his workmen "who fought for home and right to live where they had toiled so long" got the freedom of the grave.

The divisive elements that sapped labor solidarity sprang not from ethnic differences but from clashing objectives. The strikers' slogan, "we want bread and roses, too," astonished a reporter in Lawrence, Massachusetts (1912). "I shall not soon forget the curious life, the strange sudden fire of the mingled nationalities at the strike meetings when they broke into the universal language of song." But by then sharp rifts had appeared in the American labor force. Mastery of a skill distinguished some wage earners from the unskilled, and made defense of a privileged position paramount. Although the garment industry employed thousands of unskilled laborers, easily replaced, with little bargaining power, highly skilled cutters without whom the shops would close supported a union to protect their places. Since many passed training and jobs on to their sons, they sought to exclude outsiders by high initiation fees and looked askance at technological changes.

In the engineering, building, and printing trades and in the boot and shoe industry, strong craft traditions fostered narrow associations that combined concerted action against employers with mutual aid and sociability, dual functions revealed in such names as the Sons of Vulcan, the Knights of St. Crispin, and the Daughters of St. Crispin. Ethnic solidarity often reinforced these groups, as among the Irish carpenters and teamsters, the German brewery workers, and the Italian granite cutters. A monopoly of their skills allowed the Venetian mosaic workers in the Italian Marble and Mosaic Workers Union to control some branches of the industry. But the National Union of Granite Cutters (organized 1877) included Scots, Irish, English, and Yankees, as well as Italians. While excluding the Chinese, they invited all others to join.[40]

The entrenched resisted pressures to accommodate others and opposed inclusive tendencies that might dilute distinctive characters. Hence the lack of support for the National Labor Union (1866), which in any case alienated craftsmen by moving away from economic issues to politics and producer cooperatives. True, a ban of Chinese immigration and on contract labor, a ten-hour law, factory inspection, and workmen's compensation, would benefit all; but Terence Powderly's Knights of Labor, which fought for these measures, ignored actual distinctions among those it welcomed. The order, which sprang up among the Philadelphia garment cutters (1869), embraced a secret ritual and drifted toward general reform measures. As it did so, the crafts pulled away and joined the American Federation of Labor, whose leader, Samuel Gompers, assailed the class struggle and emphasized the self-interest of skilled workers in their own organizations. Peter J. McGuire of the United Brotherhood of Carpenters and Joiners explained that the American Federation of Labor had "defined the essential and radical difference between the glittering promises of the Knights of Labor and the practical every day work of the trade unions." The defeat of the Knights and the failure of the American Railway Union in the Pullman strike opened the way to unionism that emphasized limited bargaining objectives, an arrangement to the taste of employers, who hoped to return to the old idyllic closeness of boss and hand by negotiating with each craft separately rather than with the whole mass of their workers.[41]

The craft organizations held on despite technological changes that threatened their skills. In some cities, like Milwaukee, tight ethnic identity helped. During strikes and in the face of depressions, workers accepted aid from reformers like Rose Schneiderman and Leonora O'Reilly of the Women's Trade Union League and from benevolent clergymen like John Howard Melish, as well as from sympathetic socialist and coordinating labor committees. But in good times and bad they defended the lines that set them off from outsiders.[42]

Unions with a strong ethnic base, like the railway brotherhoods, which held together by excluding outsiders, thrived, for they served religious and defensive as well as collective bargaining goals. That was hardly avoidable since, in 1910, immigrants constituted 25 percent of workers in transportation, 36 percent in manufacturing, and 45 percent in mining, percentages that would have been much higher with the addition of their native-born children.[43]

Often, the union and the ethnic group overlapped. In the Pennsylvania mine fields, the secret Molly Maguires who bargained collectively through terrorism may or may not have originated among the Ribbonmen of the old country; but in the United States, active links with the Ancient Order of Hibernians gave them strength in local politics and in the courts. The Jewish character of the New York City garment workers was as pronounced as the Italian character of the New England granite cutters, and was affirmed in the formation of the United Hebrew Trades.[44]

Attitudes of withdrawal and detachment stemmed not merely from pride in their own skills and the capacity for self-defense, but also from the cultural threat mingling with strangers presented. Members who referred to themselves as brothers and to their association as a lodge could not conceive of being brothers to those who spoke a different tongue, ate outlandish foods, looked and smelled curiously. Instead, social affiliations crossed economic lines, to middle-class leaders like themselves—grocers, barkeepers, journalists, lawyers. Immigrants, in particular, remained deferential to Old World prominenti, though only slightly better off than those who worked with their hands. In addition, some enterprises, like Miller and Rhoads of Richmond, eased workforce relations by encouraging the formation of a company club (1902) and by setting aside a roof garden for members. Rudimentary pension plans and employer/employee associations aimed to create a sense of unity and to dilute class consciousness. Moreover, the *Danbury Hatters* case cast doubt upon organizations susceptible to indictment as conspiracies in restraint of trade, at least until the Clayton Act (1914) ended that uncertainty.

The unskilled, always the most precarious, remained unorganized and avoided extremes. A dollar a day was all the pay for work on the boulevard; and living standards reflected the straightened incomes. The laborers caught most of the bullets, and even peaceful strikes demanded costly sacrifices and remained measures of last resort. In the cities, long intervals without work and frequent hops from job to job and plant to plant drained away any sense of identity with fellow workers and inhibited class consciousness. Many immigrants considered themselves birds of passage, destined to return to their native villages after a few years. The prospect compensated for present hardships.

Furthermore, the foreign-born had a standard of comparison; the meager American wages seemed bountiful to those who remembered Europe. Now they lived in the golden land, in which some acquired the skills to advance; and if the withered rewards of the moment left others unfed, there remained hope in the promise that they or their children would attain a status out of reach elsewhere. In Chicago, the German Relief Society heard (1857) that people who had escaped European despotism did not look to the governing power for food and work, preferring freedom to pursue what calling they wished. Mobility upward proved actual enough to make the present tolerable despite low wages and periods of unemployment. A fluid society recognized diversities and rewarded all willing to work. The sons and daughters of the laborers and farmers found few businesses or professions closed against talent. Scores of men and women did better than parents who saw the American shore for the first time from the deck of an immigrant ship.[45]

Everywhere, spacial and social mobility complicated group life. Natives as well as immigrants reached for change and advancement. Restless people tried one occupation after another, failed to stay put; and the high level of transiency kept class and ethnicity fluid. Affiliations changed sometimes within a single generation. Middle-class people whose livelihood depended on neighborhood solidarity resisted the impulse to move. In many places the undertaker with a link to the church, the corner grocer, the saloonkeeper, and the butcher familiar with local tastes valued connections to the sources of their livelihoods. Physicians and attorneys also felt such ties. Yet districts changed and stranded the stolid practitioners and shopkeepers while the more ambitious and more venturesome moved off.

Professionals of all backgrounds, eager for stability, wished to protect their positions by excluding outsiders through licensing admission to practice. Widespread popular aversion to favoritism or privilege, however, blocked efforts to restrict the right to act as minister, physician, or attorney, so that only subtle, indirect signs of education or affiliation revealed the special status that set some apart.[46]

Distinctive ordination, garb, titles of address, and other privileges no longer defined the unique qualities of the clergy. Nor did lifelong settlement in a congregation. Pluralism and diversity obliterated special status. In the Protestant churches and among Jews, the call to a pulpit expired at the pleasure of either the flock or the shepherd.

Visitors noted the financial preoccupations. The preacher talked about "the stinginess and stubbornness of his honorable audience, of the church members who live in abundance, while he the guardian of their souls, if not left to starve still is not as well-paid as he deserves." Ministers dealt not only with listeners, but with customers, just as in the theater. To meet competition they relied on sensational oratory, as did the stars—Henry Ward Beecher, Stephen S. Wise, and Abba H. Silver. Or the pastor could gain recognition as a partisan of his laboring flock.[47]

In hierarchical churches, the power of the bishop ended when enough communicants, undismayed by accusations of heresy and schism, decided to follow a new dispensation. Class and ethnic differences persistently troubled the Catholics, as when priests from urban backgrounds sought to minister to peasants, or Irish to French Canadians, Portuguese, or Germans. Separate parishes, even in small towns, helped, as did gestures like the transfer of Jesuit operations in Buffalo from a French to a German province. But open warfare erupted over the demand of Father Peter Paul Cahensly for restructuring in national dioceses, each with its own bishop (1890), a demand the Church could not meet while it struggled to affirm its Americanism. And agitation in Scranton, Pennsylvania, led to the appearance and spread of a Polish National Catholic Church under Bishop Francis Hodur, while aggrieved Ukrainians split away in a schismatic Uniate Church.[48]

The number of sects multiplied, some clustered about economic, racial, or ethnic groups, others indiscriminate, all served by their own clergy. Even the Catholic hierarchy accommodated to the environment, retaining its unity but permitting national parishes to serve the needs of each group it embraced.

Immense social and cultural distances separated the vicar of a fashionable Park Avenue Episcopal church or the rabbi of Temple Emanuel in New York from a minister of a Birmingham, Alabama, African Methodist church or the cantor of a Harlem synagogue, each self-designated, certified by the approval of the congregation.

Directly or indirectly, the states licensed other occupations at every level of social esteem—physicians, attorneys, also plumbers, electricians, and barbers, all presumably to protect the consuming public. But no license carried with it an exclusive privilege of healing, pleading, shaving, or soldering. Attainment of the formal document, sealed by a government agency, usually required completion of a set course of study and provided a marginal advantage. But customers retained the right to select according to their own criteria, and ambitious young practitioners easily circumvented requirements. In both medicine and law, and in other trades, numerous proprietary schools offered instruction for fees; and in many areas apprenticeship still persisted.

Licensing thus proved an ineffective screening device. Instead, a more influential, less official pattern of selection recognized differences among medical and law schools, affirming the superiority of those affiliated with universities and requiring a liberal arts degree for admission. Their graduates qualified in the developing medical specialties and associated with the best hospitals, or they became partners in the most influential law firms. Others did business in the side streets, their patients and clients less likely to include corporations or names from the social register than criminals or weary housewives. Howe and Hummel of New York received an annual retainer of $5,000 from the notorious fence Mother Mandelbaum, and the firm (1869–1907) defended more than a thousand persons indicted for homicide without cutting into the business of Abraham Levy, "the Last Hope" of murderers.[49]

By the 1890s, the colleges—even Harvard and Yale—had ceased to be adequately selective in admissions; autonomous subgroupings—private clubs and fraternities—more effectively screened out their favorite types, to whom they imparted a uniformity of fashion, clothing, taste, and behavior, as much in play as in class, and especially when previous passage through a select preparatory school had established the appropriate foundation. In terms of incomes and social prestige, the elite callings thus entered differed from others—pharmacy, dentistry, accountancy, teaching, and nursing—which also required skill and training, and sometimes licensing, but lacked the leverage of medicine and law. However important their services, the less privileged occupations fell behind in social prestige and income.[50]

To further common interests and to establish uniform standards of ethical practice, all professionals created local and national associations to resist profound antielitist prejudices. "No exercise of jaw twisting India rubber law is as good as the exercise of paw on the handle of a saw, sawing wood" (1856)—the common view. The response to such critics emphasized the practical value of moot courts in the university. The American Association of Public Accountants (1887) joined counterparts in law and medicine to lobby for regulation of the professions (accountancy in New York, 1896) and to suppress proprietary "colleges" considered inadequate.[51]

Journalists faced a more complex situation. No longer journeyman artisans, but not professionals either, they depended upon an uncertain reading public. Constitutional guarantees of free speech assured any literate person the freedom to write. Some, like Edward Eggleston, shifted about from place to place and from newspapers to magazines as journalist and editor. Walt Whitman and Mark Twain also changed occupations—printer, carpenter, river pilot—before settling down to the pen. Lafcadio Hearn slept in dry goods boxes, sheds, a boiler in a vacant lot, and a hayloft, when he arrived in Cincinnati; and he worked as a servant, waiter, printer, and proofreader before finding a slot as a reporter. Others created roles for themselves either as town boosters or through an ethnic identity that gave them linguistic or national command over their readers. Charles Taylor, though himself a Yankee, gained Irish readers for *The Boston Globe* by a campaign to allow priests into local hospitals to administer last rites to the dying. Journalism provided Patrick Donahoe of *The Boston Pilot* the leverage for group leadership; his reputation among the Irish drew customers to his savings bank and his travel agency. Michael Kruszka among the Poles and Luigi Fugazi among the Italians also attracted support for their own enterprises, while Abraham Cahan's *Forward* guided Yiddish readers to his version of socialism.[52]

The most successful, however, transcended local and ethnic limitations to reach a national audience, as when Horace Greeley's *Tribune* and J. G. Bennett's *Herald* spread far beyond the boundaries of New York City. So, too, Joseph Pulitzer moved from his *Westlicher Post* to the *Post-Dispatch* in St. Louis and then to the *World* in New York City. Ethnicity survived such transitions, for the *Tribune* attracted Yankee subscribers and Pulitzer's *World* Germans, but in diluted form.

The ambitious became community leaders in any one of several ways. Emotions and self-interest moved businessmen, politicians, lawyers, and physicians toward group solidarity, like the Norwegian John Johnson, the Swedes Hans Mattson and Knute Nelson, and the Irish Patrick Collins. Patrick J. Kennedy's neighborhood saloon in east Boston provided a base for liquor dealing, local banking, and political activity fortified by a good marriage. His son Joe moved into a wider business world after study at Harvard; and a grandson John attained national office without effacing the old ties.[53]

Zeal and ambition drove on some clergymen and intellectuals. Francis A. Hoffman used the pen to stir awareness of German identity, just as some preachers exploited the pulpit. Sidney Hillman fled to Chicago after the failure of the Russian Revolution of 1905. He went to work as a tailor, then organized his fellows, and in 1910 led a successful strike. In 1914 he came to New York, and as president of the Amalgamated Clothing Workers urged members to share the responsibility for improving quality, increasing output, abolishing waste, and reducing overhead; by 1916 he had made the forty-eight-hour week general. Fan Sylian Noli, a Harvard student, united his scattered countrymen in the vicinity, founded the Albanian church of which he became bishop, formalized the language, and encouraged publication of an influential newspaper.

Such leaders sought strength by expanding countrywide. The Polish National Alliance of North America thus attempted to shift interest away from local orientations, as did the British American Association. The national German-American Alliance (formed 1901) by 1914 had enrolled some two million members. The Pan-Hellenic Union (1907), the Armenian Benevolent Union, and the United Syrian Organization shared the same aims. Aid to the old homeland, whether for relief or in the struggle for independence, drew the Irish into the Fenian Brotherhood and the American Land League and enlisted Jewish support for the Joint Distribution Committee.

But the lack of centralizing discipline and the ambitions of younger new leaders kept thousands of local organizations everlastingly sprouting, for mutual aid and sociability. At the neighborhood level they satisfied immediate desires for fraternal association—militia companies from Baxter Street to Avenue A, whether the Israelite Guards of Norfolk (1858) or the Irish brigade of Boston, revived Masonic chapters, Odd Fellows and Tall Cedars of Lebanon, and veterans' groups—some affiliated with the Grand Army of the Republic, others autonomous. The same offsetting impulses toward dispersal and concentration operated among economically based groups—state and county agricultural societies, chambers of commerce, county and city bankers' associations, trade associations, and groups urging various improvements. An unusual leader like John Mitchell of the United Mine Workers perceived the need for getting all ethnics together and persuaded Paul Pulaski to help achieve discipline and unity by conciliation; and even he did not last long.[54]

Despite elite ambitions and nationalizing tendencies, stabilizing elements long offset the effects of social mobility and preserved ethnic neighborhoods and groups, a condition which the most ambitious presidents or chairmen had to keep in mind. The ability to act as a leader depended on the ability to keep a following; and whatever the temptations of national prominence, none could forget the younger, newer strivers back in the district, each a potential rival.

Wage earners who pooled family incomes for greater security while some members sought work, remained in the areas of first settlement, or, if they moved, shifted to districts very much like those they left. The European peasants' urge for home ownership also offset the impulse to move. People who pooled small savings in building and loan associations and sank their resources into a little house, clung to it at all costs, and their immobility strengthened the ethnic communities. Where the home was, there they preferred to stay. Benevolent reformers regarded the slums as threats to American liberty, especially since they satisfied the inhabitants. Dismayed by the squalor, filth, crowding, the visitor felt "how dreadfully wretched these people ought to be. Ought to be, but are not. They are chiefly the lower class Italians." Philanthropists argued that the proper home prevented crime, immorality, anarchism, and socialism. From it proceeded citizen virtue, wrote Jacob Riis, "and nowhere else does it live." New York's first Tenement House Law (1867) legislated against the worst conditions, making ventilation mandatory and requiring a modicum of open space for each lot. But the ideal remained the privately owned, single-family detached house, the essential proof of respectability. Soon physical structures also expressed group identity— not only churches and philanthropic institutions, but also social centers like Chicago's imposing Deutsche Haus (1855).[55]

Whether of native or foreign antecedents, ethnic lines softened from one generation to another; and so did the communities they defined. Few residents of 1900 recalled the derivation of Vevey, Indiana, or Bismark, North Dakota, of Loretto or Gallitzin, Pennsylvania, or Berlin, New Hampshire. Traces of accent and intonation long identified the speech of Hoosiers and Yankees and Georgians; Vermonters and Virginians stubbornly resisted tendencies toward uniformity. On the stage and in the popular press, people for whom American English was a second language stood apart, their identity revealed by their speech. Such marks sustained communal separateness even among those who left the neighborhood of first settlement.[56]

The workplace and the school aimed to provide neutral ground for encounters transcending ethnic lines, which, however, never completely disappeared. Sometimes the wage-earners' solidarity opened communication among groups, particularly in the second generation. But education only rarely did so. Proprietary vocational institutions admitted anyone who could pay, and their self-evident utility sustained student interest. The diploma she earned from the United States School of Embalming qualified Minnie Edwards Atwood of New Hampshire to share her husband's duties as funeral director. Anyone could profit by special courses in dentistry, pharmacy, nursing, social work, veterinary medicine, accountancy, and engineering, although setting up a practice gradually led graduates back to their own groups. The public schools, however, rarely succeeded in the task of assimilation. These institutions, since the reforms of Horace Mann and Henry Barnard, expected their pupils to conform to a common Yankee Protestant mold. But whatever the attitudes of the teachers and administrators, the schools served neighborhoods with defined characteristics that determined their clientele and that set their cultural environment. Bias induced many parents to send their offspring to parochial or private schools to sustain their own ethnic heritage by way of language and faith. Catholics, in particular, insisted that only thus could they ensure the life and success of a parish. The Eliot School (Boston, 1859) provided confirmation when it punished three hundred children who refused to chant the Protestant version of the Lord's prayer. The Third Plenary Council of Baltimore (1884) commanded the devout to send offspring to Catholic parochial schools. Other groups followed a similar course. At the expense of considerable personal sacrifice, Jews and Greeks, among others, established afternoon schools where children, after having suffered mornings in English, toiled to acquire the language of their parents.[57]

At the other end of the social spectrum, the well-to-do sought to pass their advantages on to the next generation by sending them to exclusive private schools that imitated the Etons and Rugbys of the English aristocracy. Parents less well connected tucked boys away in military academies and girls in young ladies' finishing schools, there to acquire the gentility and taste to fit those aspiring for admission to a prestigious university and thence to a desirable life's calling. Such students developed intense attachments, as to a stern but affectionate parent:

> From distant Cambridge and more distant Eli
> The followers of the Crimson and the Blue
> Once more in the old Homestead are united,
> Not Yale, not Harvard but Grotonians true (1890).[58]

The public schools thus held no monopoly of education in the years of adolescence, which influenced the choice of marriage partners, the prospects of social mobility, and the ability of the ethnic group to perpetuate itself. Encounters at work, school, church, and society, reflecting neighborhood situations, operated in favor of marriages within the defined group. But the conventions of romantic love also dictated choices based on personal preference, despite the obstacles of family or of religion, as in the story (1879) in which Dorothy and Walter surmounted the Quaker prejudices against intermarriage. Unions between Catholics and Protestants or between Christians and Jews encountered even more imposing barriers.[59]

Observers who sought to describe group life in the Republic failed to capture its kaleidoscopic quality—complex, not static—ever changing in the general configuration and also in the very substance of its component bits and pieces.

Religion both unified and divided people. Distinctive creeds and practices that kept Catholics, Baptists, Jews, and Mormons from worshipping together sometimes generated prejudice and conflict, but provided a basis for organizing a complex society, enabling each individual to find an appropriate affiliation, free of interference either from others or from the government. Pluralism expanded the citizens' capacity to act, enabling each to surmount or evade the barriers of prejudice.

Particularities of belief and practice often disturbed communities by unsettling stable relationships and lines of authority, thus indirectly expanding the contours of liberty. The Roman Catholic Church early in the nineteenth century accommodated old-stock American and French communicants and the more numerous Irish immigrants, although with difficulty; and it confronted even more intricate problems in dealing with Germans, Poles, French Canadians, and Italians, all with distinct linguistic and cultural requirements. The constitutional separation of church and state prevented government intervention in these matters, and indeed, any effort to define a religion, so that Voltairine de Cleyre's American Secular Union claimed for nonbelievers all the privileges of organized faiths. Yet each church formed the nucleus of a cluster of organizations and activities—the women's Sacred Heart of Jesus Society, the altar boys and young men's clubs, a cadet corps, a dramatic group, and a choir, along with a benefit association that helped the needy, supplied a cadre of mourners at funerals, and linked communicants to their parish. Control therefore involved an important force of communal cohesion that compensated for the unsettling features of American life. Divisions therefore affected everyone.[60]

Even the imperative of self-protection failed of itself to hold groups together. Defense against attacks by outsiders almost instinctively united Jews, Irish, blacks, and other groups that considered themselves unfairly treated. The Board of Delegates of American Israelites by 1860 included representatives of thirty congregations that sought equal political rights everywhere. They considered a proposal to establish a court of arbitration to avoid recourse to law, with a panel of rabbis to introduce uniformity in services and with a superior authority for Jewish charitable institutions. But ideological differences soon split the organization apart. Narrower groups later organized the American Jewish Committee (1906), the American Jewish Congress, and the Anti-Defamation League. Meanwhile the Sephardic joined in a short-lived Federation of Oriental Jews (1912). On neither the national nor the local scale could Jews attain unity, not even in the effort to create an overarching New York Kehillah or community to rebut anti-Semitic charges and to generate a spiritual revival (1908). The socialist elements in the labor movement battled the Orthodox, and the emergence of Zionism deepened divisions. Organizations with more limited objectives succeeded better because they enlisted a single segment of the group—the Hebrew Immigrant Aid Society (1902) or the Workmen's Circle (1900), for instance. Irish organizations like the Fenian Brotherhood (1859) sometimes slipped over the line between safeguarding group interests in America and fighting for home rule or independence in Ireland.[61]

Group expansion, however desirable, often proved unexpectedly costly. Growth, whether by federation or by pressure to project local power and influence to a larger stage, revealed contradictory impulses: the desire to preserve uniqueness by excluding outsiders conflicted with the missionary impulse to spread, to become the biggest little club in town, town in the state. Furthermore, greater size complicated control, for repressive discipline only stimulated subdivision. Constitutional constraints did not apply to private as they did to government agencies; and aggrieved members could and often did secede. The bishop or vestry that disciplined a dissident clergyman faced the loss of the entire flock. Father Edward McGlynn long refused to renounce radicalism despite orders from the hierarchy. Devout Catholics though they were, Polish Americans battled the Church to the point of schism over the issue of language; and German Americans divided along religious and ideological lines in the absence of group discipline. Pacifist statements by Judah L. Magnes during World War I hastened the decline of the Kehillah and created a demand that he leave public life.[62]

So, too, a medical society could exclude unorthodox physicians but not deny them access to patients; and bar associations limited membership but not the right to practice. The law frowned equally upon all conspiracies, whether in restraint of trade or invasion of individual rights. Recurrent fear of the Masons, the Catholics, the Jews, and Wall Street limited the powers of all groups. The *Buck Stove* case thus held labor unions responsible for damages caused by boycotts, just as antitrust prosecutions under the Sherman Act set limits upon corporate growth. Similar constraints applied compulsion to voluntary associations.[63]

Loose, ill-defined forms of community organization provided an effective mechanism for pluralism. A moving testimonial to their importance came from Carl Schurz (1829–1906), a German immigrant who before he arrived had glimpsed the vision of America as the land of hope. Speaking on the eve of the Civil War, while the Know-Nothing party challenged the role of the foreign-born, his oration on "True Americanism" articulated the nation's conception of its destiny in terms of freedom and opportunity. For decades thereafter, Americans hoped to put into effect the principle "of development and perfection by voluntary standards and self-reliance," despite the increased difficulty of thus describing the national mission in the wake of the social transformations effected by industrialization, urbanization, and imperialism. In the 1880s, Josiah

Strong (1847–1916), the Congregational minister and social reformer, still wrote of the country's triumphal destiny. But some readers wondered whether that optimism expressed generally accepted views or rested on familiar slogans unrelated to actuality.[64]

Nor did other formulations describe the complexity of American communal life. Despite the popularity of Israel Zangwill's drama, reality did not match the melting-pot image; variety and freedom rather than growing homogeneity were the New World's characteristic traits. Judah L. Magnes entitled a sermon to the Kehillah, "A Republic of Nationalities," to offer a counterimage to the mistaken notions of the melting pot. However, cultural pluralism, the vision of rich potentialities inherent in a loose federation of polyglot cultures, offered no more adequate an explanation. Horace M. Kallen (born 1882), a student of William James, stimulated by the open universe of pragmatism with its varieties of human experience, argued that political autonomy liberated the individual to seek the spiritual autonomy of the group. The democratic republic allowed each nationality to express itself in its own language and in its own aesthetic and intellectual forms, although English gave them all a common means of communication. As in an orchestra every instrument had a specific timbre, so in society each ethnic group was a natural instrument, their harmony joining in a symphony of civilization. This attractive vision belied the reality of the decade in which Kallen wrote, for not all played with equal freedom; nor did each preserve its identity.[65]

The impulse toward association in the New World recognized that neither government nor other constituted authorities could do by coercion all that men and women wished to do together. People unwilling to act in solitude formed groups—for self-realization, and to express their individuality by demonstrating what voluntary rather than compulsive means could achieve. For more than a century before 1850, the dissolution of ties to the state had made religious affiliation a personal decision, and so it remained in the decades that followed; indeed, as immigration and subdivision multiplied the number of sects, uniformity became impossible. So, too, the absence of a common language in art, literature, or music deprived Americans of a single voice to answer their important questions. "Abolish the turkey," said Mr. Dooley, "an' ye desthroy th' tie that binds us as wan people. We're wan race, hitched together be a great manny languages, a rellijon apiece, thraditions that dont agree with each other, akel opporchunities f'r the rich and poor, to continue bein' rich an' poor an' a common barnyard food. When iv'rybody in a nation eats th' same things that all th' others eats, ye can't break thim up."[66]

Yet the hunger persisted, not just for turkey but for a culture not confined to a single class or limited to parlors or lecture rooms, but embracing workers and farmers and the women of all classes. And by slow stages such a culture appeared, liberating fleetingly all who imbibed it. The shrill clang of the calliope and the raucous guffaw of blackface minstrels mocked the real world, while a trip up the Hudson or down the bay, the trolley to Coney or Rockaway, provided merciful distractions. On a Sunday afternoon the squished-up crowds saw the lovers spoon and tried a dip of surf. They worked hard on Monday but one day was fun day, a better-than-none day in lives somber, uncomprehending.

Back in 1855, a hopeful poet rejoiced,

> Of the past we'll think no more,
> When our journey's end is won.
> And we'll build our house by the rocky shore
> Of the mighty Oregon.

In 1900, departures and arrivals, endings and beginnings, had lost their clarity. But the yearning for meaning endured.[67]

Not all—far from it—but many, or at least some, searched the printed page for answers to questions they did not know they asked. And certainly the columns of type multiplied, set by new machines, printed on cheap pulp paper by monster presses, speedily distributed by intricate metropolitan, indeed national, systems. Bound books in many languages, bought or borrowed from libraries, dime novels, and in 1900 more than five thousand magazines, hawked on the street or delivered by mail, satisfied the reading appetite of the nation or of particular segments of it. *The Ladies Home Journal* had a circulation of a million, and even the staid *Atlantic Monthly* reached one hundred thousand in 1905. Then a new generation of publishers, Samuel S. McClure, William Randolph Hearst, out for gigantic sales, lowered the price, and dangled the bait of massive circulation figures before national brand advertisers. Frank A. Munsey's career: "forty years—forty million," which went, at his death, to an institution far removed from his life and work, The Metropolitan Museum of Art. *Collier's* used illustrations of battle scenes and girls as well as scandal to attract buyers. The same prize attracted the owners of metropolitan daily newspapers whose bold headlines, simple language, and dramatic pictures drew pennies from the semiliterate and the foreign-born, almost twenty-eight million daily in 1920. The English critic found beyond belief the disregard for truth and soberness, the poverty of serious interest, the personality- and sensation-mongering, which he believed effaced the discipline of respect and the feeling for what was elevated. He did not understand that the stories—true or false—conveyed snatches of meaning to the readers.

The weekly *Saturday Evening Post,* led by George Horace Lorimer, sensitively reflected popular moods. Articulating the general definitions of Americanism, including neutrality and isolationism, until 1917, the *Post* then vigorously supported the war effort and shifted from a broad, expansive, tolerant, and optimistic Americanism to fierce hostility to Germany, socialists, radicals, Bolshevists, immigrants, and other subversive forces—including jazz. Editorials harangued its ten million readers to suppress the German language and alter their entertainment patterns.[68]

The pictures that moved across the comic pages escaped such control. Crude exaggerations, they made palatable the simple truths of city streets and village lanes—funny, sad, replete with wonder, like life itself. The back alley flavor emphasizing slapstick and sadism offended upper-class gentility, so Bud Fisher's Mutt, who started his life as a sportsman-hustler, evolved into a harassed suburban husband, and Jiggs of *Bringing Up Father* longed for the old ways amid newfound affluence. But the old spirit endured, offering the multitude meaningful "low-grade and trivial things"—broad incongruities mainly, grotesqueries, absurdities, evokers of the horse laugh.[69]

Off paper, in the flesh, some of the same figures passed across the stage—authentic—and particularly in the vaudeville theaters, singing, dancing, juggling, creating a world apart, a source of relief. Harrigan and Hart, Weber and Fields, Eddie Cantor and Fanny Brice, and Irving Berlin's songs. And then in culmination, by the magic of electricity, the images on a screen recreated a universe, seeming real but known as not real, as the camera reordered time and space through editing and montage. Tampering with reality formed part of the experience; the viewer, through involvement and imagination, gave depth, motion, and continuity to the flickering black-and-white shapes, no more than two-dimensional still photographs. As active participants in the experience, the audiences acquired mastery over time and motion. Edwin S. Porter's *The Great Train Robbery,* a classic tale of banditry and retribution, swiftly moved from one location to another, showing the medium's storytelling capacities based on motion and suspense. Would the firemen get to the burning building in time to save the mother and child? The film characters and events acquired an aspect, recognizable, familiar, comfortably explaining all—husbands, wives; parents, children; evil friends and generous strangers; bosses, work, police—brutality and kindness in unexpected places, illusions of success, happiness, health among the failures, the tragic, and the universal dying. Progressive reformers disapproved of the drift of popular tastes away from the values educators, clergymen, and charity workers hoped to inculcate among immigrants. At the same time the movies gave audiences access to the fantastic and the grotesque. Thus Alfred Clark in 1895 filmed the story of the execution of Mary, queen of Scots, by stopping the camera when the executioner raised his ax to strike and substituting a dummy for the actor, so that viewers could see the head chopped off. Trick films became all the rage, rearranging time and space, severing heads from bodies in a series of comic misadventures that usually ended happily.[70]

In retrospect, two trends became visible. In the 1850s, 1870s, 1890s, wherever the experience began, the reader made out the words on a small sheet in his own language, edited by one known in the neighborhood or the county. The song and dance extended from the old country place to a local hall or saloon, surmounting the distance migration created. In the play, often performed in the church, known boys and girls, scarcely costumed, took the parts. Then a more general audience took shape, reading, listening in English, the common language, less familiar to any but comprehensible to all and arranged by remote editors and impresarios, played and written by distant folk. That was one trend—the ever more impersonal general replacing the confined and intimately small.

The other trend transformed the cultural event from a human happening—understood by the likes of you and me—to a mysterious, magical machine, as accepted, though as puzzling, as was the doggie's search for the source of his master's voice. By 1920, the phonograph and the moving picture ceased to surprise. By then Jules Verne's *Twenty Thousand Leagues under the Sea* and his *Around the World in Eighty Days* had made science fiction familiar. In 1889, *The New York World* decided to beat Phileas Fogg's record and sent Nelly Bly to return in seventy-three days amid a blaze of fireworks and glory. Thomas A. Edison had already entered popular consciousness as a science fiction hero, with technology one of the salvations of the republic. The inventor who increased human power also extended the area of freedom, revealing an open-ended future with man's capacity to act potentially limitless. "In our art," he said, "impossible is an impossible word." Science; Edison as the high priest of a new faith; the light bulb its symbol—powerful at a time when isolation, individualism, and sense of powerlessness plumbed ever-new levels of meaning, the only compensation in a search for larger entities with which to identify oneself. The limitless possibilities of science would compensate for ever-greater fragmentation of social institutions. Millions throughout the nation took such wonders for granted without understanding how they functioned.[71]

Without understanding, also, that these cultural instruments had slipped out of the audience's control. Hiss, boo, applaud—it was all the same to the images on the screen. And distant directors, producers, editors, concerned only with the total measured in circulation or box office receipts, spared no time to consider particular segments of the audience. Content mattered less than appearance, just as a good actress, according to Maxine Elliott, mattered more than the play. The theaters' electric signs occasionally carried only the name of the star, without bothering to mention the title of the drama.[72]

The desire for inclusiveness thus offset the wish for particularity; the advantage lay with the larger unit. As in politics, in trade, and in the circulation of newspapers, inclusiveness—more votes, more customers, more viewers, more readers—became the source of strength, particularly when fired with patriotism. Cultural forces thus played a crucial part in developing national consciousness, in transferring some communal emotions onto a vastly larger scale, instilling in new and old citizens notions of loyalty and attachment to an entity much larger than any within their experience, except on rare occasions such as Lincoln's funeral. That traumatic loss served as a powerful symbol of a united nation. The ritualistic journey of the body, lying in state in towns through which the cortege passed, generated soaring emotions, tremendous grief, and a reaffirmation of values for which Lincoln hoped the nation stood. The travels of the Liberty Bell in a special railroad car that left Philadelphia on visits to world and regional expositions (New Orleans, 1885, Chicago, 1893, San Francisco, 1914) also generated involvement that halted only when it became clear the bell was too brittle for further peregrinations.[73]

Everyone, immigrants as well as the native-born, Southerners no less than Northerners, responded to the impulses of American nationalism. In 1850–51, when John Cox Stephens planned the great race, he named his yacht, and also the prize cup, *America.* Even as the Civil War approached, solicitous editors worried about neglect of the graves of the illustrious dead founding fathers. From Appomattox, the road led to reunion, with the passions once expended in battle later released in professions of loyalty, stimulated by veterans' organizations and by patriotic societies. For many foreign-born, the voluntary choice of destination and the gleam of opportunity displaced the old country with the new.

From the elementary readers compiled by William Holmes McGuffey, schoolchildren learned the English language and a set of meanings associated with the United States. The readers had been compiled to remedy the ignorance represented in the letter to Squire Hawkins in an effort to intimidate the court; the little books went much further than correct spelling and grammar.

> Square Haukins
> this is to Lett u no that u beter be Keerful hoo yoo an yore family tacks cides with fer peepl wont Stan it too hev the Men wat's sportin the wuns wat's robin us, sported bi yor Fokes kepin kumpne with 'em, u been a ossifer ov the Lau, yor Ha wil bern as qick as to an yor Barn tu. So take kere. No more ad pressnt.

Pious, not nationalistic in orientation, the readers taught children values McGuffey believed relevant to civilized society: punctuality, goodness, kindness, honesty, and truthfulness, with the last lesson, "We All Must Die." Later editions expanded on manners, attitudes toward parents and teachers, the poor, the aged and the animals, as well as the dangers of insolent behavior toward inferiors. The combination included enough Puritan to fit into the religious mental mode of the descendants of the Ohio Land Company; enough Cavalier to fit into the moral and mental mode of the blood of Kentucky, Virginia and North Carolina; enough economics to fit into the thrifty mental mode of the Germans and Scots. A reader that glorified the suicidal lunge of Greek soldiers against their Turkish oppressors, or venerated the Roman Rienzi, the Swiss struggle for liberty against Austria, or Henry V's address to his troops, made for very vicarious patriotism. In the United States, turkey prevailed even if but once a year.[74]

The strength of American society lay in its sensitivity to the wishes and interests of its multitudes, though some portions of them advanced far more rapidly than others. Because nationalist sentiments often remained private and local, the products of voluntary associations and communal initiatives and activities, very rarely imposed from above by governments, the country could respond effectively to a diverse populace without imposing uniform conditions on them, expanding the ability to act—hence the liberty—of all. Therefore the symbolic meaning accorded the Liberty Bell during the centennial celebrations of 1876 extended not only from the present to the past and to the future but also to all the peoples of the United States, whether or not their ancestors had once fought for American independence.

> Not to this land alone, to every clime
> Those tones of hope and prophecy were borne (1852).

The visit of the Brazilian emperor Dom Pedro II, the sole surviving New World monarch, exemplified an anachronistic age, while Count Rochambeau, grandson of the commander of the French forces during the Revolution, marked the continuities of the past. By 1893 the bell, "this precious and holy relic of our heroic age," stood for the hope that it would once more unite "the children of those fathers whom it had so often served and for whom it had so often spoken," draw together in a common sentiment those sections of the country that only a few years back had engaged in fratricidal strife. The rallying force for the future, too.

> Oh yes, if the flame on our altars should pale,
> Let its voice but be heard, and the freeman shall start
> To rekindle the fire, while he sees on the gale
> All the stars and the stripes of the flag of his heart.

The words of freedom it peeled

> blent all heart in unison,
> And made rough men and women feel
> The sacredness of common weal.
>
> . . . .
>
> Oh, better that "Red, White and Blue's" Key,
> Than all things played by Paderooskey.[75]

Out of many one—diversity thus understood enriched and strengthened American social, cultural, political, and religious life, enabling a vast, growing, and changing country to absorb many different peoples who preserved their separateness. Hatreds occasionally flared into conflict and some groups remained involuntarily apart. Yet all coexisted in a flexible structure that bent but did not break.

In the decades after the Civil War, diversity became individualism and weakened many intermediate institutions. Then dependence on the state increased, and the premise of equality before the law generated desires for uniformity. Given the lack of communal unity, only arbitrary impositions by government could gratify the urge for action. The loosely jointed community functioned well when everyone could march his or her own way; but only force could bring all in step to compel the lines to move together.[76]

I V

EQUALITY AND THE FRUITS

OF BONDAGE

FREE GROUP LIFE in the nineteenth century rested on the premise of equality. Americans could pursue happiness in their own fashions by associating with whomever they wished. Thus ran the underlying article of faith.

But as in the past, so after 1850, actual experience contradicted the easy assumption that all possessed the same ability to choose and to act. People of color felt constraints unknown to whites; and slavery and the bitter civil war that eliminated it limited the ability of blacks to associate, while others, unconcerned, shrugged off the denials of equality. In quite another fashion, red men and women encountered formidable barriers to attainment of the national ideal. And new views of race complicated the issue of liberty for all Americans.

A short simple story described the most tragic experience—then again, not so short, not so simple.

In the South, the burden of bondage grew heavier after 1850. By 1861, an Alabama court denied that a slave had a mind and therefore any will which the law need recognize. The absolute power of the master extended to every activity of his property; and a strict code of etiquette prescribed the behavior and even the dress distinctions of inferiors. Everywhere, immensely complicated cultural interactions qualified relations among blacks and whites.[1]

Already in the 1850s, Southern legislatures, anxious to control free people of color, enacted codes establishing their legal and social subordination, limiting the freedom to assemble, banning the teaching of reading and writing, forbidding employment in pharmacies that gave access to poisons. North Carolina deprived free blacks of the right to vote. Special police powers gave white patrols full legal authority to enforce the laws of slavery, thus expanding their capacity to act to protect themselves and their property. The issue extended to the federal government, which decided (1858) that a free colored man could not act as master of his own vessel in Baltimore. People like Dennis Patrick of Savannah who could pass for white (1858) threatened the integrity of a line increasingly regarded as sacrosanct: black (slave)/white (free).

Bequests by Southern whites to colored offspring generated unbearable tensions among the masters and their mistresses, wives, and daughters, since miscegenation called into question the moral capacities of the planter class. In 1856 Samuel Townsend of Madison County, Alabama, died, freeing by will some forty slaves and leaving them two hundred thousand dollars. Although white claimants shortly before had overturned a similar bequest, Townsend's was honored and the freedmen resettled in Kansas and Xenia, Ohio, whence some of the children proceeded to Wilberforce University, a black antislavery school. Miscegenation also aggravated status issues in communities like New Orleans, where blacks organized an Equal Rights League for self-defense.

Terrified observers then discerned a crisis below the Mason-Dixon Line. The bondsmen, "growing shrewder and bolder," fortified by desperate courage, would brook no delay, would fear no peril, and would soon commence open warfare. Signs of desperation: rising mortality, a falling birth rate, and the determination of runaways not to go back, as when a mother cut the throats of her children to prevent their return to bondage. An assertive Iowa convention of colored men (1857) demanded their constitutional rights.

Meanwhile other aspects of Southern society also showed signs of strain as the integration of contentious groupings proved inadequate. Mulatto children constantly reminded white women of their own precarious status, its fundamental contradictions plainly visible everywhere. At the same time, their husbands' financial commitment to the preservation of bondage grew. While the number of slaves increased slowly, their value doubled, making owners significantly better off in 1860 than a decade earlier, magnifying their ability to act, and coloring their conceptions of liberty.[2]

The varieties of black culture, North and South, shaped the contours of life for colored men and women. The interaction between slaves and their masters often generated sullen resistance on the part of the one and demands for total control on the part of the other; their attitudes to property, work, leisure, time, and self differed. The half million free blacks on the eve of the Civil War, half of them in the South, also lived in a world circumscribed by white power. Their struggle to assert their humanity in spite of their pigmentation turned their churches into ways of expressing autonomy. But whereas the limitations on whites ultimately hinged on their own needs and abilities, in the case of blacks, bond and free, skin color circumscribed individual and group liberty.

Fugitive slaves more often elicited sympathy than equality in the free states, for rising abolitionist sentiment did not lessen prejudice except among such committed radicals as William Lloyd Garrison and Wendell Phillips. The railroads in some places, but not in others, segregated colored people. Only after protest did the Boston opera house admit colored patrons (1853). A school for black girls in Washington troubled sensitive whites (1857) who like Thomas Magruder of Indianapolis (1857) praised Uncle Tom's Christian virtue, fortitude, and acceptance of life's lot. Even the tolerant Unitarians divided in 1857; and cries of "Nigger, nigger, nigger," punctuated Stephen A. Douglas's campaign meetings in 1857, despite the candidate's desperate effort to redefine the Declaration of Independence to apply to whites only. During the Illinois senatorial campaign a year later, Lincoln's supporters rejected the issues of amalgamation or equality, in favor of the defense of free as against slave labor. In the *Dred Scott* case (1857), Chief Justice Taney denied descendents of Africans the rights of citizens, excluding them forever from the American community. And what of persons with some white blood? a Chicago newspaper asked incredulously.[3]

The future of slavery preoccupied many Southerners, who considered its expansion a practical need. The yeomen eager to become great, the great ones eager to become greater, glimpsed opportunity in the West, in the farther South, and in Cuba; congressmen without a trace of irony boasted that the Bird of Liberty would lay its eggs in territories theretofore beyond United States sovereignty. In Oregon, and someday in Canada, numerous potential free states might upset the delicate balance in control of the federal government unless new slave states maintained parity. Intellectual arguments provided a foundation for the political ones. Slavery, not bad or neutral but a positive good, its apologists maintained, sustained a civilization higher than one resting on free labor. The happier bondsmen on each plantation remained free of care, blessed with moderate work and ample fare. No exiled trains of homeless peasants went in distant climes to tell their tales of woe. The cheerful song, the long loud laugh that freemen seldom shared, rang in every field. The benign institution would spread wherever determined people could take it. Meanwhile at home rumors of slave uprisings kept families on edge (1857).[4]

Their opponents could not ignore the challenge. Northerners did not agitate the question; the question agitated them. The specter of "nigger equality" conjured up by some politicians troubled some antislavery advocates. But for many, a law higher than the Constitution governed the territories, part of humanity's common heritage and dedicated to justice and liberty by the creator of the universe. In some places, public hostility impeded enforcement of stringent fugitive slave laws; elsewhere, law and order sentiments aided authority. Gradual voluntary emancipation with compensation seemed inevitable; whether peaceful or violent depended on the South's compliance with a process in its own best interest. Whatever fortified slavery complicated its ultimate extirpation. While a few Northern blacks like Martin Delaney advocated emigration and rebellion, the colored people's convention of 1853 and Frederick Douglass more characteristically called for continued agitation for freedom. Growing numbers of Northerners agreed, making the question of slavery the touchstone of their definition of liberty.[5]

War and Reconstruction profoundly affected black experience throughout the United States. The decision to enlist colored men in the Union army had symbolic virtue, but in the Massachusetts 54th and in other units, they shared in the fighting without thereby establishing their legitimacy in society. Everywhere, self-assertion encountered white opposition. And in the ten years after Appomattox, Americans learned that making peace involved as much difficulty as making war. The effects—the calamitous failures—reverberated through the following century since Union victory and the end of slavery did not resolve, indeed complicated, the issues that had led to secession.

Altogether apart from the shortcomings of federal officials, from the hatreds generated by the conflict, and from the legacies of slavery, economic and cultural distractions limited the salvage of good from the evil of war, while the loss of Lincoln's leadership compounded the difficulties. The Reconstruction attempts to reorder the South floundered. Proposed economic and social changes proved inapplicable. Unreconstructed Confederates thought their world turned upside-down and they intended to restore it to its rightful position. For the next fifty years they would consider expansion of the blacks' capacity to act so subversive as to justify any measure to reconstruct prewar social alignments.

The fighting compelled Northerners to consider the meaning of the Union they sought to preserve. The Emancipation Proclamation made a place for the freed blacks among the "one people" to whom the Declaration of Independence and the Constitution referred. But troubling ambiguities persisted. Irish laborers were not alone to resent the blood and treasure expended "just to gratify a clique of Abolitionists"; mobs attacked black job seekers in Cincinnati and Brooklyn, and fears of an invading horde of liberated slaves induced Illinois voters to reaffirm the state's exclusion law.[6]

The difficulties Thomas Jefferson foresaw years earlier remained. Neither Lincoln's Proclamation nor his mild reconstruction plan persuaded former masters and former slaves to live amicably together. Complex patterns of life dependent on bondage did not easily adjust to new conditions, particularly with the wounds of war still unhealed.[7] Black political power remained a contentious issue for whites. Some Democrats preferred to have their old Confederate allies retain control. By contrast, Republicans feared that they would have not even a toehold in the South if the rebel states returned on the basis of Lincoln's proposed plan of reconstruction. The Union's enemies would enjoy increased representation in the House of Representatives once their freed slaves counted as full, rather than as three-fifths, persons. The augmented bloc of Democratic votes would then dominate the whole nation. The remedy—black suffrage—would create voters grateful to the Grand Old Party, while widening the contours of liberty. The desire to punish the rebels added a tone of personal animus to this position.[8]

Some Northerners adhered to a radical policy out of sympathy for the freed men and women. Freedom alone would not strike the shackles from black ankles. Without help to build a new life, the emancipated would relapse into dependence; but Northern values could purify the South, corrupted by slavery. Reconstruction therefore demanded not a return to the status quo of 1860 but guarantees of civil rights and expansion of equality; federal power could bring that region into accord with the rest of the nation.[9]

Passions infused this position also. The enormously expensive war—in money, perhaps twenty billion dollars; in dead, some 620,000; in wounded, in lives wrecked, immeasurable—must all have been for some purpose! People who had grown up in the optimistic midcentury decades, who believed in progress and in human perfectibility, could not accept the brutality of the conflict without faith that some good would result in the form of redemption of the society from which the evil had sprung. Ralph Waldo Emerson considered two conditions essential (1864): emancipation so absolute as to eradicate all racial considerations; and confiscation of rebel property as in the case of the Tories during the Revolution. Neither condition materialized.

Excessive expectations contributed to the tragic failure. Nearly a million men, recently slaves, became voters before they could read, an experiment never before made by any people. The audacity of the measure explained in part the subsequent disorder, corruption, and violence. Few governments in the world would have endured the strain. Yet utter chaos did not follow this fearful combination of power and ignorance. The Republic did not collapse by this trial of its institutions; the vital spirit of liberty and broad tolerance for people's ability to act survived, which astounded contemporaries only explained by the overwhelming benevolence of divine Providence.

The sole unambiguous gain of Reconstruction for the newly freed blacks, establishment of the freedom to move, gained recognition immediately after the war—in search of kith and kin, in efforts to reconstitute broken families, to return to the place of nativity, and to recover lost wives and children. Many then sought to acquire land for their own use, resisting attempts to maintain plantation ownership in white hands. Instead, they located themselves on rented parcels to rebuild family life free from the tyranny of white control. Some of the decline in Southern agricultural output derived from insistence by black males that their wives no longer perform back-breaking outdoor labor.

But Americans lacked the strength for a bolder leap to perfection. In the South, the former masters resented the changes; in the North, self-interest and prejudice did not readily yield to appeals for reason and benevolence. Perhaps Lincoln's mediating influence might have eased adjustments; but the assassin had killed him, the Forgiver. The Avenger took his place; and none like Lincoln appeared among the statesmen after 1865. Perhaps he, too, would have failed in the postwar society, quite unlike the prewar. As old ideals faded under new conditions, the haste for growth that created the new America left the place of blacks in a white society unresolved—a dismal heritage for the future.[10]

Conditions in the prostrate South proved uncongenial to responsible attitudes. Valueless Confederate currency and bonds, plantations and towns in ruins, factories destroyed and transportation in collapse, everyone, black and white, impoverished—all faced an immense task of reconstruction. As arson and other crimes of violence seemed to increase, an observant traveler noted a truculent intransigence that boded ill for the future. "Question them as to everything for which the war was fought," wrote Whitelaw Reid, "the doctrine of secession, the rightfulness of slavery, the wrongs of the South, and they are as full as ever of the sentiments that made the rebellion."

Another Northerner observed the sullen bitterness of the vanquished toward the victors. "They hate us and despise us and all belonging to us . . . the 'nigger' they don't consider human . . . whatever harm they can do us without getting another whipping, they have got the will to do it and mean to do too." Wounded veterans and broken families wretchedly awaited aid, while civil government disintegrated and marauding bands ruled. "Smoke house broken open by the laborers and bacon stolen, corn houses robbed and the corn sold for whiskey, then the worst of crimes committed by drunken niggers . . . houses pillaged and burnt because their owners would not yield to every demand that ignorance and insolence could make, the woods full of outlaws, idleness followed by want, and the country impoverished for lack of laborers—all because fanatics . . . determined, by main force, to lift up the nigger to a level which of himself he could never attain and which, if let alone, he never would have sought."[11]

Confronting impending anarchy, the former Southern leaders reasserted themselves. Men accustomed to command gave orders; those accustomed to taking them obeyed. Personal influence counted more than law imposed by Union bayonets, resurrecting fragments of the old political system. Feeling guilt neither about their institutions nor about the war, the planters expected to rebuild their estates with some equivalent of slavery for a labor force. George Fitzhugh had earlier expressed the view to which many adhered: a rejection of laissez-faire selfishness and what they perceived as the rule of lawless mobs, in favor of a patriarchal order, uniting with bonds of affection the interests of the masters and inferiors, all in their appropriate places. An Alabama planter voiced the judgment of numerous others when he explained in 1865, "we controlled [the black's] labor in the past (at our expense) and will control it in the future (at his). . . . His condition before the war and since are almost identical."[12]

Emancipation at first markedly limited the Southerners' capacity to act, especially where the percentage of blacks was high. South Carolina whites faced the prospect of existence as a perpetual minority. Even where the racial balance favored them, the idea of sharing power with the freed bondsmen appalled the former masters. Often notions of paternalism and benevolent patriarchy disappeared, reemerging later when blacks once more sank to the bottom of the social heap. As many Southerners interpreted their capacity to act, the whites' liberty depended upon severely curtailing that of the blacks.[13]

Unaided, Blacks could not resist. The four million freed by the Emancipation Proclamation and the Thirteenth Amendment (1865) lacked land, property, and education. Without help they would starve or become violent and disruptive. On March 3, 1865, the federal government created a Freedmen's Bureau to supervise the transition from slavery. Under the leadership of General O. O. Howard, the agency supplied rations and jobs to the needy, and began to retrain and educate them. But the bureau could not provide what they most needed—land. The forty acres of which some freedmen dreamed might or might not have made them independent, but it would have broken up the great estates and thus recast the whole social system. Instead, forms of controlled labor surfaced, mitigated by Northern opposition to their harsher features and by black resistance to their shackles. For a while federal authorities provided blacks with a modicum of protection against landowners. But once control passed to local authorities, Northern notions of the marketplace gave way to simple exploitation.[14]

Desertion was the most common black assertion of newly found liberty; former slaves left their former masters and employers, belying Southern propaganda about the loyalty of domestic servants devoted to their kindly owners. Those accustomed to having their skills sold to the highest bidder preferred to do their own contracting, as mechanics, artisans, and craftsmen tried to better their lots. The initial response, in which liberty meant release from forced labor, broke down in the face of life's hardships, replaced by the desire to provide for the family on land of one's own. One maid interviewed in 1865 "had heard a woman who had bought her freedom from kind indulgent owners, say it was a very sweet thing to be able to do as she chose, to sit and do nothing, to work if she desired, or go out as she liked, and ask nobody's permission, and that was just her feeling." Initial black definitions of the capacity to act included the most rudimentary freedoms, of which slavery had deprived them.

More profound expressions of newly acquired liberty reflected the ability to ignore the myriad regulations that had once governed black lives. New forms of dress and movement without passes asserted the right to walk on the same sidewalk, ride in carriages, gather in public, form associations, parade and celebrate, behaviors that seemed insolent and insubordinate to whites. Other blacks vented their rage in looting, arson, and violence, and a few insurrections in 1865 generated nightmares in the already overwrought Southern imagination of what awaited areas under federal control. No one of either color fully comprehended the contours of black liberty.[15]

Andrew Johnson's Reconstruction policy in the end enabled Southerners to maintain several features of the old relationships. A poor white, loyal to the Union and hostile to the planter aristocracy, Johnson had once hoped to ship freedmen to Liberia. Former slaveholder, he considered blacks inferior, and unqualified for suffrage. As president, his sympathies drifted toward the well-born and respectable, who expected to resume old patterns of control in the South. He appointed civil governors in the recently subdued areas and authorized the early summons of constitutional conventions. The central issue of black suffrage he left to the states, certain that the freedmen would receive the kindliest usage from their former owners.[16]

Northerners soon observed the character of that usage. The South Carolina constitutional convention (1865) heard Benjamin F. Perry, the provisional governor, proclaim theirs "a white man's government, and intended for white men only." All the legislatures except that of Tennessee enacted Black Codes that maintained the substance of bondage within the form of emancipation. A Richmond editor explained how to extend white supremacy indefinitely by "retaining the Negro as labourer, and keeping him in a condition" that left his political influence "as indifferent as when he was a slave." Deprived of the vote, excluded from juries, prevented from testifying against whites and punished more severely for crimes, the freedmen fell into an inferior legal status. Vagrancy laws that provided for arrest for the unemployed subjected them to involuntary servitude, for hire to the highest bidder. Provisions for compulsory apprenticeship had the same effect. To complete the resemblance to prewar days, some states forbade servants to leave before the expiration of their terms and allowed the master to inflict corporal punishment. Prohibition of miscegenation and of intermarriage expressed the determination to preserve racial separateness and colored inferiority. These statutes revealed what many Northerners feared: the former Confederates sought to restore the slave order and thus to nullify the lessons they should have learned from defeat. In addition, organized violence stifled dissent.[17]

Shocked by the revelation of Southern intentions, Congress in December 1865 refused to admit the elected representatives from the seceded states and appointed a joint committee of fifteen to supervise Reconstruction. The dominant figures, Congressman Thaddeus Stevens of Pennsylvania and Senator Charles Sumner of Massachusetts—New Englanders by birth, reformers, convinced friends of the freedmen and bitter foes of the former slave owners—had suffered the agonies of a long battle for liberation and balked at moderation when evil forces threatened the fruits of past sacrifices. Sumner would not forget the "30 first rate stripes with a gutta percha cane" inflicted on him in the Senate by Congressman Preston S. Brooks (May 22, 1856), who thereupon became a Southern hero. Stevens also had had his share of pain. Scarred by their injuries and sometimes vindictive, both insisted that the Southern states, having committed political suicide by seceding, had become conquered provinces, like New Mexico in 1848. Virginia, South Carolina, and the others therefore remained subject to territorial government by acts of Congress, and needed thorough reconstruction before full readmission to the Union.[18]

The president disagreed belligerently. In February 1866, he vetoed a bill to extend the life of the Freedmen's Bureau because he believed it coddled blacks. In the same month, Johnson branded the Joint Committee on Reconstruction an irresponsible conspiratorial directory. He disapproved of acts to admit Colorado and Nebraska to statehood, to extend the suffrage to colored people in the District of Columbia and to establish racial civil rights. By March 1866, he had antagonized even moderate congressional Republicans previously uncommitted on Reconstruction. The president's uncompromising attitude created an opposition with enough votes to override vetoes. The legislators then framed a radical policy without his approval. A civil rights law aimed to complete emancipation by forbidding discrimination and by guaranteeing the protection of the courts to all, along with the freedom to acquire property, to come and go at pleasure, and to make contracts. The Fourteenth Amendment (ratified 1868) confirmed black citizenship and forbade the states to discriminate against any persons or to deprive them of civil rights, life, liberty, or property without due process of law. It also penalized those that limited the suffrage. Meanwhile the Freedmen's Bureau received an extension of two years. Congress, not the president, championed greater black liberty.[19]

Johnson's counterefforts backfired. In a long tour in 1866 campaigning for election of a more supportive Congress, he attacked the Civil Rights Act, the Fourteenth Amendment, and blacks. But a riot in Memphis and the massacre of colored people in New Orleans, perpetrated under the direction of an unreconstructed Confederate mayor, spoke more eloquently than he. Strengthened, the congressional radicals implemented their program. In March 1867, the Reconstruction Act divided the former Confederacy into five military districts under army command. Constitutions framed by conventions, once approved by universal male suffrage and by Congress, would secure states readmittance, provided they ratified the Fourteenth Amendment. Johnson's escape by one vote from the ultimate indignity of removal, his defeat in a bid for election in 1868, and the Fifteenth Amendment, designed to guarantee blacks the vote,

"Uncle Sam's bleaching powder," assured the triumph of radical reconstruction—on paper.[20]

The victory proved hollow in the absence of means to translate intentions into deeds. The Southern states met the legal requirements and wrote improved constitutions. Seven, having done so, won back their rights in 1868, the other three in 1870. None had fundamentally altered inherited patterns of race relations. The conflicts and adjustments generated by poverty, devastation, and emancipation affected liberty more than the new constitutions. The Reconstruction regimes never established the new political and social order Stevens and Sumner envisioned. The South did not solve the fundamental problems of race equity and black liberty.

High hopes, determination, and remarkable energy marked the inauguration of reform administrations, which aimed to perfect society according to ideals of justice, freedom, and equality. Dedicated Northerners, imbued with abolitionist principles, had helped even during the war—some serving as officers in black regiments, others in experimental education, as at Port Royal, South Carolina—to make the liberated self-supporting, to further "the industrial, social, intellectual, and moral and religious elevation of persons released from slavery." Such activities extended into peacetime, often carried on by disinterested and competent people, although some self-seekers among them gave a derogatory connotation to the term *carpetbagger*. Already before the war, masters like Louis Manigault of Georgia mistrusted the white who placed himself on a par with blacks, "even joining in with them in their prayer meetings" (1857). Liberation hardened mistrust into hatred. The scalawags—a term of abuse applied to white Southern Republicans—some of the section's best minds, achieved noteworthy results. An educational system supported by public and private funds made a start at narrowing the tragic gap between the South and the rest of the nation. The new regimes reorganized governments, reformed taxation, rebuilt cities, and sponsored improvements in transportation and industry.[21]

Scandals and corruption, no worse than those which then and later blemished the politics of western and Northern states, offset the positive accomplishments. "Have you seen our menagerie? Have you already been to our pigpen? You have to see our monkey theatre," said embittered whites of their black legislature. The foreign visitor saw no scandals or obscenities, with proceedings "only a bit louder and livelier" than in the House of Representatives in Washington. Occasional misdeeds provided the pretexts that justified the destruction of the Reconstruction administrations between 1870 and 1876, but did not cause the collapse. Nevertheless, the Southerners' incapacity to absorb the blacks as an equal component of their political society destroyed for the time being the chances of expanding everyone's capacity to act.[22]

Reformers failed to recognize their own limitation. Enthusiasts dwelt incessantly upon past wrongs and painted the future glowingly, but rarely took people as they were or understood their needs. Teachers who came down with great ardor lectured pupils about responsibility to the cause of liberty, attained by industrious habits, order and good conduct worthy to stand before God and man. But others complained of their students' "lack of pride of race, of esprit de corps," or of "enthusiasm for themselves as a people with a high destiny." Some reformers too often shrank from personal contact as though their pupils were black spiders. Better have a corps of colored teachers convey the importance of a free and yet disciplined life; members of their own race trained to self-respect, industry, and practical virtue would convince blacks of their capacity for the duties imposed by freedom. Perhaps the role model would succeed where others had failed.

Believing that they could deny history, reverse the past, and start from scratch, reformers ignored the sorry state of Southern agriculture before and after the war and, blinded by hopes for widening the liberty of freedmen and women, overlooked the force of persistent prejudice and entrenched interests. Unwilling to alter existing property relations, they tried to lead a mass of downtrodden followers, black and white, in one great leap to democracy and equality, and undo cultural patterns decades in the making. The liberty of all suffered the consequences.

The development of labor relations based on the discipline of work required time; even the well-intentioned Freedmen's Bureau and the army sometimes had to coerce the former slaves to get to tasks in the fields. The state governments winked at the development of peonage, while federal soldiers believed themselves "helpless lookers-on while the broken ship and crazed crew" drifted onto the rocks together. New to political power, reformers of all persuasions dissipated their energies in fruitless factional struggles or in pursuit of power or wealth, damaging the cause of liberty. Sadly one noted, "One chief trouble with us in the Negro problem as in all things, is this: we are in a great hurry about everything. But God is not in haste about anything."[23]

After 1868, disgruntled whites counterattacked, seeking to reestablish prewar labor relations with a stable work force at the lowest possible price. They wished blacks to leave their freedom over the fence when they came into the landowner's yard. A contract bound employees "to be strictly as my slaves in obeying [the overseer's] . . . instructions and

in performing all work necessary to the well organization of the plantation." Hands who voted contrary to their employer's instructions found
themselves unemployed. Whites banded together to keep wages low, to
exclude troublesome workers, to intimidate blacks unwilling to obey, and
to pay in kind rather than in scarce cash. The freedmen countered through
bargaining strategies to limit employer control. They learned the benefits
of association in seeking redress of grievances and sometimes went on
strike, which in the South smacked of insurrection.[24]

Until they recaptured the political system, former Confederates resorted to violence. Armed regulator bands terrorized blacks and their
friends. The Ku Klux Klan, a secret white order, kept colored men from
the polls and brutally punished pretensions to equality. The Klan declined
after 1872, but rifle clubs, Red Shirts, and white-liners took up the task
of intimidation; the pattern of violence endured, despite the defensive
efforts of loyal and union leagues, and however furiously GOP politicians
waved the bloody shirt. Periodic outbursts, as in the 1880s, reflected fears
lest blacks who matured without having experienced what whites considered the civilizing and restraining effects of slavery, might revert to the
bestiality of earlier stages of evolution. Occasional suggestions of new
laws to ensure fairness in elections, and an economic recession that worsened conditions for all, stirred up outbreaks of racial disorder heated by
sexual fantasies that cast all blacks as potential rapists of white womanhood.

The federal government at first attempted to assist the victims of local
lawlessness, recognizing the validity of a young freedman's answer when
asked what liberty meant to him—"citizenship, suffrage, the right to be
an American citizen." The Force Act of 1870 and the Ku Klux Klan Act
of 1871, together with the Civil Rights Acts of 1870, 1871, and 1875,
aimed to shield the Unionist minority and to preserve free elections. But
outsiders trying to maintain order in unfriendly communities labored
under heavy handicaps. Juries refused to convict and witnesses to testify,
while writs of habeas corpus easily secured from compliant judges set
wrongdoers free. "I have yet to see a white man punished in a state court
for maltreating a negro, and a negro acquitted of any crime however
small," noted an observer of Kentucky justice. The mounting number of
pending cases clogged dockets, ensuring immunity to those who defied
distant authorities in Washington.[25]

Antique patterns of representation eased the way for Redeemers who
sought a return to the prewar social order; and only the military presence
restrained them. Yet the army disliked its police duties; some officers
befriended the cultivated and well-to-do whites rather than the poor

blacks; and Northerners, tiring of the Reconstruction issue, preferred to forget the war and its extravagant hopes. Sympathetic reformers admitted that "we lovers of liberty at the North have imposed upon our colored brother all the depressing distinctions of caste that make a great part of the demoralizing influences of slavery." A few ministers harked back to the sin of slavery, but zeal subsided; peaceful reunion wore away old hatreds, while others cited instances of black improvidence—the "habit of putting off till tomorrow" what did not have to be done today. The 1872 general amnesty act permitted former Confederates to return to active political life, the courts lost interest in civil rights, and the repressive federal forces gradually shrank in size.[26]

One by one the reform governments toppled. In 1875 the radicals held only Louisiana, South Carolina, and Florida. A year later, a disputed presidential election created the opportunity for a political deal: Republicans agreed to withdraw the remaining troops from the South, Democrats conceded the election of Rutherford B. Hayes. Reconstruction ended when the last national army units departed on April 10, 1877.

The country's attention turned elsewhere. Regimes supported by force, without the consent of the governed and against dominant white local opinion, ran counter to the spirit of republican institutions, conventionally defined. Concern with equality faded in the 1870s; the desire mounted for reconciliation and business as usual, and the impulse for control from Washington vanished. Increasingly, Americans accepted a separate Southern identity, including the belief in the exceptional position of blacks in that region. Distinct sectional characteristics expressed in style of life, folkways, diet, and speech patterns justified a unique political order and an understanding of rights that excluded colored people but embraced poor whites. The South deserved charitable treatment; blacks would thrive only if the region did, in what a later generation called "the New South." Constant motion prevented stagnation, wrote a Southerner hopeful that an influx of immigrants would revolutionize the region's economy. The tempest had swept away the stem, and the excrescence which grew from it (slavery) must likewise disappear (1866).

A sentimental glow suffused survivals from the old plantation culture, so different from the grimy industrial North. Slavery, once blamed for the South's economic retardation (1860), now received the credit for having spared it the blight. Lafcadio Hearn, an immigrant, wrote affectionately about the fair, faintly exotic city New Orleans (1878). The United Daughters of the Confederacy in 1894 joined local societies in existence since 1865 and honored Varina Anne Davis, known as the

Daughter of the Confederacy, revealing the mystical devotion to the myth of the Lost Cause, potent in defining Southern identity. Objections subsided to the peculiar institutions that disenfranchised blacks and marked their inferiority through Jim Crow patterns of deference. Those people, neither thrifty nor frugal, did not know how to "lay by for a rainy day." As slaves they had received better care when sick or old than any class of laborers in the world. They therefore spent their money freely while it lasted, much as children did. The virulent racism that had festered below the surface during the Redeemer regimes erupted with the triumph of lily-white parties, producing unprecedented violence and legislation discriminating against blacks. At the same time distrust of big government extended elsewhere and to other endeavors.[27]

Meanwhile the Supreme Court contracted the scope of equal protection. In 1883, it declared the Civil Rights Act of 1875 unconstitutional. The case of *Plessy* v. *Ferguson* recognized the doctrine of *separate but equal* without providing tests of equality, so that segregation, enforced by law, became an accepted feature of life in some jurisdictions. State laws forbade intermarriage and barred contact in public places and in transportation, while the poll tax disenfranchised blacks. The court did respect the need for personal security. *Strauder* v. *West Virginia* (1879) thus reversed the murder conviction of a black tried by a statutorily all-white jury. The very fact that the law expressly denied colored people, although fully qualified citizens, the right to serve as jurors, asserted their inferiority, stimulated prejudice, and impeded equal justice. But the court also developed the doctrine of "state action," by which only overt official activity by public officials could validate complaints against unequal protection. Never mind that the Fourteenth Amendment forbade a state to "deny to any person within its jurisdiction the equal protection of the laws," without specifying whether active or passive, direct or indirect denial. Moreover, the Court determined that the implied protection of "persons" included business corporations. The cumulative result narrowed the scope of protection for human beings while potentially expanding it for business. Such sectional accommodations limited the scope of the nation's action, thereby narrowing the liberty of all.

Convinced that the cold climate and harsh living conditions would forever prove a barrier to mass black migration to the North, some Southerners resigned themselves to the thought that the problem would always be with them. Little came of the proposal to set Arizona aside as a black state—a little Africa. The scheme proved vain in view of the sorry condition of the remaining Indian tribes. Nor did anything come of dreams of shipping the problem back to Africa, so long as blacks retained the right to live where they pleased. New Orleans–born and a Confederate veteran, George Washington Cable (1844–1925), appalled at the sight of white mobs attacking blacks, moved to Massachusetts, where he argued that the United States could not tolerate a class of people less than citizens.

Blacks watched all these developments with growing dismay. Nationwide protest meetings greeted abrogation of the Civil Rights Act; Bishop Henry McNeil Turner printed copies of the Supreme Court decision at his own expense, so that everyone would know how little reliance people could place on the federal government. He swore not to die on American soil and advocated migration to Africa, where he remained but briefly. When he thought death approached, he dragged himself to Windsor, Canada, across from Detroit.

The radical Republicans had hoped that the vote would empower blacks to defend their freedom, although assertion of the right proved difficult enough even in the North, in the face of "lily white" politics. In the states of the old Confederacy, hope for improvement vanished after the populist defeat of 1896, when white Southerners united to disenfranchise blacks. Mississippi, South Carolina, and Louisiana pioneered in evading the Fifteenth Amendment. Limiting the ballot to those whose grandfathers had enjoyed it, poll and property taxes, and tests of the ability to read the Constitution, became devices to bar blacks. The tactic spread to the other former Confederate states; and the party primary served the same end. In despair the well-intentioned concluded that they had paid too much attention to the vote, and that no amount of statutory legislation would help. "The infinitely varied adjustments of human life" made such solutions impossible. The alternative, that people plant themselves "squarely and sincerely on the Sermon on the Mount," convinced few. Efforts to unite blacks and poor whites on the basis of common class interest had collapsed. Lynchings after 1896 far outnumbered those of previous years.[28]

A new generation moved into power, imbued with ideals different from those of the 1850s; none of Johnson's successors in the White House spoke up for equality, and apathy about the fate of the former slaves spread. In the North, concern for their own affairs occupied those whose business was business, but also laborers in the fields, factories, and mines. Jim Crow legislation created a bifurcated social order in a region frustrated by agricultural depression and encouraged by growing Northern willingness to acquiesce in the Southern solution of the race problem. Even reformers, driven by benevolence, ideology, or progressive commitments, expected general social improvement to solve the blacks' problems. The New South, having "fallen in love with work," focused on economic development. Cottonseed oil, iron and steel mills, paper plants, and textile factories promised to end dependence upon a single crop and its attendant difficulties.

In the distant future everyone in the region would "reach the full stature of citizenship, and in peace maintain it" (1889). Meanwhile, Booker T. Washington advised blacks to avoid agitation, train as crafts-men, and make dependable workers. By thrift and hard work they would attain more than by agitation and make the most of the region's coming industrialization. Meanwhile, they should turn inward and set their own internal affairs in order.[29]

Racist attitudes in the South had long affirmed the subordination of blacks, by nature menial and by characteristics odious. After 1859 Dar-winian scientists demonstrated the innate, biological inferiority of people of color. Already geology had vastly expanded estimates of the earth's age, effacing belief in the common descent of all humans from a single pair of ancestors; ages of evolution produced different species, with antipodal constitutions. White skin, thin lips, thick beard, brilliant eyes, strong will, and energetic mind marked the dominant whites. Sluggish molasses blood, ebony skin, protuberant lips, dull and slothful mind and body marked the inferior blacks. Easy speculations followed: Canaan's mother may have been a genuine Cushite, as black inside as out. Whatever may have been the mark set upon Cain, the "Negro," in all ages of the world, bore the mark of color. The wild Arabs and hostile American Indians invariably caught and enslaved the blacks. Taking Africans out of Africa and settling them in the United States by no means made Americans of them, wrote an ethnographer; "it would be quite as reason-able to expect zebras to turn into horses when similarly transported." Richmond P. Hobson, hero and popular lecturer, among many, spread the gospel of race.[30]

These views attracted people outside the South—Californians trou-bled by the presence of Chinese, and Yankees disquieted by tides of new immigration. As Northerners conceded the South's capacity to handle its affairs, the fearful everywhere responded favorably to racist ideas. Pon-dering the meaning of liberty in a free society, Nathaniel Southgate Shaler, dean of the Lawrence Scientific School and professor at Harvard, concluded that blacks, unlike other recent arrivals, carried a heritage that taught them nothing in the way of self-reliance, nor anything of the sense of property on which success in a free society depended. He decided that "the Negro considered as a species" could not rise above barbarism, an irremediable condition. Lack of "the peculiar quality of mind required for effective cooperation" accounted for black incapacity to act.[31]

Economic change, constantly accelerating, altered conceptions of liberty. The society then emerging nationwide expected each person to look out for his or her own welfare, the blacks like anyone else. Scientific theories explained why some races succeeded more than others and why presumed black characteristics—low intelligence, brain deficiencies, anatomical features, emotions, and patterns of thought—created deficiencies in self-reliance. Southern policies therefore expressed biological laws or natural instincts rather than bigotry and prejudice. That some should be powerful and others weak, some rich and others poor, only reflected universal rules—reassurance to politicians and the public. The storm of protest when Theodore Roosevelt invited Booker T. Washington to lunch at the White House (1901) may have influenced the severity with which the president responded to a riot of black troops in Brownsville, Texas (1906). No president repeated his open gesture of social equality. The number of black federal appointees declined after 1900, and segregation after 1908 set apart those who did hold office. It would be wrong, Shaler wrote, to appoint black officials to positions likely to exasperate whites. It was not government's business to educate people about prejudice, and any effort to do so would only increase the evil it tried to remedy.[32]

Occasional Republican Progressives objected that the white South subverted representative government by denying blacks the ballot. Victims of election frauds sometimes received a sympathetic hearing in Congress; and a Force Bill of 1890 would have employed federal officials to guarantee a free, unintimidated ballot to both races. But sympathy and good intentions bore no results, while Southern politicians manipulated electoral regulations to exclude colored people from power. Increasingly, reformers retreated to the belief that the fundamental sin of the white South lay in depriving blacks not of equality or of political rights, but of chances to become farmers, artisans, or merchants, and thus to share in the American dream. Surely the freedmen would acquire economic discipline, once they caught sight of opportunity's rewards. National harmony and unity would then prevail *"without* racial confusion," and without the dreaded amalgamation many feared should the races draw closer to each other. Total separation lay out of reach, but any measure that kept the former slaves subordinate would benefit everyone by preventing a renewed civil war which would end in the total annihilation of blacks. A woman doctor, an abolitionist, fast settled into the belief that "whatever is, is right," and drifted along with the current in the blessed assurance that "all things work together for good."

Segregation guaranteed peace, for "a contented, happy disposition" made the black masses "docile, tractable, and unambitious—with but few wants, and those easily satisfied." Inclined to idleness, with "a tendency to the commission of petty crimes," not malicious, they rarely cherished hatreds when kept in their place. Thomas Dixon's *The Leopard's Spots: A Romance of the White Man's Burden, 1865–1900* (1902) celebrated the salvation of civilization, through the Ku Klux Klan's imposition of obedience and order. The South faced fearful carnage, as insolent blacks intent on pillage and rape confronted the racial fury of Anglo-Saxons while hypocritical Northern ignoramuses denounced Southern barbarism only to recoil from miscegenation when it appeared in their own territory. "The Negro . . . no longer the ward of the Republic," had to "stand or fall on his own worth and pass under the law of the survival of the fittest." God had raised the white race to serve as trustee for civilization, for the principles of civil and religious liberty and for constitutional government. A shallow cosmopolitanism, the mask of death for the individual, obscured the burning question, Shall the future American be an Anglo-Saxon or a mulatto?

The Klansman (1905), Dixon's novel drenched in romanticism, revealed the dominant white view, widely disseminated when David W. Griffith turned it into a popular movie, *The Birth of a Nation* (1915). Thousands watched entranced as Flora, all innocence, fled through the woods and leaped to death to escape the low passion of the black Gus. This account of the violent race wars during Reconstruction, with the Klan the shield of womanhood and civilization against the bestial blacks, seemed to Woodrow Wilson an excellent way to teach history. To that extent had old hopes faded from white consciousness. As a matter of course, Dixon dedicated *The Southerner: A Romance of the Real Lincoln* (1919) to Wilson, his friend and college mate at Johns Hopkins. In that story, Abraham Lincoln, a Southerner, demanded the expulsion of blacks from the United States.[33]

In the South where most of them lived, blacks for the time being accepted conditions as they were and pursued the slow, laborious way to a better life through education and hard work, overcoming wartime disruption and evading harsh vagrancy and peonage laws. Societies for mutual help, for relieving the sick and afflicted, and for meeting the burial expenses of the poor showed signs of future improvement. With the financial and political support of influential outsiders, Booker T. Washington, through the Tuskegee Institute, urged patience and endurance. But discrimination in employment and the unwillingness of the Southern states to provide more than a trickle of support for black schools retarded even that gradual struggle; the constraints of a dual, segregated system left little for students designated inferior. The *Berea College* case (1908) affirmed a Kentucky law forbidding the teaching of more than one race in a single institution. Northern philanthropy helped somewhat in the initial struggle to reduce illiteracy. The General Education Fund (founded by John D. Rockefeller in 1903), the Rosenwald Fund (1917), and the Slater Fund provided millions in aid for the most ambitious, but not enough to improve the lot of all.[34]

The threat of violence persisted. In the 1890s in the fourteen southern states, an average of 138 lynchings each year, with 75 percent of the victims black, demonstrated the reality of power. Wide coverage and detailed, gruesome reporting assured public notice. "Savagery and barbarous acts beget savagery and barbarous acts," wrote an apologist. Riots also became a method of control, occasionally triggered in the 1890s by appointments to postmasterships in the black belt. In 1903 Senator Ben Tillman objected to naming a Negro woman to head a post office housed in Cohen's Brooklyn Bridge Store in Indianola, Mississippi, in a county where six thousand whites faced eighteen thousand blacks. The Wilmington riot of November 10, 1898, occurred in a city more black than white, threatened by a shift in political control. In addition, whites there found themselves in competition with black labor.

In Atlanta and New Orleans a black subculture in conflict with dominant white values generated friction that also erupted into riots. Rapid urban growth, weak municipal administrations, and the tide of lawlessness created tension at a time when many blacks tried to imitate whites—working, going to church, and minding their own affairs. Some riots produced positive results. In Atlanta reorganization of city management, dismissal of a fourth of the police force, and the jailing of mob leaders followed the carnage. The streetcar company rearranged its vehicles clearly to separate the races. A grand jury censored newspapers for sensationalism, and a league of leading citizens organized to promote racial harmony. Dismayed by the riot, other blacks retreated into their own world, into a community within the community, while officials blamed the violence on the lower classes—the white trash. For the majority of blacks, not much changed.

At first the riots seemed a death blow to Booker T. Washington's message of the new black—working, saving, building, advancing in spite of the color lines. Whites resurrected an older stereotype of the black as a child, a Sambo, in need of the helping hand of paternal superiors. Dr. William Lee Howard in the journal *Medicine* (1903) concluded that "the negro," untrammeled and free from control, showed atavistic tendencies. "He is returning to a state of savagery, and in his frequent attacks of sexual madness, his religious emotionalism, superstition and indolence is himself again a savage." Animalism, Howard argued, dominated black physiology and psychology. Northerners heard that there was no prospect of "redemption of the American Negro . . . none, absolutely none. It is impossible to improve the morals of a people when they have no morals to improve. . . . To endow the whole race of them in this country with a sound morality would be just as impossible as it would be to change the color of his skin and take the kink out of his hair." Liberty for such people seemed a contradiction in terms, the basic requisites for exercising its privileges inherently lacking.

Hence the answer of Senator John J. Ingalls: emancipation deepened the gulf between the races. As subordinates blacks could associate with whites, but as political equals they became strangers, taught in separate schools, worshipping in separate churches, buried in separate cemeteries. The country produced two kinds of liberty—one for whites and one for blacks, unprotected even by the rights and immunities conferred by three constitutional amendments. The future offered "no prospect of release from a bondage" imposed by "imperceptible manacles . . . forged and riveted by the tyranny of nature."[35]

Emancipation had not endowed the former slaves with equality, not even with freedom in the sense of the ability to act autonomously. The conviction spread that "you cannot emancipate a human being, he must emancipate himself. . . . You cannot legislate a people into power, they must have power to take and hold for themselves; and as little can a statute put learning or morals into individual lives." William Hannibal Thomas concluded that blacks formed a submerged class that complicated the development of American liberty, "a population in a confessedly low state of racial development, whose instincts are incompatible with, and whose acts are opposed to, American-Anglo Saxon civilization." Lacking creative qualities, they developed differently from whites. Law and government could not generate thriftiness or ordain individual success. Their own conscious sense that society believed in their racial inferiority induced blacks to desire segregation in churches, schools, and social organizations. As a result they struggled for liberty within narrow limits set by the dominant society.

Segregation, while involuntary and a burden in many respects, had the offsetting advantage of compelling blacks to become self-reliant, as did lodges of colored Odd Fellows and Masons. A short-lived National Colored Labor Union made an effort at organization in 1869. Religion proved a more cohesive force. The acceptance by Northern Methodists of racial discrimination in worship broadened the scope for separate colored churches which expressed the distinctive characteristics of their members. The number multiplied, reaching forty thousand in 1906; their ministers, as community leaders, also served as intermediaries in dealing with whites. Churches became visible manifestations of black consciousness and values, the one area in which freedom to act remained unhampered.[36]

A few sensitive listeners caught the overtones of a black culture. At the steamboat landing, juba dances and stevedore songs drew the reporter's attention. Thomas Wentworth Higginson, visiting South Carolina, felt the power of the spirituals that the Fisk Juliblee Singers later carried through the country. The sorrow songs breathed soul hunger— love, helplessness, hope, faith in the ultimate justice of things, attainable in life, or after death. Sometime, somewhere, men would judge one another by their souls and not by their skins. For W. E. B. Du Bois, racial traits justified black distinctiveness and superiority over white civilization, a level of spirituality at war with shoddy materialism. After initial indecision, he urged blacks not to assimilate but to pursue their own natures in voluntary separation and segregation. But the Niagara Movement led to the formation of the National Association for the Advancement of Colored People, a black and white alliance attacking head-on all aspects of inequality.[37]

Meanwhile, Booker T. Washington, the dominant spirit of the Tuskegee Institute, urged accommodation as the only practical strategy. Forget social and political equality; work toward improvement through useful skills. Reconstruction failed, he believed, because it "began at the top instead of at the bottom. A seat in Congress or the state legislature was more sought than real estate or industrial skill." Blacks would advance only when they found "as much dignity in tilling a field as in writing a poem." To the man in the tower, the world below looked very small, with people like hurrying ants pitifully confused and aimless. But the man in the street striving upward, however poor his plight, perceived his goal clear and distinct above him, inspiring him with hope and ambition. "The man who is down, looking up, may catch a glimpse now and then of heaven, but the man who can only look down is pretty likely to see another and quite different place." Washington compared race relations to a human hand. "In all things that are purely social we can be as separate as the fingers, yet one as the hand in all things essential to mutual progress." Friendship with white men of wealth and politicians brought him patronage and a network of influence, although W. E. B.

Du Bois and President Horace Bumstead of Atlanta University criticized his neglect of the "talented tenth" who deserved more than manual training. Washington, willing to forgo full integration and political participation in order to quiet white fears, failed to see the emergence of new hostile elements that rejected his message and regarded blacks as dangerous beasts.[38]

In 1920, a half century of effort had yielded measurable economic gains for a few black people in the South. Howard, Atlanta, and other segregated colleges offered higher education to some, along with entry to business, law, and medicine; others became independent landowners. Elias M. Wood's *The Negro in Etiquette,* preaching "the power of the gospel of civility" to overcome rudeness and intolerance, aimed at that class. But the overwhelming mass remained mired in poverty, often trapped in a sharecropping system that closed off all hopes of improvement. The situation threatened to worsen as a high birthrate pushed rural blacks off the land and into towns with their shockingly high mortality rates. In the end, the Afro-Americans, said Philip A. Bruce (1905), would perish from the face of the earth. "The word 'extermination' is gravely spoken by men who are not therefore held to be maniacs or even monomaniacs," while Du Bois described the whole area as simply an armed camp for intimidating blacks. Visions of the New South boded ill; agricultural expansion and industrial growth raised black mortality, as did relentless competition, the condition of modern life in all civilized communities. Southern economic development would sharpen the struggle for existence, while widespread notions of blacks' inferiority would leave them ever further behind. "The darkest day for the Southern whites has passed . . . the darkest day for Southern blacks has only just begun."

The New South also confronted a "new Negro," no longer restrained by slavery, too ignorant to fear the law, and exposed to the fury of the local populace should he transgress. Brutalized—according to the dominant view—by a life lacking self-discipline and self-restraint, blacks suffered from the fact that the war, having destroyed the gentry who once governed Southern society, spawned new political leaders who lacked social standing, education, and prestige and whose broadened capacity to act led to license and unbridled viciousness. The fixation on white supremacy obliterated other concerns, while petty local politicians catered to the lowest passions of constituencies that devoted their entire energies "to rendering Negro suffrage nugatory. This privilege of voting . . . thrust upon the blacks without their seeking, was destructive of every interest necessary to the welfare of the South . . . . it was destructive of the well-being of the Negroes themselves because their prosperity was inextricably bound up in peaceful relations with the white people; such relations were impossible as long as the Negroes continued to cast their ballots in a herd simply as black men, and not as citizens, regardless of color." The prevailing impression among whites that blacks just emerged from slavery were as capable of exercising the right of suffrage intelligently as the mules and oxen that drew the plows made it obligatory to suppress their votes.

George Fitzhugh, after the war, continued to urge, as earlier, that only peonage could accommodate the former slaves in Southern society; and indeed that pattern extended even to new areas in Texas where renters rarely extricated themselves from debt. The objections of blacks "to close supervision, fixed tasks and continuous labor," made tenancy the ideal solution, for it freed them entirely from supervision so that they worked with as many intervals for rest or amusement as they wished. The few who succeeded economically confronted impenetrable social and political discrimination meant to ensure their absolute inferiority. For the time being they acquiesced in Booker T. Washington's formula for separation on terms of inferiority, like the black boy Katie Rowe of Arkansas observed, chased by three or four Kluckers on horses. "He was trotting down the road ahead of them. Every time he stopped, they popped the whips at his heels and he started trotting on. He was so mad he was crying but he was getting on down the road just the same."

A half century after emancipation, the two races continued simultaneously to live together and apart, in economic solidarity but without social contact. The constant struggle to keep blacks away from political power circumscribed Southern notions of liberty; and the transformation of criminal and civil law into an instrument for subjection diminished everyone's capacity to act, as did lynching, violence, cruelty, and rioting. Literacy qualifications, designed totally to obliterate black suffrage, eliminated as well portions of the white electorate, and thus further circumscribed the liberty to act. Contemporaries acquiesced, for exclusion of the blacks from politics eliminated any special inducement for white men to go to the polls. Mississippi in 1898 cast only 27,636 ballots in congressional elections, while in 1900 the number voting for president there did not exceed 59,073.[39]

Hence, as before the war, the longing for escape; and the gradual development of an exodus, shaped at first by rural bias. For decades, the culture of an agrarian way of life defined the goals of those who departed: destinations on the soil where they could use familiar skills.

Already in the 1850s, Liberia had lost attractiveness, although the idea of a return to Africa continued to surface. *An Appeal to Pharao,* written by Carl McKinley of Charleston, South Carolina, calculated that if 12,500 child bearing women between the ages of twenty and thirty could migrate together with their husbands, the whole "maternal element" of the black race would remove within fifty years. In practice, however, movement proceeded within the United States despite the opposition of Frederick Douglass and Booker T. Washington, who regarded flight from the South as an admission of defeat. During the 1870s more than forty thousand "exodusters" left the southeast for Kansas, where a chilly welcome from the whites forced some to return to Mississippi, the chief source of this movement. Fewer than 136,000 lived in the West in 1910, mainly in Arkansas, Texas, and Oklahoma.[40]

The demand for labor to reconstruct the war-damaged cities drew others to Atlanta and Richmond and to newly industrialized places like Birmingham, where sizable black communities formed during the postwar chaos. Eager for more whites, Southern states made determined efforts to recruit transatlantic immigrants; but concern about the race problem kept Europeans away. Instead, the demand for urban workers attracted a steady stream of blacks, despite the constraints of segregation.

For many, hope shone only from the North, where abolitionists had once welcomed Sojourner Truth and Frederick Douglass as well as less famous fugitives. The growing cities there kindled a glimmer of expectation in cabins where only apathy had been before. By 1900 almost nine hundred thousand blacks lived above the Mason-Dixon Line—with significant clusters in New York (67,000), Philadelphia (79,000), Baltimore (80,000), and Boston (12,000). There and in Chicago the numbers grew thereafter. After 1915, industrial expansion, the end of European migration, and the destruction of the cotton crop by the boll weevil, set in motion a great northward migration that swelled with the economic opportunities of wartime. In 1920 more than a million blacks lived in the North, many having arrived after 1914.[41]

Migration rewarded many. Like James Weldon Johnson in New York in 1899, they glimpsed a new "alluring world, a tempting world of greatly lessened restraints, a world of fascinating perils; but above all, a world of tremendous artistic potentialities." Few shared his creative ambitions; and the city streets offered no one an easy life, but rather posed difficulties of finding a first job, of adjusting to schedules, of managing in crowds, and of coping with dense housing in a harsh climate. Release from the Southern farm nevertheless offered all new perspectives on freedom.[42]

Well-established black communities in Boston, New York, and Philadelphia, even before the Civil War, possessed their own autonomous institutions—churches, schools, and societies, as well as less formal organizations for self-defense and for sheltering fugitives. Like the crew of the *J. L. Bogart,* they resisted efforts of shipmasters to take them to Southern ports (1857), sympathized openly with John Brown, and repudiated emigration, insisting on their rights where they were (1858). They also recognized leaders, often ministers but also occasionally middle- and upper-class people. In Northern cities, as well as in Charleston, Baltimore, Richmond, Washington, and New Orleans, a light-skinned upper class maintained a distinct identity, resisting intermarriage with blacks, emphasizing education, piety, and strong family ties, and engaged in business and the professions. Their wives and daughters organized clubs and eventually joined the movement for women's suffrage. Such people found scope for economic advance and for occupational choices. The colored student refused admission to the Berkshire Medical College gained entry at Yale (1858), and William Monroe Trotter of Boston attended Harvard (1891). In Cincinnati the leaders of the variegated colored community, bent on instilling "habits of industry, economy, and sobriety," urged greater self-reliance in the struggle for material and moral improvement. Frederick Douglass, once a runaway slave, then a doughty abolitionist campaigner, tried to succeed in finance. Others with political connections developed careers in public office—two elected to the state legislature by white constituents in Boston. Business attracted still others, particularly when helped by a following held together by color and neighborhood. They joined lawyers, physicians, and ministers in a small black elite with its own character.

A sense of group solidarity suffused their activities, though the struggle for the vote long seemed paramount. All along, the ambitious made room for themselves—at a price. Mary White Ovington's *Half A Man* (1911) described the status of New York blacks whose problems rose not from innate disabilities, but rather from the denial of equal opportunity. The colored community there had its equivalent of the Four Hundred, while voluntary associations clustered around churches, old people's homes, rescue missions, Christian associations, and social settlements, which met some communal needs. Demands appeared for businesses, banks, restaurants, and factories of their own to use self-sufficiency as protection against white hostility expressed in the greed of the money shark, the lust of the landlord, and the chicanery of the cheap politician.

The black press—the *Richmond Planet,* the *Philadelphia Tribune,* the *New York Age* and *Amsterdam News,* the *Pittsburgh Courier* and the

Chicago Defender—voiced common ideals. By 1915, 450 periodicals by and for blacks in the United States corrected the biased reporting of white publications. In 1920 social scientists spoke of the New Negro, a far cry from the servility and vice ascribed to the slaves. Class consciousness, revolutionary socialism, and other ideologies penetrated the community so that the *Messenger* (1920), edited by A. Philip Randolph and Chandler Owen, maintained that "the old me-too boss, hat-in-hand, good nigger" had vanished. Under a Soviet-type system, they argued, the right to vote would rest on service and not upon race or color.[43]

Expectations rose. The 180,000 blacks who served in the Union army in time achieved equal pay, bounties, and other compensations, acquired literacy, attained a better legal status, and demanded full citizenship rights. Disappointment did not stifle the hopes of those who enlisted in the Spanish-American War or who entered the armed forces in 1917, although shunted off into segregated units or assigned menial tasks. The ironic juxtaposition of the picture of a Southern lynching with a parade of black troops returning from France (1918) lost Ernest Gruening his job as managing editor of the *New York Tribune,* an outcome that surprised few who were inured to discrimination.[44]

The rapid increase in numbers of the unskilled unfamiliar with urban life created problems for the old residents and for the larger society about them. Competition with Italian and Greek immigrants displaced black barbers, waiters, and shoe-shine men—occupations traditionally theirs. After 1890, an increasing number of women entered the wage labor force, in housework and other roles. In Philadelphia and New York, idle men slipped into a network of intrigue and bribery when they drifted into clubs with social but also political functions. And the difficulties multiplied with the sudden influx after 1914 into places already experiencing multiple shocks of economic growth and racial adjustment. The new arrivals reared in the rural South encountered formidable personal problems. More than a thousand got onto the payroll of United States Steel in Gary to explore the meaning of liberty in a dismal mill town. Since, for want of alternatives, blacks occasionally took jobs as scabs, unions offered no help—and often denied them membership or excluded them from skilled occupations. Unexpected and no less difficult communal problems proved troubling—how to form their own societies while not only cut off from the black upper class and from the white majority, but also internally divided and burdened with legal and social inequality. Nevertheless the persistent made a difference. Samuel Eason, bricklayer and plasterer, moved by the plight of black orphans and old women, in Kansas City saved enough by 1889 to rent a house as a place of refuge.

Receiving little help from others, he organized a group to help run the home; he himself carried in donated food in a wheelbarrow, and during one of these trips suffered a fatal heart attack. Still, the project survived and became a major charitable institution.[45]

Without the etiquette of slavery or of the Jim Crow South, Northern whites and blacks circled each other in an uncertain relationship. Small-town police considered innocent behavior, like hanging around Main Street, "loitering," which justified charges of disorderly conduct and arrest. Vague sexual fears erupted in stories about colored babies born to pure young mothers (1857). Down on Calvert and Sixth streets, whites formed a substantial contingent among women available in the dancing room patronized by black roustabouts. Yet respectable society quarantined the journalist who took up with Althea Foley, a mulatto, just as some blacks resented Frederick Douglass's marriage to a white woman. The subjects of passing, miscegenation, intermarriage, and race mixture, often evaded in polite discussion, nevertheless created uneasy barriers to social contacts.[46]

Success remained conditional on the goodwill of the dominant society. Few in the Northern cities forgot their own past involvement in, or stories about, abolitionism and the rescue of fugitive slaves. Up in Boston, William Monroe Trotter, fiery editor of the *Guardian,* reminded his readers how far they yet had to travel in the struggle for liberty. Unwilling to accept Booker T. Washington's neglect of political rights in favor of economic independence, Trotter and his allies called for militancy and urgency, in breaking down barriers of segregation in education and politics.[47]

William E. B. Du Bois (1868–1963) initially urged moderation. Reared in a small Massachusetts town, he first became aware of his color when he went off to college at Fisk. Like Douglass, he expected intermarriage to follow the obliteration of segregation. Experience proved harsh. A Harvard graduate, a brilliant and sometimes original thinker and a lucid writer, he nevertheless knew that he could never hold a chair in a university to which any plodder could advance with the passport of whiteness. Years of protest followed. Yet pride and the fear of rejection induced him also to look inward, to describe the soul of black folk and the unique qualities of their own culture. For a time he endorsed Booker T. Washington's views, until contact with Philadelphia blacks revealed a different reality and a need for greater efforts than in the rural South. He brooded about his "two-ness"—"an American, a Negro, two souls, two thoughts, two unreconciled strivings: two warring ideals in one dark body." Black people, deprived of fundamental freedoms whites enjoyed, also suffered from divided souls. Blacks may indeed have possessed gifts of the spirit that enriched American civilization as an offset to the cool and cautious New England reason; and the heritage of slavery forced everyone to consider, "if not wholly accept, the idea of a democracy including men of all races and colors." After 1910, he grew more extreme, less patient, as lynchings and disenfranchisement demanded more decisive social action.[48]

Mass upheavals undermined expectations of peaceful improvement. City life everywhere exposed black people to violence. In rural areas, too, they lacked recourse against abuses—beatings, lynchings, and casual acts of brutality. But there, deferential behavior and appeals to white protectors sometimes helped. Massed in town and blamed for every social ill, blacks became targets of impersonal mobs, heedless of distinctions between good and bad, between docile and uppity, intent on murderous rampages, impervious to respectable pleas for peace. Lynchings dotted the country each year and race riots in Evansville, Indiana (1903), Springfield, Illinois (1908), and East St. Louis (1917) exposed reality north of the Mason-Dixon Line. Horrible eruptions in Wilmington, North Carolina (1898), and in Chicago (1919) forced blacks to consider measures of self-defense.[49]

Some Northern state laws did attempt to improve the status of blacks by assuring them equal access to public facilities. In New York, Massachusetts, New Jersey, Maine, Pennsylvania, Michigan, Wisconsin, Illinois, Colorado, Oregon, and Washington, civil rights statutes banned discrimination. But enforcement difficulties nullified legislative intentions. Los Angeles excluded blacks from public facilities and segregated beaches, and closed some residential areas to them. Jitney buses there refused to accept colored passengers. Pasadena excluded them from parks and in 1918 set up a black playground to avoid interracial mingling.

Voluntary responses proved ineffective. Blacks, unable to join professional organizations like the Washington District Medical Society, formed their own—the Medico Chirurgical Society (1884). But that hardly compensated. The failure of the Freedmen's Bank (1874) undermined confidence in black capacity to handle finances. Few colored businessmen, merchants, restaurateurs, or barbers catered to both races; service to one clientele automatically excluded the other. Moreover, blacks persisted in patronizing white shops, no matter how discriminatory their owners in employment. Combined with class divisions, weakness of internal institutions, family difficulties, and enormous outside pressures, these impediments on the ability to act resulted directly from the slavery heritage.

Acceptance on terms of equality and freedom of association created problems for other ethnic groups also; and racism occasionally poisoned the positions of many. But the uniqueness of the black situation derived from the burden they alone bore: the heritage of slavery with its bitter history of exploitation that had culminated in the war no one forgot. That heritage affected black definitions of liberty and for a time limited their capacity to act in a white society.[50]

Almost from the very start, whites and Indians had clashed in the settlement of the New World. At first, deep cultural differences had kept the natives apart from newcomers and had impeded resistance to the advance of the English, and later of the Americans. In the 1850s the aborigines were no more ready than earlier to accommodate the dominant society, which long remained ambivalent in its attitudes toward them.

Americans revealed their lack of understanding when they applied the term *Indian* to the vastly different tribes and language groupings that dotted the continent—from the Algonquians of the eastern forest to the Sioux and Cheyennes of the plains, the transplanted Cherokees of Oklahoma, the pueblo dwellers of New Mexico and the diggers of the Pacific Coast. That view disregarded the specific identities of the peoples aggregated in a common problem defined by the conquerors—obstacles all.

Tucked away well behind the line of settlement, descendants of the aborigines did not impede migration because they had reached a stable accommodation with intruding settlers. Some red men and women mingled with whites and occasionally intermarried; others retained separate tribal forms; and still others, like the triracial isolates who lived on the margins of society, amalgamating several stocks, formed their own detached communities. Easterners anticipated a peaceful adjustment, and cheered when the Cherokees, like good capitalists, wrestled with the interest on their debt, when Jim Thorpe gained fame as an all-American, and when Charles Curtis, a Kaw, went to the United States Senate.[51]

But such eastern aberrations affected neither the image of the Indians elsewhere nor the adjustment most of the tribes made in practice. Those occurred under Western influences.

On the frontier, where recollections endured of the fate of the Oatman family at the hands of the Apaches (1851), the need to safeguard homes, farms, and ranches defined accommodations. Americans believed it a duty to remove any obstacles in their way—the tribes among them—peacefully by persuasion if possible, by force of arms if need be, acting through or by spontaneous associations. The Rogue River War in Oregon (1855) and the ruthless massacre of the Sioux in Minnesota (1862) signaled the coming bloodshed. Some whites considered the foe a wild animal. When they "found gold in the mountains around the land of winding water," an Indian leader complained, they forced war upon his people. Insulted a thousand times, their fathers and brothers killed, their mothers and wives disgraced, driven to madness by whiskey sold by white men, the homeless and desperate tribesmen took up arms. One way or another, by control, emigration, pacification, or elimination, they knew they would cease to impede settlement. Newspapers exposed General Oliver O. Howard's shameful role in the complicated moves which deprived the Nez Percé of their lands in the Pacific Northwest (1877). Yet he remained on their trail and cut off their escape into Canada, never doubting the justice of cultural extermination that facilitated settlement. That reality belied the sentimental images Americans elsewhere held of the red tribes.[52]

Back East, dime novels and lurid lithographs of Custer's last stand freshened the popular image of the skulking savages. But increasingly, a romantic glow replaced the old devilish features with benign ones, fusing the impressions of primitive nobility, courage, and chivalry from Cooper's Leatherstocking warriors and Francis Parkman's histories. If only the government would halt the liquor trade! George Bancroft and Lydia Sigourney agreed that Pocahontas's death at twenty-two in England saved her from beholding the extermination of the tribes from which she sprang.

> Forgotten race, farewell. Your haunts we tread,
> Our mighty rivers speak your words of yore,
> Our mountains wear them on their misty head,
> Our sounding cataracts hurl them to the shore
> But on the lake your flashing oar is still,
> Hush'd is your hunter's cry on dale and hill,
> Your arrow stays the eagle's flight no more
> And ye, like troubled shadows, sink to rest
> In unremember'd tombs, unpitied and unbless'd.

Generations of schoolchildren felt the pathos of Longfellow's lines in *The Song of Hiawatha* (1855). The beautiful simplicity of the Indian faith— "nothing of the dark and savage, only the mild and infantile," thrilled Henry D. Thoreau—at a distance. The glow acquired colors and depth from the eloquence and courage of Chief Joseph of the Nez Percé.

Stories of the Far West, not its brutal reality, authenticated that romantic impression. The Indians at Taos played it straight; Kit Carson's friendship kept them at peace; when he died, hostilities commenced. Unfocused images blended in a hazy picture—General Custer at the Little Big Horn, Sitting Bull and Buffalo Bill, all evidence of tribal distinctiveness. At the same time, Jim Thorpe, all-American, evidence of the capacity for assimilation. The policy of giving to all Indians a home would induce a strong incentive to labor and cause them to advance more rapidly in civilization than would the continued policy of allowing them to hold their land in common. Those in Michigan, Wisconsin, Minnesota, and Kansas willing to abandon tribal organization and create allotments in severalty, by 1870 provided evidence of the resolution of difficulties. Campaigns that gradually exterminated those who refused to adjust would kill the spirit of others. With this in mind, Buffalo Bill's highly successful play, *The Scout of the Plains,* presented "a true representation of . . . the life in that immense country . . . now gone forever." Those who did adjust realized the inevitability of it all, and asked for liberty only. "I know that my race must change," Young Joseph of the Nez Percé declared. "We cannot hold our own with the white men as we are. We only ask an even chance to live as other men live. . . . Let me be a free man, free to travel, free to stop, free to work, free to trade where I choose, free to choose my own teachers, free to follow the religion of my fathers, free to think and talk and act for myself." In the end, hopefully, "We shall be alike, brothers of one father and one mother" (1879).[53]

Confusing views impeded the formulation of a coherent national policy. After the Civil War, the federal government that sold more than seven million acres of western land annually, ever ready to hand vast tracts to the railroads, felt compelled to get the nomads out of the way. The Grant administration recognized that the United States could order no further removals, and instead undertook to confine the tribes on reservations north of Nebraska and south of Kansas, to remain permanently apart, although expectations lingered that they would somehow, sometime, ultimately mingle with the larger society about them, perhaps through educating their children at Carlisle or Hampton Institute, where they might learn the rudiments of family and home life. The Board of Indian Commissioners, the Women's National Indian Association, the Indian Rights Association, and the Lake Mohonk Conference on the Indian urged the federal government to foster a general educational system not dependent on charitable or missionary groups.

President Grant's peace policy launched in the hope of ultimately extending citizenship to the Indians rested on the assumption that assimilation guided by civilians would civilize those on reservations. But the resulting debacles, which meant loss of influence and patronage for state politicians, the army, and Congress, exacerbated the problem. The policy also called for an end to the treaty system, treating Indians as individuals responsible for their own well-being rather than as members of the tribe. Ely S. Parker, son of a Seneca chief and a graduate of the Cayuga Academy, had befriended the anthropologist Lewis Henry Morgan, who encouraged him on the road to assimilation, although outraged by the destruction of Indian culture. Morgan in time helped shape a new mythology, as inadequate as the noble savage idea; it credited the red peoples with creating communities where "liberty, equality and fraternity, though never formulated, were cardinal principles." But intimations of corruption brought Parker's resignation by 1871. He thereupon moved to New York City, where success on Wall Street brought temporary prosperity; and when he failed, he found a niche in the police department. The last "Grand Sachem of the Iroquois" died in 1895, buried in an Episcopalian service in Connecticut.[54]

Rivalry between the War and the Interior departments and among several competing missionary enterprises revealed the mismanagement of massive federal appropriations, administered by a poorly paid, corrupt, and scandal-plagued bureaucracy, an easy target for criticism. Parker also came under suspicion, branded by his successor as "but a remove from barbarism." Corruption, mismanagement, and bureaucratic feuding scarcely affected the series of Indian wars, with always enough massacres and atrocities to keep supporters of the Peace Policy in the majority, although the Indians themselves rejected Grant's proposal.

Violence followed encroachments by frontiersmen on the reservations and drew attention to such grievances as those of the Ponca, removed from the Dakota Territory in 1877. Their plight stirred public sympathy when journalists and tribal chiefs replicated the impact of pre–Civil War speaking tours of the North by former slaves. George Manypenny's *Our Indian Wards* (1880) followed the controversy, expressing optimism about assimilation if missionary endeavors received adequate support and if whites respected Indian property and other rights.[55]

Ever since Jackson's removal of the Cherokee, conscientious clergymen and other writers like the Episcopal bishop of Minnesota Henry B. Whipple and the Methodist minister and farmer John Beeson had vividly deplored the Indian lot. Helen Hunt Jackson (1830–1885) described the situation indignantly in *A Century of Dishonour* (1881); and her romantic story, *Ramona* (1884), a tale of Anglo-Saxon cruelty against an idyllic indigenous culture, generated various Indian rights associations. Critics further stirred the national conscience by the argument that Canada managed these affairs better. The Kiowa and Comanche experience confirmed the implied criticism of United States reservation policies. Though a treaty of 1867 created a reservation of nearly three million acres for them, isolation proved unenforceable. The needs of cattlemen, internal tribal divisions, and corrupt use of government funds, by 1900, left the Indians worse off than before, while agricultural leases and heavy white incursions ended the isolation policy.[56]

Some congressmen recognized a crisis. Indians, they thought, would either perish or become entirely dependent upon government. Of the total of about 250,000 to 300,000 organized in about three hundred tribes, only 130,000 supported themselves. Better they should abandon nomadic habits, learn to eat bread in the sweat of their brows, and merge with the surrounding society, assuming the duties and responsibilities of citizenship. That called for an end to tribal organization and reservations in favor of individual land ownership that would make them economically independent, like the emancipated blacks.[57]

The Dawes Severalty Act of 1887 aimed to convert a tribal culture into a farmers' society. Salvation required making the Indians citizens as fast as possible while the state in the interim protected their rights. But the laws encountered unexpected problems when its beneficiaries proved reluctant to conform, though offered no choice. Neither a tribe nor an individual could refuse to accept allotments, but progress had to be forced upon the Indians *for their own good.* The law also opened the unallotted surplus of lands to white settlements, to encourage integration. The disastrous effects soon became clear, as allotment, whatever its intentions, became a legalized fiction disguising expropriation. New battles at Little Big Horn and Wounded Knee and concern about the Ghost Dance Religion lessened the immediacy of assimilation.[58]

Red people, like blacks, raised troubling questions about the meaning of liberty, although in a different fashion. In the case of the Indians, Americans believed the answer simple—let them merge with others in the melting pot of citizenship, retaining if they wished their ethnic identity, as the Welsh or Germans or British did. The red man, once primal lord of a magnificent domain, was despoiled by craft and crime and wasting sword.

> And shall we still add wrong to wrong?
> Is this the largess of the strong—
> His need to slight, his faith to doubt,
> And thus to bar the Red Man out,
> Though welcoming all other men?

> Nay let us nobly build him in
> Nor rest till "ward" and "alien" win
> The rightful name of citizen.
> Then will the "reservation" be
> Columbia's breadth from sea to sea,
> And Sioux, Apache and Cheyenne
> Merge proudly in American. (1920)[59]

That they might reject the transformation seemed unthinkable.

Members of the Indian Rights Association sometimes argued that since "the descendants of the worst of all races are today worthy American citizens" (by which they meant blacks after the Fourteenth Amendment), Native Americans deserved equal treatment. But problems generated by black enfranchisement fueled opponents' views, including the suggestion that docile tribesmen would fall prey to unscrupulous vote manipulation and land theft. Nevertheless, by 1906 some 166,000 Indians became citizens, 65,000 through the allotment process and the rest as members of the Five Nations.

The ceremony by which the government bestowed citizenship on Indians expressed this tension. The secretary of the interior (1916) called the applicant by his white name, asked for his Indian name, gave him a bow, and requested him to shoot an arrow. Addressing him by his Indian name, the secretary said, "You have shot your last arrow. That means that you are no longer to live the life of an Indian. You are from this day forward to live the life of the white man. But you may keep that arrow; it will be to you a symbol of your noble race and of the pride you feel that you come from the first of all Americans."

Then the secretary, using the Indian's white name, told him to place his hand on a plow. "This act means that you have chosen to live the life of the white man—and the white man lives by work. Only by work do we gain a right to the land or to the enjoyment of life." The final step was presentation to the applicant of a leather purse, as a reminder that "the money you gain from your labor must be wisely kept," a flag, "the only flag you ever had or ever will have," and a gold-colored badge inscribed, A Citizen of the United States. The Supreme Court in *United States* v. *Nice* ruled citizenship compatible with tribal existence and continued guardianship and so conferrable without completely emancipating the Indians or placing them beyond the reach of congressional regulations adopted for their protection.

Yet assimilation did not work. "What is the matter with the Indian, what keeps him from assimilating with his surroundings, why cannot we absorb two hundred and fifty thousand Indians into all our millions and never know where they are?" asked Frances Campbell Sparhawk. The answer, Hamlin Garland insisted, lay in the greed and fanaticism that battled for the Indians' souls. The response, more government control, required greater paternalism. Theodore Roosevelt attacked the likes of Helen Hunt Jackson as "foolish sentimentalists" and proposed to "protect and guard [the Indians] to a certain point, but all the while . . . fitting them . . . for rough contact with the world." His commissioner of Indian affairs later maintained that the Indian had to move away from artificial restraints and protection "toward the broad area of individual liberty enjoyed by the ordinary citizen."[60]

Therein the Indians differed from the blacks, who had no choice of affiliation, but had an identity thrust upon them in a denial of equality and therefore of liberty.

Enforced ethnic identity, imposed, not voluntarily assumed, became a mark of rejection for Indians and blacks and for a few other groups set apart by color or religion—to some degree, somewhat.

Early in the nineteenth century, Americans displayed attitudes highly favorable to Orientals, and Asia long attracted missionary and business enterprise. For a time, too, its peoples promised as immigrants to relieve labor shortages, not only in California, closest to the source, but also as far away as North Adams, Massachusetts, and Louisiana. Chinese immigrants helped build the transcontinental railroad and worked in the rice fields and shoe factories. In time they established a few small independent enterprises. The coolies arrived in the United States within a well-established pattern of overseas migration, in gangs under contractual arrangements with responsible managers. Alien in appearance, language, religion, costume, and customs, these newcomers kept to themselves in labor camps and urban Chinatowns.[61]

The pattern of ethnic separateness, acceptable among Italians and Germans, evoked suspicion when it came to Asians, although often segregation resulted not from their own choice but from exclusion by others. The overland train out of Council Bluffs carried three cars, one for women and children, one for men, and the third for Chinese. No discretion allowed. A traveling Englishman remarked the "stupid ill feelings" of the "foul and malodorous Caucasians" toward the Orientals. Hostile laborers whose wages they undercut panicked at lurid tales of the vices of the little yellow rice eaters, suspected of nefarious doings in their secret Tongs. Physicians suggested that the "filthy, vicious, debased heathen" Chinese spread leprosy. The San Francisco workingmen, led by Denis

Kearney, an Irish sandlot orator, attacked the dirty Mongolians in words and acts; and later the same hateful expressions appeared in Boston. In time also the Knights of Labor and the American Federation of Labor turned the Chinese into targets of abuse. "You cannot work a man who must have beer and bread, alongside of a man who can live on rice," wrote Samuel Gompers. The result would demean the superior to the level of the lower, just as slaves degraded free labor, supplant the civilization of Christ with the civilization of Confucius. "They are with us," exclaimed the *Boston Commonwealth* upon the arrival of a group—wooden clogs and all, men of "almond eyes, pigtails, rare industry, and quick adaptation." Helpless when attacked, the Chinese fell easy victims in riots, as in the massacre at Rock Springs, Wyoming (1885), which killed twenty-eight laborers, wounded fifteen others, and chased several hundred out of town. Their irritating presence formed a useful political issue until mounting racial feelings expressed in riots led to their exclusion. Mark Twain noted that "a Chinaman had no rights that any man was bound to respect. . . . Neither his life nor his liberty was worth the purchase of a penny when a white man needed a scapegoat . . . everybody, individual, communities, the majesty of the State itself, joined in hating, abusing and persecuting these humble strangers."[62]

The favorable reception at first accorded the Japanese also turned hostile after 1900. Their color did not prevent the warm greetings accorded a diplomatic delegation in Washington in 1860; and their initially small immigration and their settlement patterns in accord with American ideals earned these newcomers acceptance. They did not cluster in slums but spread out to rural California, where they engaged in agricultural labor. Hard work brought prosperity, landownership, and education for their children. During the Russo-Japanese War the general American attitude remained favorable, and missionaries eager for converts defended them against criticism. Wallace Irwin's popular Japanese-American houseboy, Hashimura Togo, a vehicle for satirical humor, embodied this spirit when he explained that derby hat, American pants, and tuxedo overcoat rendered these immigrants completely white of complexion and able to vote for president. He wished to join "together with other patriots of star stripe banner Yankee doodle dandy, banzai" in pushing out the all-colored Yellow Perils.

But racist sentiments eventually turned against all Asians. Proposed discriminatory legislation called for higher licensing fees, the prohibition on employment of white women by Japanese, and denial of the right to inherit land. The *Sacramento Bee* in 1910 quoted a Californian, "Now the

Jap is a wily an' a crafty individual; more so than the Chink. . . . They try to buy in the neighborhoods where there are nothing but white folks. . . . They are lower in the scale of civilization than the whites and will never become our equals. They have no morals. . . . Nobody trusts a Jap." California authorities blamed the bubonic plague on immigrants, fueling union charges that the Orientals would act "as an incubus upon our industries." The clownish mayor of San Francisco and its corrupt boss abetted labor's stance, certain that the Japanese "are not the stuff of which American citizens can be made . . . as they will not assimilate with us and their social life is so different from ours, let them keep a respectful distance." If the country could keep out pauper-made goods by tariff barriers, it could do the same for the paupers themselves. Hostile legislation in California limited access to schools and to land ownership and led to a Gentlemen's Agreement (1907) that effectively ended immigration. Negative popular emotions aimed also at the small groups of Filipinos, Koreans, and East Indians ("ragheads") who had been cast on American shores by an expanding empire.

Irony—while Americans persuaded of the brotherhood of man generously supported the efforts of devoted missionaries who labored to bring Christianity to the remote peoples of Asia and Africa, those same people became the objects of venemous racial hatred within the United States. The Reverend Sidney Gulick, among other returned missionaries, defended the Japanese presence in California. Gulick had lived in the Orient for thirty years, had lectured at Doshisha University and the Imperial University at Kyoto, and consistently defended the Japanese. In 1914, the Federal Council of Churches, collaborating with the Japan Society (founded 1907), undertook to alleviate their plight, in part because missionaries in Asia complained that developments in the United States hampered their activities.[63]

Further ironies reflected the inability to apply in practice any consistent conception of race, despite efforts to grasp at scientific criteria supplied by biologists and anthropologists. Blacks, of course, and Orientals, no doubt—pigment and physical characteristics came readily to hand. Indians? Perhaps. And what about the Irish and the Italians? The Sydney Ducks, first victims of the San Francisco vigilantes, came over from Australia; and in the Andersonville prison camp, midwestern Regulators achieved order by hanging the Irish "N'Yaarkers." Such spontaneous activity after the Civil War found victims among Catholics and Jews as well as among blacks.[64]

Religion, however, provided at best but a slippery measure. Age-old suspicions directed at the Roman Catholic Church fed upon its allegiance to a foreign pontiff, but also upon the strangeness of its rituals, of its celibate institutions, and of its oath-bound orders—all exposed by the Reverend Charles Chiniquy, a lapsed priest, to the horror of the APA (1893–94), the successor to the prewar Know-Nothings. But nothing racial there, and no reflection intended upon Americans or Germans like Cardinal James Gibbon or Isaac Thomas Hecker, or even upon Edward McGlynn. However, the image of John Madden, who died in the Chicago bridewell of delirium tremens, conjured up racial sensitivities not so much Catholic as Irish, arrayed in negative features as Celts given to brutality and cruelty, to Pat-riot-ism, not patriotism, their intelligence largely low cunning, a threat to democratic political institutions.[65]

Then, too, the Jews—certainly comprehensible as a religious group, but now occasionally described in racial terms. Orthodox Christians knew that the people of the Book played a central role in the scheme of salvation, in accordance with the prophecy that their conversion would herald arrival of the millennium. English and American missionaries labored earnestly to hasten that day. Then, too, since Puritan times Americans matched their own experience to that of the ancient Israelites, pilgrim peoples both, moving to their promised lands in accord with God's will, a depiction that evoked much sympathy for Jews still trapped in less fortunate realms. Public protests in 1858 thus greeted news of the Mortara Case in Italy in which a servant surreptitiously had a child baptized against the parents' wishes. Later diplomatic intervention on behalf of Jews in Switzerland, Romania, and Russia culminated in abrogation of the commercial treaty with the czar in protest against anti-Semitic discrimination. Within the United States, also, Americans resented slurs and unintended expressions of prejudice, as when a landlord proved ignorant of what would follow when he rented rooms to a synagogue (1858), or in the case of the American minister in Lisbon who objected to "Jew interlopers" undercutting his favorites in selling supplies to the United States Navy (1869). Jews occasionally held political office of some importance, like Judah Benjamin, Francis L. Cardozo in South Carolina, Louis Brandeis, or Meyer Weil, three times mayor of Paducah, Kentucky.[66]

Nevertheless, mistrust of the strangeness lingered, fed by old and new stereotypes—of the mysterious wandering Jew and of the urban ghettos with their menacing radicals and anarchists. A War Department slur during the Civil War characterized Jewish traders as extortioners who ate up the substance of the country; and the impression persisted. Newly rich families, insecurely positioned in an ill-defined society, sought reassurance about the value of their own inclusion by excluding others, as at the Saratoga hotel that turned away a well-known Jewish financier. A controversy at Coney Island (1879) reenacted the drama at Saratoga a year earlier when the Manhattan Beach Company denied Jews access to its hotels and beaches. One of the company's managers, "personally opposed to Jews," explained, "They are a pretentious class, who expect three times as much for their money as other people. They give us more trouble on our road and in our hotel than we can stand. . . . And they are driving away the class of people who are beginning to make Coney Island the most fashionable and magnificent watering place in the World." Company officials insisted that religion had nothing to do with the matter, just "the offensiveness which they possess as a sect or nationality" with which the highest social element would not associate. Some Jews adopted "summer names" to avoid unpleasantness in making hotel reservations. Select clubs, schools, and colleges to assert their aristocratic quality also either barred or limited the number of Israelites admitted.[67]

At the same time, other fears stoked racial hostility to Jews among radicals. Shylock images surfaced in the Georgia constitutional convention (1865) during the debate over repudiation of the state war debt, and expanded with accounts of the wealth and power of the Rothschilds and other bankers, transforming international finance into the instrument of a Jewish conspiracy. The American Bimetallic League published "Shylock, as banker, bondholder, corruptionist and conspirator" (1894), dedicated to Wendell Phillips, the grandest American who liberated the black slaves. The author, Gordon Clark, certain that "the demonetization of silver was . . . the greatest crime of modern times," clearly implied that Jews were the new enslavers, amid images of Calvary and the Cross and talk of the Anglo-Jew Octopus. In Ignatius Donnelly's *Caesar's Column,* the oligarchy of wealth, led by Prince Cabano (born Jacob Isaacs), plunged all society into disaster. An anarchist newspaper wondered whether esteem for money made Jews greater cheats than Yankees. The silver question infused similar stereotypes into the Populist movement. Radicals traced Christianity's faults to a Hebrew heritage, as some Enlightenment thinkers had. The sarcastic Professor Sylvanus (1895) regarded all history as a compilation of fraudulent records, with liberty among the least understood terms. His own efforts were all part of a mission—to expose the fallacies by which a shrewd Shylock minority governed and abused humanity by foisting women's rights and high taxes on gullible citizens. Such dark suspicions sometimes turned into brutal realities, as when sixteen Philadelphians ran pins into the flesh of a Jewish boy as retaliation for the crucifixion of Christ (1856).[68]

Whether as victims or plotters, those people remained aliens in everyday life. They were nice-appearing enough, remarked a servant girl, "but the second day I found out they were Jews. I never had seen a Jew before, so I packed my bag and said to the lady, 'I beg your pardon ma'am, but I can't eat the bread of them as crucified the Saviour.' But, the lady said, 'he was a Jew.' So at that I put out." Henry Adams and other fastidious travelers resented the presence of Jews on ships. The good-hearted and educated but ignorant wife of a junior member of Wilson's administration wrote (1913) of her attendance at a party "which I'd rather be hung than seen at. Mostly Jews." Alas, two days later at a Jew Party for the Bernard Baruchs she met Felix Frankfurter, "an interesting little man, but very Jew." Meanwhile European writers like Edouard Drumont played upon some gullible intellectuals who in time swallowed whole the plot described in the forgery that exposed the conspiracy of the Elders of Zion.

For the moment, in the case of Jews and Catholics, unease did not turn racist, for conversion remained an acceptable escape from group affiliations. Persistent ethnic slurs marked off the sheeny, dago, or Mick; but equally persistent universalism—faith in the unity of mankind—kept fears and hatreds within bounds. "We are all of one blood, all descended from the same parentage," wrote the editorialist (1853); and the poet still insisted,

> All people have the same red-running blood.
> There swells and jets a heart—there all passions,
> > desires, reachings, aspirations.
>
> Do you think they are not there because they are not expressed
> > in parlors and lecture rooms?
> These are exactly the same to all, in all nations and times,
> > all over the earth.

The fears and hatreds churned beneath the surface, especially among the insecure who defined their own identity in the contrast with the excluded others.[69]

The positions of Jews and Irish Catholics remained symptomatic of the dominant tendency toward pluralism. Let them all go their own ways. Liberty called for the practical accommodation to actual diversity in a society lacking cultural or social uniformity. Let everyone associate in groups of their own choosing, all more or less to do their own things in their own fashions. Pluralism in a free society permitted that latitude—except when color, the heritage of ancient bondage, stood in the way.

Gustave Le Bon, overwhelmed by the Americans' capacity to govern themselves while existing on the verge of anarchy, noted that they had reduced "the action of the State" to such a minimum that almost no public authorities existed. Only the Anglo-Saxon could thrive in the feverish state of American society, he assumed; hence the Irishman and the Negro would vegetate in the most humble situations. "The great Republic," he concluded, "is assuredly the land of liberty. It is assuredly the land of neither equality nor of fraternity. . . . In no country on the globe has natural selection made its iron arm more rudely felt. It is unpitying. There is no room for the weak, the mediocre, the incapable. . . . By the mere fact that they are inferior, isolated individuals or entire races are destined to perish."[70]

The intrusion of race, as in the cases of blacks, Indians, and Orientals, and of racial doubts, as in the cases of Irish Catholics and Jews, culminated after 1915 in the rebirth and the spread of the Ku Klux Klan, a disturbing phenomenon in a society approaching crisis in which many people already lacked the ability to belong and drifted unattached, not quite free, not quite able to act.

V

ISOLATION

AMERICAN LIFE after 1850 incessantly conspired to detach individuals from their settings, diffusing loneliness at every level of society among men and women of every age and ethnic group. Conditions differed according to people's means and status, but dark emptiness haunted those isolated who did not fit anywhere. Mobility left many adrift. The restlessness that an earlier generation praised seemed now a symptom of social pathology, in need of treatment. Dr. George Beard diagnosed neurasthenia as an American disease (1881), part of what Emerson, still in pastoral Concord, called the age of dissociation involved in the rigors of occupational solitude, despite his praise of self-reliance.

The entrepreneurial fantasies of Mark Twain's Colonel Sellers in *The Gilded Age* and in its sequel, *The American Claimant* (1892), burlesqued the same consciousness of displacement, separation, and betrayed political birthright. That sense of chronic social crisis challenged accepted beliefs and values, and upset the balance between self and society, with a significant impact on liberty.[1]

Social mobility, sought though it was, intensified detachment. Those who rose as well as those who fell suffered sharp breaks in continuity as they climbed up or plunged down from their condition at birth. Unlucky brothers and cousins plagued Theodore Roosevelt, Stanford White, and Henry James—not bad, but failures in need of support. Andrew Carnegie reminded students of the Curry Commercial College in Pittsburgh (1885): best start at the bottom—pushing the broom around the office—but aim high. Be a king in dreams, although victory required single-minded devotion to a chosen line of work. "Put all your eggs in one basket, and then watch that basket," Carnegie advised.

Often the strivers who responded to such advice ceased to feel comfortable in their baptismal churches, and youthful companions became strangers. The discomfort of life as a dependent relation added to the pain of poverty, while removal from one context to another undermined family solidarity. Children and parents drifted apart, and early marriages ran into difficulty when the marital pair adjusted to novel circumstances at different rates and ways. The quality of adaptation varied according to wealth, ancestry, and position; but everyone to some extent felt the necessity for striking out in detachment, as an individual alone. Even Horatio Alger's Ragged Dick (1868), who became Richard Hunter, "a young gentleman," sought not riches, not a position in the unattainable elite, but respectability and contentment. Luke Larkin, son of the carpenter's widow, made just such a choice in *Struggling Upward* (1886). His new suit, with a chain that looked like gold crossing his waistcoat, was a symbol of escape from the dirty and ragged classes, the watch a token of punctuality, respect for time, and a sign of young manhood.[2]

Many Americans entered adulthood by leaving home. Apprenticeship in its earlier sense had disappeared; even in old crafts, the learner no longer became a member of the master's household. Suggestions after the Civil War to apprentice the newly freed slaves encountered opposition from blacks who saw it as another form of enslavement. In rural areas, too, sons did not wait to inherit the family farm. They viewed departure "as their education, as giving them a chance to know something" (1851). Young people continued to go off, girls as well as boys, the well-to-do for their own little communities in boarding schools and colleges where the necessary chores of books and teachers receded in importance as against athletics and fraternities, whether at the Merriwells' Yale or at good old Siwash. Gilbert Patten's nine hundred stories focused on the quest for personal excellence by heroes who neither smoked nor drank but exemplified health and vitality on the self-contained campus. A visitor to Columbia at the turn of the century sensed its aloofness from real life as he noted the contrast between the dignified, spacious grounds of the university and the "crowded tumult of New York . . . with a sense of the hooting, hurrying traffics of the wide harbor, the teeming East Side, the glitter of spending, the rush of finance, the whole headlong process of America."[3]

Although students sometimes formed lifelong attachments there, they passed through college as in a vacuum, with most relationships provisional. The promise of improved status attracted young people, for the "Christian and godly duty to attain unto riches" led to power. The lure contradicted the accepted images of success that emphasized hard work, pluck and luck, and the training best acquired in a pious home—none qualities derived from life in dormitories, fraternities, or sororities. But even the Siwash graduates, once settled in New York, joined their alumni club near Gramercy Park and gradually ascended into the king row in various lines of enterprise. "Bright young chaps with a glorious college past and a business future that you can't hock for a plate of beans a day" moved from college to the big city "like taking a high dive from the hall of fame into an ice water tank." Education complete, they confronted reality, forgot the swelled head. Experience belied Horatio Alger, Jr.'s, injunctions, revealing that the connections and manners required for advancement mattered more than classroom skills and studiousness, the moral also of Owen Wister's famous *Philosophy 4.* The aspiring did not realize, alas, that entrance into the elite rarely brought a sense of belonging in a society bent on exclusion. Only a small minority of the whole population sought secondary education; the great majority left home to work, and whatever glimmers of hope for improvement they cherished soon flickered out.[4]

Students who did not go away but continued to live at home found education in, rather than away from, the world, involving rather than isolating them. They felt the influence not only of teachers, classmates, and playmates, but also of fellow travelers on the trolley or subway and of fellow workers in the shop, as well as of parents. The continuing relationship with the family extended the tensions as well as the dependence of adolescence. Returning from the classroom or job, they picked up the continuity of earlier life and felt some of the former obligations and discipline. They could earn while they learned, could study part-time at their own pace. They were in the world.

For them, school formed just one aspect of life, not the whole of it. No matter how they performed there, they found satisfactions and esteemed themselves as persons in activities entirely unconnected with the classroom, sharing the pleasures and the pains of other urban youth. The play of the sandlot or the street, the roles performed in the gang or the club, the freedom of the loner to walk and dream, offered each opportunities to evolve a personality and draw a circle of friends that eased dependence on the family. It cost nothing to stroll in the park or listen to the band concert; and a penny, nickel, or dime would buy the pictures and stories of the newspaper or novel, or admission to the show. The church or club brought opportunities to act or sing or dance, to be on or for a team, to take excursions, to march in or cheer a parade.

Young people did not, however, escape the problems of family life. The lack of space and privacy, the daily crush of public transportation, the summer heat and winter cold, kept tempers on edge. Tight incomes called for awkward decisions on every expenditure—who contributed to the rent, the new coat, the brother's schoolbook. What jobs the youths took, how long they stayed in school, what friends they made and whom they married, concerned each and yet also all the other members of the household; to act alone was callous, to consult all, frustrating.

Life on the sidewalks, dangerous, led some to unremitting poverty, to the saloon, and to vice or crime, and others to exhausting, purposeless routines, with those who failed brothers and sisters of others who made something of themselves. Richard Connell of Poughkeepsie began as a laborer like his immigrant Irish father, then advanced from carriage-painting to newspaper reporting, won election to Congress and sent his son to Harvard. But whatever their ultimate destiny, young people growing up at home learned that they did not exist in isolation. Each was separate, but one among many also separate, and the need for living with others called for the exercise and occasional renunciation of the will. Their experience caused a thoughtful Harvard dean in 1893 to wonder whether the isolation of well-to-do students was not a mistake: whether boys would not do better to face city life by day and meet every night the counteracting influence of their own homes, rather than live cloistered and apart. Both options profoundly shaped young people's exercises of freedom.[5]

Everyone hastened on, driven by the "almost maniacal appetite for wealth prevalent in the United States." The imperative of getting rich spared few. Even to hold on required disciplined effort. George B. Green of Vermont gave an account book to Ann Elizabeth, his daughter (1857). Put down every cent received or spent. Trust no one. Mind your own business. John D. Rockefeller learned prudence from his father's tricky cheating of the children. Andrew Carnegie refused to help his friend and benefactor Thomas Scott, who went down in the panic of 1873. Self-reliance that left each master of his own destiny often ran counter to Christian notions of mutual dependence and charity.

"Why I am going away . . . I do not know myself," wrote a father to his son (1883). He had no complaint against anyone. No one had driven him away, no one had tempted him, but he could not remain. Discontent his disease, he ran away from himself. Good health, prosperous business, family—all he desired—still left him nervous, wretched, and unreasonable, filled with desperation and evil thoughts.

Goals, ever receding, denied anyone contentment. In the dark days just after the Civil War, all the Southern schoolboys interviewed hoped to be president of the United States, or at least state governors. In the nature of the case, few if any would make it. Theodore Roosevelt, only fifty when he left the White House, traveled, hunted, pontificated, and wrote, but time rested heavily on his hands. His chosen successor fell short of his expectations. The itch for action drew Roosevelt into the Bull Moose campaign in 1912. After 1913, Wilson earned his displeasure even more than Taft had. The United States should have entered the war much sooner than it did. Failure to receive a military command in 1917 disappointed Roosevelt, who died in 1919, out of it. Behind the brave and cheerful front presented to the world, an introspective and pensive man brooded, often isolated and sad—his favorite contemporary poet Edwin Arlington Robinson—his themes frustration, loneliness, and the burden of personal memory, glancingly refracted in the images of Richard Cory who suddenly "went home and put a bullet through his head," or more probably of Miniver Cheevy, born too late, who missed the medieval grace of iron clothing, cursed the commonplace, but called it fate and kept on drinking.[6]

Quite different motives drew on the health seekers who left their homes to be alone. Helen Hunt Jackson lost her husband in an accident; illness took off her children; and she believed herself at death's door in 1872. Climate was fate, she concluded, and moved from Rhode Island to Colorado Springs. Diverse in their social origins, detached by the prevalent fears of tuberculosis in the cities, invalids found hope through escape. Pure air, sunshine, and warmth reputed to have therapeutic effects drew desperate fugitives to the Colorado mountains, to Southern California, and to the coast of Florida. Others found solace in the water cure. But the results left individuals alone in isolation, more than half of them to die within the year, strangers in strange lands, coughing their lives away. At that, still better off than others back home who believed themselves victims of preserved meat or rat poison in the water or "distress of mind" responsible for President Grant's fatal cancer.[7]

Death that drove health seekers away became a refuge for others in despair. Mortality, no longer an expression of divine intention but a product of human failings or will, preoccupied those dissatisfied with traditional views. A vast mortuary literature and many tales of the supernatural titillated readers. After the Civil War, concern for lost loved ones increased fascination with the beyond. Emerson had earlier mocked the spiritualist "rat revelation, the gospel that comes by taps in the walls, and thumps in the table-drawer" (1852). But the number of adherents grew and he himself believed, "The dead live in our dreams." Death, familiar in wartime, became a foe its victims could resist or embrace.

Some sought a remedial cure by escape, even at the expense of rejecting familiar family and communal associations. Others chose suicide, the extreme form of opting out, which grew more frequent as dread of the religious consequences waned—ironic commentary on the insistence that novelists concern themselves with the smiling aspects of life because Americans breathed "a rarified and nimble air full of shining possibilities." The "mania for suicide" worried the Ohio legislature (1856). John A. Tucker of Dawson, Georgia, for more than a decade considered a step to rid the world of an existence useless to others and a burden to himself. From boyhood he had wished to be a great and good man exerting a salutary influence on mankind. Having failed, he took his life (1859) as Senator Thomas J. Rusk had.

The New York Times in 1859 warned of a suicide epidemic, attributed to urban life. Everyone assumed that closeness to the soil provided an antidote. On the farm, daily chores denied people time for mischievous thoughts, while in the cities, alcohol, leisure, rising aspirations, and temptations to vice led to self-destruction. The rich and the poor, though from opposing causes, declared Dr. Allan McLane Hamilton (1875), felt predisposed to suicide—the rich when they fell from grace, the poor because tenement houses crammed thousands into a limited space and made vice contagious. Contemporaries believed that the rate mounted remorselessly.

Whether suicides resulted from social disintegration or depended on personal incapacity to fulfill cultural expectations or were products of stresses some individuals found impossible to surmount, remained unclear. But the United States refused to follow English common law, which made suicide a felony, the body buried at midnight at a crossroad with a stake driven through it and a stone placed over the face. The 1903 Illinois case of *Burnett* v. *People* stated that "we have never seen fit to define what character of burial our citizens shall enjoy, we have never regarded the English law as to suicide as applicable to the spirit of our institutions." The 1908 Texas case of *Sanders* v. *State* held suicide innocent of criminality. But most states identified the danger of suicide as a justification for commitment in mental institutions. Changing definitions of the capacity to act thus narrowed the limits of control over one's own life.[8]

The forces that detached persons from the whole, as individuals, most often expressed a sense of separateness, of alienation, that antedated the act. A go-ahead people given to fast driving on the city streets, to reckless railroad accidents, and to boiler explosions on racing riverboats sometimes tossed life away unless livable on their own terms. The less daring thrilled to illusions of death and destruction, satisfied not only through pallid newspaper accounts but also by experiences at Coney Island in shows that re-created disasters—the eruption of Vesuvius, in which forty thousand perished, or the Galveston Flood of 1900. Heroic firemen battled the flames in buildings artificially set ablaze, leaped from upper-story windows into safety nets as spectators shuddered in fright.[9]

Often, however, the unattached, defiant, or defeated sulked silently and unobserved in homes like those of everyone else, their madness divinest sense to a discerning eye—and sense the starkest madness. Assent in the majority made them sane, dissent dangerous and handled with a chain (1862). "We are all potentially such sick men. The sanest and best of us are of one clay with lunatics and prison inmates" (Henry James).

Or the unattached moved quietly through life in lodging houses until some eruption made them visible, but leaving only meager clues to their identity. High turnover rates in factories and shops nudged employees into transiency. The unaffiliated also lived without hope in rural pockets around which the general tide of expansion swirled; or like the hired man, "off he goes when needed most," a reminder of the man in the painting who leaned upon his hoe, the emptiness of ages in his face, and on his back the burden of the world, dead to rapture and despair, a thing that grieved not and that never hoped, stolid and stunned, a brother to the ox. Such isolated men and women stayed apart from Americans who aggressively trumpeted the virtues of individualism, but found places in O. Henry stories and in John Sloan paintings.[10]

In the cities, great masses belonged to nothing—not to churches or to other groups—and therefore found no place in the data of surveys or the census. Many native by birth—for stronger forces drew the foreigners into associations of some sort—these urban isolates lived unobserved until some eruption gained them attention. Without meddling in the affairs of others, the masses of young, unattached males nursed problems of their own.

A TAWDRY MURDER. John Hollerbach (age sixteen) comes back to his room in Cincinnati (1874), hears cries for help from the nearby tannery but prudently goes to bed. The next morning police discover the remains of Herman Schilling, stabbed to death by repeated blows with a pitchfork, his body stuffed into a furnace but incompletely consumed. The blame falls on Andrew Egner, who keeps a saloon and boardinghouse in which he had rented space to the late Schilling, who had seduced young Julia Egner. Although not the first to have sexual relations with the daughter, Schilling had caused her fatal pregnancy, rousing a grieving father's wrath. The story finds its way into the press through the eloquent pen of a reporter, himself one of those isolated drifters in the urban jungle, born on an Ionian island, his mother Greek, his father Irish, his current mistress a mulatto. He would move about the country unattached and finally come to rest in Japan, where he took a wife and acquired a family. Evidence of other tragedies cropped up from time to time in the form of abandoned infants or little decomposed corpses.[11]

The number of lodging houses and boardinghouses increased steadily as did the number of tenants, sometimes two to a room—one working at night, the other by day, and many more in the mill or mining towns. Some respectable establishments accommodated proper clerks, salesmen, and skilled mechanics who could afford a good rent; others, scarcely above the level of the charity flophouses, sheltered "yeggmen" and other shady types as well as laborers. Some welcomed only Americans who looked right and spoke well; others took in immigrants unable to set up for themselves. Here the "landlady" did well in a productive calling appropriate to women as a last resort. Often her boarders, lacking links within a family or association, lived in isolation, moving frequently, getting nowhere; in the city wilderness they foraged alone.[12]

More visibly, indeed inescapably, hordes of tramps took to the roads and the rails. With the old vagrancy laws ever less stringently enforced (what jail would hold them all?), word that Jacob S. Coxey planned to lead an army of unemployed on Washington (1894) spread dread, although in the end only five hundred turned up, to be arrested for walking on the Capitol grass. Coming when the Pullman strike threatened to paralyze the railroad system until the army intervened, the march roused widespread fears of total breakdown; liberty run amok called for restraint.[13]

Still the numbers grew:

> My daddy is an engineer,
> My brother drives a hack
> My sister takes in washin'
> An' I been a wanderin'
> Early and late,
> New York City to the Golden Gate.
> An' it looks like
> I'm never gonna cease my wanderin'.

> Workin' in the army, working on the farm
> All I got to show for it
> Is the muscle in my arm.
>
> Ashes to ashes and dust to dust
> If whiskey don't get you
> Then the women must.

Enjoined to keep a trampin' or wear the ball and chain, to work like other men do, came the response:

> How the hell can I work
> When there's no work to do?
> Hallelujah I'm a bum,
> Hallelujah, bum again.

The hoboes did not suffer the solitude of the lonely backwoodsman, for they drifted usually into groups of shifting composition, for companionship or security.

> We are four bums, four jolly good chums.
> We live like royal Turks.
> We're having good luck in bumming our chuck,
> To hell with the man that works!

However, the carefree wanderers existed mainly in popular song. More often those "going on tramp" looked for work, like the cigar makers sent off with help from their union fund, or the unemployed loggers and miners who organized in Oregon to travel in groups. The poet who encountered one such band wondered what accounted for "that inexpressible scared way, those glassy eyes, and that hollow voice" of the corpse-like woman. The jolliness very likely expressed the longings of audiences pinned down to the routine of a job.[14]

Some Americans, continuing an old pattern, never came to rest, just moved on, with wife and kids or alone, in search of the something they never would find. They responded again and again to the lure of the speculator's better land out there or of the contractor or padrone, liberal in misinformation, with no redress when abandoned, entangled in mortgages or in peonage to pay off the indebtedness for fare and the commissary. At the end no better off than before, they continued the endless quest. Perceptive travelers observed the chronic migrants in broken-down wagons or later in railroad cars, who had forever lost the power of improvement but fled to the "edible gold" of the West. "Mere weak-minded restlessness, killing the power of growth, the ideal of home, the faculty of repose," drove those "dreary waifs over the West, losing possessions, love of life, love of God, slowly dragging from valley to valley till they" fell by the wayside.[15]

Others after the Civil War responded to a somewhat different call, appealing to the stubborn belief in some indefinable genius unexpectedly lurking in another Lincoln or Carnegie. Though no other in the world be aware, I exist as I am; that is enough, so wonderful! There is that in me—I do not know what it is—but I know it is in me, not a bit tamed. "Untranslatable, I sound my barbaric yawp over the roofs of the world."[16]

Irked by the settled life of stable society in country, town, or city, unwilling to accept what they could get, some matched themselves against the wild as the frontier receded. "Naked he plunges into the Maine Woods to live alone two months," ran the headline in the *Boston Post* (August, 1913). The story described how Joseph Knowles smoked his last cigarette, took no equipment, intending to live "as Adam lived." He sent back dispatches written with charcoal on birchbark, survived on berries and fish, but lured a bear into a pit, killed it with a club, and made a coat of its skin. The Maine Fish and Game Commission fined him $205 for killing the bear out of season, but twenty thousand Bostonians turned out on the Common to greet the returning hero; his book, *Alone in the Wilderness,* sold three hundred thousand copies to devotees of the cult of the wilderness.

Such people knew with Stephen Crane and Frank Norris and Jack London the survival in humans of primitive traits, the ecstasy of the primordial beast in the face of an indifferent nature; only force mattered and otherwise men were nought, all life nought. London's *Call of the Wild* (1903) described the eradication of domesticated habits through the encounter with nature that turned Buck, a huge dog, into the wolf he had originally been, more vital than the pale reflections in civilization. London became a Socialist, but clung to a vague understanding of survival of the fittest derived from Herbert Spencer. The Alaska gold rush became his fictional subject for a decade. Though *The Son of the Wolf* (1900) brought him fame, London could not put his own life in order. Married (1900), divorced (1905) and remarried, unhappiness dogged him. Alcohol early augmented recurrent depressions and frequent illnesses. He observed a savage world, in which toughness alone counted and in which mollycoddles always suffered. With man's higher nature but skin deep, only those who bit and scratched their way ahead survived. Socialism he thought would supply the iron discipline to check primitive passions.

Capitalists who flocked to hear the lectures of "a daring traveler, an original Klondiker, an experienced seaman, a prominent socialist, the American Kipling" found his tales entrancing, his theories a bore. Few knew that a Japanese valet, brought back from Korea, hovered backstage.

The badmen and train robbers who preyed upon travelers through the vast western distances merged in the popular imagination with the lone cowboys, self-sufficient, independent. Like William S. Hart and Tom Mix, the knights of the open range righted wrongs done the virtuous. Owen Wister's *The Virginian* (1902) portrayed a rebel against wealth and power, in the name of a just cause, learning from nature as did Edgar Rice Burroughs's *Tarzan of the Apes* (1914), an English baby reared in the jungle to become a superman.

In actuality the odd lot of loners included unsuccessful mining prospectors who took to robbing stages, then trains, and also some postwar Southern guerrillas who turned cowboy and engaged in those quintessentially American occupations of cattle rustling and horse stealing. Others operated on the margin of legality, like Ben Marks, a sure-thing gambler originally from Council Bluffs, Iowa, who roamed the country, carrying a board upon which to play the most popular frontier gambling game, three-card monte. But plying the trade in the street eventually became bothersome, so Ben established one of the early "big stores"—a fake brokerage establishment where the victim played in fact against the establishment, with the odds all against him. Or bespangled circus folk, out of the ordinary in their daring. Now and then a lad went off to be like them, the "kind that kinfolk can't abide," who "never did a thing so very bad," but sulked because he failed to be quite as good as anybody.[17]

Others escaped in radical fantasies. The wild Johann Most arrived in New York, at war with a world of cruelty and oppression, frustrated in his ambitions for an acting career by a disfiguring operation at the age of thirteen. He believed himself a victim of ridicule and fought back through anarchism. Tough, no sentiment. But Lucy Parsons stated the case more directly than he. She wanted every dirty lousy tramp to arm himself with a revolver or knife and lay in wait at the palaces of the rich and stab or shoot the owners. Kill them without mercy in a war of extermination, the extreme form of liberty for her, through the enslavement of everyone else.

Down in Texas, first in Austin, then in Waco, William C. Brann published the aptly named *Brann's Iconoclast,* against everything but especially the Baptists, and also blacks and atheists—to say nothing of judges and lawyers. On April 1, 1898, on a crowded street, Captain

T. E. Davis shot him from behind. Fatally wounded, Brann turned, drew his gun, and killed his assailant.[18]

More subtly, more effectively, with humor, the kat in the comics and the tramp on the screen persisted in defiant individualism. Every day the tough mouse let fly at the cat with a brick; then the cop/dog chased after him—jail. But this was the joke: the cat was on his side and both of them hated the cop/dog. Krazy Kat!

The cop/dog, the law, had to keep others from doing what they wanted to do. He guarded the encrusted rules by which parents, church, friends, and the state prevented cats and mice from being themselves, while the tough mouse refused to let the law push him around. And the cat brought cake to the jail—knowing that tomorrow the mouse would again throw the brick—because she loved him. Together they fought to be free, to retain the ability to express themselves. At war with the ludicrous conventions of their society (Krazy!), they kept their own standards and sought fulfillment through doing what they thought right, just as the cowboy did in the movie. Against odds, they pursued their own causes and considered the effort worth making though they might lose in the end, for victory lay not in the reward but in the striving.

In their society, everyone ran—the boss in his avarice, the brutal fellow worker in his greed, and the law, brandishing its nightstick. And the little fellow ran, too, with all after him.

They chased him as the outsider, alone, who belonged to no one. Often he had no name, but always he had an identity and fought back, using their own rules to defeat them. At the end, the prize usually was not worth having, and he walked jauntily off, disdaining the reward, preserving the individuality for which he fought.[19]

The less introspective drifted away because they found no job where they were, hoped to land something in construction elsewhere, intended to come back, then put off the return to irksome responsibilities as they glimpsed the dead end of toil that awaited them back there, where home had been, preferred to drift on. They thereby attained the goal of the familiar minstrel ditty,

> I wish I was single again,
> For when I was single,
> My money did jingle,
> I wish I was single again.[20]

A blend of motives induced millions to follow the road or ride the rails.

*

The mobile, wandering, unsettled population raised the grim prospect of national decline.

Civil War separations pained those who stayed, worried, sitting and weeping all the time, unable to work. The miraculous escape of the young Georgia private shot in the left breast by a ball that lodged in his Bible consoled few. Nor did the jokes: "Dear Mother, don't grieve about me. If I get killed, I'll only be dead."

Losses created a serious deficit in the cohort of men available as husbands and fathers, and any further drain would cause irreparable damage. Add the aimless drifters to the drummers and business travelers like David Levinsky, and the threat to survival became clear. Toward the end of the century, American intellectuals influenced by European warnings about degeneracy recognized the symptoms at home. The fact that the world's population had successfully reproduced itself since creation offered no assurance about the future. President Theodore Roosevelt (1901) made women's willingness to bear children and men's readiness to work and fight requisites of a healthy race. All other problems, however important, paled in comparison with that of the diminishing birthrate that led to race suicide.[21]

Danger lurked everywhere. Wives lonely in the absence of husbands became prey for the seducer, a perfect fop, showy and dandy in dress, who always at night put his pantaloons in a stretcher and kept his boots treed. Passion might sway women, considered more emotional than men, and draw betrayed spouses into misguided retaliation, as it did the Reverend George W. Carawan. Scandal sullied even the reputation of the silver-toned Henry Ward Beecher, too solicitous about the loneliness of the wife of the traveling Theodore Tilton. Many cautionary tales detailed the fate of those whose conception of liberty outdistanced accepted conventions, and who paid with their reputations and often their lives for passing beyond the boundaries of the permissible. Those fun-loving girls foreign travelers admired grew up to become dangerous females.[22]

The resulting moral damage—beyond the most lurid imagining—would undermine the home, society's mainstay. The bride entered this sanctuary "to become a priestess at its altar," its privileges far from confining. Home remained the antithesis of the outside world, where those who battled in the struggles of life found the refuge in which higher values, more humane relations, and gentler virtues reigned. Without the place "you somehow haven't to deserve" but need, the "place where, when you have to go there, they have to take you in," everyone would drift about, unmoored. Elihu Root suggested that the national bird of

America be not the wild turkey, nor the predatory eagle, but the homing pigeon—the wise creature attached to the nest. Without the sheltering home, everyone young and old would slide into the same dependent situation. "Home, Sweet Home," a brutal assault upon the feelings of those always departing; pathos unrelieved by dignity, it seemed to an English traveler.[23]

Emphasis on the home altered women's self-perception, especially when household chores eased and left them more free time. As men's lives outside grew more demanding and troublesome, the image of the home as refuge acquired greater urgency, the haven from a world increasingly heartless. "Little do we know of the agony our husbands are experiencing," wrote the wife of a New York merchant after the panic of 1857. Make his home "bright and cheerful in spite of his worried anxious face. . . . Fold his aching head to your bosom and begin the duty of cheerful economy." A considerable literature elevated the homemaker's above all other occupations, implying that the ability to act of wives and mothers, seemingly circumscribed, in actuality formed a powerful force for good when employed cautiously.[24]

Tough chaps did not mind detachment from home and welcomed the lack of ties; in their longing for the wild, they disregarded the penalties that gave most young people pause and shook off the enfeebling love that made men effete. But the plight of the elderly flashed a warning. Not abandoned but left behind by the young, the survivors of an earlier and once-vigorous generation discovered they could no longer keep a house, a farm, a country store. Even mowing the field and gathering in the aftermath in the silence and the gloom, brought them not sweet new grass, but tangled tufts. Dreading the poorhouse's complete loss of liberty, they kept up a show of spirit, aware of the plight of those like Polly who all her life had gotten little more out of the world than simply standing ground. She had never had anything but saw other folks a-clawin' an' gettin' other things an' actin' as if they was worth havin'. The former veneration of the aged, as sources of wisdom, experience, and guidance, shifted to a new view of maturity, the time of retirement, serenity, calmness, and removal from action. Old age was "not disgraceful but immensely disadvantageous," Emerson noted. But in this as in other matters, he did not quite understand why, and gave the simplest answer. Old age meant decay and death. Yet the proportion of the elderly in the population grew, mostly from falling birthrates, but also from falling death rates. Old age, once the experience of a few, became the lot of many.[25]

*

Decade after decade, observers perceived the damaging effects on the family of decisions to go it alone, which weakened supports for social stability. In the 1850s, Americans still regarded marriage primarily as a rationally-based undertaking to satisfy common needs and attain common objectives, as it did for the young lady whose newspaper advertisement publicized her wish to form a matrimonial engagement. Though attitudes toward sexuality and domesticity changed after 1900, the centrality of the home persisted. Even women who gloried in the freedom a single state promised perceived the tensions between marriage and loss of independence, as Lucy Sprague did.

> Free, I'm neither daughter, mother, wife,
> But oh, the treasured freedom costs me dear.
> And I who've welcomed other burdens, fear
> To bear the burden of this unbound life.

Matchmaking agencies did a thriving business; and communities tolerated common law alliances that established stable households. But Mormon polygamy deferred Utah's admission to the Union as long as it preserved its peculiar institution, even though some women maintained that their liberty expanded in households where "sisters" shared wifely duties and where the emotional and physical needs of large family units circumscribed men's authority.[26]

The gender bias created by Civil War losses condemned many women to spinsterhood. Some rebuilt their lives when the intended died on the battlefield or wandered off to the West for years; like Louisa Ellis they avoided family responsibilities and learned to live alone. The number of women who never married rose steadily with the cohort born in 1860, particularly among those with a college education. Louisa May Alcott in the *Ladies' Home Journal* (1887) described the spinsters as a "very useful, happy independent race, never more so than now when all professions are open to them and honor, fame, and fortune are bravely won by many gifted members of the sisterhood." But the vast majority accepted the social norm, regarded "life, alone and especially for a woman" as incomplete, no matter how full of other interests and work. Fear lingered of being an old maid with the remorseless progression from dutiful daughter to genteel woman to maiden aunt.

Others nevertheless welcomed the escape from matrimony, as did Emily Dickinson, who had trembled lest at some time she, too, would be yielded up. She had seen flowers at morning "satisfied with the dew, and those same sweet flowers at noon with heads bowed in anguish before the mighty sun"; and she knew that her whole life would be henceforth to the man of noon, mightier than the morning. She would no doubt have accepted either of those to whom she gave her heart, but since that would not be, better not.

> To make a prairie it takes a clover and one bee.
> One clover, and a bee,
> And revery.
> The revery alone will do,
> If bees are few. (1896)

Few enjoyed her capacity for equanimity, although others heard echoes in the popular refrain,

> Before I was married, I lived at my ease,
> But now I am married, I have a husband to please,
> Four small children and them to maintain.
> Oh, how I wish I was single again.[27]

Yet the single state, whether a matter of preference or resignation, had disquieting consequences, particularly when the divorce rate soared from one of every sixteen marriages in 1890 to one in every twelve in 1900—to say nothing of desertions, more numerous still. Edward A. Ross related the trend to the decline of the old economic framework of the family and to the relaxation of the authority of social institutions. Any policy that deprived the individual of choices and diminished freedoms harked back to darker times. The recognition of happiness, the end of human institutions, required allowing the unhappy to unlock the chains of matrimony. Rank individualism, by-product of women's liberation from tradition, weakened lasting union and thus defeated the ends of marriage; not moral decay, but the modern social situation caused the change.

The diffusion of birth control practices at the same time gave substance to trepidations about the country's population; the term *race suicide* ever more frequently appeared in discussions of the future. A book appropriately entitled *Race Suicide* (1912) warned American wives to become mothers if they wanted to sustain the civilization of the West. The fault in part lay with men willing to "place the yoke of industrial serviture" upon women's necks in the mills, from which "blighted and fallow" females emerged. "The barbarians are swarming at our gates," the author cried, while lawmakers, state and national, frittered their time away bickering over spoils, tariffs, and trust issues, not realizing that a new race would conquer not by the sword or spear, but by its cradles.[28]

Family size, once governed by God's will and by luck, increasingly became a matter of choice. A highly competitive economy required a good start; and too many offspring, draining common resources, deprived all of the skills or capital to advance. Considerations of purity, prudence, and restraint produced various ill-informed experiments with birth control, blamed by some for the spread of prostitution. Contraception no doubt enlarged women's control over their lives, despite the lack of significant technological improvements. Smaller families augmented their leisure, while mass entertainment, department stores, and clubs redefined motherhood and the home. The bungalows stretching eastward from California demonstrated in their modest dimensions the shrinking scope of family life. The birthrate among native families may have fallen as much as 30 percent in the half century after 1860. Smaller households significantly expanded women's capacity to act and in the middle and upper classes made free time available for public activities.[29]

Changes in family size emanated from the ability to make choices. Once the number of offspring had seemed beyond individual control and the household could expand indefinitely—the more children, the more hands at work. An equilibrium balanced survival and mortality. But when the family lost cohesion as a household, the number of offspring became important, no longer taken for granted. In the cities, living space determined comfort and status. More children strained incomes, lowered standards of living, and narrowed everyone's opportunities; John Stuart Mill in England had argued that restricting the number of babies could secure workers a greater share of the national income. Size then became an issue, with the burden of decision on the individual couple. Since midcentury, the birthrate in the United States had declined. In the cities, widening avenues for amusement took people outside the home; begetting children ceased to be the poor man's only pleasure. Furthermore, offspring less often contributed to family income after laws progressively deferred the age at which they could become breadwinners.[30]

Speculation about birth control remained covert. People hesitated to discuss openly a subject deemed indecent. Besides, the law frowned on any consideration of the issue, and churches condemned the practice as sin. Vagueness and self-consciousness generated tension in the relationships of husbands and wives; the unspoken issue shadowed any discourse connected with attitudes toward sex and love. Compelled to reconsider their mutual obligations, family members as individuals no longer relied on habits or old ways in relationships connected with profound religious and emotional drives. Anxiety and guilt accompanied the formation of new ties. Exhortation by birth control advocates after 1900 did not help, for even well-intentioned, like Margaret Sanger, swayed by eugenicists, stressed the duty of restraint by impoverished slum dwellers to elevate their living standards. The president of the American Medical Association (1912) urged the government to deny marriage to couples unable to obtain a clean bill of health, in order to prevent excessive offspring. This harsh view of the freedom to act, with its racist overtones, persuaded few and threatened many with loneliness.[31]

The sense of isolation also affected people not literally alone. Marriage and immersal in a family remained the norm to which all expected to conform. The stories, the plays, the songs, informed women that love would hold the family together. Poor and lowly though they be in a world that riches ruled, gold, they consoled themselves, would buy almost anything but a true girl's heart. Whoever disregarded that injunction might present

> a beautiful sight to see—
> Appear happy and free from care.
> [But] she's not though she seems to be.
> For her beauty was sold for an old man's gold.
> She's a bird in a gilded cage. (1900)

The hummed lyrics provided satisfaction of a sort. In romantic novels, the tale ended at the altar: and they lived happily ever after.

Or did they? Not all of them. Unchastity, adultery, intemperance, and cruelty made many unions a living death. According to some pious critics, child rearing, no longer a woman's major task in life, among the better off fell to foreigners or, in the South, to blacks. Even in the rural communities, a minister complained, there was "a prevalent and growing intention, even at the cost, if need be, both of good morals and law, to let the inferior classes rear most of the children." The wealthy chose to be unfruitful while the "dangerous classes" multiplied.

In palatial dwellings like that of Charles Perrin Smith in Trenton, men and women surrounded by servants amid expensive statuary and silk curtains had nothing to say to each other; in row houses and suburban cottages, in crowded tenement flats, uncommunicative people pushed against one another, but hugged their loneliness.[32]

The older integrated household with the husband-father its head survived in self-contained groups unaffected by the dominant trends of American life. On the family farm, old relationships had a fighting chance, while it remained intact as a rural unit of production as well as a home. So long as the family's head retained title to the land, directed operations, and controlled the children who shared the labor, he could preserve its coherence. In stable agricultural communities, where change did not disorder personal relationships, the father's role as family law-giver persisted, although sons like John Peter Altgeld (1847–1902) bitterly resented parental brutality. Mechanized, rationalized, and integrated into the larger economy, however, the farm lost its isolation and ceased to be entirely a unified household enterprise; opportunities for alternative work and the influences of schools, books, and popular culture pulled youngsters away from parental authority.

Similar pressures swayed the lives of rural wives, who had never played a purely static role within a sphere bounded by barnyard and kitchen. By the end of the century they became more visible partners in all decisions, responsibilities, and power, their lives more autonomous than the misleading prescriptive literature implied. The image of the lady on the pedestal rarely reflected reality; unofficial exercise of powers and influences they were not supposed to possess, according to some ideologists, spurred women into public action. The women's rights movement had large followings in western rural regions, where states first legally recognized women's transformed position. The changing structure of rural families added to the sense of detachment and isolation of husbands and wives.[33]

Conditions elsewhere varied. In small towns and cities, among clerks, managers, artisans, and shopkeepers—the heterogeneous middle classes—the father remained the sole breadwinner whose income sustained the whole family. Other members rarely worked outside the home, and indeed, if they did, neighbors regarded it as a sign of precarious status. Responsibility for sustaining the family rested on the husband, who provided for immediate needs and also fixed the status of all his dependents. Whether his wife and children lived respectably, rose to a higher social level, or sank to a lower one depended on his effort, which determined the fortune or disaster of all. Success acquired a wide connotation encompassing not merely material well-being but the happiness of the entire family. Making good brought a solid income and also the capacity to shape the style of life of the wife and children. Dwight Eisenhower's father, who failed as a merchant, wound up in a marginal night watchman's job, and when his son requested an education, responded "Go get it." The ability to perform tested the personality, affected all relationships within and outside the family, and caused enormous emotional tensions. Every man with reason to believe that he had not accomplished enough hid the humiliation in small business affairs, in quarrels about the Bible, and in aspiration to some local office.[34]

In the small towns and in the suburbs of larger cities, most people tolerated these burdens. There, in relative stability, neither the way up nor the way down passed over dangerously steep slopes. When the spreading streetcar networks opened up acre upon acre, little houses, stuccoed or thrown up on balloon frames with cheap nails after widely used pattern books, put self-contained homeownership within the reach of many. There and in towns that neither expanded rapidly nor declined precipitously, offering neither great opportunities nor great perils, established positions remained in relative equilibrium.

But more dynamic areas in expanding cities created both opportunities and dangers. The guilt for business failures and bank closings during the economic downswings of the 1890s fell on personal incompetence, extravagance, or ignorance, and justified a host of reform movements, including temperance, directed primarily against male habits. Elizabeth Willard had earlier blamed masculine "law of division and antagonisms, the law of discord, combat and destruction," for throwing the world into a mess. An order under women's sway would improve, especially if feminine values, institutionalized in domesticity, could apply to public affairs. The warfare between the sexes seemed to worried bystanders yet another symbol of disintegration, reflecting the isolation and loneliness of human beings thrown back upon their own capacities for action, without support or sustenance from wider units in families or communities. In response, men blamed women—spendthrift status seekers who drove dispirited husbands to ever-harder labor merely to satisfy whims.[35]

Futile arguments could not obscure the essential point. An economy operating totally by monetary calculations gave no weight to worth in any other terms—neither piety, learning, nor generosity counted. Success depended on the ability to transform life by making a fortune. A man of business who tried one thing after another until he found the right one always, like a cat, landed on his feet. Courageous, patient, and responsible, he attended to details. He let speculators make their thousands in a day, but stuck to his regular trade, never taking great hazards, knowing that prosperity resulted mainly from perseverance. Without careful means for conserving capital, even the lucky strikes of gold, silver, copper, or oil would simply not take care of themselves. Such unexpected and unpredictable windfalls called for prudent investment in order to garner the rewards. Great opportunities carried with them great risks. At stake was the necessity for proving oneself, Calvinist in origin, but also romantically heroic, and incongruously mingled with Darwinist conceptions of survival of the fittest.

True, popular novels and muckraking journalists exposed the corruption that lurked in the metropolitan cities, either through entanglement in politics, excessive ambition, or the disregard of traditional precepts. Silas Lapham, a man of humble origins, forgot the morality of the Old Testament and of Poor Richard's Almanac when he gained wealth; his fortune went up in smoke in the effort to build a fashionable home in Boston. David Levinsky (1916) scrambled up from the slums to wealth as a clothing manufacturer only to discover the spiritual losses he had suffered. Levinsky and Lapham represented the price exacted by capacities for action.[36]

The potential multiplication of Laphams and Levinskys renewed emphasis on the paternal role of the household's head. The image sharpened at the end of the century; perception of father as king, not only in his work but also in his home, became more elaborate precisely when it diverged from reality. Upper-class tastes affected the imagination of broader circles, and the symbol at first evolved for a small part of society, spread outward because it met emotional needs and filled psychic gaps among wider segments of the population.

Family life then acquired a monarchial quality. Use of the royal figure of speech reflected the well-to-do estimation of their own position. Though not absolute, the husband-father commanded the resources by which to reorder everything. He could indulge in symbols and actions that displayed his quality as one who had made it, turn his wife into a queen and transform the home into a court. He could make his children princes or princesses in style of life, expected to equal their parents in success. Awesome—Alice (born 1867) never forgot how her mother forced her to sit and look at the photograph of Father, then away in Europe, saying, "See how sad he is, with a naughty daughter." And indeed the face grew sadder and sadder till tears filled his eyes and ran down his cheeks and reduced Alice herself to weeping and bitter lamentation. Fear of the father: "Terror dominated my youth," wrote William Carlos Williams.[37]

The image of the man made king in his home by his own efforts attracted the dynamic social elements. Success brought immediate rewards and totally transformed character. Aspirations varied; few expected to install themselves in the baronial, indeed regal, settings of Newport or Fifth Avenue. But many merchants, lawyers, physicians, and shopkeepers realistically expected to occupy a neat single-family home surrounded by its own yard or garden, at a respectable address that marked their achievements. Neither Willa Cather nor Sherwood Anderson understood such people, and hence each portrayed them as small-minded, greedy, unimaginative, incapable of appreciating creativity, conformist, repressive, and insensitive, hostile to art, all culminating in Ezra Pound's Hugh Selwyn Mauberly:

> the "age demanded" chiefly a mould in plaster,
> made with no loss of time,
> a prose kinema, not, not assuredly, alabaster
> or the "sculpture" of rhyme.[38]

The undesirable life-style created by individual haste for success complicated definitions of the role of the head of the family. The hierarchical model, never a true reflection of reality, seemed increasingly false. The good man, by contrast, appeared in S. Weir Mitchell's portrayal of George Washington and his aide-de-camp Hugh Wynne, as well as in the heroes of Booth Tarkington's *Monsieur Beaucaire* (1900), Paul Leicester Ford's *Janice Meredith* (1899), and Mary Johnston's *To Have and to Hold* (1900)—big, but not aggressive; quiet, efficient, humbly in command—models difficult to emulate in the shops, farms, and offices, or in the homes. Fiction masked the realities of loneliness and isolation, the burdens of growing capacities to act.

The wife-mother in the monarchical household retained her sanctified, almost religious, aura as provider of love and nurture and the transmitter of moral values to offspring. White and black shared the characteristics, each responding to its own sets of tensions. Black mothers bore the same moral responsibilities as white, but in segregated environments, though many supplemented family income by working as nurses, laundresses, household helpers, hairdressers, seamstresses, and midwives. In black families as well as in white, the father, ever more often away from home at work, served primarily to apply discipline, to reinforce by strength his wife's authority. From the 1850s onward, also, judicial solicitude for dower rights and divorce law reform improved women's legal position and their rights of property, as if to exempt them from the grimy dealings of the husband-father and spare the family the consequences of his increasingly fateful misjudgments.[39]

Appraisals of the family's prospects shaped the choice of a marriage partner. Prudent people postponed the day—Bernard Baruch till age twenty-seven, Frances Perkins to thirty-one, John Hay to thirty-eight. Sensible young women behaved as fashion expected:

> Corseted to the bursting point,
> With unguents nightly we anoint;
> List to the opera they call grand
> We neither like nor understand. (1899)

Sensible young women gave their hands to respectable, upright, and industrious young men capable of creating a desirable future. By contrast, headstrong girls swayed by notions of freedom and love thrilled to stories about Lord Byron's adultery and interpreted Robert Browning to enjoin "a disregard for all rights" that clashed with their own—individualism carried to its extreme. Some even longed for acting careers and slipped to a tragic end, as in the novels written by Louisa May Alcott when she tired of concocting "moral pap for the young."

The New Woman of the turn of the century, better educated and freer in her morals and behavior than earlier generations, did not turn her back upon the ideal mate framed by her predecessors, though less tense in her interaction with men and thus more aware of what marriage entailed. Broadening contours of liberty had altered her position considerably by 1900. The greater responsibility that accompanied her freer choice also augmented the burdens upon her. She alone paid the price for wrong decisions that depended less on parental approval or societal sanctions, and more on her.

The scope of change widened swiftly after 1900, for by then some 30 percent of employed women held clerical or sales positions, white collar, respectable, mostly native white and educated. The secretary became the quintessential modern working girl, old inhibitions released, seeking autonomous satisfaction in freedom of behavior, and not only in the choice of marriage partners. These changes accelerated for all segments of the population, from the liberated society girl to the daughters of immigrants, loosening the bonds holding them to parental homes and indirectly shaping the kind of marriages and homes they envisioned for themselves.

Changes in sexual mores after 1900 began on the fringes of society; dance crazes, rising hemlines, and slimmer silhouettes, public amusements, jazz, and bohemian culture, all affected the behavior of marriageable young women. Freudian ideas spread from Greenwich Village to college campuses, where rouge, powder, and eyeshadow, once marks of prostitution, became signals of the emergence of the respectable flapper. Child labor laws increased the number of young people in schools and colleges, environments where they experimented with greater freedom and challenged tradition. The growth of coeducation in state universities provided new settings for courtship rituals, new patterns for heterosexual relations, seeking pleasure in petting, dancing, smoking, and drinking.

Open discussions of female sexuality, once confined to radicals like Emma Goldman, Andrew Jackson Davis and his wives, or itinerant lecturers and spiritualists, became more common after 1900 as Freudians declared war on society's outlook, labeling it unscientific, repressive, and unhealthful. They wished to liberate sexual pleasure, separate from procreation, as a positive, energy-producing force. Marketing experts, aware of women as consumers, used sexuality to sell all kinds of products, while young women tutored by magazines on the "attractive" personality learned to market themselves as products. Their vision of motherhood changed as well, buttressed by social scientists and physicians who declared motherhood a job to be scientifically managed. A flood of expert advice warned against too much emotional involvement, prescribed schedules, and regulated what was once a more spontaneous relationship.[40]

Young men felt as confused as their female counterparts in the face of conflicting guidelines. "There is an upheaval of old traditions and conventionalities," a distraught male complained; "with no firm ground to stand upon, the self confidence of the past has vanished. Disbelief in everything involves disbelief in one's self." The choice of a marriage partner became one more obstacle to overcome.[41]

The great mass of laborers, industrial workers and blacks, lacking choices, suffered from disorderly family lives. The husband–father lost his importance and respect, for poverty demonstrated his shortcomings. Everyone else's lowly status stemmed from his failure in his most important function and therefore reflected upon his manhood. When he ceased to be the only or even the most important breadwinner, his role shrank; the resulting tensions accounted for desertions, intemperance, and outbreaks of criminality—the desperate rejoinders of men informed by the circumstances of their lives, by the relationships with their wives and children, that they had not made it. Wife-whipping was commonplace, brutal beatings frequent, conjugal murder not unknown. Still, Mrs. Henry Maidland came to her husband's defense, though he had her on the floor, choking, when the police burst in; the family could ill afford the twenty-five-dollar fine (1859). Child abuse: Shem Lewis beat his eleven-year-old son with a shovel; but what good would it do the boy to have Pa off in the penitentiary for three years (1856)? Such homes had become no more than the father's lodging house and the mother's theater of operations.[42]

The narrowing role of the man as breadwinner created problems among the poor, those endowed with the least resilience. The patriarch held the economic keys to the larder. But instead of deciding on equitable distribution, he drifted into the saloon or the gambling den. Coercion failed; imprisonment for him meant a respite from toil while dependents suffered from lack of income. Warfare in the home ran counter to the current of nature. The observer noticed that communities thrived, multiplied, and prevailed among immigrants, in spite of drinking, because they held "closely to the old time-honored bonds and obligations of the family."

The more prosperous suffered not so much from desertion or intemperance as from consistent tension among women unable to determine their own futures and among men driven to strive, yet fearful that failure would plunge them downward and demonstrate their inadequacy as husbands and fathers. "Greed, greed. The spirit of greed had eaten" the architect through and through. In his world this passion had a dignified name—*enterprise*—and justified knavery by *success,* although his ruthlessness appalled his wife. Many novels, however, focused on husbands driven into bankruptcy or adultery by overly demanding, discontented women, willing to assume neither motherhood nor domestic responsibilities. A sizable literature blamed them for putting the "home in peril," another cause of the race suicide scare. Frank Hagar (1905) suggested that only paternal power would save the Christian family, already endangered when incessant demands and frivolities drove husbands to an excess of hard work, resulting in general nervousness. The entrance of women into the labor force in ever-larger numbers also caused disarray and worried Arthur W. Calhoun (1917), who regarded it as implicit criticism of the American male, no longer deemed able, during a revolution of rising expectations, to support the household as in the past.

Good fortune, alas, did not solve all problems. Mary Stillwell Edison got everything—a nice house, lavish gifts, growing wealth, and a loving husband who worked day and night—everything except something to do besides visit the family in Brooklyn and summer at the shore. She stuffed herself on chocolates, sickened, and died at the age of twenty-nine—an extreme case of the mysterious maladies that plagued middle- and upper-class women like Alice James and Elizabeth Bancroft, whose emotional strains, labeled neurasthenia and insomnia, fear of responsibility, morbid self-consciousness and paralysis of the will, neither water cures nor caring brothers nor solicitous husbands alleviated.[43]

The wife's position nevertheless usually retained greater stability than the husband's, for though subject to his physical and fiscal power, she drew strength from her role as mother that attached the children to her.

> Always take mother's advice
> She knows what is best for your good:—
> Remember that she is the nearest,—

> To you in this world she is dearest
> Let her kind words then suffice
> And always take mother's advice!
> On earth you will ne'er have another
> In this weary world there's no other,
> And God only gives you one mother!
> So cherish and love her most dear. (1884)

The dying soldier:

> Just break the news to mother.
> She knows how dear I love her
> And tell her not to wait for me
> For I'm not coming home;
> Just say there is no other,
> Can take the place of mother. (1896)

Defeated by the grasshoppers, farmers emblazoned on the eastward-bound wagons: "Going home to mother." And the matriarchs would not let go: Mrs. MacArthur took up lodgings at West Point (1899) and Mrs. Roosevelt at Cambridge, the better to keep their eyes on Douglas and Franklin. Andrew Carnegie, in his fifties and hard as the steel from his mills, would not marry the woman he loved until his mother died. Arthur W. Calhoun, appropriately enough, dedicated three massive tomes on the American family "to Mother."[44]

At all social levels, some power slipped into mama's hands. The immigrant husband who came in advance, leaving his wife in temporary charge of the household, sometimes never regained domestic authority. Reunited and settled down, she managed all aspects of family life while he went off to the job. A Boston settlement worker heard Mrs. Murphy refer to her newborn twins as "more insurance for me old age." As the father's role declined, Irishwomen grew in stature. Observers often praised the self-sacrificing, responsible wife who held the home together while taking care of an inebriated husband.

Black women also struggled to keep their families intact. Once slavery ended, they withdrew from field labor to confront a more private universe than that of the plantation, with their labor solitary, without the support of kin or friends, their incomes crucial. Many did double duty, in and out of the home, a pattern that continued in northern cities, where they found places as domestics even when their husbands remained unemployed.

Toward the end of the century, middle-class and professional black women organized clubs like those of their white counterparts. Ida B. Wells Barnett of Memphis, daughter of Mississippi slaves and a former teacher, edited her own newspaper. When three friends lost their lives to mobs, not for raping a white lady but for success in business, she urged the black community to demonstrate its muscle and resist by boycotting white enterprises. Driven from town, she played a key role in the national and international crusade against lynching. Helped by Mary Church Terrell, an Oberlin College graduate, she formed the National Association of Colored Women in part because white clubs refused to admit blacks to membership. The fight for dignity and rights and public health campaigns emphasized self-help and community responsibility, supporting welfare institutions and providing child care and homes for the elderly.[45]

The law adjusted but slowly to change among all Americans. Internal hostilities unsettled the rights and obligations of the married pair. The common law regarded husband and wife as one person, while civil law accepted the personal independence of both and protected each in the enjoyment of property rights, the home the primary school of virtues, sexual indulgence under healthy restraints. Dissolution of the bond of marriage, contemporaries feared, would open fully the floodgates of licentiousness.

Yet somehow the power of love endured, however the statutes changed or practices altered. Roger B. Taney on his wedding anniversary (1852) renewed the pledges of love made to his wife forty-six years earlier. His constant affection had never wavered. Whatever forces changed about them, Abe and Mary (Lincoln), Al and Katie (Smith), remained constant in their attachment.[46]

Wavering standards and uncertain discipline encouraged independence in children subject to wayward fits of pride and temper. On thousands of popular stages, Little Eve rose nightly to her reward, clad in white, so good in her purity. Ah well, at least she did not survive for the soiling like poor Mary Fagan in Cairo and poor Mary Phelan in Atlanta and poor Ellen in the Griffith movie. And Evelyn Nesbit in the newspaper, the heroine of the scandal starring the famous architect Stanford B. White.

Proper families hedged their little girls about with safeguards, and very proper families sent theirs to St. Timothy's or Miss Hall's or Madeira to get by the most difficult years. In rural communities domestic service offered young women an interval between confirmation and marriage during which to gather a dowry and learn domestic skills. But even good little girls rebelled, unable to govern thoughts and feelings well. Passionate, headstrong, and sometimes selfish, they often made incorrect choices. More than one enraged father, like M. H. Bowyer, otherwise gentle, peaceful, and courteous, killed the seducer of his daughter (1858). Fanny Brice, having quit whatever schools did not expel her, learned to act by pilfering and begging as a child and walked onto the stage at thirteen to live unhappily ever after.

The family preference—better that a girl marry, but well and not just for wealth, lest she end up a bird in a gilded cage, her beauty sold for an old man's gold and the smile on her face only the mask of an aching heart. The readers who wrote to ask the author whom the little women would marry conceived of no other aim in life. The alternative for most: recurrent childbirth and a domineering husband or the job in the mill. In the dance hall, the social worker noted (1909) the overworked girls, lonely, in search of fun, condemned to frustration, or trapped by cadets, on the road to prostitution.[47]

Boys, more fortunate, early on accepted the discipline of wage-earning, immediate or prospective. From Sylvester Graham, William Alcott, and numerous male and female itinerant lecturers who illustrated their discourses with titillating models, paintings, and mannequins, fathers knew the sexual dangers their sons encountered. Useful work, "occupying many hours through each day," left them "wearied bodies at night for their safe passage from yielding youth to firm resisting manhood." Some expended energy on the scouts (1910) or in YMCA gymnastics or sandlot athletics. The job came first, whether peddling newspapers or shining shoes or running errands, or working at the mill or mine, because everyone preferred any kind of family to the alternative—an institution of some sort. The thousands who dragged grimy bodies up the tenement steps each night returned to a home and knew that their exhausting labor had a comprehensible purpose: to bring bread to the family. Hence the pride in his task of even the "nipper" or door boy in the anthracite mine. Then, too, for a favored few the discipline of work instilled virtue and, as *Barriers Burned Away* revealed, ensured triumph over the perils of the great cities.[48]

Sooner or later, the bad boys who moved mischievously through the stories of George Peck and Booth Tarkington impatiently felt the stirrings of men's powers at that provisional stage in life that G. Stanley Hall would soon call adolescence (1904). They had to cut loose, break out, and would not wait for the discovery of manhood in battle as Henry Fleming did. Wild William, Billy Black McCullough, had no need to leave the aunt and uncle good to him but did not wish to be controlled.

Off he went at age sixteen to drink, swear, chew tobacco, and slobber around "full of dirt and filth and foolish talk" till a wife took him in hand. Eugene Debs, one of ten children, went to work at fifteen in a railroad shop and could have advanced to fireman or engineer, but he escaped the routine to work as grocery clerk, then editor. William Sidney Porter modeled the characters in his stories on himself. Left home at fifteen for a job as drugstore clerk, shuffled around, did a little jail time, and never got his feet down on the ground except as a writer. Billy Sunday tasted a little learning in Nevada High School while he janitored there, then found an opening in a furniture store. From tossing the ball around with the boys, he landed a position with the pros and flashed across American League infields until the spirit of God got to him. From the pulpit he soared in the great cities as a revivalist, helping thousands overcome their sense of weakness and isolation through union with God.[49]

Children faced easier problems, when long-standing patterns of lax behavior (1857) and lapses in traditional discipline eased acceptance of liberated roles. During their minorities, they passed through home as transient guests due to depart, not totally locked into the family situation by birth. Childhood became a time of preparation for the exit, while they developed their own personalities, skills, and talents for the break-away moment. Adult commentators worried (1905) about signs of approaching anarchy: youngsters seemed more independent, insubordinate, resistant to authority, because fathers no longer ruled and feminine tenderness suffused schools. Wild boys and less modest, less well-mannered girls, suffered for lack of discipline.[50]

Boys and girls appraised the situation differently. Sometimes their sadness sprang from generational contrasts, as when little Mary Antin went from success to success in the public school while her father sank from failure to failure in feeble efforts to establish a little business. For young people, frustrations, inhibitions, and anxieties derived not so much from their immediate roles as from the status they expected to achieve after leaving home.[51]

Youngsters reared in placid, sanitized suburbs, where school and church extended parental influence, lacked exposure to contrasting neighborhoods and the strange cultures of settlement houses in the inner city. They proceeded like Penrod and Sam through the round of boyhood/girlhood adventures, left ill-prepared for the bruising contacts of adulthood unless they found some post that promised a safe, undemanding extension of the familiar. Whether they succeeded or failed, either way many lost; and the emptiness of life subjected numerous Americans to depressions few could analyze.[52]

Those raised in less favored circumstances made everyone pay the price. Without proper training, a boy of ten unable to distinguish good from evil would not be responsible even for a murder (1860). Orphans, particularly vulnerable, could forgo deadening incarceration in the asylum only by running away or by escape to the care of relatives or of some Aunt Lizzie willing to act as surrogate parent, teaching habits of thrift and stoicism along with social inhibitions and the willingness to work hard, dread waste, and submit to authority. Childish shyness and reticence then characteristically hardened into a defensive shell.[53]

Concern about the number of offspring and changing roles reflected the transformation of the family from an institution based upon the activities of a unified household to one which increasingly tested the utility of relationships to the self-realization and self-fulfillment of individual members. Observers worried about the prevalence of theories that ignored reproduction and the principles of love and domestic association and thus led to avoidance of parenthood. Selfishness reigned while equality, independence, competition, and warfare between the sexes, the new norms, made victims of children. Procreation, now a factor of personal desires, and marriage, now a relationship of individuals to fulfill each other, focused on the criterion of the extent to which roles, actions, or obligations served self-realization. The family ceased to be an end in itself; it became an instrument that served individuals, thus redefining the liberty, that is, the ability to act, of all.

Changes in family life profoundly affected religious rituals and traditions. The wisdom of the church, in explaining these relationships, had once supplied the discipline by which members met their fixed obligations.

The hallmarks of married life blurred when no longer sanctified by rituals that gave them communal approval. Marriage became a civil rite, despite an ongoing struggle to preserve the sacred against corrosive environmental effects. The number of clergy increased, but not enough to match population growth. Despite continuous countereffort, the disregard of traditional forms prevailed. The journalist William Allen White worried about the modern conception of religion and its emasculated Christ, a "pale, feminine, wishy washy, otherworldly" figure "grown out of the monkish idea of religion" (1912).[54]

Liberated spirits questioned the relevance of supernatural rites to events that called for no more than a public record. Civil registry without benefit of clergy became the important evidence of family formation. Nevertheless, a routine gesture in a government office did not satisfy the emotional hunger of Americans who lacked the alternative celebrations other societies provided in the round of festivals that accompanied the changing seasons of the year as well as family events. The desire to affix a religious mark on these occasions persisted. Childbirth, no longer a providential incident over which individuals lacked control, but the outcome of an affirmative parental decision, called for celebration, particularly when the birth rate and maternal deaths both declined. The emotional weight of these events required formal recognition. So, too, marriage, regarded as the end result of romantic love rather than of a family arrangement, needed greater approval than the mere signing of a paper.

The longing for ritual deepened as concern about health and medical developments transformed attitudes toward disease. Death became less a providential event determined by God's will, than one over which individuals had a measure of control. Some Americans refused to concede its finality—"just away":

> With a cheery smile and a wave of the hand,
> He has stepped away to the better land,
> And left us wondering how very fair
> It needs must be since he lingers there.

Mark Twain refused to recognize a soul but believed that his "dream self" would endure forever. And the spirits rapping out consoling messages met the characteristic response, "I do not believe, but I do not disbelieve," hardly less credible than the invisible germs striking their victims in space. With resignation no longer adequate, death became a dramatic and climactic event, deserving ceremonial recognition with some degree of authenticity to satisfy emotional demands.[55]

The traditionally faithful knew the answer. Immigrants, blacks, and adherents of stable religions faced minimal difficulties because their creeds provided them with meanings in rituals, the sacred character of which they took for granted. Hence too the attractiveness of Catholicism for those repelled by Mammonism and by the contemporary spirit in art. Strange rites and customs also survived in the Southwest, where Mexican Americans stoned a local witch to death for turning a respectable citizen into a woman for three months. The flourishing sect of Penitents attracted nationwide attention for resurrecting flagellant rites in accord with the verse, "Without shedding blood there is no remission of sins"; and rumors of actual crucifixions titillated readers back East. Eastern cults and other esoteric faiths attracted those dissatisfied with established creeds and searching for meaning in an anonymous society where the increased capacity to act failed to compensate for unexpected losses and difficulties. Altogether new faiths emerged. In the 1870s Charles Taze Russell expanded upon the Adventist legacy by revealing to Jehovah's Witnesses the continuing need to battle Satan for rule of the world. In that decade, too, experiments in faith healing and the laying on of hands culminated in the definition of Christian Science by Mary Baker Eddy.[56]

Experimentation with new forms reflected the weakened confidence in rituals that left participants bereft of the desired emotional relief. Intellectual developments that undermined traditional faith wreaked further havoc at a time when external blows profoundly transformed religious thought. Students still read *Pippa's Song:*

God's in his heaven—
All's right with the world!

But the conception of an orderly Newtonian universe, in which a remote God did not interfere, had faded away, as had the old vision of a cosmic drama of salvation in which man played a central role.[57]

Americans had learned from geology that the earth was far older than traditionally thought, and had begun to question accepted accounts of Creation and the whole body of Scripture. Darwin's *On the Origin of Species by Means of Natural Selection* (1859) set forth ideas widely popularized during the next decade. Evolutionary thought conceived of a developmental and purposeless universe, further undermining inherited beliefs, and denied Judeo-Christianity its central significance in world history. Man became an entirely material object, subject to the same laws that operated throughout nature. Astronomy probed the unknown distances of the universe, generating speculation about earthly and solar spheres and therefore about the uniqueness of humans and their position in the universe. People confronting such challenges in seventy years of excited speculation no longer attached significance to ritual events formerly justified by religious truth. Intensified loneliness qualified the individual's ability to act; without faith, each could only cling to hope in the midst of despair. In response, theologian Walter Rauschenbusch defined the mission of Christianity as the transformation of "human society into the Kingdom of God, by regenerating all human relations and reconstituting them in accordance with the will of God."[58]

Subtle changes that isolated individuals from the family and the community developed in a context that altered all relationships in the productive system. In 1850, many households still operated as coherent economic and social units, whether in free farming or in trade, in the handicrafts or in the first manufacturing enterprises. Only plantations deviated in organizing individual hands rather than families as the units of labor. They foreshadowed a new world that destroyed the household as a functioning productive entity, replaced by the wage-earner, whose rewards bore no relationship to family life except for the home work that endured in garment manufacture.

Great cities drew together large numbers of people and made jobs available on an individual basis. In the industrial labor force, men did not always occupy the most advantageous positions; sometimes employers preferred women and children, who performed better and more cheaply at many unskilled tasks. Each person sought an income as an individual. The boy did not tag along to work with his father, but took his own place on the payroll regardless of age or family ties. Scale proved critical. In the 1830s, in mills with about a hundred hands, the employer knew them as husbands and fathers, not only as entries on the payroll. A generation later, when thousands and tens of thousands passed through the gates, the personal element vanished. Managers treated workers in a disciplined, impersonal manner, as abstract entries in the cost of production, disregarding family, church, or ethnic identity, utilizing labor in a fashion entirely detached from the human quality of its components. Entering the factory, people shed other identities and merged in a mass that disregarded origins, needs, or desires. Leaving, they lacked any relationship with each other outside the plant, dispersing to distant homes to encounter family members returned from other employments. The wage, the only link between job and household, bore no relationship to needs or to family position. The husband might earn less than the wife, the father less than the children, anomalies that altered the meaning of *head of the family*. The disorientation spread before long to clerical and managerial positions, so that in time, work and income acquired the same abstract quality, unrelated to the earner as a person.

The older order survived among shopkeepers and petty enterprisers and in traditional crafts such as mining, tailoring, building, and printing. It persisted also in some professions, as when home still housed the physician's consulting room. But more generally, changes in the productive system tore labor away from the family context, with the effect of destroying the household of the past.[59]

While it remained intact as an economic unit as well as a home, the family farm sustained old relationships. So long as its head retained title to the land, directed operations, and controlled the children who shared the labor, its coherence survived. There also the child's intimate association with the parents remained the natural means of developing character and guarding against temptation. With both mother and father around, the youngster could still learn from them and develop habits of obedience, the only basis for strong and free manhood and womanhood, educators pointed out. The restraints of civil and divine law bore heavily only on those undisciplined in youth.

But farmers always struggled against disquieting impulses to expansion. Urban growth increased markets and made goods and services available so that country people increasingly depended on the town where they sold their products and bought necessities. The city, the source of temptations, also drew children away and shattered household solidarity. Young people left home not only to seek their fortunes there but also to escape drudgery and tradition, to struggle for wealth, to satisfy the appetite for excitement, and to assuage personal tastes and needs. The prospect of individual freedom, as attractive as money, threatened the integrity of the home and roused farmers' resentment. "Urban life," wrote a worried contemporary (1887), "through its variety and intensity of interests, tends to develop individualism; rural life, each home removed from its neighbor, tends to develop the family."[60]

Expansion also offered young men opportunities to set up on their own. *Where there's a will, there's a way;* and Horace Greeley pointed it out. *Go west, young man* (1863). Homesteading and easy credit tempted them to strike out for themselves rather than await inheritances while remaining in subordinate positions. The father dependent upon his sons for labor faced a crisis when they departed, obliging him either to hire hands or reduce operations. Even on the farm, therefore, individual goals posed serious threats to unity.

The family had already shrunk to the nuptial pair and their offspring, losing connections with community. The pressure of further changes required a reconsideration of obligations and rights no one could take for granted. The family ceased to be coherent, fixed, or permanent; many of its aspects turned provisional and temporary. It thus ceased to function as expected, particularly when most needed. Sympathy expended on animals or on some half-barbarians in a distant clime did not extend to unfortunates at the door. Fads brought people together in clubs for pleasure or for culture, but the beaming rays of love fell only on those first nurtured in the home.[61]

The erosion of old relationships created what some regarded as pathological social conditions. Down through the eighteenth century, when breakdowns occurred in the aftermath of great disasters—Indian attack or epidemic, adults killed, orphans without shelter—the communal response had absorbed the shock when family resources proved insufficient to meet the aftereffects of calamity, fire, theft, and delinquency. Relatives or neighbors cared for the orphans, elderly, and disabled, sometimes reimbursed by the county or town. By the standards of the time, dependents received adequate support.

After 1850, such arrangements no longer sufficed. The growing number of unsupported elderly people, orphans, insane, and others exposed the fragility of older solutions. Increasingly, observers commented on the large number of unattached youngsters in the cities, many no more than children, totally independent and earning their own living. Efforts to deal with homeless boys and girls originated in charitable impulses but soon acquired a punitive form. Unattached youths threatened order; communities responded by locking them up in orphanages or reform schools. Frequent rhetorical appeals to benevolence and charity mingled with practical steps to protect society, which took precedence over service to inmates.

Desertions also revealed the family's vulnerability. The husband-father, the putative head of the family, shook off some burdens by skipping out, sometimes hitting the road, sometimes moving to another part of town, shielded by urban anonymity. Lax states like Indiana long made more institutionalized separations available through divorce. But toward the end of the century, wealthier families followed that course everywhere—at rates highest in New England, lowest in the South. The variety of possibilities created problems that led some to argue for legislation granting Congress the power to establish uniform laws on the subjects of bankruptcy, marriage, and divorce. Liberal legislation enabled some couples to separate who would not otherwise have done so. By the turn of the century, among the acceptable causes were "smothered hatred, love turned to the reverse, jealousies which no reason can allay, an indefinite jarring of natures in collision and other purely mental causes."[62]

The role of wife and mother subtly changed. The very poor, of course, set domesticity aside, for they required the earnings of all to survive. Others, relieved of the round of successive pregnancies and child rearing, acquired additional functions and occupations. The complex forces that united to demand complete equality of legal and social rights for women won a partial victory by 1920. This political conflict, however, obscured many heavy social pressures. A new college-educated generation pushed to the fore, impatient of old restraints in dress as in employment and organized in associations that pursued its own goals.

Prewar involvement in temperance and abolition widened to take in labor and social reform; and behavior patterns changed to accommodate athletics and the bicycle. The rebellious minority did not directly affect the wives of immigrant laborers or of frontier farmers, whose lives fell within harsh external confines, but they did shape the ideal image of what women should be.[63]

Two contradictory conceptions of womanhood struggled for supremacy. One, personified in the image of the Southern lady, defined her as custodian of civilization, which she transmitted to the oncoming generation. Freed of dreary household tasks and dedicated to the finer impulses and "higher arts," she cultivated piety, gentility, and manners, unlike the "petticoated despisers of their sex—would-be men" who plunged into reform movements. Before the Civil War, control of the household and the management of domestic slave labor and tasks around the idealized mansion placed her in a strategic position to mold her own little empire, ruling the family's physical and emotional needs. After 1865 that role changed in practice, though the ideal remained intact.[64]

By contrast, domesticity, one of the key conceptions of the New England woman, defined her image as homemaker and mother, imparting traditional virtues to her children, cared for by her and not by black nannies. Her moral precepts and the quality of life she perpetuated assured the success and salvation of her offspring. In addition, some, like Louisa Ellis, valued their work for its own sake, taking pleasure in order and cleanliness, ripping a seam "for the mere delight of sewing it together again," surrounding visitors by a hedge of lace.[65]

The conflicting images persisted through the nineteenth century, running into each other and overlapping. Women who read the stylized, literary descriptions did not recognize themselves in those pages. Others, from economic and social backgrounds that made a sound home life, however defined, difficult, posed challenges to the privileged in search of different agendas. All confronted a sense of isolation, loss, and loneliness that reflected their imperfect capacities to act.

The shifting positions of women, the altered contours of households, and novel social pressures induced occasional Americans to reject everything traditionally associated with the home, whether in the cities or the countryside, in town houses or on farms. Unable to attain the ideal and despairing of finding alternative frameworks within which to unite humans, a few took refuge in utopian notions that conflicted with accepted wisdom, opting for totally new ways to organize society. Edward Bellamy's *Looking Backward* outlined an alternative to the home. Housework disappeared, along with domestic servants; the state took care of basic needs, such as laundering, cooking, and cleaning. Public kitchens provided food. Organized into industrial armies, men and women no longer toiled for self-support. Civilization meant interdependence and specialization in a vast industrial partnership that made the home irrelevant.

Already utopian experiments tried to eliminate the private household. In 1869 forty bold experimenters in Cambridge, Massachusetts, for one year tried to live cooperatively. The experiment collapsed because few women wished to work hard enough for the common good. Meanwhile, technology expanded traditional arrangements and complicated daily life. Wood stoves, replacing open hearths, increased the variety cooked simultaneously while a temperature gauge in the oven door after 1890 facilitated procedures. Commercial canneries appeared in the 1870s and the new icebox helped preserve foods. Improved sewing machines eased other tasks, and the introduction of electricity into moderate-income homes powered washing and ironing machines. Higher standards of living expressed in greater variety of clothing, more complex diets, and better housing, generated a host of new anxieties that no number of etiquette books seemed able to assuage.

Not accidentally, the brave new world constructed in Bellamy's *Looking Backward* lacked affection. In his world, mothers had long ceased making pies, while the father, son, and husband more often dined at the club or restaurant than at home. Once the dinner table disappeared, so did the setting for the man as paterfamilias. The household Bellamy described worked harmoneously because it had banished passion, by no means a radical change among Americans and particularly among Yankees committed to reserve.[66]

Laments on the loss of traditional standards and moralistic reflections on the absence of personal warmth and of intimacy exposed a sense of something missing, something popular culture made central to the family relationship, that is, love—a sentiment taken for granted, scarcely worth mentioning. " 'Tis easy to be alone," said the old widower, his wife eight years dead, but "I miss her just the same every day"; or that other who wore a "cross of snow" upon his breast

> These eighteen years, through all the changing scenes
> And seasons, changeless since the day she died.

All those romantic historical novels, like the poetry and songs, conveyed the same message of constancy of affection, through thick and thin, for better or worse. And indeed the majority of Americans did not divorce or desert, but accepted the burden of relationship and paid a price for doing so.[67]

A short life expectancy deepened the austerity. The debilitating effects of long working days and of stretches of unemployment weakened resistance to disease. Pneumonia, tuberculosis, typhoid, malaria, diphtheria, and intermittent malnutrition brought thoughts of death nearer, reminding even the young of the tentative, provisional character of family ties. Emotional reserve, still a necessity in the face of relentless mortality, set limits to sentimental attachments. When her friend, a devoted Christian, went to her long-sought home, Rachel wished also to get to heaven to live nearer her Savior. "Why did I not die when a child," she complained. "I am all alone. Oh! how lonely it is to be alone away out in the country at night" (1865, 1866). Some sought consolation or at least acceptance in thoughts of an afterlife but meanwhile hardened themselves to go it alone as individuals.[68]

Those who found the burden too heavy sought escape or at least momentary relief in sensations that obliterated feelings, although all such indulgences contributed to the pathologies that troubled society. Decades of temperance agitation had made Americans familiar with the evils of alcohol. The histrionic orators, the lurid tracts, the tearful pledges, the laws, and the sermons had not lessened the attractions of the dram of rum, of the growler of beer, that brought a moment's ease, whatever remorse it left behind. During the Civil War, men, away from home and from their wives' oversight, slipped and then regretted it. "My feelings are almost insupportable," wrote one of them in his diary (1865). "O whiskey! Thou demon! May I never put thee to my lips again." And his wife, in whom he confided, prayed to God for grace to overcome. It took all the powers of her mind and soul to bear up under her sorrow and to hide the anguish of her heart. She resolved to try and forget it. "He seems almost heartbroken over his missteps & I feel that it needs an effort to save him from despair. He has vowed to me that henceforth no such missteps shall befall him."[69]

Good resolutions rarely sufficed, even among well-known athletes like Rube Waddell. Jack London, after marching to join Coxey's army, became the hard-drinking tramp that he described in *John Barleycorn* (1913). In town, saloons appeared in the neighborhoods and at the termini of streetcar lines to serve the Tin Bucket Brigade on the way to and from work. Such establishments welcomed societies and labor unions, which often had difficulties in securing other meeting places. Use of the upstairs rooms, free of charge, attracted a steady clientele. The saloon also functioned as a labor exchange; and efforts by temperance reformers to offer free, dry alternatives failed. The saloon also served as a bank where workers cashed paychecks. Temperance advocates complained that the paycheck rarely found its way home intact. The breweries cooperated by providing saloonkeepers with cash on hand to change checks.

After 1900, employer attitudes changed with the discovery that the drunken worker threatened himself and others, damaging efficiency and profits. Public concern about wrecks and passenger injuries forced railroads to check on employee sobriety. Aaron Montgomery Ward, owner of the Chicago mail order house, furious that his employees drank unnoticed, had the city council vote the territory around his new plant dry, then forbade workers to visit bars within half a mile of the dry district. Spies photographed saloon crowds, with any employee recognized liable to instant dismissal. At the same time he merchandized liquor in his catalog.

Some temperance advocates believed that the only solution was to give drinkers a choice by substitutes for the saloon, at strategically placed coffee wagons. In Boston, Mrs. Annie Adams Fields, wife of James T. Fields, publisher of the *Atlantic Monthly,* devoted much time and money to establishing coffeehouses in tenement districts. The Oriental Tea Company, the YMCA, reading rooms, and employment agencies also sought to divert men from the fleshpots. Chicago's home saloon, started in 1895 by Episcopal Bishop Samuel Fallows, preserved all the features of the barroom except the drink—barmaids, spitoons, even the nickel lunch, and bishop's beer, a watered-down near beer. The Health Department, however, closed the experiment when it discovered that bishop's beer had enough alcoholic content to require a license.[70]

More insidious, because less visible, were the inroads of drug addiction, as with Willie the Weeper, who had the dope habit and had it bad. And Cocaine Lill—too far gone, like scores of women dependent on discreet helpings of morphine. The opium devotee, at once the most abject of slaves and the most hopeless of unfortunates, rushed along toward that slippery verge where the fanciful merged into the dark real, and then tumbled irrevocably. The ultimate liberation, the liberation of the dark forces in humanity, when a deranged moral sense released man's worst propensities, was a disease of the wealthy, driven to enliven the hours of ennui after giddy rounds of pleasure by aching heads, jaded appetites, and flagging spirits, the result of a debauched life. "The woman of elegant leisure, the woman of fashion," unable to meet the exhausting demands of dissipation, fortified herself with morphia powder (1872). The New England Watch and Ward Society (founded 1878) in three years dragged 178 persons into court in Boston for illegally selling and distributing opium, cocaine, morphine, heroin, and hasheesh, which transformed men and women into ghosts, magnifying their "evil tendencies," changing them almost into incarnate devils. Blindness and insanity were among the lesser effects; reason dethroned transformed intelligent women into maudlin maniacs, filthy in body, shattered in nerves, shrieking "give me a hypo, I want a hypo." S. Weir Mitchell, an eminent neurologist, experimented on himself, using the mescal buttons of the peyote cactus. He felt "as if the unseen millions of the Milky Way" flowed in a sparkling river before his eyes so that he feared "a perilous reign of the mescal habit when the agent becomes attainable." Meanwhile, hundreds of thousands found relief—of a sort—for what ailed them, in the great American fraud, patent medicines, their brand names made familiar through national distribution and through extensive advertising in newspapers and magazines, their contents unknown. No disclosure requirements informed those they relieved of the alcohol, opium, or digitalis in the contents, or for that matter of the caffeine (or perhaps cocaine) in the increasingly popular Coca Cola.[71]

In vain, the World's Parliament of Religions (1892) called on all faiths to unite against alcohol and drugs, perceived by the turn of the century as a worldwide problem requiring unorthodox measures, another mission for a Christian nation bearing a special responsibility for such "child races" as the Chinese. Mrs. S. L. Baldwin, president of New York Branch Methodist Women's Foreign Missionary Society, after many years in China concluded that the opium traffic posed a more deadly obstacle to uplifting the people than their idolatry and superstition. Besides, to educate and Christianize a people would immediately multiply their wants and open the door for Western products. The Pittsburgh Chamber of Commerce urged President Theodore Roosevelt to induce Great Britain to release China from treaty provisions tolerating this traffic that pauperized and demoralized the people and diminished foreign commerce.

Fantasy provided an escape, if not in the haze induced by drugs then in cloudy outlines of popular stories. Generations of girls identified with Jo March of *Little Women* (1868), coping with wistful and genteel poverty as its author had—Christmas with only makeshift presents, going to a ball with only one glove. Young married couples tearfully empathized with O. Henry's Magi in love's sacrifice. Zane Grey and the dime novels gave boys their fill of the tidy violence in cowboy stories and of crime on the city streets, neatly solved by Nick Carter. Alternatively, the grotesque mirrors of Luna Park reflected a world completely unreal.[72]

P. T. Barnum understood that his countrymen did not know how to entertain themselves; he hoped to get rich by elevating their tastes and spreading information or misinformation about nature. He anticipated the sensationalism of nineteenth-century fiction that emphasized morbid failings and cravings, taste for fiery sauces and strongly seasoned meats and drinks. Barnum gave his customers a wide variety of thrills. At the same time, popular fiction in circulating libraries and railway bookstalls usurped the role formerly played by preachers and teachers, molding minds and tastes, aiming at constant excitement, the craving of diseased appetites. Illustrations, which Emerson feared (1851) would turn "literature into a sensual pleasure," heightened the effects. Weekly serialization called for frequent and rapid recurrence of piquant incidents and startling situations to sustain interest. Stories elaborated out of morbid feelings and overwrought sensibilities shifted toward a materialistic supernaturalism, terror growing out of realistic psychological and physiological devices and processes—the theme often the gradual unraveling of some carefully prepared enigma, leading to disclosure of transgression or villainy, the tearing off of a mask, lifting of a veil, with the tension hinging on things not being what they seemed as people assumed false selves for gain.

The fascination with the pathological, the repeated use of madness as a crucial narrative convention, bridged fiction and reality. Imaginings turned often to Lizzie Borden, her of the forty whacks whose tale supplied the rhythms to which generations of girls jumped rope. Aged thirty-two, unmarried, passionately devoted to her father but not to her stepmother, active in good causes, teacher of a Sunday school class for Chinese children, Lizzie won acquittal in her trial for the double murder of her parents but never laid to rest the fantasies of childhood revenge— an American Electra murdering the mother who had stolen the father's love.

Many a woman and some men shuddered fondly at the vampire image, female, all in white as in the painting, beside the drained body of her prey, whom she hunted for sex, not for love. On the New York stage, in the drama, *A Fool There Was* (1914), a woman enslaved and ruined a diplomat encountered on an ocean voyage. Film version (1915)—the vamp, Theda Goodman, a Cincinnati tailor's daughter, renamed Theda Bara for publicity's sake and endowed with a romantic, fictitious past. In four years she turned out thirty-nine films, taking revenge, she said, on all the evil men had done to women.[73]

Sexual fantasies left more literary than social or police records. The techniques of sublimation usually concealed women's emotions. *The Scarlet Letter* (1850) pointed out that "the virgins of Dimsdale's church group grew pale around him, victims of a passion so imbued with religious sentiment that they imagined it to be all religion and brought it openly, in their white bosoms, as their most acceptable sacrifice before the altar." But the unbuttoned poet did not hesitate. Without shame the man he liked knew and avowed the deliciousness of sex; and without shame the woman he liked knew and avowed hers. But the poet sang only for himself; not even his readers avowed their emotions or left evidence of whether they satisfied them within or outside the marriage bed, in homosexuality or in lesbianism, or in cash transactions. Some men took pride in reputations as great libertines, for they never had any other, and although pretending to deny the charge, really hoped neighbors would continue to accuse them. People watched each other so closely, however, that there was no opportunity to be other than honest and circumspect in this respect. Close friendships among men lent themselves to the nudity of clubs and camps, as well as to endearing modes of address, as did the ambiguous huggings, squeezings, and kissings of intimate female friends. On the other hand, there was no doubt about the forthright amatory declarations in Godfrey Lowell Cabot's letters to his wife. Oh, you wouldn't believe the things he made me do, complained an aggrieved spouse. Still, Oliver Wendell Holmes for years maintained a discreet relationship with Lady Clare Castletown.[74]

The existence of brothels and red light districts implied the existence of patrons, but the prevailing view sentimentalized the prostitute—more to be pitied than censured, more to be helped than despised, only a lassie who ventured on life's stormy path ill advised. Every door is closed against her, not a soul for her will mourn, she has fallen by the wayside, she has gone beyond recall. At her home there's a name that's never spoken, and a mother's heart half-broken. There is still a memory living, there's a father unforgiving, and a picture that is turned toward the wall.

> Do not scorn her with words fierce and bitter,—
> Do not laugh at her shame and down-fall;
> For a moment just stop and consider—
> That a man was the cause of it all.

Hence the shock at Dreiser's more realistic *Sister Carrie* (1900) and *Jennie Gerhard* (1911).[75]

Diligent investigators puzzled over the phenomenon. The American Purity Alliance (1895), its president Aaron N. Powell, a distinguished New York Committee of Fifteen (1900–1902), and the Philadelphia Vice

Commission (1913), in the end blamed it all on poverty and family looseness. The remedies usually called for coercion—incarceration of the debauched in asylums or reformatories and creation of moral police for surveillance and repression. The American Vigilance Association and the New York Bureau of Social Hygiene set themselves the tasks.[76]

Pity or censure, envy or admire—no matter! Individuals all, trying to make out, each a law unto himself, even the ostensible failures. Heroes all, evidence of human determination: Helen Keller and Lizzie Borden and Theda Bara and Annie Oakley—see what they could do.[77]

The prize ring, once the disgraceful scene of fiendish passions (1853), the setting for masculine heroics, became spiced with violence. Throw him down, McCloskey, you can lick him if you try, so that future generations with wonder and delight would read on history's pages of the great McCloskey fight: from John L. Sullivan onward to Jack Johnson and Jack Dempsey, the champs strode across the popular consciousness.[78]

Even in team sports where the common effort counted, still one stood out from the rest, or appeared to do so, or could be made to appear so, able to do more, hence freer than the others.

Baseball, the great American pastime, sank to an inglorious low point in 1919 when the White Sox threw the World Series in the interest of gamblers. Still, it had its share of heroes. The memory at least lingered of Christy Mathewson—tall, blond, blue-eyed, religious, an intelligent college graduate who refused to play on Sundays and lived clean. A nice man, too bad he died young of tuberculosis.

None more competent than Ty Cobb. Yet the terror of the diamond died alone at the age of seventy-three, a bitter old man, always a loner, who never forgave his vindictive father and hated everyone. "I had to fight all my life to survive. They were all against me . . . but I beat the bastards and left them in the ditch." When they build a triumphal arch for a hero, Mr. Dooley suggested, let them build it of bricks, so they'll have something to throw.[79]

Many more people shared the excitement by reading or hearing about it than by actually getting to the diamond, the ring, or the gridiron. Others found pleasure in recollections of a tune heard at the dance hall or the park concert or the vaudeville show; the more fortunate, gathered around the parlor piano, sang from the sheet music or heard it on the Victrola. Whatever the setting, however slight the acquaintanceships, voices lifted together provided a kind of pleasure, as if the easy jingly phrases expressed genuine emotions that the singers felt or felt they should have felt. Tin Pan Alley churned out the tunes and lyrics; the prolific

Harry von Tilzer alone wrote more than three thousand songs. At the show also the spectators found occasions for wonder and laughter in the nonsense of grotesque clowns and freaks, the acrobats and comics; and they took pleasure in magical hoaxes and psychological thrillers laden with implicit violence, mystery, deception, and intrigue, and charged with love, hate, loyalty, and revenge.

Americans paid the price of liberty in isolation, as Harriet Beecher Stowe's novel pointed out. Nobody, said a character in *Dred,* "is absolutely free, except Robinson Crusoe, in the desolate island; and he tears all his shirts to pieces and hangs them up as signals of distress, that he may get back into slavery again."[80]

No more than Crusoe did they like the costs of liberty.

Residents of a reality so detached from past experience that it made no sense, people in isolation repeatedly thrust back on inadequate inner resources, scarcely hoped for meaning in life, sought rather the relief of ironic commentary on their own situations. In time they found what they sought not in the world of actuality, not even on the live stage, but on the flickering screen where the comic tramp repeatedly, gallantly, survived the blows of a hostile environment—a character much like themselves, without a name, without a family, detached from all sense of belonging, from all faith other than his own effort to go on.

The little men and women, isolated individuals because detached from family, church, and all other intermediate institutions, reached out to one another but all too often lacked the means of making contact in a world of strangers. Increasingly, the detached people sought to satisfy the emotional need for belonging and to establish relationships with others through the one big national entity of which all were part.

The unattended consequences of patriotism and expanded government power significantly contracted the liberty all sought.

V I

GOODNESS

ALL BUT THE MOST HARDENED recoiled from the metaphors individualism evoked: of the jungle, with the fangs of each bared against the others; of the ocean in which the bigger, more powerful, more agile, devoured those too weak for self-defense or escape; of some great force at work "throwing vast masses of people into life" who could not all succeed.[1]

Inherited precepts rejected these dismal images of human destiny. The brotherhood ordained by the one God of the Christians and Jews called for loving-kindness among all who shared the same fate by virtue of common descent from Adam and Eve. And the legacy of the American enlightenment kindled reminders of phrases about progress, improvement, and everyone's capacity for reform. Emerson's hope that his country would take pride "in being a nation of servants, and not of the served," struck many as reasonable. It would break down prisons, end capital punishment, abolish the laws against atheism, and establish the pure religion of justice and asceticism (1865). Moreover, the citizens of the Republic tried to refute the common European criticism of America as a great money-making machine, lacking heart and given over to materialism. Still a new country, "untrammeled by ages of tradition," its progressive society ceaselessly advanced ideals of social justice and satisfied material wants. Then, too, the revolutionary promise of equality formed a legacy yet unexplored, incongruous with the jungle image. People needed to acknowledge their solidarity and join others; "men's tracks cover the whole world, and there ain't standin' room outside of 'em."[2]

The jungle image also emptied freedom of meaning. The brute struggle for survival mocked *life, liberty, and the pursuit of happiness,* words venerated since the forefathers' time. Few sought authority over others; each expected to remain free of control except by consent. Yet the formal ability to act meant little when each person battled all others merely to survive.

Did man deserve confidence? Not according to Herman Melville.[3]

The issue shadowed the life of Mark Twain (Samuel Langhorne Clemens, 1835–1910), now amused, now dismayed by the changes he ruefully observed about him. His disappointed father, who never found the fortune for which he left Kentucky, died when Sam was twelve; and the boy drifted—for a while as a journeyman printer and then as a pilot of a Mississippi riverboat. Years of wandering gave him acute insight into his countrymen's character. When he began to write and lecture after the Civil War, humor made him a success. He enjoyed the popularity of amusing books like *Tom Sawyer* (1876) and the pleasant home his wife provided; get-rich-quick schemes tempted him, as they did other Americans. Yet he remained deeply critical of his society. Not consistently, but often enough to be disturbing, he wondered what had happened to its moral values, rejecting as he did William Lecky's flaccid assurance that an innate moral sense governed people. In *Huckleberry Finn* (1884), a bitter book beneath its humorous coating, Twain probed the meaning of conscience for his readers. In time, personal grief and disillusion about the United States and the world brought first despair, then the bitter resignation that clouded the years until his death. Men, he knew, needed no hell other than that they occupied from the cradle to the grave; only release from the bonds of their odious flesh could end their meanness and misery. "Whoever has lived long enough to find out what life is, knows how deep a debt of gratitude we owe to Adam, the first great benefactor of our race. He brought death into the world."[4]

The implications of doing good in an imperfect world emerged but slowly. People who sought to escape the jungle by creating a virtuous society of moral beings confronted unexpected problems, the resolution of which determined the future of liberty in the United States.

In the middle of the nineteenth century, the abundant means available to attain desired ends generated confidence. The benevolent had recourse to the state and to numerous voluntary associations, as well as to personal endeavor; and such instruments endured after 1850. Indeed, the immense increase of government power during the Civil War revealed unexpected potentials, not only for the deployment of military force but also for matters only indirectly connected with the conflict. Congress reorganized the currency and the banking system, encouraged education, improved transportation, expanded agricultural settlement, and advanced sanitation and medical practice on the battlefields. The national legislature thereby set precedents for responding to demands that the federal government and the states act to further progress.

But the failure to recast Southern society during the Civil War and Reconstruction left a bitter residue of frustration that shadowed calls for positive action. Later revelations of corruption at all levels raised doubts about the ability of elected officials disinterestedly to execute even the best-intentioned policies. Editors continued to call for action on behalf of the self-governing. But a long way remained to fulfillment of the duty to further everyone's welfare and prosperity. "Representative assemblies," a Harvard president noted, had not proved "senates of unfailing wisdom, guided only by desire for the public good." As a result, the disappointed drifted toward a general loss of faith in government. Anyone "with ordinary perception of human nature" should have expected that party politics would overshadow the welfare of the whole community in the legislators' calculation. Attention shifted to voluntary or even individual action induced by exhortation, though the sheer magnitude of some ills required compulsion and therefore some political involvement.[5]

Whatever means Americans chose after 1850, their responses remained inconsistent, for imposing difficulties persisted. In the absence of a clear definition of evil, they fumbled about uncertainly in the wish to do good. Retaining faith in the capacity of autonomous human beings to decide and choose on their own, they continued to expect that self-supporting families, satisfying all their own needs, would remain independent.

But if not, then what?

In the face of that question, certainty faded. The community had to intervene to control behavior when people failed to earn their own livelihoods or squandered what they had, or infringed upon the rights of others. How?

In the past, on smaller scales, all-knowing neighbors glimpsed what went on in the vicinity; rough judgments took form of who was good and who bad, of what acts were right and what wrong. Opinion, approximate and informal, then rendered verdicts, whether by way of juries or mobs or arbitration panels, with recourse to the formal apparatus of law a last resort. Since Americans regarded the certainty, not the severity, of punishment as the chief deterrent to crime, they remained impatient with procedural delays by which lawyers displayed their virtuosity and inflated their fees. Indictments quashed because of inadvertent misuse of a word and other unreasonable niceties made the law a contrivance to defeat justice. The effort to simplify some forms in Pennsylvania's revised code (1860) and in other states had little effect, hence the general preference for informal mechanisms that reduced both the cost and the length of proceedings. Veneration for the right to trial by jury inhibited expansion of the power of justices of the peace and of other magistrates but did not narrow the willingness to accept confessions and other forms of plea bargaining.[6]

As the nineteenth century advanced, the confidence in retribution for criminal acts dwindled and criticism of the lax administration of the laws mounted. The fault lay not so much in the feeble mechanism for detecting and apprehending lawbreakers, nor yet in the corruption of some police officials, nor even in abuse of the pardoning power; the problem arose from transformation of the context. In the large impersonal metropolitan cities and in the vast spaces of the newly settled West, the hastening concourse of strangers could not oversee each other's affairs as readily as formerly, while the old clarity about right and wrong, worthy and unworthy, faded. Therefore deviations from the ideal expectations of autonomy and self-sufficiency everywhere grew more pronounced, and, despite repeated failures, called for intervention, whether by public or by private agencies—all unprepared.

"The degeneracy which afflicts civilization," wrote an analyst in 1913, originated in social maladjustments. Abnormal arrangements and functions, acting upon individuals, induced personal and social misconduct. The increasing dissociation of the better off from their civic obligations and the withdrawal of the traditional guardians of society and morals into their own havens, left control to others. Officeholding became a source of personal aggrandizement with no supervisory moral function. Respect for officials and for the laws then faded. The more the crooks prevailed, the less the incentive to honesty. Opinions that engendered contempt for the rights of property followed naturally from the spectacle of men grown rich by plunder, making all converts to the doctrine of Rob Roy,

> They should take who have the power
> And they should keep who can.

In addition to the old-time corruption, collusion between the police and criminals and overly zealous legislation also contributed—too many laws on the books, governing too many jurisdictions. Altogether too many public and private matters had become subjects of complex statutes often irrelevant to life—all of which eroded the average citizen's respect for the law. The propensity to lawmaking led to the countervailing propensity to lawbreaking, the ruling maxim being that "the average man can never be legislated into . . . temporal or spiritual well-being nor will he willingly obey laws for which he cares nothing and which he cannot understand."

Paradoxically, serious crime—murder, armed robbery, rape, and burglary—declined nationwide. In no imminent danger, therefore, society could expend the energy of criminal justice on other purposes—order, discipline, upholding a moral code. Alameda County, California, thus quieted down, with sneak thieves and rowdies the main problems in Oakland. Gas lamps extended into remote parts of the cities added to security. "Crime is committed in the darkness, its opportunities are dispelled by the light."[7]

Imprisonment for debt, once the most visible sign of dependency, disappeared from the list of offenses. But poverty persisted, and often in more acute forms than ever before—not only in the countryside, where some means of coping existed, but even more dramatically in the totally unprepared great cities.

Evident urban poverty discredited denials of its existence. No one wished "to constitute the whole community the equalizer of the great law of supply and demand" (1857). "It is all wrong to be poor, anyhow," said a popular preacher. To sympathize with a man whom God had punished for his sins, thus to help him when God would still continue a just punishment, was an error, for there was not a poor person in the United States not made poor by his own shortcomings. However, being a Christian, even the preacher conceded some sympathy appropriate, though it became ever more difficult to draw the traditional distinction between the worthy and the unworthy; between the honest poor, whom intelligence offices would direct to employment, and vagrant paupers fit only for incarceration in the workhouse. Nor did the blame rest, as it had early on, with unskilled foreigners, for in Detroit and other cities the most numerous recipients of aid consisted of native Protestants. Dependency sprang not from some failing of character but often from forces beyond personal control, and therefore beyond remedy by such spasmodic charity as allowing the needy to take wood for fuel from a burned-out building (1859). The poor would always be there, but they need not suffer for the necessities of life. However benevolent the intentions, merely to feed the hungry and clothe the naked damaged society by encouraging imposters; true assistance demanded rather creation among the sufferers of the self-respect and industry to ward off future want (1860). How?[8]

Almshouses ceased to house indiscriminately vagrants, disorderly persons, children, and the insane, all now more usually accommodated in specialized establishments. The state provided for those who needed control or restraint, served by education and by professional treatment, as well as for miscellaneous dependent types not aided by private charities. Voluntary and religious organizations operated orphan asylums, hospitals, and homes for the aged as well as breadlines, soup kitchens, and temporary shelters. Still other societies assisted the needy in their own homes and helped the ill through visiting nurses.[9]

These varied expressions of benevolence reflected changing attitudes to the dependent. American travelers in southern Europe invariably condemned the persistent beggars seen in the streets. Their negative comments revealed a misunderstanding of traditional Christian charity as a demonstration of the virtue of the giver rather than a response to the receiver's need. *Virtue* reflected the donor's sentiment, not the remote prospect of correcting the recipient, with philanthropy valid whether the object was deserving or not, redeemable or not. A quite different concept appeared in the United States. Doing good became a means of reforming the needy. The obligation to expend limited resources carefully to generate the greatest improvement shifted emphasis to examining the worthiness of those aided, judged by unemotional scientific means, a view that seemed to the traditional-minded charity scrimped and iced in the name of a cautious, statistical Christ.[10]

New problems confronted the benevolent after 1850. The number of dependents seemed to increase. The aged, the poor, the insane, the orphans, the blind, grew more numerous, partly through the way in which society defined the self-sustaining. With everyone capable of rational behavior expected to further his or her individual interests, whoever did not swelled the number of dependents. Increased longevity and the decline of mortality had the same effect. In addition, migration and the strain of absorption diminished the family's ability to care for its own. The remote cousin, nephew, even son, could not count on help when needed. Mobile individuals, cast adrift in the effort to better themselves, enjoyed a dubious freedom.

Dramatic examples revealed the extent of the need. In Salem, Massachusetts, two brothers alternated in school attendance because they had only one pair of shoes between them (1881). The numerous deaths in New York's infant boarding houses (1868) called attention to the helplessness of parents who lacked the means of caring for their babies. Whoever ventured or blundered into the slums confronted "disgusting and demoralizing scenes of little beggar boys and girls . . . soliciting alms from every passer by," and saw or smelled dirty streets, inadequate lighting, miserable paving, stables side by side with houses unconnected with sewers. A Chicago nursery cared for the offspring of working mothers (1860), and the Five Points Mission in New York valiantly but vainly tried to place children in homes (1856). But packs of wild youths long mingled with tramps, hoboes, and other vagrants on the road or in the alleys. Starving babes, dying orphans, shoeless beggars in the cold, no one to help, no one to pity, none to caress, drifted through the popular lyrics:

> Mister, please give me a penny
> for I've not got any Pa—
> Please sir, give me just one penny—
> I want to buy some bread for Ma!

Later, journalists armed with cameras revealed how the other half lived, and realistic novels traced the degradation wrought by poverty on young women, more defenseless than their brothers (1893). A reformer denounced the "error and disappointment" of the easy assumption that his was a civilized age, and asked his audience "to begin with the frank concession that we live in a pretty barbarous old world."[11]

Individual examples provided graphic testimony. Strolling the beach at Coney Island one night, a New York music critic stumbled on a family huddled helplessly in the space beneath a bathhouse. The father, out of work, had pawned, piece by piece, bit by bit, everything in the house, while the children lived in the streets, feeding at garbage cans. Neighbors could not help, for they had difficulty assembling one meal a day for themselves. Then, lacking the money for rent, the homeless family drifted away from the stifling street, to this final refuge. Now they were hungry. That is, they had eaten nothing at all for days on end.[12]

Efforts to understand poverty revealed that the inadequate earnings of even the hard-working poor lay at the heart of the matter. Personal deficiency had nothing to do with it.

> Look up the land, look down the land,
> The poor, the poor, the poor, they stand
> Wedged by the pressing of Trade's hand
> Against an inward-opening door
>
> . . . .
>
> The kilns and the curt-tongued mills say go!
> There's plenty that can, if you can't; we know.

Move out, if you think you're underpaid.
The poor are prolific; we're not afraid;
Trade is Trade.

Radical critics who shifted the blame for poverty from the victims
to the victimizers, from the families with inadequate earnings to the
wealthy and the social system that tolerated inequalities and indulgence
in luxuries (1857), stirred audience sympathies but rarely won power.
Their grand explanations promised the poor pie in the sky but failed to
address the immediate needs, greater in depression, less in prosperity,
always leaving many at the edge of destitution.[13]

Older definitions of crime also proved inadequate. Earlier, damage
to one person affected all and obliged the whole society to punish
transgressions. As that sense of obligation faded, puzzling questions remained. Belief in a communal stake in preserving order persisted. But
without the authority of inherited codes that defined sin and sinfulness,
people disagreed about the nature of criminality and about the appropriate treatment of its perpetrators. Entangled in procedural matters, the law
administered in the courts did not further the understanding of justice and
moreover did not seem to do so. New York's reformatory at Elmira
(1876), imitated in other states, assumed that juvenile delinquents required
not punishment but education. Separate courts for children (1899), probation, and suspended sentences began to treat the young offenders by
reeducation, although the impulse to retribution lingered on.[14]

Some offenses once deemed of general concern gradually ceased to
be so, with injured individuals instead expected to seek their own remedies. The arrest of the editor of an indecent publication, *The Town Talk*
(1857), gave the citizen defamed no satisfaction, for slanders less often
became criminal misdemeanors, more often personal private offenses for
which victims could seek relief in civil actions, as they could also with
regard to libel and frauds and an expanding category of torts. Persons so
injured could try to secure redress of their own accord; the community
did not act for them.[15]

Discussions of murder, larceny, and other heinous acts revealed disagreements about the offenders' natures and therefore about the appropriate punishments. Contemporary penologists wandered off into all-pur-
pose theories of rapid moral deterioration after social disturbances, with
war a form of neurosis, spreading venereal disease, unfitting man for
civilian life, depriving him of industrious habits, and bringing aggressive
instincts to the forefront, so that he abandoned self-reliance and became

totally dependent. The theories did not convince. Eliminate the devil and the forces of evil, then how explain James B. Kirk, an intelligent young teacher who opened school each morning with prayer only to emerge exposed as a member of a counterfeiters gang (1859)? Or the notorious Jumpertz, first found guilty of murdering a woman and stuffing her body in a trunk, then released because the evidence was only circumstantial (1859)? Insanity, domestic violence, or emotional distress as in the case of Congressman Daniel Sickles (1859), or the passions of Italians and Chinese accounted for some homicides. But the causes puzzled observers, as did the spectacles of public executions, "these worse than heathenish exhibitions," that social scientists argued cheapened human life and dissolved inhibitions against capital crimes.[16]

No dispute about it: murderers deserved punishment. But questions of proof and of the evaluation of evidence persisted; and the performance of skilled attorneys in lurid cases raised doubts about the evenhandedness of justice. Clarence S. Darrow lost only one of the fifty murder cases in which he acted for the defense. A radical almost from birth (1857), he acted for well-paying corporate clients, but also for labor leaders and Wobblies. Commanding the usual lawyer tricks, he also kept on good terms with judges, built up favorable publicity in the press, and sprinkled his oratory with familiar jokes. He denied the fault of the accused without control over their actions, behaving in response to hidden social, biological, and psychological forces for which they were not responsible.

Extensive newspaper coverage of gruesome murders satisfied readers' morbid curiosity but may have encouraged others to imitate the crimes and weakened resistance to lawless and immoral activities. The decline of religion had the same effect. That left only the coercive authority of penal statutes to impress upon the weak that obedience to moral obligation so necessary to righteous society. Inhibitions dissolved without faith to offset the danger in the environment. Where nine persons of both sexes shared the same room, rape and incest were the natural result.

Evil impulses lurked also at the opposite end of the social scale. The acquittal of Ned Stokes, caught red-handed killing Jim Fisk in a battle for the favors of the voluptuous Josie Mansfield, followed as a matter of course and inspired the cynical ditty:

> If you've plenty of stamps, you can hold up your head
> And walk away from your own prison door.
> But they'll hang you up high, if you've no friends or gold.
> Let the rich go, but hang up the poor.

Harry Thaw and Stanny White would reenact the drama.

Persistent questions focused on the death penalty. The society that depended on the gallows manifestly sought only retribution for the wrong—a response appropriate for an evil beyond remedy. Yet that judgment always bothered those who held reform the purpose of punishment, an instrument of social improvement. Illinois built a new state prison in 1858 designed to house eleven hundred inmates for generations to come. Vain intention. It soon proved inadequate.

How define grand larceny? Five dollars.

And all the efforts at incarceration and prevention eroded the issue of guilt, as deviants of every sort used confessions of their dismal pasts to deny responsibility for their derelictions. They drew support from the persistent popular belief that bandits did good for the poor, that the rich had it coming to them. Contemporary Robin Hoods emerged not just as hoods who robbed, but as avengers of the downtrodden, defenders of the defenseless who redressed the balance always in favor of the high and mighty. Hence the tendency to glorify Jesse James (1847–1881) and other bad men. In *Roughing It,* Mark Twain found romance in sitting face-to-face with the gentlemanly-appearing, quiet, and affable person "who in fights and brawls and various ways, had taken the lives of twenty-six human beings."[17]

Anxiety about the family blurred distinctions between private and personal matters, between those that concerned the community and those that did not, yet of which government took cognizance because defined as criminal. Violations of some accepted sexual conventions and taboos earned swift and unequivocal condemnation. Seventy-year-old Edward Wilson and his forty-year-old daughter Eliza injured no one by incestuous cohabitation; but their infamy offended their neighbors, so, too, an uncle and a niece in Detroit (1858). But other conventions lost their binding quality. Seduction, once a serious crime, ceased to earn punishment even as a misdemeanor. At most, like other torts, it became subject to a civil suit for damages, often brought by the father deprived of the benefit of his daughter's labor, with a twofold purpose in view—"the redress of an injury and the punishment of a wrongdoer." Ambiguity, however, suffused attitudes toward the man guilty of sexual misbehavior. True, he ruined her, dragged her down until her soul within her died, shattered each and ev'ry dream.

> You fooled me from the start,—
> And though you're not true

May God bless you.
That's the curse of an aching heart. (1913)

In January 1875, when Henry Ward Beecher took the stand to defend himself against the charge that he had seduced Mrs. Elizabeth Tilton, the ladies of his congregation sent him a huge bouquet—"a dunghill covered with flowers," commented the editor of the *Louisville Courier Journal*. Few Americans doubted his guilt; what to do in such cases remained unclear.[18]

Confusion also explained the inability to decide whether prostitution was a private transaction between client and provider or an offense against public order. The men involved rarely earned blame or censure, while the women, judged guilty of vice, faced punishment. But some situations remained ambiguous. Everyone standing by had a tear in his eye (for some had a daughter at home) and all knew that the woman in tears from the crowd's angry jeers was once someone's joy. Cast aside like a toy, abandoned forsaken, unknown, she once may have seen better days. Yet citizens who objected to police brutality and pitied the neglected, wretched female children turned vagrant, living on the streets, doubted the possibility of reformation.

The initial response: let them do what they liked, only out of sight and not in good residential neighborhoods. Regulate the activities that exposed helpless young women, wearied by monotonous work or by the lack of work, to the wiles of the unscrupulous—dance halls where the liquor flowed freely, cheap theaters, "bohemian resorts" that trapped unwary college students, and brothels. From 1880 onward, the Civic Federation of Chicago, the Massachusetts Civil League, and the Watch and Ward Society of Boston pointed to the spread of venereal disease as a result of these far-from-victimless crimes.[19]

The angry sermons of the Reverend Charles H. Parkhurst, a Presbyterian minister and president of the New York Society for the Prevention of Crime, touched off the probing investigations of the Lexow committee and revealed what many citizens knew: that prostitution flourished with the collusion of the police and of the political machines. Indignation ousted Tammany temporarily from power and installed a short-lived reform administration. But spasmodic moral outbursts did not clarify attitudes toward sexual behavior, while proposals to close the brothels got nowhere. Nor did Margaret Sanger's indignant reports. More telling results followed from the fury about white slave rings exposed in newspaper stories, novels, and in the movie *Traffic in Souls* (1913). Gangs that shipped cargoes of girls to bordellos in Panama and South America infuriated voters, whose protests broke up Maurice Van Bever's notorious levee operation in Chicago and led to the federal Mann Act making it an offense to take females across state lines for immoral purposes (1910). On the local level, police sometimes persecuted women in short skirts or transparent gowns or those who openly solicited from doorways. Jail terms and high conviction rates also aimed to discourage. Mechanization, however, restored liberty to favored prostitutes when the discreet telephone replaced older tactics of arrangement.[20]

Local efforts to maintain communal standards of purity early required reinforcement because indecency spread nationwide from remote sources. Lewd pictures and pornographic books might fall into innocent hands, do the work of corruption, anywhere; freedom of the press surely did not extend to these materials. Anthony Comstock, long YMCA agent, and John S. Sumner of the New York Vice Society sought to exclude offensive matter from the mail; and the law of 1873 took a step in that direction. Furthermore, the Watch and Ward Society in Boston and elsewhere maintained a vigilant but inadequate guard against transgressors. The League of American Authors, however, proved no more effective in resistance. In time, Comstock took credit for the seizure of 134,000 pounds of books, 143,000 pounds of printing plates, 5,500 decks of indecent playing cards, 3,150 boxes of contraceptive pills and powders, and 60,300 illegal rubber objects. He also had the Woodhull and Claflin sisters jailed for sending obscene newspapers through the mail.[21]

These matters affected primarily those directly involved and therefore fell within a realm deemed private. Nevertheless, in a fashion not quite understood or articulated, they also bore some relationship to social order because of their connection with family life, in which the community had a stake. Children deserved protection from such as Charles B. Brigham, daguerreotype artist, who used his Sunday school connection to lure little girls into his studio where he took indecent liberties with their persons (1858). So, too, when it came to the welfare of infants unable to protect themselves, only a vague line separated what the government could do from what lay beyond its competence. Abortion, considered akin to murder, partook of a criminal character, although difficult to detect or punish. Public indifference shocked medical crusaders; perfectly respectable and proper women knew all about self-induced abortions or got advice from gypsies, part of a general disregard for human life. The president of the Philadelphia County Medical Society (1870) reflected that the staggering infant mortality figures and the large number of stillbirths could not possibly result from accidental or unavoidable causes, but must be the product of criminal acts by the mother and her abettors. Comstock undertook to destroy New York's most famous abortionist, Madame Restell, who numbered the rich and famous among her clients; she cut her own throat when he tricked her into exposing her trade.[22]

Infanticide raised quite different issues; destitute babies sent to the Chicago poorhouse rarely survived three weeks (1858); and New Yorkers who tucked away their offspring in Madame Parselle's infant boarding house (1868) for a single flat fee until adoption or death, hardly expected ever to see them again. At the foundling hospital on Randall's Island, municipally operated, the mortality rate rose to ninety-six percent in 1889. So, too, the City did nothing for decades while swill milk killed thousands of children (eight thousand in 1858 alone). Not until 1905 did the state affirm the authority of the Board of Health to regulate the whole milkshed.[23]

Attitudes toward gambling suffered from ambivalence. A nation prone to risk-taking rewarded those willing to take a chance—Diamond Jim Brady and Bet-A-Million Gates, for instance. Investments in the hazards of the unknown, as in railroads and factories, earned great returns and attendant social esteem. Yet those who allowed the frenzy of speculation to get the best of them plunged to their ruin and dragged others along with them. Repeatedly, in the midst of booms, moralists warned that "the greatest land speculation in history" could not go on forever. The day of reckoning approached, when inflated values would collapse, as indeed they did. It did no good. Every crash taught the same unlearned lesson. A society given to speculation and risk-taking sought—not always successfully—to distinguish investment in productive enterprises from taking chances on the turn of a card or the cast of the dice. Yet the hint of admiration that tinged the condemnation in 1919, when gamblers corrupted the Chicago White Sox in the World Series, reflected conflicting attitudes. More characteristically, Arnold Rothstein would bet on anything, on horses, on ball games, elections, fights—on anything but the weather, which he conceded he could not fix. In the cities, even in the nation's capital, gambling houses offered players poker, faro, and keno with scarcely a need for concealment; and the numbers game involved thousands who staked as little as three cents in a network linked to a central office by telegraph. Over in the tenderloin on New York's West Side, amid the dance halls and peep shows, the venturesome could play any game.[24]

The madness spread to smaller places without the cloak of business. Hotels, markets, riverboats, and railroad cars abounded with sharpers playing with shinplasters, dice and chuck-a-luck; and many towns had their share of discreet houses given over to various forms of excitement. Bogus lotteries long remained impervious to prosecution and publicity. Newspaper exposés of J. M. Patee's swindlings only attracted additional customers until the federal government shut him down for violating the postal laws by sending his nefarious circulars through the mail. The cautionary career of the villainous Harvey Green in *Ten Nights in a Bar-Room* showed the insidious effects on everyone. Certainly numerous statutes in California and elsewhere forbade these activities; but only rarely did officials enforce the law. More often the police and the gamblers worked hand in hand, for their mutual profit. Those gentry did not differ from the quacks selling worthless nostrums, the medical colleges that covered up shady activities, the bankers who milked their clients with untrustworthy claims, the jewelers who sold gullible customers shards of glass instead of diamonds. And in some places, as in Nevada, "the lawyer, the editor, the banker, the chief desperado, the chief gambler, and the saloonkeeper, occupied the same level in society, and it was the highest."[25]

In the face of abounding evil, the struggle to achieve goodness needed help, and above all, the sanctions of religion. The wrongs—sins as well as crimes—offended not only the civil codes but also the moral injunctions of inherited faith, often identified in the United States with Americanism; it made sense therefore to expect clerical support. The time had certainly come, wrote Walt Whitman (1872), "to discharge the idea of religion," from "mere ecclesiasticism," to consign it to democracy en masse, in a country in which history and humanity seemed to culminate. His own poems, he hoped, would plant the seeds of a greater religion, regarded by ever more Americans not as a body of dogma but as a rule of conduct focused on ethics, not theology. The fatherhood of God and the brotherhood of man formed their simple creed.[26]

Not everyone wanted an activist faith; and in a pluralistic society, churches supplied a variety of needs, accommodated by the multiplying sects. For the bereaved, they provided means of expression for deprivation, commemoration, and continuity. They also offered consolation, and recompense in the hereafter for earthly sorrows. Various Adventists and millenarians meanwhile anticipated an early providential solution to all mundane problems. Ellen Gould Harmon (born 1827) had heard William Miller preach on Christ's return to earth, and in 1844 began to receive visions that continued until her death in 1915. She and her husband, James Springer White, became itinerant ministers but established headquarters in Battle Creek, Michigan. Known after 1860 as Seventh Day Adventists, the couple developed health institutions, colleges, and missions, especially in the cities. She provided constant contact with God, urging spiritual preparation for the ultimate end of the world by individual temperance and self-control.

Charles Taze Russell, the first president of the Watch Tower Bible and Tract Society, had followed George Storrs, who taught that those who had died without knowledge of Christ would receive an opportunity to learn of his sacrifice for them after an earthly resurrection, and if faithful would earn the gift of everlasting life in a restored paradise on earth. The idea of Christ's ransom, atonement, and the return of mankind to a paradise on earth attracted Russell, who argued that those dying in the Lord from 1878 onward would have immediate heavenly resurrection rather than sleeping in their graves. He did not at first consider himself a prophet or divinely inspired, but in time assumed the mantle under his wife's pressure. Bitterly attacked by the press, the Jehovah's Witnesses steadily gained strength and resisted the war in 1917.[27]

By contrast, conservatives fearful of social change sought to exclude all traces of millenarianism and enthusiasm from worship. Recognizing that the American Revolution had undermined the sense of hierarchy and authority, they turned to the Scriptures to learn how to live and what to do, trying to keep apart the religious and the social.[28]

But persistent if inchoate calls for ethical enthusiasm reverberated everywhere. The perilous experiment of American liberty, with its breaking up and passing away of old creeds and usages (1857), touched off the quest for religion. The United States, ran the complaints, lacked "genuine fountains of fervid beliefs" from which moral results could flow. Its churches and pulpits existed not by solid conviction, but by a "sort of tacit, supercilious, scornful sufferance." Few spoke openly—none officially—against them. But powerful, soul-shattering belief had utterly departed from people's minds. They lacked something greater than all the science and poems of the world: "the intuitive blending of divine love and faith in a human emotional character—blending for all, for the unlearn'd, the common, and the poor." Instead, the flaccid notion prevailed that "if men would only devote themselves to doing good, they would remove all the sufferings of the world." Service to humanity or the development of ethical systems replaced adherence to creeds and formularies of devotion. Some critics worried about the assumption that people would continue to behave unselfishly when they had forgotten the religious grounds for self-denial. Could a philanthropy that rested on no moral sanction contribute to social progress, particularly "a weak and sentimental pseudophilanthropy" that looked upon criminals as heroes?

Others argued that the state had no right to punish offenders, since all restrictive laws encroached on human liberty, with wrongdoers regarded as victims of unfortunate environments. To control the disturbing and divisive forces of brutish selfishness and irrational self-will, the state needed the power of educating its citizens and the right to threaten and to inflict punishment. Men would not recognize an absolute law, without an absolute lawgiver or an eternal right.[29]

Nevertheless, without creedal subtleties, only as a matter of common sense, many Americans felt a religious imperative to meliorate social problems. "I was wondering as I sat there under the gallery," asked a jobless printer, "if what you call following Jesus is the same thing as what He taught. What did He mean when He said, 'Follow me'? . . . What do you Christians mean by following the steps of Jesus? . . . What do you mean when you sing, 'I'll go with Him, with Him all the way'? Do you mean that you are suffering and denying yourselves and trying to save lost, suffering humanity just as I understand Jesus did?" The challenge stirred the little story's thousands of readers. Already in 1871 Joseph Cook, in Lynn, Massachusetts, had struggled to apply practical Christianity to industrial conditions. Within the next decade the Salvation Army appeared in the New World, speaking and singing on street corners.[30]

The social gospel drew support from many elements, but more particularly from preachers attracted less by the rituals and consolatory functions of the churches than by the prospect of bettering the world. Drawing upon the Lutheran tradition, Walter Rauschenbusch, unwilling to wait for the remote Kingdom of God in the afterlife, insisted on seeking it in the present. He called on "the mighty spirit of Christ" to battle "on a gigantic scale" the sin that pervaded the nation. He also attacked inequality in the distribution of property. Men abjectly dependent for the very chance of work were not free. The church, involved in politics, would ask nothing for itself but "demand protection for the moral safety of the people." From quite different points of departure, the Catholics John A. Ryan and Edward McGlynn did the same, as did Cyrus Adler's Ethical Culture Society. The Congregationalist Washington Gladden exposed the hollow right to contract with a great corporation; individuals could make their voices heard only through collective bargaining by their unions (1911). Like Lyman Abbott and Richard T. Ely, he called for industrial partnerships, as an economic expression of human brotherhood and as recognition of the heavy debt to society due from everyone who accumulated property. Workers wanted economic freedom, not the protection of the state or the paternalism of an employer, but industrial

democracy, giving them through collective bargaining a voice in determining their share of the joint product.[31]

The shift of emphasis from the salvation of one soul to social service
for whole communities influenced all the Protestant sects—Methodists,
Baptists, Congregationalists, Presbyterians, and Episcopalians—as well as
Catholics and Jews.

Viewing Chicago, "this ocean of smoke," a critic asked, "Are filth
in the air, and slime underfoot, or dust in the nostrils, indices of enlightenment?" That human swamp seemed to him a city of indifference. But he
erred in concluding that nobody cared. On the contrary, the obligation
to do good drove men and women into numerous movements to improve
the lives of their fellow human beings. With so much to do, the whole
realm of social experience lay open to those who wished to make others
better. Although sometimes related, these endeavors differed among
themselves in methods and intensity. People of all sorts turned to righting
wrongs, as did San Francisco's James King of William, who failed as a
barber and editor before entering a reform career. But in general such
efforts fell into two separate though related categories: those moved by
emotions and those moved by science.[32]

Often, the felt wish to do good extended movements initiated earlier
in the century. The missionary impulse attracted orthodox Christians
convinced of the inerrancy of the Bible and devoted to converting the
unenlightened in remote parts of the world—to knock the daylight into
China (1857), for instance. But increasingly among such people, awareness spread of the misery in the darkness close to home. Charles Stelzle
found work enough in the Bowery; and the Judsons in the 1870s formed
the Brotherhood of the Kingdom in downtown New York, an effort that
later spread nationwide. The Episcopal Church Association for the Advancement of the Interests of Labor addressed a wide array of reform
concerns.[33]

Emotion suffused people of conscience who contemplated the immense task before them—the millions on the spot waiting for redemption, the millions more around the globe in need of the succor Americans
could give "unless devitalized by alcohol and tobacco." Again and again
the readers of popular sentimental novels learned of the redemptive
power of a pure child's death—Little Eve, Mary Morgan, and many
others—which demonstrated the general need for preparatory purity.
Converts to spiritualism like Abby Ann Judson (1890) heard the same
eloquent message from their departed dear ones, which made them understand their own unworthiness to impose on others restrictions they did

not impose upon themselves. And that inadequacy conveyed a sense of the believers' immense delinquency. Overwhelmed by their own sinfulness, they surrendered to the call of revivalist preachers, no longer in the fields and forest clearings but after 1857 increasingly in great, highly organized urban crusades, brought to a pitch of intensity by the dramatic staging of Ira Sankey and Dwight L. Moody and by Billy Sunday's histrionics. Moody held in silent attention some of the largest assemblies addressed in America. His Philadelphia campaign (1875–76), six months in preparation, daily attracted twelve thousand persons crowded into a freight depot donated by John Wanamaker. The New York campaign (1876), sponsored by J. Pierpont Morgan and Cornelius Vanderbilt, Jr., in Barnum's great Roman hippodrome, convinced *The New York Times* that the drunken had become sober, the vicious virtuous, the worldly and self-seeking unselfish, the ignoble noble, and the impure pure. Moody's simple message: We are a bad lot by nature, blinded by the devil. "The first man born of woman was a murderer. Sin leaped into the world full grown." Repeated warnings from less theatrical clerics that unnatural excitement produced a great crop of rascalities went unheeded.[34]

Ever more often the same emotional wish to be good, to do good, attracted support for the preachers of the social gospel. Horace Bushnell explained that the Civil War had freed the United States to play its millennial role by forging a sacredly heroic, providentially tragic unity that converted the sense of nationality into a kind of religion. Josiah Strong's *Our Country* called attention to the universal American mission of redemption at home and abroad, and animated the formation of the Federal Council of the Churches of Christ in America (1905), joined within a few years by thirty-three sects. Under the influence of John A. Ryan, the Bishop's Program for Social Reconstruction launched a parallel Catholic effort. A separate though related messianic impulse drew others to socialism and anarchism, not out of scientific persuasion but out of spiritual longing for an alternative world free of oppressive exploitation.[35]

Again and again Americans sought some total solution to their ills. They subscribed to such general statements of ultimate benevolence as those formulated for the Universal Peace Union (1866) or the later foundations directed toward ending battlefield carnage established by Edwin Ginn and Andrew Carnegie (1910). But happy pacifist intentions had little impact on events in the Crimea and South Africa, or on the conflict that tore the nation apart in 1861, or on the splendid little war that in 1898 engaged the United States in Cuba. So, too, environmental faith in the redemptive power of green spaces, of parks drawing together all classes, with a common purpose, each individual adding to the pleasure of all, had little relation to the actuality of plans dominated by carriageways for the well-to-do, although the fresh air and openness benefited many. The influence of German reformers and planners, the desire to lure working people away from saloons and their children into orderly playgrounds, the argument that contact with nature would prevent mental disorders and counteract materialistic tendencies, the attractiveness of the impulse to the primitive, all made nature a source of spiritual truth and beauty.[36]

More important were the intimate, narrower undertakings with a direct bearing on everyday life. London's Toynbee Hall inspired some troubled and rebellious young people, often women who escaped the prescribed roles of dutiful daughter and, in time, obliging maiden aunt, by helping the slum dwellers, as Jane Addams and Lillian Wald did. Settlement workers meant well—"white mice," the people called them—misguided busybodies, so starched and clean, with their notebooks and all, pry, pry, pry, asking insulting questions and given to condescension, but also ready to aid the hungry. Agents of the charitable aid societies suffered from the same faults, wanting to change people, understanding little, but able to help—at least until various municipal boards and commissions took over the task after 1880, along with more rigid professional social workers.[37]

Reformers who sought to alter long-standing habits encountered bitter opposition, however benevolent their intentions. The battle over some issues reached back well before 1850 and extended on into the twentieth century. Enforcement of the old laws governing Sabbath behavior now garnered secular as well as religious support. Statutes forbidding Sunday work not only sustained the Old Testament commandment, but also provided a regular day of rest devoted to religious contemplation. Yet already before the Civil War large cities like Chicago confronted ingrained differences in habits. With one-third of the residents Yankees loyal to the old blue laws and another third Germans who used the time off not for devotion but for relaxation in the beer garden or park, an imposed uniformity of attitudes lay out of reach. Only mutual toleration made civic peace possible. The inherited legislation remained on the books, its severity tempered by corrupt police who learned to look the other way.[38]

Success more visibly crowned the temperance crusade, although difficulties of enforcement there, too, drained victory of satisfaction. From early in the nineteenth century, reformers had made the evil effects of indulgence in alcoholic beverages amply familiar. Yet the efforts at persuasion failed. The urgings of redeemed drunkards from hundreds of lecture platforms, reinforced by thousands of tracts, periodicals, and sermons, had persuaded many voluntarily to take the pledge of total abstinence but had nevertheless somehow failed to limit the consumption of intoxicating beverages. General U. S. Grant considered his alcoholism a sign of moral weakness that he struggled to overcome, not always successfully; and many shared his plight. The reverend and learned president of Indiana University forced to resign because of drunkenness and lewdness illustrated the peril. Nor had licensing laws and restrictions on the conditions of sale helped. Gary, Indiana, in 1910 supported 210 saloons, one for every hundred in its population, and the $50,712 in license fees they paid formed a substantial part of the municipal budget.[39]

The focus of agitation early shifted from moral suasion to compulsion. Neal Dow, mayor of Portland, secured the enactment of the Maine Law (1851)—total prohibition; and twelve other states followed in the next five years, hoping to overcome by force of law the difficulty of reforming individuals by persuading them to be free. *Death by Inebriety on Van Buren Street:* Edward Miles discovered two lodgers (each shared a bed with four others) dead from an overdose of whiskey taken to help them sleep.

Legislation would eliminate the evil influence of the grog shop. Bitter opposition inflamed political passions and influenced party alignments so that often local option provided the only escape, with wet and dry communities existing uneasily side by side. The traditional jolly innkeeper had become the vicious saloonkeeper corrupting the community, as *Ten Nights in a Bar-Room* explained. The village, once an idyllic, orderly place of satisfied families guided by a benevolent squire, fell into disarray, with everyone corrupted by the tavern's influence. The owner, once a good, hard-working miller, yielded to the desire for gain which corrupted first him and then the rest of the community. His downfall followed. Yet his ambition was precisely the impulse that led some people west and gave others the capacity to create new economic forms.[40]

Those who would not compromise took direct action, as when the ladies of Mansfield, Ohio (1857), or the citizens in Greencastle, Indiana, destroyed every liquor shop in town (1859). Licensing having failed to check the evil, zealots hoped that legislative prohibition could control people's habits. The Prohibition party made a local appearance in 1866 and slowly moved to a national organization that asserted itself in the 1880s. Ethnic and ideological elements shaped divisions over the issue, with Yankees in favor and Germans and Irish opposed to controls. Political debate also arrayed those who argued that no civil power had the right to say what others could eat or drink and that only education could promote order, virtue, and sobriety, against the simple, emotional cry of fanatical ultraists: "Thousands are falling. Your sons are not safe!"

The Prohibition party, however, failed to attract voters loyal to traditional political affiliations. Many fought intemperance through the Anti-Saloon League, which in 1916 made an all-out effort to elect only dry members to Congress and won enough support to have the prohibition amendment submitted to the states.

The Supreme Court helped when in 1917 it upheld the constitutionality of the Webb Kenyon Law, which granted the states power to prevent the importation of liquor for personal use. The alcoholic content of beer fell to 2.7 percent by weight, and the amount of foodstuffs used in its manufacture declined. Home brew came next, in an effort to prohibit personal consumption. Though some argued that prohibition would decrease federal revenue, that the liquor interests were about to have their property confiscated without just compensation, setting a bad precedent, the drys replied that protection of the health, welfare, morals, and safety of the people took precedence.[41]

Intemperance brought with it a train of other evils, leading its victims into improvidence so that they wasted their resources and impoverished themselves and their families. Many a sigh responded to Henry Clay Work's ballad:

> Father dear father come home with me now!
> Our house is all dark, and mother's been watching since tea—
> With poor brother Benny so sick in her arms
> And no one to help but me.

Or relief at the sign of reformation:

> I'll soon be home mother, don't feel bad—
> I've led the wrong life, I know that you are sad.
> I'll heed your gentle warning
> So I'm home with you tonight.

By 1900, almost every state required temperance instruction in the schools.

The injunctions to thrift and purity in inherited precepts ceased, however, to ring true, acquired a slightly comic tone.

> Waste not, want not is a maxim I would teach
> Let your watchword be dispatch and practice what you preach.
> Do not let your chances like sunbeams pass you by
> For you never miss the water till the well runs dry.

Any good American lass could hold off a marquis or an earl on the stage.

> Then to him the girl did say:
> Stand back villain go your way! Here I will no longer stay.
> You may tempt the upper classes with your villainous
>   demi-tasses,
> But heaven will protect the working girl.[42]

The discrepancies between preachings and practice tended to discredit all efforts to reform morals. The crude and unscrupulous, though effective, pressure tactics of the Anti-Saloon League (1893ff) left smoldering resentments, especially its use of anti-German slogans and its efforts to limit alcohol through the wartime food control law. People grumbled but went along, for the moment at least. Saloonkeepers vainly outdid themselves in patriotism, bought liberty bonds, and removed all traces of alien connections from menus. Chicago Mayor William Hale Thompson earned the nickname "Kaiser Bill" for insufficient zeal. Revulsion would come later.

The spreading use of narcotics, often with the encouragement of physicians, received less attention, although in 1900 the country contained some 250,000 known addicts. Association with the Chinese drew attention to the evils of opium, and some state laws regulated the use of morphine despite the resistance of patent medicine makers. But cocaine, cheaper and more widely accepted, escaped oversight because commercially distributed in popular compounds. Efforts to establish federal control ran up against constitutional barriers; reliance upon the revenue and interstate commerce clauses to tax or regulate sales proved futile when *Hammer* v. *Dagenhart* (1918) denied the power of Congress to limit the interstate shipment of goods made by child labor, therefore also of drugs.[43]

Efforts to manage behavior on scientific medical grounds as yet found little support, although addiction would later fall into the category of mental diseases. A classification (1888) of forms of insanity listed masturbation, but not intoxication or addiction. Personal judgment or common sense also imposed restraint on the reformers. Harvey W. Wiley, who developed the Agriculture Department's Bureau of Chemistry, launched a campaign to bar products containing caffeine. The idea intrigued President Theodore Roosevelt, who invited Wiley to the White House. Wiley, however, blew the opportunity by going on to propose a ban on saccharin, Teddy's favorite sweetener. The more usual moral exhortation against the evil of drugs, as by the Reverend Charles Brent, and muckraking exposés by Samuel Hopkins Adams meshed with other campaigns against cigarettes—coffin nails, little white slavers—without appreciable effect.

Ironically, just when prohibition won its greatest national victory in the enactment of the Eighteenth Amendment and the Volstead Act, the doubts grew into certainty, as in Charlie Chaplin's film *The Pilgrim,* an acid satire on the genteel piety of the religious hypocrite. The intuitive goodness of the social pariah exposed the flaws in the respectable folk of such small towns as Edgar Arlington Robinson and Sherwood Anderson also described. The dishonesty and hypocrisy of the temperance deacon who kept a whiskey bottle in his back pocket provided a bitter commentary on the pretensions to reform.[44]

In the ceaseless battle for goodness, women bore, as expected, a particularly heavy responsibility. Identified as the finer, more sensitive sex, guaranteed respect by the Christian Bible, judged more responsive to faith than men begrimed by involvement in the workaday world, they had long assumed the task of uplifting the degraded and the heathen, whether overseas or in the United States. Dorothea L. Dix had already immersed herself in reform, and others in the 1840s had launched the struggle for political equality.

Many obstacles lined the way. In the 1850s serious debates treated the question of whether St. Paul's injunction that women be silent in the house of God applied to the right to sing in the church choir; and some members talked of resigning their seats in the Nebraska legislature when the lower house passed a bill permitting women to vote. But the legal problems of female citizenship did not prevent women from becoming vigorous pioneer participants in the crusades for abolition, temperance, peace, education, and health reform. Catherine Beecher, one of the architects of the rationale for settling women in their own sphere, also believed that the values they upheld at home qualified them to become the final arbiters of morality. Orphanages, tract societies, homes for the aged and help for widows, and direct relief for the city poor, all reflected the faith that female sensibilities provided the proper alternative to competitive individualism and materialism in the immoral society outside the American home. Support for such activities occupied Mormon, Jewish, and Catholic as well as Protestant ladies—their exemplar Harriet Ryan, a Boston hairdresser who devoted all her earnings to a home she established for incurables.[45]

As the century moved through its second half, other issues generated growing problems. Clearly women enjoyed the rights of citizenship and even of naturalization (1858). But that innocent proposition became susceptible to two divergent implications. One argued that all citizens, male and female, enjoyed natural legal and political equality as individuals, regardless of sex, thus emphasizing personhood rather than gender; the other argued that distinctive attributes required special consideration and increased the value of female civic contributions. In practice the two positions often blended, though based on logically opposed premises. Thus Catherine Beecher, the early advocate of domesticity, argued that "obedience in the family to the 'higher power' held by man" was no more humiliating than obedience to a civil ruler (1872). She emerged as an opponent of female suffrage, while her sister, Harriet Beecher Stowe, wished to have it both ways, demanding legal and political rights for women on the grounds of their special mission as social reformers but also because all humans shared similar responsibilities.[46]

Small steps forward did not require resolution of the basic issue. Jokes about female fashions and about the cost of a lady's dress ceased to seem appropriate. A New York bill allowed women married to drunkards to transact business in their own names. Professor Joseph Henry defended the ability of ladies to take part in philosophical discussions—but it was he, of course, who read the paper written by one of them to the American Association for the Advancement of Science. "A girl fit for These States must be free, capable, dauntless just the same as a boy," wrote Walt Whitman. Although the availability of servants and of labor-saving devices detached some wives from active involvement in running their homes, most took pride in mastery of the household skills, whether considered crafts or domestic science. Harriet Beecher Stowe, who glorified the home as woman's anointed sphere, "more holy than cloister, more saintly and pure than church and altar," knew by her own experience how sharply reality diverged from the ideal, how often the husband proved incompetent to fulfill his role. Her life, as woman, wife, and mother, often conflicted with the portrayals of these functions in her books; but she could afford invalidism and rest cures, escapes beyond the reach of most Americans.

Involvement in the industrial labor force altered perceptions. In the 1860s, a poem still referred to "the naughty-haughty stitching girls" (1869); and some who came in by train complained of indecent hoodlums who stared at them "like great, idiotic, grinning country school boys."

But however discreet and fastidious the operatives remained, they organized, formed unions, went on strike and marched on picket lines, out of some imagined standard of goodness as well as out of self-interest.[47]

Perceptions of self subtly changed along with the willingness to speak out boldly and publicly. The female shoeworkers of Lynn understood their vulnerability, with half-supported wives and girls ready to work at any wage, but nevertheless fought back (1879). Denied admission to the Knights of St. Crispin, they formed their own union, the Daughters of St. Crispin. One young woman who dismissed the pious hypocrisy of Henry Ward Beecher—ignorant, overfed, and overpaid—always thought Eve "entitled to a little more mercy than she received, in consideration of the poor material from which she was made."

Factory work created solidarity among female employees guided not only by issues of gender and by grievances about hours of work and wages, but also by a sense of goodness and fairness. Tough, they formed associations, went on strike, experimented with cooperatives, and often proved more militant than men burdened with families to support. Humanitarian sympathizers like Moses Beach of the *New York Sun* set up protective unions to provide them legal aid; and Grace M. Dodge established working girls' societies to make education available. An outgrowth of one such group, the National Consumer's League long agitated for factory legislation and improved working conditions. But discrepancies in personality and objectives defeated overtures for alliance by the Women's Suffrage Association. Efforts to enter the well-paying skilled trades like cigarmaking and printing failed; entrenched unions limited the entry of any newcomers and saw no reason to share the work with females. On the other hand, Mary E. Kenney, appointed organizer by the American Federation of Labor (1891), successfully unionized laundresses and garment and bindery workers.[48]

Working women at least had the consolation of shared problems and of day-to-day contact with neighbors. Not so the farm wives on isolated homesteads who tried to sleep with their eyes open, out of fear of what they might see in their dreams. Reviewing the day's chores, the wife-mother-housekeeper knew

> If men to such a task were set,
> They'd lock their doors and swear and fret.
>
> . . . .
>
> And say an age were time too short,
> To learn this trade, perfect this art.
> But we must learn a hundred trades

> Without apprenticeship or aids,
> And practice all with equal skill,
> Tis their good pleasure, our good will. (Texas, 1855?)[49]

After 1848, mothers like Cady Stanton, others unmarried like Susan Anthony, altered the terms of the debate. Educated, energetic, and determined, like Frances Willard or Jane Addams, they made careers of reform, in part as a means of self-assertion in a society uneasy with their demands. They enlisted supporters from among leisured women of means, idled by the invention of the sewing machine and other domestic appliances, less occupied with children as family size shrank and boarding schools took over, fearful of neurasthenia worsened by the standard prescribed rest cures, and impatient with crude husbands yet inhibited when it came to affairs with interesting men, able to talk and sing and dance. Commonly such women came from New England and the Mid-Atlantic states and usually had a strong religious background, trained, like Amelia Bloomer, by a truly Christian mother. Native-born Protestants from professional families moved by a strong social conscience, such leaders as Stanton, Anthony, Lucy Stone, Lucretia Mott, and Amelia Bloomer early became involved in church work and other activities outside the home. They, and many like them, needed occupation and outlets for their energy and ability outside the boundaries of domesticity.

The cause of womanhood added meanings to their lives. The wives and daughters of immigrants and blacks, of the working poor and of farmers, did not occupy their time with political issues in the public domain. But the affluent had traditionally been more involved in a church or a charity, in an art or activity. The educated sought a life commensurate with their abilities and wished to do something significant outside the home and family. Not every woman had the luxury of having a Susan B. Anthony to help out. Other cultures that lived by different rules and morals, despite poverty, attracted such people as Vida Scudder, who suspected that the poor led a more real existence than those in her own class. *Gestures of Defiance:* a Sausalito belle and a member of its smart set enter San Francisco's St. Francis Hotel, recline in its luxurious chairs, and begin to smoke cigarettes in violation of the city ordinance. The more earnest, like Florence Kelley, found in the settlement house an escape from a failed marriage, help in arranging care for her three children, and the opening to a long and varied career in doing good. For many educated young women, a stint in the slums became the start of social and political activism—some, like Lois Rantoul or Frances Perkins, enlisting in the battle for temperance and labor reform and other benevolent movements.

The Boston Women's Trade Union League (1903) thus encouraged organization and worked for protective legislation. Other associations, formed initially for self-development and literary activities, entered broad social campaigns. The Chicago Women's Club became an ally of the settlement workers and helped found the legal aid society, the public art association, and the protective agency for families. The General Federation of Women's Clubs (1890) by 1900 had 150,000 members and later claimed to represent a million women.[50]

The campaigns for goodness proceeded on several fronts, not quite distinct from one another but often overlapping and sometimes interlaced with struggles for other improvements. Abolition, emancipation, and the effort to extend the vote to freedmen stimulated the demand for equal rights for women. Stanton made her first speech on behalf of temperance, organized a Sunday school for black children, and helped lobby the New York State legislature for a married women's property act. And she insisted on her own name, not her husband's. "Ask your colored brethren if there is nothing in a name? Why are the slaves nameless unless they take that of their master? Simply because they have no independent existence. They are mere chattels, with no civil or social rights. Even so with women" (1847). This was not quite the case, but Lucy Stone agreed. In 1860 Stanton boldly proclaimed "the prejudice against sex . . . more deeply rooted and more unreasonably maintained than that against color." Her efforts deepened in intensity as the century advanced. On the other hand, dress reform initiated by Amelia Bloomer faded away, as a distraction. Bloomer, temperance crusader, editor of *The Lily,* one of the earliest women's rights journals in the United States, condemned feminine garments as cumbersome, unwholesome, and unsanitary, part of a masculine conspiracy to hamper women's activities. The Turkish pantaloons and knee-length dress she adopted gained national attention. Although ridiculed as immodest, the outfit seemed important to Bloomer, for it drew attention to other issues like education, wider fields of employment, more equitable wages, and the ballot.[51]

Temperance became the preeminent cause after the Civil War, uniting as it did religious impulses and concern with sound family life. Unions for Christian Work, prayer meetings, and periodic crusades manifested concern and culminated (1874) in the Women's Christian Temperance Union, "organized mother love," to wrestle with the demon rum. Its White Ribboners boldly confronted the purveyors of the poison. Frances Willard, their leader, considered temperance the pivotal issue, with the right to vote a means of mobilizing support for eradication of the liquor evil. Moreover, abstinence would encourage workingmen to use their funds advantageously and thus help their families. Hence she participated actively in the Prohibition party in 1882 and in the People's party in 1892, and served for a time as president of the National Council of Women. For her, as for others, the crusade served as a "baptism of power and liberty"; the issue bridged the private and public domains inhabited by womanhood and hence justified their public stand. Their capacity to act and hence their liberty in no way conflicted with female attributes and virtues, preservation of which depended upon defeat of the demon rum that would protect the liberty of all. Few went so far as to emulate the direct action of Carry A. Nation (1900), who believed herself the recipient of heavenly instructions. Singing her favorite temperance song,

> Who hath sorrow? Who hath woe?
> They that dare not answer no;
> They whose feet to sin incline,
> While they tarry at the wine.
>
> . . . .
>
> Touch not, taste not, handle not;
> Drink will make the dark, dark blot.
> Like an adder it will sting,
> And at last to ruin bring
> They who tarry at the drink,

she smashed her way through Wichita, Kansas, saloons, infuriated by pictures of nude women on the walls, their sole purpose to stir up the male animal.

Direct action also took less dramatic but equally effective form, Mark Twain reported. The saloonkeeper had to stand "meekly behind his bar, under the eyes of a great concourse of ladies" better than he and aware of their social superiority, "and hear all the iniquities of his business divulged to the angels above, accompanied by the sharp sting of wishes for his regeneration." Those who considered women powerless ignored decades of self-assertion on the part of an aggrieved group demanding to be heard. Their capacity to act, hence their liberty, though circumscribed when compared with that of some men, found numerous outlets, with temperance the most visible.

The inadequate legal rights of married women, "unjust and subversive of human happiness" (1859), long attracted attention, although corrective legislation appeared only slowly. Slower still was action on an intimate matter close to women's interests, control of their own pregnancy. Abigail Scott Duniway took offense when an Ohio minister called on his colleagues to examine women's responsibility for abortion and infanticide. Regarding enforced maternity as an evil, she publicized incidents like the death of an unwed mother at the Portland Medical Dispensary and fraudulent ads aimed at curing feminine diseases. Influenced by the growing eugenics movement, she even held infanticide sometimes justifiable. One of her novels described a brain-damaged baby whose aunt advocated a sleeping potion to end its misery, implying that the day would come when such children would not live out their years in pain.

Margaret Higgins Sanger, champion of women who had "nothing at which to laugh," never forgot that her tubercular Irish mother had died after bearing eleven children. As a nurse in a New York City hospital, Margaret decided that reformist efforts to relieve the misery about her would fail without enough order in families to control pregnancy. In 1914 she established a birth control league, her slogan "No gods; no masters." Although the Comstock Act of 1873 declared any information about contraception obscene, she set up a clinic and published *What Every Girl Should Know* (1916) and *What Every Mother Should Know* (1917); and she persisted in agitation despite opposition from conservative churches and also from doctrinaire socialists who feared a palliative that would dull revolutionary zeal.[52]

Women fought the battles over alcohol, abortion, property rights, divorce, and civil custody despite their own uncertain political status. For Stanton and Anthony, those causes blended well with wider political objectives. Their efforts to do good became instruments for attaining their salient objective, political rights. A vast campaign took form after the foundation of the American Woman Suffrage Association (1890). Dedication to the cause then covered over internal disagreements and inconsistencies. To the old question of whether the claim to the vote rested on equality to men or differences from them, the answer was: BOTH. Rheta Childe Dorr (1912) "wanted all the freedom, all the opportunity, all the equality there was in the world," to belong to the "human race, not to a ladies' aid society." Yet Anna G. Spencer in 1898 explained that by involvement in education and philanthropy, government entered the area of distinctive feminine training and power and therefore needed the service of women. She thereupon unwittingly recapitulated the views of Catherine Beecher, just as she anticipated the argument of Jane Addams in 1906 that cities had failed as housekeepers because they had not consulted the traditional custodians of domesticity. To advance goodness and liberty society required women's full participation.

The suffrage movement made no effort to resolve the strategic question of whether to campaign on the local or the federal and even international levels. It generated enthusiasm among thousands who canvassed door-to-door and won support among the poor and the working class. After 1910 the drive gained steam not through more effective tactics but through popular acceptance of the vision anticipated by the poet, of equality as an index of government purification. When the populace would rise against "the never-ending audacity of elected persons," and the citizen became the head and ideal, with president, mayor, governor, and what not mere agents for pay, then women would "walk in public processions in the streets, the same as men," and "enter the public assembly and take places the same as the men," be "appealed to by the orators, the same as the men." Carrie Chapman Catt organized the woman suffrage party of greater New York (1909) to reach across class and ethnic boundaries. A ten-month campaign in 1915 enrolled sixty thousand new members, organized thousands of meetings, distributed three million leaflets, and sponsored street dances, religious services, and outdoor concerts. Democratic and Republican national conventions the next year endorsed women's right to vote. Ceaseless agitation brought victory, first in the western states, then in the East, and finally by a constitutional amendment everywhere in the country. Not by coincidence, the Prohibition Amendment came into effect at almost the same time (1919, 1920).[53]

The Seneca Falls Convention (1848) had already formulated a full array of grievances for a generation of female reformers. Although wives in some states had gained the right to hold their own property, they had no legal claim to their earnings or to the custody of their children. Nor could they testify against their husbands in court. Discrimination kept their wages below those of men—even for the same work—and excluded them from the professions. Only Oberlin and some state universities admitted them to higher education until Smith, Vassar, and other institutions provided segregated alternatives to the young ladies' finishing schools. Efforts to wedge open the doors of opportunity made only slow progress.[54]

More general issues also attracted attention. Dramatic portrayals of the conditions of female domestic and factory labor stirred the emotions of well-to-do readers, and a few theorists began to consider the wider social implications. Charlotte Perkins Gilman, great-granddaughter of Lyman Beecher and great-niece of Catherine Beecher and Harriet Beecher Stowe, emerged from the depression that followed her marriage and the birth of a daughter to argue for the professionalization of housework as a step toward economic independence. But however widely read, such proposals had little effect. Nor did Cady Stanton's proposal for defining marriage as a civil contract entered into and dissolved by the simple agreement of the partners prove acceptable at the time, although several states broadened the grounds for separation.[55]

Such reforms left untouched the discontent created by dissolution of the household's unity. Most people's concerns turned about immediate problems, such as loss of the breadwinner's earning power, potentially ruinous to his dependents. The feverish excitement after a train collision revealed the agony of apprehension about the victims' identity (1853). No such uncertainty followed industrial accidents, as when Alexander Brumbach, caught on the belt of a machine in the sugar refinery, had his skull crushed and his face beaten to a pulp (1903). To ease the consequences, foresighted individuals secured insurance if they could afford it; and some fraternal and benevolent associations provided limited benefits. The Metropolitan Life Insurance Company, among others, believed the highest humanity good business and built a sanatorium for its tubercular employees. The expenditure survived a stockholder's challenge when the New York State Supreme Court held that "the enlightened spirit of the age" made such care a duty very much in line with the normal business conduct of corporations. But those palliatives did not satisfy critics who sought workmen's compensation laws. Efforts of the injured or their survivors to sue the employers ran afoul of complex requirements of proof of negligence, and in any case proved expensive and time-consuming.[56]

The blameless victims silently demanded more than the drop of a tear. So young, they engaged not in a game or in a maidenly stroll, but in work to support themselves, parents, brothers, sisters, as was appropriate. The paper told the story—143 dead. Not in some old dilapidated mill, but trapped by fire in the modern Triangle Shirtwaist Factory (March 25, 1911). An accident. Need it have happened? Public outcry led to creation of the New York State Factory Investigating Commission, with Samuel Gompers one of its members. The commission proposed legislation to improve safety and sanitary conditions and more stringent inspection to ensure the health and welfare of workers. The horror also galvanized Rose Schneiderman's unionization efforts.[57]

Earlier, laws had limited the labor of women and children in factories and had forbidden the fabrication of cigars in tenements. Now campaigners for women's rights, labor reformers, socialists, settlement house workers and other crusaders wanted more. Women, worst exploited and lowest paid, deserved special protection in view of their tasks as wives and mothers. Florence Kelley explained the need to offset the burdens of maternity, and Josephine Goldmark supplied Louis D. Brandeis the evidence to demonstrate the health hazards of overwork. Besides, her book *Fatigue and Efficiency* explained that shorter hours would also raise productivity.

Child labor still found defenders who argued that the factory taught industry and punctuality and provided better schooling than homes in disarray and life on the streets. But the proposal to ban by federal legislation the shipment in interstate commerce of articles produced by child labor in excess of eight hours a day (1916) seemed an abuse of power, and the courts held those constraints unconstitutional impairment of the rights of employees to make their own contracts. Since a Pennsylvania decision of 1886, the courts had rejected any such insulting attempts to put the laborer under a legislative tutelage not only degrading but subversive of his privileges as a citizen. Campaigns to circumvent limitations on the protection of women and children continued, however, drawing on the common law tradition that allowed differential treatment for specific incapacities, as in laws prohibiting usury that recognized the helplessness of the borrower at the mercy of the lender.[58]

The growing distance of the workplace from the residence increased the importance of hours. Long days and nights devoted to labor blunted affections and dwarfed the moral nature, leading to neglect of husbands, wives, and children. "Good homes make good workers," wrote Ida Tarbell; the welfare of all, including the capitalists, required well-fed and well-housed employees whose efficiency and stability depended also on reasonable hours on the job, where they could develop a sense of camaraderie and an awareness of the utility of their labor. On the other hand, excessively long days produced a truly toxic fatigue that led to accidents and curtailed productivity. Hence demands for early closing, and the efforts of labor to secure state-by-state enactment of ten-hour laws.[59]

The immense number of youthful vagabonds on city streets and rural roads revealed the consequences of the narrowing ability to meet family expectations. By the end of the century boys made up some three-quarters of the nation's tramps. Staying put, however, did not always help. Benevolent visitors discovered children of five made habitually drunk by mothers to keep them quiet. Charles Loring Brace and the Children's Aid Society had long been at work in New York City and had counterparts elsewhere. But when goals shifted away from making the child a productive family member, toward giving each an equal chance for the future, they increasingly focused on the evil of child labor, calling not merely for limited hours but for prohibition of work by boys and girls under the age of thirteen and also requiring school attendance for at least twelve weeks a year for those between seven and fourteen.

That battle, fought out state by state, gained a signal victory with enactment of such a law in Wisconsin in 1888. But Judge Ben Lindsey's Denver children's court and busy probation officers everywhere revealed that a long way remained to go. Lindsey, refusing to despair, suggested that the whole nation required psychoanalysis, "to bring the art of self knowledge to the American people." He attributed the problems of youth to an "instinctive reaction against our system of taboos, tribal superstitions, intolerance and hypocrisies." Coercion, hostility, and intolerance would surely produce counterdefiance and intolerance. Brutal wardens, the Simon Legrees of the prison system, only degraded and destroyed human beings. In the end he hoped parents would impart to their children "that gift of rational freedom which carries with it its own valid restraints, its sane and cultural preferences and legitimate and healthful aspirations."[60]

The wearisome battle for goodness on front after front produced a longing for general redemption, for some encompassing solution to put all goals within reach. Something had gone wrong in the national spirit, had corrupted the public and its officials; and the ill called for the restoration of power to the people. Each group identified its interests with those of the aggrieved, and ambitious individuals pushed themselves ahead as champions of the oppressed. Decade after decade, discontent focused on the economic grievances of monopoly and money. Men and women who worked hard and lived frugally nevertheless often found themselves destitute while exorbitant rewards went to a few. Discontent mounted and gave protest political form.

Farmers, hard hit when prices entered a disheartening slide after the Civil War, mobilized for cooperation. Oliver H. Kelley, too ambitious to scratch away at the soil, slipped through a variety of ventures in the search for success. Born in Boston (1826), the fifth child of a tailor, he changed jobs and residences frequently, working in Illinois, Iowa, and Minnesota as a clerk, reporter, telegraph operator, farmer, and Indian trader. In 1864 he landed in the Bureau of Agriculture in Washington, and while traveling around conceived the idea of a fraternal association of agriculturists. In 1867 he persuaded six people to join the Grange, which thereupon began a spectacular growth. Signing his letters "yours on the sickle," the indefatigable organizer considered his Patrons of Husbandry the most beneficent and useful secular institution in the country. Patterned after the Masonic order in rituals, secrecy, and mutual benefits, the Grange held impressive initiation ceremonies and admitted women and young people who might thereby feel tempted to stay on the farm, away from precarious urban life. Kelley, however, pressed onward. In 1878 his interests shifted to Florida land speculation and he resigned from the Grange. Alas, his business flyers failed, but the organization he established survived.[61]

Aggrieved urban workers also reached out for power to help themselves. The willingness to admit anyone to membership enabled the Knights of Labor to capture political control of some mill towns. But the order's ranks thinned after the failure of the great strikes of 1877 while the stronger craft unions in the American Federation of Labor stood apart.

Many workers supported Henry George's campaign for the New York mayoralty. George (1839–1897), once a seaman and a journalist, in *Progress and Poverty* (1879) exposed the paradox of want and depression in the midst of technological progress and material abundance. A single tax on the unearned rent received by speculators who held an unnatural monopoly arising from possession of land would relieve the burden on enterprise and make all other government action unnecessary. Otherwise wages and interest would fall, rents rise, the rich become richer, the poor more helpless and hopeless. The unscrupulous would stoke blind popular desires and passions; carnivals of destruction would follow; brute force and wild frenzy would alternate with the lethargy of declining civilization. Industrial depressions, which caused as much waste and suffering as famines or war, like the twinges of shock which preceded paralysis would sweep civilization into that downward path easy to enter and hard to abandon, annihilating liberty.

George's ideas remained amorphous but attractive; mind he considered the instrument by which humans advanced through cooperation in free and equal associations. Occasionally attached to socialist trade unions in New York, he also squinted in the direction of the Democratic party, which he indeed rejoined in 1892 in support of the hard money policies of Grover Cleveland.[62]

Defeat and the decline of the Knights of Labor temporarily ended labor's reach for political power, just as the farmers returned to the arena. Agriculture did well in the closing decades of the century, for interest rates fell and made credit available. At the same time, favorable terms of trade drove down the prices of goods the farmers bought more drastically than those of the products they sold. These happy conditions did not however cheer those who expected more abundant rewards for the painful human sacrifices involved in settlement. The dreary, lonely life in the open space, romanticized by urban dwellers removed from its hardships, cast shadows over all economic developments. Wheat dipped to its low point in 1894, corn in 1896, and cotton in 1898. Returns on tobacco, beef, and sheep told the same dismal story. One-crop areas suffered most. The number of mortgaged holdings climbed, while foreclosed farms depressed land values. Men and women who had hopefully taken on debts saw the future close in about them, their homes at stake, their personal sacrifices going for nought. America had no place for failures.[63]

Blame the grasshoppers who laid thousands of acres waste and even gnawed up the carpets (1857)? Or the rust that blackened the stalks of wheat? No. The fault, as in the past, lay with human adversaries such as nonresident speculators. Now those endangered organized in self-defense. The Granges, by the 1890s, particularly in the older, better-settled parts of the country, had become social associations, inappropriate for vigorous protest. But more energetic Farmers' Alliances spread in a broad band from Kansas northward into the recently settled plains of Minnesota and South Dakota, where the hardships of becoming established made failures disastrous. "God's country," the men had called each new district to which they advanced. (Who else would want it? the women wondered.) Now the dreams turned to dust.

> We've reached the land of hills and stones
> Where all is strewn with buffalo bones.
> We have no wheat, we have no oats,
> We have no corn to feed our shoats;
> Our chickens are so very poor
> They beg for crumbs outside the door,
> We do not live we only stay;
> We are too poor to get away.[64]

Confronting a blank future, many farmers with nothing to lose and nothing to gain, nothing to eat and nothing to wear, formed attentive audiences when glib lawyers, wordy county sales agents, and preachers explained why.

> Here I am stuck and here I must stay
> My money's all gone and I can't get away;
> There's nothing will make a man so hard and profane
> Like starving to death on a government claim.

In the scattered homesteads people isolated from one another through much of the year valued occasions for meetings to discuss common grievances. Seasoned politicians believed farm associations, like those of business and labor, products more "of social hunger than political thought or action" in areas with little communal life, no secret societies, nothing of clubs, scarcely a church social (1891). Farmers' Alliances also mushroomed in the South, gradually spreading eastward from Texas and Arkansas to Georgia and South Carolina, appealing mostly to marginal farmers adversely affected by falling prices and by the competition of new methods. Their experience belied the hackneyed proposition that those who labored in the earth were the chosen people of God, with agriculture "the art of all arts, the science of all sciences, and the life of all life, the true basis of all wealth and of substantial progress." Worsening times convinced many that only group action could sustain them. Membership swelled.[65]

Restless promoters like Charles W. Macune (1851–1940) supplied the leadership for a time. Variously a farmhand, rancher, cattle driver, house painter, physician, lawyer, journalist, and Methodist preacher, Macune drifted through Texas, organizing Alliance lodges. He often discussed cooperation as a solution to agrarian problems. His subtreasury scheme proposed that the federal government help farmers by providing warehouses and loans at low interest so that they could store their crops until prices rose. A flexible currency would allow them to resist unfavorable market fluctuations. With the United States, rather than merchants and bankers, the source of cheap capital, the scheme would end the profits for the few at the expense of the many and transform the social order. Extremes of wealth and poverty would disappear and all wages would rise, while consumers would pay less for needed goods. Middlemen and moneylenders would suffer, and justly so. Such proposals aroused old fears that promiscuous goodness, disregarding constitutional provisions, might give the government new functions "such as making 'good times for the people,' largely by robbing the haves for the benefit of the have nots."[66]

Macune opposed talk of a third party. "Under our system of government, we should not resort to a new political movement to carry out every reform necessary. . . . In partisan politics, the members of our order should participate, not as Alliancemen, but as citizens, because politics is for the citizen" (1887). But the proposal to mobilize government authority on behalf of the farmers required political support, damaged his nonpartisan position, and implied that if neither of the two major parties took up the cause, the Alliance would have to generate its own force.

Alliance members usually held two factors responsible for their plight: the excessive toll taken by middlemen, and the money shortage, which artificially depressed prices. The state could correct both conditions. The railroads—the most visible intermediaries between farm and city—seemed great monopolies able to exact from the little man what rates they wished. Under government ownership, the lines would serve anyone. Fiscal stringency sprang from the power of the money changers. By making money dear, Wall Street controlled railroad rates, cornered agricultural markets, drove down the value of commodities, and undermined popular liberties. The remedy was to increase the supply of currency by eliminating the bankers' control over paper emission and by free coinage of silver. The prohibition of speculation and a system that gave farmers credit against the security of their crops would also help them control the prices they received. They could thus realign the economy in the interest of the whole population.[67]

These objectives called for political power, either, as in the South, through the Democratic party or, as in the West, with the help of independent organizations. Massive Farmer's Alliance activity already produced results in 1888 and 1889, when the organization claimed millions in membership. Then in 1890, the Alliances seized five southern state legislatures and demonstrated notable strength in Kansas, Nebraska, and South Dakota. In addition, they elected about fifty congressmen—suddenly a force to reckon with.

As they gained prominence, the Alliances reached outward, appealing not to self-interest but to goodness. The farmers regarded themselves as *the people* and identified their causes with those of all who labored honestly in a nation that still considered itself close to the soil. They therefore attracted the surviving Knights of Labor. The demand for government ownership of railroads struck a responsive chord among some socialists, although Daniel de Leon and the Socialist Labor party recoiled from collaboration with middle-class landowners. On the other hand, journalists like Milton George and Leonidas Polk, intellectuals, and other reformers outraged by the contrast between farm poverty and capitalist wealth lent their support—Edward Bellamy and Henry Demarest Lloyd, among others. Temperance campaigners who wished to divert the workers' dollars from the saloon to the bakery, and many women's rights and good government advocates impatient with the two major parties, identified their own battles with those of the farmers and enlisted under the banner of reform in a crusade for moral redemption. They thereby created a new core of power.[68]

For six years after 1890 the movement gained strength, animated by a distinctive style that summoned its forces to battle, by nationalism, and by hostility to the existing social order entrenched in the cities. Populists' techniques owed much to religious revivalism. Addressing those enlisting in the crusade, Leonidas Polk said, "I know you are asking today, 'How long will it take?' Not long, because no lie can live forever. How long? . . . Not long, because the arm of the moral universe is long, but it bends toward justice." Tracts like W. H. Harvey's *Coin's Financial School* (1894) and Ignatius Donnelly's *American People's Money* (1895), as well as didactic novels like Donnelly's *Caesar's Column* (1890), delivered a simple message: In the greed of the wicked lay the source of evil, and damnation awaited those who failed to repent, while redemption lay within reach of those who sought it. Borrowing from an earlier political tradition, no longer in style for the major parties, the campaigns recalled the cider barrel days of another generation, with wagon trains, parades, ballads, and songs, in a folksy dialect that drew upon older electioneering tactics. Bands of fiery orators called upon their audiences to save society, their speeches and songs enlivened with biblical phrases, laced with the language of the people.

> O, the farmer is the man who feeds them all!
> The farmer is the man,
> The farmer is the man,
> Buys on credit till the fall;
> Then they take him by the hand,
> And they lead him to the land,
> And the merchant is the man who gets it all.[69]

The rasping voice of the irascible Ben Tillman of South Carolina (1847–1918) laid it on to lawyers, merchants, and blacks. Brutal rhetoric laced his 1894 canvass for the Senate. President Cleveland, he charged, was "either dishonest or the most damnable traitor ever known." "When Judas betrayed Christ, his heart was not blacker than this scoundrel, Cleveland, in deceiving the Democracy. . . . He is an old bag of beef and I am going to Washington with a pitchfork and prod him in his old fat ribs." The pitchfork, a basic farming tool, became the means to attack the vipers who polluted public life; and Tillman supporters took to wearing miniature pitchforks on their lapels. Mary Elizabeth Lease (1853–1933), "the Kansas Pythoness" or "the People's Joan of Arc," warned the bloodhounds of money to beware, while she urged the farmers to raise less corn and more hell, as she herself did. The daughter of an Irish political exile, the mother of four and reared as a Catholic, she gained admission to the Kansas bar in 1885 but preferred oratory to legal practice. In the campaign of 1890 she delivered some hundred and sixty speeches, attacking national inconsistencies. "We wiped out slavery and by our tariff laws and national banks began a system of white wage slavery worse than the first.

Wall Street owns the country," with the common people slaves and monopoly the master. Arrayed against the gigantic octopus of Wall Street, the corporate vultures, stood the horny-handed sons of labor. In Kansas, the Santa Fe Railroad and the loan companies robbed the common people to enrich their masters. "Go home and figure how many paupers you must make" to support the thirty thousand millionaires in the United States. Her opponents perceived "a miserable caricature upon womanhood, hideously ugly in feature and foul of tongue," spouting vulgarity at ten dollars a night, her venomous tongue the only thing marketable about the old harpy. She argued also for women's suffrage, prohibition, evolution, and birth control, and achieved her own climactic liberation by a divorce (1902).[70]

The Populists emphasized America's unique role in human development. Corrupt institutions enabled greedy rulers to control other nations; the United States stood apart, destined for purity, its duty to fulfill the mission of the founding fathers—to ensure liberty and justice for all. The "real wealth of the nation," a North Carolina Populist explained, lay in "the capacity to produce," that is, in land and people, activated by cheap money issued directly by government, which an Alabaman maintained should supersede avaricious bankers and blind nature in the creation of currency. Nurturing the vision of a golden past, Populists turned to the state to reassert American distinctiveness. They had no reasonable doubt that "this race, unless devitalized by alcohol and tobacco," would dispossess the weaker ones, assimilate others, and mold the remainder, until it Anglo-Saxonized humankind.

Existing conditions, however, betrayed the nation's heritage and its promise. In a millennial vision buttressed by Protestant evangelicalism, the believers made out a time when "the great rush and hurry" will have disappeared, with food and space for all, the earth "home for God's children," no longer despised or defrauded by cunning laws and sharp practice. The people themselves would then rule. Beggars would disappear and also crime, war, and murder, for with rivalry and hatred gone, all would live peacefully.

"A man tha'd expict to thrain lobsters to fly in a year is called a loonytic; but a man tha thinks men can be tur-rned into angels be an illiction is called a rayformer an' remains at large," commented Mr. Dooley.[71]

Tom Watson (1856–1922), a red-headed, studious, but undereducated Georgia lawyer attracted by romantic poetry and French history, puzzled it out and everywhere found evidence of treachery. An evangelical persuasion provided appropriate imagery. He invited farmers to contrast the pittance they received for a year's labor with the rewards of fortunate urban residents whose sybaritic life neared retribution. "Belshassar is repeated at every epoch. . . . The pampered Aristocrats will listen to no warning, until Daniel strides into the Hall and the laugh of the voluptuary freezes on the lips of the quaking crowd." Watson also indicted Congress. "Drunken members have reeled about the aisles—a disgrace to the Republic. Drunken speakers have debated great issues on the floor, and in the midst of maudlin ramblings have been heard to ask, 'Mr. Speaker, where was I at?' Useless employees crowd every corridor. Pledged to reform, they have not reformed, pledged to economy, they have not economized, pledged to legislate, they have not legislated."

Farmers responded to these cries. To suffer from the winter's blizzards and the summer's heat, never to glimpse other folk in the loneliness of the Great Plains, always to stifle in the crowded tenant's shack of the South, then to lose all to plagues or insects—that was the lot of the tiller of the soil.

> De merchant got half de cotton,
> De boll weevil got de res'.

The life of ease, the unconfined luxury of the gilded mansions, depended on wealth drawn from the labor of others. So Farmer Stebbins discovered on the Bowery; so it always was. Cheats! No surprise that the fleshpots of Babylon tempted young men and women who deserted their families to go off to the metropolis.[72]

Corruption of the Republic—not the people's fault! The bloated plutocrats who had engrossed the nation's wealth bore the guilt. Their grip on all aspects of life threatened, unless loosened, to subject the entire country to their will. Like the "profligate nobles" of prerevolutionary France, who sneered contemptuously at Rousseau's social contract, then suffered when the second edition "was bound in their skins," the Americans also would face retribution—thus Tom Watson citing Carlyle (1892). The common men and women—in whom a divine spark dwelt—could solve every difficulty by taking control through the direct election of senators, the primary, cooperatives, and government ownership, thus regaining their capacity to act.

Farmers unable to contend with high-interest loans grasped at a simple though imaginary explanation of the means by which the few subjugated the many. The plutocrats gained power through an insidious conspiracy of international bankers—particularly the British and the Jews—who mastered the whole economy by manipulating money. The gold standard enabled them to raise and lower prices, to create trusts, and to oppress the toilers of field and factory as well as honest small business-men. A revived democracy that restored power to the people would counter the threat and save the nation's heritage of liberty. The "vast streaming endless swarms . . . marching noiselessly as shades to unavoid-able and everlasting misery" could escape not by revolution—"a crawling silent beast . . . with bloodshot, glaring eyes, and tense drawn limbs of steel, ready for the fatal spring"—but by goodness through the state's philanthropic action.[73]

Local success emboldened the reformers in 1892 to reach for national power. The existing political organizations offered no genuine choice, with the Democrat Grover Cleveland and the Republican Benjamin Harrison unresponsive to demands by the Farmers' Alliance. Only a new third party would suffice. The People's party that year nominated for the presidency James B. Weaver of Iowa (1833–1912). One of thirteen children, he had slipped into the practice of law after a desultory educa-tion. Hostility to slavery drew him into the Civil War, from which he emerged a brigadier general. A devout Methodist and an ardent prohibi-tionist, he refused to play the political game with Republican leaders; and sympathy with hard-pressed farmers and laborers led him into the Green-back party, on whose ticket he ran for the presidency in 1880 after serving in Congress. The 1892 Populist platform, adopted as "women shrieked and wept, men embraced and kissed their neighbors, locked arms, marched back and forth and leaped upon tables and chairs in ecstasy of their delirium," voiced the objectives of the aggrieved, promising unlim-ited coinage of silver and gold at a ratio of sixteen to one to constitute a national currency, to ease the burden of debt, and to raise miners' prices. Some restriction of immigration, controls over strikebreaking detective agencies, and the eight-hour day on government projects sought to attract labor, while nationalization of railroad, telegraph, and telephone lines, a graduated income tax, and postal savings banks would undermine mo-nopolies. A single term for the president, direct election of senators, and the initiative, referendum, and recall would restore the people's control over politics. Considering the Populists the new abolitionists, the capital-ists the old planters, Weaver's campaign aimed to overthrow the oligar-chy and expand liberty through the wise employment of sovereign political authority for everyone's benefit. Campaign clubs, parades and rallies, glee clubs, bands and firework displays, as well as farmers' proces-sions along with their wagons and buttons with the motto "One Country and one Flag, Equal rights to all, special privileges to none," loosened the bonds that tied voters to the two major alignments. The Democrats won, but Weaver gained a respectable vote and took twenty-two places in the electoral college, showing particular strength in the Great Plains, the silver states, and the South. Populist prospects for the future seemed excellent.[74]

In the next four years, national attention focused on fiscal problems. The Sherman Silver Purchase Act (1890) had directed the Treasury to buy four and a half million ounces of silver monthly in order to maintain parity with gold. Since the prohibitory rates of the McKinley Tariff at about the same time lowered customs receipts, the nation's gold supply drained away. By 1891, silver worth only 84.76 cents as bullion commanded one dollar in gold from the government. Whoever could, profited from the spread by paying silver into the Treasury and drawing out gold. Depressed federal revenues after the panic of 1893 along with hoarding and withdrawals to Europe produced a crisis. Operating within an international economy, Americans could not alone sustain the use of silver as money. Only international bimetalism could have saved the situation, and the Brussels Monetary Conference (1893) rejected that course. Since the United States paid out valuable gold for the silver no one else wanted, its net reserve dropped from more than $190 million in 1890 to less than $65 million in 1894. President Cleveland in 1893 persuaded Congress to repeal the Silver Purchase Act; but his efforts to replenish the reserve failed until a syndicate led by J. P. Morgan, at a handsome profit, took a large issue of bonds for gold bullion, half of it drawn from overseas.[75]

Farmers, debtors, speculators, and silver miners eager for inflation then brought the struggle over monetary policy to a head; Populists urged the great free nation of industrious, enterprising citizens to undo the wrong inflicted by monopolists and end the injustice and inhumanity that pervaded the cities and profited only merchants, creditors, professionals, and other recipients of fixed incomes. But voters rarely aligned themselves solely by a simple calculation of interests, and many rejected the evangelical millenarianism of Populism. People supported or opposed a stable currency in the light of their total attitude to the economic and social system, of their own definitions of the capacity to act. In Nebraska, agrarian Populists confronted antiprohibition Democrats and Presbyterian or Episcopalian Republicans, while in Georgia blacks disappointed the People's party by casting their ballots for the old-line organization. And some voters evaded the choice entirely through refuge in the anti-Catholic American Protective Association, which enrolled almost a million members by 1896, recalling the Know-Nothing pattern of forty years earlier.[76]

In the congressional elections of 1894 the Populists made notable gains, electing six senators and seven representatives. However the major parties adopted some reforms and for the sake of victory threw out feelers for fusion. Committed Populists resisted the temptation, knowing that coalition would sound the death knell of their own organization. They still hoped that enough aggrieved voters would turn against any gold candidate, either Republican or Democrat, to sweep the third party into national office. In Texas, popular grievances brought confidence; and in Oklahoma Populists enjoyed the support of twenty-one newspapers, while the "Enid Railroad War" touched off by differences with the Rock Island substantiated warnings of arbitrary government. Drought, debt, and poverty made many sure of victory.

But the prospect of capturing the presidency in 1896 created irresistible pressure for alliance among middle-of-the-roaders. The Republicans rejected the bait of coalition. Their convention, carefully manipulated by Marcus A. Hanna, the Ohio coal and oil millionaire, nominated William McKinley and ratified a plank opposing any measure to debase the currency. The Democrats, unwilling to defend Cleveland's unpopular administration, repudiated the bond sale to the bankers and demanded stronger antitrust legislation. But William Jennings Bryan of Nebraska overshadowed other considerations when he roused the delegates with the religious imagery of his Cross of Gold speech, unleashing a wave of emotion at the reminder of the people's martyrdom. No matter what other countries did, "You shall not press down upon the brow of labor this crown of thorns, you shall not crucify mankind upon a cross of gold." The platform took an unequivocal stand in favor of the free and unlimited coinage of silver at a ratio of sixteen to one with gold and Bryan secured the nomination, although accepting a respectable banker as his running mate.[77]

The choice boxed in the Populists. In Texas the local People's party leaders rejected fusion. "Bryan means death," said a telegram from Dallas County, while one delegate avowed that he "would not go to heaven" if he "had to go in Democratic company." A Georgia Populist declared, "If the Savior of mankind himself was nominated by the Democratic Party on a platform of the Ten Commandments, I would vote against him. That is how I feel about the Democratic Party." Yet to have run their own candidate, as some wished, would have divided the silver vote. Accepting Bryan as the head of their ticket, they nominated Tom Watson of Georgia for the vice-presidency as a token of independence.[78]

The issue, clearer to the electorate than in any campaign since 1860, arrayed McKinley against what were considered wild experiments that might hamper industrial development, while his own agenda gave Americans the full dinner pail. Careful organization and ample funds got his message across. Bryan, by contrast, frenetically traversed thousands of miles for scores of speeches to voice the protests of wealth-producing farmers against subjection to the great cities. McKinley's clear victory revealed where the balance of strength now lay. Without support in the industrial regions, alien to Bryan, no candidate could carry the presidency.

The Populists never recovered. They held out for a time in Nebraska and Kansas, but the major parties drew away their strength by appropriating some of their proposals. Traces of influence survived in the South, where many members turned racist in resentful disappointment that instead of cooperating, the blacks had become tools of the Bourbons. Whites of all classes then united to disenfranchise the colored men. Tom Watson, for one, grew more bitter, parochial, and prejudiced as his world plunged hellward, directing his animosity at the Catholics, Jews, socialists, and blacks, who had corrupted the nation.

Everywhere agricultural recovery altered political orientations; the return of prosperity restored most farmers to their Republican loyalties. The silver issue died when discoveries of gold in Alaska and South Africa and more efficient mining and refining methods raised the supply of specie. An improvement in the balance of trade relieved monetary stringency, and the United States formally adhered to the gold standard in 1900. The revolt subsided; and the longing for goodness and the reform impulse moved into other channels less infused with passion, guided by less emotional leaders.[79]

People left out moved toward the IWW, not "I Won't Work," but Industrial Workers of the World, which inherited the inspirational Populist style. The solitary drifters had celebrated a land that's fair and bright,

> Where the handouts grow on bushes
> And you sleep out every night,
> Where the boxcars are all empty,
> And the sun shines every day
> On the birds and the bees and the cigarette trees
> And the lemonade springs where the blue bird sings,
> In the Big Rock Candy Mountains.

Now Big Bill Haywood summoned the migratory laborers, the men in the timber and mining camps, to an apocalyptic future—"God's goin' to set this world on fire, One o' these days!" Soon the rebels would wrest

America's heritage from "the grip of corporation bribery, and tear national legislation from the hands of swollen provincial Dogberries, upstart mushroom tradesmen, an aristocracy of greedy shopkeepers, an abortive spawn of tax-born riches, mountebank money jugglers . . . cowering over their gold, all floating scum-like uppermost."

> No more tradition's chains shall bind us;
> Arise, ye slaves, no more in thrall.
> The earth shall stand on new foundations;
> We have been naught—we shall be All.
> 'Tis the final conflict.
> Let each stand in place
> The Industrial Union
> Shall be the Human Race.

Emma Goldman, transformed into a celebrity upon her release from jail and lionized like a prize fighter, baseball player, matinee idol, or decrepit European aristocrat, poured out the rhetoric in attacks on religion and marriage and in advocacy of free love for women as well as men. Mary Harris ("Mother") Jones summoned the toilers out to battle.

An anarchic vision of one big union to unite the whole working class, for a time, required interpreters in forty-five languages. Pleas for solidarity, combined with violent, direct action in strikes, attracted the lonely and hopeless, terrifying respectable citizens, but staking out no permanent position, nor even suggesting any prospect of advancing goodness. In towns of which no one in New York had ever heard, thousands voted for dangerous doctrines, turning to anarchism as a new faith. "Sick and sickening" disorders of capitalism combined with feelings of sympathy for the "tired and sleeping masses of men," stirred a craving which no existing church satisfied, for it stemmed from "nearness to and sympathy with that most heavy laden and long enduring mass of common toilers." These redefinitions of liberty failed, however, to replace more deeply rooted versions of the capacity to act.[80]

All along, earnest men and women had explored alternative paths toward improvement, not by appeals to sensibility but by reasoned appraisals. Everyone suffered from the universal pangs of avarice, workers and middle-class people alike; but everyone also responded to appeals to trust and fellowship. Journalists and other intellectuals more often than preachers or politicians called attention to the possibility of improving the human condition by the appropriate intercession of government or by other institutional means. Vida Scudder, founder of Boston's Dennison

House, and Jane Addams, of Chicago's Hull House, responded to social disarray not by calls for return to simpler days, but by accepting economic growth and dealing with its maladjustments. The same impulse that transferred individuals from private homes to hospitals and then transformed the function of hospitals from custody of the ill to effecting cures could alleviate other social disorders.[81]

Since the eighteenth century, the states had experimented with the use of prisons not only to incarcerate but to reform wrongdoers, to diminish criminality. The case was even clearer when it came to juveniles. Communities needed some better remedy than to send a ten-year-old boy to jail for petty thieving, there to come into contact with vice and to imbibe a fixed hatred of all organized society (1853). The president of the National Conference of Jewish Charities at the turn of the century demanded elimination of old-fashioned institutions "marked by repression if not atrophy of the impulse to act independently." Decade after decade each new generation of penologists exposed the faults of its predecessor, in a never-ending search for new, more effective techniques out of the unquenchable desire to do good. Americans wished prisons to serve either as communities in which criminals readjusted to social norms, or as schools where they would learn new ways, or as hospitals to cure, or even as self-sustaining businesses, paying their own way. None succeeded, but the absence of alternatives provided the decisive if unarticulated consideration in favor of continuing the search. With any return to eighteenth-century barbarism unthinkable, every glimmer of a new way to handle deviants proved attractive, as it had in the cases of the insane, the orphaned, and the aged.[82]

The hope also persisted, however scant the evidence for it, that more effective compulsion would impose order on the populace. Self-evident needs and the failure of less formal means of control justified a vast expansion of police power. In 1897 the president of the American Bar Association estimated that 90 percent of state legislation rested on police power, which worried contemporaries regarded as a disturbing extension of the active state, for its intervention ranged all the way from expanding the authority of the local Boards of Health to antimargarine laws, the latter, as one judge maintained, because "in a complex society, the tendency necessarily must be toward affirmative exercise of governmental powers."

To advance individuals toward goodness, toward freedom from vice, communities sought to limit people's capacity to act, that is, their liberty. When persuasion did not end intemperance, poverty, and crime, coercion would compel people to behave for their own good and for other people's. Cady Stanton even proposed that the state prevent the physically and mentally handicapped from marrying. Men and women who did horrible things deserved electrocution, according to the chairwoman of the Good Government Club's suffrage literature committee (1911). The force of law had to replace such milder measures as education, workmen's compensation, licensing, and the setting of standards, as in regulation of industrial safety and the hours of labor.[83]

Public health justified the most wide-ranging state activity because of the rapid growth of the nation's population and particularly of its urban sectors. True, objective measurement revealed steady improvement in the factors affecting freedom from disease. In New York City, for instance, the crude death rate per thousand dropped steadily from 31.68 in the decade 1860–69, to 15.0 in the decade 1910–19. Such changes did not cause complacency. Rather, greater sensitivity after midcentury to the sights, odors, and sounds of life on the expanded urban scale heightened the itch to do something. What men and women once tolerated in the unpaved lanes and undrained privies became intolerable in the new setting of growing towns and even more so in the tidy suburbs. Certainly sewers—improvisation would no longer do when wastes had to move long distances for disposal. Volunteer fire companies had already proven their inadequacy; and disastrous conflagrations in Nashville, Chicago, and Boston as well as the San Francisco earthquake showed that densely-crowded, high buildings demanded large professional fire-fighting companies and expensive equipment.[84]

The most vigorous government action at the local level came through efforts to advance public health. Fear created anxiety about the consequences and causes of disease. Matters rarely reached the extreme they did during the outbreak of yellow fever in New Orleans (1858), where survivors barely endured the stench when floods inundated the shallow graves used when the cemeteries ran out of space. In Chicago, epidemics of cholera, typhus, scarlet fever, and diphtheria revealed the inadequacies of the water and sewer systems after 1849, and led to the creation of a board of water commissioners with the approval of the Board of Health. Municipalities always, though rarely successfully, tried to regulate the nuisances created by the mounting heaps of manure and garbage, the inadequacy of sewerage, and the wastes left by butchers' fat, bone boilers, and rag dealers. Quarantine regulations, well-established by 1850, nevertheless led to local clashes, as in the war on Staten Island in 1858.

Municipalities acted directly to meet these demands, as they did also in creating public parks. But responses to other needs varied. Some cities lit up the streets, at first using whale oil. But during the transition to gas and later to electricity, heavy capital investment led to a call on private corporations for illumination. Confusion also marked the response to the need for pure water, clearly related to intestinal disorders. New York City, Philadelphia, and Boston built their own systems of aqueducts and reservoirs, but others allowed regulated profit-making enterprises to do so. Complaints against Croton water (1859) revealed that deficiencies arose in one type as in another.

Each city followed its own course. Nashville borrowed fifty thousand dollars, which it invested in slaves to dig trenches for pipes from the Cumberland River to the hydrants in town, part of the cost made up by the rise in value of the slaves. San Franciscans for a while relied on water brought in sacks from Sausalito Spring, then peddled door-to-door on the backs of mules, one dollar a bucket or more until 1858, when the San Francisco Water Works Company began operations. An attempt at municipal ownership failed at the polls in 1875. Conflicts between supporters of public and private ownership ended only with passage of the Raker Act (1913), granting the city the power and land use needed to ensure its inhabitants a steady supply.

Until 1882 Tucson residents obtained water from private wells or from carriers who sold it for five cents a bucket. Though for the time being water was available for all, a lawsuit in 1885 threatened to split the Anglo community and caused bad feelings among the Mexicans. For centuries, the Santa Cruz flowed unhampered—until more people arrived in the valley. Settlers cut down the mesquite timber and overgrazed the bottomlands, bringing on quick runoffs and floods which lowered the riverbed. In the 1880s, a group of Chinese immigrant truck farmers with high water requirements successfully fended off a lawsuit by Anglos.[85]

Other matters remained marginal, imbued with public interest yet persistently regarded as private. Milk, a necessity of life for infants and dependent upon rural distribution methods, early and demonstrably became hazardous to health. In Chicago (1857) a demand for licensing of milkmen followed the revelation of adulteration, but for a half-century the abuses grew steadily worse. Ineffective policing of private distributers continued until the creation of free milk clinics as private charities.

The publication of *What We Eat* (Boston, 1861) suggested that corrupt politicians subverted food regulation and that consumers protect their dearest rights by mob law. Thomas Hoskins, its author, demanded "government interference to protect the lives and pockets of the public." Professional associations of pharmacologists and others opposed regulation of their disciplines, except insofar as it would destroy the amateur or charlatan. As Americans moved away from blind faith in the common law doctrine of *caveat emptor,* and toward a view that sanctioned and encouraged governmental intervention, courts found reasons to read express warranties into a seller's word, spreading the idea of implied warranty in commercial transactions.

Housing remained entirely the province of entrepreneurial builders, contractors, and developers, who supplied what the market could afford and speedily threw up multiple-family dwellings that provided shelter for vast numbers through the economical use of space. The American homes on which republican citizenship depended turned out small spaces in which human beings could barely exist—crowded together in dark, ill-ventilated rooms, into many of which the sun never entered and in most of which fresh air was unknown. Some observers marveled not that children grew up thieves, drunkards, and prostitutes in these centers of disease, poverty, vice, and crime, but that so many grew up decent and self-respecting. Reformers, shocked at the crowding and consequent disorder, secured laws for the inspection and regulation of tenement houses, and some private experiments with model dwellings cropped up from time to time, like Alfred T. White's in Brooklyn, but proved no equal in efficiency to the New York dumbbell building and its counterparts elsewhere.

Increasingly, slum overcrowding aligned zealous reformers interested in social utility against the property rights of owners interested in profit. In 1866, some fifteen to twenty thousand people lived in cellars in New York City. Get them out, called the physicians. Where shall they go? asked the landlords. A tenement house law the next year satisfied neither party. But the widespread belief in a connection between poor housing and the spread of disease induced some cities to establish minimum standards and provide for regular inspection.[86] Only in 1901 did New York City finally get a new Tenement House Department, proposed much earlier (1884) by a legislative commission chaired by Felix Adler. Zoning began in that city in 1916. The fuel supply suffered even more casual neglect, although vital in the northern winters when scarcity enabled monopolists to exact extortionate prices and deliver short measure at that (1857, 1888).[87]

No clear conceptual line divided activities considered appropriate for direct government operation from those performed for profit, although subject to state regulation, and from those immune from all intervention. One critic attacked enterprises that began by saying, "We know what is good for you better than you know yourself and we are going to make you do it." They violated liberty, which demanded that people "live out their own lives in their own way." The wish for goodness did not justify a Spanish policy of dominion and regulation, which required a coherent set of principles to guide the rule makers. Man born to struggle against nature and others survived only with the aid of societal institutions, explained William Graham Sumner. But those institutions developed historically and led a life of their own, governed by unconscious sentiments that made it useless to discuss state interference as planned social change. Organization produced inequality because some adapted their individual efforts more intelligently than others and an intellectual could do nothing worse than set up some abstract ideal of society and then try to implement it. Sumner and other critics questioned the utility of expanding the state's capacity to act and its consequent restriction of personal liberty.[88]

Usually reformers lacked popular support and depended on an elite bureaucracy without a firm position in the political system yet claiming to act on behalf of the citizen's welfare, thus justifying questionable expansions of government authority. The voters did not always see eye-to-eye with them, even in the absence of direct conflicts of interest. Common sense as well as traditional practices and dissenting advice often ran counter to proposals advocated by the boards of health. Already in 1852 a surgeon at the Massachusetts General Hospital demanded "more rational means" to prevent the spread of disease by modern sanitary reform. The vast majority of people required "a preventive medical police" as well as model dwellings. He asked the medical profession to shape the opinions and practices of those who made the laws relating to public health. Nevertheless, the Anti-Vaccination League (1882) wished to make parental consent a requirement and gained some judicial support. *The Medical Record* (1883) declared compulsory vaccination of infants on immigrant steamers dangerous. The Anti-Vaccination movement became a vehicle to strike back at efforts by the American Medical Association to control licensing. By 1888, Dr. E. B. Foote called vaccination "rape with a venereal taint," while the homeopath Dr. Alice Campbell employed the preventive "varioline" when a smallpox outbreak in the winter of 1893–94 led the Brooklyn commissioner of health to vaccinate all individuals coming in contact with the disease, threatening them with forcible detainment if they did not submit. Dr. Campbell and her supporters formed the Anti-Compulsory Vaccination League, which instituted legal proceedings. In 1894 a local judge ruled that the health department had no right to vaccinate anyone against their will. Individuals sued for damages on the grounds that they had either been quarantined or forcibly vaccinated, while others told of being seized, handcuffed, vaccinated, and made ill, thus losing work time. By 1897 the New York health commissioner declared that the Board of Health had never favored compulsion.

But more generally, the calm assurance of established physicians usually carried conviction in a society increasingly aware of the benefits of modern science. "Public Health is purchasable," proclaimed the New York Board of Health (1915), implying that well-being lay within everyone's reach if only prudently governed. "Within natural limitations, a city can determine its own death rate." Few laymen challenged that confident assertion. Yet the emphasis on dramatic epidemics left untouched the major causes of death in the cities: tuberculosis, pneumonia, and respiratory, enteric, or diarrheic disorders. Often the citizens took matters into their own hands, as did the members of the Newark Dog Poisoners' Association, worried about the spread of rabies. And journalists' exposures of existing deficiencies led the campaigns for a pure food and drug act. Broadening everyone's choices paradoxically depended on limiting people's capacity to act.[89]

The conflicting requirements of rational living under new conditions generated unresolved tensions. The longing for panaceas received expression in some two hundred utopian tracts and proposals, as if escape through fantasy were a proper antidote to reality. Mary Elizabeth Lease's *The Problem of Civilization Solved* (1895) suggested that Caucasian planters and black and yellow tillers of the soil colonize the tropics. William Dean Howells's *Traveler from Altruria* and *Through the Eye of the Needle* exposed some of the contradictions of American civilization, the ideal of physical labor in attractive surroundings a message for the idle rich as well as for the starving poor. Universal suffrage had enabled Altrurians to vote monopoly capitalism out of existence along with the inequality and competition that conflicted with Christian doctrine and the Declaration of Independence. In lovely villages that replaced the teeming cities, the state owned all buildings including homes, and a few daily hours of labor supplied all needs.

King Camp Gillette (1855–1932), a self-made man, having risen from the position of hardware salesman to inventor of the safety razor, called for a revolution against the disease of individualism. To replace capitalism, "the most damnable system ever devised by man or devil," he called for the migration of all Americans to one glorious megalopolis where a single corporation, owned and directed by the people, would control the world's production. Himself associated with such concepts as disposable products, mass production, clever advertising, and planned obsolescence, Gillette called for a gigantic people's corporation to control the world's output of goods and services. Everyone would serve a few years in the labor force organized into huge industrial armies directed by an international bureau. The corporation would end chaos, duplication, and waste, along with the fragmenting, diversified, overspecialized, and confused world of the twentieth century, returning human existence to a comprehensible wholeness. Individuals would live their lives and pass into the great beyond; but the great Corporate Mind would survive through the ages, always absorbing and perfecting itself for the benefit of all the earth's inhabitants.[90]

However titillating such fantasies, the most constructive efforts responded locally to immediate, specific problems. Abstract global theories about cooperatives, communal ownership, and direct democracy, or the future of the proletariat, provided little comfort in confronting death-dealing milk and water, increased transit fares, and the rising costs of bread and coal. A few political leaders spoke directly to these ineluctable issues, and their efforts at goodness expanded local liberties. John Peter Altgeld, for instance, had come to the governor's mansion in Illinois from the bitter poverty of a harsh youth, bringing with him a sympathetic understanding of the underdog. He worried when he studied the state's penal system and when he reviewed the Haymarket Riot convictions. Convinced of the injustice of the trials, he pardoned the surviving anarchists and took labor's part in the great Pullman strike.[91]

Samuel Milton Jones (1846–1904), another self-made man loyal to his origins, had migrated with his parents from Wales in 1849. At the age of ten he went to work to contribute to the family income. The discovery of oil brought him to Pennsylvania in 1865, where he saved enough to get up his own business in Toledo. There he prospered by manufacturing machinery.

In his factory he hung a placard—"Golden Rule"—a reminder of what each ought to do unto others. "For thousands of years men have said, 'self-preservation is the first law of nature,' forgetting that it is a still more important law of nature that you make yourself worth preserving." The answer, the Golden Rule, said to men, "this rule is a double acting rule; it works both ways. It means that you are to do your work as you would want us to do it, if you were in the office and we were in the shop." Jones used no timekeeper but instead installed an eight-hour day, refused to cut wages or employ children, favored trade unions, gave his workers paid vacations, Christmas bonuses, and the opportunity to buy stock, and encouraged a medical insurance plan. The hall, park, and playground he supported all bore the title Golden Rule. In the 1890s he crusaded for a cooperative commonwealth in which the state owned the trusts and operated industry for the benefit of all.

Elected mayor of Toledo in 1897, he brought to government the same principles that had helped him in business. The merit system, the eight-hour day, and decent wages raised the morale of municipal employees. He took clubs away from the police and forbade them to make arrests on suspicion. He gave the people kindergartens, playgrounds, and free concerts and fought the traction company that ran the street railways. The politicians writhed, but Jones kept the support of labor and of the mass of voters and demonstrated the progress possible on the local level.[92]

Goodness also called attention to the backcountry Southern poor whites—dull, shiftless, improvident rednecks and clay-eaters. Their plight attracted Joseph Goldberger, who had spent his earliest years in a tiny Austrian village, then came to New York with his family in 1880. Hard work brought him to medical school and to the United States Public Health Service where he investigated the causes of yellow fever and typhus. In 1914 he began a field investigation into pellagra in the South. He exposed himself yet did not fall ill; not contagious therefore. He noted also that this malady of the poor spared the well-to-do. Suspecting diet as the source of the difficulty, he observed that hospital inmates fell ill, nurses did not. The disease struck older children in orphanages, not babies or the very young. He concluded that some element in milk and fresh food preserved good health. A later generation would use the term *vitamin*. As important as the cure for pellagra, Goldberger called attention to proper diet—a signal as valuable as any achievement in elite modern medicine.[93]

Nevertheless, organized medicine gained steadily in prestige and dramatized the utility of knowledge, that is, of science. Emphasis shifted from the heart to the head and redirected the efforts of reformers away from goodness, that all humans shared, to efficiency, assured by experts. Doubts grew about the benevolent instincts of the people. Never mind those who joined in lynchings or committed murders; consider the cruelty of small-town mobs that poured turpentine on a stray dog to set him on fire. Cowardly, sheeplike beings made a mockery of the very concepts of free will and sacrifice and responded only to coercion.[94]

The successors of Jones and Goldberger therefore ceased to focus on the lovingkindness that eased people's lots and shifted instead to making individuals function better. The culture that shaped the determined effort to apply to the great problems of the economic and social system the best knowledge available determined its success and its limitations. Mary

Foote Henderson bluntly declared the human race ill, anemic, and the world converted by man into a hospital seen and judged through the eyes of the invalid. Her formula promised to reclaim humanity through pure habits and untainted heredity. The men and women of the future would become "the aristocracy of health," ashamed of weak nerves and poor digestion. Herbert Wescott Fisher declared war upon disease through commercial efficiency. "Eleemosynary institutions have been rescuing many lives unfit to survive even in a valley." At the same time, Dr. Luther H. Gulick, author of *The Efficient Life,* dedicated to Theodore Roosevelt, suggested that the savage "had only a moderate control over his purely physical faculties." His limited power of endurance left him helpless in an emergency. The answer was to increase human efficiency while decreasing those periods of depression and low vitality when snap and enthusiasm were absent from daily life. It was the "business" of every citizen "to ascertain" how to do so and comply with the demands.[95]

Faith gone, hope flickers.

In the ambiguous conclusion to *Moby Dick* (1851), Herman Melville vaguely grasped the beginnings of that change.

One seaman escapes total disaster when Ahab wrecks the *Pequod* in the reckless pursuit of a personal goal. Inured to loneliness, Ishmael finds another chance on the *Rachel,* whose captain had lost his own beloved sons.

The novelist did not reveal the consequences of the transition.[96]

VII

REVERIES

OF UNSHACKLED MINDS

THE EVENTS OF THE SECOND HALF of the nineteenth century challenged but did not destroy the inherited faith in progress. The Civil War and Reconstruction showed Americans that they could not solve all problems rationally; and thereafter, industrial, urban, and agricultural expansion created imposing new difficulties. Streaks of pessimism, therefore, surfaced in intellectuals as different from one another as Mark Twain and Henry Adams. Since the Middle Ages, wrote the former, Christianity and civilization had marched hand in hand, "leaving famine and death and desolation in their wake, and other signs of the progress of the human race."[1]

Yet most Americans, of whatever antecedents or status, remained confident. Their republican society had faults, more evident in tenant cabins or tenement slums than in suburban homes. But neither the rebellious nor the content drifted toward conservative traditions, as the would-be aristocrats urged them to. Reform remained possible. In the vague balance sheet that people commonly kept in their minds, the gains outweighed the costs; the depressed neighborhoods of the cities and the difficulties of life on the Great Plains formed but temporary inconveniences on the road to improvement—witness the Hoe printing press and the linotype, the sewing machine, the telephone, and the electric light. True, users had to speak distinctly and not too loudly, with mouth near the transmitter and receiver pressed against the ear, and they had to refrain from eavesdropping on the conversations of others, a new challenge to privacy rights. Still, Alexander Graham Bell had put humanity on the verge of "strange developments in the philosophy of life." Niagara Falls, harnessed to supply electricity for Buffalo (1896), demonstrated men's triumph over nature. The Garden of Eden lay in the past, paradise in the

253

future. Knowledge to some degree offset the penalty that followed the first disobedience by injecting a new power into life and transforming mere innocence, but a passive state without merit or reward, into a positive virtue.[2]

Confidence in the power of reason to answer every important question dissolved both complacency and despair about social and personal difficulties. People who believed that they could solve all problems eagerly faced challenging situations, determined to apply the intellect to society's needs. Science and technology had produced immensely beneficial results. The correct use of intelligence would also show how to improve all the conditions of life. Minds unshackled indulged in the amplest dreams.

The great Philadelphia Centennial Exposition of 1876, a paean to progress, demonstrated the national growth, material and also cultural, in the century since Independence. Visitors left confident that still more impressive results lay ahead. Thoroughgoing environmentalists, they believed that proper training would enable them successfully to overcome every obstacle. Hence many states had displayed, in addition to industrial and agricultural achievements, the evidence of their educational advances. The whole exhibition, "the grandest scene ever exhibited upon earth," drew together "a museum of the arts, a library of knowledge, a convocation of nations, a Babylon of tongues, a Paris of fashion, and a London of business" in the centennial of "the greatest republic which ever existed upon earth." With that national celebration over, the country went "quietly, surely, and confidently to work upon her second century."

The continued popularity of the lecture platform illustrated learning's utility. The Chautauqua movement, after 1874, gave adults who could afford it a variety of extended courses amid the rustic environment of upstate New York; there the National Sunday School Association gathered over one hundred thousand people to view a diagram of Palestine, representing all the interesting points of the holy land. The 1898 season did indeed offer a stellar roster of orators, including Murat Halstead, Jane Addams, and William R. Harper, as well as illustrated talks on mountain climbing, the Klondike, the Weather Bureau, and China. Entertainment by E. P. Ransom (sleight of hand), Jennie Pratt Cobb (plantation melodies), and other musicians eased the burden of classes in psychology, musical theory, oratory, letter writing, and parliamentary law. A wholesome community not given to crazes and fads drew together earnest people interested in philanthropy, education, and religion, but not easily swept away by unthinking emotion. Evening courses in the cities extended learning to those who worked by day. Meanwhile, the spread of public libraries put books within everyone's reach, "the one safe investment," Emerson wrote, from which all could profit.[3]

Increasingly, however, Americans identified education with the formal school system, intended to equip children with the information and skills needed for life. Despite lip service to the ideal of universal instruction, wide variations, as always, marked actuality. The elementary levels lagged after the Civil War despite the reforms initiated earlier in the century by Horace Mann and his followers. The South, particularly slow before 1850, after the war had to accommodate blacks as well as whites and failed both. Hopefully, time would permit a catch-up.

The optimistic intellectual outlook drew support from the impact of science on thought. In the 1880s, Charles S. Peirce reconsidered long-accepted philosophical premises about the nature of knowledge, which, he asserted, emanated not by deductions from abstract or ideal systems, but by encounters with facts and events, that is, by induction from experience.

William James, physician turned philosopher, had before 1890 begun to convert psychology from a cluster of subjective theories into a laboratory science. He realized that the investigator could best understand an organ in terms of its function, which explained its structure and its relationship to the rest of the body—comprehend the eye, for example, by considering it a tool of vision. Then James generalized: the scholar could know all phenomena by the way in which they worked. The insights of Peirce and James suggested that experiments always yielded knowledge. The searcher could discover the truth of a concept from its consequences rather than from the extent to which it matched any abstract proposition. James's widely read books *The Will to Believe* (1897) and *The Varieties of Religious Experience* (1902) related his assumption to the troubling conflict between religion and science. The two, he explained, served different functions, both valid: one providing emotional satisfaction, the other organizing information about the natural world, a distinction that created the outlines of a pluralistic universe in which diverse ideas, attitudes, and cultures coexisted. Never, a younger colleague observed, "was the human mind the master of so many facts and sure of so few principles."[4]

James thereby lessened the impact of the clash between Darwinian evolution and the literal biblical account of the origin of the universe and of humanity's place in it. Scientists ceased to accept the idea of an instantaneous creation designed by God to provide the stage on which people would act out the drama of salvation. Under the new dispensation, the world developed gradually and all creatures stemmed from a blind process of natural selection. The sense of uniqueness and of a known beginning and a known end to history vanished. An animal past reached back through the dim eons of time, prologue to an unpredictable future. While evolution could square with an argument from design, natural selection made chance formative—beyond reconciliation with divine foresight and goodness. Robert Chambers's *Vestiges of Creation,* published with the hope of improving "the knowledge of mankind and through that medium, their happiness," claimed to "connect the natural sciences with the history of creation" without upsetting existing beliefs. Chambers had no doubt that Revelation would square with the new scientific discoveries, just as the Copernican and new geological concepts had. He did not however confront the issue of natural selection.

Darwinism, moreover, bore a still more frightening aspect. With the Bible deemed inaccurate, faith no longer supported any authority, not even that of science. All absolute propositions became questionable, for knowledge itself developed and had validity only within a given, evanescent context. While the old certainties disintegrated, no new ones replaced them. In the United States not merely traditional orthodoxy but the doctrinal basis of all religious belief faced a threat.

The initial reaction of the devout, a frontal attack on the whole theory of evolution, failed to persuade Americans swayed by the practical prestige of science. In vain Francis Bowen, editor of the *North American Review,* argued that Chambers left no need for God. "If there is no need of a bricklayer," Bowen said, "we might as well discard also the brickmaker." Scientists like Asa Gray also criticized Chambers. William Barton Rogers, soon to be first president of the Massachusetts Institute of Technology, debated origins with Louis Agassiz in a more illuminating fashion than the argument at Oxford between Thomas H. Huxley and Samuel Wilberforce. Handsome, impetuous, eloquent but unguarded in his speech, Agassiz got the worst of it.

Controversy paved the way for the acceptance of Darwin. Once concede that two kinds of knowledge coexisted, then a metaphoric reading of the Scriptures and support for the claims of science in the areas of its competence enabled the triumph of the will to believe; use of the telephone and of modern surgery did not conflict with inherited ideas of heaven and hell. Henry Ward Beecher and Lyman Abbott explained from their pulpits that evolution displayed in a new, sublime form the mysterious ways in which God worked his wonders. His hosts in the United States baffled the English agnostic Thomas H. Huxley by assuring him that they would dine once more beyond the grave in that great banquet hall in heaven. The American Institute of Christian Philosophy devoted itself to distributing literature that proved science and religion indeed in accord. The redemptive system of Christianity curbed the mighty tendencies to evil that modern technology and science unwittingly encouraged, and secured the steady progress of human society toward its destined end of blessedness and glory. The pastor of the Central Congregational Church in Brooklyn assured his flock, "the future will have its expanding revelations," which would yet march together with reason to the beat of a common drummer. Professor Charles B. Warring did not doubt that "However much scientists may differ as to the mode of the being and character of God, they unite, with scarcely an exception, in recognizing His existence."[5]

The understanding of knowledge as evolving through experience permitted John Dewey (1859–1952) to reconcile his Hegelian commitment to the dialectic of progress with Darwinian evolution. By emphasizing the connection between truths and their uses, Peirce and James provided him an intellectual foundation for the argument that the constantly changing environment left all statements tentative, all therefore requiring frequent reconsideration. Rethinking education, Dewey rejected the formal curricula that imposed a fixed body of information upon the student. *On the Influence of Darwinism* (1910) and *Democracy and Education* (1916) argued that learning came through doing—through activities related to the external world, with schools a setting for life and not a preparation for future living. They could therefore train their products for social progress and reform in an open, pluralistic world. Secure in reputation and the beneficiary of intimate contacts with numerous figures in public life and in cultural affairs, Dewey enjoyed easy access to the pages of scholarly and educational journals as well as to the broader audiences of *The Dial, The Nation, The New Republic* and *The Independent.*[6]

Pragmatic ideas exerted an influence far beyond philosophic circles; they corresponded with long-term tendencies in American thought and fitted the world outlook of a generation raised on Darwinian controversies. A constantly changing universe gave scope to the creative freedom of intelligence, while the social results provided tests of the validity of experiments. Since the eighteenth century, people who regarded religion as ethics and education as a means of getting ahead accepted practicality as a test of knowledge. Moreover, evolutionary theories suggested that ideas and institutions evolved through time, so that those appropriate in one age lost validity in another. Pragmatic methods justified change and explained how to direct it intelligently. Hence Dewey argued for the "freedom of social inquiry and of distribution of its conclusions," to bring "a desired state of society into existence" by building up a body of knowledge implemented by social planning.[7]

Pragmatism did not propound a homogeneous progressive doctrine or program. The challenge to unite knowledge and action stimulated scientists, technicians, clergymen, and journalists to examine the world about them critically. Each group responded in terms of its own experience and thus contributed its definition of the capacity to act to the meanings of liberty in subsequent years.

Social scientists, increasingly self-confident and aware that they stood apart from philosophers of older schools, sought knowledge to improve the human condition. The influence of American pragmatists meshed with that of Auguste Comte in directing attention away from introspection and imagination and toward observation and analysis. The universities of Chicago (1891) and Wisconsin added significantly to the available resources for research and teaching. The operations of the productive system, once the province of political philosophers, now fell to systematic economists; and Arthur F. Bentley (1908) called for empirical quantitative methods to assess the impact of group pressure and public opinion on politics. President A. Lawrence Lowell of Harvard considered the most difficult and most momentous question of American government that of transmitting individual opinion into public action, and he searched for the psychological forces that led to states of mind eventually translated into statutes and decisions. Older economists, political scientists, and sociologists like Richard T. Ely and Lester Ward found themselves in accord with younger men like John R. Commons, Edward A. Ross, Thorstein Veblen, and J. Allen Smith. Ross spoke for many in rejecting exhortation as a means to reform, preferring to mold the individual into conformity by psychological and sociological techniques.[8]

Classification, the first step in all research, led scientists to sort people out into groups, some inferior to others; to preserve racial superiority, Ross argued, called for "pride of blood and an uncompromising attitude toward" lesser breeds. Madison Grant doubted that improvement lay within the reach of "racial nondescripts." The European governments had unloaded on the United States the sweepings of their jails and asylums, an increasing number of the weak, the broken, and the mentally crippled. These immigrants adopted the language of the American, wore his clothes, stole his name, and began to take his women, but seldom understood his ideals. Intelligence tests, however, provided objective and infallible instruments for arranging individuals in appropriate places. Scholars did not hesitate to predict the approaching moment when intellect would "rise to the mastery over property, and define the relations of the state to the property it protects, as well as the obligations and the limits of the rights of its owners." Democracy in government, brotherhood in society, equality in rights, and universal education foreshadowed the next-higher plane of society that would recreate in a superior form the liberty, equality, and fraternity of the ancient tribes. From her vantage point at Hull House, Jane Addams actively supported the scientific method, arguing that education would somehow advance social progress.[9]

Most social scientists therefore vigorously rejected the idea, sustained by William Graham Sumner, that evolution proceeded by laws beyond human control and that only free competition assured the survival of the fittest. Sumner considered "mores" and group differences immutable, not subject to change "by any artifice." The greatest human folly was "to sit down with a slate and pencil to plan out a new social world." The "overbearing disposition, the greed of gain, the ruthlessness in methods, which are the faults of the master of industry at his worst," would persist were he a functionary of the state. Evolution would enhance the prosperity of all unless nations allowed speculations about the future of civilization and humanity to sway their actions. All human arrangements involved a measure of evil; the true gains came by slow and difficult steps and consisted only in better adjustments of people to circumstances.[10]

More optimistic social scientists held that human will and intelligence could influence development, with education and propaganda shaping opinion in the desired direction. Lester Frank Ward (1841–1913) explained that society suffered from undergovernment, from the failure to keep pace with expanding intellectual resources. Evolution operated not only through "the unconscious forces of nature, but also through conscious and deliberate control by man." Governmental planning, preferably under the aegis of an intelligent social science, would advance the human condition. Sociology mattered "for the purpose of determining in what ways and to what extent social phenomena may, with a knowledge of their laws, be modified and directed toward social ideals. . . . The knowledge is the important thing, the action will then take care of itself."

Since many held deficiencies in the system of production responsible for all social shortcomings, readers took heart when Simon N. Patten demonstrated the adequacy of existing resources to produce an abundance of goods and abolish poverty. Political and social reform would follow. It only remained for science to work out the appropriate mechanisms for distinguishing the universal qualities of man and nature from societal accretions. The process would reveal that everything good resulted from enduring general laws, while everything evil resulted from economic conditions that could be isolated and overcome.

Confident observers thus believed in a peaceable adjustment of the labor problem, and from the 1860s onward made efforts to collect the information about working conditions that would enlighten the public and lead to a solution. Patten's central thesis—the transition from scarcity to abundance and the need for restraints on behavior justified by modern science—won the praise of fellow economists (1892) by providing "a scientific basis of an optimistic faith that is in all of us." Its promoters had earlier formed the American Economic Association (1886) to develop a system of social ethics to restrain the greed of combinations and monopolies through the great collaborative society called the state.

The data social science required could not take the form of impressionistic observations; it could meet the requirements of validity and reliability, as Elizur Wright explained, only if organized with the precision of the actuarial tables on which insurance companies increasingly depended. Statistics therefore crowded the pages of social science.

Statisticians, however, quickly discovered the inadequacy of actual numbers and embarked on a search for more satisfactory modes of measurement. Insurers learned that crude mortality rates could not tell them the odds of an individual's death unless they knew the distribution of the population among various age groups. Price computations exposed a similar problem—how to find an average that would trace the changing relationship of commodities to gold. Ultimately an index number pinned to a specific time provided an abstract reference point against which to measure changes in relative value. Such numbers replaced actual ones in many computations that sought to separate short- from long-term and primary from secondary reactions. Meanwhile mathematicians and logicians explored the usefulness of partial numbers. Charles Saunders Peirce noted the utility of reasoning from samples; and empirically manufacturers of hats and shoes for mass markets learned that a few sizes would fit most heads and feet. A decisive shift came when geneticists dealing with very large quantities began to work out sampling techniques with the aid of the calculus of probability. Ever more often, discussion focused not on specific persons, but on samples and averages, abstractions that crowded men and women into uniform rows—all alike.[11]

The task of diffusing and applying the new scientific knowledge fell to various engineers now identifying themselves in self-conscious professional terms. Improvisation would no longer do. In planning a power plant, Charles Stone and Edwin Webster had to know enough about concrete structures, electrical equipment, and interest rates to predict immediate and long-term cost, utilization, and rate structures. Herbert C. Hoover, a partner of Bewick, Moreing and Company of London, reorganized mines all over the world and then maintained his own consulting offices in London, New York, San Francisco, Petrograd, and Paris. So, too, when it came to the social order. Just as in factories, technicians organized the machines that raised output, so other specialists would use their skills to manage production and staff the law-enforcing regulatory bodies. Lord Bryce noted that Theodore Roosevelt consulted academics on railroad control, meat inspection, immigration, housing, and other problems. Bryce had "never in any country seen a more eager, high minded and efficient set of public servants, men more useful and creditable to their country, than the men doing the work of the American government in Washington and in the field." They could thus reorganize the basic institutions of society. Hence the resentment they evoked. The Chicago meat packer, Thomas E. Wilson, fighting a proposed pure food and drug measure (1906), appealed to a congressional committee "for protection against . . . a bill that will put our business in the hands of theorists, chemists, sociologists, etc. and the management and control taken away from the men who have devoted their lives to the upbuilding and perfecting of this great American industry."

The imperative to know bore as heavily on commercial and civic as upon technological pursuits. The orators at the opening of Bryant and Stratton's commercial college (1858) envisaged a national chain of institutions transmitting specific business skills—far from the traditional education of older institutions. The Connecticut Yankee in King Arthur's court made it clear: "Training—training was everything; training was all there was to a person." Not nature, but society shaped the personality. Twain told his illustrator, "This Yankee of mine has neither the refinement nor the weakness of a college education; he is a perfect ignoramus; he is boss of a machine shop; he can build a locomotive or a Colt's revolver, he can put up and run a telegraph line, but he is an ignoramus nevertheless." In increasing numbers such paraprofessionals joined government and corporate bureaucracies.[12]

To educated progressives, the moral innocence of earlier self-assured reformers, deficient in knowledge, who acted out of goodness and uninformed sympathy, masked a vain desire for power. Their failures revealed the need for method and expertise in dealing with social disorder, and for tax support to replace promiscuous, indiscriminate, voluntary contributions. Trained social workers eagerly shouldered tasks once performed by clergy and voluntary female associations. Women determined to have careers, like Jane Addams and Lillian Wald, found this a satisfactory life's calling. Widespread recognition of social work as a profession generated confidence that scientific rules, properly applied, would correct all social ills.[13]

Progressive ideas also suffused the activities of ministers no longer content with a primarily sacramental or teaching role. Washington Gladden and others, determined to prove the worth of religion by its works, preached the social gospel and directed renewed attention to the poor. Walter Rauschenbusch made reform the central conception of Christianity. Since God constantly perfected his creation, each generation had to find and implement its own divine truth, with the clergy in the vanguard of the revolutionary mission, the living spirits by which new truths entered humanity. Industrialism had destroyed established institutions and traditions but also made possible a more perfect community, burying individual self-interest and establishing the Christian virtues of cooperation, love, and equality.[14] Some clergymen, instead of preaching individual regeneration, actually went down to work in the slums, as Charles Stelzle did, denying that he had abandoned the Gospel in favor of sociology, insisting that he merely reinterpreted the Christian message in workingmen's terms. Stephen S. Wise among the Jews and John A. Ryan among the Catholics spread a similar message outside the Protestant denominations. Ryan calculated that excessive consumption only increased "pride, vanity, waste of time and unsocial feelings of superiority," prevented performance of the works of charity Catholicism demanded, and undermined "the clean, vigorous, healthy lives" for which reformers agitated.[15]

Active journalists enlisted in the cause, out of conviction and out of the awareness that sensational exposés attracted attention, raised circulations, and earned substantial rewards. Henry D. Lloyd's *Wealth against Commonwealth* (1894) and Ida Tarbell's history of Standard Oil (1904) called attention to the misdeeds of big business; while Burton J. Hendrick's story of life insurance (1906) warned potential purchasers of the corruption and speculation that infused those enterprises. *Frank Leslie's* and *Harper's* had early published critical articles. But now *McClure's, Everybody's,* and *Collier's* provided outlets for muckrakers who exposed to public indignation the shady activities of politicians and businessmen. They did so either in fictional form, as did Upton Sinclair, or in reports of careful research and observation like Lincoln Steffens's and Ray S. Baker's. Progressives valued such writings as legitimate levers to steer public opinion along desirable tracks. Dewey respected Hobbes and the utilitarians for their stimulus to a science of human nature operating through social controls on behalf of the common good, a consciously manipulative view then also approaching a peak of development in commercial advertising.[16]

The disparate groups that termed themselves *progressive* did not produce a unified, coherent program except insofar as all assumed the feasibility and desirability of improvement. Sympathy for farmers and industrial workers drew some to populism; others became adherents of socialism of one sort or another. Still others, shaking off party discipline, termed themselves insurgents. But the progressive agenda encompassed remedies for numerous social ills, mingling inherited general reforms with responses to immediate local conditions, without unanimity upon detailed proposals.

Moreover, transatlantic influences kept progressive ideas in ferment. Britain, France, and Germany also faced difficulties in the wake of industrial and urban growth; and theories evoked by their experience and elaborated by their thinkers filtered over to the United States. Americans rarely adopted intact the propositions of Marx or the Fabians, of Auguste Comte or William Morris; but the reactions, critical or uncritical, destroyed complacency and strengthened the determination to act. The influence of the German historical schools and of the imperial government—whether exemplified in Bismarck's social legislation or in urban planning—rippled through the United States, and particularly as carried by Edward A. Ross and others who had studied in Berlin.[17]

Formal education became the necessary instrument for developing and transmitting the knowledge experts required. Critics like Jonathan Baldwin Turner (1853), who wished a curriculum for the people rather than one for the unequal and inordinate culture of the professions, could not prevail against the impulse to develop counterparts of the German universities, where serious scholars pursued advanced studies. Americans eager to supply a firm scientific foundation for the professions sought to cut away from the schools, which devoted their energies to the rudimentary teaching of teenagers. By 1888 admission requirements had become complicated enough to turn holding pens for unruly adolescents into "universities in fact as well as in name." The introduction of the elective system to all Harvard classes required a new mode of preparation for which memorizing orations of Cicero or books of Homer and Xenophon no longer sufficed. Established as graduate institutions, with an explicit intention of avoiding undergraduate instruction, Johns Hopkins and Clark universities aimed to become centers for the disinterested pursuit of knowledge. At Johns Hopkins and its hospital, from the painstaking study of many cases, researchers drew the data on the basis of which they arrived at general formulas for solving problems, for testing and perfecting cures, so that the continuing interplay of science and practice both advanced understanding and helped the patient. What was true in medicine was equally true in other fields of knowledge.

Whatever the intentions of their founders, the graduate universities did not remain a species apart, where the passion for pure knowledge burned without flickering. A Wisconsin University professor complained in 1910 that students strained after the doctorate not to carry forward the gospel of education, but because all "had been reared from babyhood in the atmosphere of the struggle for success." Harvard and Yale among the older colleges and Michigan and California among the state institutions pursued similar objectives; the university became a holding company that simultaneously carried on a variety of different and sometimes contradictory activities. The 1887 Columbia School of Mines admission examination included questions in geometry and algebra, American and English history, bookkeeping, and physics, as well as in French and German. Control rested somewhat incongruously with boards of trustees designated by the state or by the wealthy who contributed financial support and who regarded scientific pursuits and academic freedom with mingled faith and distrust. Ceaseless lobbying and cajoling by harried administrators squeezed the necessary funds from niggardly state legislators representing rural constituencies and from dubious businessmen. The pleas of benefits ran without end, as at the University of Illinois, whose professors of agriculture helped the farmer, whose professors of engineering increased public ease and security by improving building ventilation, and whose professors of chemistry, biology, medicine, and commerce rendered practical services to the state and the nation worth conservatively one hundred million dollars annually. Moreover, while the universities purported to seek knowledge for its own sake, and to develop "unselfishness, loyalty and industry . . . to form a rich cream of social altruism" with education nothing but "an adventure in practical idealism," their stability rested on students' expectation that degrees helped in the race for success. "The ruling passions just now" (1921), complained Nicholas Murray Butler, was "not to know and to understand, but to get ahead," to apply some bit of information or some acquired skill in ways that bring material advantage. College had taken their minds off the true business of education—to prepare to live—and "fixed them upon something which is very subordinate," namely how to make a living.[18]

The university's role remained ambiguous, for it sought to serve society both by training youth and by nurturing science, which ceased to be the avocation of amateurs and became a profession, organized by specialized disciplines and subject to its own rules of inquiry and discovery. Americans regarded science with both hope and fear—hope that knowledge would hasten progress, fear about the unsettling questions it might raise. Academic freedom therefore remained conditional on respect for the social order, as occasional dissidents like Edward A. Ross, Thorstein Veblen, and Scott Nearing discovered. Francis Bowen and John Fiske, who held unorthodox values, received no appointments, for the findings of great research institutions, attached to universities, would pass to the public through the colleges and schools. True, Lester F. Ward had attained his degree by studies at night. But ever more often, a four-year college provided the normal channel for disseminating learning. Harvard's President Charles W. Eliot cogently stated the need: all sorts of quacks and imposters thrived. The astrologer, a rare personage in the Middle Ages, now "advertises in the public newspapers and flourishes as never before." Men and women of all classes "seek advice . . . from clairvoyants, seers, Christian Scientists, mind-cure practitioners . . . and fortune tellers. The ship of state barely escapes from one cyclone of popular folly like the fiat-money delusion or the granger legislation of the seventies, when another blast of ill-informed opinion comes down on it, like the actual legislation which compels the buying and storing of silver by the Government." The university's learning would define the correct answers to all such issues.[19]

The number of such institutions, public and private, multiplied. Their purpose gleamed in the rhetoric: to develop "all the powers and faculties of the human being" (1853); to produce manhood and men, not mushrooms and monks. Yet endless controversy followed efforts to attain the objectives. Chancellor John H. Lathrop's decade of struggle at the University of Wisconsin finally led to his resignation (1858), but the battle continued.

A network of secondary schools received children from elementary grades and prepared young people for institutions of higher learning. Ambitious citizens, however, demanded more, despite problems in fiscal support and qualified instruction. Normal schools after the Prussian model aimed to train teachers, but few states or municipalities provided adequate funds.[20]

In theory, the educational system acted as a filter, sorting out the most talented for service to society. Admitting all children at the lowest grade, the schools, step-by-step, selected those best qualified to advance to the highest level. Practice diverged from that surviving Jeffersonian ideal. The high schools in towns like Decorah, Indiana, offered only a two-year course of studies, so ambitious youngsters like Arthur Patrick Redfield boarded in Indianapolis to prepare for college. Admission to high school generally required completion of an eight-year elementary course, although not all who did so qualified, with the offspring of comfortably-off middle-class parents most likely to get in. In suburban Staten Island, for instance, most young people did not attend. Boys from large families with low incomes preferred to learn a trade and earn their keep. In addition, a high drop-out rate further distorted the schools' task as selectors of future leaders.[21]

Of the graduates, only a minority went on to college. Those willing to pay the costs of tuition and of an expensive life-style passed through institutions that linked their studies with gentlemanly or ladylike behavior—in literary tastes as in athletics, manners, and social intercourse. A durable circle of friends prepared them for elite positions in the professions or for lives of cultivated leisure. Other young men and women acquired useful skills in state or municipal universities, to earn livelihoods in trade or as accountants, pharmacists, engineers, and farmers. For those who could not afford the four years or more such education required, a growing number of junior colleges provided more focused opportunities.[22]

The many meanings of *education* reflected America's social diversity. The free public library, suggested as early as 1851, would offset social differences "by the self-culture that resulted from reading." Cheap publications had by then gradually raised tastes from such poor trash as novels up to the excellent and valuable works of all sorts read by the middling classes everywhere, and in New England even by a majority of the people. Successful businessmen enjoyed the praise of publishers like Freeman Hunt in his *Merchant's Magazine* and in books like *Worth and Wealth* (New York, 1856); and John Jacob Astor, though hardly generous in his lifetime, left five hundred thousand dollars for a library (1848).[23]

That aspiration also moved Andrew Carnegie (born November 25, 1835), who had come with his family in 1848 to Allegheny City, Pennsylvania, from the Scottish village of Dunfermline. Years of hard labor by day and study by night enabled him to move from a job in a cotton factory to a position as private secretary to T. A. Scott, division superintendent of the Pennsylvania Railroad; then Andrew climbed to an executive post when Scott became president, and during the Civil War helped organize the transportation and telegraph systems of the Union armies. At the age of thirty-three, with an annual income of fifty thousand dollars, he considered making no further "effort to increase fortune but spend the surplus each year for benevolent purposes . . . the amassing of wealth is one of the worst species of idolatry—no idol more debasing than the worship of money." However, he perceived the opportunities in steel and in 1885, at the age of fifty, controlled the mines that produced the raw materials, the ships and railroads that carried them, and the fabricating plants that worked them into finished products. Pondering the meaning of his migration and success, he concluded that the vast wealth accumulated through free enterprise posed a danger unless periodically redistributed. A great inheritance encumbered striving and hard work—life's true objects. Those who had earned riches bore the obligation to use them while still alive, devoting as much time to disposing of fortunes as to assembling them. He who dies rich dies disgraced, Carnegie wrote. Shocked at the bitterness of the Homestead strike and anxious to withdraw from business, he sold his assets and systematically gave his wealth away for education, research, and peace. About $56 million went for construction of 2,509 libraries throughout the English-speaking world, including buildings in 1,412 communities in the United States. In all, Carnegie distributed more than $350 million; and his will left most of the residue to public purposes. Similar concerns occupied John D. Rockefeller although not yet on so wide a scale. Both hoped thereby to increase individual mastery of the environment—the extension of knowledge developed human powers by augmenting self-reliance. Although Washington Gladden's *Tainted Money* attacked organizations that accepted ill-gotten gains extorted by industrialists from their workers, the bitter rhetoric did not stay the outstretched hands. Libraries, research, schools, and peace—the chief objects of beneficence—revealed the social concerns of the immensely rich.[24]

Education would help rational citizens apply science to solve their problems. Hence the confidence of Progressives in their ability to implement the reform agenda through their command of knowledge. *The Smart Set,* a magazine of cleverness (1914), announced that one civilized reader was worth a thousand boneheads; and the college grads had no doubt who was who. Professor Edward A. Ross, who flaunted his year's study in Berlin and his Hopkins Ph.D., boasted that the University of Wisconsin stood outside the social system and indeed formed "a most determined enemy of it." His *Social Psychology* undertook to shape the individual into conformity with progressive principles.[25]

His views had much in common with those of practitioners of public relations like Ivy Lee, who considered publicity a means of molding human nature. Commercial advertising had developed the necessary manipulative techniques; as goods flooded the market and as urban life broke down neighborly relations between producers and consumers, merchants had to persuade buyers of the superiority of one product over others. The agent who canvassed orders for newspapers and incidentally sold advertising space spread out from patent remedies to mattresses that alleviated rheumatic and neuralgic pains, to antifat pills, and to psychomancy—"how either sex may fascinate and gain the love and affection of any person they choose, instantly." By 1912, some 235 agencies in the United States had made advertising "as much a part of life as electricity, antiseptic surgery or trolley traction." They no longer catered to needs, but created and determined patterns of consumption, behavior, and cultural values, breaking down preferences acquired early in life. Scientific selling, the counterpart of scientific management, aimed at "greater efficiency and greater economy in production" through manipulation of the public.

A University of Michigan psychologist explained in "Advertising and Its Mental Laws" (1916) that scientific data on attention, memory, and response would enable the advertiser to plan his campaign for an assault on the public consciousness, exploiting the foibles of sexual difference and industrial and occupational groups. Similar techniques, employing appropriate words and slogans, could modify behavior and rectify evils through publicity, taking account of innate hereditary and racial differences in intelligence. The task of exercising social control would fall to educated bureaucrats. *The Springfield Union* (1877) did not doubt that "Here we should have a civil service to stagger the immortals."[26]

The confident smarties embarked on the adventure to make the world over—and better.

After 1910, their determination forged a consistent progressive attitude. Intelligence tests showed wide disparities in the level of personal competence, creating doubts deepened by theories that held that reason exerted only a limited influence on human actions. In *Behavior* (1914), John B. Watson explained how to condition humans to make unreflective responses to predetermined stimuli, and advertising applied the techniques he suggested. William McDougall, in *The Group Mind* (1920), called into question the rationality of behavior by pointing out that people responded less often to logical precepts than to instincts, a concept that entered also into the thinking of Thorstein Veblen, who emphasized the nonrational elements in society. Popular, unreasoning resistance to change created a cultural lag, and made it the duty of technologists and engineers to manipulate development in the proper direction. Walter Lippmann went further. In *A Preface to Politics* (1913) and in *Drift and Mastery* (1914), he combined ideas derived from Graham Wallas with Freudian concepts and with instinct psychology to argue that people did not make decisions rationally on isolated issues but responded according to preconceived opinions or stereotypes based on emotion and interest. The influence of intelligence seemed insignificant in comparison with brute forces and natural catastrophes. People drifted into their work without knowing why. Mastery demanded the substitution of conscious intention for unconscious striving, to introduce plan and purpose into the jungles of disordered growth. Citizens had to substitute purpose for tradition, treat life rationally, change its social organization, alter its tools, and control it. They therefore needed the guidance of exceptional individuals to make correct policy choices in government, not a distinct area set off from other human experience but part of the total life of the community.

Momentum from the past carried some causes forward—temperance and women's rights, for instance. Others acquired a new urgency from the increased stakes of economic change. Harvard Professor Thomas Nixon Carver (1915) held the rich responsible for the condition of the poor. People of means set the pace of competitive consumption, which always worked to the disadvantage of the less fortunate, unwilling to fall behind their neighbors in dress, food, and general appearance. The remedy, moderation in all things. Political corruption now involved not only great sums of money but also franchises and control of enterprises that affected the whole economy. Sensational journalists exposed the costs: erosion of respect for law and destruction of popular liberty. A widespread progressive assumption held the party system at fault for the ills of government; the remedy—place power directly in the hands of the people by enabling them to review judicial decisions, to bypass the legislature through the initiative and referendum, and to remove offensive officials through recall. The primary and the direct elections of senators would also broaden the popular role in the electoral process.[27]

Reformers did not expect those changes to increase the power of the majority of blockheads but rather to replace crude politicians with informed, educated leaders, people like themselves, they hoped. However, Oregon reformers pointed out (1907) that unexpected results followed the abolition of party bosses and political machines. Though such alterations increased the legislature's respect for the Constitution, reduced logrolling, and increased the power and responsibility of the legislature and governor, the people still remained in the background. To get the best results, skeptics argued, the voters had to do their own governing every day. To steer a straight course, they had to hold the helm and control their officers all the time. Such phrases reassured those fearful of change. Comforted by the natural conservatism of Americans, Woodrow

Wilson thought they desired not a revolution but a readjustment, to serve the common and public interest (1911).

Twentieth-century alterations in the rules of the game bore unanticipated fruits. The primary initiated in Mississippi in 1903 and Wisconsin in 1904 had deleterious long-term effects insofar as it reinforced one-party systems and replaced durable collective political structures with *ad hoc* personal electoral choices, thus insulating the elite from the populace, a trend extreme in the South but not unique to that region. The referendum and recall rarely fulfilled expectations. Imports from Switzerland pushed on theoretical grounds, the new procedures rested not so much on faith in democracy as on dissatisfaction with party control of legislatures. Often the innovations made public officials nervous, irresolute and inactive, avoiding any discussion at all. The direct election of United States senators (1912-13), proposed with the hope that transferring the choice from state legislatures to the people would eliminate corruption and make for a more representative body, had very limited effects other than to consolidate the legitimacy of the nonapportioned second chamber. Personal registration laws reflected the absence of any way to keep track of potential voters in anonymous urban environments, while antipartisan legislation that tried to rationalize politics, ended up by replacing the electoral campaign with administrative bargaining among bureaucrats.[28]

Rule changes increasing the volatility and complexity of electoral politics excluded many citizens from participation. Going to the polls after 1900 ceased to be a simple expression of group loyalty, a festive occasion directed by a recognized leader, and instead demanded decisions about complex issues remote from the concerns of most voters. The percentage of the potential electorate that cast ballots for members of Congress dropped. Mistrust of the legislative process, touched off by exposures of big business corruption and competing forms of government through the courts and bureaucratic agencies, made the ballot seem less important than the mobilization of interest groups by industrialists, workers, farmers, do-gooders, intellectuals, health reformers, and worriers, competing for influence in administrative and judicial proceedings.[29]

No simple solution, moreover, could dispose of the aggrieved masses who owned no property, nothing—out of it all. The certainty that individuals controlled their own destinies, that poverty, disease, and unemployment reflected personal weakness and failure, had given way to the belief that environmental forces determined all; credit and blame had nothing to do with it. When it occurred to a man that Nature did not regard him as important, and that she would not maim the universe by disposing of him, he at first wished to throw bricks at the temple and hated the fact that there were no bricks and no temple. The only recourse, to recognize that interdependence in a civilized society called for surrender of the selfishness of private responsibility, as inappropriate as each man in a crowd in the rain holding his umbrella over himself and his wife and giving neighbors the drippings. Only comprehensive social remedies could help the underprivileged against the massive impersonal forces that ruled nature and society.[30]

Nor could any easy formula dissolve discriminatory practices that conflicted with the ideal of equal opportunity. Progressives divided on the issue of whether to restrict immigration or to continue the traditional policy of open gates. But they agreed on the desirability of assimilating newcomers and outsiders, like the Indians, and broadening all avenues for advancement. Some, accepting the racist view, denied that everyone could become fully American; and even those not overtly racist ascribed the virtues of the United States to its Anglo-Saxon heritage, as did the historian John B. McMaster (1883). Generally, however, the progressives considered all social difficulties subsidiary to the economic one. Just as Booker T. Washington argued that blacks could advance through acquisition of skills, so whites maintained that a more efficient productive system would increase social justice. Steam and electricity, an influential book explained, should have raised output enough to satisfy all wants. If instead unemployment and poverty accompanied material progress, the fault lay in inequities in land ownership, as a result of which improvements forced rents up and wages down. Alleviation of abuses would begin a golden age and expand liberty and virtue.[31]

Economic reform focused on efficiency for two distinct but related objectives, conservation and planning, both requiring increased government control. Before the Civil War had ended, George Perkins Marsh had complained that humans extirpated thousands of organic forms without even consuming them. Destructiveness advanced with civilization— with the forest gone and its vegetable mold converted into parched dust, its reservoir of moisture evaporated and returned only in deluges of rain to wash the soil away. The well-wooded and humid hills turned to ridges of dry rock. The partial reversal of this process—reforestation, draining swamps, and checking the drift of coastal dunes—did not offset the damage. Geographical regeneration lay beyond the means and the political power of the places that needed it most. Yet humans held the earth for use alone, not for consumption, still less for profligate waste. The organic and inorganic worlds, bound together by mutual adaptations, had ensured the continuation of the established conditions of each, or at most a very gradual succession of changes. But man, everywhere a disturbing agent, turned the harmonies of nature to discord wherever he appeared. The time had come for a change, to protect present and future generations against the waste of nature's bounty, whether by actual destruction or by making it unusable.[32]

As events validated Marsh's predictions, Ellen Churchill Semple, Charles R. Van Hise, and other geographers and geologists explained the necessity for prudence. In the past, a unique combination of vast size, abundance, superior industrial organization, and "Anglo Saxon vigor of character and tenacity of purpose," had made the United States the world's greatest producer; but to continue, required wise conservation of resources that did not spontaneously renew themselves. The historian Frederick Jackson Turner pointed out that the end of the wilderness frontier, critical in the nation's past, compelled Americans to explore new frontiers of science. Naturalist John Muir deplored the disappearance of the country's wildlife, founded the Sierra Club, and pushed through creation of great national forests against outcries by wealthy thieves allowed to steal timber wholesale (1890). The United States had earlier expanded without direction, by a process neither inevitable, natural, nor rational. But the accelerating pace of change had destroyed the capacity to resolve difficulties after they appeared. To deal with future problems before they occurred required planning in order to employ scarce material and expensive labor to best advantage. Foresight and the intelligent arrangement of tasks would maximize results, whether in the household, in the manufacturing plant, or indeed in the whole country. Experts would direct the process from a central location, displacing legislative bodies and the existing civil bureaucracy.[33]

Conservation and planning depended on action by government, which alone possessed the required power. Lester F. Ward had called for sociocracy as an alternative to democracy, with important questions "considered in a non-partisan spirit based on scientifically settled information." Edward Alsworth Ross's Social Control (1912), dedicated appropriately enough to Lester F. Ward and read with approval by Oliver Wendell Holmes and Theodore Roosevelt, regarded order as a "fabric, rather than a growth," and thus amenable to manipulation and planning, in accord with the corporate will. To ascertain that will, Henry Laurence Gantt wished to replace theories or opinions by hard evidence and social data. Heavily influenced by Veblen, he founded "the New Machine," which counted among its members engineers and sympathetic reformers.

Their agenda: higher wages, the elimination of plutocracy, technical surveys of cities, and greater power to the experts.

In the interest of conservation and planning, the Newlands Reclamation Act (1902) set aside funds from the sale of public lands for irrigation and established a reclamation service in the Department of the Interior. Between 1901 and 1908 the size of the national forest grew from forty-three million to a hundred ninety-four million acres and was supervised by the United States Forest Service. Meanwhile, protective state legislation could conserve human resources, as in laws to limit the work hours of women and children. Josephine Goldmark's brief in *Muller* v. *Oregon* argued for shorter working hours for women on the grounds of greater job efficiency. By relating scientific data and legal reasonableness, she and Louis D. Brandeis justified the expansion of legislative power when economic conditions required the state to intervene on behalf of the demonstrably weaker party.[34]

Efficiency, attained through good management, furthered industrial safety and also conservation and planning. Thorstein Veblen criticized predatory businessmen interested only in short-term profits, disregarding the common man's instinct for workmanship. The old-timers who had come out on top had learned from experience and had maintained control by close attention to detail. Later they talked freely about the qualities of the successful entrepreneur—keen observation, rapid reasoning, trained imagination—all aspects of mental efficiency that prepared the mind for every decision business required. The manager so equipped made the profits that kept him in capital; he held down the costs of labor and of supplies, and he outsold competitors. That self-serving view lost persuasiveness in the light of evidence from the marketplace that other qualities also entered into competitive victories. Edward Page, lecturing at Yale in 1911, defined moral conduct as a social phenomenon, arguing that righteousness and success ought to be the twin ideals of business life. In a time of large enterprises and quick trades that emphasized efficiency, businessmen faced painful conflicts between moral and economic impulses. Page urged them to turn away from the fetish of competition and recall the chain of evolution that linked all life and conduct, men and animals, civilization and savagery, volitions and instincts, conduct and behavior in a universe of elemental motion and change.

Louis D. Brandeis, among others, considered efficiency increasingly dependent on specialized training and information, "the hope of democracy." The size and complexity of enterprises made trial and error risky. The entrepreneur required the counsel of educated experts, and technology became the realm of the engineer. Early on, Andrew Carnegie had relied on the advice of Alexander L. Holley, whose work on steam engines and locomotives had led him into the design of Bessemer steel plants. No amateur tinkerer could keep abreast of new patents and new processes in chemistry, metallurgy, and geology, in France, England, and Germany as well as in the United States. Holley had learned from experience; but after 1870 formal instruction seemed ever more desirable. Technical schools expanded rapidly; the graduates of Stevens and Cooper Union, of R.P.I. and M.I.T. and V.P.I., organized societies of mining, mechanical, and civil engineers, began to publish journals and acquired professional status. Viewed in the light of these developments, the metropolis also required technically competent management. Mayor Josiah Quincy of Boston thus entrusted the construction of a subway tunnel to a transit commission (1894).[35]

A few managers, at the end of the century, agreed with some engineers that plants might arrange human beings more efficiently than in the past. Already blueprints determined the location of the machines. A plan ought also to marshal workers who handled expensive machinery and labored in large groups, all performing their own tasks, but all parts of a whole. The craftsmen's improvisation could not cope with the problems of fabricating complex products; the sheets of steel or miles of tubing fitted into a twelve-wheel six-hundred-ton locomotive, or a battleship of fourteen thousands tons clad in up to eighteen inches of armor, demanded precise design and execution. Yet the owner or superintendent could not keep thousands of employees under his constant oversight. Only rational organization could control their performance, bring them to their appointed places at the appointed times, calculate the cost and value of their labor, and pass commands along to them through a hierarchy of foremen, department overseers, and first hands. From 1895 onward, Frederick W. Taylor occupied himself with devising such systems and persuading industrialists of the utility of adopting them. In the process, scientific management destroyed faith in tradition and in the individual judgment of the craftsman.

Alert and imaginative managers struggled to cope. Ruin awaited the business that failed to meet the challenge. The appearance of prosperity might temporarily hide inner rot, but not indefinitely. The mills of the American Woolen Company, scattered in a dozen towns, its central selling office in New York, operated under the direction of William Wood in Boston, who rewarded himself with a fabulous salary. Even had he willed it, he could not be everywhere. Nor could he supervise all those to whom he delegated power, which left horrendous opportunities for pilferage, for kickbacks, for private deals at company expense, for graft by the foremen, for error, and for miscalculation. Each factory produced whatever quantity of cloth for which its superintendent guessed the selling office would find purchasers. Not until the end of the year, if then, did Wood know whether he had made a profit or suffered a loss, and later still before he could add up the figures to know why; far too late then to learn where the credit or the blame lay, or even to judge the numbers' accuracy. Besides, variations in conditions and costs made comparisons among the totals for each mill imprecise.[36]

Size imposed efficiency on some enterprises. Hotels in the United States, far larger than their European counterparts, had to operate systematically; unable to count upon skilled servants, the managers had to calculate the supplies that their guests would require and plan to provide regular services, as well as deal with the unexpected. The London journalist George A. Sala commented that the American hotel was to an English hotel what an elephant was to a periwinkle. Brass buttons and gold braid appeared on bellboys, elevator men, and doormen in livery (1877). Modern plumbing by the 1890s made common the advertisement, "every room with a bath." A. D. Pelton's radiator, invented in 1855, by the 1870s permitted centralized steam heat to reach every floor. The Fifth Avenue Hotel in New York in 1859 installed the "vertical railway," otherwise known as the elevator. In 1882 the Hotel Everett in New York blazed forth with 101 of Edison's incandescents in its main public rooms; and Chicago's Palmer House that year installed a small plant that provided electricity for 96 lamps in two dining rooms. It took another decade, however, before the telephone became a standard hotel feature. The intricate system by which department stores moved hundreds of items to and from their shelves also called for elaborate planning and management.[37]

The railroads early experimented with accounting and controls. Though Charles Francis Adams, Jr., assured riders that they would find more safety inside the first-class carriage of a train in full motion than out in the street, he wanted accurate statistics on accident rates. Managers depended on precise information. Since their cash dribbled in and out through numerous hands, from fares and freight, for supplies and services, they needed means of verifying receipts and governing expenditures if they were not to be robbed blind. Transit and gas and electric companies as well as chain stores felt the same needs, met by skilled accountants replacing old-time cashiers. In addition, snooping state and later federal regulatory agencies, commissions, and investigating committees like the Armstrong and Pujo demanded accurate records. Charles E. Russell and other critics envied the centralized German railway system, unaware of the price in bureaucracy there and in France. While working for the Pennsylvania Railroad, Carnegie learned the utility of a flow of data to keep management informed, a lesson he applied at every stage of his subsequent career. Merciless to partners and employees who deviated from the rule, he demanded universal accountability. Others learned from him.[38]

Gusts of paper fluttered through the business world. The old clerk on his stool gave way to a battery of shorthand secretaries; the letterpress yielded to the typewriter; and piles of ruled blanks and books, printed forms and memorandums, accumulated in the files. Additional employees handled these documents under the supervision of an array of new officers. A spreading bureaucracy interposed itself between the entrepreneur and the enterprise, all for the sake of efficiency.

Leadership thereafter called for administrative talents to master the data and to act upon the reports of such engineers as Stone and Webster or Arthur D. Little. Elbert H. Gary, for instance, commanded with precision the far-flung empire of United States Steel. But he operated for a salary by rules set by a board of directors, rather than by his own judgment based on personal ownership.[39]

Most industrialists before 1900 started without formal preparation, one-time grocers, clerks, drummers, telegraph boys, mechanics, learning across the counter to buy and sell, becoming familiar with methods by copying letters or delivering messages, knowing the machine from the feel of grease on their hands, dealing with laborers as foremen on the job, advancing by saving and scheming. Few took the time out for college, or even to wait for a high school diploma. But young Henry Ford, while still in the machine shop, studied at night in a business school because the accounting skills taught by books and lectures would help him get ahead. Later, when he enjoyed personal profits of about $50 million a year, popular imagination fixed on the image of the puttering mechanic who built a small steam engine on a forge in a schoolyard and who delved into mechanical journals during the winter, when farm work was slack. But the ability to calculate had equal importance. Private proprietary courses such as Ford attended appeared in various cities, while commercial instruction also intruded into more traditional academic institutions.[40]

The new administrators followed career patterns different from those of the old entrepreneurs. The boards that entrusted them with great enterprises sought convincing credentials of reliability and training. Furthermore, the unwillingness of some wealthy heirs to carry on made room for the professionals. Ernest L. Thayer, for instance, could have stepped into his father's place in command of several Massachusetts woolen mills.

But a Harvard education spoiled the young man for the dreary life in trade; he toured Europe, wrote a column for a San Francisco newspaper, and finally settled into leisurely gentility in Santa Barbara. An outsider took his place.[41]

To hold the interest of such heirs as well as to develop and transmit ever more complex commercial skills, the nation's oldest university in 1908 opened a graduate school of business administration, an indication that making and dealing approached the status of a profession to which a formal course of education offered entry. Louis D. Brandeis attacked the "practical businessman," the "narrow money maker without either vision or ideals." Big business had to lose its sinister meaning to be revealed for what it truly was—a profession, "as distinguished from the occupation of petty trafficking or mere money making." As a profession, business would resolve the great industrial and social problems expressed in current unrest by using knowledge, organized as science, to increase efficiency. This aspiration, not yet an actuality, formed part of an extended quest for orderly forms of production to offset the tremendous hazards of private enterprise. The quest had begun much earlier, when the government had ceased its attempt to direct the economy. Industrialization increased the urgency for developing a systematic alternative.[42]

The old ways simply could not go on. In the 1890s, Carnegie Steel owned iron mines, coke works, barge fleets, railroads, blast furnaces, Bessemer converters, open-hearths, rolling mills, and finishing plants worth well over $250 million. The firm operated as a partnership held together by a sloppy "iron-clad" agreement of dubious legality and subject to the imperious will of an aging man whose death or disability might put the whole enterprise up for grabs. Much better to achieve order, stability, and increased profit through incorporation, just as competing companies did better by joining forces than by bloody struggles.[43]

Even the successful tired of the grind of unrelenting competition. In a popular parable they rode in comfort atop a coach dragged up a hilly road by the toiling masses. Even the fortunate remained insecure, for an unexpected jolt could throw them off and deprive them of their seats. They would then join the toiling draggers, lashed on by the driver, hunger. "The apprehension that this might happen was a constant cloud upon the happiness of those who rode." Hence the willingness to exchange the joys of strenuous competition for security through accommodation, by way of agreements, pools, informal understandings, trusts and holding companies. The Sherman and the Clayton antitrust laws frowned upon such restraints upon trade, as did the independents in oil, Pennsylvania anthracite, and Michigan copper. But the United States Chamber of Commerce, formed in 1912, aimed to ease that hostility enough to permit some degree of self-regulation, as on the New York Stock Exchange and the Chicago Board of Trade.[44]

Some progressives, like Thorstein Veblen, wanted to eliminate all wasteful features by government controls (within the Anglo-Saxon constitutional tradition, of course). Others, like Louis D. Brandeis, considered bigness a curse and wished to attain efficiency by liberating industry from rapacious trusts such as held 121 separate corporations within the grip of the New Haven Railroad. Still other progressives, like Herbert Croly, thought greater integration desirable, but regulated in the community's interest. His book *The Promise of American Life* (1909) grappled with the problems confronting a nation whose governmental organization and social life coexisted with an inherited outlook out of step with the needs of the times. The answer called for new techniques to further general progress, even at the cost of curtailing the individual freedom to pursue self-interest. Croly urged hard-headed reformers to accept the industrial revolution for what it was, and to harness it in desirable directions instead of harkening back to a nonexistent golden age. Whatever the means advocated, progressives agreed that increased efficiency in the productive system, in government, and in society, would make more goods available, advance the position of labor, and solve the problems of the underprivileged.[45]

A utopian novel that sold more than a million copies and touched off a nationwide flurry of organization summed up the longing for an encompassing, abundance-providing association. Edward Bellamy's *Looking Backward* put into American terms Saint-Simon's ideal of government by technical managers. But the idea's attractiveness sprang from indigenous sources—formation of an industrial army to produce all the goods society wanted. The vision of mobilized men acting with a common purpose proved irresistible. Bellamy earlier could see the troops, "a blue river sweeping along, the polished bayonets rising and falling with the swinging tread of the men, like interminable waves rolling in upon the shore, giving the impression of a single organism, a mighty whole, a great dragon terrible in its beauty." Such an army, he wrote of Shays's Rebellion, formed a "school of democratic ideas" that converted the son of a poor farmer into a leader of men. The nation's industry under a single control, all its processes interlocked, would multiply the total product, just as disciplined troops under one general performed more efficiently than a horde of barbarians with a thousand petty chiefs. Society would function by persuasion, for the laborers worked for their own welfare, and that excluded the need for compulsion. The vision attracted forward-looking people of all classes.[46]

Progressives employed both private and governmental means to further their agenda. Older philanthropic organizations broadened their scope, attracted professional personnel, and shifted emphasis from charity to reform. New agencies rose to deal with the urban poor and particularly with youth, the hope for the future. The Neighborhood Guild of New York (1886) and Hull House of Chicago (1889) transplanted from England the techniques of the settlement house; there college women and men like Lillian Wald, Jane Addams, and Robert A. Woods attempted to learn about and help the poor by living among them. By 1895, fifty such groups operated throughout the country, and the number grew thereafter. In the Hull House drawing rooms emotional needs, intellectual sympathy, and professional ideals converged for Sophonisba Breckinridge, Edith Abbott, and other activists. City officials like Charles Ball approached the staff for help in surveying housing—a chance for social research to advance science and to discover the grim features of immigrant lives, and also to improve conditions. Therefore workers in the slums behaved as good neighbors should, aiming to develop social cohesion as well as civic welfare.[47]

Such enterprises remained poor while philanthropy depended upon the generosity of individual donors with narrow notions of the amounts necessary. Attitudes changed, however, at the turn of the century. Carnegie and Rockefeller did not long remain isolated figures. In 1907 the Russell Sage Foundation awarded a grant for a program of social research, a practical training center for progressives. Leading public figures, people of wealth and businessmen, as well as sociologists, participated. Women more often than men shared in activities that required time and effort as well as money, and perhaps a special sensitivity to issues affecting family life. Those sponsored by the Junior League also earned prestige. The rich slowly learned the obligations of their positions, although they continued to give according to their own tastes rather than according to any abstract definition of society's needs. Libraries and medical research, however useful, left untouched the issues progressives considered most urgent.

Some private organizations therefore altered their focus from directly administering programs to urging them upon government, lobbying both for regulatory laws and for the expenditure of public funds. Most of these groups remained nonpartisan, concentrating upon some particular cause, like the National Consumer's League (1898) or the National Child Labor Committee (1904) or the American Association of Labor Legislation

(1906). Robert C. Chapin's report on the standard of living of working-men's families in New York City (1909) to the New York State Conference of Charities and Corrections revealed the depressing effect of wage and price changes. A year later Florence Kelley, general secretary of the National Consumer's League, suggested a partnership between producers and consumers to better conditions among workers.[48]

Such well-intentioned campaigns lacked focus. In addition to its other concerns, the National Consumer's League worried about the adequacy of the federal food and drug law and about the slave labor used to produce cocoa. Apart from a general desire for fairness, the reformers shied away from any open assertion that the community had an interest of its own, linked to any system of morality. Instead, the emphasis fell upon the use of science to further individual welfare. Progressives therefore spread their efforts among local, state, and federal levels.

Municipalities at first presented the greatest challenge, for government there functioned least successfully and most directly affected everyone. However attractive rural ideals remained, improvement in the quality of urban life became urgent. Nice little articles on the joys of agriculture failed to return the thronging millions to the prairies. Young men and women like Henry Ford who forced their way to the large towns rejected farming in favor of commerce and industry. Reformers gradually recognized that reality and along with it the obligation to make the city congenial to those who yet valued the yeomen's virtues, as through the YMCA and its counterparts. In addition they wished to address more general issues. Chicago academics and social workers used their credentials to challenge the political machine, although the busy world still regarded them as something between dealers in scientific magic and cranks. By 1895, organizations devoted to municipal reform operated in 150 cities in thirty-one American states. Within a few years, the National Municipal Association, the American Society for Municipal Improvement, and the League of American Municipalities coordinated efforts and exchanged information. In some places also local research bureaus investigated operations with an eye to reform. William H. Tolman, who defined himself as a social engineer, counted among his activities the Museum of Safety, the International Congress of Improved Dwellings, the Imperial Technological Museum, and the International Committee on Social Insurance, evidence of expertise.[49]

At first the old political machines, entangled in subtle distinctions between honest and dishonest graft and allied with crime, vice, and intemperance, seemed the main obstacles to progress. Occasionally progressives attracted a following by showing the extent to which corruption injured even slum residents, as the Lexow investigation (1894) had revealed. The revelations permitted Republicans to promise cleaner administration in an appeal to independent voters and also stirred up intellectuals. Lincoln Steffens, who had covered the hearings for *The New York Evening Post,* went on to examine Boston, Philadelphia, Pittsburgh, and Chicago, finding none well governed. Jacob Riis, working for *The Evening Sun,* traced the corruption the committee uncovered to poverty. Fiorello H. La Guardia, then in Prescott, Arizona, read accounts of the disclosures in the *New York World.* Shocked, he "could not understand how the people of the greatest city in the country could put up with the vice and crime that existed there." Resentment against Tammany became a life-long obsession. But the failure of reform administrations to win reelection convinced Steffens and others that in politics corrupt government often represented what the people wanted. The United States stood for business, not for human welfare.[50]

To consolidate temporary gains, progressives tried to restructure administration on an efficient basis, free of political distractions. The mismanagement of Washington, Boston, New York, and Philadelphia had shocked and dismayed Delos F. Wilcox, who assumed that cities were unnatural, fit mainly for transients, certainly not for children. Bryce had already pointed to municipal government as the nation's one conspicuous failure, and the years since his *American Commonwealth* only made matters worse. But Wilcox also considered cities ideal social laboratories, where people depended on each other, where gigantic public utilities and other great enterprises fostered civic spirit and efficiency, both deemed essential to democracy. Cities, he thought, nurtured great enterprises, outward manifestations of the spirit of cooperation.[51]

In the aftermath of a disastrous flood, Galveston, Texas, in 1900 put control of all departments in the hands of a small commission; in the next twelve years, more than two hundred places did the same, and Staunton, Virginia, and Sumter, South Carolina, experimented with managers patterned after corporation presidents. Experienced men of high character and training, chosen for merit and fitness, would ensure a day's work for a day's pay, clean streets, better security, and public health, with contracts honestly made and strictly carried out. William H. Tolman's *Social Engineering* (1909) argued that improved men for improved machines had economic value, with colossal opportunities for guiding and uplifting millions, not an issue of altruism or philanthropy, but of good business. Engineers, encouraged to accept careers in municipal employment, would impose strict accounting methods, continuity of policies, definite responsibility, and the elimination of all political plunder. Local self-government, the exploitation of municipal property and franchises for the public good, and administration by trained officials fully accountable to the people, would enforce the law and preserve order.[52]

Measures aimed only at efficiency by eliminating corruption and lowering costs could not long sustain the loyalties of the masses who paid no taxes. Insofar as they eschewed conventional political methods and divorced themselves from party connections, the progressives served more effectively as critics in opposition than as administrators in power. Furthermore, the link to Sunday closing laws and prohibition cast them in the role of gloomy puritans forbidding citizens to enjoy their little intervals of leisure.

Like Samuel M. ("Golden Rule") Jones, however, Brand Whitlock of Toledo, Josiah Quincy of Boston, and Thomas L. Johnson and Newton D. Baker of Cleveland demonstrated that progressive city administrations could achieve more than mere economy. Specialized agencies assumed responsibility for welfare, water, and garbage removal, releasing the police for the detection of criminals. Municipal ownership, or at least strict regulation, of public utilities, lowered costs; and cheap ice and better milk improved diets. Monumental but also functional structures like Boston's South Station served thousands without cost to taxpayers. Tenement house inspection laws, park concerts, baths, playgrounds and kindergartens offset the brutishness of slum life. Such measures stirred the enthusiasm of social workers, who became intermediaries to the poor, and in alliance with muckraking journalists, developed political power in some places that rivaled that of the machines. The progressive vision embraced efficient cooperation to replace the unity of subordination and dependence by the unity of interdependence and coordination, the binding obligation of law by the binding obligation of accord.

The full costs manifested themselves later, when excessively low transit fares drove carriers into bankruptcy. Grandiose schemes for universal public education, to produce a morally and politically homogeneous people out of a heterogeneous mix, also showed the deleterious results of doing good. The innovations of the juvenile court system, "all light and no darkness," in the best interests of the child and society, exposed the gulf between the reformers' expectations and practical results. Progressive designs for criminal justice and mental health reform met a similar fate.[53]

Moreover, with municipalities mere instruments of the states, crucial decisions fell to governors and legislatures rather than to mayors and councils. Transactions in Albany, Harrisburg, Annapolis, Springfield, and Baton Rouge generally escaped the scrutiny of big city journalists; and there uninhibited lobbyists, franchise seekers, and hunters after patronage operated freely.[54]

On this level, too, progressives attempted to bring the machinery of government into tune with the times. The tripartite structure—executive, legislative, judicial—remained intact. But when new states joined the union (Utah in 1896, Oklahoma in 1907, and New Mexico and Arizona in 1912) or when old ones revised their constitutions, determined drives aimed for the adoption of initiative and referendum; and by 1912 twenty-nine had provided for the direct election of United States senators.

More substantive reforms followed. Although progressives some-times filtered into positions of influence in the legislatures, control of those bodies usually remained in the hands of rural political organizations hostile to change. Governors who owed their places to popular election proved more responsive, among them Altgeld in Illinois, Roosevelt and Hughes in New York, LaFollette in Wisconsin, U'Ren in Oregon, Folk in Missouri, Cummins in Iowa, and Johnson in California. The climactic election of 1910, which brought Woodrow Wilson to power in New Jersey and John Dix in New York, revealed the extent of political realignment. Using patronage to keep legislatures in line, these chief executives drew upon the universities and free-lance intellectuals for ideas and administrative talent. The University of Wisconsin served as a nerve center of government, with thirty-five of its professors in service to the state. It also became a model for efforts to reach out to the localities for power and influence. Its extension division under Edward J. Ward went beyond the provision of agricultural information, sending out social engineers to reshape rural society.[55]

The power thus mobilized produced laws to conserve natural re-sources, to develop water power, to guard against impure foods, and to expand public education. Other statutes reflected concern for public health and for conditions in tenements and factories, and experimented with workmen's compensation and limits to the labor of women and children. Stronger railroad and public utility commissions fixed rates in the consumers' interest. Wisconsin created an industrial commission and introduced an income tax. Some states also took tentative steps to protect labor against exploitation, despite the inclination of courts to hold uncon-stitutional statutes infringing upon the rights of contract and of private property, grounds on which the Ritchie (1895) and the Lochner (1905) cases had invalidated limitation of the hours of certain wage earners. The death of Thomas C. Platt in 1910 and the state elections that year marked the passing of an era. Bosses like Platt had enabled the polity to adjust to profound social changes after the Civil War. Now, government-regulated party operations and corporate campaign contributions had reduced the influence of patronage by tightening rules for appointments to public office. The decline in voter turnout and widespread ticket splitting revealed the weakened role of the party, while legislatures became increasingly responsive to opinion mobilized by specialized interests speaking through experts—not so much to the party clubhouse to which the masses turned as to the progressive societies in which the educated and well-to-do enlisted.[56]

Important problems remained beyond the scope of state action. Only the federal government could deal with the great interstate trusts or control an economy continental in scope. Yet the Washington of the 1890s took a narrow view of the role of government. Stale controversies over the currency, the tariff, and civil service reform focused attention on inessentials; and emotion dominated the election of 1896. Endless hours spent debating tariff rates produced one, unintended, result. In the effort to create an alternative source of revenue, a constitutional amendment (1913) authorized an income tax, but at a minuscule level; not until decades later would the implications of that power emerge.

The federal electoral system, however, did not change. Since 1888, when the parties began to collect national war chests, campaigns had grown more expensive and increasingly dependent on great donors like John Wanamaker and August Belmont. The elections of the 1860s had cost Belmont at least eighty thousand dollars out of his own pocket. He continued to subsidize the Democratic party, fearing lest the organization sink "between the weight of the billions of the monopolistic money kings, and the socialistic heresies preached by unscrupulous demagogues" (1888). Behind McKinley stood Marcus A. Hanna. Deaf to calls for reform, Czar Thomas B. Reed, Speaker of the House, and Senator Nelson Aldrich and their allies in both parties kept firm hands on the machinery of Congress.[57]

Occasional efforts to revise the copyright and the patent laws touched only tangentially on the issue of monopoly. And the only direct response to the spread of industrial combinations, the Sherman Antitrust Act (1890), which declared illegal any combination or conspiracy in restraint of trade, only implemented old common-law provisions. It avoided the risk of a judicial ruling of unconstitutionality; but a justice department short of manpower found it difficult to enforce. Although any person injured by illegal acts could recover from the guilty threefold damages plus costs, the measure hardly affected the economic trends toward concentration.[58]

Those problems lingered on into the twentieth century to plague a generation of college men who trickled into practical politics. Theodore Roosevelt (1858–1919), the most notable of them, never shook off the need to prove himself. As a boy asthmatic and nearsighted, he strove to impress his father. A Harvard graduate fascinated by history, he decided not to go on lest he become one of the little men who taught in colleges. Instead he entered politics, served in the New York State Assembly, and ran a creditable though unsuccessful race for the mayoralty in 1886. He went on from membership in the Civil Service Commission to become president of the New York City Board of Police Commissioners, acquiring a reputation, publicized by Jacob A. Riis, as an honest and competent reformer. Widely read, he had opinions on everything and a self-confidence that erased the initial impression of his stubby figure and squeaky voice. Trained not as a lawyer but as a historian and writer, he drew freely on the outpouring of new ideas that emanated from the universities and from the press; and some intellectuals eagerly responded to the invitation to share power in order to put their thoughts into action. He threw himself with zest into every conflict, whether for simplified spelling or the exposure of nature fakers. But though he never doubted the correctness of his own position, he learned to compromise for the sake of the possible. Assertive, he cherished his own ability to act and in politics that required the grasp of power which he determined to use for communal improvement in accord with his developing understanding of the good society. But aware of the need to enlist the cooperation of men and women moved by dreams of their own, who also cherished the capacity to act, he tried, with varied success, to share power and to work with, rather than against, others.

Coming home from the Spanish American War, in which he served in the field at the head of a cavalry regiment, the Rough Riders,

> a lovely regiment whose men wus strong and stout
> Fer some they had diplomas and fer some wus warrants out

Teddy maneuvered the Republican party into nominating him for the New York governorship. Annoyed party leaders thrust him into the vice-presidency to be rid of him, but McKinley's assassination brought him into the White House. Roosevelt, eager to play a historic role at home and abroad, loved every minute of his strenuous terms of office.[59]

*

Roosevelt considered himself an intellectual, capable of solving problems rationally, scientifically. Government he regarded as a referee in the great game of life—its first obligation a square deal for all, fairness, so that no competitor could violate the rules or gain an undue advantage over antagonists. Each person judged on his or her merits deserved an opportunity to do his or her best. The state thus expanded the liberty, that is, the ability to act, of all.

In pursuit of his reveries, Roosevelt rarely went beyond the line of the politically feasible and most readily sponsored reforms free of controversy. Journalistic exposures of the meat-packing industry created a wave of popular sentiment in favor of government inspection. Since the larger and more respectable packers sought standards to protect them against less scrupulous competitors, he got easy enactment of the Pure Food and Drug and the Meat Inspection acts (1906) designed to protect consumers against adulterated and unsafe processed foods and patent medicines. Characteristically, he evaded such uncomfortable issues as responsibility for payment of the costs of inspection.

Again and again, practical considerations intruded in Roosevelt's reveries about ordered liberty and moved him to compromise. He took a mediating position on the problems of labor, seeking to "guard as zealously the rights of the striker as those of the employer," but resolved that order prevail at whatever cost. In a riot there would be no "blank cartridges or firing over the head of anybody" (1895). In the end, he considered the corporate looters and the reckless agitators equally enemies of orderly liberty (1895). Concerned about the shortage of fuel as winter approached, he intervened in the coal strike of 1902. In an effort at impartiality, he refused the owners' request for federal troops to police the mines and urged labor to moderate its demands. But by the time he got J. P. Morgan to persuade the mine owners to compromise he had gained additional insight into the hardships of the workers and the stubbornness of the industrialists. In his second term, therefore, he displayed the federal government's concern with the lot of the toilers in the mills and the mines, by asking for an investigation of child labor and by approving a law providing compensation for accidents on common carriers. In 1908, an act of Congress took the first step toward regulating the hours of trainmen on interstate railways.[60]

The problems of industrial integration proved less amenable to compromise. Roosevelt took office as popular sentiment against the trusts rose to fever heat, kept glowing by the muckrakers. Professional people, small businessmen and farmers—numerically the weightiest elements in the Republican party—demanded something more than the inadequate Sherman Act of 1890, which outlawed the pools and trusts of the preceding two decades, a sentiment Roosevelt's public utterances frequently echoed. Yet he opposed government ownership and considered it unrealistic to attempt to break the great business aggregations into smaller units. Insofar as they strengthened the economy, he wished to tolerate the trusts, subject to strict oversight in the public interest. Preferring publicity to prosecution, he formed the Bureau of Corporations in the Department of Commerce (1903) to collect information about large enterprises in the hope that exposure would exert restraint. But he enforced the laws when necessary. A suit against the Northern Securities Company, a mammoth effort by James J. Hill and J. P. Morgan to unite the Northwest railways, led to a Supreme Court order (1904) to dissolve the company, deemed an illegal restraint of trade. In the next four years, indictments followed against twenty-five trusts, including those in beef, oil, and tobacco. Yet Roosevelt did not attack indiscriminately. His attitude adjusted to the occasion. "Th' trusts," says he to himself, "are heejous monsthers built up be th'inlightened intheprise iv th' men that have done so much to advance progress in our beloved counthry," he says. "On wan hand I wud stamp thim undher fut; on th' other hand not so fast." Cartoonists outdid themselves in mocking the president clubbing corporations with a tiny stick, and Upton Sinclair portrayed him as the tool of monster commercialism spreading corruption and death (1907). The president, however, considered the big aggregations inevitable; the effort to destroy them might do the utmost mischief to the body politic. He drew the line against misconduct, not against wealth or size (1902); in 1907 therefore he acquiesced in Morgan's acquisition of the Tennessee Coal and Iron Company for United States Steel, out of fear of a deepening financial crisis.

Simply to proceed against monopolies did not ease complaints against the railroads, whose rates determined everyone's competitive position. The carriers owed their very existence to charters and privileges; yet their managers governed their little principalities much as petty German despots had a century earlier, making more enemies than friends. Competition remained the preferable means of furthering efficiency and lowering costs, with regulation the proper function of government. State railroad commissions served advisory functions, with publicity their chief sanction until Illinois (1870) set up an agency that actually fixed rates and operating conditions. In *Munn* v. *Illinois* (1877) the Supreme Court upheld its constitutionality.

Increasingly, however, transportation passed across state lines and thus escaped local supervision. Then the *Wabash* case (1886) made national action imperative by ruling that only Congress, acting under the commerce clause, could control the interstate movement of passengers and goods. Shippers and railroads thereafter favored a federal solution that would spare them the burden of dealing with numerous, and sometimes conflicting, state commissions. In response, the Interstate Commerce Act of 1887 forbade rebates, discrimination between long and short hauls, and pooling arrangements. However, the commission created to investigate abuses had to seek redress through the courts, which soon circumscribed the new agency's limited powers. The desire for order had brought the railroads and their users to a point at which they acknowledged the utility of regulation, but not to the point of surrendering faith in expansive free competition. Tension persisted in every transaction between the liberty of one party and that of the others.

Two laws passed with Roosevelt's support took the first steps toward reform. The Elkins Act (1903) ordered the railroads not to depart from their published rates. The carriers had no objections, for they hoped that the measure would shield them against the piratical practices of large shippers. The president doggedly prosecuted corporations that accepted rebates. A fine of $300,000 imposed on the American Sugar Refining Company showed the seriousness of government intentions. Yet the highly competitive atmosphere encouraged evasion; with each firm out to get what it could, the decisive power to set rates remained in the hands of the individual roads. Roosevelt's maneuvers resulted in the Hepburn Act (1906), which extended the Interstate Commerce Commission's jurisdiction to cover storage facilities, pipelines, express companies, and refrigerated and sleeping cars, and permitted it to set maximum rates on the basis of the carriers' valuation of railroad properties. However, the courts could entertain appeals—on procedural grounds—from commission decisions and delay enforcement by injunctions. The act thus struck a balance between the roads and the users, between vigorous action and passive acquiescence.[61]

In some matters, Roosevelt considered discretion the better part of valor. He spared himself the political turmoil of efforts to change the tariff—a maze of contradictory provisions for serving special interests with little economic justification. In his more successful conservation efforts, Roosevelt avoided head-on collisions with the opposition. He judiciously labored for both efficient utilization of the soil, minerals, and forests, and protection of wildlife and scenic areas. But he did not stir up the speculators who favored quick and easy exploitation. Conferences publicized his position, and he requested legislation that did not damage existing vested interests. The president increased the size of the national forests, but characteristically did not make an issue of the matter when an amendment to the agricultural appropriation bill in 1907 forbade him to add to the holdings; instead he hastened to complete the transfers before the measure became law.

Summing up in 1910, Roosevelt condemned efforts to divide Americans "on the line that separates class from class, occupation from occupation, men of wealth from men of less wealth, instead of remembering that the only safe standard is that which judges each man on his worth as a man, whether he be rich or poor, without regard to his profession or his occupation in life." He did not like "the dull purblind folly of the very rich men; their greed and arrogance," which produced excitement and irritation in the popular mind expressed "in the great increase in socialistic propaganda" (1906). Impatient also with facile chatter about a classless society, he pursued his own vision of ordered liberty, the safeguard of everyone's capacity to act. Therein he remained the interpreter of public sentiment, totally spontaneous in his reactions to it.

The tasks of compromise lay beyond the abilities of Roosevelt's chosen successor, William Howard Taft (1857–1930), who lacked the imagination to cope with rising progressive demands or to satisfy his predecessor. He, too, wished to advance orderly liberty but did not command the necessary political skills to do so. Taft believed that recent college graduates carried away with them, together with the diploma, "a spirit of criticism and impatience" and "little understanding of the fundamental rules upon which all public affairs ought to be conducted." He reserved his sharpest barbs for wealthy university graduates who preached socialism. "The spectacle of men who enjoy all the luxuries of life, with trained servants and costly establishments of all kinds, declaiming against the social order and the injustice done to the poor and suffering in the community, is not one to attract the sympathy of sensible men." Satisfied by the balance between efficient administration and democracy, Taft wished to take into account popular prejudices and emotions while formulating policy. Experience showed that government could better provide some services than private enterprise, and should control others through regulation because of the probability of abuse. Impressed by the tremendous advances made under the guarantees of life, liberty, and property, he had little understanding of yearnings for radical change and emphasized postponement of gratification in order to preserve that which the future could enjoy. Above all, he believed in the sanctity of the law, no matter what the human costs of sustaining it. During the Pullman strike he deplored the fact that the military had killed only six of the mob—hardly enough to make an impression!

Taft had great faith in the party system, the essential mechanism for reducing the varying wishes and views of the population of eighty million to one resultant executive force. He carried Roosevelt's square deal further by extending the merit system in the Civil Service and by calling for an income tax. He set up the Children's Bureau in the Department of Labor. And he approved the creation of parcel post and postal saving systems, both desired by the rural population. But the corrosive effects of progressive ideas eroded the discipline and cohesion essential to any popular government. As a result the Taft administration's reform efforts often backfired.

Taft created the Bureau of Mines and set aside substantial forest and oil reserves. But the conservationists rose up in arms when Secretary of the Interior Richard A. Ballinger leased some northwest water sites and Alaska lands to private interests, as the law directed him to. Whatever the wisdom of those arrangements, no one suggested irregularities; and Ballinger had supported conservation, initiating the creation of petroleum reserves on public lands, for example. Nevertheless, Gifford Pinchot, chief of the Bureau of Forestry, attacked the leases, hinting at corruption. An opinionated bureaucrat, proud of his education and expertise, the kind of boy who had flinched when servants called him by his first name, Pinchot considered anyone who disagreed a villain and refused to let the issue die after the president exonerated Ballinger. Besides, Taft had dropped Pinchot's pet project for international collaboration to protect nature in the less developed parts of the world. Because Taft served as honorary vice-president of the Conservation League of America, Pinchot formed his own rival National Conservation Association. When the outcry continued the president finally dismissed Pinchot, thus upholding civilian authority over the bureaucracy.[62]

Taft also bore the blame for softness in antitrust actions, although as vigorous in prosecutions as his predecessor. In dissolving the Standard Oil Trust, and in a judgment against the American Tobacco Company (1911), the Supreme Court held that combinations arising from the desire for more efficient operations, although they had the effect of reducing competition, did not illegally restrain trade, as did others that achieved dominant positions through rebates, unfair price wars, and other predatory practices revealing an intent to monopolize the market. In practice, this Rule of Reason permitted action against offensive trusts without excluding every form of economic combination. "The freedom of the individual right to contract when not improperly exercised" remained "the most efficient means for the prevention of monopoly." The crucial question remained, Who was to administer the rule? Taft, like the Court but unlike Roosevelt, believed that the decision should lie in the hands of the judiciary as ultimate arbiter.

Taft faced trouble in Congress and did not enjoy his predecessor's popularity and therefore his immunity to attack. Good intentions, moreover, led him to a dead end when it came to finance and the tariff. To relieve the stringency caused by the panic of 1907, the Aldrich-Vreeland Act (1908) had loosened the conditions under which banks could issue notes and had authorized the appointment of a National Monetary Commission to recommend reform of the currency system. That body proposed to give the currency elasticity through a central bank controlled by financiers. Congress refused to enact the Aldrich Bill (1912), based on the commission's report, and left the impression that the president had wished to hand control of the nation's money over to the bankers.[63]

Nor could Taft maneuver to safety through the tariff issue as Roosevelt had. Progressive criticism of the excessively high rates of the Dingley Act persuaded Taft to call a special session of Congress in 1909, hoping for downward revision and for an inheritance tax to offset the expected loss of revenue. The old guard, entrenched in the Senate, where each economic interest lobbied to protect its own products, enacted the Payne-Aldrich Act with higher rates than the Dingley; and when Taft signed it he gained the enmity of the progressives, who made impressive gains in the congressional and state elections of 1910. A successful rebellion by Norris and other Republicans in the House of Representatives stripped the speaker, Joe Cannon, of control of committee assignments. Although in the long run the result was a seniority system no more progressive than the one it replaced, the uprising showed the strength of the forces mobilized against the old guard identified with Taft in 1912.

Taft's reveries ran to order, enforced by law. Without the popular support and the tactical skill of Theodore Roosevelt, he could not evade awkward decisions. Roosevelt could follow a middle course, antagonizing neither the conservatives nor the progressives, because his administration only began to bring federal action to bear upon national economic and social dilemmas. Taft had to face problems squarely. By the time he entered the White House, progressives with more than a decade's experience in the states and municipalities as well as in Congress made demands not as susceptible of compromise as in 1901.

The presidential election of 1912 clearly revealed how progressive sentiment had grown. A major party split produced a four-cornered campaign and projected a relatively unknown personality to prominence. The outcome, which went a long way toward shaping national institutions in the twentieth century, hinged upon two decisions. One showed that the developing progressive movement had enlisted majority support; the other clarified the vague and undefined features of reform and pointed the direction of future developments.

Looking Backward had explained that there was no such thing in a civilized society as self-support. From the moment when human beings began to live together, self-support became impossible. Liberty no longer meant personal autonomy. The subdivision of occupations and services made mutual dependence the universal rule, along with the duty and guarantee of mutual support. Elihu Root's The Citizen's Part in Government described the dependency of the urban family for every article of life upon products from faraway places. It exercised no control at all over the things absolutely necessary to its daily life. Paradoxically, such a family could overcome its utter dependency only by joining others equally dependent and gaining control by common organization, that is, by government. People could either govern or be governed, control their own lives or lead subject lives. Citizenship, the product of intensive training, required destruction of that individualistic tendency which made people conscious of responsibilities to their own families, personal interests and pursuits, while neglecting obligations to the larger community.[64]

Perhaps not directly but nonetheless decisively, these ideas impinged upon politics. After he left the White House, Roosevelt's judgments on the important economic issues before the nation expanded, reshaped by new friends. George W. Perkins, a Morgan partner and formerly head of New York Life Insurance Company, Frank A. Munsey, the newspaper publisher, and T. C. Du Pont argued that the day of free competition and of the individual entrepreneur had ended. Only the great corporations could organize modern business effectively; and society would benefit so long as these entities behaved in an orderly, responsible manner. Roosevelt had also read Herbert Croly's Promise of American Life (1909), which treated the corporation as the central agency of modern times while it served as an instrument for attaining goals set by the state. Calling for a new nationalism, Roosevelt explained that efforts to restore competition as it had existed sixty years earlier were as foolish as a return to the flintlocks of Washington's army. Government ought not to strangle but to regulate business.[65]

*

Progressives, emboldened by success in the election of 1910, believed that their moment had come. In January 1911 they formed the National Progressive Republican League, to work within the GOP for the nomination of Senator Robert M. LaFollette, who called for a more vigorous antitrust policy among other objectives. But he collapsed on February 12, 1912, and a nervous breakdown took him out of the running. With the organization adrift, Theodore Roosevelt became convinced of his duty to take over.

He had tired of big game hunting and of desultory travel. Only fifty-four in 1912, he could not reconcile himself to the end of his career. Furthermore, his resentment against Taft, caused by differences over patronage and pique over the Ballinger-Pinchot controversy, intensified. Prosecution of the United States Steel Corporation increased T.R.'s emotional conviction that the country was in improper hands; after all, he had assured J. P. Morgan that acquisition of Tennessee Coal and Iron would lead to no reprisals. Roosevelt also feared that William Jennings Bryan or some other wild Democrat would win, to the infinite damage of the Republic.

Above all, Roosevelt had a cause no one else articulated. Although many discussed the importance of the corporation, no responsible politician had given it adequate recognition, and Progressive antitrust clamor drowned out the most valuable answer to the problem. He alone could make the people listen. In August 1910, in a speech widely interpreted as an attack on Taft, he issued a call for a New Nationalism, its theme the use of Hamiltonian means (a strong, directing government) for Jeffersonian ends (the common welfare). Large organizations he deemed necessary and useful if controlled by a corresponding increase in government power. Therefore muckrakers' babbling obscured as many dangers as industrialists' stubbornness. Roosevelt proposed neither to smash nor yield to the trusts, but safely to harness them to socially useful purposes, thus use them to expand everyone's liberty to act.

This conviction animated his activities in 1912, first in the unsuccessful quest for the Republican nomination and then in the losing Progressive campaign for the presidency. All his life a regular, who had spurned the mugwumps and independents for their lack of realism, he formed a new party to crusade for national redemption, out of personal rage and out of the conviction that he alone could lead the nation in the correct direction. Herbert Croly bluntly described Roosevelt's agenda in 1912: a "drastic reorganization of the American political and economic system, the substitution of a frank social policy for the individualism of the past"—and "the realization of this policy, if necessary, by the use of efficient governmental instruments." T.R., in victory, would triumph over primitive democratic politics, with their excessive concern for popular rights, limited government, and "the protection of specific individual and local liberties." Roosevelt represented to his supporters an end to a democracy "socially and nationally irresponsible . . . interested not in the people as a whole . . . [but] in the people as divided into local groups and supposed individuals."[66]

The Democrats nominated a progressive to draw votes away from the two GOP wings. William Jennings Bryan, the peerless loser, having by then gone down to defeat three times, opted for Woodrow Wilson of New Jersey, who had earned a reform reputation as president of Princeton University and governor of New Jersey.

The new Progressive party convention welcomed a host of strange delegates—relatively few politicians, but a great many reformers and social workers—not the comrades-in-arms with whom their nominee, Roosevelt, had worked earlier. Nor did the platform altogether express his views. Calling for social justice, a living wage for an eight-hour day, insurance against sickness, accidents, unemployment, and old age, and for a commission to regulate industry, he summoned the hosts to stand at Armaggeddon and battle for the Lord.[67]

The Socialists put a fourth candidate in the field and for the first time seriously challenged the dominant political groups. The number of votes they had gained had risen from about a hundred thousand in 1900 to about four hundred thousand in 1904 and 1908. Eugene V. Debs, however, by 1912 enjoyed a devoted national following impressed by his personal decency and ideological pragmatism, "so genial and charming as a human being" that Emma Goldman "did not mind the lack of political clarity which made him reach out at one and the same time for opposite poles." Furthermore, honest and efficient Socialist municipal administrations in Milwaukee and Bridgeport left the impression that this party, too, was progressive, merely more advanced than the others. Debs would poll 6 percent of the popular vote after blasting the major parties as tools of oppression and slaves of greed, and espousing an alternative system that would conduct industry for the common good in a vision of ordered liberty that would effect "the transition from economic individualism to Socialism, from wage slavery to free cooperation, from capitalist oligarchy to industrial democracy."[68]

Four progressive candidates thus contested the presidential election of 1912. The marked differences among Taft, Roosevelt, Wilson, and Debs did not conceal the common assumption that the use of intelligence by government could correct society's ills and improve people's lives. However, beyond the surface similarity of calls for control of the trusts and for broadened responsibilities of government lay vital disagreements about the future of industrial organization, particularly between Roosevelt and Wilson.

Roosevelt sought increased use of centralized governmental authority in domestic as well as in foreign affairs. Distrusting the established political processes and the courts, he preferred greater executive action, using men of intelligence, education, and wealth, whose wisdom and disinterestedness could best serve the country. His experience as president and the doctrines of the New Nationalism convinced him that a powerful bureau of corporations overseeing the whole economy could best judge the reasonableness of combinations and guard the public welfare by the licensing power. Quick action on behalf of labor could also avoid divisive class conflicts. The state could thus expand the ability to act of all its citizens.

Therein the Progressives and the Democrats differed fundamentally. Roosevelt accepted a degree of economic concentration under government control unthinkable to Wilson, who feared that the paternalistic combination between money and government, which T.R. envisioned, would enslave the people. Only free enterprise could preserve American liberty. Wilson had not given much thought to these issues until August 1912, when he met Louis D. Brandeis, a lawyer who had spent much of the previous decade fighting the public utilities. Brandeis persuaded the Democratic candidate that bigness, itself an evil, a source of inefficiency and corruption, tended naturally toward monopoly. The remedy, contraction of the role of government except as a means of maintaining competition and protecting the weak against the strong. That message of the New Freedom attracted agrarians in the South and the West to the Democratic standard-bearer.

In sending Wilson to the White House, the voters rejected the course Theodore Roosevelt advocated. The new president and the agrarians who staffed his administration judged social policy from the viewpoint of the small proprietor and the independent farmer. Jeffersonians not only in ends but in means, they considered restraint on bigness the most effective protection for individual liberties. The New Freedom aimed to rectify the injustices industrialization had caused by a return to the earlier values of economic and political democracy. The attempt to shape policy according to those values formed the primary task of Wilson's first years in office.

He entered the White House without legal training, strongly persuaded of the power of correct ideas; but he lacked T.R.'s knack for compromise. His first inaugural called for a New Freedom, for laws to look after men on the make, those seeking to advance. Critics like Herbert Croly saw in it a general "revival of Jeffersonian individualism," a backward-looking orientation, essentially a negative set of policies, disparaging expert contribution to the business of government, opposing the extension of national responsibility, and entrusting the future of democracy to cooperation between an individualistic legal system and a fundamentally competitive economic system. Advice from congressional Democrats and academics and other intellectuals helped frame Wilson's agenda. The income tax provided revenue that permitted downward revision of the tariff (1913) and delegation to the Tariff Commission of authority to make future adjustments (1916). The Federal Reserve Act (1913) created a central banking system dominated not by bankers, as the 1912 monetary commission had recommended, but by government boards. These measures created a positive, directing, but limited role for government. Others strengthened regulatory powers, as did the Clayton Antitrust Act, which empowered the Federal Trade Commission to halt practices it deemed illegal by cease-and-desist orders. Still other measures protected vulnerable members of society, providing loans to farmers through land banks, aiding the construction of rural post roads, and setting standards for the labor of seamen, railroad workers, and children under fourteen.[69]

Not deliberately or consciously but nonetheless consistently, Wilson approached Lester Ward's vision of sociocracy, replacing parties and politicians with a unified nation acting as a single individual and guided by the social intellect. "To the influence of intelligence in artificially modifying the environment of man in his own interest there is scarcely any limit," Ward had written, and the world needed only "vigorous action in this direction." The result would, Herbert Croly explained, end the discrepancy between democracy and nationalism. The country would cease to be "a democracy of indiscriminate individualism, and become one of selected individuals" united by a sense of "joint responsibility for the success of their political and social ideals."[70]

Soon the war to make the world safe for democracy opened new opportunities for the experiment in sociocracy, as the federal government embarked on the railroad and shipping business, raised the minimum income tax from 2 to 12 percent, and took control of industrial production. Contemplating the need to define peace terms, Colonel House set up "The Inquiry" staffed by intellectuals and scholars. Art also enlisted. James Montgomery Flagg's best-known Uncle Sam poster—"I Want You for the U.S. Army," with its compelling design, pointing finger, and eyes that seemed to follow passersby, paralleled the work of the Bureau of Cartoons, set up under the auspices of George Creel's Committee on Public Information, which published a weekly bulletin advising artists how to serve the war effort. The government took these steps casually, without considering their fateful effect on the future of liberty in America.[71]

Their minds unfettered by knowledge acquired at Harvard, Yale, Princeton, and Hopkins, the twentieth-century presidents dreamed of expanding liberty by remolding the intractable masses. But unanticipated implications followed from the appeal to common action. Americans had cause to worry about the trend to treat individual liberty not as the goal of human progress but as a means to advance public morality; the courts remained one check on partisan attempts by the majority to abridge the freedom of the minority (1903). Yet guarantees of personal liberty could not stand against reassertion of the dogma of absolute sovereignty (1915).

The people called to unity gave their own meanings to nationalism, and revived the concept of *mission,* dormant during the post–Civil War decades while Americans concentrated their energies on internal problems. In the desire to strengthen the federal government, progressives often appealed to national solidarity, linking patriotism and reform as *Looking Backward* had already done. The association of nationalism and progress proved particularly effective in the decades when the final reconciliation of North and South generated a strong emotional upswell of loyalty. The splendid little war against Spain excited widespread patriotism, and entry in the world war did even more. Citizens could not calmly prate

> Of great deeds that our sires had done,
> And take the name of Washington
> Upon our lips unworthily,
> While Cuba fights for liberty.

Americans who read a popular novel learned that they "were not worse than the old nations," but had a right to be very much better. Free to grow great, they could be the richest, if only they took care not to be the most sordid.

Internal problems persisted. The Populist revolt had subsided, but economic reorganization still proceeded, with its economic, cultural, and social effects still unclear. And the freedom described in progressive dreams evoked troubling thoughts. Whither? Would all those improvements envisioned by the smarties station the mass of men and women like automatons at the service of the machines, or arrange them in the lines of industrial or military armies?[72]

VIII

ON LINE, IN STEP

MORE, MORE! Bigger, bigger! Of everything.

The incessant clamor beat upon everyone—men, women, and children; rich and poor; manufacturers, merchants, bankers, planters, artisans, and farmers.

All responded—and out of the best of motives.

Everything swelled in size: schools, business offices, skyscrapers, bonanza farms, government, and yachts and hotels. San Francisco's Palace Hotel (1876), by its own claim the biggest in the world, boasted 755 rooms, with 2,042 ventilating tubes, four artesian wells, thermostatic bulbs that formed a complete fire alarm guard, five elevators, and a gigantic bill of fare. Promoters of the 1893 Chicago exhibition emphasized its location "in one of the vastest park systems in the world"—created by months of titanic toil and the expenditure of vast sums in "the greatest enterprise of modern times." Only the most skilled builders could "grasp its immensity, the intricacy of the executive machinery . . . the enormous daily outlay required to keep in harmonious and perfect rhythm the many thousand of picks and shovels and hammers" that enabled "the enchanted white city—the city of alladin's palaces" magically to spring from the mud of a primeval prairie. And not only capitalists out for profit, but also reformers seeking goodness and efficiency by way of hospitals and universities, by way of regulatory bureaucracies and of fattening statute books—almost everyone proclaimed expansion the supreme law of the land. At the opening of the New York Metropolitan Opera House (1883), the nouveaux riches, the Goulds and the Vanderbilts, the Morgans and the Whitneys, perfumed the air with the odor of crisp greenbacks.

Only a few craftsmen, left behind, complained, unheeded, against the forces that devalued their skills. "It's America, the land of machines and of 'hurry up.'"

Even fewer Americans wondered why expansion in these decades took the form it did.[1]

After 1850, as earlier, territorial spread, population growth, and soaring outputs of agriculture and industry altered the social structure and shaped cultural patterns. Goods made available in once-unimaginable abundance generated an environment of perpetual boom and occasional bust, and encouraged efforts to arrive at ever-higher degrees of rationality, efficiency, and order. The steady upward movement of the gross national product interested few; but visible evidence of another sort did. Twenty-seven million visitors at the Chicago Exposition of 1893, twenty million more at the St. Louis Exposition in 1904, surveyed a record of progress, including the achievements of women. The electric light, a sensational novelty in Chicago, had become commonplace in St. Louis. Hundreds of exhibits displayed the limitless resources of minerals and oil and confirmed the certainty of continuing growth. The output of anthracite, of bituminous coal, of iron ore, of copper and of aluminum, as well as the continued increase of agricultural goods, testified to progress. While in outward form expansion continued as before—more land, more rails, more factories—anxiety tinged the exuberance lest the mighty powers now created get totally out of control. Although the orators did not cease to recall contributions to religious and civil liberty, growth, once a self-evidently desirable force through the opportunities it created and the goods it provided—more for all—now displayed hideous aspects threatening to shackle helpless humans to impersonal machines, to destroy the freedom to act unless contained within reasonable limits. Irony: efforts to establish such limits only tightened the restraints on individuals.[2]

Few objected that a national transportation system stimulated the immense expansion of settlement and of manufacturing between 1850 and 1920, easing the advance along the frontier, lowering the cost of agricultural and industrial products, and creating a national economy. The spread of population and the rise in farm and factory output presented opportunities to entrepreneurs who promoted ventures to tie together the "exceedingly new" country that had "advanced by leaps to the Pacific, and left many a lesser Oregon and California unexplored." Railroads extended across the continent, forming an integrated pattern of communication that held everyone in place, although wasteful construction—

boilers bursting, rails snapping, and bridges breaking—squandered human life and resources.[3]

The railroads built before 1850 excited popular fantasies about the wonders of the iron horse. Flying across the plains or trundling gallantly up the hillsides, locomotives stirred the romantic dreams of onlookers, fostered by the man-made machine's conquest of space. In many localities the manufacturer's mind's eye made out an endless line of freight cars loaded with his products; the farmer saw loads of grain hauled to eager, distant purchasers; land speculators firmly believed that the cars would return crammed with settlers; and promoters and investors had no doubt that the value of securities would skyrocket. Periodic panics and depressions when the boom burst did not halt the general expansion. The miles of track multiplied five-fold in the two decades after 1850 and then tripled in the twenty years after that.

In a great burst of construction, four bands of iron thrust out from the Mississippi to the Pacific. The project had raised political questions in the 1850s, but in 1862 the federal government encouraged the Union Pacific to move westward from Omaha and the Central Pacific to build eastward from Sacramento. "We have drawn the elephant. Now let us see if we can harness him up," wired the engineer Theodore Dehone Judah when President Lincoln approved. The term *elephant* connoted bigness, strangeness, and a hint of the ominous. Construction began in 1865; and after four laborious years the two lines met in Utah, where women learned to bolt the doors and windows of their homes as the crews approached.

Rival promoters secured charters for other transcontinentals. The Northern Pacific planned to reach from Chicago and Milwaukee to Portland and Seattle, the Southern Pacific from Los Angeles to El Paso and thence eastward, while the Santa Fe took off from San Diego. A fifth competitor appeared in 1890 when James J. Hill combined a number of smaller corporations to form the Great Northern from St. Paul to the west coast. In addition, the Chicago, Burlington, and Quincy developed extensive routes beyond the Mississippi. A half-dozen guidebooks testified to the popularity of transcontinental touring.[4]

Fully as important, four great east-west railroad networks linked the Atlantic seaports with the Mississippi valley. By the 1870s, the New York Central, the Erie, the Pennsylvania, and the Baltimore and Ohio had consolidated smaller lines and drew traffic from thousands of miles of feeders. The process, at first slower in the South, accelerated with a flurry of construction in the 1880s. With each road built by its own promoter, track widths, locomotives, rolling stock, and types of coupling varied widely, constricting the movement of freight over long distances. Only decades of gradual standardization enabled the cars of one line to move over the tracks of another, avoiding transshipment costs. Meanwhile, cooperation depended on common operational practices while fast freight and express companies expedited the movement of goods and ended the romance of the pony express and the overland stage.

Physical improvements helped. Iron and steel bridges, capable of bearing greater loads, replaced primitive wooden spans and crossed many rivers for the first time in the 1870s. George Westinghouse's air brake, Eli Janney's coupler, automatic block signals, steel instead of iron rails, and better techniques for laying roadbeds carried heavier equipment at greater speed and lower cost. Hotel cars, palace cars, and finally the Pullman car added touches of luxury to travel by rail.[5]

The volume of freight and the number of passengers climbed. Conceivably more traffic could have moved by the canals and waterways still in use, along with additional ones that might have appeared in the absence of railroads. Highways might also have escaped the neglect from which they suffered until 1890, when the appearance of millions of bicycles created demands for improved roads. But even making allowances for these hypothetical alternatives, the railroads in actuality expanded communications and created a net saving in transportation costs.[6]

In the twentieth century a new figure of speech replaced the old image of the iron horse creeping across the Massachusetts countryside (1850); increasingly critics referred to "the octopus"—tentacles reaching everywhere, irresistible, intentions mysterious but sinister, able to crush any human who fell within its grip, called into being by that "perpetual and restless desire of power after power that ceaseth only in death" described by Thomas Hobbes in his *Leviathan*. The fury of ambition, the lust for success in disregard of reason and morality, drove on the promoters depicted by journalists and by novelists like Frank Norris, who aimed to expose injustice, crime, and inequality in everyday life. Like the sheep crushed by a passing train on the track onto which they had wandered, individuals counted for nothing. But beyond the clash between them and centralized, rapacious power lay the wheat, the land itself, unchanged, and the spirit of the people that would triumph in the end.[7]

Nevertheless, Edward H. Harriman, a romantic, dreamed of circling the globe with his railroads and steamships. His lines extended from New York to San Francisco and Mexico, and his Pacific Mail Steamship Company operated between American and Asian ports. From Japan, he expected to move through Manchuria, Siberia, and Russia to the Baltic whence his steamers would proceed to New York. But the Japanese would not grant him control of the South Manchuria Railroad just acquired from Russia. Foiled! The market did not let such types get away with it, either in mobilizing the investment capital or in attracting the freight-paying shippers. A narrower logic moved the competitive combinations: gobble up feeder lines or be gobbled up.[8]

The capital invested in railroads in 1890 stood at well over $10 billion (at a time when the total national debt amounted to $1 billion). To accumulate funds of this magnitude, promoters counted on a long tradition of government assistance for internal improvements. A federal land grant to aid construction of the Illinois Central Railroad (1850) became a precedent for similar benefactions to the transcontinentals after 1862. Generally, in return for undertaking to complete their roads in ten or twelve years, the corporations received a specified number of sections along their rights of way. Some states, like Maine and Texas, also used their domains to stimulate construction; others guaranteed the railroad bonds. And many a city or town, persuaded that the arrival of the rails would turn it into a metropolis, willingly made donations or loans or, more usually, subscribed to securities. The coming of the Northern Pacific, which made it the Lake Superior terminus, thus transformed Duluth from a remote hamlet to a bustling metropolis.[9]

The broad bands of land the grants marked out on the map looked substantial, but provided less assistance than appeared on paper. Since few railroads met the conditions imposed by law, their agents in the federal and state capitals had to cajole or bribe legislators to secure extensions and prevent forfeitures. By 1881, for instance, of almost 180 million acres set aside for this purpose, the grantees had actually patented only 33 million and had sold less than half of that, for a total of $71 million. Divided among the competing corporations, the immediate value of such aid proved dubious, apart from the psychological stimulus it gave to private investment. With every new road a speculation, innocents took heart from the belief that the government stood behind the venture. Although they sometimes learned, to their grief, that a state could default on its obligations, for the moment involvement seemed a token of added security.

Private investment supplied most of the funds, and some roads like Hill's Great Northern received no aid at all. Since sales of stock rarely brought in more than the cash for organization and surveys, construction depended on bonds floated among the public. Some promoters persuaded banks to make loans against the bonds as security; others operated through intermediary construction companies, which raised their own capital on the strength of lucrative building contracts. About one-fifth of the amount needed came from English, Dutch, and German investors; the balance emanated from the savings of Americans.

Returns proved uneven. In the 1870s and 1880s both interest and dividend payments plunged downward; and some ventures never paid off. Securities found an ample market in prosperous times but no takers in periods of financial stress. Roads, overbuilt at high cost during booms, reeled under heavy charges for debt when the economy contracted. All too often, also, dishonest promoters and excessive payments to construction companies controlled by insiders added to the handicaps under which the enterprises labored. Hard-hit New York farmers complained of rates that favored western products at the expense of eastern growers. A militant Farmers' Alliance called on the people to dethrone the arrogant railway magnates.[10]

The transportation pattern followed no coherent plan as did the French, but operated by competitive trial and error, with key decisions by speculative entrepreneurs. Two routes connected New York to Washington, four to Chicago, and three to Boston. Keen rivalry gave rise to unfair tactics in the absence of recognized pricing policies. A road that bid against a rival for through traffic but monopolized the business between intermediate points charged more for the short haul than for the long haul. Aggressive companies seduced big shippers by rebates and sought favors from politicians by the liberal use of passes. To eliminate such costly practices and to keep rates high, competing roads divided the market by pooling arrangements. Some railroad men, unhappy about excessive competition, tried self-regulation. In 1875, twenty-two southern roads, and a few years later, groups of eastern and western lines, set up associations to govern rates. But these devices, subject to evasion, evoked the protests of users.

Popular approval quickly became popular dislike. Citizens who had eagerly persuaded the railroad to pass through town, within a few years felt aggrieved by unpaid interest on the bonds and by rates that drained off the returns from sales of corn and wheat. The gallant iron horse became a devouring monster threatening to enslave commerce and endangering free government. When the Hall of Transportation opened at the Chicago World's Fair (1893), commentators also hoped that the railroad, upon which the happiness and prosperity of so many depended, would pass to the state, where the control rightfully belonged. Americans, however, lacked the faith in government to make the transfer, and therefore evaded the issue of the relation to liberty.[11]

Other forms of communication survived in the interstices railways did not serve. Although the volume of overseas trade continued to mount, the percentage borne in American carriers declined after 1860. Severe foreign competition made alternative investments more attractive to merchants. Traffic on the inland waterways expanded; but the canals and coastal shipping lost ground to the railway. By contrast, the telegraph network grew rapidly; and Alexander Graham Bell's invention, the telephone (1876), entered into widespread use in the 1880s, privately operated unlike its counterparts in other countries. The ingenuity of Theodore N. Vail (1845–1920) devised a system of interdependent exchanges providing universal service without state intervention; and dealings with the politically controlled post office stifled any thought of nationalization. Meanwhile Cyrus Field's cable had opened communication across the Atlantic in 1866.

The demand for improved transportation within the growing cities long remained unmet. Compared to Babylon's hanging gardens, the Egyptian pyramids, and the Acropolis of Athens, the Brooklyn Bridge, an engineering triumph completed in 1883 after fifteen years of effort at a cost of $10 million, eased the pressure on ferries. The "motionless mass of masonry and metal" seemed to Mayor Abram Hewitt a symbol of "organized intelligence," producing absolute stability out of unstable elements. Conflict remained the law of the city, but intelligence, guided by science, commerce, and courage could transform it into harmony.

Washington and Buffalo then had adequately paved streets. But in the 1880s Chicago, more typical of the country at large, left two-thirds of its roads unsurfaced, and rapid transit still depended on horse cars and on the hundred thousand animals who drew them. New York, Kansas City, and Brooklyn experimented with elevated railways, but relied on steam locomotives for traction at heavy expense and with considerable inconvenience. Some municipalities turned to cars conveyed by grappling through a slotted trench to an endless, moving steel cable. The urban population could not move about conveniently, swiftly, or cheaply, however, until Thomas A. Edison developed the technique for transmitting power from a distant central station (1882), which enabled Frank J. Sprague in Richmond, Virginia, to operate a line drawing electricity from an overhead trolley wire supplied from such a source (1888). In the next two years, fifty cities adopted the system. Soon the new arrangement ran elevated and underground cars in a true rapid transit system.[12]

Effective communications depended not only on the rails and wires that carried people, things, and messages, but also upon a dependable set of relationships among passengers, dispatchers, and receivers—connections largely personal until 1850. Owners had until then set the approximate schedules and the rates; and travelers transacted their business with the driver or the station agent. But arrivals and departures fluctuated with the weather and with road conditions. In 1870 some eighty different times prevailed in the United States. Flexibility, a condition of smallness, fewness, became ever less tolerable.

On the continental or metropolitan scale, time became precise and measured in seconds within zones that divided the country (1883) to avoid collisions on routes with dense traffic and to ensure close connections at transfer points. The payment of fares became mechanical, just as machines stamped on a card the worker's moment of arrival and departure. Some observers blamed that precision for American nervousness. But most people adapted with little strain. The thousands of voyagers who thronged Grand Central or Penn or Union station or who shuffled from one subway platform to another avoided collisions by accepting inflexible rules. Wondrous to behold, in the winter's chill or the stifling summer heat, the Calabrian and the Cantonese, the starched-up clerk and the tattered tailor keeping to the right, walking not running, jostling not shoving, arrived at their destinations as they crowded out of consciousness the mingled odors of garlic and sweat, of still uneaten fish or of bread yet hot. The movements of bicycles and automobiles also fell into line— keep to the right, the rule of the road.[13]

Every feature of the productive system depended upon disciplined behavior. Controlled traffic determined the performance of all people and things, and all the more so in a system without switching points to guide the direction of individual impulses.

Education trained citizens in the proper responses. The one-room schoolhouse disappeared, along with its casual instructors and haphazard subject matter imparted to students of all ages proceeding at their own pace according to ability. New buildings served the much larger numbers of a city neighborhood or a consolidated rural district, with pupils sorted out into arbitrary grades in a three-tier system—primary, secondary, collegiate—each articulated with the others and all directed by professional teachers and administrators. A uniform curriculum, dominated by the requirements for passage to the next tier, set the terms for learning. At thousands of desks boys and girls practiced penmanship according to the Palmer method in the expectation that correct handwriting would get them ahead. In the twentieth century reformers devoted much effort to setting national standards so that every diploma or degree would have the same value.[14]

Those who arrived too late to enter the first grade or had to take jobs before graduation could go on in vocational, continuation, or night schools in an earnest effort to catch up. Adults, and particularly the foreign-born, toiled away, not knowing what the school expected of them.

Writing lessons for steel workers aged twenty-five to thirty, wearily making the effort to stay awake: they copy, "I am a yellow bird. I can sing. I can fly. I can sing to you." More to the point, the first lesson in English for employees at the International Harvester Company:

I hear the whistle. I must hurry.
I hear the five minute whistle.
It is time to go into the shop.
I take my check from the gateboard and hang it on the department board.
I change my clothes and get ready to work.
The starting whistle blows. I eat my lunch.
It is forbidden to eat until then.
The whistle blows at five minutes to starting time.
I get ready to work.
I work until the whistle blows to quit.
I leave my place nice and clean.
I put all my clothes in my locker.
I go home.

Thus they learned to stay in line.[15]

American society regarded knowledge as a great thing—the ability to use it, apply it, even greater.

Never mind the knowledge people: the scientists, agronomists, the engineers, the architects. Consider the intermediaries: the organizers, the people with schedules and lists who followed the plans and got the work done by manipulating time, hands, and materials.

George J. Adams and the hundred Maine farmers who sailed off to raise oranges in Jaffa (1866) failed not from want of vision but from neglect of the mechanism for getting the product to market. The groves in Florida and California did better because linked to a distribution network that also took perishable fruit and vegetables from the irrigated southwest to the sidewalks of New York and Chicago.

The middlemen, contractors vilified in reform polemics because they siphoned profits off the top simply for moving, rather than creating, goods, performed essential services. James Kyner, one of them, took on jobs for the western railroads. He did not himself swing an ax or shovel the intractable rocks. But at a fixed point in an empty wilderness he assembled the men, the horses, the rails and timber, the tents for the camps and the supplies for the commissary—and all on time and in place; otherwise expenses soared to the failure point.

Before 1850, danger had ended when the ship arrived in port; the master had only to pass through the formalities of quarantine and customs, then tie up and unload. Then traffic in the great harbors—New York, New Orleans, Baltimore, and San Francisco—grew more complex. Enormous steel-hulled vessels could not maneuver alone, amid insistent ferries and other craft, by the bridges and through the narrow spaces to their docks, but required tugs and local pilots, intermediaries, to nudge them into places—on schedule and not simply when convenient.

New York City cherished its superlatives—busiest, highest, largest— all earned, but tenuous because utterly dependent upon precision in bringing together thousands of human and material components. In 1910 the Pennsylvania Station opened, and in 1913 the Woolworth Building—one with its tunnels under the Hudson and East Rivers making it the largest structure in the country, the other, a 792-foot cathedral of commerce, the highest in the world. Each rested on a frame of structural steel, braced against wind and fastened by rivets such as experience with fabricating boilers had developed. Concrete walls curtained the interior; and elaborate electrical systems provided power for light and for the elevators. McKim, Mead, and White and Cass Gilbert, the architects, gave one a classical, the other a Gothic veneer; and Charles W. Raymond and Gunvald Aus Company did the engineering calculations. But success in the ventures depended upon contractors who got the steel beams, the lumber, concrete, rivets, wires, and pipes for plumbing through the narrow Manhattan streets, on drays, in time, when needed, and neither too late nor too early.

Similar feats of organization, if not of architectural artistry, went into the speedy erection of thousands of tenements and three-deckers as well as of endless rows of suburban one-family houses. And modern factories required the efficient assembly of numerous parts and the prompt removal of the finished products. Whatever waited around caused needless expense.[16]

Discipline therefore regulated the movement of goods as it did of people. Once the merchant or manufacturer had acted through trusted agents, or consigned goods to factors or to the ship's captain or supercargo who made sales on the owner's behalf. Modifications of this system continued to convey agricultural products from farmers to processors or consumers. Perishable crops went to commission merchants who sold them at prices established by fluctuations of local supply and demand. In the more orderly market for the great staples, brokers in the important towns bought up the cotton or wheat, paying a price determined on central commodity exchanges.

A more elaborate pattern developed for manufacturers. At the chief regional distribution points, wholesalers or jobbers bought goods, which they divided into smaller quantities to stock the retailers' shelves throughout the country, thereby linking the manufacturer with every crossroad shop. The wholesalers also supplied three to six months' credit to their customers, thus easing capital requirements. A corps of traveling salesmen made the rounds of neighborhood stores or passed from village to village, carrying in their sample cases the offerings of distant factories.

Retail shopkeepers, the building blocks of the distribution system, completed the ultimate transactions that transferred products to consumers. A slight investment enabled the ambitious to enter this channel of trade, often by making a start in peddling. Thousands of rural general stores carried a variety of products; in the cities, more specialized enterprises handled food, dry goods (textiles), and hardware. The shopkeeper who knew his customers extended them a year's credit and acted as intermediary between their tastes and the outpouring of goods from the factory. He could also adjust prices by bargaining, while loose accounting methods often postponed settlements.

Measured by the ability to distribute the products of industry, these arrangements worked and explained the abundance that some Europeans believed accounted for the failure of socialism to attract Americans. But the system required the services of thousands, and increased costs paid by the final purchasers persuaded aggrieved consumers that the hucksters' prices reflected not the "commercial law of supply and demand" but speculative greed. However, proposals to establish "protection Unions, or people's grocery stores" (1857) came to nothing, leaving scope for the ingenuity of entrepreneurs whose efforts to economize regulated distribution patterns.[17]

George Francis Gilman, a New York City hide and leather dealer, began in 1860 to dabble in tea, and kept scheming for some way to make it big. He devised a club plan through which he sold bargains directly to groups, and he added units to his chain of retail stores. By 1871 his Great Atlantic and Pacific Tea Company had outlets scattered from Saxton's River, Vermont, to Baton Rouge, Louisiana, and also did a mail order business that aimed at high-volume distribution of a few items, like tea. In 1878, when his business got too large, he entered into a partnership with George Huntington Hartford, who systematized the enterprise, expanded the number of stores, and added a full range of grocery items.

Band concerts, parades, and prizes advertised the A&P virtues and expanded its clientele. When Gilman died in 1901, he left—along with a young widow who lived in his house and claimed she was his adopted daughter—his affairs in a tangle. But he had launched retailing upon a modern course that made the old-fashioned trader anachronistic. James Butler, an Irish immigrant, did the same.

In 1879, F. W. Woolworth of Lancaster, Pennsylvania, started to sell five- and ten-cent items in his shop, then developed a chain of more than three hundred outlets despite competition from S. S. Kresge. James E. Scripps, publisher of a cheap evening newspaper in Detroit, also spread out. Improved transportation, lowered postal rates, and rural free delivery created other opportunities for innovation. In 1872, Aaron Montgomery Ward's mail order business sent its tempting catalogues to thousands of farm households; shortly Sears, Roebuck joined it and the sales of both firms grew steadily. One Price for All, the slogan of these ventures, attracted customers insecure about their haggling talents.[18]

Expanding cities created new opportunities. Enterprising dry goods dealers added other items—crockery, kitchen utensils, furniture, clothing—to tempt women who made the family purchases when they came to buy muslin or woolens at Stewart's or Macy's or Wanamaker's. At the central point of the streetcar network, department stores pulled growing numbers through their doors, offering shoppers bargains at fixed prices. Lavish display advertisements persuaded customers to buy articles they did not know they wanted. In the marble palace Field and Leiter opened in Chicago (1868), anyone could ride the steam elevator or stroll by the walnut counters lit by gas fixtures, or acquire a lady's walking suit for $160—underskirt of blue and black satin, top skirt of black velvet with five puffings, open back to allow piping and heavy fringe to protrude. The customer—always right—could return goods that failed to satisfy and find comfort in lavatories, lounges, soda fountains, and restaurants, all organized on a large scale. Christmas exhibitions and periodic sales sustained interest.[19]

Some manufacturers developed their own distribution organizations. In the hope of controlling its market, the Standard Oil Company dealt with retailers through subsidiaries rather than through wholesalers who also handled the kerosene of its competitors. The need for servicing a complicated mechanism led the Singer Sewing Machine Company to establish outlets in every corner of the country. Gustavus F. Swift (born 1839 on a Cape Cod farm) at fourteen went to work for his brother, the village butcher. At twenty he drove cattle to Boston and discerned the inefficiency of transporting livestock for slaughter close to market, when it would be far cheaper to slaughter the animals near the source and ship only the meat. He moved to Chicago, whence in 1875 he sent carloads of dressed beef to Boston under refrigeration. To offset conservative local dealers, Swift set up his own national sales organization and arranged for expeditious transportation from his packing plants in Kansas City, Omaha, St. Louis, St. Paul, and Fort Worth. Local millers also lost out to a few great firms, operating technologically advanced plants close to the source of the wheat, but distributing standardized products through thousands of outlets.

Changes in advertising techniques helped such manufacturers. With newspapers still the primary medium, the large displays of department stores gradually preempted the prime columns formerly given over to many notices a few lines long. Agencies like N. W. Ayer bought space on behalf of clients; and James Walter Thompson designed the whole layout. They and others could insert descriptions of the producer's wares in hundreds of newspapers at once; and magazines with national circulation also opened their pages to this material. Merchants discovered that a "newsy style" reminiscent of light romantic novels increased sales without creating an image of cheapness.

> *Should my daughter wear corsets?*
> This is a question many a mother asks herself.
> Several years ago we thought out the problem and prepared
> girdles and corsets . . . several styles and kinds . . .
> including
> the corset with smallest hip and bust proportions to prevent
> the figure
> spreading.

By 1890, in addition, billboards plastered the blank spaces along roads and streets. National advertising took the power of choice out of the hands of the retailer when his customers ceased to ask for soap or cocoa and learned to demand Pear's or Baker's.[20]

Imperceptibly, gently, scores of products enmeshed the welcoming Americans, Elisha Otis's elevator (1854), Melville Bissell's carpet sweeper (1876), and Lewis Waterman's fountain pen (1884)—machines better than servants, as *The Confidence Man* had explained. Certainly few women preferred to boil their own soap or spin their own thread; few men, even on the farm, wished to butcher their own hogs, as grandpa had, when local shops offered almost as good. Yet the change involved a surrender of autonomy, created dependence on a remote, impersonal A&P

or five-and-dime—no credit, no neighborly chatter, pure business transactions.[21]

The city, focal point for much of this activity, housed some manufacturing but remained primarily a transportation, distribution, and management center. Its population swelled far beyond the midcentury limits. In
1890 almost 30 percent of Americans resided in places with eight thousand
or more inhabitants. Twenty-five cities in 1870 had boasted populations
of fifty thousand or more; fifty-eight did so in 1890. Fewer than five
million people had lived in such communities at the earlier date; almost
twelve million did so at the later, and by then three cities had gone above
the million mark.

Complex life there demanded numerous daily contacts of such sensitivity that they could not depend, as in the past, upon well-established,
static connections among stable households. Instead the residents had to
behave individually and impersonally, achieving regularity of contacts by
rigid allocations of space and time. That order permitted factories and
department stores to function.

Growth magnified inherited unsolved urban problems—the additional residents needed housing, water, and light; they created wastes, and
they commuted to their jobs. The problems of establishing order through
democratic government, of providing protection against fire and violence, and of satisfying heterogeneous social and cultural needs, complicated the physical difficulties. In the painful effort to respond to these
challenges, Americans paid the price for creation of a national distribution
system to move goods and people about.

Individuals shrank in the new scale of things, so that Mark Twain
considered humans sheep, who followed the handful making the most
noise.[22] The massive cities, factories, even farms, operated by mechanical,
impersonal rules, demanding that men and women adjust, whatever their
wish or preference. In the 1880s, in western Nebraska, a railroad contractor remained unmoved when he saw "an almost unbroken stream of
emigrants from horizon to horizon—a distance of not less than eight
miles or ten. Teams of covered wagons, horsemen, little bunches of cows,
more wagons, some drawn by cows, men walking, women and children
riding"—hardy, optimistic folk going west to seek their fortunes and to
settle an empire. So they willed it. According to Montana rancher Gran-
ville Steward, who experienced *Forty Years on the Frontier,* thousands of
buffalo then darkened the rolling Montana plains and every hill sheltered
deer, elk, wolves and coyotes. In the fall of 1883, not a buffalo remained

on the range and six hundred thousand head of cattle had replaced the scarce antelope, elk, and deer.[23]

By the end of the century will had little to do with journeys that had become less hazardous, physically more comfortable, more orderly, but arranged by the mechanics of timetables and machines. As in other aspects of modern life, the ability of participants to act seemed to grow, yet paradoxically also dwindled.

Expansion, whether of the communications network, of agriculture, or of industry, depended upon substantial investments. Other societies that made the transition at the same time and later, used force to diminish consumption and thus to make savings available. Popular government in the United States blocked that expedient; decisions to spend or invest remained voluntary, with the risks and rewards personal. Ability or luck earned profits, which prudent entrepreneurs refrained from using but instead plowed back into business. Their proper concern, to keep profits rising and costs falling, explained why the less able and the less cautious failed. So ran the commonly accepted belief; the popular literature of the 1870s and 1880s expounded the maxim that with luck, pluck would win out.

Special conditions in the social environment permitted managers to keep expenses low and save the surplus for reinvestment. Minuscule taxes, assessed mainly on property, fell most heavily on landowners. The levy on incomes (and on liquor) imposed in the North during the Civil War disappeared in 1871 and did not reappear permanently until ratification of the Sixteenth Amendment. In the interim, federal revenues came mostly from the tariff, a charge ultimately borne by consumers—enough to pay for the tiny army and even for the growing navy. Businessmen, therefore, suffered little from the burden of either state or federal government. Economists argued for a scientific method of allocating costs (1915), which some believed ought to reflect ability to pay. But until 1918, charges remained substantially lower than in other countries.[24]

Entrepreneurs also escaped other costs. The unemployed during depressions generally heeded advice to maintain law and order (1857). The factory owner who laid off laborers bore no charge for their support; if they became dependent, he could contribute to the charity that fed them but did not have to do so. Yet he knew that he would find other hands to tend his machines when needed. The future of land and water use troubled only a few scientists like John Wesley Powell. The mills could take water from the streams and pour back waste as they wished without charge; and proprietors did not worry when smoke befouled a whole valley. Restrictive judicial decisions long limited the power of municipalities to control the nuisance despite its damage to public health.[25]

The costs of the failures did not fall upon the shoulders of the successful. Competition by trial and error that took traffic away from canals and riverboats injured their owners but created no obligation for the successful railroads. A new route or a new invention ruined some to make others rich. The law of economics and of life impelled each individual to pursue his own welfare, seeking only to outdistance rivals, an attitude that infuriated Hjalmer H. Boyesen, whose *Mammon of Unrighteousness* (1891) excoriated the dehumanizing effects of the struggle for wealth and power. The impact on rural areas formed the background of Hamlin Garland's *Main Travelled Roads* (1891), while Henry Demarest Lloyd's *Wealth against Commonwealth* (1894) indicted the entire system as exemplified in the Standard Oil Company.

The growing demand for capital broadened the ranks of participants and forced promoters to compete against alternative uses for cash. Repeated injunctions to frugality urged people not to expend in consumption what they might save; even advertising stressed the economy as well as the desirability of the product. The portrayal of women and children in illustrated advertisements strengthened the message and also suggested the need for savings, for their sake and for family unity. And while overemphasis on the "bargain" aspect of sales gave an establishment a cheap image, advertisers shied away from the impression that they aimed only to part individuals from their money, and not always for essentials, either. A revolving inkwell paid for itself, the ad explained, because it prevented evaporation, dust or rust, and could not tip over (1910). Words like *value, sanitary, efficiency, time, durability, scientific, bargain,* and *economize* became staples in the jargon, appealing particularly to the money-saving propensities of women, presumed more prudent than men. The spendthrift not only wasted his own substance, he kept it from productive use. The cultural environment, congenial to enterprise, set a premium on work and investment, that is, it encouraged accumulation of the capital the economy wanted.[26]

The sums saved could not, however, flow simply to meet the expanding requirements of trade. Per capita income did increase steadily, leaving a surplus above the demands of consumption. But businessmen asked to buy stocks or bonds had to divert the money from their own operations. What flowed into one channel did not flow into another. Caution balanced prudence against the temptations of gain. Even great windfalls, as in the discoveries of gold, silver, coal, copper, and iron, rarely generated investment capital.

International commerce more often increased the supply of funds. Exports only partially offset the rising volume of American imports. Cotton continued to find a gratifying market abroad. But in the 1880s foodstuffs met increasing competition from central Europe, the Ukraine, and Australia; and down to 1875 the sales of some processed and manufactured goods outside the United States did not compensate. The overall pattern of trade therefore created deficits in the balance of payments, which enabled Europeans to invest in America.[27]

Capital, not spontaneously generated but laboriously assembled, took one form in the currency held by the public in specie and paper. After 1880, the totals multiplied. Gold, the established legal tender, created no problem, but silver had become so rare that the government had ceased to mint it in 1873. Ironically, discoveries immediately thereafter increased the amount extracted to such a degree that the coinage mandated by the Bland–Allison Act of 1878 by 1890 added about $375 million to the currency.[28]

The amount of paper in circulation changed little. Gold and silver certificates, simply equivalents for the metal, depended on the quantity of specie available. During the war, the government had also issued about $450 million in greenbacks, notes backed only by its promise to pay, an act of desperation justified by the emergency and intended to terminate at the peace. In 1875 the Treasury redeemed all but $350 million. Their future became a political issue when the Greenback parties (1876, 1878) sought to halt further redemptions. Speculators and other debtors, as well as farmers, had long believed that the government need only disregard the accidental limits set by the amount of gold or silver available to manage the currency by emissions of paper to encourage investment and raise prices. Craftsmen, professionals, and people on fixed incomes, who resisted inflation, usually won out after 1865. In the 1880s, cheap money hopes shifted to silver when new mines flooded the market, lowering the price of the metal so that demonitization seemed a bankers' plot, part of the mysterious manipulation of the money trust. That campaign collapsed in the vain crusade of 1896.[29]

Furious currency debates obscured the deeper mystery of credit and capital controlled by invisible exchanges among private financial institutions. The federal law of 1864 had taxed the notes issued by state banks out of existence and had limited the amount printed by national banks to 90 percent of their holdings of federal bonds, a quantity that actually diminished as the national debt declined after 1865. Most transactions therefore involved some form of credit, and most savings rested in account books rather than in cash. The number of banks and the amount of their assets soared when they lost their former note-issuing function and became instruments for managing credit. Deposits rose steadily, and the ability to make loans and investments increased correspondingly. Meanwhile savings banks, first established before the Civil War to encourage thrift among workingmen, also multiplied, and their accumulations soared. Clearings—the sums transferred on paper from one account to another—climbed in a fashion not quite understood by the depositors whose property depended on the accuracy and reliability of the bookkeeping. Substantial amounts also rested in the hands of insurance companies; and whether they paid over large life premiums or the little weekly sums accepted by door-to-door agents, people required assurance of the judicious safeguarding of the reserves out of which ultimate payments would come.[30]

The funds' custodians dealt with bankers of another sort, more concerned with investment than with day-to-day commercial deposits and loans. The activities of Jay Cooke, J. P. Morgan, and Jacob Schiff evolved out of the business of the great international merchants of an earlier day. J. & W. Seligman had actually begun by buying and selling dry goods. Like their predecessors, these firms remained private and emphasized family connections, personal judgment, and ties with a foreign house. Morgan began his career with George Peabody and Company of London; August Belmont arrived as an agent of the Rothschilds. Jay Cooke held jobs in St. Louis and Philadelphia before he succeeded as fiscal agent of the Treasury Department during the Civil War. But when he embarked on a general banking business, he opened a branch in London, and lack of European contacts may have contributed to his later failure. Sometimes such men still handled commodities; but they had also acquired skills now put to more profitable uses. Mr. Dooley considered Morgan more powerful than any president or king. "Pierpont Morgan calls in wan iv his office boys, th' prisidint iv a naytional bank an says . . . 'James . . . take some change . . . an' run out an' buy Europe f'r me,' he says. 'I intend to re-organize it an' put it on a paying basis,' he says" (1901).[31]

The overseas merchant of the past had always known the price of gold and the cost of bills of exchange, and frequently made loans to princes. His successors did the same; they traded in money and purchased the bonds of governments. They found opportunities as well in railroad securities. When William H. Vanderbilt decided to sell his 250,000 shares of New York Central stock for $30 million, he asked Morgan to make the arrangements. So, too, Jay Cooke undertook to float the securities of the Northern Pacific; and when he failed, Drexel Morgan and Company organized a syndicate to distribute $40 million of that road's bonds.[32]

Bankers could pass such securities on to financial institutions with surpluses. Corporate bonds formed less than 1 percent of the assets of a sample of life insurance companies in 1860; in 1890 the amount had risen to 22 percent. By 1890 the investment houses held a key position in the economy. They took an interest in the corporations whose securities they sold and as a matter of course became directors of commercial banks, life insurance companies, and railroads, adding to their resources and strength by those interlocking roles.[33]

Their operations centered in New York City, which became the nation's financial capital. For a time, Philadelphia and Boston still held their own; Tampa Electric and other power companies found their capital there. But those stodgy cities rebuffed outsiders and clung to conservative methods, applied by "the same clerks on the same wharves, in the same counting houses with the same threadbare coats on." In 1890 the great port on the Hudson stood unrivaled. Preponderant in transatlantic trade, it handled the related fiscal transactions and its cosmopolitan society proved more receptive to newcomers than did other eastern cities. Above all, the process by which corporate securities passed into the hands of individuals turned about operations on Wall Street, where eleven hundred members of the stock exchange and many other brokers on the curb acted for customers throughout the country.[34]

Business-minded Americans before 1860 knew something about how to buy and sell stocks and bonds, usually in local enterprises. The Civil War spread the habit among professional people, farmers, small entrepreneurs, and clerks when the Union's financial needs touched off vast bond drives; Jay Cooke at one time employed twenty-five hundred salesmen to dispose of the paper, appealing to patriotism, self-interest, and piety. Men of modest means then learned to invest their savings in paper, expecting secure returns of interest and principal. They remained willing customers for railroad, and later for industrial, securities. The telegraph, the tickertape, and the telephone made the market for stocks and bonds national. Brokers in New York acted on behalf of customers anywhere and developed a country-wide network of correspondents.[35]

Investors showed little concern with interest or dividends; the average yield of corporate securities, low to begin with, tended to decline. Purchasers reached for fortune through a rapid and dramatic appreciation of

al values. To speculate on a rise they needed little cash, say 10 percent
wn. They could borrow the rest until the price went up enough to
liquidate the debt. In a decline, alas, they lost the 10 percent.

Although almost all states made gambling illegal, the venturesome in
every city could take a chance in numbers games, keno parlors, pool halls,
and other establishments. Stock speculation offered respectable citizens
thrilling risks without the odium of breaking the law, and indeed with
the virtuous assurance that they thriftily helped develop the country's
transportation, mining, and industry. Speculation created losers as well as
winners; but the outcome, everyone believed, resulted from shrewd calculation rather than from the accidental turn of a card. The men who did
business on Wall Street had a prematurely gray look, and died at a
comparatively early age, said a guide book (1872). They lived too fast,
passing their days in great excitement, elated or depressed by every little
fluctuation of the market. Frequently a broker rose and fell three or four
times in his career.[36]

No doubt abuses existed. Charles Yerkes, a Philadelphian, embezzled
millions before his exposure. The Credit Mobilier scandal (1873) impli-
cated scores of statesmen, including the vice-president, Schuyler Colfax,
and future president James Garfield. Democrats and Republicans shared
the loot; Alden Stockwell's Pacific Mail Steamship Company gained
lucrative government contracts by bribing politicians in Washington
until outbid by Jay Gould in 1873. Bucket shops never executed their
customers' orders; if the price went down they pocketed the sum invested.
If the price rose they cheerfully credited the victim's balance until his
fortune turned. When their obligations became too heavy, they simply
absconded. The law rarely caught up with them unless a murder drew
attention to them. Edward Stokes used Josie Mansfield, Jim Fisk's mistress, for tips and blackmail. Later Josie testified to what the press called
Fisk's oriental tastes and desires, but society shunned Stokes, who shot him
(1873). Two trials led to a brief term in Sing Sing but also to abundant
publicity. Meanwhile Vanderbilt, friendly with Victoria Woodhull and
her sister Tennessee, set them both up as brokers and hired a spiritualist
medium to get information about stocks from Jim Fisk's spirit beyond
the grave.[37]

Perfectly legal—if not precisely honest—ways permitted the shrewd
to profit by manipulating supply and demand. The exchanges dealt not
only in present but also in future deliveries. The bears sold short securities
they did not yet own and tried to depress the price; the bulls bought long
and tried to raise the level. To gain from the fluctuations, groups pooled
their resources to change the price either by throwing large blocks of

securities on the market or by concerted heavy purchases. Th[ ]
goal, a corner, control of the whole available supply, perm[ ]
speculator to set what price he wished for stocks due him. It helped in
these maneuvers to have influence within the corporations; Daniel Drew,
as treasurer of the Erie Railroad, could print off as many shares as he
wished when he sought to lower the price. It helped also to own a
newspaper, as Jay Gould did, to plant strategic rumors to sway the
gullible. Access to presidents, as Fisk thought he had, and owning a few
judges and legislators kept the limits of the law flexible. Eugene V. Debs
noted the familiarity with such expressions as "money talks" and "money
rules." Never before in the country's history had people seen wealth grasp
with paws and jaws the government of the United States and bend it to
its will.[38]

Sensational books and articles told the story of frenzied finance but
did not long reduce the number of hopeful customers. Those who lost
heavily in Wall Street yowled in protest but kept coming back for
another try, just as patrons of the keno parlors did. Daniel Drew, Jay
Gould, and Jim Fisk—scoundrels all; but many an American felt scarcely
concealed admiration for their escapades and dreamed of emulating
them—sharp chaps, not quite as likable as the swindlers in O. Henry's
stories; still you had to hand it to them (before they grabbed it). Uncle
Daniel Drew, who made a pretense of bucolic illiteracy, built a $13
million fortune by engineering market ups and downs, remaining inside
with everyone else outside; then lost control, and the thirteen millions
melted like snow in a ditch, leaving him in debt and heartbroken. The
plunger's way of making a fortune beat that of frugality, punctuality, and
hard work. Therefore Mrs. Hettie Green, alone among women, succeeded
as a speculator. The number of investors grew, although not the number
who succeeded.[39]

Occasionally panics plunged hundreds of unwary speculators to ruin
although the culprit responsible escaped unharmed, as on the Black Friday
in September 1869, when Jim Fisk's effort to corner the gold market
failed. Albert Speyer, the demoralized broker, then wandered across the
floor, begging to be shot. Lesser incidents also dragged down the unwise
or the unlucky. Panic became depression when the effects penetrated the
whole economy. Inadequate bankruptcy laws made matters worse, and
plaintive pleas for reform went unheeded. In September 1873 Jay Cooke's
firm crashed, overextended in the effort to build the Northern Pacific.
Greedy financial institutions had not heeded the *Bankers Magazine* advice
(May 1873) "to keep a healthy reserve at home, and not to trust too large
a sum in Wall Street." Now depositors everywhere made demands on

banks, which called in short-term loans. Failures multiplied, confidence
dwindled, security prices dropped as hard-pressed investors dumped their
holdings on unreceptive markets. Lack of money paralyzed fall crop
movements and blocked foreign exchange. Hoarded cash further contracted credit. Factories cut production and railroad and building construction halted. Unemployment grew and consumer purchasing power
declined. For six years the country knew the meaning of depression.
Recovery came in 1879. But the events of 1873 revealed a vulnerability
that would recur in 1893 and 1907 as long as growth depended not on
coordinated calculations but upon speculative capital drawn from thousands of individual investors.[40]

Unease affected every level of society. "No sane man can be happy,
for to him life is real, and he sees what a fearful thing it is. Only the mad
can be happy"—thus Mark Twain. Executives regarded the little empires
they ruled and found them not altogether good. Few considered rural life
any more satisfying. Equanimity rewarded neither the yeoman nor the
tenant nor the great landowners. However large or small the number of
their acres, none enjoyed confidence in the morrow. Certainly the sharecroppers lived from one year's debt to another; and owners, squeezed by
mortgages incurred in the good times and by payments for expensive
machines, just about got by. Farming bound a man right down to the
grindstone, so that he got nothing out of it, simply wallowed around in
the manure, helpless like a fly in a pan of molasses. "The more he tears
around the more liable he is to rip his legs off." Wives hated the
life—nothing but fret and work, never going any place, fighting flies and
washing dishes and churning. On the great bonanza holdings of twenty
to thirty thousand acres where the corn grew eighteen feet high and
where in harvest times an army worked with military precision and order
to keep pace with the steam harvester and binder, the larger stakes, win
or lose, raised the level of anxiety. On the million-acre ranch and during
the long drive that moved hundreds of thousands of cattle to the railhead,
the same question prevailed: What price? The agriculturist, altogether
different from what he was a generation before, sold his hogs and bought
bacon and pork, sold cattle and bought beef, sold apples and peaches and
bought them back in cans. Instead of making clothing in his own house,
he purchased it from the town tailor. Nearly everything he once produced
for himself ever more often involved commercial transactions.

In the bucolic small towns, shopkeepers, country lawyers and doctors,
bankers and public officials and their employees, always seeking, never
finding, developed contemptible views of themselves, humiliated at not

having accomplished more. They and their wives watched each other like hawks so that none had much opportunity for cheating. Sinclair Lewis grew up in such a place, a physician's son, stifled by comfort, by pervasive dullness, dissatisfied but lacking a vision of what he wanted to find over the horizon toward which he strained. All blamed their discontent on that which they most avidly desired—money. Money dictated financial policy; money controlled the business of the country; money despoiled the people.[41]

Promoters and speculators rarely found rest. Colonel Berea Sellers, whose wife worried "we live in the future too much," had railroads and city plans a plenty, all in the planning stage, including his favorite city, Corruptionville, where good soil and much sinfulness made an ideal place for missionaries. Panics drove such people over the edge. From the stock exchange gallery, the observer saw brokers begging people to take their property from them at any price, moved by brute terror like that which devours a horse tormented by a pair of broken shafts hanging to his heels, or a dog fleeing from a tin pan tied to his tail.

Manufacturers had no easier time of it. Large output, quick sales, and keen competition drove processors into a general steeplechase for preeminence. The thousand-barrel mill forced the competitor to bet on a two-thousand-barrel mill. Stockyards, dairies, and bakeries raced ahead under the same compulsion.[42]

Critics regarded the captains of industry as ingenious and pecuniary masters of soulless corporations, who left details of production and organization to subordinates. That facile generalization disregarded the great variety of corporations—large, small; mutual, stock; family firms or individually owned; and it did not apply to Andrew Carnegie, the Du Pont and Mellon families, to Henry Ford, Thomas A. Edison, and James B. Duke, venturers who aggressively made their firms what they were— and who regarded their enterprises as extensions of themselves, projections of their personalities. Often poor boys from the countryside, they had scrabbled up by hard work and luck. The plants and all within them, their property, they possessed in their own names or in partnerships or in closely held corporations controlled by friends or family members. What they created, they jealously guarded and frantically sought to expand. Ruthlessly they eliminated competitors, as a chieftain would the strays of an enemy clan.[43]

Caught up in a productive system constantly in flux, the wealthy could not relax. Joking and boyish pranks sometimes provided their only safety valve. They knew the danger of toppling as they reached forward;

yet no perch offered security enough to enable them to sit back in contentment. Regarded from below by the men in his plant and his city, Pullman seemed the "King," in absolute control; none knew the depth of his uneasiness. Competitors stalked the business jungle. Already in 1865, John Sherman in New York met English capitalists intent on investments in railroads, iron works, locomotive and machine shops. Someone would do it, leaving bystanders behind. Charles F. Woerishoffer speculated upon the ruination of others. A furious and unrelenting bear, he made enormous profits until a wrong guess on the wheat crop in 1885 brought on a heart attack that killed him at the age of forty-three.

Nightmare: "Just fancy yourself a banker—and discovering outside your plate glass facade an ever lengthening column of men and women, all having bankbooks and checks clutched in their hands. . . . Fancy those . . . best known to you, the ones with the biggest balances pushing to the head of the line. . . . Heighten the effect with a swarm of hoarse throated newsboys, each with his cry pitched to an hysterical scream, and then give the hideous concert an overtone of sound from the scuffling feet of a mob" (1907).[44]

Facile critics of the money power and the trusts little understood the compulsions to combination in large units.

Change awaited no one's convenience. The Civil War had accustomed business people to nationwide operations and mass production, and stimulated the complex transition from the early Lowell cotton mills to the great steel plants of Gary and Homestead, which drew together enormous sums of capital, whole armies of labor, and great skill in organization. Iron masters and clothing makers felt the immediate stimulus of big orders and high profits; costs did not count when it came to supplying men at arms with boots or uniforms or guns. Wartime inflation further encouraged the enterprising, as rising prices eased repayment of sums borrowed for expansion. The boom pointed the way to mass production in textiles and in boot and shoe manufacturing but not to the hazards of changes in fashion or of the sudden impact of a novel machine or process, or of a lucky discovery of new technology.[45]

Always one thing led to another and even windfalls proved mixed blessings. When the McKay stitcher transformed the shoe industry, manufacturers changed over or went under. Coal in the ground had worth, though not so much as at the pithead, and certainly not so much as when carried to market; therefore the Reading Railroad controlled the anthracite mines whether it owned them or not. Andrew Carnegie held on to the old verities: pioneering don't pay; plow back the profits. He could junk tools, machines, and whole factories when new ones appeared and raised productivity. He believed himself securely perched in his Pittsburgh stronghold until the need for coke entangled him with Henry Clay Frick in an embrace he could not readily shake off. Pennsylvania continued to yield iron ore down to the end of the century. But new fields in the Lake Superior region added to the supply and drew Carnegie into an unwelcome relationship with the Rockefellers. To fortify his position he invested in railroads and barge lines. Meanwhile rich deposits opened up between Chattanooga, Tennessee, and Birmingham, Alabama. He did stand off from the vast bituminous field that stretched from Lake Erie down to northern Alabama, and he stayed away from petroleum, still used mainly for lubrication and, as kerosene, for illumination. But the Lima field in northern Ohio and Indiana also hinted at the potential of natural gas, and John D. Rockefeller showed no such restraint although he, too, felt the pressure to integrate, not always gracefully and sometimes slowly. Ridiculous to ship the oil to and from the refinery barrel by barrel; better use a pipeline, and storage tanks to adjust supply and demand and high volume for cheapness and by-products and new technology—all causes for unease.[46]

No such concerns troubled fortunate discoverers who supplied the cities' demand for lumber from the abundant stands of timber in Wisconsin, the Pacific Northwest, or the southern uplands, or who stumbled on rich lodes of gold, silver, or copper in the mountain states, any more than the character who raked in the jackpot at poker—except, of course, what to do with the take. Then they, too, fell victims of anxiety and one and all sought some dependable order. Positions on top, while more comfortable than at the bottom, also limited the ability to act.

In 1920 as in 1850, new men continued to battle for places. But those who succeeded, tiring of endless competition, also wished to institutionalize their achievements and therefore found unperceived values in order and predictability. They looked about for surrogates to keep things going, leaving the owner time for other interests. Let Charlie Schwab take over! Carnegie's thoughts turned to the castle in Scotland and the cause of peace; Frick collected art, as did Mellon, who also wished to play the statesman; and even Ford, in time, dabbled in politics and antiques. Looking at the painting he had bought, however, Stillman saw dollar signs, "in plain figures on the canvas the annual interest figured upon the cost of the picture."

Irony: Men who spent their whole lives in accumulation found unexpected pleasure, even power, in giving God's gold away, each in his own fashion. Andrew Mellon, having read *The Chemistry of Commerce* by Robert Kennedy Duncan, wanted fellowships so that industry could utilize the services of scientists to increase production, lower costs, and raise wages; university presidents eagerly encouraged the belief. Even Henry M. Flagler became involved in Florida colleges. Jay Gould, by contrast, rarely yielded to impulses to generosity. Still, philanthropy posed fewer hazards than business. Pullman, Homestead, Cripple Creek— let others wrangle with labor and lawyers while the benefactors basked in the approval of fawning clergymen and professors and while Ivy Lee and other P.R. types spread it on thick for the masses. Thus the most fortunate found unexpected liberty to act.

Of course, age also took its toll, with the old zip less often there every morning. Remembering how they had shoved falterers aside, many tycoons wondered what obscure young buck down in the organization would some day brashly seize command. Better arrange to pass the power so that it would at least memorialize its creator.

Even in the process of pushing out or swallowing up rivals, the venturers had recognized the utility of figurers and arrangers, of experts whose minds ran to statutes and blueprints, who found the ways to get it done. Andrew Carnegie, amazed at the advance of specialization in watchmaking, shoemaking, and textiles, understood the trend. Sooner or later, the decisions came to let the lawyer or engineer or salesman take charge as executive.[47]

Administrators approached positions of control racked by anxiety. They had not fought their way up through the plant but had come laterally, by invitation, often from the outside, especially the lawyers. Calvin S. Brice, for instance, practiced in Cincinnati until clients involved him in managing some regional railroads. He ran the Lake Erie and Western and promoted, planned, and helped build the Nickel Plate. So, too, Elbert H. Gary had been attorney for midwestern railroads and industries before becoming a director of the Illinois Steel Company, then president of Federal Steel, and ultimately head of United States Steel.[48]

Certainly such people wished to succeed by enlarging their enterprises, taking advantage of technological breakthroughs, of opportunities for mergers and acquisitions on a national and multinational scale. But they had to make public reports of earnings and operations and answer stockholders' questions; and they knew that they held their posts on approval; the old men who had voted them in, never distant enough, could vote them out—and not only on the basis of the balance sheet, but also on judgments of style of life, what the church, what the wife, what the tailor, where the home. The competitive spirit that moved the officeholders, therefore, differed from that of the man on the make. Not owners of property taking pleasure in aggrandizement, but salaried officials finding satisfaction or security in a job well done, they valued order, regularity, and predictability, that is, planning. Unlimited rivalry they considered chaotic, wasteful, and uncertain. Like the engineers, the administrators prized efficiency and hoped to attain it by emerging from the jungle where each clawed the others. More civilized, mutually advantageous relationships might follow from integration that drew the savagely individualistic entrepreneurs into large units, controlled for the benefit of all by competent, disinterested managers. In an age of steam, electricity, and machinery, such necessary aggregations yielded the greatest good to the greatest number.

The serried ranks of a vast industrial army, never at ease, steadily expanded. The sergeants followed the rules, rarely made decisions calling for judgment. They stood at counters or sat at desks, reading, writing, counting—their credentials earned by study—none secure enough to neglect the starch of collar, cuffs, dickey, or shirtwaist. These gentlemen and ladies (who might equally well have taught school) rode the cars to buttoned-up homes, for their conduct at or away from the job affected chances for promotion to a managerial post, even a vice-presidency, or a raise, layoff, or dismissal. They scrimped for enough to buy the house that would keep a roof over their heads, no matter what, or in order to save for the inevitable rainy day—unless, that is, a needy sibling or parent presented some insistent plea for help. Constant anxiety accompanied every decision to spend, lingered with every effort to enjoy, shadowed by awareness of espionage as part of the system.[49]

Many enterprises remained small and independent, managed by their owners, and successfully resisted efforts of big fellows to gobble them up, like the copper mines that only became part of Phelps, Dodge and Company in 1917. Local markets limited the operations of bakeries and dairies; almost all construction work fell to contractors on the spot; and a similar pattern survived in garment manufacturing. Other firms also remained tightly owned although large. In 1887, Ball Brothers moved from Buffalo to Muncie, Indiana, and began to turn out trademarked fruit jars; they never yielded control of the growing enterprise, though constantly improving sales and fabrication methods.

Such small, owner-managed companies depended on ready credit from friends, countrymen, coreligionists, or relatives when commercial sources tightened. The owner with a surplus in hand could afford to make judicious investments, even take moderate risks, perhaps now and then be

game for a flyer. The moral was plain: Have a surplus. Get it by underconsumption, by frugality, by taking less out of the business than it yielded,
that is, by plowing back the profits, by keeping costs low, by adhering
to the iron necessity of economizing.

Many men and some women drifted about in the interstices of a
loosely articulated economic system, restlessly slipping from one slot to
another, clerks, salespeople, drummers, agents, teachers, journalists, now
salaried, now working for fees or commissions, loosely disciplined,
largely on their own, a passing breed that had not yet outlived its time.

Still, all these people counted themselves more fortunate than the
overalled men and women in the ranks who stood at the scaffolding or
machines and worked by the hour or the piece. Leave aside the common
laborers who had nothing and earned little, or the laundresses who
starched those shirts. Consider instead the hands with jobs, who worried
about more than the pay packet—shifting seasons and falling orders and
fairness in the plant. They sank into a mass—30,000 of them at the
Homestead mill in 1890 seemed exceptional, but a generation later United
States Steel had 168,000 employees. Five hundred names appeared on
many a payroll. Those workers no longer moved informally under the
owner's oversight, but labored at intricate machines in large gangs, their
tasks part of a dimly perceived whole accounted for by the same abstract
calculations as any other element of the factory. How did such a one
esteem himself regarding the Jones mixer, a huge iron chest lined with
refractory bricks, capable of holding 250 tons of liquid pig iron? Hung
on trunnions, so that it could swing to and fro, it received ladle after ladle
of molten metal flowing clean and creamy, with fairy lights dancing over
the surface. A boy of thirteen or fourteen, his implike face black with
soot, stood near the flaming funnel, shouting shrill directions to his fellow
demon, who reversed the five-ton ladles with the ease of a society woman
emptying her cup of tea. At night the flashing fireworks, the terrific gusts
of heat, the gaping, glowing mouth of the giant container, the quivering
light from the liquid, the roar of a nearby converter, the weird figure
of the child and the pipings of his shrill voice, the smoke and fumes and
confusion, produced an effect bewildering to the stranger, but matter-of-
course to the employee. Pittsburgh no doubt struck visitors as hell with
the lid off—smoke-begrimed, dirty, darkened by steam and soot. And the
Chicago slaughterhouses, as efficient, made no more favorable an impression though blood red, not black. Uniform discipline brought the workers to their appointed places at the appointed times; and rigid appraisals
of costs determined their wages and hours. Yet observed at the exits they

proved men; and they joined unions in the hope of attaining a more humane system.[50]

Benevolent intentions did not count. Experiments in housing, no matter how well conceived, turned out instruments of control, whether in model tenements or in Pullman and Granite City, Illinois, or Gary, Indiana—efforts to reshape people into more efficient workers, *for their own good,* whether they willed it or not, everything subdivided by the company, which also specified use and architecture. Men who had to go up over the line to Mobtown or the Patch for a beer, in the end preferred the old neighborhoods, slums and all, where they felt human, not adjuncts of the machines.[51]

Henry Ford wished to transform the automobile from a pleasure vehicle for the well-to-do into a mass commodity so low in price that anyone could own one "and enjoy with his family the blessing of hours of pleasure in God's open spaces." A continuous integrated process generated the economies. In Flint, Michigan (1905), a reporter observed the factory: the orderly process of an assembly room where engines moved along from one group of men to another until ready. Ford elaborated the process. On sixty acres in Highland Park, he built a large new factory extending Eli Whitney's old principle of replaceable parts to the assembly line. His cars contained about five thousand units, brought to the men instead of the men to the work (1913), like the overhead trolleys the Chicago packers used in dressing beef. With the tools and the workmen located in the sequence of the operation, slides carried the components the least possible distance, from one to the next. As a result, each person could do more than four earlier, but at a pace determined by the machine. The 690 employees in 1908 turned out 6,000 vehicles; 44,000 in 1919 produced 775,000. Ford denied that repetitive work had damaging effects, but the laborers felt no better when scientific personnel systems mysteriously assigned each to a job.[52]

The assembly line established order of a sort at a price few wished to pay. Yet in a productive system ever in flux, no one possessed the power to set or enforce binding alternatives. Since early in the nineteenth century, the state refrained from directing economic growth, and, subject to popular control, remained capricious in its attitude toward concentration and regulation.

Persistently, though inconsistently, Americans sought to minimize political action, not only to lower expenditures and taxes but also to fend off avaricious spoilsmen and to ensure the victory of the most efficient. In practice, however, an imperfect world required some governmental intervention, as to protect infant industries in the United States against competition with cheap European labor; whatever the attitude in theory, each particular interest struggled for higher tariffs on its products and lower ones on its raw materials, but the general level crept steadily upward after 1872. By the 1880s also businessmen grudgingly recognized that fair competition depended upon acceptance of general rules such as those established by the Interstate Commerce Commission, which, however, did not constrain entrepreneurs in the pursuit of profit.

To protect that quest without interfering with it, uniformed and disciplined police defended the natural right to property, the saved earnings of labor, not only against thieves but also against agitators and unruly workingmen. The state also secured individuals against more subtle threats, as in impairment—whether by conspiracies or by governmental meddling—of the right freely to form contracts. Each person could ply what trade he or she wished, buy and sell, hire and take employment, with the total assurance that the courts would uphold any voluntary agreement. Judges struck down limitations on that liberty. The *Slaughterhouse* cases (1873) extended that protection to corporations and threw out offending state regulatory schemes; and the *Wabash* case (1886) explained that the Fourteenth Amendment's guarantee of due process forbade not only arbitrary procedures, but any substantive act that diminished the right to property, a tricky proposition when it came, for instance, to weighing the claims of butter producers for protection against margarine (1888).

In Europe, voluntary associations portioned out the market and ruled many branches of industry with the government's benevolent approval. But in the United States, every cry of *monopoly* mobilized voters, legislators, and judges and prevented the formation of cartels. To no avail did speakers justify Western Union's consolidation of telegraph lines and its withdrawal from the telephone business. American industrialists fumbled along for years, experimenting with schemes for sharing markets and for consolidation, all on the margin of the law, often mystifying the public and evoking angry popular reactions. Every effort at business accommodation remained vulnerable to the accusation of conspiracy, if not under a statute then under some vague provision of the common law. Investment bankers discovered the limits of their power to induce integration; and federal and state governments, unable to clarify their own attitudes, acted in a negative fashion. Wealth grew luxuriantly but according to no deliberate plan.[53]

Woodrow Wilson in 1913 recognized that the United States had entered an age that submerged the individual. Men worked, not for themselves, not as partners in the old way, but generally as employees of great corporations. He perceived something very new and very big and very complex about the altered relations of capital and laborer. American industry was not as free as it once was; the man with only a little capital found it harder to compete with the big fellow because the laws did not prevent the strong from crushing the weak. Finger ever ready for the dyke, he proposed his remedy: legislation to look after the men on the make, treating business not as exploitation or as a quest for profit, but as service to society.[54]

The effort to rationalize industry drew fierce retaliation. No matter how clever the lawyers, how secret the documents, how mum the collaborators, no matter what persuasive bribes or political pressures passed to prosecutors and legislators, high prices and restrictive terms gave the game away. Effective controls made themselves felt; that was their purpose. To secure an orderly flow of freight, railroads for a time gave large shippers rebates, until the spread of such discounts wiped out their competitive advantages and reduced the carriers' profits. Voluntary agreements among producers more effectively aimed to establish order.

All the issues of order, control, and law surfaced in the process of exploiting the nation's untapped petroleum resources. Amid alternating periods of shortage and glut, the refiners battled for shares of the market. One of them, John D. Rockefeller, warily maneuvered for advantage from his strategic location in Cleveland, a city linked by rail and lake to the fields and to markets. He built up his defenses by vertical integration; he manufactured the barrels and acid used in his plants and owned a fleet of lighters and tankers and a drayage service. He also bought out competitors but preferred amicable coexistence, live and let live—in the abstract, at least. Railroads that ruinously reduced rates to take traffic from each other already understood that they would all prosper by sharing the business, reducing the number of trains, and increasing the charges. So, too, Rockefeller and some of his rivals in 1871 formed the South Improvement Company to allot quotas to its participants and to assign agreed-on percentages to the railroads that served them. In return, the Rockefeller allies expected a rebate on every barrel of oil transported, whether by members or nonmembers. Refiners who refused to cooperate therefore indirectly subsidized those who did. During its brief existence, the company thus controlled competition. In 1885, the producers of steel rails also voluntarily curtailed production; and in 1887 they set up a pool to limit the output of each mill to stabilize prices by removing the incentive for competition.

The merger of competing firms was an alternative to the pool. In 1870, John D. Rockefeller and his associates formed the Standard Oil Company of Ohio, which bought up a cluster of refineries in Cleveland and its vicinity. In the 1880s the Edison General Electric Company united a number of small producers.

But the law and popular opinion set limits to such combinations. Illegality tainted even the informal pools vulnerable to prosecution as conspiracies in restraint of trade under the common law.

In 1882, Rockefeller's attorney, S. T. C. Dodd, proposed a way out. The stockholders of Standard Oil of Ohio, in return for trust certificates, assigned all the property of the corporation to a board of nine trustees that managed the enterprise free from public scrutiny and without legal restrictions. In the next few years the same nine men by the same process acquired control of almost all the country's important oil refineries, each of which continued its own operations under the general direction of the trustees. Other ingenious entrepreneurs also experimented to achieve the control they could not attain through open combination. Whatever the device used, small excluded competitors and consumers ran screaming to the state for redress, reviving the old battle cries of the Tea Party and of Jackson's war on the monster bank. Monopoly! Popular opinion frowned upon the bullying goliaths, particularly when the visible result was the concentration in a few hands of great fortunes lavishly thrown away in orgiastic living, while the virtuous little men lost all.

Before the Civil War, a hundred thousand dollars counted as a substantial fortune; only twenty-five New Yorkers and nine Philadelphians had possessed a million dollars each, with Stephen Girards's $6 million estate altogether unusual. The biographies then published in *Hunt's Merchant's Magazine,* the editor believed, reflected a setting in which "talent is free, and where . . . stupid restrictive laws enacted in ages of feudal barbarism" did not check enterprise, ingenuity, or industry. After 1870, the scale changed radically. By 1890, the Vanderbilts worth $300 million, the Astors $250 million, and Carnegie, Marshall Field, and Jay Gould well over $100 million each revealed the scope of new riches. Ordinary millionaires numbered three thousand, of whom a hundred enjoyed annual incomes—untaxed—of more than a million dollars. Few believed that the exercise of traditional virtues earned these monstrous accumulations, although some apologists argued that vast fortunes came from "backing the country."

Americans regarded these amazing figures with admiration, envy, and mistrust. They enjoyed the convenient transportation and the cheap goods the railroad and the factory made possible; but comparing the fortunate few with other citizens, they wondered about the effect on society of such enormous disparities among its members, and they feared lest the masters of wealth become masters of the Republic. The concentration of wealth regulated the living standards of rich and poor, worked beneath the forms of government and the press, and affected the fiber of churches, colleges, and homes. Any hint of conspiracy therefore touched off a wave of mistrust along with demands for prosecution. An investigation into the Union Pacific "unchained a veritable cyclone of criticism" upon E. H. Harriman, "anathematized as a horrible example of capitalistic greed and lawbreaking" (1907). The demand that government do something mounted from the 1880s onward.[55]

Americans responded favorably to suggestions of radical solutions by writers and politicians, as scandal rocked the petroleum, sugar, beef, insurance, and banking industries. Behind the scenes, men of great wealth manipulated bosses to protect vice and block child labor, conservation, and tariff legislation. The mechanics, the unions, the country merchants, among others, demanded an end to barbaric and piratical competition which relentlessly suppressed the weak, and its replacement by abstract appeals to communal solidarity, either out of goodness or out of faith that knowledge would lead to progress, enabling all to share in correcting the prevailing abuses.

But the legal system obstructed effective action against the masters of capital. Interpretations of the right of contract had shifted from emphasis on the relationship among individuals to emphasis on their relationship to government. The federal Constitution and the Fourteenth Amendment had forbidden the states to pass any statute impairing the obligations of contract or depriving any person of his property without due process of law; and the courts had held corporations persons protected by the same provisions. A line of judicial decisions beginning with the *Dred Scott* case (1857) went further, declaring the guarantees substantive and prohibiting not only arbitrary procedures but any action that diminished the ability to make agreements or use property, in effect, any meddling by government in the economy. The inviolability of property and contract created a climate congenial to enterprise but also shackled the polity. The feeble Reconstruction efforts to exert some influence faded, along with the possibility of using politics to establish goals for the economy or for the society. Federal, state, and municipal governments thereafter confined themselves to policing and regulatory functions.

The distinction between "public" and "private" sharpened. The former word denoted those affairs involving no private property and directly subject to government—the maintenance of roads, streets, and bridges, for instance. Railroads, however, built by investment, sustained by profits from fares, and free from interference, fell into the *private* category. The distinction reflected the circumstances of origin rather than any abstract principle. The public, indeed national, postal system differed from the private telegraph and later telephone lines not by clear-cut, defined spheres in which they operated but by specific accommodation to pressures exerted at particular moments.

The government acted positively toward communal goals only on the public side of the line. In all other matters the self-regulating economy developed by its own rules, curing its occasional imperfections and finding its own equilibrium through forces generated internally. Nature knew best and yielded maximum benefits for the whole population when free of interference. The phrase *natural selection,* reminiscent of Darwin, replaced the older references to a providential guiding force. The state stood by—neutral, a passive policeman—acting only to forestall meddling with the finely balanced mechanism.

Few accepted government ownership as a solution. Democracy bred familiarity with the uses of power, and familiarity dispelled illusion. People knew the cop on the beat, the legislator in the lobby, the mayor in his office, the judge on the bench—palms crossed one and all—none evil by nature but all pliable, one party or the other, as anyone might be, when violation of an ordinance, or award of a franchise or contract, or revision of a tax assessment, gave them the chance. The remedy: reduce the chances to a minimum. The daily press regularly confirmed the validity of William Graham Sumner's prediction that "when the politician and the master of industry were joined in one," the country would "have the vices of both unchecked by the restraints of either."[56]

Therefore no significant group clamored for a takeover by the state. Benign competition remained the preferable means of assuring equity to consumers and users, of furthering efficiency, and of lowering costs. Government properly prevented artificial interference with the incessant combat of one against all others, and did no more. Unrelaxing vigilance, the price of security, kept the pressure on everyone.

The antitrust laws raised the pressure; by excluding any collusion to soften competition, they left consolidation the only escape. The purchase of one corporation by another involved millions, sometimes hundreds of millions, of dollars; and few businessmen possessed ready cash in those amounts. But some enjoyed access to mammoth financial resources, composed of small savings, responding to opportunity. Surplus funds in free

and fluid movement coursed unpredictably through the economy, usually
with constructive, but sometimes also with disruptive, consequences. The
turbulence bothered some industrialists and administrators; and it infuriated investment bankers. Risky investment (theirs), yes; rampant
speculation (others'), no. The heavings and plungings of the stock market
betrayed the presence of streaks of irrationality perilous to the economy.

The Sherman Antitrust Law certainly seemed disruptive. It meant
different things to different people and, in any event, conceived in a spirit
of repression not expansion, took no account of the fact that the times
created the trusts. By contrast with the common law ban on restraint of
trade only if unreasonable, its verbiage about conspiracy exposed the
economy to unsettling raids by speculating freebooters, to disorderly
pricing and marketing practices, and to costly cycles of panic and boom.
The statute left only the escape of merger, for one company buying the
assets of another did not conspire with itself. The modern corporation,
a fact and not a theory, sprang from the desire for organization, its
underlying cause not the greed of men for wealth and power but the
natural working of evolution, said George W. Perkins (1908).[57]

The number of recorded mergers in manufacturing and mining
mounted rapidly after 1890. Simple combinations, as when the American
Tobacco Company, which had manufactured cigarettes, acquired the
factories of Marburg Brothers and the Gail and Ax Company in return
for cash and some of its own common stock (1891), required no large
outlays and no significant dilution of control. But the availability of
substantial capital in the security markets enabled promoters of larger
combinations to use the procedures of the New Jersey Corporation Act
of 1889. The holding companies chartered under that law operated no
plants but simply held the stock of other corporations doing business
anywhere. Extensive multilayered pyramids took shape, with each stra-
tum of subsidiaries owning or controlling numerous smaller firms. The
device offered some of the advantages of the trust yet escaped the taint
of illegality. Combinations controlled kerosene; cottonseed oil; sugar;
oatmeal; starch; cornmeal; barley; coal; castor oil; linseed oil; lard; oil-
cloth; salt; street railways; whiskey; rubber; steel; steel rails and beams;
nails; wrought-iron pipes; envelopes; paper bags; cordage; coke; reaping,
binding, mowing, and threshing machines; glass and water works.

The American Sugar Refining Company (organized 1891), itself
successor to a trust that had held twenty refineries, took over its five
leading competitors and for a time accounted for almost 90 percent of
the national output. Competition vanished, prices rose, and production
declined. President Henry Havemeyer bluntly stated: "Let the buyer

beware, that covers the whole business. You cannot wetnurse people from the time they are born until the time they die. They have got to wade in and get stuck and that is the way men are educated." A year later, Standard Oil, under attack in the state courts, abandoned the trust form and secured a New Jersey charter, which survived the fierce onslaughts of critics and rivals until dissolved by the Supreme Court. After 1891 the holding company spread, with some combinations, once formed, themselves assimilated in larger groupings. By 1904, 318 holding companies capitalized at well over $7 billion, controlled 5,288 plants in the United States. "The most stupendous revolution ever accomplished in the history of the world's industrial growth" abruptly overturned the natural law of competition, almost without forethought, certainly with slight consideration for trade moralities or for the weightiest of human liberties and with little regard for the perils to public order.

The resources for these audacious combinations came from the stock of savings by individuals and by financial institutions. The more frightened the public of trusts and rapacious oligarchs, the more it invested to get in with the winners. In the aftermath of the panic of 1907, the number of Great Northern Railroad stockholders increased from 2,800 to 11,000, of the Pennsylvania from 40,000 to 57,000. The number of individuals holding stock in United States Steel exceeded 100,000, the average holding about 98 shares. The assets of commercial banks soared from less than $5 billion in 1890 to $18 billion in 1910. Deposits in savings banks almost doubled in that period, while the assets of life insurance companies rose in the same twenty years from $771 million to $4,400 million.[58]

Investment bankers, eager for the business of floating new issues, managed the orderly flow of capital. Familiar with the securities of competing companies and able to provide the necessary funds, they often took places on the boards of firms they created, partly out of responsibility to the investors who followed their advice, partly out of the desire for power. As directors of railroads, commercial banks, life insurance firms, and manufacturing companies, they influenced policy, planned further mergers, and gave financial counsel. Since they often sat on the boards of several corporations, interlocking the directorates, they provided a means of coordination; in return they secured tremendous rewards. J. P. Morgan and Company directly or indirectly received some $150 million for promoting and underwriting the United States Steel Company.

Such payments added water to the holding company stocks. The capitalization usually included an amount large enough to cover the estimated value of the component companies and also the expenses of floating and managing the consolidation. The shares therefore often bore a market price far higher than the worth of the assets. The components of United States Shipbuilding (formed in 1902) owned plants valued at $12 million, with a working capital of only about $5 million. Yet the new company issued stocks and bonds to the amount of almost $68 million—a substantial overestimation, magnified still further when a receivership later revealed the inflation of even the values originally stated. More moderate promoters also left themselves ample margins. Pirates—one and all—charged the critic, producing nothing but higher prices and lower wages, all for the purpose of manipulating Wall Street securities.[59]

The enormous stakes involved in holding companies engendered intense rivalry, as competing capitalists carved out empires and established alliances to mobilize maximum strength. Several complex groupings took form at the opening of the twentieth century although their boundaries remained vague.

John D. Rockefeller and his Standard Oil associates had the longest experience in manipulating great enterprises, and control of 80 to 90 percent of the nation's oil business put vast sums at their disposal. Connections with the National City Bank and the Equitable and Mutual Life Insurance companies added to their power. An understanding with the Widener and Elkins interests involved them in United Gas Improvement of Philadelphia and other public utilities. An association with Jay Gould gave them a voice in the Missouri Pacific, the Wabash, and the Chicago, Milwaukee, and St. Paul railroad systems, and in American Telephone and Western Union. The Standard Oil crowd also dominated the great copper, smelting, mining, and tobacco corporations, and they had a share in United States Steel.

Their only peer was J. P. Morgan and Company, tightly connected with the First National and Chase National banks, the Guaranty Trust, and the New York Life Insurance Company. Solidly entrenched in the New Haven, Chicago, Burlington and Quincy, Northern Pacific, Southern and Atlantic Coast Line railroads, the group also claimed preeminence in steel, shipping, and rubber. Morgan, educated in Europe, profited from influential connections in London and Paris. His ability to sell to transatlantic investors gave him the leverage in the 1880s to reorganize the Philadelphia and Reading, the Chesapeake and Ohio, and other railroads. Imperious, confident, tough, he knew how to use power. His yacht he called *Corsair* and he acted the part. Annoyed by the disorderly economy, he preferred calculable rules, just as he wished firm values in another of his zealous pursuits, art.

Smaller bands held positions of lesser influence; and scores of capitalists in Boston, Philadelphia, Chicago, and San Francisco as well as in New York orbited as satellites around the great financial stars, contributing local resources to one or another, deriving some share of profits as rewards, but not upsetting order and stability.[60]

Political force partly offset economic power and set limits to concentration. Mutual mistrust troubled the uneasy relationships between government and business. In the rough-and-tumble decades after the Civil War, the bagman trotted between legislative halls and corporate offices; in those days, a critic said, Standard Oil could do anything it wished with the Pennsylvania legislature except refine it. Collis Porter Huntington (born 1821), tall, impressive, liberal in the use of profanity and cash, thus lobbied for the Central Pacific Railroad in Washington and New York, effectively enough to have acquired a Fifth Avenue mansion and a princely son-in-law by the time he died in 1900. Ubiquitous corruption extended also to adulteration of foodstuffs, to sweatshop clothing, patent medicines, unsanitary tenement houses, and unsafe theaters and excursion steamers. Buyer beware, in every transaction. In time, however, the glare of publicity, the fear of exposure, and the sense of corrupter and corrupted that each fell victim to the greed of the other, diminished open influence peddling. But enough buyers and sellers of votes remained to ruffle the order bankers and reformers desired.[61]

Trust-busting, the popular term for any attack on big business, therefore clouded every operation with uncertainty. The accusation that the holding company was a conspiracy in restraint of trade drew an audience for any politician, sold magazines for any scribbler. On this issue, however, the law remained resolutely ambiguous. Nothing in the rhetoric, legislation, or judicial decisions informed the rational businessman who wanted to know how far he could go. Imagination and ignorance fed hostility toward corporations although the tendency toward centralization affected all modern institutions.[62]

In any case, internal forces slowed consolidation. Some integrated enterprises toppled because they lacked a firm base to support top-heavy capitalization. Lack of orders thus washed out profits from shipbuilding. Nor could every activity sustain a holding company pyramid. Furthermore, the cleverest of potentates enjoyed no immunity from expensive errors of judgment. Morgan in 1902 established the International Mercantile Marine with the expectation of uniting all the North Atlantic shipping companies. But the Cunard Line refused to join and maintained its independence with a British government subsidy. As a result, the International controlled only about 40 percent of the traffic, lost out in the competition, and paid no dividends.

The efficient management of very large enterprises also called for complex arrangements beyond available techniques and skills. The great life insurance companies, for instance, wrote policies for millions of customers in all the states and in many foreign countries. They dealt with numerous governments and operated through thousands of agents. They invested reserves of hundreds of millions of dollars and maintained connections with dozens of banks and trust companies. Lacking computers or even calculators, they did everything by hand, kept enormous files of records on punched cards, depended upon primitive controls over subordinates, and suffered from the want of qualified personnel. The magnitude of the task set a brake on inclinations to consolidate.[63]

Above all, unforeseen changes scuttled the best-laid plans. In the 1890s the American Sugar Refining Company commanded almost 90 percent of the national output. Then the development of beet sugar reduced its share to less than half. William Wrigley, Jr.'s, promotional maneuvers shook the chicle trust; and western wells after 1900 undermined the Standard Oil monopoly. The exuberant Californian who named his son Carbon Petroleum Dubbs revealed his expectations of the course future development would take. The automobile and aluminum industries, which grew in importance after 1900, escaped the control of the old barons, whose empires did not widen to encompass the new areas of production. Morgan's haughty rebuff allowed William C. Durant to follow his own erratic hunches in pulling together twenty-five firms as General Motors to make automobiles, taxi cabs, trucks, and accessories. The Morgans and the Rockefellers lacked the power or the will to push concentration any further. A balance developed between the tendencies toward integration and dispersal.[64]

The prospect pleased few observers, however. Calling for control by "an intelligent and active public conscience," President Hadley of Yale (1901) insisted that only public sentiment to regulate the trusts would slow the trend to empire in Washington. In the absence of assurance that the developing equilibrium would hold, bigness more seriously threatened democracy after the Sherman Act than before, and war prevented a trial of the corrective Clayton Act. Not only workers and farmers but also shopkeepers, craftsmen, manufacturers, and professionals considered themselves enmeshed in a vast, impersonal apparatus, operating according to ill-understood forces that substantially diminished their liberty to act, crushing their individuality. "To be socialized into an average and placed under the tutelage of the mass of us would be an irreparable loss," wrote the historian of the frontier as the chain store replaced the familiar crossroads emporium, the railroads operated by their own schedules, and remote markets determined prices and wages, that is, the welfare of all.[65]

Often anger focused on the factory—certainly already commonplace in 1850, yet somehow growing ever more strange and ominous thereafter, and not only in scale but in a transformation of the place of humans in it. The clock tower of the old village cotton mill had formed a familiar element of the landscape. Carnegie's Lucy mill (1872) stood seventy-five feet high and twenty across and processed thirteen thousand tons of iron in its first year. A volcano in eruption masked the daily and nightly operation of the south Chicago rolling mills, set in "a forlorn, dirty, muddy, smoky, unkempt district." In the Richmond Tobacco Factory, employing thirty-five hundred, the cigarette girls, all models of young womanhood, frugal in habits, proved susceptible to fainting and coughing spells (from the dust and smell); but the black men sang as they stripped the leaves in an area with the strongest, most biting odor. From an endless belt carrying the tobacco under knives that fell eight or ten strokes to the second, little boys of ten or twelve carried off the chopped leaves.

In such places, the visible water power of the past ever less often turned the wheels, replaced first by steam and then by electricity, each less comprehensible than its predecessor. Electricity, strange and mysterious in the eighteenth century, seemed no less so in the twentieth; the immense force flowing through a wire made sense only as a kind of magic, thus different from water or steam. Furthermore, electricity permitted much more flexible organization of plants. General Electric in Schenectady covered 135 acres and employed six thousand men and women in ninety buildings linked by freight trolley trucks on which the heavy castings moved around. Electric cranes and electric lights testified to the force behind it all, the current generated in Mechanicsville miles away.

The ability to rearrange equipment and dispose of the labor force for efficiency further reduced the comprehensibility of operations and removed the machine from the control of the individual who tended it. Everything rested in an abstract productive flow only engineers understood. The telephone switchboard generated "a continuous sound of many voices; a steady cadence in which no individual note dominated." "In a long line, perched on high stools, they sat before the black panels which rose behind their narrow desk. Into the transmitters—hung from their necks, they articulated their strange confused chorus . . . a hundred pairs of hands reached back and forth across the panels, weaving interminably a never-to-be-completed pattern on its finely checkered face," while "a thousand little lights blinked white and disappeared. . . . Outside under the gray sky of a rainy day . . . over slim wires, buried in conduits below the trampled street, or high strung, swinging in the rising wind, the voices of a thousand people told their thousand messages to waiting ears."[66]

In 1920, the new plants had taken on a totally strange appearance. No longer exposed, visible, often sheathed in steel, the machines gave no indication of their function or mode of operation. The job for most laborers became a prescribed task only incompletely understood, part of a larger obscure process guided for efficiency by professionally skilled experts who planned production. Henry Ford put it concisely: "We measure on each job the exact amount of room that a man needs; he must not be cramped—that would be a waste. But if he and his machine occupy more space than is required, that also is waste. This brings our machines closer together than in any other factory in the world . . . scientifically arranged not only in the sequence of operations but to give every man and every machine every square inch that he requires and, if possible, not a square inch . . . more. . . . Our factory buildings are not intended to be used as parks." Assembly-line techniques spread rapidly from Ford to ever-widening sectors of industry, taking advantage of technological change in the most effective manner, utilizing each machine and each employee most lucratively. Manufacturing therefore employed masses of unskilled, ununionized labor, many formerly on the margin of destitution. Each simplified step in production made the craftsmen and skilled laborers of the past superfluous.[67]

For the moment, the process worked. The factories appeared. Trains of freight and passengers moved across the continent. The nation grew in population, wealth, and power. But it paid a price in painful adjustments to the new conditions.

The widespread application of assembly-line techniques raised questions, not at first among the laborers, mainly concerned with income, but among social critics troubled by the effects of work within the new plants. "Our business grows faster than those within it. The men do not keep up with the changes," a manager complained of the inability of hands to cope, a phenomenon psychologists explained as a fundamental human tendency to adjust to the lowest level of efficiency that would carry. Few wished to confront a deeper question: Was it proper to put humans in positions totally dependent on a machine? Delighted when the workers referred to him as Andy, Carnegie thought that understanding would dissolve the problems of management and labor. Could that expectation hold when labor itself became a replaceable part, a minor element in the productive system, disposable in the sense that one body could do exactly what another did in the same position? Americans could not casually dismiss the observation of a character in an English novel, "What you organize you kill. . . . Yet some organization you must have. . . . What can be ruled about can be machined and there is always a tendency to organize and then to automate." Henry Ford denied that increasing power, machinery, and industry created "a cold, metallic sort of world in which great factories will drive away the trees, the flowers, the birds, and the green fields, and that then we shall have a world composed of metal machines and human machines." He refused to tear up a whole shirt because the collar button did not fit the button hole. He could not wish away the forces that compelled people to stand in line, march in step.[68]

No doubt, the world of making, buying, using, bore contradictory appearances. The consumer-oriented economy depended upon growing markets; yet investment required underconsumption to accumulate savings that became capital—the sums put in the bank fell beyond the reach of the sellers of coats and Kodaks. Considered a factor in the cost of production, labor received as low a price as possible; but with wage earners also potential purchasers of the goods industry produced, low pay, or none, meant skimpy spending, or none. Each entrepreneur sought orderly planning in his plant, yet fiercely fought as monopolies the like efforts of others—what some considered free enterprise others considered restraint of trade.

A common, abstract formula resolved all such apparent contradictions. The rational choices of men pursuing their own interests through the free operation of the market would establish an equilibrium at the optimal point between savings and spending, between earnings and purchasing power, between concentration and fragmentation. Nature's method advanced man by forcing him to depend upon himself. Every effort to relieve him of that responsibility would lead to his deterioration. So ran the theories.[69]

The ingenious projections did not work out in practice, not so much because of defects in reasoning but because they never fitted precisely the concrete cases and because they took no account of extraneous political and social forces that perversely intruded in life as in the school, however insistently exorcised in theory.

By 1900, the lessons of the dialectic had percolated down through parts of the educational system through the influence of W. T. Harris, John Dewey, and others. A gratifying development had spread progressive instruction from its seedbed, Chicago. True, the dominant trend ran in the counterdirection—toward large, more formal institutions and rigid curricula. The philosopher argued, however, that humans and society played upon one another. Individuals free to find their own way influenced the world about them, which in turn shaped their character. Only—each person needed help to stay within the lines, to proceed in step as on the subway platform, compulsion by law for his or her own good, just as all the books in the public library had their places in rows established by Melvil Dewey's classification. In 1916, John Dewey wondered whether the state could operate an educational system without restriction, constraint, and corruption, and cheerfully concluded that it could do so by teaching what bound people together in cooperative human pursuits. The press of numbers thrust everyone in the same direction, in schools as in factories.[70]

Persistently, therefore, injured Americans chose life over logarithms, set science aside and called upon the state to become a more active policeman than prevailing theory dictated, to intervene not for some purpose of its own but to help people along. Perhaps the waxing and waning of industrial crises followed rules as regular as those of the planets; but the worker knew the meanwhile pain of joblessness and hunger. Perhaps nature intended the great manufacturer to swallow his marginal rival, as the shark the minnow; but the small businessman—with customers vanished, debts soon due, investments dead, new ventures hazardous— refused to be digested. Perhaps some tamper-proof universal calculator would of itself set the charges for elevators and railroads; but the farmers wanted to pay less, get more. Perhaps the waste of competition was a small price for expansion; but corporation executives who arranged thousands "in order according to their character and education," wished to plan with confidence, and earn their due esteem. They had done more for the community than teachers, preachers, statesmen, artists, and orators, yet never appeared as statues in the park or as faces on postage stamps or paper money. By contrast, "women agitators, ministers, socialists, labor leaders, editors" and missionaries who gained fame by claiming devotion to public service achieved nothing.

Not yet simply digits filed away in numbered flats on numbered streets, they bore names that revealed whose sons and daughters or wives they were; and they belonged in neighborhoods that revealed what kind they were. They listened to the cylinders or disks on phonographs and watched the films at movie houses; but the mechanical marvels had not yet stilled the evening voices round the parlor piano or on the porch or at the bar; and the curtain rising at the vaudeville show or theater still touched sparks of magic anticipation. That is, most Americans still possessed identities to which they clung, lest they slip in among the drifting, placeless integers. Everyone aggrieved yelled for help, and their notion of democracy required the state to respond.[71]

The war intervened before any test of the effectiveness of the reactions. And as in 1861, military needs expanded governmental authority and brought still other regulatory bureaucracies into being in an effort to organize and discipline the whole population. Shape up! Get in line! March in step! The commands responded not simply to the emergency of 1917. They had resounded earlier in response to the urgency of work in a mechanized economy and of life in huge metropolitan cities. Hence the fears about the loss of personality and the impingement on individual liberties.

IX

BATTLEFIELDS

THE GREAT WARS INTRUDED, unanticipated, unwanted.

Soldiers in 1859 still considered service a frolic. That year, Louisa May Alcott, visiting a militia encampment, longed for the sight of uniforms in combat. Governor William Gilpin (1860) saw the people achieve incredible conquests, self-governed, self-fed, self-armed, self-commanded—stupendous fresh new forces unveiled.

They had much to learn, both of them. Her *Hospital Sketches* described another reality; and machines did not spread the "unstinted enjoyment" he imagined.

So, too, their grandsons in 1917.

> For we are the same our fathers have been.
> We see the same sights our fathers have seen.
>
> . . . .
>
> To the life we are clinging, they also would cling,
> But it speeds from us all like a bird on the wing.

Baptized with blood and fire, free in death, they proclaimed the new gospel: the cannon giveth peace, Christ rides upon the warship his army to increase.

In 1861, a few Southern fire-eaters, oblivious to reality, lusted after glory. They did not envision the relation of their actions to the unfolding drama, as an English traveler had when he described the decay of public virtue as the greatest danger. "In despotic countries the people may be virtuous though the government is vicious, but a corrupt republic is tainted in its blood and bears the seeds of death in every pulsation." Nor in 1917 did the bellicose warriors who joined Teddy Roosevelt's call to

343

arms, in the search for fresh opportunities for strenuous daring and doing, foresee the unknown totality that would follow.[1]

Abraham Lincoln and Woodrow Wilson and the great majority of their countrymen flinched from the prospect of armed conflict—irrational, wasteful. Yet in the one case, as in the other, when the guns boomed the presidents summoned thousands to march off in response to the echoing roar, none knowing what they would find there. They never would make the discovery, not the commanders or the obedient.

Great modern conflicts kept participants ignorant. No longer, as in the eighteenth century, did a brief exchange of desultory fire precede a wait of months before the next battle. Here the soldiers confronted each other in trenches for days on end; and they shot to kill. The monstrous toll of civil war—360,000 dead on the Union side, 258,000 dead on the Confederate side—heaped up, a stupendous mound of corpses, all American. When the need mounted,

> thay ware not so perticular Who they got to fight the foe . . .
> Among the bravest of the brave was the irish volinters. (1865)

Not by design, but in the nature of the case, the vast scale of operations reaching across whole counties, whole states, the tens of thousands involved, permitted few to glimpse more than their own small share of mud and blood, of heedless rain, of boredom interspersed with bursts of violence.[2]

The real war, that many-threaded drama that left "an unending, universal mourning-wail of women, parents, orphans," would never get into the books, wrote the poet. Everywhere among the countless graves of the soldier cemeteries, he saw on monuments and stones, singly or in masses, the significant word UNKNOWN. Amid the beauties of nature, the wounded awaited treatment as in a slaughterhouse, like James Kyner at Shiloh, "all mutilated, sickening, torn, gouged out," except those who remained unnamed. "Likely one of them crawls aside to some bush-clump, or ferny tuft on receiving his death shot there sheltering a little while, soaking roots, grass, and soil with red blood and there with pain and suffering, the last lethargy winds like a serpent round him and there at last crumbles in mother earth, unburied and unknown."

The poet's elegy

> Saw the ships how they sail'd,
> And the summer approaching winter richness, and the fields all
> busy with labor,

And the infinite separate houses, how they all went on, each
    with its meals and minutia of daily usages,
And the streets, how their throbbings throbb'd, and the cities
    pent, lo then and there,
Falling upon them all and among them all, and enveloping me with
    the rest,
Appear'd the cloud, appear'd the long black trail,
And I knew death, its thought, and the sacred knowledge of
    death.[3]

In time, other images crowded out the memories, transformed the bitter conflict into an episode of high adventure. Never marred by dishonor or betrayal, the glorious pageant had strengthened the Union.

That splendid little war in the Caribbean (1898) occasioned little grief; brief, decisive, with most of the casualties foreigners, it swirled out of public consciousness in the end-of-the-century euphoria. But the anguish returned in 1918. Though American troops saw much less combat than did Europeans and suffered fewer casualties by far, the intensity of the impact matched that of a half century earlier. And in big numbers: 107,000 dead and 237,000 wounded of the 4,750,000 under arms—two million of them volunteers, the others drafted from among the twenty-four million registered under the Selective Service Act of May 18, 1917, this time no substitutes accepted. "Look out of the window," said Judge Martin J. Wade of St. Paul, Minnesota, "and see the boys marching by, in step with the drum beat, following the flag . . . side by side, the boy from the German home, the boy from the Swedish home, the boy from the home of Irish parents, and Scotch parents, and French parents, and Norwegian parents, the sons of every race . . . the banker's boy, and the son of the street cleaner, the lawyer's boy and the farmer's boy, the Methodist boy, the Jewish boy, the Catholic boy." Down in the trenches, many will die, and "in the mingled blood of those boys of different creeds and races and classes, we are going to build a new America, stronger, more powerful, more just and more free than ever before." Fought on battlefields remote from hometown rhetoric, beneath the sea and in the air, encased in armor, aflame with guns machined by science, the First World War deprived the doughboys of romantic cavalry self-images and left a sense of incompleteness, which in the 1920s led on the one hand to the jingoistic patriotism of the legionnaires and on the other to the black disillusionment of the generation that considered itself lost.[4]

With neither conflict—not that of 1861 nor that of 1917—acceptable as a good in itself, people came to terms with both for their service to an ennobling cause. Liberty and slavery, explained the abolitionist Samuel J. May, could not abide in peace in the same country, utterly irreconcilable, like good and evil, Christ and Belial—eternal antagonists. Marching to battle or exulting in victory, love of liberty fired the citizen with antique heroism. Surveying the grounds of the bitter fighting in 1863, Lincoln summoned Americans to "dedicate themselves to the great task remaining—to take from these honored dead increased devotion to that cause for which they gave the last full measure of devotion, highly to resolve that those dead shall not have died in vain—that this nation, under God, shall have a new birth of freedom, and that government of the people, by the people, for the people, shall not perish from the earth." *The New York Herald* that year recognized an age of miracles of a positive, real, tangible character, proofs of man's status little lower than the angels. Ralph Waldo Emerson saw in 1865 the dawn of a new era, worth to mankind all the treasure and all the lives it had cost, yes, worth to the world a whole generation of American men, had it been demanded. Manifestly "God's doing," the war formed the final and most dramatic stage of the corrective process that eradicated the national flaw of slavery. To parents whose son died in battle in 1863 he explained that some crises claimed the sacrifices of nations, as well as of individuals; and "one whole generation might well consent to perish if, by their fall, political liberty and clean and just life could be made sure to the generations that follow." "We are drifting upon the currents of a destiny under the control of a power higher than human agencies," wrote *The New York Times* editorialist.

Put into the long perspective, the blood and mud receded into the background as the living atoned for the guilt of having survived. In anticipation, they confronted the memory of the "young figures of the fallen with their arrested expressions, with the indefinable shining stigmata exquisitely for all our time, facing us out, quite blandly ignoring us, looking through us or straight over us at something they partake of together but that we mayn't pretend to know." Those heroes had died for liberty. They rested, asleep in the land they had made free. The consoling sorrow cherished year after year, at innumerable Decoration Day celebrations, marked escape from the pressure of a general nightmare. Difficulties great and novel remained, but Reason no longer waited for Passion to spend itself. From 1868 onward, the war became an element of a significant ritual, an occasion for mobilizing and displaying the unity and solidarity of communities in their heroic dead. They all loved a parade, and the marching band replaced the sung hymn in the procession to the cemetery—stars and stripes forever. Small towns where every family had some direct or indirect connection with the casualties imparted an almost sacred quality to memorialization of the war. In a nation committed to nonsectarianism, one in which nationalism displaced the desire for religious communion, the ceremony gave different kinds of people an opportunity to draw together, as did the Fourth of July, in the shared recollection of losses. The dear departed who "died for the rights of man, for the perpetuity of a government founded on liberty," became a binding element in American experience.[5]

In time, the war's symbolic function served ever-broader strata of the population. The great conflict that had torn the nation apart became a token of national reunion, its theme free labor exemplified in the Homestead Act and the rejection of speculation and monopoly. Decoration Day lost its exclusively Northern character; as acrimony diminished it became usual for Confederates and Yankees to commemorate the occasion together, with "the mutual sorrows of the past" spreading goodwill and forbearance and making the names of Robert Lee and Ulysses Grant the loved inheritance of one common people, one common country. The readers who peeped through *The Gates Ajar* could see the mingled Union and Confederate dead (80,000 copies sold). In the eye of heaven the bereavement of mourners who brought flowers to the mounds of the fallen Virginians and Georgians was as sacred as the tender grief of offerings to Northern martyrs. Liberty

> united
> One mingled flood of braided light—
> The red that fires the Southern rose
> With spotless white from Northern snows.[6]

And therefore, worthwhile!

> Not a grave of the murdered for freedom, but grows
> seed for freedom, in its turn to bear seed,
> Which the winds carry afar and re-sow, and the rains
> and the snows nourish.
> Not a disembodied spirit can the weapons of tyrants let loose,
> But it stalks invisibly over the earth, whispering, counselling,
> cautioning,
> Liberty! Let others despair of you! I never despair of you.

For years, Oliver Wendell Holmes, Sr., could not bear to read anything about the war, but later justified it as a necessary episode in the evolutionary struggle. His son, Justice Oliver Wendell Holmes, Jr., reflecting on his own experience and the two wounds he took, in 1884 explained that the war had set apart his generation, touched it by fire, stimulated it to a capacity for emotion and feeling, taught it that life was a profound and passionate thing, "a national act of enthusiasm and faith," a condition of greatness. To fight required belief and a willingness to commit oneself to a course without being able to foresee exactly where it would come out. Transmuted from the bitter conflict it had been, the war became an episode of high adventure; every base element vanished; only nobility remained. In "The Moral Equivalent of War" (1910), William James recognized combat as inherent in human nature; everlasting battle gave the outside world its moral style. To bind Americans in unity, both sides had to seem right, no villains, only heroes, everyone gallant in the glorious pageant that strengthened the Union.

By 1917, concern with degeneration and loss of virility suffused thoughts of war. In the 1880s Daniel Beard began to champion the strenuous life to save overly civilized children from loss of the frontier skills of survival. In 1910, the American Boy Scouts set up summer camps to teach outdoor life, sleeping in tepees and cooking outdoors, imparting also progressive ideals of efficiency and fairness. Seven years later some 450,000 had enrolled.

Popular literature idealized natural, aggressive male models like Tarzan and Owen Wister's Virginian. A military uniform offset the soft office life of modern times. Better for America "a policy of blood and iron" rather than "milk and water," insisted Theodore Roosevelt; and younger men like Henry Stimson and Franklin Roosevelt agreed on the need to fend off youthful decadence. One of the war's heroes, Sergeant Alvin York out of the Tennessee mountains, initially opposed killing human beings. Devoid of book-learning, he acted as the need arose. Ernest Hemingway, who enlisted in the Italian army to get close to action, rejected William James's suggestion that fighting poverty was a satisfactory moral equivalent of war. John Dos Passos, horrified on the French battlefields in 1917, nevertheless felt more alive the closer shells landed. Charles Thwing, president of Western Reserve University, noted that many students enlisted in service organizations that took them close to the battles long before the United States entered the war.

Dissenters who objected that liberty remained only a name, not a reality, without material equality to end misery, poverty, and crime, also urged creation of an army of intelligent labor of millions of men and women with a common focus in view to build a great central city. Their energy could serve an idealistic end.

Woodrow Wilson attempted to cast a similar sunny light on that later conflict—a war to end war and to make the world safe for democracy. Reverberations from remote European battlefields, however, conjured up the image of a mourning figure walking, unable to rest, near "the old court-house pacing up and down . . . bronzed, lank man!"

> He cannot sleep upon his hillside now,
> He is among us; as in times before!
>
> . . . . : . .
>
> His head is bowed. He thinks on men and kings.
> Yes, when the sick world cries, how can he sleep?
> Too many peasants fight, they know not why,
> Too many homesteads in black terror weep.
>
> . . . .
>
> He cannot rest until a spirit-dawn
> Shall come;—the shining hope of Europe free;
> The league of sober folk, the worker's earth,
> Bringing long peace to cornland, alp and sea
>
> . . . .
>
> That he may sleep upon his hill again.

In the case of one conflict as of the other, doubts intruded, when the nation slipped into the excesses of the gilded age and of imperialism, ironic commentaries upon the new birth of freedom for which thousands died at Gettysburg and at Château-Thierry.

> Whats about "Christ" and "feller men,"
> And "doin' as ye would be done by"?
> Time isn't now as they was then;
> We now need all that we can come by.
> Don't you suppose Christ sometimes spoke in figgers?
> And didn't mean by "men" half-breeds and niggers.

In 1919, the battle shifted to the "wolf at the gates of civilized Europe," bolshevism, maddened by hunger; and only the veterans could stem its insidious guile.

Francis Lieber, James Russell Lowell, and Herman Melville had looked forward to a nation rededicated by the Civil War. Orestes A. Brownson envisioned a vastly stronger central government, with obedient citizens replacing the misty theories of the Declaration of Independence. But civil liberty, that freedom of action man enjoyed as a social being, had not produced as expected "the utmost variety, as all untrammeled life and unfettered individual action necessarily" should have. To some degree anarchistic, such liberty rested upon the intention of giving personal differences the freest play possible without mutual destruction. But only the saints in paradise enjoyed that condition, on earth unknown. The need for order engendered intolerance of opposition and blind obedience, the lockstep of chained convicts, the mechanical arrangement of military movements.

Professor Arnold Bennett Hall of the University of Wisconsin (1920) complacently noted that the war had demonstrated how to utilize and harness organized patriotic sentiment, under the driving impulse of which people gloriously accepted burdens and sacrifice. Proper education would mobilize the instinctive and emotional life of the nation to solve domestic problems also. New ideals and aspirations, a new morality, and a new patriotism, both social and constructive, would bring victory in peace as in war. The test of practice would validate the truth.

A younger thinker attacked the inadequacy of John Dewey's pragmatism as a philosophy of life. More alarmed by the excesses of pacifists than by those of the military, the pragmatists ignored efforts to conscript thought, and assumed that the war techniques need not generate mob fanaticism, injustice, and hatred, indeed hoped to use those techniques as raw material for remaking the world in an exquisite, rare, liberal political structure. The optimism-haunted unwearily maintained that all would yet work for the best in a mad and half-destroyed world. Perhaps William James in the face of such a disaster would have abandoned his moral equivalent of war for an immoral equivalent which, in swift and periodic saturnalias, would have acted as vaccination against the sure pestilence of war. Yet that unthinkable alternative pointed only downward to the fiery cataclysm described in lurid popular novels.[7]

On the Slope. What would the world's future be like? Doubts troubled Americans for the first time since the seventeenth century. They had assumed that the old Europe and its decadent monarchies would shortly expire. But in 1900, Europe displayed vigorous expansive power. Cartels created formidable competitive economic empires, and each nation carved out for itself spheres of influence and colonies in remote parts of the world. By contrast, the United States had seemed incapable of action.

In Hawaii, Samoa, even Tangier and Morocco, it had to decide not whether to annex or intervene, or whether these areas should remain independent. If the United States did not intervene, they would come under the control of Germany, France, Japan, or Britain.

The American stake in the Pacific and Asia had mounted after the acquisition of California. Expressions of concern warned the French and English away from Hawaii, long a field for merchants and missionaries from the United States. The conservative Japanese empire, until then impenetrably closed to foreigners, yielded in July 1854 when Commodore Matthew C. Perry entered Tokyo Bay, demanded recognition, and thus brought the islands into contact with the modern world. Three years later, Townsend Harris, the American consul, by friendly methods secured a more favorable arrangement.

The Caribbean also attracted expansionist interest. The United States, while recognizing Spanish sovereignty over Cuba, had clearly indicated that it would not permit its transfer to any other power. In 1854, a statement by James Buchanan, John Y. Mason, and Pierre Soulé, the ministers to England, France, and Spain, respectively, proclaimed the readiness to purchase Cuba, with the option of taking it by force if Spain refused. Meanwhile, however, Cuban revolutionists in New York agitated for independence; and filibustering expeditions under William Walker, who held power in Nicaragua between 1855 and 1857, diverted attention to Central America.

But it was difficult to think of expansion in the terms earlier popular. William Henry Seward, deeply committed to Manifest Destiny, in 1867 negotiated the purchase of Alaska, which ultimately deepened the country's Pacific role. Remoteness and sparse population removed the complications that impeded other proposed acquisitions. Santo Domingo, for instance, though available for the taking, seemed indigestible, for Americans could not conceive its status in the Union. Union troops occupying Louisiana during Reconstruction had not altered that state's basic institutions. They would do no better on a distant island. Every political tradition rejected the suggestion that the United States hold a possession in simple imitation of the aggressive Europeans. The country, born in a revolution, could not imagine itself the ruler of colonies, like those who rode round the earth

> To see what they may gain,
> And ever the road they ride runs red
> With the blood of martyrs slain;
> And ever God's name is on their lips
> Whatever the deed to be done;
> And ever the psalm of the sabre rings
> With the gospel of the gun.

Yet neither could Americans conceive of Santo Domingo as a territory in the sense that New Mexico had been, its status temporary, in preparation for equal statehood. The difficulty of assimilating such racially mixed populations persuaded the United States to avoid additions of territory and in effect to halt expansion at its existing continental limits. There they could cherish liberty, "an elevated condition, the offspring of a sublime principle implanted in the human breast which being cultivated and fostered renders man capable of self-government and makes a state which is but an aggregate of individuals, able to endure perils from without and from within." The problem arose once more in the 1880s in the case of Hawaii, when the Congress refused to ratify annexation on essentially the same grounds, although in that case, opinion later shifted.[8]

The issue would not disappear; indeed, the acquisitions from Spain inflated it at a time when many Americans thought the Filipinos a new brand of canned goods. The massive campaign to sell a $200 million war bond issue (1898) familiarized some with the setting. But old benevolent attitudes persisted.

> Little Brown Brothers across the sea,
> Running your race for liberty,
> Here's to you.
> We've been there ourselves.
>
> . . . .
>
> Little Brown Brothers across the blue sea,
> Battling so bravely for liberty,
> Here's to you.
> We've been there ourselves and won. (1899)

The contrast remained vivid.

> Tortures of dearth and war our Fathers bore,
> To live and serve their God, in liberty.
> We lift His cross upon a far-off shore,
> And 'neath its arms slay those who would be free.

The liberty songs celebrated the foolish Tagal who pitted naked spear and bow against death on land and sea.

> What futile school
> Has taught the fool
> The fatal word of Liberty?
> Lo God is with us and our guns.
> Pile up his bleeding flesh in tons.
> So beat him back.
> And shoot him down.
> And run him through.

They mocked the jingoes.

> And here's a Jingo song;
> The flag is right in any fight;
> Our country, right or wrong.

Massachusetts Senator George F. Hoar reminded the Senate of one symbol more potent even than the American flag—the bread and wine which represented the body and blood of the Savior of mankind. "A man who would use an appeal to the flag in aid of the subjugation of an unwilling people, would be capable of using the sacramental wine for a debauch." He appealed "from the Present, bloated with material prosperity, drunk with the lust of empire, to another and a better age . . . from the Present to the Future and to the Past" (1900).

Whatever the outcome of verbal, musical, or military battles, the ambiguous concept of citizenship remained alive and troubling. The Constitution and the rights it guaranteed followed the flag. Squirm as the courts would over the implications, every resident of the United States became eligible for citizenship and for the equality ensured by the Fourteenth Amendment. Those offended could avoid further massive dilutions of the original stock only by assuming that some possessions were not territories on the way to statehood but simply held temporarily in preparation for ultimate independence. Cuba, the Philippines, and Puerto Rico, occupied after the Spanish-American War, fell into that ambiguous status. Professor John W. Burgess, among others, who had once considered the drive to empire expression of a divine impulse, changed his mind out of concern lest unlimited rule in the colonies demoralize constitutional government at home.

By the end of the century, war and racism had clarified the issue. Americans could shut themselves up between the oceans and sink from among the great powers of the world, heaping up riches that stronger, bolder people would gather. Let the pacifist but regard the growing armies of the others—never mind the kaiser and the czar, look at Serbia and Belgium! Or alternatively, Americans could follow the true laws of their being, retain and develop the Philippines, and expand Asian trade "to the very edge of the cradle of the Aryans," whence their far-distant ancestors had started on the march which had then girdled the world. In that event, an imperial state had to control and discipline subject peoples *for their own good.* The democratic social system of the United States had developed individual self-control and self-direction in the citizen not found elsewhere and responsible for Anglo-Saxon superiority (1900). Imperialism, which William James branded enslavement, became the end result of the aim to attain a new birth of freedom on the battlefield.[9]

Power ruled at home also, certainly after 1917. Patriotic bodies sprouted all over the country, arousing the emotions by attack and hysteria, their love of country expressed in screams, violence, and extremes, their savage intolerance reeking of the burn of acid. Seeking to stoke fervor essential to unity of thought and action, the California Sons of the Revolution called (1917) for a new, purely national air, not like the Star-Spangled Banner borrowed from another land. The American Legion, infuriated by the Centralia massacre, embarked on a campaign to develop and maintain correct thought.[10]

Everyone knew the need for strenuous outdoor activity to offset the effeminacy, flabbiness, raw tensions and nerves, generated by life in unhealthy urban environments. "Weakness is a crime," Bernarr MacFadden's *Physical Culture* proclaimed; and preparedness aimed to ready men for the trenches. In 1915 and 1916, twenty thousand volunteers exercised their manhood in Business Men's Military Training Camps in Plattsburg, New York. In 1917 a network of state councils coordinated such activities, not only in the field but also in molding opinion through makers of public sentiment—bankers, clergy, employers, and ethnic leaders. War rallies followed to save food and to stimulate industrial and agricultural efficiency. Clamor for a female role compelled the Council of National Defense to form a women's committee to join suffrage activities to patriotism. Baby Weeks emphasized public health, also for the war service. Massive liberty sings and liberty loan campaigns drew these efforts together, while some Progressive reformers sought to shape the participants in a "conscious corporate existence."

The press willingly went along and failed miserably in criticism. In the urgency to emphasize homogeneity, it ignored Polish loyalty meetings; and Czechs, Hungarians, Yugoslavs, Croatians, along with the Scandinavian organizations and Dutch groups who supported the war, got no notice. Theodore Roosevelt (1915) insisted that the country had no room for hyphenated Americans, in a tangle of squabbling nationalities. As a result, the chauvinists had the field to themselves, "singing their hymns of hate and damning officials for inefficiency and spinelessness when they failed to produce traitors to be put before a firing squad."[11]

Passion infused the old, gentler, nineteenth-century patriotism. The Sons of the Revolution suggested (1915) that as part of daily schoolwork, pupils every morning salute the American flag and sing the national hymn. Pilgrims traveled to Mount Vernon, Monticello, and other sacred shrines:

> O dearest country of my heart, home of the high desire,
> Make clean thy soul for sacrifice on Freedom's altar fire;

For thou must suffer, thou must fight until the war lords cease,
And all the peoples lift their hands in liberty and peace.

Breathes there a man with soul so dead—this is my own, my native
land—may it always be right but my country right or wrong.

And not only the all-engulfing Americanism, but the lesser national-
isms also of Irish-, Italo-, Czech-, Polish-, Slovak-, Anglo-, Zionist-
Americans—as if intermediate institutions having failed, floundering individuals required some *patria* to which to cling. In Boston, Fan Sylian
Noli, a Harvard student, and Faik Bey Konitza, an editor, fanned into
life a movement that would make Albania an independent nation. In
Nebraska, Alexander Bilmanis prepared to become the first president of
an independent Latvia. In Pittsburgh, Czechs and Slovaks agreed on the
form of a new Czechoslovakia.

The dissenters who hoped, with Mary Antin, that America would be
what the immigrants would have a hand in making it, and not what a
ruling class decided, who resisted the reduction of all distinctive qualities
into a tasteless, colorless fluid of uniformity, nevertheless also recognized
the imperatives of patriotism. America required before anything applied
religion, a new outlook on life, a spiritual revival expressed in 1000
percent pure Americanism. It had no tolerance for anarchist snickering
at the land "of that proud bird which steals everything it can from smaller
birds and then sits gloating with its victorious eye fixed on vacancy
dreaming of what it will eat next" (1899).[12]

In this respect as in others, ideals, however fair in prospect, turned
ugly in realization. The happy ending for which everyone longed slipped
away into the tragic, sinister, or at best comic modes. The somber fruits
of the great abolition crusade displayed themselves among the shoeless
sharecroppers and in the lynchings of the un-Reconstructed South as well
as in the race riots of segregated northern cities. And all the efforts
reformers had lavished on temperance approached fulfillment in enactment of the Eighteenth Amendment only to give way to immense
disappointment with Prohibition. So the endeavors to purify politics
undermined the popular control asserted in the local urban machine or
in the People's party. Materialism, improvidence, and indifference resulted in "hush money and bought policemen, bought legislatures, special
privilege, corporation joy riding and dollar votes, venality and stupidity
in office, unemployment, strikes, misery and want, child labor, waste of
public funds and public lands and public resources of power, filth and
disease, robbery and murder." Newspapers increased their circulations and
journalists their name recognition by generating an insatiable public

appetite for exposure and denunciation which, though accurate, amounted sometimes "to a positive mania" that added to the burden of responsibility upon the citizen. Meanwhile, private associations swelled into massive national bureaucratic federations remote from individual members, a trend particularly worrisome when people doubted that experts could keep in touch with popular thought.[13]

The need of cooperation and compromise between public opinion and expert knowledge remained vital. Improvements hurt—whether they resulted in great uncontrollable rail, transit, telephone, and utility lines, or replaced the cracker-barrel grocer with the shining identical but impersonal units of the chain. The dreamers who wanted every human being free proposed to eliminate competition and ensure equality, but also cried out against the efficiency of the machine, destitute of adaptability of means to ends—the essence of true reason. In H. G. Wells's novel, popular in the United States, a man who on earth embodied "coldly scientific reason" went insane when exposed to the antlike superbeing who had transformed "the lunar world into one efficient socialized and soulless state" (1917).

In the hundreds of thousands, the autos trundled off the assembly lines, the bushels emptied into the elevators. But the workers responsible, who toiled in the factory or the farm or the executive office, did not become the happier thereby. Nor did the buyers able to get a Ford of any color as long as it was black, able to take home any bread but not fresh-baked. The fruits of so much labor too often rotted before they yielded anyone enjoyment—rich or poor, old or young, male or female. Doomed to defeat, the tramp endlessly battled the malfunctioning inanimate objects he possessed but did not need. The wealthy, "just as much slaves to circumstances as the poorest beggar," suffered under the constant strain of anxiety in guarding their property and labored night and day from early years to old age. Women, promised such freedom and happiness as their most ardent advocates never dreamed of, sharing "with equal right the material benefit derived from progress and no longer restricted by laws to a limited field of action," shared also the burden of insecurity. Work leveled all social conditions, the fulcrum from which to arrive, individually and collectively, at a superior plane of existence, but also the source of responsibility and obligations and therefore of tension.[14]

Immobility spelled death. To keep alive, churches as well as the entire population of the United States sought new fields of endeavor. Visitors commented that even in leisure Americans engaged in strenuous activities. "Repose, in the sense it hitherto had for humanity," remained unknown in America. Relaxation from labor came only in games, in which formidable energy exploded with an intensity theretofore unknown. The popularity of ragtime or syncopation, a music of contrasts in which the irregular accents of the melody went against the regular accents of the beat, sprang from its inherent instabilities. It sounded nervous and steam-powered, jagged and pulsing, echoing the rhythms of manufacturing and conveying a sense of activity and conflict to ears conditioned by European waltzes. Arnold Bennett (1913) called it "the music of the hustler, of the feverishly active speculator, of the skyscraper and the grain elevator."

The twentieth century defined sport as a masculinity-validating experience, an essential test of manhood once acquiring a farm, starting a business, or moving to the frontier had become less challenging. Elaborate rules and rituals helped define heroes, illustrated the meaning of life, and suggested core values, building strong and decent men, marking national character, and defining wholesome international rivalry. The emphasis on athletics meshed with progressive ideas of education and of play. Richard T. Ely and others supported the establishment of playgrounds and parks where young men's animal spirits might find release, and Lillian Wald and Jacob Riis championed recreation facilities as a deterrent to gang activity. Thorstein Veblen saw the attention to sport as "emulative ferocity," its goal the restoration of a lost sense of male prowess, conjuring up a make-believe world of participation in the serious but lost art of human survival. It developed ferocity and cunning, precisely the qualities needed in modern competition.

Ernest Hemingway failed to make the football team at Oak Park High in Chicago because of his puny stature; a spurt of growth between his freshman and sophomore years still left him clumsy and slow, only good enough for substitute tackle. Then he took up boxing, and found a streak of the bully in his nature. Football, explained Percy Haughton, Harvard's coach, like war, entailed discipline, hard work, sacrifice and strain, and cultivated spiritual togetherness.

> Heavy the work that waits our hands;
> Our single strength but small,
> United here for common tasks,
> Each finds the might of all.

Savage hatred, violence, and disappointment also infused sport. No joy in Mudville, but passionate fury—

> "Kill him, Kill the umpire" shouted
> Someone in the stand.

And it's likely they'd have killed him had
Not Casey raised his hand.

Fraud cried the maddened thousands,
And the echo answered "Fraud,"
But one scornful look from Casey and
The audience was awed;
They saw his face grow stern and cold, they
Saw his muscles strain,
And they knew that Casey wouldn't let that
Ball go by again.

The sneer is gone from Casey's lip,
His teeth are clenched with hate;
He pounds with cruel violence his
Bat upon the plate.

Cries of "Kill the umpire" jarred a French visitor astounded by the
authority of those officials over crowds electrified by the excitement of
the game.

Was nothing any longer sacred?

The national game exhibited its character not only in the corrupt
White Sox, but also in its crooked owners, in the misuse of rules, and
in anointment of a czar, K. M. Landis, famous for having imprisoned a
dissenting Socialist congressman. The fans were about to venerate their
supreme hero—"the Sultan of Swat," Babe Ruth, a notorious boozer and
fornicator who would hit fifty-nine home runs in 1921 when his nearest
rival had but twenty-four and who visited dying children.

Yet every sovereign individual carried about indelible beliefs displayed in vast newspaper advertisements devoted to spiritualism, healing,
voodoo, fortune-telling, astrology, and necromancy.[15]

"Thought you greatness was to ripen for you like a pear?" asked the
poet, observing the traitors, the wily officeholders, the scrofulous wealth,
greed, passion, decay of faith, and fossilelike lethargy about him. "Pride,
competition, segregation, vicious willfulness and license" brooded over
the nation, made manifest in the lack of leaders and the meanness of the
masses.

The corruption exploded also during the Great War, and not only
in the businessmen's profits or the inflated wages of laborers and the
farmers' soaring prices, but also in the puffed-up prominence of scientists

and other intellectuals who enlisted for the opportunity to remake the world, among them Walter Lippmann, Thorstein Veblen, and Herbert Hoover, who abrogated the antitrust laws and fixed prices to feed the world. Daylight saving (1918) to promote efficiency, after all, reordered nature's irregularity.

A few younger writers, Randolph Bourne, among others, had expected to make John Dewey's philosophy the foundation stone of a thoroughgoing social and cultural revolution. They painfully discovered that he would not lead where they wished to go, with the Treaty of Versailles the final betrayal. By unleashing forces unamenable to social control, the critics feared that war would subvert to unintended ends Dewey's much-vaunted creative intelligence and reveal the emptiness of his assumptions about human rationality. The critics would not concede that association with the dominant trends would enable intellectuals to control events any more than the child on the back of a mad elephant could stop the beast.

Realists, on the other hand, could not escape the choice of alternatives, what Lincoln called necessity: in 1861, a divided Union and slavery perpetuated; in the 1890s, Hawaii and the Philippines Japanese; in 1917, Prussian militarism spreading from Europe to Baghdad.

The incorrigible optimists of the older generation counseled patience. Keep on! Liberty would triumph, whatever occurred. One or two failures, the indifference or ingratitude of the people, the brutality of soldiers, the belching of cannons, the penal statutes, would not defeat the end in which the hopeful believed, which would patiently await its time—a year, a century, a hundred centuries. The faithful promised to search carefully in defeat, poverty, imprisonment, not knowing what shape the liberty they would find would take.[16]

Ominously often, they looked in the wrong places: in the democratized armies, in the marching uniformed troops, in the assembly lines of new factories, in every type of mechanized order, lavish in promises that concealed repression.[17]

In 1861, the Zouaves had gone gaily off to war—crimson trousers sparkling in the sun, perfect targets one and all. That year also the Illinois "Woodpeckers" had formed ranks, each in scarlet fez and bloomers, yellow tassel, blue jacket trimmed with braid, and white leggings— hardly appropriate to trench warfare. They had come back—some of them—unobtrusively clothed in somber blue and gray. In 1917, drab khaki dressed all the soldiers. By then, too, the kids had learned to wear Boy Scout uniforms. Civilian attire also changed. Colors disappeared from the waistcoats and jackets in which men once decked themselves, replaced by sober black or gray suits, whether factory-made or bespoke. Railroad conductors, postmen, and the police appeared in uniforms. And the A&P and Woolworth storefronts effaced all signs of individuality.[18]

The wars had revealed a democratic society amenable to intelligent controls, beyond the wildest hopes of progressive social scientists. John Dewey expected to liquidate unemployment, the parasitical leisure class, inefficient production and distribution, drift and lack of organization, by-products of the past, alterable with the application of will, determination, and force. He foresaw science applied to communal purposes, national boundaries obliterated by air navigation, and world unity strengthened by the economic interdependence of all countries. Purely personal relationships, under the old aristocratic code of honor and dignity, would give way to the management of international affairs along lines similar to those in industry and modern commerce. The army's alpha test revealed how to sort out individuals by intelligence, each into an appropriate place. Thousands of men in identical dress, marching in step to the blare of brass, by one will directed toward a single destination: no individual goal perceived but that which national destiny dictated, just as each shaved with an identical Gillette. National destiny required elimination of any who got out of line, who failed to hold the common beliefs the common schools taught, who wandered away from jobs and stated places to pursue goals of their own choosing.[19]

Henry Ford, the dissenter who sponsored the Peace Ship (1916), to persuade the belligerents to lay down their arms, conformed once the United States entered the war, and set his plant to turning out Liberty Motors. *The New Republic,* self-defined organ of applied pragmatic realism, pointed out how soon "mastery" became "drift," tangled in the fatal drive toward victory as its own end, how soon the well-intentioned became mere agents and expositors of forces as they were.

But then, everything tended to even itself out. In December 1914 at the opening of *Watch Your Step,* Irving Berlin sat with his mother, who had come from the Bronx and spoke no English. They watched the curtain rise on a law office in which stenographers typed in syncopated time. A group of country folk awaited the reading of a will that bequeathed $2 million to any relative who managed to avoid falling in love. One of the hits, "Let's Settle Down in a One-Horse Town," a Tin Pan Alley staple, expressed rural nostalgia, the yearning for a simpler life. The ghost of Verdi turned up. Angered by the chorus singing in syncopation, he urged them not to "hurdy gurdy Mr. Verdi." Anything went.[20]

*

What then happened to the ability to act, that is, to liberty?

Liberty became conditioned by the willingness to stay in line, to march with the others. The campaign against venereal disease showed that young men who behaved in approved fashion left happily for the front, while back in the hospital "the useless slackers" who disobeyed became a burden upon the government. *The End of the Road* (1919), prepared by the War Department, followed two young women who moved to New York, one to take up nursing, the other to work in a department store. The nurse, strengthened by high ideals, refuses an unworthy man's advances and serves in the army, while the shop assistant gives in, thus taking the first step on the road that "leads in the end to disease, desertion and disgrace." The massive power arrayed in the serried ranks, whether asserted through government or through voluntary associations of the like-minded or through churches, communities, or mobs, brushed aside those like Emma Goldman who refused to go along with the others, who remained therefore impotently apart.

The war and its outcome provided a vantage point for criticism of the values of the preceding half century, when unwillingness to take vigorous action left America rudderless. The challenge of battle became the last best effort to restore purpose in national life. However, Wilson's peace, the Senate decided, embodied the mistaken ideas of the college-bred internationalists who took the country down the path to moral emasculation. Therewith perished for a time that gorgeous humanitarian optimism of the nineteenth century, once immortal, now dead. The organization for material interest essential to modern human society proved ruinous when applied to intellectual interests. The United States (1918) prized a petty efficiency above liberty, party loyalty above justice, subservience to mob expression over the exercise of individual reason, all symptoms of deep disease.[21]

Even pageantry, an expression of social rituals, harnessed a collective effort to rally the nation by exploiting history. Herbert Croly and others demanded an end to individual and collective irresponsibility, and called for "organizing the soul of America." Douglas Fairbanks's *Swat the Kaiser,* Mary Pickford's *100% American,* and Charlie Chaplin's *The Bond* rallied support for the war; and stock scenes compressed the nation's icons into clearly identifiable tableaux that foreshortened time and space—as when Washington, Wilson, and Lincoln together saluted the Statue of Liberty. Mass demonstrations of national loyalty glossed over historical, local, and regional divergences.[22]

Indeed, some insisted on the need for greater controls. Associate

Justice M. F. Morris of the court of appeals saw the chief dangers from within, from the socialist, the anarchist, the assassin, allied to secret organizations that controlled a vast global network, stretching its tentacles into every country through secret lodges, which would drive the United States into the arms of military despotism, invariably the refuge from such intolerable violations of individuals' rights as agrarianism and communism entailed. To preserve the temple, to sustain it and perpetuate it, required heroic effort. Peace transformed war agencies into organs of pressure, as when the Playground and Recreation Association of America reorganized the War Camp Community Service into a civilian community service. Hundreds of towns that had once built Civil War sculptures to honor the Union and Confederate dead now constructed community center buildings for its chapters, described as "power plant[s] for the generation of civil happiness," designed to draw together people from diverse backgrounds and to channel leisure into socially approved activities. Fearful of unrest, a community service brochure explained, "A Sarajevo starts a world war; a Seattle strike rocks a continent. A local blaze may set the world on fire. Tomorrow." Community service provided social insurance against that fire (1919).

President Frank Goodnow of Johns Hopkins University (1916) denied that stress on rights could secure a good social organization. Emphasis had shifted to social duties. Humans, under modern conditions, could secure the greatest opportunities as individuals only as they recognized their duties as members of society and limited their rights by considerations of social justice and expedience. They could thus develop that social efficiency necessary for both personal happiness and the public welfare (1916). Already an imaginative novel had described the citizenship card, evidence of membership in the state, entitling the holder to food and lodging subject to the oversight of an army of inspectors (1906).[23]

The narrowed scope of the ability to act by 1920 had put the liberty of all in peril, though those who stayed in line did not yet realize it. A long, hard process of discovery would occupy the decades that followed.

NOTES

PREFACE

1. Benedetto Croce, *The History of Europe in the Nineteenth Century,* trans. Henry Furst (1931; London, 1934), pp. 10 ff., 15 ff.
2. Oscar and Lilian Handlin, *Liberty and Power* (New York, 1986); Robert W. Landis, *Liberty's Triumph: A Poem* (New York, 1849), p. xi.
3. Oscar and Lilian Handlin, *Liberty in Expansion* (New York, 1989).
4. Robert Underwood Johnson, *Poems of War and Peace* (New York, 1917), p. 99.
5. Johan Huizinga, *America,* trans. Herbert H. Rowen (New York, 1972), p. 110.
6. *Liberty Poems* (Boston, 1900), p. 22.
7. Alan Trachtenberg, *The Incorporation of America: Culture and Society in the Gilded Age* (New York, 1982), pp. 4–5.

I: REPRESSION

1. Emma Goldman, *Living My Life* (Salt Lake City, Utah, 1934); Richard Drinnon, *Rebel in Paradise* (New York, 1976); Mary Antin, *The Promised Land* (1912; ed. Oscar Handlin, Boston, 1985); Louis F. Post, *The Deportations Delirium of Nineteen-Twenty* (Chicago, 1923), pp. 3–4.
2. Goldman, *Living My Life,* pp. 88, 92, 95, 100.
3. *The Independent,* Jan. 3, 1920; Oscar and Lilian Handlin, *Liberty and Power* (New York, 1986), pp. 205 ff.; Oscar and Lilian Handlin, *Liberty in Expansion* (New York, 1989), pp. 336 ff.; Sidney Howard, *The Labor Spy: A Survey of Industrial Espionage* (New York, 1921).
4. Barbara M. Solomon, *Ancestors and Immigrants* (Cambridge, Mass., 1956), passim. See also below, chap. 4.
5. Edward P. Hutchinson, *Legislative History of American Immigration Policy, 1798–1865* (Philadelphia, 1981).
6. *Chicago Daily Tribune,* Jan. 31, Apr. 10, 1856; Jan. 20, 29, 1858; Dickson J. Preston, *Talbot County* (Centerville, Md., 1983), pp. 204 ff.; James M. McPherson, *Battle Cry of Freedom: The Civil War Era* (New York, 1988), p. 168.
7. Henry Hughes, *Treatise on Sociology* (Philadelphia, 1854; reprinted New York,

1968), pp. 185, 222, 289–291; R. Jackson Wilson, "In Quest of Community," *Social Philosophy in the United States, 1860–1920* (New York, 1968), pp. 23–25.

8. Joel Porte, *Emerson in His Journals* (Cambridge, Mass., 1982), pp. 421, 429; Thomas D. Morris, *Free Men All* (Baltimore, 1974), pp. 130 ff., 151 ff., 156 ff., 160 ff., 166 ff.; McPherson, *Battle Cry of Freedom,* p. 79; Harold Hyman, *A More Perfect Union: The Impact of the Civil War and Reconstruction on the Constitution* (New York, 1973), pp. 25, 27.

9. *Chicago Daily Tribune,* Oct. 25, 1859, Mar. 29, 1860.

10. *Chicago Daily Tribune,* Feb. 14, Mar. 13, 15, 17, Sept. 22, 1854, Jan. 29, Apr. 25, Dec. 27, 1855, Jan. 24, 28, Feb. 7, 8, May 5, Aug. 22, 1856, Jan. 24, Mar. 7, 20, 26, Apr. 1, June 26, Oct. 5, 1857, Apr. 1, 1858; Paul Finkelman, ed., *Slavery, Race, and the American Legal System 1700–1872,* 2 ser., 16 vols. (New York, 1988), 1: 573 ff., 617 ff.; Jonathan Katz, *Resistance at Christiana* (New York, 1974), pp. 81 ff., 140; Oscar and Lilian Handlin, *Liberty in Expansion,* pp. 86 ff.; Hyman, *A More Perfect Union,* p. 95.

11. Goldman, *Living My Life,* p. 150; Jonathan Baxter Harrison, *Certain Dangerous Tendencies in American Life* (Boston, 1880), pp. 24–25; Evelyn Geller, *Forbidden Books in American Public Libraries, 1876–1939* (Westport, Conn., 1984), p. 41.

12. *Chicago Daily Tribune,* May 12, Aug. 1, 1856; Carl Schurz, "True Americanism," in *Speeches, Correspondence, and Political Papers,* 6 vols. (New York, 1913), 1: 48 ff.; Oscar and Lilian Handlin, *Liberty and Power,* pp. 213 ff.; Oscar and Lilian Handlin, *Liberty in Expansion,* pp. 68 ff., 177 ff.; Hyman, *A More Perfect Union,* pp. 4–7; Alan Trachtenberg, *The Incorporation of America: Culture and Society in the Gilded Age* (New York, 1982), p. 165; Harrison, *Certain Dangerous Tendencies in American Life,* p. 23; see also below, chap. 2, n. 38.

13. Hiel Hollister, *Pawlet* (Albany, N.Y., 1867), p. 121; Lilian Handlin, *George Bancroft* (New York, 1984); Walt Whitman, "Proto-Leaf," in *Leaves of Grass,* verse 20; Wilson, *In Quest of Community,* pp. 12–13; John Bach McMaster, *A History of the People of the United States during the Lincoln Administration* (New York, 1927), pp. 29–32; also *Chicago Daily Tribune,* Feb. 11, 1861.

14. Zechariah Chafee, Jr., *Free Speech in the United States* (Cambridge, Mass., 1948), p. 263; Hyman, *A More Perfect Union,* pp. 61 ff., 72, 77, 93 ff., 171, 176, 177.

15. Walt Whitman, "Specimen Days," in *Complete Prose Works* (New York, 1914), pp. 16 ff.; Preston, *Talbot County,* p. 215; 4 wallace, 2, 75; Hyman, *A More Perfect Union,* pp. 83 ff.; Ella Lonn, *Desertion during the Civil War* (New York, 1928); Thomas D. Hamm, *The Transformation of American Quakerism* (Bloomington, Ind., 1988), pp. 66 ff.; Eric Foner, *Reconstruction* (New York, 1988), p. 15; John Bach McMaster, *A History of the People of the United States during Lincoln's Administration,* pp. 226–227, 417–418; 474–475; *Chicago Tribune,* Aug. 9, 1862; Harold Earl Hammond, ed., *Diary of a Union Lady, 1861–1865* (New York, 1962), pp. 354, 357, 358. See also below, chap. 4.

16. *Chicago Daily Tribune,* Mar. 1, Oct. 13, 1859; see also Handlins, *Liberty in Expansion,* chap. 2.

17. *Chicago Daily Tribune,* June 28, 1854, Apr. 2, 16, 24, 26, 29, 1856, Mar. 6, May 18, 19, 28, June 2, July 4, Aug. 6, 1857, Feb. 6, Mar. 11, Apr. 6, 28, 1858; Aleksandr Borisovich Lakier, *A Russian Looks at America,* ed. Arnold Shrier and Joyce Story (Chicago, 1979), p. 162; Mary Floyd Williams, *History of the San Francisco Committee of Vigilance of 1851: A Study of Social Control on the California Frontier in the Days of the Gold Rush* (Berkeley, 1921), pp. 162 ff., 417 ff.; also Richard Bernheimer, *Wild Men in the Middle Ages* (Cambridge, Mass., 1952), pp. 58 ff.

18. *Chicago Daily Tribune,* June 6, 1857, Jan. 25, June 4, 7, 8, 9, 1858; J[ohn]. Thomas Scharf, *The Chronicles of Baltimore* (Baltimore, 1874), pp. 550 ff.; Richard Maxwell Brown, *American Violence* (New York, 1970), pp. 42 ff.

19. Herman Melville, "The House-top," in *Battle-Pieces* (New York, 1866), pp. 86, 87; Hyman, *A More Perfect Union,* pp. 67 ff.; McPherson, *Battle Cry of Freedom,* pp. 610, 611, 613.

20. David M. Chalmers, *Hooded Americanism* (Chicago, 1968); Elliot M. Rudwick, *Race Riot at E. St. Louis,* July 2, 1917 (Carbondale, Ill., 1964); Brown, *American Violence,* pp. 126 ff.; see chap. 4, n. 17.

21. Humbert S. Nelli, *From Immigrants to Ethnics* (New York, 1983), p. 40; Hartmann, *Bald Knobbers,* pp. 8, 15, 23, 32, 67; Gunther Barth, *Bitter Strength: A History of the Chinese in the United States, 1850–1870* (Cambridge, Mass., 1964); Theodore Saloutos, *The Greeks in the United States* (Cambridge, Mass., 1964); Leonard Dinnerstein, *The Leo Frank Case* (Athens, Georgia, 1987).

22. *Chicago Daily Tribune,* Jan. 18, Dec. 5, 1857, Jan. 25, Feb. 10, May 25, Oct. 8, 1858, Apr. 1, 1859; Chafee, *Free Speech,* p. 264; Walter Blair, *Mark Twain and Huck Finn* (Berkeley, Calif., 1960), pp. 3 ff.; Geller, *Forbidden Books,* pp. 22 ff.

23. Humphrey Desmond, *The American Protective Association Movement: A Sketch* (1912; New York, 1969), pp. 35–44; Donald L. Kinzer, *An Episode in Anti-Catholicism: The American Protective Association* (Seattle, Wash., 1964), pp. 33–57.

24. Roger A. Bruns, *Knights of the Road* (Methuen, N.J., 1980), p. 11; Roger A. Bruns, *The Damnest Radical: The Life and World of Ben Reitman* (Urbana, Ill., 1987), p. 36; Andrew Sinclair, *Jack: A Biography of Jack London* (New York, 1977); Goldman, *Living My Life,* p. 191.

25. *Chicago Daily Tribune,* May 3, 1859; James D. McCabe (pseud., Edward W. Martin), *History of the Great Riots* (Philadelphia, 1877), pp. 91 ff.; Charles Fein, "Centennial New York," M. M. Klein, ed., *New York* (Port Washington, N.Y., 1976), p. 89; Paul Avrich, *The Haymarket Tragedy* (Princeton, N.J., 1984), pp. 16, 17; Brown, *American Violence,* pp. 85 ff.; Henry F. Pringle, *The Life and Times of William Howard Taft,* 2 vols. (New York, 1939), 1:128; Henry David, *The History of the Haymarket Affair,* 2 vols. (New York, 1936); Harry Barnard, *"Eagle Forgotten": The Life of John Peter Altgeld* (New York, 1938); Leon Wolff, *Lockout: The Story of the Homestead Strike* (New York, 1965).

26. Brown, *American Violence,* pp. 122 ff.; Albert E. Horsley (Harry Orchard), *The Confessions and Autobiography of Harry Orchard* (New York, 1907), passim.

27. *Robertson v. Baldwin,* 165 U.S. 275, 281 (1897); J. B. Thayer, *Legal Essays* (Boston, 1908), p. 38; Chafee, *Free Speech,* pp. 163 ff.; Geller, *Forbidden Books,* pp. 111 ff.; Frederic Trautmann, *The Voice of Terror: A Biography of Johann Most* (Westport, Conn., 1980); Nicholas Murray Butler, *A World in Ferment* (New York, 1917), pp. 245–249.

28. Woodrow Wilson, *History of the American People,* 5 vols. (New York, 1902), 3: 153 ff.; Samuel L. Clemens, *Mark Twain's Mysterious Stranger Manuscripts,* ed. William M. Gibson (Berkeley, Calif., 1969), p. 155; Timothy W. Gleason, *The Watchdog Concept* (Ames, Iowa, 1990), p. 99.

29. Paul H. Buck, *The Road to Reunion* (Boston, 1937); Wallace E. Davies, *Patriotism on Parade* (Cambridge, Mass., 1955); Handlins, *Liberty in Expansion,* pp. 170 ff.; Isaac J. Quillen, *Industrial City: A History of Gary, Indiana* (New York, 1986), pp. 298 ff.; see also below, chap. 9, n. 5.

30. Chafee, *Free Speech,* pp. 11–13, 34, 35, 38 ff., 42 ff., 497 ff.; Walter Nelles, *Espionage Act Cases* (New York, 1918); William Preston, *Aliens and Dissenters* (Cambridge, Mass., 1963).

31. Zechariah Chafee, Jr., *Free Speech in the United States* (Cambridge, Mass., 1948), pp. 25, 51 ff., 75 ff., 97 ff., 100 ff., 247 ff., 286, 287; Theodore Dreiser, *Letters,* Robert H. Elias, ed. (Philadelphia, 1959), 1:205, 208; *People* v. *Hoffer,* 94 (Washington): 136 (1916); *Abrams et al.* v. *United States,* 250 U.S. 616 ff. (1919); John L. O'Brien, *New York Bar Association Report,* 281 (1919): 279, 292, 297; B. F.

Shambaugh, ed., *Iowa and War* (Iowa City, 1919), passim; M. R. Montgomery, *Saying Goodbye* (New York, 1989); Arthur and Pearl Zipser, *Fire and Grace: The Life of Rose Pastor Stokes* (Athens, Ga., 1989), p. 189; James Weinstein, ed., *The Trial of Scott Nearing and the American Socialist Society* (New York, 1972), p. 7; Sally M. Miller, *Victor Berger and the Promise of Constructive Socialism, 1910–1920* (Westport, Conn., 1973), pp. 193–194.

32. Chafee, *Free Speech,* pp. 30, 70, 80, 95, 108 ff., 126, 128 ff.; *Schenck* v. *United States,* 249 U.S. 50–52 (1919); Jeremy Cohen, *Congress Shall Make No Law: Oliver Wendell Holmes, The First Amendment, and Judicial Decision Making* (Ames, Iowa, 1989); Sara Alpern, *Freda Kirchwey: A Woman of the Nation* (Cambridge, Mass., 1987), p. 32; Miller, *Victor Berger and the Promise of Constructive Socialism,* pp. 199, 200–202.

33. George Creel, *How We Advertised America* (New York, 1920), pp. 200–207; Ray H. Abrams, *Preachers Present Arms* (New York, 1933); Hermann Hagedorn, *The Hyphenated Family* (New York, 1960), pp. 233 ff.; James R. Mock, *Words That Won the War* (Princeton, N.J., 1939); Gerd Korman, *Industrialization, Immigrants and Americanizers* (Madison, Wis., 1967), pp. 170 ff.

34. *The Independent,* Jan. 24, May 1, 1920; Francis Russell, *City in Terror 1919* (New York, 1975); Thomas O'Connor, *South Boston* (Boston, 1988), pp. 165 ff.; Chafee, *Free Speech,* pp. 3 ff., 143 ff., 202 ff., 228; Samuel Walker, *In Defense of American Liberties: A History of the ACLU* (New York, 1990), pp. 25, 26, 43; Preston William Slosson, *The Great Crusade and After, 1914–1928* (New York, 1930), pp. 79–88.

35. Chafee, *Free Speech,* pp. 159 ff., 575 ff.; Richard D. Ware, *Politics Adjourned* (Amherst, N.H., 1920), p. 54; Richard D. Ware, *Politics Regained* (Amherst, N.H., 1920), p. 22.

36. *Chicago Daily Tribune,* June 23, Aug. 7, 1857.

37. *Chicago Daily Tribune,* Apr. 15, 1856, Mar. 5, 1857; Gunther Barth, *Bitter Strength: A History of the Chinese in the United States* (Cambridge, Mass., 1964); Brown, *American Violence,* pp. 92 ff. See also below, chap. 4, n. 62.

38. *Nishimura Ekin* v. *United States,* 36 U.S. 651, 659 (1892); *Turner* v. *Williams,* 194 U.S. 279 (1904); *Lopez* v. *Howe,* 259 Fed.: 401 (1919); Charles Recht, *American Deportation and Exclusion Law* (New York, 1919), p. 9; Finley Peter Dunne, *Observations by Mr. Dooley* (New York, 1906), pp. 53–54; Ware, *Politics Regained,* p. 27.

39. Oscar Handlin, *American People in the Twentieth Century* (Cambridge, Mass., 1954), p. 121; see also Oscar Handlin, *Race and Nationality in American Life* (Boston, 1957), pp. 71 ff.; William E. D. Stokes, *The Right to Be Well-Born; or, Horse-Breeding in Its Relation to Eugenics* (New York, 1917), pp. 5–8, 48–49; see below, chaps. 4, 7.

40. John Bukowczyk, *And My Children Did Not Know Me* (Bloomington, 1987); Stokes, *Right to Be Well-Born,* pp. 155–156, 173–174, 249; Theodore Roosevelt, *The Letters of Theodore Roosevelt,* ed. Elting E. Morrison, 8 vols. (Cambridge, Mass., 1954), 8: 1422; Robert J. Rusnak, *Walter Hines Page and the World's Work* (Washington, D.C., 1982), pp. 75–99; Handlin, *American People in the Twentieth Century,* p. 121.

41. Brown, *American Violence,* pp. 63 ff., 96 ff.; Knight Dunlap, *Personal Beauty and Racial Betterment* (St. Louis, 1920), pp. 54–55, 58–59; Stokes, *Right to Be Well-Born,* pp. 155–156, 173–174, 249.

II: POWER IN A DEMOCRATIC POLITY

1. Harold M. Hyman, *A More Perfect Union* (New York, 1947), pp. 309 ff.
2. Finley Peter Dunne, *Dissertations by Mr. Dooley* (New York, 1906), p. 271; Thomas

Schick, *The New York State Constitutional Convention of 1915 and the Modern State Governor* (Lebanon, Pa., 1978), pp. 10, 17.

3. *Chicago Daily Tribune,* Aug. 23, Nov. 10, 1858; Feb. 16, 1860; Oscar and Lilian Handlin, *Abraham Lincoln and the Union* (Boston, 1980).

4. *Chicago Daily Tribune,* May 13, 1857; Michael O'Brien and David Moltke-Hansen, *Intellectual Life in Antebellum Charleston* (Knoxville, Tenn., 1986), p. 153; James M. McPherson, *Battle Cry of Freedom* (New York, 1988), pp. 68 ff.; Hyman, *A More Perfect Union,* pp. 121, 129; Robert Hendrickson, *Sumter: The First Day of the Civil War* (Chelsea, Mich., 1990), p. 187; Mary P. Coulling, *The Lee Girls* (Winston Salem, N.C., 1987), pp. 80 ff.

5. Daniel Webster, *Papers,* 7 vols., ed. Charles M. Wiltse (Hanover, N.H., 1974–90), 7:59; *Chicago Daily Tribune,* Apr. 16, 1858; Oct. 25, 1859, Mar. 31, Nov. 7, 26, Dec. 1, 1860; McPherson, *Battle Cry of Freedom,* p. 258; John R. McKivigan, *The War against Proslavery Religion* (Ithaca, N.Y., 1984); Hyman, *A More Perfect Union,* p. 277.

6. *Chicago Daily Tribune,* May 9, 1859; Homer E. Socolofsky and Allan B. Spetter, *The Presidency of Benjamin Harrison* (Lawrence, Kans., 1987), p. 9; M. J. Heale, *The Presidential Quest* (London, 1982), pp. 133 ff.; Elizabeth Frost, ed., *The Bully Pulpit* (New York, 1988), p. 15.

7. Socolofsky and Spetter, *Presidency of Harrison,* p. 34; Finley Peter Dunne, *Mr. Dooley's Opinions* (New York, 1901), pp. 96–97.

8. Abraham Lincoln, "Chicago Speech, July 10, 1858," in Roy P. Basler, ed., *The Collected Works of Abraham Lincoln,* 10 vols. (New Brunswick, N.J., 1953–55), 2: 484–502; *Chicago Daily Tribune,* Mar. 12, Apr. 30, May 1, 1857.

9. Hinton R. Helper, *The Impending Crisis of the South* (New York, 1960); Brian P. Damiani, *Advocates of Empire* (New York, 1987); Frank B. Freidel, ed., *Union Pamphlets of the Civil War,* 2 vols. (Cambridge, Mass., 1967); McPherson, *Battle Cry of Freedom,* p. 199.

10. Herman Melville, "Poems," in *Works* (London, 1920), 16: 5; Webster, *Papers,* 7: 51 ff.; *Chicago Daily Tribune,* Oct. 21, 22, 24, 29, Nov. 4, Dec. 2, 1859; *Richmond Examiner,* Dec. 3, 1859; Willie Lee Rose, *Slavery and Freedom* (New York, 1982); Jeffrey S. Rossbach, *Ambivalent Conspirators* (Philadelphia, 1982).

11. William H. Seward, "Speech at Auburn, Oct. 21, 1856," *Works,* 5 vols. (Boston, 1884), 4: 277–281; Carl Schurz, *Speeches, Correspondence, and Political Papers,* 6 vols. (New York, 1913), 1: 14 ff.; McPherson, *Battle Cry of Freedom,* p. 133; William E. Gienapp, *The Origins of the Republican Party, 1852–1856* (New York, 1987), pp. 35, 38 ff., 64 ff.; W. Darrel Overdyke, *The Know-Nothing Party in the South* (Baton Rouge, La., 1950), pp. 240 ff. See also Alicia E. Carroll, *The Great American Battle* (New York, 1856); *The Origin, Principles and Purposes of the American Party* (n.p., 1855), pp. 5–7; John Bach McMaster, *With the Fathers: Studies in the History of the United States* (New York, 1896), pp. 87–106; see below, chaps. 4, 6.

12. Andrew Johnson, *Papers,* ed. Leroy P. Graf et al., 7 vols. (Knoxville, Tenn., 1970), 2: 281 ff.; *The Origin, Principles and Purposes of the American Party,* pp. 11–12; An American, *The Sons of the Sires: A History of the Rise, Progress, and Destiny of the American Party* (Philadelphia, 1855), p. 46; Oscar Handlin, *Boston's Immigrants,* rev. ed. (Cambridge, Mass., 1979), pp. 191 ff., 199. See also Jean H. Baker, *Ambivalent Americans: The Know-Nothing Party in Maryland* (Baltimore, 1977); McPherson, *Battle Cry of Freedom,* pp. 135 ff.

13. *Chicago Daily Tribune,* Mar. 15, 1858, Apr. 29, 1859; Eric Foner, *Reconstruction: America's Unfinished Revolution* (New York, 1988); Drew Gilpin Faust, *A Sacred Circle: The Dilemma of the Intellectual in the Old South, 1840–1860* (Baltimore, Md., 1977), pp. 104–107; Drew Gilpin Faust, *The Creation of Confederate Nationalism* (Baton Rouge, 1988).

14. *Chicago Daily Tribune,* May 4, 1860; Oscar Handlin, *Truth in History* (Cambridge, Mass., 1979), pp. 353 ff.
15. Woodrow Wilson, *Congressional Government* (Boston, 1885), p. 318; Michael F. Holt, *Forging a Majority: The Formation of the Republican Party in Pittsburgh* (New Haven, 1969), pp. 84 ff., 263; Paul Kleppner et al., *The Evolution of American Electoral Systems* (Westport, Conn., 1981), pp. 10, 24; Ernest Samuels, *Henry Adams* (Cambridge, 1989); Nicholas Murray Butler, *Is America Worth Saving?* (New York, 1920); Montague Vernon Ponsonby, Esq., *The Preposterous Yankee* (London, 1903), pp. 20, 71; Allan Nevins, ed., *America through British Eyes* (Gloucester, Mass., 1968), p. 375; Paul Kleppner, *The Cross of Culture* (New York, 1970).
16. *Chicago Daily Tribune,* Feb. 25, 1856; Victoria C. Woodhull, "A Speech on the Impending Revolution," in *The Victoria Woodhull Reader,* ed. Madeleine B. Stern (Weston, Mass., 1974), p. 32; Ray Ginger, *Age of Excess: The United States from 1877 to 1914* (New York, 1965), pp. 98–128; Leonard White, *The Republican Era, 1869–1901* (New York, 1958), pp. 278–302; John G. Sproat, *"The Best Men"* (New York, 1968).
17. Gideon Welles, *Diary,* ed. John T. Morse, Jr., 3 vols. (Boston, 1911), 3: 97; Samuel Walker McCall, *The Liberty of Citizenship* (New Haven, 1915), pp. 21, 24–25; Kleppner, *Evolution of American Electoral Systems,* pp. 10 ff., 24–27, 114 ff.; Paul Kleppner, *Third Electoral System* (Chapel Hill, N.C., 1979), pp. 48 ff., 144 ff.; J. Morgan Kousser, *The Shaping of Southern Politics* (New Haven, 1974); Woodhull, "Speech on the Impending Revolution," p. 32.
18. Allan Nevins, *Grover Cleveland; A Study in Courage* (New York, 1933); John M. Blum, *The Republican Roosevelt* (Cambridge, Mass., 1964); John M. Blum, *Joe Timilty and the Wilson Era* (Hamden, 1961); Theodore C. Smith, *The Life and Letters of James Abram Garfield* (New Haven, 1925), pp. 726 ff.; Allan Peskin, *Garfield, a Biography* (Kent State, Ohio, 1978), p. 551; Justus D. Doenecke, *The Presidencies of James A. Garfield and Chester A. Arthur* (Lawrence, Kansas, 1981), p. 99; Socolofsky and Spetter, *Presidency of Benjamin Harrison,* p. 212.
19. Elihu Root, *Addresses on Government and Citizenship* (Cambridge, Mass., 1916), pp. 3–4; see also below, chap. 7.
20. *Chicago Daily Tribune,* Apr. 11, 1856; James A. Kehl, *Boss Rule in the Gilded Age* (Pittsburgh, 1981), pp. 139 ff.; Morton Keller, *The Art and Politics of Thomas Nast* (New York, 1968); Madeleine B. Stern, ed., *The Victoria Woodhull Reader* (Weston, Mass., 1974), pp. 4–6; Finley Peter Dunne, *Mr. Dooley at His Best,* ed. Elmer Ellis (New York, 1938), pp. 190, 227, 230, 231; Simon Michael Bessie, *Jazz Journalism: The Story of the Tabloid Newspapers* (New York, 1938), pp. 33, 40, 64; Joyce Milton, *The Yellow Kids: Foreign Correspondents in the Heyday of Yellow Journalism* (Harper and Row, 1989), pp. xii, 293.
21. *Chicago Daily Tribune,* July 16, 1858, Aug. 6, 1860; Rollo Ogden, ed., *The Life and Letters of Edwin Lawrence Godkin,* 2 vols. (New York, 1907), 2: 202–203; Oliver Gramling, *AP: The Story of the News* (New York, 1940); Upton Sinclair, *The Brass Check* (Pasadena, 1919).
22. Finley Peter Dunne, *Mr. Dooley's Philosophy* (New York, 1900), p. 102; Dunne, *Mr. Dooley's Opinions,* p. 98; Theodore Roosevelt, *Letters,* ed. Elting E. Morison, 8 vols. (Cambridge, Mass., 1954), 8: 835.
23. *Chicago Daily Tribune,* Mar 24, 1854; Aug. 7, 1858; Andrew Johnson, *Papers,* ed. Leroy P. Graf et al., 7 vols. (Knoxville, Tenn., 1970), 2: 425 ff.; Finley Peter Dunne, *Dissertations by Mr. Dooley* (New York, 1906), p. 116; Walton Bean, *California: An Interpretive History* (New York, 1973), pp. 236–243, 335–336; J. P. Young, *San Francisco,* 2 vols. (San Francisco, 1912), 1: 535, 538; Donald T. Critchlow, *Socialism in the Heartland* (Notre Dame, Ind., 1986); David A. Shannon, *The Socialist Party of America* (New York, 1955); Garin Burbank, *When Farmers Voted Red* (Westport,

Conn., 1976); Kleppner, *Third Electoral System*, pp. 239, 252 ff., 298 ff.; Steven Rosenstone et al., *Third Parties in America: Citizen Response to Major Party Failure* (Princeton, N.J., 1984), pp. 4, 8.

24. *Chicago Daily Tribune*, May 3, 4, Aug. 1, 1860; Robert G. Ingersoll, *Works*, 12 vols. (New York, 1900), 9: 56 ff.; Peskin, *Garfield*, p. 493; McPherson, *Battle Cry of Freedom*, p. 162; George Fitch, *Sizing Up Uncle Sam* (New York, 1914), p. 107.

25. Richard Jensen, *The Winning of the Midwest* (Chicago, 1971); Richard E. Welch, *The Presidencies of Grover Cleveland* (Lawrence, Kansas, 1988), p. 102; Samuel P. Hays, "Political Parties," in *The American Party System*, ed. William N. Chambers and Walter Dean Burnham (New York, 1967), pp. 152 ff.

26. Dunne, *Dissertations by Mr. Dooley*, pp. 117, 200–202; Clinton R. Woodruff, "Philadelphia's Election Frauds," *Arena*, 24 (1900): 397 ff.; Kehl, *Boss Rule in the Gilded Age*, pp. 28 ff.; Clifton K. Yearley, *Money Machines* (Albany, 1970).

27. Kleppner, *Third Electoral System*, pp. 225 ff., 238 ff., 345; see also below, chap. 4. See also, William Gillette, *Retreat from Reconstruction, 1869–1879* (Baton Rouge, La., 1979), pp. 363–380.

28. *Chicago Daily Tribune*, Jan. 21, 1860; Kleppner, *Third Electoral System*, p. 333; Peskin, *Garfield*, p. 503; Welch, *Presidencies of Grover Cleveland*, p. 102; Root, *Addresses on Government*, pp. 201–202.

29. Kehl, *Boss Rule in the Gilded Age*, p. 70; Hyman, *A More Perfect Union*, pp. 96, 179, 194; Thomas C. Reeves, *Gentleman Boss: The Life of Chester Alan Arthur* (New York, 1975), pp. 257–259; William S. McFeely, *Grant* (New York, 1981), pp. 292–294.

30. *Chicago Daily Tribune*, Jan. 10, 17, Mar. 2, 28, 1857, Feb. 1, 1858; Henry Adams, *Democracy* (1880; New York, 1908), pp. 307–310, 350–355, 357–358; Dunne, *Dissertations*, pp. 258, 261; Welles, *Diary*, 3: 551, 571, 576. See also David B. Truman, *The Congressional Party* (New York, 1959); Reeves, *Gentleman Boss*, pp. 257–259; McFeely, *Grant*, pp. 292–294; M. A. Richter, *The Municipalist* (New York, 1858), pp. 7, 26–27, 49, 64, 81; Moncure D. Conway, *Republican Superstitions as Illustrated in the Political History of America* (London, 1872), p. 50.

31. Welles, *Diary*, 3: 14; Elihu Root, *Miscellaneous Addresses* (Cambridge, Mass., 1917), p. 265; David Rothman, *Politics and Power: The United States Senate, 1869–1901* (Cambridge, Mass., 1966). See also Donald R. Matthews, *United States Senators and Their World* (Chapel Hill, N.C., 1960).

32. Arthur Mann, *Fiorello La Guardia*, 2 vols. (Philadelphia, 1959–65), 1: 73–108; James Holt, *Congressional Insurgents and the Party System* (Cambridge, Mass., 1967), pp. 16 ff.; William E. Gienapp, *The Origins of the Republican Party, 1852–1856* (New York, 1987), pp. 240–241; L. White Busbey, *Uncle Joe Cannon* (New York, 1970), p. 247.

33. Holt, *Congressional Insurgents*, pp. 41 ff.

34. *Chicago Daily Tribune*, Jan. 25, 1859; Welles, *Diary*, 3: 73, 317, 362, 366; Eric L. McKitrick, *Andrew Johnson and Reconstruction* (Chicago, 1960).

35. Busbey, *Uncle Joe Cannon*, pp. 355–356.

36. *Chicago Daily Tribune*, Mar. 12, July 9, 15, Oct. 20, 1857; Don Fehrenbacher, *The Dred Scott Case* (New York, 1978).

37. *Chicago Daily Tribune*, Feb. 16, 1858; Holt, *Congressional Insurgents*, p. 59.

38. See below, chap. 3; Welch, *Presidencies of Grover Cleveland*, pp. 151–153; Benjamin R. Twiss, *Lawyers and the Constitution* (Princeton, 1942); Carl Bent Swisher, *Roger B. Taney* (Hamden, Conn., 1961), p. 372.

39. Oscar O. Winther, *The Transportation Frontier 1865–1890* (New York, 1964), pp. 5 ff., 99 ff.; Carlene E. Stephens, "Partners in Time," *Harvard Library Bulletin*, 35 (1987): 375 ff.; Grace S. Woodward, *The Man Who Conquered Pain* (Boston, 1962); Hyman, *A More Perfect Union*, pp. 99, 101, 108 ff., 112 ff., 135 ff., 551; McPherson,

Battle Cry of Freedom, pp. 500 ff., 594, 616 ff.; E. L. Godkin, "The Constitution and Its Defects," *North American Review,* 99 (1864): 120, 123; James B. Bryce, *American Commonwealth,* 2 vols. (New York, 1889), 2: 904–905; William H. Goetzmann, *Exploration and Empire* (New York, 1966); Paul W. Gates, *The Illinois Central Railroad and Its Colonization Work* (Cambridge, Mass., 1934); Robert S. Hunt, *Law and Locomotives* (Madison, Wis., 1958); J. B. Edmond, *The Magnificent Charter* (Hicksville, N.Y., 1978).

40. Welles, *Diary,* 3: 137; Lawrence Grossman, *The Democratic Party and the Negro* (Urbana, Ill, 1976); McPherson, *Battle Cry of Freedom,* pp. 857 ff.; Hyman, *A More Perfect Union,* pp. 160 ff.; see below, chap. 4.

41. Welles, *Diary,* 3: 523; William Gillette, *Retreat from Reconstruction* (Baton Rouge, La., 1979), p. 6; Michael Perman, *The Road to Redemption: Southern Politics 1869–1879* (Chapel Hill, N.C., 1984); McPherson, *Battle Cry of Freedom,* pp. 700 ff.; see below, chaps. 4, 9.

42. E.g., House Committee on Expenditures in the Department of Justice, *Report 2164,* 48th Cong., 1st sess., 1864, p. 1; also James Willard Hurst, *Law and Social Process in the United States* (Ann Arbor, Mich., 1960); William R. Brock, *Investigation and Responsibility* (Cambridge, Mass., 1984), pp. 42–43.

43. Alexander H. Stephens, *A Constitutional View of the Late War between the States,* 2 vols. (Philadelphia, 1867), 1: 12; Martya Lockett Avery, ed., *Recollections of Alexander H. Stephens* (New York, 1910), pp. 32, 71–72; Alexander H. Stephens, *The Reviewers Reviewed* (New York, 1872), pp. 190–191; Hyman, *A More Perfect Union,* pp. 306–310.

44. Dan T. Carter, *When the War Was Over: The Failure of Self-Reconstruction in the South* (Baton Rouge, La., 1985); Eric L. McKitrick, *Andrew Johnson and Reconstruction* (Chicago, 1960), pp. 97–119; also Welles, *Diary,* 3: 22 ff.

45. Welles, *Diary,* 3: 10 ff.; Michael Perman, *Reunion without Compromise* (Cambridge, England, 1973), pp. 57–109; LaWanda Cox, *Lincoln and Black Freedom* (Columbia, S.C., 1981); Hyman, *A More Perfect Union,* p. 267.

46. Daniel Y. Elazar, *The American Partnership: Intergovernmental Cooperation in the Nineteenth Century* (Chicago, 1962).

47. [Francis Fellows,] *Youth's Manual of the Constitution of the United States Adapted to Classes in Schools* (Hartford, Conn., 1835), pp. viii–x; Israel Ward Andrews, *Manual of the Constitution of the United States* (New York, 1887), pp. 12–13; Walter S. Clark, *The Government Class Book* (New York, 1882), pp. 14–15; Charles Nordhoff, *Politics for Young Americans* (New York, 1876), pp. 12–15, 24–25; James M. Walker, *A Tract on Government* (Boston, 1853), pp. 20, 21, 26; Albert Stickney, *A True Republic* (New York, 1879), pp. 12–13, 258–259.

48. John S. Hittell, *Reform or Revolution* (San Francisco, 1900), pp. 3–15, 183–196; Conway, *Republican Superstitions;* Peter H. Burnett, *American Theory of Government* (New York, 1863), 77–78; Gustave Le Bon, *Psychology of Socialism* (New Brunswick, N.Y., 1982), p. 337; *The Psychology of Peoples* (New York, 1974), p. 148.

49. William R. Brock, *The American Crisis: Congress and Reconstruction* (New York, 1963); John Shelton Reed, *Southerners: The Social Psychology of Regionalism* (Chapel Hill, N.C., 1983), pp. 70–94.

50. *Chicago Daily Tribune,* Feb. 12, 1856, Mar. 2, 4, 5, Apr. 2, 1857; Kleppner, *Third Electoral System,* pp. 198 ff.; Richard F. Bensel, *Sectionalism and American Political Development* (Madison, Wis., 1984), pp. 22–59; Richard E. Engler, *The Challenge of Diversity* (New York, 1964); Conway, *Republican Superstitions,* p. 17; Le Bon, *Psychology of Socialism,* pp. 336–337.

51. *Chicago Daily Tribune,* Feb. 16, 1856, Feb. 25, 1860; Paul Goodman, "The Politics

of Industrialism: Massachusetts, 1830–1870," in *Uprooted Americans,* ed. Richard L. Bushman et al. (Boston, 1979), pp. 181 ff.; McPherson, *Battle Cry of Freedom,* pp. 692 ff.; Gienapp, *Origins of the Republican Party,* p. 105.

52. *Chicago Daily Tribune,* Feb. 26, 1859; Andrew Johnson, *Papers,* 2: xxvii, 357 ff.; Conway, *Republican Superstitions,* p. 2; Richard S. West, *Lincoln's Scapegoat General* (Cambridge, Mass., 1965), pp. 366–378; Harry Barnard, *Eagle Forgotten: The Life of John Peter Altgeld* (New York, 1938), pp. 173–177; Mary Hartman, *Bald Knobbers* (Gretna, La., 1988), pp. 117, 146, 187.

53. James H. Kyner, *End of Track,* ed. Hawthorne Daniel (Caldwell, Idaho, 1937), p. 95; Martin Ridge, *Ignatius Donnelley* (Chicago, 1962), p. 2; Clifton K. Yearley, *The Money Machines* (Albany, N.Y., 1970).

54. Jerome Mushkat, *The Reconstruction of the New York Democracy 1861–1874* (Rutherford, N.J., 1981), pp. 36, 41, 54; Herbert J. Bass, *"I Am a Democrat": The Political Career of David Bennett Hill* (Syracuse, N.Y., 1961), pp. 1–18; Frederick A. Cleveland et al., eds., *Democracy in Reconstruction* (Boston, 1919).

55. Harry Barnard, *Eagle Forgotten: The Life of John Peter Altgeld* (New York, 1938), p. 262; Hartman, *Bald Knobbers,* pp. 218 ff.; McPherson, *Battle Cry of Freedom,* p. 106; *Chicago Daily Tribune,* Feb. 21, 25, 1856.

56. *Chicago Daily Tribune,* July 11, 1857, Feb. 2, 1858; Frank Marryatt, *Mountains and Molehills* (London, 1855), p. 202; Mary F. Williams, *History of the San Francisco Vigilance Committee* (Berkeley, Calif., 1921), p. 156; Theodore Dreiser, *The Financier* (New York, 1912), pp. 583 ff.; Howard R. Lamar, *Dakota Territory, 1861–1889* (New Haven, 1956), p. 138; Howard R. Lamar, *The Far Southwest, 1846–1912* (New Haven, 1966), pp. 192–196, 214–215, 300; Seymour J. Mandelbaum, *Boss Tweed's New York* (New York, 1965), p. 52.

57. Barnard, *Eagle Forgotten,* pp. 261–262; Robert F. Wesser, *Charles Evans Hughes: Politics and Reform in New York, 1905–1910* (Ithaca, N.Y., 1967), pp. 1–17; Nancy Joan Weiss, *Charles Francis Murphy, 1858–1924: Respectability and Responsibility in Tammany Politics* (Northampton, Mass., 1968); Conway, *Republican Superstitions,* p. x.

58. *Chicago Daily Tribune,* Feb. 10, 1858; Lamar, *The Far Southwest,* pp. 214, 215, 299–300; Robert Silverman, *Law and Urban Growth: Civil Litigation in the Boston Trial Courts, 1880–1900* (Princeton, N.J., 1981).

59. Elisha Douglass Perkins, *Gold Rush Diary,* ed. Thomas D. Clark (Lexington, Ky., 1967), pp. 145, 159; *Chicago Daily Tribune,* Nov. 5, 1858; Samuel A. Foot, *Autobiography,* 2 vols. (New York, 1873), 2: 323 ff., 335 ff.; McPherson, *Battle Cry of Freedom,* pp. 172 ff.; Richard S. Skolnik, "The Crystalization of Reform in New York City, 1890–1917" (Yale Doctoral diss., 1971), 378–413.

60. *Chicago Daily Tribune,* Nov. 7, 1853, Jan. 31, 1856; Kenneth T. Jackson, *Crabgrass Frontier* (New York, 1985), pp. 140 ff.

61. Kehl, *Boss Rule,* p. 76.

62. *Chicago Daily Tribune,* Mar. 1, 1856, Mar. 9, 11, Apr. 17, 1857; Ari Hoogenboom, *Outlawing the Spoils* (Urbana, Ill., 1961), pp. 260–261.

63. J. Joseph Huthmacher, *Massachusetts People and Politics* (Cambridge, Mass., 1959); J. Joseph Huthmacher, *Senator Robert Wagner* (New York, 1968); Oscar Handlin, *Al Smith and His America* (Boston, 1958), pp. 18 ff.; Harold Zink, *Government of the Cities in the United States* (New York, 1948), pp. 196–211; Leo Hershkowitz, *Tweed's New York* (Garden City, N.Y., 1978).

64. Henry Bruére, *A Plan of Organization for New York City* (New York, 1917); Henry Bruére, *The New City Government: A Discussion of Municipal Administration Based on a Survey of Ten Commission-Governed Cities* (New York, 1912); Richard J. Sillman, *The Rise of the City Manager* (Albuquerque, N.Mex., 1974); *Chicago Daily Tribune,* Mar. 5, 1856, July 9, 1857, Jan. 20, 1858; Edith Abbott, *Historical Aspects*

of the Immigration Problem (Chicago, 1926), p. 649; Olivier Zunz, *The Changing Face of Inequality* (Chicago, 1982), pp. 109 ff., 323; Bessie Louise Pierce, *A History of Chicago,* 3 vols. (New York, 1940), 2: 190–245; T. De Witt Talmage, *T. De Witt Talmage As I Knew Him* (London, 1912), pp. 69–70, 175.

65. *Chicago Daily Tribune,* Mar. 5, 6, July 1, 4, 8, 9, 10, 11, 15, 22, Dec. 12, 1857, Nov. 13, 1858; Handlin, *Al Smith and His America,* pp. 19 ff., 31 ff.; Sigmund S. Spaeth, *Read 'Em and Weep* (Garden City, N.Y., 1927), p. 231; Lewis L. Gould, *Wyoming, A Political History 1868–1896* (New Haven, 1968), pp. 171–172; Kehl, *Boss Rule,* p. 75; also Oscar and Lilian Handlin, *Liberty in Expansion* (New York, 1989), p. 67.

66. *Chicago Daily Tribune,* Mar. 8, 1856, Apr. 27, 1858; Kehl, *Boss Rule,* p. 102; Albert Fein, "Centennial New York, 1876," in *New York,* ed. M. M. Klein (Port Washington, N.Y., 1976), p. 98; Lyle W. Dorset, *The Pendergast Machine* (New York, 1968), p. 60; Alexander Callow, "San Francisco's Blind Boss," *Pacific Historical Review,* 25 (August 1956): 277; Spaeth, *Read 'Em and Weep,* pp. 230, 231; Quillen, *Industrial City,* p. 211; Donald Spivey, ed., *Sports in America: New Historical Perspectives* (Westport, Conn., 1985), p. 96.

67. James McGurrin, *Bourke Cockran: A Free Lance in American Politics* (New York, 1948); L. Wendt and H. Kogan, *Lords of the Levee* (Indianapolis, 1943); Roger W. Lotchin, *San Francisco* (New York, 1974), p. 247.

68. *Century Magazine,* 52 (1896): 632 ff.; William H. Taft, *The President and His Powers* (New York, 1916); Walt Whitman, *Complete Prose Works* (New York, 1914), pp. 110, 204, 227; Dunne, *Dissertations,* p. 277; John Bruce, *Gaudy Century* (New York, 1948), p. 175; Darrell Garwood, *Crossroads of America: The Story of Kansas City* (New York, 1948), pp. 172–173.

69. *Chicago Daily Tribune,* Oct. 18, 1858; Lately Thomas, *Delmonico's: A Century of Splendor* (Boston, 1967), pp. 303 ff.; William L. Riordon, *Plunkitt of Tammany Hall* (New York, 1963), p. xxvi; Rudyard Kipling, *From Sea to Sea,* 2 vols. (London, 1900), 2: 2; Paul P. Van Riper, *History of the United States Civil Service* (Evanston, Ill., 1958), p. 166.

70. Riordon, *Plunkitt of Tammany Hall,* pp. xx, 11; James J. Bryce, *The American Commonwealth* (New York, 1908); *Chicago Daily Tribune,* Mar. 6, 7, 1854; William R. Brock, *Investigation and Responsibility,* pp. 116–147; Thomas, *Delmonico's,* pp. 303–318; Finley Peter Dunne, *Mr. Dooley Says* (New York, 1910), p. 38.

71. Henry Bruére, *New City Government,* pp. ix–xiii, 13; Willoughby Jones, *The Life of James Fisk, Jr.* (New York, 1872), pp. 223–236, 242.

72. *Chicago Daily Tribune,* June 30, 1854, Feb. 21, 22, Mar. 29, 1856, Mar. 31, 1858; William R. Hunt, *Distant Justice: Policing the Alaskan Frontier* (Norman, Okla., 1987), pp. 52–62; Jones, *The Life of James Fisk, Jr.,* pp. 255–257.

73. *Chicago Daily Tribune,* May 16, 17, 1853, Apr. 23, 1856, May 28, 1857, Apr. 23, 1858, Apr. 5, 15, 1859; Theodore Roosevelt, *Letters,* 1: 453 ff., 2: 925 ff.; G. M. Roe, *Our Police: A History of the Cincinnati Police Force, from the Earliest Period until the Present Day* (Cincinnati, Ohio, 1890), pp. iii, 43; Pierce, *History of Chicago,* 2: 310–311; Henry Bruére, *New City Government,* pp. 272–275.

74. Larry D. Ball, *The United States Marshals of New Mexico and Arizona Territories, 1846–1912* (Albuquerque, N.Mex., 1978), pp. 238–244.

75. John J. Bukowczyk, *And My Children Did Not Know Me* (Bloomington, Ind., 1987); Henry Bruére, *New City Government,* p. 265; James H. Kyner, *End of Track,* ed. Hawthorne Daniel (Caldwell, Idaho, 1937), pp. 246 ff.

76. *Chicago Daily Tribune,* June 26, 1847, Jan. 15, Feb. 24, Oct. 6, 1858, Aug. 7, 1860; William J. Mathias et al., *Horse to Helicopter: First Century of the Atlanta Police Department* (Atlanta, 1973), pp. 15–64; G. W. Hosmer, *The People and Politics; or, The Structure of States and the Significance and Relation of Political Forms* (Boston,

1883), pp. 277, 281–283; E. Kimbark MacColl, *Merchants, Money and Power: The Portland Establishment, 1843–1913* (n.p., Georgian Press, 1988), pp. 289–290.

77. *Chicago Daily Tribune,* Sept. 16, 1856, Oct. 23, 1857, Mar. 4, 19, 1858; Whitman, *Poetical Works,* p. 192; Georg A. Sala, *America Revisited* (London, 1883), 2: 125 ff.; Pierce, *History of Chicago,* 2: 313–314, 476–478; James W. Sheahan and George B. Upton, *The Great Conflagration* (Chicago, 1871); Lotchin, *San Francisco,* pp. 18 ff.; Frederic May Holland, *Liberty in the Nineteenth Century* (New York, 1899), pp. 203, 206–208; Orestes A. Brownson, *The American Republic: Its Constitution, Tendencies, and Destiny* (New York, 1866), p. 72.

78. Stuart Galishoff, *Newark: The Nation's Unhealthiest City, 1832–1895* (New Brunswick, N.J., 1988), pp. 143 ff.; Brock, *Investigation and Responsibility,* pp. 116–147; Barbara G. Rosenkrantz, ed., *Selections from Public Health Reports and Papers* (New York, 1977), pp. 56–67; George Rosen, *Preventive Medicine in the United States* (New York, 1977), pp. 3–13.

79. *Chicago Daily Tribune,* Aug. 22, 1856; Galishoff, *Newark,* pp. 128 ff.; Zachary Gussow, *Leprosy, Racism, and Public Health* (Boulder, Colo., 1989), p. 38; Rosen, *Preventive Medicine,* pp. 36–37; Galishoff, *Newark,* pp. 87–90.

80. *Chicago Daily Tribune,* Jan. 5, 1860; Frederick Ratzel, *Sketches of Urban and Cultural Life in North America,* ed. Stewart A. Stehlin (New Brunswick, N.J., 1988), p. 9; Barbara G. Rosenkrantz, ed., *Selections from Public Health Reports 1873–1883* (New York, 1970), p. ix; Henry I. Bowditch, *Public Hygiene in America* (Boston, 1877), pp. 51; Bruére, *New City Government,* pp. 315–316.

81. Ratzel, *Sketches of Urban and Cultural Life,* pp. 31 ff.; John Duffy, *A History of Public Health in New York City, 1866–1966* (New York, 1974), pp. 32, 81; Gussow, *Leprosy, Racism, and Public Health,* pp. 39, 41, 42; Bruére, *New City Government,* pp. 318–319; H. G. Bowditch, *Public Hygiene in America* (Boston, 1877), p. 328.

82. Herman R. Lantz, *A Community in Search of Itself: A Case History of Cairo, Illinois* (Carbondale, Ill., 1972), p. 145; Rosenkrantz, *Selections from Public Health Reports 1873–1883,* p. 281.

83. *Chicago Daily Tribune,* Feb. 22, 1856, Aug. 10, 1857; Stuart Galishoff, *Safeguarding the Public Health: Newark, 1895–1918* (Westport, Conn., 1975), pp. 81 ff.; Nelson M. Blake, *Water for the Cities* (Syracuse, N.Y., 1956); Joel A. Tarr et al., "Water and Wastes," *Technology and Culture,* 25 (1984), pp. 226–263; Joel A. Tarr, "From City to Farm," *Agricultural History,* 49 (1975): 598 ff.; Eustace Miles, *Prevention and Cure* (New York, 1912), p. 236; Margaret Ripley Wolfe, *Lucius Polk Brown and Progressive Food and Drug Control,* pp. 83–84; Mitchell Okun, *Fair Play in the Marketplace* (Dekalb, Ill., 1986).

84. *Chicago Daily Tribune,* May 2, 1856, Mar. 28, May 21, June 26, 1857, June 10, 1859; Galishoff, *Newark,* pp. 5, 82, 185; Aleksandr Borisovich Lakier, *A Russian Looks at America,* ed. Arnold Schrier and Joyce Story (Chicago, 1979), pp. 90 ff., 99 ff.; *Fighting Venereal Diseases* (Washington, D.C., 1920), pp. 1–9; Duffy, *History of Public Health in New York,* pp. 37 ff., 44; Dan E. Beauchamp, *The Health of the Republic,* pp. 103, 112–113; Judith Waltzer Leavitt, *The Healthiest City, Milwaukee* (Princeton, N.J., 1982), pp. 122–127; see below, chap. 9.

85. Harry F. Dowling, *Fighting Infection: Conquests of the Twentieth Century* (Cambridge, Mass., 1977), pp. 17–18.

86. *Historical Statistics of the United States, 1789–1945* (Washington, D.C., 1949), p. 294; Morton G. Keller, *Affairs of State: Public Life in Nineteenth-Century America* (Cambridge, Mass., 1977).

87. *Chicago Daily Tribune,* Oct. 1, 1858; Van Riper, *History of the United States Civil Service,* p. 225.

88. Edward N. Doan, *The La Follettes and the Wisconsin Idea* (New York, 1947); Fola Belle La Follette, *Robert M. La Follette* (New York, 1953); *Chicago Daily Tribune,*

Feb. 25, 1859; Walt Whitman, "Democratic Vistas," *Complete Prose Works,* p. 204; Dan E. Beauchamp, *Health of the Republic,* p. 118; see below, chaps. 7, 8.

89. *Chicago Daily Tribune,* May 5, 1857, Jan. 14, Apr. 9, 1859; Samuel Swift, *History of the Town of Middlebury, Vermont* (Middlebury, 1859), pp. 371 ff.; also Josiah F. Goodhue, *History of the Town of Shoreham, Vermont* (Middlebury, 1861), p. 83; Lotchin, *San Francisco,* pp. 150 ff.; Johnson, *Papers,* 2: 191 ff., 207; James H. Canfield, *Taxation* (New York, 1883), p. 30.

90. Lanz, *A Community in Search of Itself,* pp. 163–164.

91. Whitman, "Democratic Vistas," *Complete Prose Works,* pp. 210 ff., 219 ff.

III: COMMUNITIES UNDER PRESSURE

1. Calvin Townsend, *Analysis of Civil Government* (New York, 1869), p. 247; Robert H. Fuller, *Government by the People* (New York, 1908), pp. 2–3; Frederick A. Cleveland et al., eds., *Democracy in Reconstruction* (Boston, 1919), pp. 424 ff.; H. G. Wells, *The Future in America* (New York, 1906), pp. 43, 47; James Huneker, *New Cosmopolis: A Book of Images* (New York, 1915), p. 147.

2. Wells, *Future in America,* pp. 153, 154.

3. Cleveland, *Democracy in Reconstruction,* p. 425.

4. Rosalie Ross, *Travels in America* (Carbondale, Ill., 1982), pp. 109, 115; George Horace Lorimer, *Letters from a Self-Made Merchant to His Son* (Albany, 1902), p. 235; Paul R. Baker, *Stanny: The Gilded Life of Stanford White* (New York, 1989), pp. 108 ff., 291 ff.

5. J. Marion Sims, *The Story of My Life* (New York, 1884), pp. 192 ff.; Walt Whitman, *Complete Prose Works* (New York, 1914), p. 322.

6. Jan Cohn, *The Palace or the Poorhouse: The American House as a Cultural Symbol* (East Lansing, Mich., 1979), pp. 53–54.

7. *Chicago Daily Tribune,* Apr. 11, 1856; William Dean Howells, *The Rise of Silas Lapham* (Boston, 1885); Charles E. A. Gayarré, *Louisiana* (New York, 1851), pp. 1197 ff.; Giuseppe Giacosa, *Impressioni d'America* (Milano, 1908), pp. 53–68, 85–89, 173–192; Baker, *Stanny,* p. 118; Cohn, *The Palace or the Poorhouse,* pp. 60–61; Mark Sullivan, *Our Times: The United States, 1900–1925,* 6 vols. (New York, 1929), 2: 250; Milton Rugoff, *America's Gilded Age* (New York, 1989), pp. 68–95; Eliza Potter, *A Hairdresser's Experience in High Life* (New York, 1980), p. iv.

8. *Chicago Daily Tribune,* Dec. 3, 1860; Ezra Stiles Gannett, *The Prince's Visit* (Boston, 1860); *The New England Tour of His Royal Highness the Prince of Wales* (Boston, 1860); Rafael J. De Cordova, *The Prince's Visit* (New York, 1861); Kenahan Cornwallis, *Royalty in the New World* (New York, 1960); Rufus Griswold, *The Republican Court; or, American Society in the Days of Washington* (New York, 1854), pp. 366–370; Maureen E. Montgomery, *Gilded Prostitution: Status, Money, and Transatlantic Marriages* (London, 1989).

9. James Parton, *Triumphs of Enterprise, Ingenuity and Public Spirit* (New York, 1872), pp. 323–352.

10. Ward McAllister, *Society as I Have Found It* (New York, 1890), pp. 157 ff., 212 ff., 216 ff.; Maud Howe Elliott, *Uncle Sam Ward and His Circle* (New York, 1938), p. 423; Clare Brandt, *An American Aristocracy: The Livingstons* (New York, 1986), pp. 203–204.

11. Mrs. E. F. Ellet, *The Court Circles of the Republic; or, The Beauties and Celebrities of the Nation* (Hartford, Conn., 1869), pp. 524–525, 550–564, 581–586; Oscar Handlin, *Al Smith and His America* (Boston, 1958), p. 16; John F. Kasson, *Rudeness and Civility: Manners in Nineteenth-Century America* (New York, 1990); Francis Parkman, "The Failure of Universal Suffrage," *North American Review,* 129 (1878):

4–5, 16–17, 20; Edward Chase Kirkland, *Dream and Thought in the Business Community* (Chicago, 1964), pp. 35, 36; L. A. Gobright, *Recollections of Men and Things at Washington, during a Third of a Century* (Philadelphia, 1869), p. 400.

12. Andrew Johnson, *Papers,* 7 vols., eds. Leroy P. Graf et al. (Knoxville, Tenn., 1970), 2: 215 ff., 235 ff.; Brandt, *American Aristocracy,* pp. 204–205; Finley Peter Dunne, *Mr. Dooley at His Best* (New York, 1938), p. 249.

13. Lorimer, *Letters from a Self-Made Merchant,* pp. 230–231; Wells, *Future in America,* pp. 72–73, 80–81.

14. Robert Louis Stevenson, *The Amateur Emigrant,* ed. Roger G. Swearingen (Ashland, 1976), passim; Wells, *Future in America,* pp. 60–61, 72–73; Alan Trachtenberg, *The Incorporation of America: Culture and Society in the Gilded Age* (New York, 1982), pp. 117–118; Parton, *Triumphs of Enterprise,* pp. 64, 65; Huneker, *New Cosmopolis,* pp. 158, 162.

15. *Quarter-Century of the New England Society of Orange, New Jersey* (Orange, N.J., 1895), pp. 38 ff.; Charles T. Morrissey, *Vermont* (New York, 1981), p. 133; *Chicago Daily Tribune,* Feb. 6, 18, 1856, Jan. 15, 1858; Baker, *Stanny,* p. 4; Lotchin, *San Francisco,* pp. 127; Stewart Holbrook, *The Yankee Exodus: An Account of Migration from New England* (New York, 1950); Parton, *Triumphs of Enterprise,* p. 632; Jan Cohn, *Creating America: George Horace Lorimer and the Saturday Evening Post* (Pittsburgh, 1989), pp. 7–10.

16. Gordon O. Hendrickson, ed., *Peopling the High Plains* (Cheyenne, Wyo., 1977), pp. 169–171.

17. Johnson, *Papers,* 2: 53 ff.; Henry C. Tracy, *American Naturalist* (New York, 1930), p. 110; Stanley Buder, *Pullman: An Experiment in Industrial Order* (New York, 1967), pp. 46–74; Parton, *Triumphs of Enterprise,* pp. 39–41.

18. *Chicago Daily Tribune,* Mar. 6, 1857; Newell G. Bringhurst, *Brigham Young and the Expanding American Frontier* (Boston, 1986), pp. 199 ff.; Ira L. Mandelker, *Religion, Society, and Utopia in Nineteenth-Century America* (Amherst, Mass., 1984); William R. Perkins and Barthinius L. Wick, *History of the Amana Society* (New York, 1975); Ia'acov Oved, *Two Hundred Years of American Communes* (New Brunswick, N.J., 1988); Parton, *Triumphs of Enterprise,* pp. 63–64.

19. Arthur Mann, "The Melting Pot," Richard L. Bushman, et al., eds. *Uprooted Americans* (Boston, 1979), pp. 291 ff.; Lotchin, *San Francisco,* pp. 108 ff.; Olivier Zunz, *The Changing Face of Inequality* (Chicago, 1982), pp. 309 ff.; Israel Zangwill, *The Melting Pot* (New York, 1911); Booker T. Washington, *Up from Slavery* (New York, 1901); Mary Antin, *The Promised Land* (Boston, 1912); Walt Whitman, "Chants Democratic," *Complete Poetical Works,* pp. 81, 83; Joel Porte, *Emerson in His Journals* (Cambridge, 1982), p. 539; Henry Adams, *Education* (Boston, 1974), preface; Henry James, *Letters,* 2 vols. (New York, 1970), 2: 495.

20. Henry James, *The American Scene* (New York, 1907; 1946), pp. 116 ff.; Parton, *Triumphs of Enterprise,* p. 616; Peter Conn, *The Divided Mind* (Cambridge, 1983), p. 44.

21. Edward N. Saveth, *American Historians and European Immigrants* (New York, 1948), p. 123.

22. Rena C. Gropper, *Gypsies in the City* (Princeton, N.J., 1975), p. 38; Parton, *Triumphs of Enterprise,* p. 634.

23. Theodor Griesinger, *Lebende Bilder aus Amerika* (Stuttgart, 1858), pp. 113 ff.; Paul Fox, *The Poles in America* (New York, 1922), pp. 73 ff.; Thomas H. Gladsley, "The Immigrant on the Land," *New England Quarterly,* 56 (1988): 429 ff.; Joshua Fishman, *Language Loyalty in the United States* (New York, 1978); *Chicago Daily Tribune,* Dec. 2, 1859; Joseph F. Wall, *Andrew Carnegie* (New York, 1970), pp.

174 ff.; Frederick C. Luebke, *Germans in the New World* (Urbana, Ill., 1990), pp. 31–47; Gerd Korman, *Industrialization, Immigration, and Americanizers* (Madison, Wis., 1967), pp. 167 ff.

24. Pascal d'Angelo, *Son of Italy* (New York, 1924), pp. 99 ff.

25. Louis H. Sullivan, *Kindergarten Chats* (New York, 1947), pp. 138–141; Carl Sandburg, *Smoke and Steel* (New York, 1941), pp. 4, 5; Carl Sandburg, *Chicago Poems* (New York, 1916); Walt Whitman, "Leaves of Grass," *Complete Poetical Works,* pp. 283, 288; Whitman, *Complete Prose Works,* pp. 11, 110, 118; Finley Peter Dunne, *Mr. Dooley's Opinions* (New York, 1901), pp. 118–129; Richard Sennett, *Families against the City* (Cambridge, Mass., 1970).

26. *Chicago Daily Tribune,* July 9, 1857; Kenneth T. Jackson, *Crabgrass Frontier* (New York, 1985); Henry Binford, *The First Suburbs: Residential Communities on the Boston Periphery* (Chicago, 1985); Sam Bass Warner, Jr., *The Private City: Philadelphia in Three Periods of Its Growth* (Philadelphia, 1968), pp. 194–197; Sam Bass Warner, Jr., *Street Car Suburbs: The Process of Growth in Boston, 1870–1900* (Cambridge, Mass., 1978); Jean F. Block, *Hyde Park Houses* (Chicago, 1978), pp. 1 ff., 25 ff.

27. *Chicago Daily Tribune,* Apr. 9, 1856; Giacosa, *Impressioni,* pp. 173–192; Kate H. Claghorn, "Foreign Immigrants in New York City," United States Industrial Commission, *Reports,* 15: 476; Oscar Handlin, *The Newcomers* (Cambridge, Mass., 1959), p. 29. Cf. Fernando Devoto, "The Origins of an Italian Neighborhood in Buenos Aires," *Journal of European Economic History,* 18 (1989): 37 ff.

28. Sigmund Spaeth, *Read 'Em and Weep* (Garden City, 1927), pp. 115, 131; Jane Addams, *Twenty Years at Hull House* (New York, 1911), pp. 97 ff.; Hutchins Hapgood, *The Spirit of the Ghetto* (New York, 1966); Irving Howe, *The World of Our Fathers* (New York, 1976); Cohn, *Palace or Poorhouse,* pp. 160–161.

29. *Chicago Daily Tribune,* Nov. 13, 1858, Apr. 9, 13, 1859; Jane Addams, *Twenty Years at Hull House,* pp. 97 ff.; Griesinger, *Lebende Bilder aus Amerika,* pp. 26 ff., 113 ff., 204 ff.; Ernst Otto Hopp, *Transatlantisches Skizzenbuch* (Berlin, 1876), pp. 199 ff., 209 ff., 214, 227 ff.; Roy Rosenzweig, *Eight Hours for What We Will* (Cambridge, 1983), pp. 13 ff., 35–64; Henry George, *Social Problems* (New York, 1883), p. 12; John H. Mollenkopf, ed., *Power, Culture, and Place* (New York, 1988), pp. 53–69; Jacob A. Riis, *How the Other Half Lives* (New York, 1890), pp. 43, 74, 229, 235, 237.

30. Edward W. Howe, *Story of a Country Town* (1882; New York, 1907), pp. 228 ff., 237 ff.

31. Jerome Mushkat, *Tammany: The Evolution of a Political Machine, 1789–1865* (Syracuse, N.Y., 1971), pp. 364–380; Mary F. Williams, *History of the San Francisco Committee of Vigilance* (Berkeley, Calif., 1921), pp. 323 ff.

32. Ednah D. Cheney, *Louisa May Alcott* (Boston, 1890), p. 82; Mollenkopf, *Power, Culture, and Place,* pp. 107–130; John E. Kasson, *Amusing the Millions* (New York, 1978), pp. 3–9, 38; Lewis A. Erenberg, *Steppin' Out: New York Nightlife and the Transformation of American Culture, 1890–1930* (Westport, Conn., 1981); Abram Dayton, *Last Days of Knickerbocker Life in New York* (New York, 1896). See also Oscar and Mary F. Handlin, *Dimensions of Liberty* (Cambridge, Mass., 1961), pp. 91 ff.

33. Frederika Bremer, *The Homes of the New World,* 2 vols. (New York, 1853), 2: 152 ff.; Lakier, pp. xxxv, 86; Handlins, *Dimensions of Liberty,* pp. 89 ff.

34. Whitman, "Chants Democratic," p. 129; Lafcadio Hearn, *An American Miscellany,* ed. Albert Mordell, 2 vols. (New York, 1924), 2: 89 ff.

35. Ellery Sedgwick, "Walter Hines Page at the *Atlantic Monthly,*" *Harvard Library Bulletin,* 35 (1987): 427 ff.; Donald R. Taft, *Two Portuguese Communities in New England* (New York, 1923); August M. Vaz, *The Portuguese in California* (San Francisco, 1965); Theodore Saloutos, *The Greeks in the United States* (Cambridge,

Mass., 1964), p. 278; Antanas J. Van Reenan, *Lithuanian Diaspora: Königsberg to Chicago* (Lanham, Md., 1990); Anne Blasig, *The Wends of Texas* (San Antonio, 1954); George R. Nielsen, *In Search of a Home* (College Station, Tex., 1989); *Chicago Daily Tribune,* Mar. 4, 1858, July 23, 1860; Oscar Handlin, *The Uprooted* (Boston, 1990); Marc Angel, *La America* (Philadelphia, 1982); Albert J. Arnoteau, "The Sephardic Immigrant from Bulgaria," *American Jewish Archives,* 42 (1990): 57 ff.; Walter P. Zenner, "Chicago's Sephardim," *American Jewish History,* 79 (1989): 221 ff.; Wells, *Future in America,* pp. 141–143; Ray S. Baker, "Hull House and the Ward Boss," *The Outlook,* 58 (1898): 770–771; Rosenzweig, *Eight Hours for What We Will,* p. 32; Baker, *Stanny,* p. 156.

36. Walt Whitman, "Leaves of Grass," *Complete Poetical Works,* p. 64; *Chicago Daily Tribune,* June 25, 1857, Apr. 16, 1858; Aug. 11, 17, 1860; Welles, *Diary,* 3: 426; Albert Robbins, *Coming to America* (New York, 1981), pp. 108–109; Shelly Tenenbaum, "Culture and Context: The Emergence of Hebrew Free Loan Societies in the United States," *Social Science History,* 13 (1989): 211 ff.

37. Jeffrey S. Gurock, "A Stage in the Emergence of the Americanized Synagogue," *Journal of American Ethnic History,* 9 (1990): 8 ff.; Thomas N. Brown, *Irish-American Nationalism* (Philadelphia, 1966); Victor Greene, *The Slavic Community on Strike: Immigrant Labor in Pennsylvania* (Notre Dame, Ind., 1968).

38. Sam Bass Warner, Jr., *Province of Reason* (Cambridge, Mass., 1984), pp. 124 ff.

39. *Chicago Daily Tribune,* May 3, 4, 1853, Feb. 6, 1856, Apr. 5, 1858, June 7, 13, 1859, Apr. 2, May 14, 1860; Rosenzweig, *Eight Hours for What We Will,* pp. 27–32; James R. Green, *The World of the Worker* (New York, 1980), p. 85; Zunz, *Changing Face of Inequality,* pp. 50, 327 ff.; W. J. Rorabaugh, *The Craft Apprentice* (New York, 1986), pp. 133 ff., 155.

40. Sigmund Spaeth, *Weep Some More* (New York, 1927), pp. 235 ff.; David Brody, *The Butcher Workermen: A Study in Unionism* (Cambridge, Mass., 1964); David Montgomery, *The Fall of the House of Labor* (Cambridge, 1987), pp. 6 ff.; Edwin Fenton, *Immigrants and Unions* (New York, 1975), pp. 382, 435, 461; Mary H. Blewett, *Men, Women, and Work: Class, Gender, and Protest in the New England Shoe Industry* (Urbana, Ill., 1988); Brian Greenberg, *Work and Community* (Albany, N.Y., 1985), pp. 119–140.

41. *Chicago Daily Tribune,* Mar. 24, 1860; Terence V. Powderly, *Thirty Years of Labor* (Columbus, Ohio, 1889), pp. 131 ff.; J. C. Schonfarber, "Testimony," U.S. Industrial Commission on the Relations and Conditions of Capital and Labor, *Report* (Washington, D.C., 1901), 7: 423 ff.; Lotchin, *San Francisco,* pp. 92 ff.; Walter Galenson, *The United Brotherhood of Carpenters* (Cambridge, Mass., 1983), p. 53; Harold C. Livesay, *Samuel Gompers and Organized Labor in America* (Boston, 1984); Leon Fink, *Workingmen's Democracy: The Knights of Labor and American Politics* (Urbana, Ill., 1983).

42. Korman, *Industrialization, Immigration, and Americanizers,* pp. 41 ff., 52; John J. Buckowczyk, *Steeples and Smokestacks: Class, Religion, and Ideology in the Polish Immigrant Settlements* (Harvard dissertation, 1980); John J. Buckowczyk, *And My Children Did Not Know Me* (Bloomington, Ind., 1987); Herbert G. Gutmann and Donald H. Bell, eds., *The New England Working Class and the New Labor History* (Urbana, Ill., 1987), pp. 137–152; Zunz, *Changing Face of Inequality,* pp. 224 ff.

43. David Brody, "Labor," in *Harvard Encyclopedia of American Ethnic Groups,* ed. Stephan Thernstrom et al. (Cambridge, Mass., 1981), pp. 609 ff.

44. Franklin B. Gowen, *The Lives and Crimes of the Molly Maguires* (Philadelphia, 1877); Edwin Fenton, *Immigrants and Unions* (New York, 1975); Wayne G. Broehl, *The Molly Maguires* (Cambridge, Mass., 1965); Anthony Bimba, *The Molly Ma-*

guires (New York, 1932); Roger David Waldinger, *Through the Eye of the Needle* (New York, 1986); Donald Miller and Richard E. Sharpless, *The Kingdom of Coal* (Philadelphia, 1985), pp. 136 ff.

45. Stephan Thernstrom, *Poverty and Progress* (Cambridge, Mass., 1964); *Chicago Daily Tribune,* Nov. 16, 1857; Edith Abbott, *Historical Aspects of the Immigration Problem* (Chicago, 1926), pp. 325–326.

46. Oscar and Lilian Handlin, *Liberty in Expansion* (New York, 1989), pp. 184 ff.

47. Griesinger, *Lebende Bilder,* pp. 26, 65, 113, 204; Robert D. Shapiro, *A Reform Rabbi in the Progressive Era: The Early Career of Stephen S. Wise* (New York, 1988); Melvin Urofsky, *A Voice That Spoke for Justice: The Life and Times of Stephen S. Wise* (Albany, 1982); Marc L. Raphael, *Abba Hillel Silver* (New York, 1989); John Hick, *Problems of Religious Pluralism* (New York, 1985), pp. 96–101; Korman, *Industrialization, Immigrants, and Americanizers,* p. 55; Martin E. Marty, *A Nation of Believers* (Chicago, 1976), pp. 18–79; Mark A. Noll, ed., *Religion and American Politics* (New York, 1990), pp. 146–163.

48. Anthony J. Kuzniewski, *Faith and Fatherland: The Polish Church War in Wisconsin, 1896–1918* (Notre Dame, Ind. 1980), pp. 70–89; Victor Greene, *For God and Country* (Madison, Wis., 1975), pp. 97 ff.; Stephen Wlodarski, *The Origin and Growth of the Polish National Catholic Church* (Scranton, Pa., 1974); Fox, *Poles in America,* p. 113; see also Arthur E. Sutherland, "Private Government," *Yale Review,* 41 (1952): 407 ff.

49. Richard H. Rovere, *Howe and Hummel* (New York, 1947), pp. 25 ff.

50. Donald Fleming, *William Welch and the Rise of Modern Medicine* (Baltimore, Md., 1987); Howard L. Holley, *The History of Medicine in Alabama* (Birmingham, Ala., 1982), pp. 260–262; Lawrence M. Friedman, *A History of American Law,* 2nd ed. (New York, 1985), pp. 606 ff., 633 ff.; Martin W. Sandler, *This Was Connecticut* (Boston, 1977), p. 100.

51. *Chicago Daily Tribune,* Feb. 14, 20, 1856; Abraham Flexner, *Medical Education in the United States* (New York, 1910); Kenneth M. Ludmerer, *Learning to Heal: The Development of American Medical Education* (New York, 1985), pp. 166–190.

52. Lafcadio Hearn, *An American Miscellany,* ed. Albert Mordell, 2 vols. (New York, 1924), 1: 7; Jules Chemetzky, *From the Ghetto: The Fiction of Abraham Cahan* (Amherst, Mass., 1977), p. 125; Anthony J. Kuzniewski, *Faith and Fatherland,* passim; Victor R. Greene, *American Immigrant Leaders 1800–1910,* pp. 126 ff.; Louis M. Lyons, *Newspaper Story: One Hundred Years of the Boston Globe* (Cambridge, Mass., 1971), pp. 47–50.

53. Greene, *American Immigrant Leaders 1800–1910,* pp. 33 ff., 36 ff., 56 ff., 71 ff.

54. Oscar Handlin, *The American People in the Twentieth Century* (Cambridge, Mass., 1954), pp. 49 ff.; *Chicago Daily Tribune,* Oct. 6, 1858, Jan. 11, 1859; Robert H. Wiebe, *Businessmen and Reform* (Cambridge, Mass., 1962), pp. 18 ff., 24; Miller and Sharpless, *The Kingdom of Coal,* pp. 245 ff.; Clifton J. Child, *The German Americans in Politics* (Madison, Wis., 1939); Philip Gleason, *The Conservative Reformers: German-American Catholics* (Notre Dame, Ind., 1968); Fox, *Poles in America,* p. 90; Handlin, *Boston's Immigrants,* p. 209; Gerald Sorin, *The Prophetic Minority* (Bloomington, Ind., 1985).

55. Zunz, *Changing Face of Inequality,* pp. 130 ff., 152 ff., 178 ff., 220, 238; Cohn, *Palace or Poorhouse,* pp. 146–147, 151, 156.

56. Aleksandr B. Lakier, *A Russian Looks at America* (Chicago, 1979), p. 136.

57. Alice Scourby, *The Greek Americans* (Boston, 1984), pp. 23–60; Saloutos, *Greeks in the United States;* Steven Bela Vardy, *The Hungarian Americans* (Boston, 1985), pp. 57–58; Robert James Ulrich, *The Bennett Law of 1889: Education and Politics in Wisconsin* (New York, 1980); Herbert A. Miller, *The School and the Community* (Cleveland, 1916), pp. 33 ff.; McPherson, *Battle Cry of Freedom,* p. 133.

58. George St. John, *Forty Years at School* (New York, 1959); William A. Gardner, *Groton School Verses, 1886–1903* (Boston, 1904), p. 63; Louise L. Stevenson, *Miss Porter's School,* 2 vols. (New York, 1987).

59. Mary Hallock Foote, "Friend Barton's Concern," *Scribner's Magazine* (July 1879); Israel Zangwill, *The Melting Pot* (New York, 1911); Richard M. Bernard, *The Melting Pot and the Altar* (Minneapolis, Minn., 1980); Aharon G. Aharonian, *Intermarriage and the Armenian-American Community* (Shrewsbury, Mass., 1983); Egon Mayer, *Love and Tradition: Marriage between Christians and Jews* (New York, 1985).

60. James Turner, *Without God, Without Creed* (Baltimore, 1985); Paul Avrich, *An American Anarchist: The Life of Voltairine de Cleyre* (Princeton, N.J., 1978).

61. *Chicago Daily Tribune,* Nov. 22, 1859, Feb. 24, 1860; Handlin, *Boston's Immigrants,* pp. 205 ff., 218; Wilfried Neidhardt, *Fenianism in North America* (University Park, Pa., 1975), pp. 7–15; Allon Gal, "The Zionist Influence in American Jewish Life," *American Jewish Archives,* 41 (1989): 173 ff.; Arthur A. Goren, *New York Jews and the Quest for Community: The Kehillah Experiment, 1908–1922* (New York, 1970), pp. 1–24; Judah J. Shapiro, *The Friendly Society* (New York, 1970), pp. 35 ff.; Diane Matza, "Sephardic Jews," *American Jewish History,* 79 (1990): 348.

62. Sutherland, "Private Government," *Yale Review,* 41 (1952): 407 ff.; Robert Cross, *The Emergence of Liberal Catholicism in the United States* (Cambridge, Mass., 1958).

63. Leo Wolman, *The Boycott in American Trade Unions* (Baltimore, 1916), pp. 79–82; Harry W. Laidler, *Boycotts and the Labor Struggle* (New York, 1913), pp. 134–150.

64. Walt Whitman, "Democratic Vistas," *Complete Prose Works* (New York, 1902), 2: 50 ff., 61, 143; Josiah Strong, *The New Era; or, The Coming Kingdom* (New York, 1893); Hans L. Treffousse, *Carl Schurz* (Knoxville, Tenn., 1982), pp. 74–75.

65. Zangwill, *The Melting Pot;* Horace M. Kallen, "Democracy *versus* the Melting Pot," *The Nation,* 100 (1915): 200 ff.; Edwin E. Slosson, "What Is Americanism?" *The Independent,* 101 (Mar. 20, 1920); Arthur Mann, *The One and the Many: Reflections on the American Identity* (Chicago, 1979).

66. Finley Peter Dunne, *Mr. Dooley's Opinions* (New York, 1901), pp. 128–129.

67. Walt Whitman, "Democratic Vistas," *Complete Prose Works,* pp. 197, 224; Spaeth, *Read 'Em,* pp. 218, 237; John Howard Bryant, *Poems* (New York, 1855), p. 84; Hans Nathan, *Dan Emmet and the Rise of Early Negro Minstrelsy* (Norman, Okla., 1977); Robert C. Toll, *Blacking Up: The Minstrel Show* (New York, 1974); John F. Kasson, *Amusing the Millions: Coney Island at the Turn of the Century* (New York, 1978).

68. Matthew Arnold, *Civilization in the United States* (Boston, 1888), pp. 169 ff.; Alan Trachtenberg, *The Incorporation of America: Culture and Society in the Gilded Age* (New York, 1982); George Britt, *Forty Years—Forty Millions: The Career of Frank A. Munsey* (New York, 1935), pp. 300–301; Cohn, *Creating America,* pp. 100–103; Edward Wagenknecht, *American Profile, 1900–1909* (Amherst, Mass., 1982), p. 209; Melvin L. De Fleur, "How Massive Are the Mass Media?" *Syracuse Scholar,* 10 (1990): 17 ff.; Frank L. Mott, *A History of American Magazines, 1885–1905* (Cambridge, Mass., 1957), 3: 460 ff., 494.

69. Samuel Clemens, *The Mysterious Stranger,* pp. 164 ff.; Robert Sklar, *Movie Made America: A Social History of American Movies* (New York, 1975), pp. 16–17.

70. Sklar, *Movie Made America,* pp. 18–19, 21–29.

71. Wyn Wachhorst, *Thomas Alva Edison: An American Myth* (Cambridge, Mass., 1981), pp. 89–112; Leo Marx, *The Machine in the Garden: Technology and the Pastoral Ideal in America* (New York, 1967).

72. Wagenknecht, *American Profile, 1900–1909,* p. 242.

73. Wilbur Zelinsky, *Nation into State: The Shifting Symbolic Foundations of American Nationalism* (Chapel Hill, N.C., 1988), pp. 89–93.

74. *Chicago Daily Tribune,* Mar. 2, 1957; Paul H. Buck, *Road to Reunion* (Boston, 1937); Edward Eggleston, *Hoosier Schoolmaster: A Story of Backwoods Life in Indiana* (New York, 1871), p. 220; see also below, chap. 9.
75. Victor Rosewater, *The Liberty Bell: Its History and Significance* (New York, 1926), pp. 130–138, 203–209, 219–220.
76. Yehoshua Arieli, *Individualism and Nationalism in American Ideology* (Cambridge, Mass., 1964).

IV: EQUALITY AND THE FRUITS OF BONDAGE

1. *Chicago Daily Tribune,* Nov. 4, 1859.
2. Joel Williamson, *A Rage for Order: Black/White Relations in the American South since Emancipation* (New York, 1986), pp. 9–11, 28, 35; Gavin Wright, *The Political Economy of the Cotton South: Households, Mobility, and Wealth in the Nineteenth Century* (New York, 1978); *Chicago Daily Tribune,* Aug. 20, 1858.
3. *Chicago Daily Tribune,* May 16, 27, 31, 1853, Jan. 27, 1854, Jan. 29, 31, Feb. 2, 7, 16, 18, 28, 1856, Feb. 14, Mar. 7, 11, 12, 18, 30, Apr. 6, May 4, 13, 21, June 25, Aug. 21, Nov. 12, 1857, Feb. 4, Oct. 9, 27, Nov. 1, 1858, Oct. 26, Dec. 9, 1859, Jan. 24, Mar. 28, 1860; 17 Howard, 393; Theodore B. Wilson, *The Black Codes of the South* (University, Ala., 1965), pp. 13 ff.; John W. Blassingame, *Black New Orleans, 1860–1880* (Chicago, 1973), pp. 17 ff., 51 ff.; Harold M. Hyman, *A More Perfect Union* (New York, 1973), p. 22; Daniel J. Flanigan, *The Criminal Law of Slavery and Freedom* (New York, 1987), pp. 1, 21 ff., 31 ff., 117 ff., 215; Aleksandr Borisovich Lakier, *A Russian Looks at America,* ed. Arnold Shrier and Joyce Story (Chicago, 1979), p. 58; Joel Williamson, *New People: Miscegenation and Mullatoes in the United States* (New York, 1980); James Kinney, *Amalgamation: Race, Sex, and Rhetoric in the Nineteenth Century American Novel* (Westport, Conn., 1985), pp. 54–101; Eric Foner, *Free Soil, Free Labor, Free Men: The Ideology of the Republican Party before the Civil War* (New York, 1970); Roger W. Lotchin, *San Francisco* (New York, 1974), pp. 130 ff.; Paul Finkelman, ed., *Slavery, Race, and the American Legal System, 1700–1872,* Ser. 2, 16 vols. (New York, 1988), 1: 299 ff., 407 ff., 534; see also above, chap. 2.
4. William J. Grayson, *The Hireling and the Slave* (Charleston, S.C., 1854), pp. 19 ff.; *Chicago Daily Tribune,* Sept. 30, Oct. 11, 1853, Mar. 27, Apr. 3, 1857, Sept. 28, 1858.
5. *Chicago Daily Tribune,* Sept. 4, 1857; Nathan I. Huggins, *Slave and Citizen: The Life of Frederick Douglass* (Boston, 1980); David W. Blight, *Frederick Douglass' Civil War* (Baton Rouge, La., 1989).
6. James M. McPherson, *Battle Cry of Freedom* (New York, 1988), pp. 507, 563 ff.
7. Oscar and Lilian Handlin, *Liberty in Expansion* (New York, 1989), pp. 309 ff.; Peyton McCrary, *Abraham Lincoln and Reconstruction: The Louisiana Experiment* (Princeton, N.J., 1970); McPherson, *Battle Cry of Freedom,* pp. 509, 558; Williamson, *Rage for Order,* pp. 53–54.
8. See above, chap. 2; McPherson, *Battle Cry of Freedom,* p. 560; William R. Brock, *An American Crisis: Congress and Reconstruction, 1865–1867* (New York, 1963); Richard H. Abbott, *The Republican Party and the South, 1855–1877* (Chapel Hill, N.C., 1986), pp. 20–74; Richard H. Sewell, *Ballots for Freedom: Antislavery Politics in the United States, 1837–1860* (New York, 1976), pp. 321–365.
9. Michael Les Benedict, *The Fruits of Victory* (Philadelphia, 1975), pp. 20 ff.; Hyman, *A More Perfect Union,* p. 492.
10. Herman Melville, *Poems* (London, 1924), p. 103; Joel Porte, *Emerson in His Journals* (Cambridge, Mass., 1982), p. 525; Gary Collison, "Anti-Slavery, Blacks, and the

Boston Elite," *New England Quarterly,* 61 (1988): 419 ff.; Hodding Carter, *The Angry Scar* (Garden City, N.Y., 1959); Atticus Green Haygood, *Our Brother in Black: His Freedom and His Future* (New York, 1881), pp. 80–81.

11. *Chicago Daily Tribune,* Aug. 3, 1860; Whitlaw Reid, *After the War: A Tour of the Southern States* (New York, 1965), p. xvii; John Richard Dennett, *The South as It Is* (New York, 1965), pp. x, 84; James L. Roark, *Masters without Slaves* (New York, 1977); Dan T. Carter, *When the War Was Over* (Baton Rouge, La., 1985), p. 23; Sidney Andrews, *The South since the War* (New York, 1969), p. 63.

12. George Fitzhugh, *Cannibals All! or, Slaves without Masters* (1857; Cambridge, Mass., 1960), pp. 52 ff., 65 ff., 204 ff.; Wilson, *Black Codes,* p. 148; Peter Kolchin, *First Freedom: The Responses of Alabama's Blacks to Emancipation and Reconstruction* (Westport, Conn., 1972), p. xviii; William Gillette, *Retreat from Reconstruction* (Baton Rouge, La., 1979), pp. 97 ff.

13. Williamson, *Rage for Order,* pp. 40–43; Joel Williamson, *After Slavery: The Negro in South Carolina during Reconstruction* (Chapel Hill, N.C., 1965).

14. Flanigan, *The Criminal Law of Slavery and Freedom,* pp. 284 ff.; Dickson J. Preston, *Talbot County: A History* (Centreville, Md., 1983), pp. 247 ff.; William S. McFeely, *Yankee Stepfather: General O. O. Howard and the Freedmen's Bureau* (New Haven, Conn., 1968); Robert Charles Morris, *Reading, 'Riting, and Reconstruction* (Chicago, 1981); Claude F. Oubre, *Forty Acres and a Mule: The Freedmen's Bureau and Black Land Ownership* (Baton Rouge, La., 1978), pp. 181–198; Edward Magdol, *A Right to the Land: Essays on the Freedmen's Community* (Westport, Conn., 1977), pp. 139–173; Hyman, *A More Perfect Union,* p. 287.

15. Williamson, *After Slavery,* pp. 35–49.

16. Andrew Johnson, *Papers,* ed. Le Roy P. Graf, et al. 8 vols. (Knoxville, Tenn., 1967–1989), 1: 354, 2: 360 ff.; 395 ff., 477; Hans L. Trefousse, *Andrew Johnson, A Biography* (New York, 1989); Carter, *When the War Was Over,* pp. 29 ff.

17. *Laws of Mississippi, 1865* (Jackson, Miss., 1866), pp. 91–93; Edward A. Pollard, *The Lost Cause Regained* (New York, 1868), p. 14; Andrews, *South since the War,* p. 46; Wilson, *Black Codes,* pp. 61 ff., 67 ff., 90 ff., 96 ff.; Flanigan, *Criminal Law of Slavery and Freedom,* pp. 165, 191 ff., 217 ff., 223 ff., 275, 284 ff., 304 ff.; Lewis N. Wynne, *The Continuity of Cotton-Planter Politics in Georgia, 1865–1892* (Macon, Ga., 1986), pp. 7–29; George C. Rable, *The Role of Violence in the Politics of Reconstruction* (Athens, Ga., 1984); Carter, *When the War Was Over,* pp. 39 ff.; Benedict, *The Fruits of Victory,* pp. 81, 86 ff.; also *Chicago Daily Tribune,* Dec. 2, 1858; Gerald Schwartz, ed., *A Woman Doctor's Civil War: Esther Hill Hawk's Diary* (Columbia, S.C., 1984), pp. 189, 190, 199, 233.

18. Orville V. Burton, *In My Father's House Are Many Mansions* (Chapel Hill, N.C., 1985), pp. 93 ff.; Herman Belz, *Reconstructing the Union: Theory and Policy during the Civil War* (Ithaca, N.Y., 1969); Michael Les Benedict, *A Compromise of Principles: Congressional Republicans and Reconstruction, 1863–1869* (New York, 1974); David Donald, *The Politics of Reconstruction, 1863–1867* (Baton Rouge, La., 1965); Ralph Korngold, *Thaddeus Stevens: A Being Darkly Wise and Rudely Great* (New York, 1955); David Donald, *Charles Sumner and the Rights of Man* (New York, 1970).

19. Flanigan, *Criminal Law of Slavery and Freedom,* pp. 320 ff.; La Wanda and John Cox, *Politics, Principles, and Prejudice, 1865–1866: Dilemma of Reconstruction America* (New York, 1963); Eric L. McKitrick, *Andrew Johnson and Reconstruction* (Chicago, 1960); Hyman, *A More Perfect Union,* pp. 449 ff.

20. Gillette, *Retreat from Reconstruction,* pp. 18–24; Wilson, *Black Codes,* pp. 134 ff.; Leon Edel, *Henry James, The Untried Years* (London, 1953), p. 172; Jane Maher, *Biography of Broken Fortunes* (Hamden, Conn., 1986) p. 33; Hyman, *A More Perfect Union,* p. 477.

21. Willie Lee Rose, *Rehearsal for Reconstruction: The Port Royal Experiment* (New York, 1967), p. 35; Alruthius Ambush Taylor, *The Negro in South Carolina during the Reconstruction* (Washington, D.C., 1924), pp. 153 ff.; W. E. Burghardt Du Bois, *Black Reconstruction* (New York, 1935); Paul Lewinson, *Race, Class, and Party* (New York, 1932), pp. 17 ff.; William C. Harris, *The Day of the Carpetbagger: Republican Reconstruction in Mississippi* (Baton Rouge, La., 1979); Sarah Woolfolk Wiggins, *The Scalawag in Alabama Politics, 1865–1881* (University, Ala., 1977); Otto H. Olsen, *Carpetbagger's Crusade: The Life of Albion Winegar Tourgee* (Baltimore, Md., 1965); Michael Perman, *Reunion without Compromise: The South and Reconstruction, 1865–1868* (Cambridge, Eng., 1973); Richard N. Current, *Those Terrible Carpetbaggers* (New York, 1988).

22. Friedrick Ratzel, *Sketches of Urban and Cultural Life* (New Brunswick, N.J., 1988), pp. 167 ff.; John Hammond Moore, ed., *The Juhl Letters to the Charleston Courier* (Athens, Ga., 1974), pp. 81, 82.

23. Schwartz, *A Woman Doctor's Civil War*, p. 116; John R. Commons, ed., *Documentary History of American Industrial Society*, 10 vols. (New York, 1958), 1: 141 ff.; Wilson, *Black Codes*, p. 58; Sherman, *Republican Party*, p. 70; Flanigan, *Criminal Law of Slavery and Freedom*, p. 287; Otto H. Olsen, ed., *Reconstruction and Redemption in the South* (Baton Rouge, La., 1980), pp. 78–108; Edward Magdol, *A Right to the Land*, pp. 109–138; Roger W. Shugg, *Origins of Class Struggle in Louisiana* (University, La., 1939), pp. 234 ff.; Williamson, *Rage for Order*, p. 76; Mary F. Armstrong, *Hampton and Its Students* (Philadelphia, 1874), pp. 15, 23, 76, 80.

24. Williamson, *After Slavery*, pp. 96–103.

25. David M. Chalmers, *Hooded Americanism* (Chicago, 1968); Flanigan, *Criminal Law of Slavery and Freedom*, pp. 232 ff., 265 ff., 316, 350 ff., 360, 552 ff.; Dan T. Carter, *When the War Was Over*, pp. 11–13; Gillette, *Retreat from Reconstruction*, pp. 23, 34, 43 ff.; Allen W. Trelease, *White Terror: The KKK Conspiracy and Southern Reconstruction* (New York, 1971); Everette Swinney, *Suppressing the Klan: The Enforcement of the Reconstruction Amendments, 1870–1877* (New York, 1987); Hyman, *A More Perfect Union*, pp. 455 ff.; Williamson, *Rage for Order*, pp. 78–86; Armstrong, *Hampton and Its Students*, p. 85; Benedict, *Fruits of Victory*, pp. 137 ff.; George C. Wright, *Racial Violence in Kentucky, 1865–1940* (Baton Rouge, La., 1990), p. 53.

26. Wilson, *Black Codes*, pp. 123 ff.; Andrews, *The South since the War*, pp. 24, 69; Armstrong, *Hampton and Its Students*, p. 96; Benedict, *Fruits of Victory*, pp. 137 ff.; Haygood, *Our Brother in Black*, p. 11; C. Vann Woodward, *Origins of the New South, 1877–1912* (Baton Rouge, La., 1951), p. 211; Gillette, *Retreat from Reconstruction*, pp. 101 ff.

27. George W. Cable, *The Silent South* (New York, 1885), pp. 16 ff., 30 ff.; H. R. Helper, *Impending Crisis of the South* (New York, 1860), pp. 21 ff., 25, 59, 120 ff.; Melville, *Poems*, pp. 181 ff.; Rollin G. Osterweis, *The Myth of the Lost Cause* (New York, 1973), pp. 92–101; Carter, *When the War Was Over*, p. 20; Lewinson, *Race, Class, and Party*, pp. 79 ff.; Haygood, *Our Brother in Black*, pp. 12, 15–16; I. A. Newby, *Jim Crow's Defense: Anti-Negro Thought in America, 1900–1930* (Westport, Conn., 1965); Shugg, *Origins of Class Struggle*, pp. 274 ff.

28. *Chicago Daily Tribune*, Mar. 11, 1857; Oscar Handlin, *Race and Nationality in American Life* (Boston, 1957), pp. 46–47; Haygood, *Our Brother in Black*, pp. 17–18, 185–186; Gillette, *Retreat from Reconstruction*, p. 14; Gideon Welles, *Diary*, J. T. Morse, ed., 3 vols. (Boston, 1911), 3: 8; Paul Kleppner, *Third Electoral System, 1853–1872* (Chapel Hill, N.C., 1979), pp. 92 ff.; Benjamin R. Twiss, *Lawyers and the Constitution: How Laissez-Faire Came to the Supreme Court* (Princeton, N.J., 1942); Hyman, *A More Perfect Union*, pp. 461 ff., 467 ff.; Charles G. Sellers, ed., *The Southerner as American* (Chapel Hill, N.C., 1960), pp. 138, 140; Neil R.

McMillen, *Dark Journey: Black Mississippians in the Age of Jim Crow* (Urbana, Ill., 1989), pp. 1–8; Gillette, *Retreat from Reconstruction,* pp. 41 ff.; Edward A. Pollard, *The Lost Cause Regained* (New York, 1868), p. 14; Richard B. Sherman, *The Republican Party and Black America* (Charlottesville, Va., 1973), pp. 91, 105; Andrews, *The South since the War,* pp. 70 ff.

29. Henry W. Grady, *Life and Labors* (New York, 1890), pp. 240 ff.; Henry W. Grady, *The Complete Orations and Speeches* (New York, 1910), pp. 14 ff.; Booker T. Washington, *Up from Slavery* (Boston, 1901), pp. 14 ff.; Woodward, *Origins of the New South;* Rayford W. Logan, *The Negro in American Life and Thought: The Nadir, 1877–1902* (New York, 1954); Stanley P. Hirshson, *Farewell to the Bloody Shirt: Northern Republicans and the Southern Negro, 1877–1893* (Bloomington, Ind., 1963).

30. Handlin, *Race and Nationality in American Life;* William Stanton, *The Leopard's Spots* (Chicago, 1960); R. W. Shufeldt, *The Negro: A Menace to American Civilization* (Boston, 1907), p. 11.

31. Nathaniel Southgate Shaler, *The Citizen: A Study of the Individual and the Government* (New York, 1904), pp. 26–43, 230; Nathaniel Southgate Shaler, *The Neighbor: The Natural History of Human Contacts* (Boston, 1904), pp. 138, 140; Cable, *The Silent South* (New York, 1885), pp. 6–11, 15–20, 35; Allen Tullos, *Habits of Industry: White Culture and the Transformation of the Carolina Piedmont* (Chapel Hill, N.C., 1989), pp. 134–171; Dwight B. Billings, *Planters and the Making of a New South* (Chapel Hill, N.C., 1979).

32. Sherman, *Republican Party,* pp. 27, 38 ff., 56 ff., 113 ff.; August Meier and Elliott Rudwick, "The Rise of Segregation in the Federal Bureaucracy, 1900–1930," *Phylon,* 28 (1967): 178–184; Newby, *Jim Crow's Defense,* pp. 27–49; Shaler, *The Neighbor,* p. 185.

33. Cable, *Silent South,* pp. 109 ff.; Alfred H. Stone, *Studies in the American Race Problem* (New York, 1908), pp. 221, 241, 431; Thomas Dixon, Jr., *The Clansmen* (New York, 1905), pp. 341 ff.; Nancy J. Weiss, "The Negro and the New Freedom: Fighting Wilsonian Segregation," *Political Science Quarterly,* 84 (1969): 61–79; Kathleen Long Wolgemuth, "Woodrow Wilson and Federal Segregation," *Journal of Negro History,* 44 (1959): 158–173; Thomas Dixon, *The Leopard's Spots: A Romance of the White Man's Burden, 1865–1900* (New York, 1902), pp. 159, 382, 414, 435, 441; Thomas Dixon, *The Southerner: A Romance of the Real Lincoln* (New York, 1919); Schwartz, *A Woman Doctor's Civil War,* pp. 225 ff.

34. Sherman, *Republican Party,* p. 99; Joseph F. Wall, *Andrew Carnegie* (New York, 1979), pp. 973 ff.; Henry A. Bullock, *A History of Negro Education in the South* (Cambridge, Mass., 1967), pp. 117–146; James D. Anderson, *The Education of Blacks in the South* (Chapel Hill, N.C., 1988); Robert A. Margo, *Disenfranchisement, School Finance, and the Economics of Segregated Schools in the United States South, 1890–1910* (New York, 1985).

35. Williamson, *Rage for Order,* pp. 120–125, 127–151; Shufeldt, *The Negro,* pp. 13, 114, 131, 196–197; *Chicago Tribune,* May 28, 1893.

36. George W. Cable, *The Silent South* (New York, 1885), pp. 72 ff., 76; Edward L. Wheeler, *Uplifting the Race: The Black Minister in the New South, 1865–1902* (Lanham, Md., 1986); Charles H. Wesley, *Negro Labor in the United States* (New York, 1927), p. 171; William Holcombe Thomas, *The New South: An Inside View* (Montgomery, Ala., 1908), p. 3; William Hannibal Thomas, *The American Negro: What He Was, What He Is, and What He May Become* (New York, 1901), pp. 398–406; also *Chicago Daily Tribune,* June 29, 1854.

37. W. E. B. Du Bois, *The Souls of Black Folk* (1903; New York, 1913), pp. 251 ff.; Lafcadio Hearn, *American Miscellany,* 2 vols. (New York, 1924), 1: xv., 147 ff.

38. Booker T. Washington, *Selected Speeches,* ed. E. Davidson Washington (New York, 1932), pp. 31–36; Booker T. Washington and Robert E. Park, *The Man Farthest Down* (1911; New Brunswick, N.J., 1984), p. 390.

39. W. E. B. Du Bois, *The College-Bred Negro* (Nashville, Tenn., 1898); George Fitzhugh, *Sociology for the South* (Richmond, Va., 1854); Fitzhugh, *Cannibals All!;* George Fitzhugh, "The Freedman and His Future," *Lippincott's Magazine,* 4 (1869): 436 ff.; *Final Report of the Industrial Commission, 1902* (Washington, D.C., 1902), 19: 97 ff.; Benjamin A. Botkin, *Lay My Burden Down* (Chicago, 1945), pp. 116–117; William Archer, *Through Afro America* (New York, 1910), pp. 191–192, 207–208; Philip Alexander Bruce, *Rise of the New South* (Philadelphia, 1905), pp. 31, 439–451; John F. Kasson, *Rudeness and Civility* (New York, 1990), p. 54.

40. *Chicago Daily Tribune,* May 13, 1858; Nell I. Painter, *Exodusters: Black Migration to Kansas after Reconstruction* (Lawrence, Kan., 1986); Jimmie L. Franklin, *Journey toward Hope: A History of Blacks in Oklahoma* (Norman, Okla., 1982); also Alruthius A. Taylor, *The Negro in Tennessee* (Washington, D.C., 1941), pp. 106 ff.

41. Wilson, *Black Codes,* pp. 44 ff., 51 ff.; Rowland T. Berthoff, *An Unsettled People: Social Order and Disorder in American History* (New York, 1971); *Chicago Daily Tribune,* Nov. 14, 1853, Mar. 7, 1854.

42. James Weldon Johnson, *Along This Way* (New York, 1935), p. 152.

43. *Chicago Daily Tribune,* Feb. 13, 1857, Aug. 16, Dec. 25, 1858, Feb. 14, Dec. 2, 1859; Jonathan Katz, *Resistance at Christiana* (New York, 1974), pp. 27 ff., 50 ff., 60 ff.; John W. Blassingame, *Black New Orleans, 1860–1880* (Chicago, 1973), pp. 52 ff.; Sarah Lawrence Lightfoot, *Balm in Gilead* (Reading, Mass., 1988), pp. 20 ff.; Nancy Cott, *The Grounding of Modern Feminism* (New Haven, Conn., 1987), pp. 30, 32; Adelaide C. Hill, *The Negro Upper Class in Boston* (Radcliffe Doctoral diss., 1952); David A. Gerber, *Black Ohio and the Color Line, 1860–1915* (Urbana, Ill., 1976), pp. 170–174; Stephen R. Fox, *The Guardian of Boston: William M. Trotter* (New York, 1971), pp. 3–30; Mary White Ovington, *Half A Man: The Status of the Negro in New York* (New York, 1969), pp. 170–187; Herbert J. Seligmann, *The Negro Faces America* (New York, 1920), pp. 11–12, 28, 286, 293; Benjamin Quarles, *Frederick Douglass* (Washington, D.C., 1948); Oscar Handlin, *Boston's Immigrants* (Cambridge, Mass., 1959), p. 212.

44. Eric Foner, *Reconstruction,* pp. 8–10; Sara Alpern, *Freda Kirchwey* (Cambridge, Mass., 1987), p. 29; Walter J. Stevens, *Chip on My Shoulder* (Boston, 1946), p. 52; Ely Green, *Ely: Too Black, Too White* (Amherst, Mass., 1970); Gerber, *Black Ohio,* pp. 277–283.

45. Oscar Handlin, *The Newcomers: Negroes and Puerto Ricans in a Changing Metropolis* (Cambridge, Mass., 1959); Gilbert Osofsky, *Harlem: The Making of a Ghetto* (New York, 1966), p. 32; Quillen, *Industrial City,* p. 267; "The Black Voter of Philadelphia," *Charities,* 15 (1905): 31 ff.; A. T. Brown and Lyle W. Dorsett, *K.C.: A History of Kansas City* (Boulder, Colo., 1978), pp. 93–94; Lawrence Brooks de Graaf, *Negro Migration to Los Angeles, 1930–1950* (Univ. of Calif., L.A., Doctoral diss., 1962), p. 7.

46. *Chicago Daily Tribune,* Aug. 7, 1857, Jan. 18, 1859; Hearn, *American Miscellany,* 1: 1xvii, 1, 161; Gerber, *Black Ohio,* pp. 284–285.

47. Fox, *Guardian of Boston.*

48. Francis L. Broderick, *W. E. B. Du Bois* (Stanford, Calif., 1959); Elliott M. Rudwick, *W. E. B. Du Bois: Propagandist of the Negro Protest* (Philadelphia, 1968); Robert Michael Franklin, *Liberating Visions* (Minneapolis, Minn., 1990), pp. 36–37, 45, 57.

49. Ray S. Baker, *Following the Color Line: American Negro Citizenship in the Progressive*

Era (New York, 1964); Richard Sherman, *Republican Party and the Blacks,* p. 12; Elliott M. Rudwick, *Race Riot at East St. Louis* (Carbondale, Ill., 1964); Zunz, *Changing Face of Inequality,* pp. 373 ff.

50. Constance McLaughlin Green, *The Secret City: A History of Race Relations in the Nation's Capital* (Princeton, N.J., 1967), pp. 126, 131–132.

51. *Chicago Daily Tribune,* Dec. 19, 1859; Marvin Ewy, *Charles Curtis of Kansas* (Emporia, Kan., 1961).

52. *Chicago Daily Tribune,* Jan. 29, Mar. 7, 1857, Aug. 24, 1858; Richard M. Brown, *American Violence* (Englewood Cliffs, N.J., 1970), pp. 55 ff.; Oliver O. Howard, *My Life and Experiences among Our Hostile Indians* (New York, 1972), pp. xii–xv; Carlos E. Cortes et al., *Three Perspectives on Ethnicity* (New York, 1976), pp. 155–169; also Herman Melville, *The Confidence-Man* (New York, 1963), pp. 192 ff.

53. *Chicago Daily Tribune,* Aug. 10, 1857, Nov. 24, 1859; William Howarth, *Thoreau in the Mountains* (New York, 1982), p. 178; *Annual Report of the United States Commissioner of Indian Affairs for the Year 1870* (Washington, D.C., 1870), pp. 8–9; William Cody, *The Adventures of Buffalo Bill* (New York, 1904), pp. 145, 150–151; Cortes et al., *Three Perspectives on Ethnicity,* pp. 168–169; Lydia H. Sigourney, *Pocahontas and Other Poems* (New York, 1855), p. 32.

54. Henry E. Fritz, *The Movement for Indian Assimilation, 1860–1890* (Philadelphia, 1963), p. 165; Christine Bolt, *American Indian Policy and American Reform* (London, 1987), pp. 205–230; William McFeely, *Grant* (New York, 1981), pp. 308–317; Alan Trachtenberg, *The Incorporation of America* (New York, 1982), p. 36.

55. Fritz, *Movement for Indian Assimilation,* pp. 24 ff., 56 ff., 87 ff., 109 ff., 151 ff.; McFeely, *Grant,* p. 316; Bolt, *American Indian Policy,* pp. 86–87.

56. Fritz, *Movement for Indian Assimilation,* pp. 34 ff., 198 ff.; Bolt, *American Indian Policy,* p. 87; Robert W. Mardock, *The Reformers and the American Indians* (Columbia, Mo., 1971); Francis P. Prucha, *American Indian Policy in Crisis: Christian Reformers and the Indian, 1865–1900* (Norman, Okla., 1976).

57. *Congressional Record,* 49th Cong., 2nd sess. (Washington, 1887), 18: 190 ff.; John Beeson, *Plea for the Indians* (New York, 1858); Fritz, *Movement for Indian Assimilation,* pp. 34 ff.; Loring B. Priest, *Uncle Sam's Stepchildren: The Reformation of United States Indian Policy, 1865–1887* (New Brunswick, N.J., 1942), pp. 5 ff.; Norris Hundley, Jr., ed., *The American Indian* (Santa Barbara, Calif., 1974), pp. 77–100.

58. Fritz, *Movement for Indian Assimilation,* pp. 281 ff.; Leonard A. Carlson, *Indians, Bureaucrats, and Land: The Dawes Act and the Decline of American Farming* (Westport, Conn., 1981), pp. 3–22.

59. Brian W. Dippie, *The Vanishing American: White Attitudes and United States Indian Policy* (Middletown, Conn., 1982), p. 195.

60. Dippie, *Vanishing American,* pp. 117–196; William T. Hagan, *The Indian Rights Association: The Herbert Welsh Years, 1882–1904* (Tucson, Ariz., 1985).

61. Gunther Barth, *Bitter Strength: A History of the Chinese in the United States, 1850–1870* (Cambridge, Mass., 1964); Rose Hum Lee, *The Chinese in the United States of America* (Hong Kong, 1960).

62. Isaac H. Bromley, *The Chinese Massacre at Rock Springs, Wyoming* (Boston, 1886), pp. 50 ff.; *Boston Pilot,* Apr. 15, 1882; Samuel Gompers, *Meat versus Rice* (San Francisco, 1908); Samuel Gompers, *The American Federationist,* 12 (1905): 940 ff.; Frank Marryat, *Mountains and Molehills* (London, 1855), pp. 96 ff., 172 ff.; Robert Louis Stevenson, *Amateur Emigrant,* ed. Roger G. Swearingen, 2 vols. (Ashland, Ore., 1976), 2: 61, 92, 93; Arthur Mann, *The One and the Many* (Chicago, 1979); Roger Daniels, ed., *Anti-Chinese Violence in North America* (New York, 1978), pp. 18, 47–55, 103–129, 291; Janet Smith, ed., *Mark Twain on the Damned Human Race* (New York, 1962), p. 80; Roger W. Lotchin, *San Francisco, 1846–1856: From*

Hamlet to City (New York, 1974), pp. 123 ff.; Shih-Shan Henry Tsai, *China and the Overseas Chinese in the United States, 1868–1911* (Fayetteville, Ark., 1983), pp. 60–80; Zachary Gussow, *Leprosy, Racism and Public Health* (Boulder, Colo., 1989), p. 56.

63. *Chicago Daily Tribune,* May 5, 1860; Sidney L. Gulick, *American Japanese Problem* (New York, 1914); *Report of the Commissioner General of Immigration, 1908,* pp. 221–222; John Modell, *The Economics and Politics of Racial Accommodation* (Urbana, Ill., 1977), pp. 34; Harry H. L. Kitano, *Japanese Americans: The Evolution of a Subculture* (Englewood Cliffs, N.J., 1969), pp. 10–24; Roger Daniels, *The Politics of Prejudice: The Anti-Japanese Movement in California and the Struggle for Japanese Exclusion* (Berkeley, Calif., 1977), pp. 16–64; William R. Hutchison, *Errand to the World: American Protestant Thought and Foreign Missions* (Chicago, 1987); Carey McWilliams, *Prejudice: Japanese Americans, Symbol of Racial Intolerance* (New York, 1971), pp. 55–57.

64. See below, chap. 7, Daniels, *Politics of Prejudice,* pp. 65–67; Lotchin, *San Francisco,* pp. 191 ff.; Williams, *San Francisco,* pp. 121 ff., 241 ff.; John McElroy, *Andersonville* (Toledo, Ohio, 1879), pp. 220 ff.

65. *Chicago Daily Tribune,* Oct. 12, 1853, May 8, 1857, Jan. 23, Feb. 3, 1858, July 4, 1859; Charles Chiniquy, *Fifty Years in the Church of Rome* (Chicago, 1887); "The Power of the Irish in American Politics," *Littell's Living Age,* 171 (Oct. 30, 1986): 382 ff.; Paul Bocock, "The Irish Conquest of Our Cities," *The Forum,* 17 (April, 1894): 186 ff.

66. *Chicago Daily Tribune,* Dec. 1, 5, 7, 11, 1858; Welles, *Diary,* 3: 514; Oscar Handlin, *Adventure in Freedom* (New York, 1954); Oscar Handlin, *Danger in Discord: Origins of Anti-Semitism in the United States* (New York, 1948); Schwartz, *A Woman Doctor's Civil War Diary,* p. 157; Shai Weisbach, "Stability and Mobility in the Small Jewish Community," *American Jewish History,* 79 (1990): 355 ff.

67. Carlo Gardini, *Gli Stati Uniti,* 2 vols. (Bologna, Italy, 1887); Jules Chametzky, *From the Ghetto: The Fiction of Abraham Cahan* (Amherst, Mass., 1977), p. 35; McPherson, *Battle Cry of Freedom,* pp. 441, 623; *Coney Island and the Jews: A History of the Development and Success of This Famous Seaside Resort* (New York, 1879), pp. 20–21; Pal Sylvanus, *Tit for Tat: Satirical Universal History* (Chicago, 1895), pp. 74, 93–94; Louise A. Mayo, *The Ambivalent Image: Nineteenth-Century America's Perception of the Jew* (Rutherford, N.J., 1980).

68. *Chicago Daily Tribune,* May 7, 1856; Dan T. Carter, *When the War Was Over* (Baton Rouge, La., 1985), p. 80; Oscar Handlin, "American Views of the Jew," American Jewish Historical Society, *Publications, 40* (1951): 323 ff.; Paul Avrich, *The Haymarket Tragedy* (Princeton, N.J., 1984), p. 127; Gordon Clark, *Shylock as Banker, Bondholder, Corruptionist, Conspirator* (American Bimetallic League, Washington, D.C., 1894); *Coney Island and the Jews: A History of the Development and Success of This Famous Seaside Resort* (New York, 1879).

69. *Chicago Daily Tribune,* Apr. 28, 1853; editorial, *Independent,* 58 (1905): 716; William T. Youngs, *Eleanor Roosevelt* (Boston, 1985), pp. 106, 107; Walt Whitman, "Leaves of Grass," *Poems* (New York, 1902), pp. 24, 30.

70. Gustave Le Bon, *The Psychology of Peoples* (New York, 1974), pp. 145–147.

V: ISOLATION

1. Kenneth S. Lynn, *The Dream of Success* (Boston, 1955); Moses Rischin, ed., *The American Gospel of Success: Individualism and Beyond* (Chicago, 1965), pp. 91–97; Richard Weiss, *The American Myth of Success* (New York, 1969); Emory Elliott, ed., *Columbia Literary History of the United States* (New York, 1988), pp. 482–498.

2. John G. Cawelti, *Apostles of Self-Made Man: Changing Concepts of Success in America* (Chicago, 1965), p. 118; Richard M. Huber, *The American Idea of Success* (New York, 1971); Gary Scharnhorst, *Horatio Alger, Jr.* (Boston, 1980), pp. 68–69.

3. George Fitch, *At Good Old Siwash* (Boston, 1911); Joel Porte, *Emerson in His Journals* (Cambridge, 1982), p. 419; Gilbert Patten, *Frank Merriwell's "Father"* (Norman, Okla., 1964); H. G. Wells, *The Future in America: A Search after Realities* (New York, 1906), pp. 212–213.

4. Russell H. Conwell, *Acres of Diamonds* (1890; New York, 1943); Fitch, *At Good Old Siwash,* pp. 285–289.

5. Clyde and Sally Griffen, *Natives and Newcomers: The Ordering of Opportunity in Mid-Nineteenth-Century Poughkeepsie* (Cambridge, Mass., 1978), p. 223; Bernard Bailyn et al., eds., *Glimpses of the Harvard Past* (Cambridge, Mass., 1986).

6. Charles T. Morrissey, *Vermont* (New York, 1981), p. 153; Joseph F. Wall, *Andrew Carnegie* (New York, 1970), pp. 267 ff.; Edward W. Howe, *Story of a Country Town* (New York, 1917); David McCullough, *Mornings on Horseback* (New York, 1981), pp. 355–367; Gerald Schwartz, ed., *A Woman Doctor's Civil War Diary* (Columbia, S.C., 1984), p. 157; also Edwin A. Robinson, *Children of the Night* (New York, 1910).

7. Aleksandr Borisovich Lakier, *A Russian Looks at America,* ed. Arnold Schrier and Joyce Story (Chicago, 1979), p. 168; *Chicago Daily Tribune,* Apr. 6, 1857; Billy M. Jones, *Health-Seekers in the Southwest, 1817–1900* (Norman, Okla., 1967), pp. 92, 97, 99, 180; J. H. Beadle, *The Undeveloped West; or, Five Years in the Territories,* 2 vols. (Philadelphia, 1873); Susan E. Cayleff, *Wash and Be Healed: The Water Cure Movement* (Philadelphia, 1987); Leslie Dorsey and Janice Devine, *Fare Thee Well: A Backward Look at Two Centuries of Historic American Hostelries* (New York, 1964); James Wharton, *Crusaders for Fitness: The History of American Health Reformers* (Princeton, N.J., 1982).

8. *Chicago Daily Tribune,* Apr. 2, 1856, Aug. 10, 1857, Jan. 8, 1859; William D. Howells, *Criticism and Fiction* (New York, 1891), pp. 123–140; Lafcadio Hearn, *An American Miscellany,* ed. Albert Mordell, 2 vols. (New York, 1924), 1: xx ff., xxiv–xxv; Porte, *Emerson in His Journals,* pp. 434, 435, 558; Martha Banta, *Failures and Success in America* (Princeton, N.J., 1978), p. 505; James T. Patterson, *The Dread Disease: Cancer and Modern American Culture* (Cambridge, Mass., 1987), pp. 1–11; Herbert Hendin, *Suicide in America* (New York, 1982), pp. 13–25; R. Laurence Moore, *In Search of White Crows* (New York, 1977); Elizabeth Stuart Phelps, *The Gates Ajar* (Cambridge, Mass., 1964); Howard I. Kushner, *Self-Destruction in the Promised Land: A Psychocultural Biology of American Suicide* (New Brunswick, N.J., 1989), pp. 35–62.

9. *Chicago Daily Tribune,* Apr. 28, 29, 1853; Roger W. Lotchin, *San Francisco, 1846–1856: From Hamlet to City* (New York, 1974), pp. 100 ff.; John F. Kasson, *Amusing the Millions: Coney Island at the Turn of the Century* (New York, 1978), pp. 71–72.

10. Emily Dickinson, *Poems,* ed. Thomas H. Johnson, 3 vols. (Cambridge, Mass., 1955), 2: 255; Robert Frost, *North of Boston* (New York, 1914); Rischin, *American Gospel of Success,* p. 167; Albert B. Wolfe, *The Lodging House Problem in Boston* (Boston, 1906).

11. Hearn, *An American Miscellany,* 1: 29 ff.; *Chicago Daily Tribune,* July 20, 1858, Aug. 7, 1860; Paul S. Boyer, *Urban Masses and Moral Order in America, 1820–1920* (Cambridge, 1978).

12. Wolfe, *Lodging House Problem,* pp. 1–10.

13. Roger A. Bruns, *Knights of the Road* (New York, 1980), pp. 21, 49, 56; Donald Le Crone McMurry, *Coxey's Army* (Boston, 1929), pp. 1–20; Robert L. Stevenson, *Amateur Emigrant,* 2 vols. (Ashland, Oreg., 1976), 2: 98.

14. Carl Sandburg, *The American Songbag* (New York, 1927), pp. 185, 189, 192; Herman Melville, *The Confidence-Man* (New York, 1963), pp. 192 ff.; Walt Whitman, *Complete Prose Works,* pp. 198, 199; Wolfe, *Lodging House Problem,* p. 9; McMurry, *Coxey's Army,* p. 16.

15. Clarence King, *Mountaineering in the Sierra Nevada* (Boston, 1886), pp. 95–106, 110–111; Pascal d'Angelo, *Son of Italy* (New York, 1924), pp. 99 ff.; Stevenson, *Amateur Emigrant,* 2: 88–91; Upton Sinclair, *The Jungle* (New York, 1906).

16. Walt Whitman, "Leaves of Grass," 106, 153, 354, 367, in *Poems,* pp. 35, 41, 76, 78; *Chicago Daily Tribune,* July 20, 1858.

17. Stephen Crane, *Complete Short Stories* (Garden City, N.Y., 1963), pp. 339–359; Frank Norris, *McTeague* (New York, 1899), and *Octopus* (Garden City, N.Y., 1901); Jack London, *The Call of the Wild* (1903; New York, 1923), pp. 82, 83; Robert Frost, "The Death of the Hired Man," in *North of Boston;* O. O. Winther, *The Transportation Frontier* (New York, 1964), pp. 140 ff.; James O. Kaler, *Toby Tyler* (1881; Philadelphia, 1937); David W. Maurer, *The American Confidence Man* (Urbana, Ill., 1974), pp. 8–22; Roderick Nash, *Wilderness and the American Mind* (New Haven, Conn., 1982), pp. 141–143; John Perry, *Jack London, An American Myth* (Chicago, 1981), pp. 201–216; David A. Shannon, *The Socialist Party of America* (New York, 1955), pp. 56–57; Andrew Sinclair, *Jack: A Biography of Jack London* (New York, 1977); William W. Savage, *The Cowboy Hero: His Image in American History and Culture* (Norman, Okla., 1979), pp. 3–23; Ramon F. Adams, *The Cowman and His Code of Ethics* (Austin, Tex., 1969); William A. Pinkerton, *Train Robberies, Train Robbers, and the Hold-Up Men* (New York, 1974).

18. Paul Avrich, *The Haymarket Tragedy* (Princeton, N.J., 1984), pp. 62 ff., 89, 91; Carolyn Ashbaugh, *Lucy Parsons: An American Revolutionary* (Chicago, 1976); Frank L. Mott, *A History of American Magazines, 1885–1905* (Cambridge, Mass., 1957), pp. 440 ff., 446.

19. Gilbert V. Seldes, *The Seven Lively Arts* (New York, 1924); Paul Bourget, *Outre-Mer* (New York, 1895), 2: 142, 157; Bruns, *Knights of the Road,* pp. 6, 11; Arthur A. Berger, *The Comic Stripped American* (New York, 1973), pp. 60–78; David Manning White and Robert H. Abel, *The Funnies: An American Idiom* (New York, 1963), pp. 1–35, 131–141.

20. Sandburg, *The American Songbag,* p. 47.

21. James C. Mohr, ed., *The Cormany Diaries* (Pittsburgh, Pa., 1982), pp. 440, 442; Theodore Roosevelt to Hugo Munsterberg, June 3, 1901, *Letters,* 3: 86; Max Nordau, *Degeneration* (New York, 1895); Mills Lane, *Dear Mother: Letters from Georgia Soldiers in the Civil War* (Savannah, Ga., 1977), p. xxi; Sydney Barrington Elliot, *Aedoeology: A Treatise on Generative Life* (New York, 1892), pp. xiv, 8.

22. Louisa May Alcott, "The Rival Prima Donnas," in *Louisa May Alcott,* ed. E. D. Cheney (Boston, 1890), p. 63; *Chicago Daily Tribune,* Dec. 13, 1853, Mar. 6, Nov. 12, 13, 1857, May 24, 1858; Bourget, *Outre-Mer,* pp. 142, 157; Lakier, *A Russian Looks at America,* p. 25.

23. Frost, "The Death of the Hired Man," in *North of Boston* (London, 1914); Ellen K. Rothman, *Hands and Hearts: A History of Courtship in America* (New York, 1984), p. 114; Elihu Root, *Miscellaneous Addresses* (Cambridge, Mass., 1917), p. 63; Stevenson, *Amateur Emigrant,* 2: 65.

24. *Chicago Daily Tribune,* Oct. 26, 1857; Carl Degler, *At Odds: Women and the Family, 1776 to the Present* (New York, 1980); David M. Katzman, *Seven Days a Week: Women and Domestic Service in Industrializing America* (New York, 1976), pp. 241 ff.

25. Mary E. Wilkins Freeman, "Sister Liddy," in *Humble Romance and Other Stories* (New York, 1887), p. 93; Sarah Orne Jewett, "Along Shore," in *The Country of the Pointed Firs* (Boston, 1896); Robert Frost, *An Old Man's Winter Night* (New

York, 1916); David Hackett Fischer, *Growing Old in America* (New York, 1978), pp. 114–117.

26. *Chicago Daily Tribune,* June 24, 1854, Feb. 25, May 7, 1856, Feb. 19, Apr. 20, May 2, 22, 23, 1857; Theodor Griesinger, *Lebende Bilder aus Amerika* (Stuttgart, 1858), pp. 113 ff.; Newell G. Bringhurst, *Brigham Young* (Boston, 1986), pp. 163 ff.; Rothman, *Hands and Hearts,* pp. 246–248, 254.

27. Mary E. Wilkins Freeman, *A New England Nun* (New York, 1891); Emily Dickinson, *Letters,* ed. Thomas H. Johnson (Cambridge, 1958), 1: 93; Sigmund Spaeth, *Read 'Em and Weep* (New York, 1945), p. 26; Rothman, *Hands and Hearts,* pp. 249, 252; Jules Chametzky, *From the Ghetto: The Fiction of Abraham Cahan* (Amherst, 1977), p. 110.

28. David J. Rothman and Sheila M. Rothman, eds., *Women and Children First* (New York, 1987), pp. 149–152; M. S. Iseman, *Race Suicide* (New York, 1912), pp. 5–6.

29. Rothman, *Hands and Hearts,* pp. 282–284; Olivier Zunz, *Changing Face of Inequality* (Chicago, 1982), p. 74.

30. Eden and Cedar Paul, eds., *Population and Birth Control: A Symposium* (New York, 1917), pp. 163–167; William J. Robinson, *Birth Control, or, The Limitation of Offspring by Prevenception* (1917; New York, 1928), pp. 14–18; David Kennedy, *Birth Control in America: The Career of Margaret Sanger* (New Haven, Conn., 1971), pp. 108–126.

31. Mohr, *Cormany Diaries,* p. 131; Margaret Sanger, *An Autobiography* (New York, 1939), pp. 128; Margaret Sanger, *Woman and the New Race* (New York, 1920).

32. Spaeth, *Read 'Em and Weep,* pp. 205, 225; Rothman and Rothman, *Women and Children First,* pp. 1–4; Herman K. Platt, *Charles Perrin Smith* (New Brunswick, N.J., 1965).

33. Nancy Cott, *The Grounding of Modern Feminism* (New Haven, Conn., 1987).

34. Edward W. Howe, *Story of a Country Town* (1882; New York, 1907), pp. 228 ff., 237 ff.

35. Joe L. Dubbert, *A Man's Place: Masculinity in Transition* (Englewood Cliffs, N.J., 1979), pp. 80–95.

36. Freeman Hunt, *Worth and Wealth: A Collection of Maxims, Morals, and Miscellanies for Merchants and Men of Business* (New York, 1857), pp. 82 ff., 103 ff., 120, 503 ff.; William Dean Howells, *The Rise of Silas Lapham* (Boston, 1884); Abraham Cahan, *The Rise of David Levinsky* (New York, 1917); Robert Herrick, *The Memoirs of an American Citizen,* ed. Daniel Aaron (Cambridge, Mass., 1963); Frank Norris, *The Pit* (New York, 1903); Kenneth T. Jackson, *Crabgrass Frontier* (New York, 1985), pp. 121 ff.; Emily Stipps Watts, *The Businessman in American Literature* (Athens, Ga., 1982), pp. 55–59.

37. Alice Foote MacDougall, *The Autobiography of a Business-Woman* (Boston, 1928); William Carlos Williams, *Autobiography* (New York, 1951); Charles Franklin Thwing and Carrie Butler Thwing, *The Family: An Historical and Social Study* (Boston, 1887), p. 124.

38. Willa Cather, "The Sculptor's Funeral," *Collected Short Stories,* ed. Mildred R. Bennet, 3 vols. (Lincoln, Nebr., 1965), 2: 173–185; Sherwood Anderson, *Winesburg, Ohio* (New York, 1919); Ezra Pound, *Personae: The Collected Poems* (New York, 1926), p. 188.

39. *Chicago Daily Tribune,* Feb. 22, 1856, Apr. 1, 1859; Catherine E. Beecher and Harriet Beecher Stowe, *The American Woman's Home* (New York, 1970); Ruth Schwartz Cowan, *More Work for Mother: The Ironies of Household Technology from the Open Hearth to the Microwave* (New York, 1983); Susan Strasser, *Never Done: A History of American Housework* (New York, 1982); Barbara Miller Solomon, *In the Company of Educated Women* (New Haven, Conn., 1985); Paula Fass, *The Damned and the Beautiful: American Youth in the 1920s* (New York, 1977); Sheila

Rothman, *Woman's Proper Place* (New York, 1978); Margery W. Davies, *Woman's Place is at the Typewriter: Office Work and Office Workers, 1870–1930* (Philadelphia, 1982); Sara M. Evans, *Born for Liberty: A History of Women in America* (New York, 1989), pp. 175–196; Barbara M. Wertheimer, *We Were There* (New York, 1977), pp. 176–177, 227–232; Gerda Lerner, ed., *Black Women in America: A Documentary History* (New York, 1972).

40. Evans, *Born for Liberty,* p. 182; Cheney, *Louisa May Alcott,* pp. 63 ff., 82, 196 ff.
41. *Chicago Daily Tribune,* Mar. 9, 1857; Cheney, *Louisa May Alcott,* p. 269; Joe I. Dubbert, *A Man's Place,* pp. 100–101; Frank L. Mott, *A History of American Magazines, 1885–1905,* 5 vols. (Cambridge, Mass., 1938–68), 4: 325 ff.; Norman B. Crowell, *The Mind of Robert Browning* (Albuquerque, N.Mex., 1968), pp. 2, 3.
42. *Chicago Daily Tribune,* Jan. 21, 23, Feb. 27, 1856, Mar. 7, 1857, June 24, 1859; Thwing and Thwing, *Family,* p. 124; Frank Hagar, *The American Family* (New York, 1905), pp. 129–133; Arthur W. Calhoun, *Social History of the American Family* (New York, 1917), 1: 10–12; Christopher Lasch, *The New Radicalism in America, 1889–1963* (New York, 1965), pp. 39–46.
43. Robert Herrick, *The Common Lot* (New York, 1904); Robert Herrick, *The Memoirs of an American Citizen,* ed. Daniel Aaron (Cambridge, Mass., 1963), pp. xiv, xxiv; Louis J. Budd, *Robert Herrick* (New York, 1971), pp. 50–55; Mott, *History of American Magazines,* 4: 401 ff.
44. Spaeth, *Read 'Em and Weep,* pp. 127, 176; James H. Kyner, *End of Track* (Caldwell, Idaho, 1937), p. 92; Wall, *Carnegie,* pp. 398 ff.
45. Hasia A. Diner, *Erin's Daughters in America* (Baltimore, 1983), pp. 62–69; Evans, *Born for Liberty,* pp. 119–122, 151–152; Dorothy Sterling, ed., *We Are Your Sisters: Black Women in the Nineteenth Century* (New York, 1984), pp. 479–495; Jacqueline Jones, *Labor of Love, Labor of Sorrow* (New York, 1985); Leon Litwack, *Been in the Storm So Long: The Aftermath of Slavery* (New York, 1979), pp. 229–247; Paula Giddings, *When and Where I Enter: The Impact of Black Women on Race and Sex in America* (New York, 1984); Katzman, *Seven Days a Week,* pp. 184 ff.
46. James Schouler, *A Treatise on the Law of Domestic Relations* (Boston, 1889), pp. 3–11; Carl B. Swisher, *Roger B. Taney* (Hamden, Conn., 1961), p. 469.
47. Cheney, *Alcott,* pp. 25, 32; *Chicago Daily Tribune,* Sept. 4, 1858; Joel Myerson and Daniel Shedy, "The Sale of Louisa Alcott's Books," *Harvard Library Bulletin,* n.s. 1 (1990): 47 ff.; Spaeth, *Read 'Em and Weep,* p. 206; Jane Addams, *The Spirit of Youth* (New York, 1909), pp. 3–21; George G. Turner, "The Daughters of the Poor," *McClure's,* 34 (Nov. 1909): 45 ff.; Lauren A. Kattner, "Growing Up Female in New Braunfels," *Journal of American Ethnic History,* 9 (1990): 49 ff.; Norman Katkov, *The Fabulous Fanny* (New York, 1953).
48. Timothy J. Arthur, *Ten Nights in a Bar Room* (Cambridge, Mass., 1964), p. 42; Louisa May Alcott, *The Fatal Love Chase; or, A Modern Mephistopheles* (Boston, 1877); James O. Kaler, *Jenny Wren's Boarding House* (Boston, 1902); *Chicago Daily Tribune,* Dec. 12, 1853, May 6, 1857; Edward P. Roe, *Barriers Burned Away* (1872; New York, 1970); Donald L. Miller and Richard E. Sharpless, *The Kingdom of Coal* (Philadelphia, 1985), pp. 84 ff.
49. Stephen Crane, *The Red Badge of Courage* (New York, 1895); Miller and Sharpless, *Kingdom of Coal,* p. 44; William G. McLoughlin, *Billy Sunday Was His Real Name* (Chicago, 1955).
50. Hagar, *The American Family,* pp. 170–172.
51. *Chicago Daily Tribune,* Aug. 4, 1857; Mary Antin, *Promised Land,* ed. Oscar Handlin (Princeton, N.J., 1985), pp. 277 ff., 292 ff.; Sam B. Warner, *Streetcar Suburbs: The Process of Growth in Boston* (Cambridge, Mass., 1962).
52. Booth Tarkington, *Penrod* (Garden City, N.Y., 1914); George M. Beard, *American Nervousness* (New York, 1881).

53. *Chicago Daily Tribune,* Aug. 20, 1860; George H. Nash, *The Life of Herbert Hoover,* 2 vols. (New York, 1983); E. A. Ross, *Seventy Years of It* (New York, 1977), pp. 2 ff.
54. William Allen White, *Selected Letters,* ed. Walter Johnson (New York, 1947), p. 130.
55. Samuel M. Jones, *The New Right* (1899; Westport, Conn., 1975), p. 55; Lakier, *A Russian Looks at America,* p. 79; Francis and Theresa Pulszky, *White Red Black,* 3 vols. (London, 1853): 1: 77 ff., 234 ff., 2: 120 ff., 269, 3: 72–88.
56. Charles F. Lummis, *The Land of Poco Tiempo* (London, 1893); Ralph Adams Cram, *The Gothic Quest* (Garden City, N.Y., 1915); Walter Blair, *Mark Twain and Huck Finn* (Berkeley, Calif., 1960), pp. 21, 306 ff., 350 ff.
57. Norman B. Crowell, *The Convex Glass: The Mind of Robert Browning* (Albuquerque, N.Mex., 1968), p. 24.
58. David Noble, *The Progressive Mind* (Chicago, 1970), p. 77.
59. Fred C. Jaher, ed., *The Age of Industrialism: Essays in Social Structure and Cultural Values* (New York, 1968).
60. Thwing and Thwing, *Family,* p. 110.
61. Hagar, *American Family,* pp. 156–157, 167–171.
62. *Chicago Daily Tribune,* July 10, Nov. 4, 1858; Herman R. Lantz, *Marital Incompatibility and Social Change in Early America* (Beverly Hills, Calif., 1976), pp. 24 ff.; Thwing and Thwing, *Family,* p. 186.
63. Cott, *Grounding of Modern Feminism,* pp. 21, 23; Mott, *History of American Magazines,* 4: 358 ff.
64. Louisa S. McCord, "Enfranchisement of Women," *Southern Quarterly Review,* 5 (April, 1852): 322 ff.; Anne F. Scott, *The Southern Lady: From Pedestal to Politics, 1830–1930* (Chicago, 1970); Karen Blair, *The Clubwoman as Feminist: True Womanhood Redefined* (New York, 1980); William O'Neill, *Everyone Was Brave: The Rise and Fall of Feminism in America* (Chicago, 1969), pp. 3–106; Susan Porter Benson, *Counter Cultures: Saleswomen, Managers, and Customers in American Department Stores, 1890–1940* (Urbana, Ill., 1986).
65. Freeman, *New England Nun,* pp. 6, 9; Nancy A. Hewitt, *Women's Activism and Social Change: Rochester, New York, 1822–1872* (Ithaca, N.Y., 1984), pp. 177–258; Mary Elizabeth Massey, *Bonnett Brigades* (New York, 1966); Barbara Wertheimer, *We Were There: The Story of Working Women in America* (New York, 1977), pp. 249–261; Ruth Bordin, *Women and Temperance: The Quest for Power and Liberty, 1873–1900* (Philadelphia, 1980); Glenna Matthews, *Just a Housewife: The Rise and Fall of Domesticity in America* (New York, 1987), pp. 92–116.
66. Edward Bellamy, *Looking Backwards, 2000–1887* (New York, 1951); Dolores Hayden, *The Grand Domestic Revolution: A History of Feminist Designs for American Homes, Neighborhoods, and Cities* (Cambridge, 1981); David Handlin, *The American Home* (Boston, 1979); David M. Katzman, *Seven Days a Week: Women and Domestic Service in Industrializing America* (New York, 1973); Faye E. Dudden, *Serving Women: Household Service in Nineteenth-Century America* (Middletown, Conn., 1983); John Thomas, *Alternative America: Henry George, Edward Bellamy, Henry Demarest Lloyd, and the Adversary Tradition* (Cambridge, 1983), p. 255.
67. Sarah Orne Jewett, "Along Shore," *The Country of Pointed Firs* (Boston, 1896); Henry Wadsworth Longfellow, "The Cross of Snow" (1879) in *Poetical Works,* 6 vols. (Boston, 1886), 3: 220; Joseph P. Lovering, *S. Weir Mitchell* (New York, 1971), pp. 134–144; S. Weir Mitchell, *The Youth of Washington* (New York, 1904) and *Hugh Wynne* (New York, 1909); Charles Major, *When Knighthood Was in Flower* (Indianapolis, 1899); George B. McCutcheon, *Beverly of Graustark* (New York, 1904); Barton Levi St. Armand, "Your Prodigal," *New England Quarterly,* 61 (1988): 367 ff., 372.

68. Mohr, *Cormany Diaries,* pp. 549, 584.
69. Mohr, *Cormany Diaries,* pp. 571, 582.
70. Harold Seymour, *Baseball* (New York, 1960), p. 105; Perry R. Duis, *The Saloon: Public Drinking in Chicago and Boston* (Urbana, Ill., 1983), pp. 172–203.
71. Samuel Hopkins Adams, "The Great American Fraud," *Colliers,* 36 (Oct. 7, 1905): 14 ff.; Hearn, *American Miscellany,* 1: 169; James Harvey Young, *The Toadstool Millionaires* (Princeton, N.J., 1961); Sarah Stage, *Female Complaints: Lydia Pinkham and the Business of Women's Medicine* (New York, 1979); Lovering, *S. Weir Mitchell,* pp. 124–125; Gerald Grob, ed., *American Perceptions of Drug Addiction* (New York, 1981), pp. 9, 15; Wilbur F. Crafts et al., *Intoxicating Drinks and Drugs in All Lands and Times* (Washington, D.C., 1911), pp. 14–15, 240–243; David S. Musto, *The American Disease: Origins of Narcotic Control* (New York, 1987).
72. Louisa May Alcott, *Little Women* (Boston, 1880); J. G. Huneker, *The New Cosmopolis: Intimate New York* (New York, 1915), pp. 162 ff.; P. T. Barnum, *The Life of P. T. Barnum* (New York, 1855), pp. 339 ff.; William Sydney Porter [O. Henry], *Complete Works,* 2 vols. (Garden City, N.Y., 1953), 1: 7 ff.
73. Joyce C. Williams et al., eds. *Lizzie Borden: A Case Book of Family and Crime in the 1890s* (Bloomington, Ind., 1980); Ethan Mordden, *Movie Star* (New York, 1983), pp. 1–10; Porte, *Emerson's Journals,* pp. 418, 433.
74. Whitman, *Complete Poetical Works,* p. 225; Spaeth, *Read 'Em and Weep,* pp. 152, 161, 191; Theodore Dreiser, *Letters,* 3 vols. (Philadelphia, 1959), 1: 50 ff.; Paul R. Baker, *Stanny: The Gilded Life of Stanford White* (New York, 1989), pp. 273 ff.; John S. Monagan, *The Grand Panjandrum: Mellow Years of Justice Holmes* (Lanham, Md., 1988).
75. Spaeth, *Read 'Em and Weep,* pp. 238, 239; Spaeth, *Weep Some More,* p. 214.
76. James Marchant, *The Master Problem* (New York, 1979), pp. xiv–xv, 1–17, 20; Edwin R. A. Seligman, ed., *The Social Evil* (New York, 1912), pp. 2, 151.
77. Whitman, "Democratic Vistas," *Complete Prose Works,* p. 208.
78. *Chicago Daily Tribune,* Dec. 15, 1853.
79. Ty Cobb, *My Life in Baseball* (Garden City, N.Y., 1961); Seymour, *Baseball,* pp. 75 ff., 107 ff., 111, 115; Spaeth, *Read 'Em and Weep,* p. 140
80. Alice Crozier, *The Novels of Harriet Beecher Stowe* (New York, 1961), p. 51.

VI: GOODNESS

1. Theodore Dreiser, *The Financier* (New York, 1912), p. 40.
2. Ralph Waldo Emerson, "The Fortune of the Republic," in *Miscellanies* (Concord, Mass., 1904), pp. 541–542; Joel Porte, *Emerson in His Journals* (Cambridge, Mass., 1982), p. 527; Mary Eleanor Wilkins Freeman, "A Solitary," in *A New England Nun and Other Stories* (New York, 1903), p. 232; Henry Reed Burch and S. Howard Patterson, *Problems of American Democracy* (New York, 1922), pp. 2, 5.
3. Helen P. Trimpi, *Melville's Confidence Man* (Hamden, Conn., 1987), p. 250.
4. Samuel L. Clemens, *Mark Twain's Mysterious Stranger Manuscripts,* ed. William M. Gibson (Berkeley, Calif., 1969), pp. 11, 19; Walter Blair, *Mark Twain and Huck Finn* (Berkeley, Calif., 1960), pp. 135 ff.; Paul M. Zall, ed., *Mark Twain Laughing* (Knoxville, Tenn., 1985), p. 65; Sherwood Cummings, *Mark Twain and Science* (Baton Rouge, La., 1988).
5. Bruce Palmer, *Man over Money: The Southern Populist Critique of American Capitalism* (Chapel Hill, N.C., 1980), pp. 40–41; A. Lawrence Lowell, *Public Opinion and Popular Government* (New York, 1914), pp. 130–133.
6. *Mills* v. *Commonwealth* (Pa., 1850); *Commonwealth* v. *Rogers* (Bucks, 1854); Arthur

F. Bentley, *Process of Government,* ed. Peter H. Odegard (Cambridge, Mass., 1967), p. 276.

7. Thomas Speed Mosby, *Causes and Cures of Crime* (St. Louis, 1913), pp. 14–22; Lawrence M. Friedman and Robert V. Percival, *The Roots of Justice: Crime and Punishment in Alameda County, California, 1870–1910* (Chapel Hill, N.C., 1981), pp. 27–33.

8. Russell H. Conwell, *Acres of Diamonds* (New York, 1915), pp. 17–22; *Chicago Daily Tribune,* Feb. 20, 1856, Jan. 18, Dec. 2, 1857, Aug. 27, 1858, Mar. 31, 1859, Nov. 27, 1860; New York Association for Improving the Condition of the Poor, *Ninth Annual Report, 1852,* pp. 25–27; Jane Addams, *Twenty Years at Hull House* (New York, 1911), pp. 173 ff.; Olivier Zunz, *The Changing Face of Inequality* (Chicago, 1982), p. 272; Roger A. Bruns, *The Damndest Radical: The Life and Work of Ben Reitman* (Urbana, Ill., 1987), p. 39; Jacob A. Riis, *How the Other Half Lives* (New York, 1968); Stephen Crane, *Maggie, A Girl of the Streets* (Gainesville, Fla., 1966).

9. Edward T. Devine and Lilian Brandt, *American Social Work in the Twentieth Century* (New York, 1921), pp. 4–8; Josiah Flynt, *Tramping with Tramps* (New York, 1901).

10. John Duffy, *A History of Public Health in New York City, 1866–1966* (New York, 1974), p. 41; Bruns, *The Damndest Radical,* p. 43.

11. *Annual Report of the Salem School Committee,* Dec. 1882, p. 24; *Chicago Daily Tribune,* Apr. 27, 1853, Sept. 5, 1856, Mar. 14, 1857, Apr. 26, 1860; Charles F. Dole, *The Burden of Poverty* (New York, 1912), p. 9; Sigmund Spaeth, *Weep Some More, My Lady* (Garden City, N.Y., 1927), pp. 25, 40, 168, 250; Jacob A. Riis, *The Children of the Poor* (New York, 1892); Gerald W. Brace, *Days That Were* (New York, 1976), pp. 27 ff.

12. James Huneker, *New Cosmopolis* (New York, 1915), pp. 169 ff.

13. Sidney Lanier, *The Symphony* (New York, 1875); Samuel M. Jones, *The New Right* (New York, 1899), p. 15; *Chicago Daily Tribune,* Mar. 27, 1857.

14. Devine and Brandt, *American Social Work,* pp. 8–14; Robert M. Mennel, *Thorns and Thistles* (Hanover, N.H., 1973), p. 32 ff.; David Rothman, *Conscience and Convenience* (Boston, 1980).

15. E.g., *Chicago Daily Tribune,* Sept. 23, 1857, Mar. 31, 1859; Devine and Brandt, *American Social Work,* pp. 8–12.

16. *Chicago Daily Tribune,* Feb. 7, 1856, Jan. 25, Apr. 21, 23, Dec. 2, 1858, Mar. 2, 3, 4, Apr. 2, May 6, 9, Dec. 14, 1859; Mosby, *Causes and Cures of Crime,* pp. 23 ff.

17. *Chicago Daily Tribune,* May 6, 1858, Jan. 5, 1859; Carl Sandburg, *The American Songbag* (New York, 1927), p. 418; Mark Twain, *Roughing It* (New York, 1899); Marvin B. Scott and Stanford M. Lyman, "Accounts," *American Sociological Review,* 33 (1968): 46–62; Mosby, *Causes and Cures of Crime,* pp. 24–47, 222–233; Arthur and Lila Weinberg, *Clarence Darrow: A Sentimental Rebel* (New York, 1980); Richard Garett, *Famous Characters of the Wild West* (New York, 1971), pp. 128–156.

18. *Phelin* v. *Kenderdine* (Pennsylvania, 1853); *Chicago Daily Tribune,* Apr. 2, Oct. 6, 1858, Apr. 4, June 14, 1859; Sigmund Spaeth, *Read 'Em and Weep* (New York, 1945), pp. 259, 260; *The Great Scandal: History of the Famous Beecher-Tilton Case* (New York, 1874); Altima L. Waller, *Reverend Beecher and Mrs. Tilton* (Amherst, Mass., 1982); *The Veil Removed: H. W. Beecher's Trial and Acquittal Investigated: Love Demonstrated in Plain Dealing* (New York, 1874).

19. Spaeth, *Read 'Em,* pp. 124, 170, 210; Perry Duis, *The Saloon: Public Drinking in Chicago and Boston* (Urbana, Ill., 1983), pp. 262–273; Paul Boyer, *Urban Masses and Moral Order in America, 1820–1910* (Cambridge, 1978), pp. 162–219; Mark Thomas Connelly, *The Response to Prostitution in the Progressive Era* (Chapel Hill, N.C., 1980); see also below, chap 9.

20. F. M. Lehman, *The White Slave Hell; or, With Christ at Midnight in the Slums of Chicago* (Chicago, 1910).

21. *Chicago Daily Tribune,* May 7, 1856; Charles H. Parkhurst, *Our Fight with Tammany* (New York, 1895); and *My Forty Years in New York* (New York, 1923); Anthony Comstock, *Frauds Exposed; or, How the People Are Deceived and Robbed and Youth Corrupted* (Patterson, N.J., 1969); Heywood Broun and Margaret Leech, *Anthony Comstock, Roundsman of the Lord* (New York, 1927); Margaret Sanger, *The Woman Rebel,* 1, nos. 1–2 (Mar.–Oct., 1914); Theodore Dreiser, *Letters,* ed. Robert H. Elias, 2 vols. (Philadelphia, 1959), 1: 227.

22. *Chicago Daily Tribune,* Oct. 1, 1858; Allan Keller, *Scandalous Lady: The Life and Times of Madame Restell* (New York, 1981), pp. 126–187.

23. *Chicago Daily Tribune,* May 27, Sept. 3, Nov. 19, 1858; Duffy, *Public Health in New York City,* pp. 208 ff., 255; Keller, *Scandalous Lady,* pp. 177–186; Charles Rosenberg and Carroll Smith Rosenberg, eds., *Abortion in Nineteenth-Century America* (New York, 1974), pp. 27, 28, 35 ff.

24. *Chicago Daily Tribune,* Apr. 29, Aug. 28, Sept. 4, 1857; Apr. 27, 1858; Nelson Algren, *The Man with the Golden Arm* (Garden City, N.Y., 1949); Harold Seymour, *Baseball: The Golden Age* (New York, 1971), pp. 276 ff., 308; Helen Campbell, *Darkness and Daylight; or, Lights and Shadows of New York Life* (Hartford, Conn., 1892), pp. 639 ff.; Ernst Otto Hopp, *Transatlantisches Skizzenbuch* (Berlin, 1876), pp. 199 ff., 209 ff., 214, 227 ff.

25. *Chicago Daily Tribune,* Aug. 26, 27, 28, 1857; Mark Twain, *Roughing It* (New York, 1899); John M. Findlay, *People of Chance: Gambling in American Society from Jamestown to Las Vegas* (New York, 1986), pp. 98–110; Comstock, *Frauds Exposed,* pp. 132–145.

26. Walt Whitman, *Leaves of Grass,* 1872 preface (New York, 1902), verse 33; Jones, *New Right,* p. 5.

27. Roy E. Graham, *Ellen G. White, Co-Founder of the Seventh Day Adventist Church* (New York, 1986), pp. 13–39; James M. Penton, *Apocalypse Delayed: The Story of Jehovah's Witnesses* (Toronto, Canada, 1981), pp. 13–46.

28. Samuel Seabury III, *Moneygripe's Apprentice,* ed. Robert B. Mullin (New Haven, 1989), p. 23.

29. *Chicago Daily Tribune,* Jan. 30, 1857; Walt Whitman, *Complete Prose Works* (Boston, 1888), pp. 473, 477; Mrs. D. P. Wells et al., *Conservation of National Ideals* (New York, 1911), pp. 102, 107, 110, 112, 122; Charles Howard Hopkins, *The Rise of the Social Gospel in American Protestantism, 1865–1915* (New Haven, Conn., 1940); Donald K. Gorrell, *The Age of Responsibility: The Social Gospel in the Progressive Era, 1900–1920* (Macon, Ga., 1988), pp. 11–88; Henry F. May, *Protestant Churches and Industrial America* (New York, 1949); Jacob Henry Dorn, *Washington Gladden: Prophet of the Social Gospel* (Ohio State, 1967), pp. 203–235.

30. C. M. Sheldon, *In His Steps* (New York, 1889), pp. 7–12; Mary Blewett, *Men, Women, and Work* (Urbana, Ill., 1988), pp. 179 ff.

31. Washington Gladden, *The Labor Question* (New York, 1911), pp. 86 ff.; Robert Cross, *The Emergence of Liberal Catholicism in America* (Cambridge, Mass., 1958); Edward H. McKinley, *Marching to Glory: The History of the Salvation Army in the United States* (New York, 1980), pp. 1–31; Jane Addams et al., *Philanthropy and Social Progress* (Boston, 1893), pp. 157–158, 183–186, 203–204; Francis Broderick, *Right Rev. New Dealer, John A. Ryan* (New York, 1963).

32. Louis H. Sullivan, *Kindergarten Chats* (New York, 1947), pp. 138 ff.; Roger W. Lotchin, *San Francisco, 1846–1856* (New York, 1974), pp. 250 ff.

33. *Chicago Daily Tribune,* Feb. 5, 1857; Joan Jacobs Brumberg, *Mission for Life* (New

York, 1980), p. 15; Charles Stelzle, *A Son of the Bowery* (New York, 1926); Ronald C. White, Jr., and C. Howard Hopkins, *The Social Gospel: Religion and Reform in Changing America* (Philadelphia, 1976), pp. 70–79.

34. *Chicago Daily Tribune,* Apr. 19, 1858; Josiah Strong, *Our Country* (New York, 1885), pp. 172–178; Brumberg, *Mission for Life,* pp. 158 ff.; James F. Findlay, *Dwight L. Moody* (Chicago, 1969); Jane Addams, *Philanthropy and Social Progress,* pp. 157–158, 183–186, 203–204; Abby Ann Judson, *The Bridge between Two Worlds* (Minneapolis, 1894); William G. McLoughlin, Jr., *Billy Sunday Was His Real Name* (Chicago, 1955); J. C. Pollock, *Moody: A Biographical Portrait* (New York, 1963), pp. 180–191; Gamaliel Bradford, *D. L. Moody: A Worker in Souls* (Garden City, N.Y., 1928), p. 89.

35. Horace Bushnell, *Building Eras in Religion* (New York, 1881), pp. 292, 329; Jules Chametzky, "From the Ghetto," *The Fiction of Abraham Cahan* (Amherst, Mass., 1977), pp. 5 ff., 108 ff.

36. Frederick Law Olmstead, *Public Parks* (Brookline, Mass., 1902), p. 75; George L. Schepler, "The Reformist Vision of Frederick L. Olmstead," *New England Quarterly,* 62 (1989): 387; Roy Rosenzweig, *Eight Hours for What We Will* (Cambridge, 1983), pp. 127–152; Roderick Nash, *Wilderness and the American Mind* (New Haven, Conn., 1982), pp. 106–107, 155–158; Norman Foerster, *Nature in American Literature* (New York, 1923), pp. 264–305; Larry L. Fabian, *Andrew Carnegie's Peace Endowment: The Tycoon, the President and Their Bargain of 1910* (Washington, D.C., 1985).

37. Huneker, *New Cosmopolis,* p. 15; Chametzky, *From the Ghetto,* p. 94; Zunz, *Changing Face of Inequality,* p. 268; Ross Terrill, *R. H. Tawney and His Times* (Cambridge, Mass., 1973), pp. 28 ff.; Roy Lubove, *The Professional Altruist: The Emergence of Social Work as a Career* (Cambridge, Mass., 1965); John C. Farrell, *Beloved Lady: A History of Jane Addams's Ideas on Reform and Peace* (Baltimore, Md., 1967).

38. *Chicago Daily Tribune,* July 13, 1858; Timothy S. Arthur, *Ten Nights in a Bar-Room,* ed. Donald Koch (Cambridge, Mass., 1964), p. 231; Oscar and Lilian Handlin, *Liberty in Expansion* (New York, 1989), p. 345; Andrew Sinclair, *Prohibition* (Boston, 1962); Rosenzweig, *Eight Hours for What We Will,* pp. 93–126; *Chicago Daily Tribune,* July 4, 1859; Roger Lane, *Policing the City* (Cambridge, Mass., 1967); Theodor Griesinger, *Lebende Bilder aus Amerika* (Stuttgart, 1858), pp. 26 ff., 65 ff., 113 ff., 204 ff.; Duis, *The Saloon,* pp. 114–171.

39. *Chicago Daily Tribune,* Jan. 26, 1859; James McPherson, *Battle Cry of Freedom* (New York, 1988), p. 589; Isaac J. Quillen, *Industrial City: A History of Gary, Indiana* (New York, 1986), p. 220.

40. Andrew Johnson, *Papers,* ed. LeRoy P. Graf, et al., 8 vols. (Knoxville, Tenn., 1967–89), 2: 266 ff.; *Chicago Daily Tribune,* Feb. 2, 1858, Jan. 21, 1860; Arthur, *Ten Nights in a Bar-Room,* passim.

41. *Chicago Daily Tribune,* Apr. 3, 1857, Feb. 2, 1859; Arthur, *Ten Nights in a Bar-Room,* pp. 138, 160; Paul Kleppner, *Third Electoral System* (Chapel Hill, N.C., 1979), pp. 240, 254; Jack S. Blocker, *Retreat from Reform: The Prohibition Movement in the United States, 1890–1913* (Westport, Conn., 1976); James H. Timberlake, *Prohibition and the Progressive Movement, 1900–1920* (Cambridge, Mass., 1963), pp. 172–181; McPherson, *Battle Cry of Freedom,* p. 134.

42. Spaeth, *Read 'Em,* pp. 57, 143, 198, 212.

43. Spaeth, *Weep Some More,* pp. 121 ff., 148 ff.

44. André Bazin, *What Is Cinema?* (Berkeley, Calif., 1967), p. 152; David F. Musto, *The American Disease: Origins of Narcotic Control* (New York, 1987), pp. 1–68; Duis, *The Saloon,* pp. 298–303; Thomas Szasz, *Ceremonial Chemistry: The Ritual Persecution of Drugs, Addicts, and Pushers* (Holmes Beach, Fl., 1985), pp. 3–68; Charles J. Marland, *Chaplin and American Culture* (Princeton, N.J., 1989), pp. 60–62.

45. The Channing Home (Boston), *Report No. 1* (Boston, 1869), p. 5; William H. Mahoney, "Benevolent Hospitals in Metropolitan Boston," American Statistical Association, *Quarterly Publications,* 13 (1913): 419 ff.; Leonard J. Arrington, *Great Basin Kingdom* (Cambridge, Mass., 1958), pp. 251 ff.; Charlotte Baum et al., *The Jewish Woman in America* (New York, 1975); June Sochen, *Consecrate Every Day* (Albany, N.Y., 1981).

46. *Chicago Daily Tribune,* Oct. 3, 1853, Feb. 21, 1856, Jan. 19, 1857; Handlins, *Liberty in Expansion,* pp. 192 ff., 240 ff.; Joan J. Brumberg, *Mission for Life* (New York, 1980), pp. 81 ff.; Glenna Matthews, *"Just a Housewife"* (New York, 1987), pp. 66 ff.; Nina Baym, "Onward Christian Women," *New England Quarterly,* 63 (1990): 249 ff.; Jeanne Boydston et al., eds., *The Limits of Sisterhood: The Beecher Sisters on Women's Rights and Woman's Sphere* (Chapel Hill, N.C., 1988), pp. 1–8; William Leach, *True Love and Perfect Union* (New York, 1980), p. 10.

47. *Chicago Daily Tribune,* Feb. 2, Mar. 22, 1856, Aug. 20, 1857, Jan. 23, 1858; Matthews, *"Just a Housewife,"* pp. 15 ff., 35 ff.; Mary H. Blewett, *Men, Women, and Work: Class, Gender, and Protest in the New England Shoe Industry, 1780–1910* (Urbana, Ill., 1988), pp. 120 ff., 159, 223; Whitman, *Poetical Works,* p. 130; Catharine E. Beecher, *Woman's Profession as Mother and Educator, with Views in Opposition to Woman Suffrage* (Philadelphia, 1872), pp. 180–181; Kathryn Kish Sklar, *Catharine Beecher: A Study in American Domesticity* (New Haven, Conn., 1973); Mary Kelly, ed., *Woman's Being, Woman's Place: Female Identity and Vocation in American History* (Boston, 1979), pp. 201–215.

48. Blewett, *Men, Women, and Work,* pp. 167, 191, 207, 212; Norbert C. Soldon, ed., *The World of Women's Trade Unionism* (Westport, Conn., 1985), pp. 57–72.

49. Wright Morris, *God's Country and My People* (New York, 1968); Sandra L. Myers, *Women and the Frontier Experience, 1800–1915* (Albuquerque, N.Mex., 1982), p. 147.

50. *Chicago Daily Tribune,* Mar. 30, 1858; Dexter C. Bloomer, *Life and Writings of Amelia Bloomer* (New York, 1975), pp. vi–vii; Roger A. Bruns, *The Damndest Radical* (Urbana, Ill., 1987), p. 75; Sheila Rothman, *Woman's Place,* p. 112.

51. *Chicago Daily Tribune,* Oct. 8, 10, 1853, Mar. 7, 1856; Bloomer, *Life and Writings of Amelia Bloomer,* pp. 70–71; Blanche Glassman Hersh, *The Slavery of Sex: Feminist-Abolitionists in America* (Urbana, Ill., 1978); Gerda Lerner, *The Grimké Sisters of South Carolina, Pioneers for Women's Rights and Abolition* (New York, 1967); Ellen DuBois, *Feminism and Suffrage: The Emergence of an Independent Movement in America, 1848–1869* (Ithaca, N.Y., 1981); Kelly, *Woman's Being, Woman's Place,* pp. 233–245; Alice Stone Blackwell, *Lucy Stone: Pioneer of Woman's Rights* (Boston, 1930), pp. 171–178.

52. Carry A. Nation, *The Use and the Need of the Life of Carry A. Nation* (Topeka, Kans., 1909); Herbert Asbury, *Carry Nation* (New York, 1929), pp. 45–47, 65; Ruth Barnes Moynihan, *Rebel for Rights: Abigail Scott Duniway* (New Haven, Conn., 1983), pp. 114–115; Ruth Bordin, *Woman and Temperance* (Philadelphia, 1981); Barbara Leslie Epstein, *The Politics of Domesticity: Women, Evangelism, and Temperance in Nineteenth-Century America* (Middletown, Conn., 1981); Kelly, *Woman's Being, Woman's Place,* pp. 283, 285.

53. Lois W. Banner, *Elizabeth Cady Stanton* (Boston, 1980); *Chicago Daily Tribune,* Jan. 19, 1857, July 4, 1859; Matthews, *"Just a Housewife,"* pp. 74 ff.; Walt Whitman, "Chants Democratic," in *Complete Poetical Works,* p. 100 (verse II/10); Walt Whitman, *Complete Prose Works,* pp. 227, 228; Sara M. Evans, *Born for Liberty: A History of Women in America,* pp. 152–156, 167, 170; Karen Blair, *The Clubwoman as Feminist: True Womanhood Redefined, 1868–1914* (New York, 1980); Aileen Kraditor, *Ideas of the Woman Suffrage Movement, 1890–1920* (Garden City, N.Y., 1971); Cathleen Barry, *Susan B. Anthony: A Biography of a Singular Feminist* (New

York, 1988), pp. 275–335; Robert Booth Fowler, *Carrie Catt: Feminist Politician* (Boston, 1986), pp. 137–154; Steven M. Buechler, *The Transformation of the Woman Suffrage Movement* (New Brunswick, N.J., 1983), p. 8; Cott, *Grounding of Modern Feminism*, p. 28.

54. *Chicago Daily Tribune*, Mar. 30, Oct. 16, 1858; Barbara M. Solomon, *In the Company of Educated Women* (New Haven, 1985).

55. Elizabeth Griffith, *In Her Own Right: The Life of Elizabeth Cady Stanton* (New York, 1984).

56. *Chicago Daily Tribune*, Apr. 26, 27, May 12, 1853, Oct. 22, 1857; New York State Department of Labor, *Third Annual Report of the Commissioner* (Albany, N.Y., 1903), part 3, p. xxxi; John Joseph Buckowczyk, *Smokestacks and Steeples* (Harvard Doctoral diss., 1980); Ida M. Tarbell, *New Ideals in Business: An Account of Their Practice and Their Effects upon Men and Profits* (New York, 1916), pp. 86–89; Donald L. Miller and Richard E. Sharpless, *The Kingdom of Coal* (Philadelphia, 1985), pp. 106 ff.

57. Oscar Handlin, *Al Smith and His America* (Boston, 1987), pp. 53 ff.

58. Albert Fein, "Centennial New York, 1876," in *New York,* ed. Milton M. Klein (Port Washington, N.Y., 1976), p. 90; Susan Lehrer, *Origins of Protective Labor Legislation for Women, 1905–1925* (Albany, N.Y., 1987), pp. 3–50, 198; Benjamin R. Twiss, *Lawyers and the Constitution: How Laissez-Faire Came to the Supreme Court* (Princeton, N.J., 1942), p. 128; David M. Katzman, *Seven Days a Week* (New York, 1976), pp. 96 ff.

59. Tarbell, *New Ideals in Business,* pp. 134, 163–192.

60. Francis and Theresa Pulszky, *White, Red, Black,* 3 vols. (London, 1853), 1: 77–83, 85–86, 234 ff., 2: 120 ff., 128, 269, 3: 72, 81, 88; Arthur Holitscher, *Amerika* (Berlin, 1912), pp. 251 ff., 274 ff., 287 ff., 375 ff.; *Chicago Daily Tribune,* Dec. 27, 1855, Mar. 13, 1857; Ben B. Lindsey and Wainwright Evans, *The Revolt of Modern Youth* (Seattle, Wash. 1973), pp. 14–19, 362; Bruns, *Damndest Radical,* p. 46.

61. Oliver H. Kelley, *Origins and Progress of the Order of the Patrons of Husbandry in the United States: A History from 1866 to 1873* (Philadelphia, 1875), pp. vii, 22–26, 125–131; Jonathan Periam, *The Groundswell: A History of the Origins, Aims, and Progress of the Farmers' Movement* (Cincinnati, 1874), pp. 286–289.

62. Rosenzweig, *Eight Hours for What We Will,* pp. 30 ff.; Henry George, *Progress and Poverty* (New York, 1881), pp. 455 ff., 465 ff., 475 ff., 483, 486 ff.; Morton Keller, *Affairs of State: Public Life in Nineteenth-Century America* (Cambridge, Mass., 1977), p. 182.

63. W. A. Peffer, *The Farmer's Side* (New York, 1891), pp. 42, 56, 58 ff., 121; Allan G. Bogue, *Money at Interest: Farm Mortgages on the Middle Border* (New York, 1955); Douglas C. North, *Growth and Welfare in the American Past* (Englewood Cliffs, N.J., 1966), p. 286; Robert Kleppner, *The Economic Bases for Agrarian Protest Movements in the United States, 1870–1900* (New York, 1978), pp. 7–55; Stuart Bruchey, *Enterprise: The Dynamic Economy of a Free People* (Cambridge, Mass., 1990), pp. 301–303. By contrast, see John D. Hicks, *The Populist Revolt* (Minneapolis, 1931).

64. *Chicago Daily Tribune,* Jan. 17, Aug. 10, 1857; Herbert Quick, *One Man's Life* (Indianapolis, 1925), pp. 207–209, 212–217; Wright Morris, *God's Country and My People* (New York, 1968); Carl Sandburg, *The American Songbag* (New York, 1927), pp. 122, 281.

65. Francis B. Simkins, *The Tillman Movement in South Carolina* (Durham, N.C., 1926); A. M. Arnett, *The Populist Movement in Georgia* (New York, 1922); A. D. Kirwan, *Revolt of the Rednecks* (Lexington, Ky., 1951); also, James C. Malin, *A Concern about Humanity* (Lawrence, Kans., 1964); Bruce Palmer, *Man over Money: The Southern*

Populist Critique of American Capitalism (Chapel Hill, N.C., 1980), p. 15; Michael E. McGerr, *The Decline of Popular Politics: The American North, 1865–1928* (New York, 1986), p. 93.

66. Jonathan B. Harrison, *Certain Dangerous Tendencies in American Life* (Boston, 1880), pp. 27 ff.

67. Palmer, *Man over Money,* pp. 105–108.

68. Peffer, *Farmer's Side,* pp. 121–123; Kleppner, *Evolution,* pp. 196, 291; Morton Keller, *Affairs of State,* pp. 385, 572–573. By contrast, see the romantic vision of Lawrence Goodwyn, *Democratic Promise: The Populist Movement in America* (New York, 1976), pp. 146–149, 168–169.

69. Sandburg, *American Songbag,* p. 283; Goodwyn, *Democratic Promise,* pp. 553–554; McGerr, *Decline of Popular Politics,* pp. 211–219; Oscar Handlin, *Truth in History* (Cambridge, Mass., 1979), pp. 346 ff.

70. Francis B. Simkins, *Pitchfork Ben Tillman* (Baton Rouge, La., 1944), pp. 315–316; Scott G. McNall, *The Road to Rebellion: Class Formation and Kansas Populism* (Chicago, 1988), pp. 172–173, 214–215.

71. Josiah Strong, *Our Country* (New York, 1885), pp. 171 ff.; Bruce Palmer, *Men over Money,* pp. 86, 88–89, 125–126; McNall, *Road to Rebellion,* pp. 214–215; Finley Peter Dunne, *Mr. Dooley's Philosophy* (New York, 1900), p. 255.

72. *Harper's Weekly,* 27 (Mar. 17, 1883): 161; Carl Sandburg, *American Songbag,* p. 10; Theodore Soloutos, *Farmer Movements in the South, 1865–1933* (Berkeley, Calif., 1960); C. Vann Woodward, *Origins of the New South* (Baton Rouge, La., 1951). See also the uncritical version of Norman Pollack, *The Just Polity: Populism, Law, and Human Welfare* (Urbana, Ill., 1987), pp. 210 ff.

73. Oscar Handlin, "American Views of the Jew," American Jewish Historical Society, *Publications,* 40 (June 1951): 323 ff.; Oscar Handlin, "Reconsidering the Populists," *Agricultural History,* 39 (April 1965): 10 ff.; Pollack, *Just Polity,* pp. 209, 233–243.

74. J. M. H. Frederick, comp., *National Party Platforms* (Akron, Ohio, 1892), pp. 82 ff.; Fred E. Hayes, *Third Party Movements since the Civil War* (Iowa City, 1916), p. 263; Pollack, *Just Polity,* pp. 62, 336; McGerr, *Decline of Popular Politics,* pp. 216–217.

75. Milton Friedman and Anna J. Schwartz, *A Monetary History of the United States, 1867–1960* (Princeton, N.J., 1963).

76. Richard P. Bland, "Present Status of the Silver Question," *North American Review,* 165 (Oct. 1897): 475; Palmer, *Men over Money,* pp. 111–112; Robert W. Cherny, *Populism, Progressivism, and the Transformation of Nebraska Politics, 1885–1915* (Lincoln, Neb., 1981), p. 71; Barton C. Shaw, *The Wool Hat Boys: Georgia's Populist Party* (Baton Rouge, La., 1984), pp. 71, 77, 92–96.

77. William Jennings Bryan, *Speeches,* 2 vols. (New York, 1909), 1: 248–249; "Government by Hysteria," *Century Magazine,* 102 (Sept. 1896); Worth Robert Miller, *Oklahoma Populism: A History of the People's Party in the Oklahoma Territory* (Norman, Okla., 1987), pp. 98–121; Donna A. Barnes, *Farmers in Rebellion: The Rise and Fall of the Southern Farmers Alliance and People's Party in Texas* (Austin, Tex., 1984), pp. 136–159; Thomas Beer, *Hanna* (New York, 1929), p. 155.

78. Paolo E. Coletta, *William Jennings Bryan* (Lincoln, Neb., 1964); Shaw, *Wool Hat Boys,* pp. 142–161; Cherny, *Populism, Progressivism, and the Transformation of Nebraska Politics,* pp. 74–77; Barnes, *Farmers in Rebellion,* pp. 164–188.

79. C. Vann Woodward, *Tom Watson, Agrarian Rebel* (Savannah, Ga., 1973); McNall, *Road to Rebellion,* pp. 291–301; Paul W. Glad, *McKinley, Bryan and the People* (Philadelphia, 1964).

80. Marie Louise Berneri, *Journey through Utopia* (Boston, 1950), p. 318; Emma Goldman, *Living My Life* (Salt Lake City, Utah, 1982), p. 154; W. D. Heywood, *Bill Heywood's Book* (New York, 1929), p. 177; Sandburg, *American Songbag,* p. 478;

The Power-Holding Class (Newport, R.I., 1900), p. vi; Elizabeth Gurley Flynn, *Memories of the Industrial Workers of the World* (New York, 1977), pp. 2, 10; Melvyn Dubofsky, *We Shall Be All: A History of the Industrial Workers of the World* (Urbana, Ill., 1988), p. 154; John Graham Brooks, *American Syndicalism: The I.W.W.* (New York, 1913), pp. 1–12, 168–178, 242–243.

81. J. Marion Sims, *The Story of My Life* (New York, 1884), p. 268; Dreiser, *Letters*, 1: 209; Terrill, *Tawney*, pp. 190 ff.; David Rothman, *Conscience and Convenience: The Asylum and Its Alternatives* (Boston, 1980), pp. 47–48.

82. *Chicago Daily Tribune*, Feb. 15, 1853; Rothman, *Conscience and Convenience*, pp. 143, 209.

83. Marlene Springer and Hashell Springer, eds., *Plains Woman: The Diary of Martha Farnsworth, 1882–1922* (Bloomington, Ind., 1986), p. 209; Keller, *Affairs of State*, pp. 409–413; Leach, *True Love and Perfect Union*, p. 35; Miller and Sharpless, *Kingdom of Coal*, pp. 113 ff.

84. *Chicago Daily Tribune*, Apr. 7, 1858; John Duffy, *A History of Public Health in New York City 1866–1966* (New York, 1974), p. 643; Handlins, *Liberty in Expansion*, pp. 227 ff.; Zunz, *Changing Face of Inequality*, pp. 113 ff.; Leach, *True Love and Perfect Union*, p. 36.

85. *Chicago Daily Tribune*, Aug. 18, 1859; Albert Fein, "Centennial New York, 1876," in *New York*, ed. M. M. Klein (Port Washington, N.Y., 1976), p. 102; Sims, *Story of My Life*, pp. 246 ff.; C. L. Sonnichsen, *Tucson: The Life and Times of an American City* (Norman, Okla., 1982), pp. 110–111, 141; John Bernard McGloin, *San Francisco: The Story of a City* (San Rafael, Calif., 1978), pp. 218–220; Anita Shafer Goodstein, *Nashville, 1780–1869: From Frontier to City* (Gainesville, Fla., 1989), pp. 186–189.

86. *Chicago Daily Tribune*, Aug. 28, 1858; Duffy, *Public Health*, pp. 5 ff., 17 ff.; Edith Abbott, *The Tenements of Chicago, 1908–1935* (Chicago, 1936), pp. 34–61; *Housing and Town Planning* (Philadelphia, 1914), pp. 140–141; Zunz, *Changing Face of Inequality*, p. 95.

87. *Chicago Daily Tribune*, Jan. 17, 31, 1857; *Boston Pilot*, Jan. 28, 1888; Mitchell Okun, *Fair Play in the Marketplace: The First Battle for Pure Food and Drugs* (Dekalb, Ill., 1986), pp. 8–31; Lawrence M. Friedman, *A History of American Law* (New York, 1973), pp. 232–235, 384–385; Jacob A. Riis, *The Peril and the Preservation of the Home* (Philadelphia, 1903), pp. 24–34; *Housing and Town Planning*, pp. 8–16; Roy Lubove, *The Progressives and the Slums* (Pittsburgh, 1962); George L. Schepler, "The Reformist Vision of Frederick Law Olmstead," *New England Quarterly*, 62 (1989): 387 ff.

88. William G. Sumner, "Conquest of the United States by Spain" (1898), *War and Other Essays* (New Haven, 1911), pp. 303 ff.; Ellsworth R. Fuhrman, *The Sociology of Knowledge in America, 1883–1915* (Charlottesville, Va., 1980), pp. 50–51; Harrison, *Certain Dangerous Tendencies*, pp. 2–22.

89. New York City Board of Health, *Annual Report*, 1915, p. 25; Duffy, *Public Health*, pp. 143 ff., 148 ff., 238, 268 ff.; Stuart Galishoff, *Safeguarding the Public Health: Newark* (Westport, Conn., 1975), pp. 31 ff.; Charles E. Rosenberg, ed., *Origins of Public Health in America: Selected Essays, 1820–1855* (New York, 1972), pp. 5, 25, 28, 37, 39; Upton Sinclair, *The Jungle* (Pasadena, Calif., 1920), pp. 113–114.

90. Kenneth M. Roemer, *The Obsolete Necessity: America in Utopian Writings, 1888–1900* (Kent, Ohio, 1976); Elizabeth Hansot, *Perfection and Progress: Two Modes of Utopian Thought* (Cambridge, Mass., 1974), pp. 169–192; King C. Gillette, *The Human Drift* (1894); Kenneth M. Roemer, ed., *Delmar* (New York, 1976), pp. iii–xx; John F. Kasson, *Civilizing the Machine: Technology and Republican Values in America, 1776–1900* (New York, 1976), pp. 225–230.

91. Harry Barnard, *Eagle Forgotten* (New York, 1938).

92. Samuel M. Jones, *The New Right: A Plea for Fair Play through a More Just Social Order* (New York, 1899), pp. 397, 401; John Chamberlain, *Farewell to Reform* (New York, 1932), pp. 57 ff.
93. Robert P. Parsons, *Trail to Light* (New York, 1943).
94. Blair, *Mark Twain and Huck Finn,* pp. 309 ff., 337; Keller, *Affairs of State,* p. 412.
95. Mary Foote Henderson, *The Aristocracy of Health* (New York, 1906), pp. 1–14; Herbert Wescott Fisher, *Making Life Worth While: A Book on Health, and More* (New York, 1910), pp. 41, 51; Luther H. Gulick, *The Efficient Life* (New York, 1907), pp. 1–19.
96. Pearl C. Solomon, *Dickens and Melville in Their Time* (New York, 1975), p. 4.

VII: REVERIES OF UNSHACKLED MINDS

1. Samuel L. Clemens, *Mark Twain's Mysterious Stranger Manuscripts,* ed. William M. Gibson (Berkeley, Calif., 1969), p. 135.
2. Robert V. Bruce, *The Launching of American Science, 1846–1876* (New York, 1987); *Massachusetts Telephone Company* (South Framingham, Mass., 1881), pp. 1–2; James H. Chapin, *The Creation and the Early Developments of Society* (New York, 1880), pp. 145–146; *The Telephone in America* (New York, 1936), p. 8; Neil Harris, "Utopian Fiction and Its Discontents," Richard L. Bushman et al., eds., *Uprooted Americans* (Boston, 1979), p. 220.
3. Daisy Shortcut and Arry O'Pagus, *One Hundred Years a Republic: Our Show* (Philadelphia, 1876), pp. 9–82; *Railroad Tourists Guide to the Centennial Exhibition* (Cincinnati, 1876), pp. 1–6, 11–17; *Chautauqua: The Famous Summer Town on Chautauqua Lake, New York* (New York, 1898), pp. 1–2; Joel Porte, *Emerson in His Journals* (Cambridge, Mass., 1982), p. 553.
4. George Santayana, *Character and Opinion in the United States* (New York, 1934), p. 163; Howard M. Feinstein, *Becoming William James* (Ithaca, N.Y., 1984); William James, *Pragmatism* (New York, 1907), pp. 45 ff.; Bruce Kuklick, *The Rise of American Philosophy* (New Haven, Conn., 1977).
5. Joseph F. Wall, *Andrew Carnegie* (New York, 1970), p. 388; Robert Chambers, *Vestiges of the Natural History of Creation, with a Sequel* (New York, 1868), pp. 199–200; Benjamin N. Martin, "The Recent Scientific Philosophy of Society," *Journal of Christian Philosophy,* 2 (April 1883): 269; A. J. F. Behrends, "Reason and Revelation," *The Journal of Christian Philosophy* 3 (April 1884), p. 304; Charles B. Warring, "The Agreement of Science with Genesis," *Journal of Christian Philosophy,* 3 (Jan. 1884): 177; John Fiske, "Agassiz and Darwinism," *Popular Science Monthly,* 3 (1873): 692 ff.; Thomas F. Glick, ed., *The Comparative Reception of Darwinism* (Austin, Tex., 1972), pp. 168–183; Edward Lurie, *Louis Agassiz: A Life in Science* (Chicago, 1960), pp. 295–297; James Turner, *Without God, Without Creed* (Baltimore, 1985).
6. John Dewey, *Intelligence in the Modern World* (New York, 1939), pp. 391, 951, 954; David W. Noble, *The Paradox of Progressive Thought* (Minneapolis, 1958), pp. 174–198.
7. John Dewey, *The Middle Works,* ed. Jo Ann Boylston, 15 vols. (Carbondale, Ill., 1976–83): 11, passim; Oscar Handlin, *John Dewey's Challenge to Education* (New York, 1959), passim.
8. Arthur F. Bentley, *Process of Government,* ed. Peter H. Odegard (Cambridge, Mass., 1967), p. 276; Edward A. Ross, *Seventy Years of It* (New York, 1936), pp. 106, 113; A. Lawrence Lowell, *Public Opinion and Popular Government* (New York, 1914), pp. vii ff.
9. Alfred H. Stone, *Studies in the American Race Problem* (New York, 1908), p. 241;

Lewis H. Morgan, *Ancient Society* (New York, 1877), pp. 551–552; Mary Jo Deegan, *Jane Addams and the Men of the Chicago School* (New Brunswick, N.J., 1988), p. 248; Ellsworth R. Fuhrman, *The Sociology of Knowledge in America* (Charlottesville, Va., 1980), pp. 75–83, 93; Madison Grant, *The Passing of the Great Race*, rev. ed. (New York, 1918), pp. 86–92; E. A. Ross, *Seventy Years of It*, p. 93; Lawrence A. Cremin, *American Education: The Metropolitan Experience* (New York, 1988), pp. 233 ff.

10. William Graham Sumner, "The Absurd Effort to Make the World Over," *Forum*, 17 (1894): 98–102; William Graham Sumner, "Reply to a Socialist," *Collier's Weekly* (October 29, 1904): 123 ff.; William Graham Sumner, *Folkways* (1906; New York, 1940); Fuhrman, *Sociology of Knowledge*, pp. 64–65.

11. Félix Klein, *Au Pays de la Vie Intense* (Paris, 1905), pp. 191–211, 331–336; Lester Frank Ward, *Dynamic Sociology*, 2 vols. (New York, 1883); Lester Frank Ward, *The Psychic Factors of Civilization* (1893; Boston, 1906); Samuel Chugarman, *Lester Ward, American Aristotle* (Durham, N.C., 1939); Richard T. Ely, "Report of the Organization of the American Economic Association," *Publications of the American Economic Association*, 1 (1886): 15–17; Daniel Fox, *The Discovery of Abundance* (Ithaca, N.Y., 1967), pp. 145–146; James R. Leiby, *Carroll Wright and Labor Reform* (Cambridge, Mass., 1960); Oscar Handlin, *Truth in History* (Cambridge, Mass., 1979), pp. 201 ff.

12. *Chicago Daily Tribune*, May 6, 1858; Henry Nash Smith, *Mark Twain: The Development of a Writer* (Cambridge, Mass., 1962); David W. Noble, *The Paradox of Progressive Thought*, pp. 196–198; George H. Nash, *The Life of Herbert Hoover*, 2 vols. (New York, 1983); Richard Hofstadter, *Anti-Intellectualism in American Life* (New York, 1963), pp. 206, 207; Sam Bass Warner, *The Province of Reason* (Cambridge, Mass., 1984).

13. Edward Bellamy, "The Boy Orator," in *Looking Backward*, ed. John L. Thomas (Cambridge, Mass., 1967), pp. 7 ff.; Herman Melville, *The Confidence Man* (New York, 1963), p. 51; Leiby, *Carroll Wright*, passim.

14. Washington Gladden, *Plain Thoughts on the Art of Living* (Boston, 1868); Charles M. Sheldon, *In His Steps* (New York, 1935); Walter Rauschenbusch, *Christianity and the Social Crisis* (New York, 1907); Walter Rauschenbusch, *Christianizing the Social Order* (Boston, 1912); Henry F. May, *Protestant Churches and Industrial America* (New York, 1949); David W. Noble, *The Paradox of Progressive Thought*, pp. 232, 238; see also above, chap. 6.

15. Charles Stelzle, *A Son of the Bowery* (New York, 1926), pp. 49, 66, 96, 109, 190; John A. Ryan, "The church and the Working Man," *Catholic World*, 89 (1909): 776 ff.; Francis L. Broderick, *Right Rev. New Dealer* (New York, 1963), pp. 48–76.

16. Louis Filler, *Crusaders for American Liberalism* (Yellow Springs, Ohio, 1939), pp. 197–199.

17. Jurgen Herbst, *The German Historical School in American Scholarship* (Ithaca, N.Y., 1965); Edward A. Ross, *Seventy Years of It*, pp. 26 ff.

18. John S. White, *Recent Examination Papers for Admission to Harvard, Yale, Princeton, Sheffield Scientific School, and Columbia School of Mines* (Boston, 1888), pp. iii–iv, 310–319; Nelson Antrim Crawford, *A Man of Learning: A Half Century of Educational Services as Exemplified by Arthur Patrick Redfield* (Boston, 1928), pp. 34, 84, 85; F. C. Howe, *Wisconsin: An Experiment in Democracy* (New York, 1912), p. 189; Norman Foerster, *The American State University: Its Relation to Democracy* (Chapel Hill, N.C., 1937), pp. 24–25, 68, 84–85; Grant Showerman, *With the Professor* (New York, 1910).

19. Lightner Witmer, *The Nearing Case* (New York, 1915); Ross, *Seventy Years of It*, pp. 64 ff.; C. W. Eliot, "Wherein Public Education Has Failed," *Forum*, 14 (1892): 411, 412; Cremin, *American Education*, pp. 379 ff.

20. Lawrence A. Cremin, *The Transformation of the School: Progressivism in American Education, 1876–1956* (New York, 1969); Foerster, *American State University*, p. 25.
21. Maurice Denzil Hodgen, "A High School in Perspective: The Characteristics of High-School Life on Staten Island, 1881–1926" (Teacher's College Doctoral diss., 1959), pp. 67, 147; Crawford, *A Man of Learning*, p. 27; George F. Counts, *Selective Character of American Secondary Education* (Chicago, 1920), passim.
22. Frederick Rudolph, *The American College and University: A History* (New York, 1962).
23. George Ticknor to Edward Everett, July 14, 1851, in *Life, Letters and Journals, George Ticknor*, 2 vols. (Boston, 1876), 1: 300–302; Sigmund Diamond, *The Reputation of the American Businessman* (Cambridge, Mass., 1955); Cremin, *American Education*, pp. 445 ff.
24. Wall, *Andrew Carnegie*, pp. 828 ff.; George S. Bobinsky, *The Carnegie Libraries: Their History and Impact* (Chicago, 1969), p. 3; Burton J. Hendrick, *The Life of Andrew Carnegie* (Garden City, N.Y., 1932), 2 vols., 2: 146, 147; Andrew Carnegie, *Autobiography* (Boston, 1920), p. 48; Washington Gladden, "Tainted Money," *Outlook*, 52 (Nov. 30, 1895): 886.
25. Carl R. Dolmetsch, *The Smart Set* (New York, 1960); Ross, *Seventy Years of It*, pp. 101 ff.
26. Ivy Lee, *Human Nature and Railroads* (Philadelphia, 1915), p. 49; Ray E. Hiebert, *Courtier to the Crowd* (Ames, Iowa, 1966); Ralph M. Hower, *The History of an Advertising Agency: N. W. Ayer and Son* (Cambridge, Mass., 1939); *The Ayer Idea in Advertising* (Philadelphia, 1912), pp. 10–12, 21–33; Henry Foster Adams, *Advertising and Its Mental Laws* (New York, 1916), pp. 1–17, 317–319; Clifford Kirkpatrick, *Intelligence and Immigration* (Baltimore, 1926), pp. 7 ff., 16 ff.; Bellamy, *Looking Backward*, p. 34; Lee W. Huebner, "The Discovery of Propaganda" (Harvard Doctoral diss., 1968); Robert A. Nye, *The Origins of Crowd Psychology* (London, 1975).
27. Thomas Nixon Carver, *Essays in Social Justice* (Cambridge, 1915), pp. 376–383; C. B. Galbreath, *Initiative and Referendum* (Columbus, Ohio, 1911), pp. 56–58; William Bennett Munro, ed., *The Initiative, Referendum, and Recall* (New York, 1912), pp. 52–60, 69–91, 126–134; Thomas E. Cronin, *Direct Democracy: The Politics of Initiative, Referendum, and Recall* (Cambridge, Mass., 1989), pp. 125–133.
28. Lincoln Steffens, "The Shame of Minneapolis," *McClure's*, 20 (January 1903): 227–239; William Howard Taft, *Popular Government: Its Essence, Its Permanence, and Its Perils* (New Haven, Conn., 1913), p. 83; George F. Mowry, *California Progressives* (Berkeley, Calif., 1951).
29. Grant McConnell, *Private Power and American Democracy* (New York, 1966), pp. 30–50; Theodore J. Lowi, *The End of Liberalism: Ideology, Policy, and the Crisis of Public Authority* (New York, 1969), pp. 3 ff.; Robert D. Marcus, *Grand Old Party: Political Structure in the Gilded Age, 1880–1896* (New York, 1971), pp. 251–265; Richard L. McCormick, *From Realignment to Reform* (Ithaca, N.Y., 1981), pp. 270–272.
30. Stephen Crane, "The Open Boat," in *Complete Short Stories*, ed. Thomas A. Gullison (Garden City, N.Y., 1963), p. 353; Bellamy, *Looking Backward*, pp. 178, 193.
31. Henry George, *Progress and Poverty* (New York, 1881), pp. 3 ff., 254 ff., 265 ff., 295, 489 ff.
32. George Perkins Marsh, *Man and Nature* (1864; rev. ed., New York, 1885), pp. 33 ff.; Charles T. Morrissey, *Vermont* (New York, 1981), p. 185; Roderick Nash, *Wilderness and the American Mind* (New Haven, Conn., 1967); Theodore Roosevelt, *Governor's Conference, Proceedings of the Conference of Governors in the White House, Washington, D.C., May 13–15, 1908* (Washington, D.C., 1909), p. 10.
33. Ellen Churchill Semple, *American History and Its Geographic Conditions* (Boston,

1903), pp. 434–435; Frederick Jackson Turner, *The Frontier in American History* (New York, 1920), pp. 293 ff.; Samuel Haber, *Efficiency and Uplift: Scientific Management in the Progressive Era, 1890–1920* (Chicago, 1964), pp. 42–49; Samuel P. Hayes, *Conservation and the Gospel of Efficiency* (Cambridge, Mass., 1959); James Mitchell Clarke, *The Life and Adventures of John Muir* (San Diego, Calif., 1980), p. 292.

34. Mary Blewett, *Men, Women, and Work* (Urbana, Ill., 1988), p. 249; Guy Benveniste, *The Politics of Expertise* (Berkeley, Calif., 1973), pp. 23–24, 48–49; Lester F. Ward, *Psychic Factors in Civilization* (Boston, 1897), pp. 323 ff.; Edward A. Ross, *Social Control: A Survey of the Foundations of Order* (New York, 1912), pp. 4–5, 395; Ross, *Seventy Years of It,* p. 100; Susan Lehrer, *Origins of Protective Labor Legislation for Women, 1905–1925* (Albany, N.Y., 1987). pp. 20, 54–55.

35. Edward D. Page, *Trade Morals: Their Relation to the Science of Society* (New Haven, Conn., 1914), pp. 213–274; Gerd Korman, *Industrialization, Immigrants, and Americanizers* (Madison, Wis., 1967), pp. 110 ff.; Jeanne McHugh, *Alexander Holley and the Makers of Steel* (Baltimore, Md., 1980), pp. 244–258; Josiah Quincy, *American Review of Reviews,* 19 (May 1899): 515.

36. Arthur H. Cole, *The American Wool Manufacture,* 2 vols. (Cambridge, Mass., 1926), 2: 231 ff.

37. Lakier, *A Russian Looks at America,* pp. 19, 22; Jefferson Williamson, *The American Hotel* (New York, 1975), pp. 38–72; Peter Conn, *The Divided Mind* (Cambridge, 1983), p. 40.

38. Charles Francis Adams, *Notes on Railroad Accidents* (New York, 1879), pp. 241, 270–271; Julius Grodinsky, *Iowa Pool* (Chicago, 1950); B. M. Ratcliffe, "Bureaucracy and Early French Railroads," *Journal of European Economic History,* 18 (1989): 331 ff.

39. Warner, *Province of Reason,* pp. 52 ff.; Irving S. Olds, *Judge Elbert H. Gary* (New York, 1947); Ida M. Tarbell, *The Life of Elbert H. Gary: The Story of Steel* (New York, 1925); Alfred D. Chandler, Jr., *Scale and Scope: The Dynamics of Industrial Capitalism* (Cambridge, Mass., 1990).

40. Burton J. Hendrick, *The Age of Big Business* (New Haven, 1921), pp. 171–187; Carol Gelderman, *Henry Ford: The Wayward Capitalist* (New York, 1981), pp. 1–15.

41. Allan Nevins, *Ford,* 3 vols. (New York, 1954–63), 1: 74 ff.; Wall, *Andrew Carnegie,* p. 834.

42. Louis D. Brandeis, *Business—A Profession* (Boston, 1914), pp. liii, 11–12.

43. Wall, *Andrew Carnegie,* pp. 747 ff.

44. Bellamy, *Looking Backward,* p. 97; Lee Benson, *Merchants, Farmers, and Railroads* (Cambridge, Mass., 1955).

45. Louis D. Brandeis, *Other People's Money* (1913; repr. New York, 1932), pp. 203–206; Louis D. Brandeis, *The Curse of Bigness* (New York, 1935); Herbert Croly, *The Promise of American Life* (New York, 1909); Eric Goldman, *Rendezvous with Destiny* (New York, 1952); Joseph Dorfman, *Thorstein Veblen and His America* (New York, 1947); Noble, *Paradox of Progressive Thought,* pp. 209–211.

46. Edward Bellamy, "An Echo of Antietam," *Century Magazine* (July 1889); Edward Bellamy, *The Blindman's World* (Boston, 1898); Edward Bellamy, *The Duke of Stockbridge* (Cambridge, Mass., 1962); Bellamy, *Looking Backward,* pp. 11, 37; Warner, *Province of Reason.*

47. David J. Rothman, *Conscience and Convenience,* pp. 53–54, 65; Ellen Fitzpatrick, *Endless Crusade: Women Social Scientists and Progressive Reform* (New York, 1990), pp. 74–76.

48. Robert Coin Chapin, *The Standard of Living among Workingmen's Families in New York City* (New York, 1909), pp. 249–250; *Annals of the American Academy of*

Political and Social Science, Supplement, September 1910; The Work of the National Consumer's League during the Year Ending March 1, 1910 (Philadelphia, 1910); Fitzpatrick, *Endless Crusade,* pp. 174–175.

49. Edward E. Hale, *Sybaris* (Boston, 1869), pp. 123, 127 ff.; H. G. Wells, *The Future in America* (New York, 1906), pp. 212–213; Fitzpatrick, *Endless Crusade,* pp. 192–193; Jane Addams, "Why the Ward Boss Rules," *Outlook,* 58 (April, 1898): 879–882; William B. Whiteside, *The Boston Young Men's Christian Association* (New York, 1951); William H. Tolman, *Social Engineering: A Record of Things Done by American Industrialists Employing Upwards of One and One Half Million of People* (New York, 1909), pp. 1–47.

50. Lincoln Steffens, *The Shame of the Cities* (New York, 1904), pp. 2–6; Lincoln Steffens, *The Struggle for Self-Government* (New York, 1906), pp. v–xxiii; Isabelle K. Savell, *Politics in the Gilded Age in New York State and Rockland County* (New York, 1984), pp. 9–21; Richard L. McCormick, *From Realignment to Reform,* pp. 50–53.

51. Delos F. Wilcox, *Great Cities in America* (New York, 1910), pp. 2–14, 402–416; Jackson, *Crab Grass Frontier,* pp. 168 ff.; David B. Tyack, *The One Best System* (Cambridge, Mass., 1974); William A. Bullough, *Cities and Schools in the Gilded Age* (Port Washington, N.Y., 1974); Selwyn K. Troen, *The Public and the Schools* (Columbia, Mo., 1975); Kleppner, *The Third Electoral System,* pp. 198 ff., 225 ff.; Rothman, *Conscience and Convenience,* p. 235; Edward J. Ward, *The Social Center* (New York, 1913), pp. 1–6.

52. Clinton R. Woodruff, ed., *A New Municipal Program* (New York, 1919), pp. 10–11.

53. Croly, *Promise of American Life,* pp. 213 ff.; Morton Keller, *Regulating a New Economy* (Cambridge, Mass., 1990), pp. 171 ff.

54. Steffens, *Struggle for Self-Government;* see also above, chap. 2.

55. G. Wallace Chessman, *Governor Roosevelt: The Albany Apprenticeship* (Cambridge, Mass., 1965); John Blum, *Joe Tumulty and the Wilson Era* (Boston, 1951); F. C. Howe, *Wisconsin: An Experiment in Democracy* (New York, 1912), pp. 46, 50, 184, 190.

56. *Chicago Daily Tribune,* May 3, 1853; *The Independent,* 81 (Jan. 14, 1915): 4, 5; Paul Kens, *Judicial Power and Reform Politics: The Anatomy of Lochner v. New York* (Lawrence, Kans., 1990); McCormick, *From Realignment to Reform,* pp. 251–254; Bentley, *Process of Government;* A. Lawrence Lowell, *Public Opinion and Popular Government* (New York, 1914).

57. Nathaniel Wright Stephenson, *Nelson W. Aldrich: A Leader in American Politics* (New York, 1930), pp. 404–425; David Black, *The King of Fifth Avenue: The Fortunes of August Belmont* (New York, 1981), pp. 309, 711.

58. Morton Keller, *Affairs of State,* pp. 436–437.

59. Gregory Mason, "College Men in Practical Politics," *Outlook,* 99 (1911): 85 ff.; Theodore Roosevelt, "American Ideals," in *American Ideals and Other Essays* (New York, 1900), pp. 25–45; David Francis Sadler, "Theodore Roosevelt: A Symbol to Americans" (University of Minnesota Doctoral diss., 1954), pp. 150–157, 162, 165; Chessman, *Governor Theodore Roosevelt;* Stephen F. Whitman, "Ballad of Teddy's Terrors," in *Spanish American War Songs,* ed. Sidney A. Witherbee (Detroit, 1898), pp. 947–948; Burton J. Hendrick, "The Battle Against the Sherman Law," *McClure's Magazine,* 31 (October 1908): 670–671; Upton Sinclair, *The Industrial Republic: A Study of the America of Ten Years Hence* (New York, 1907), pp. 192–195; Morton Keller, ed., *Theodore Roosevelt: A Profile* (New York, 1967), pp. 113, 135, 140, 143; David M. Chalmers, *Neither Socialism nor Monopoly: Theodore Roosevelt and the Decision to Regulate the Railroads* (Philadelphia, 1976), pp. 1–32.

60. Keller, *Regulating a New Economy,* pp. 115 ff.; Robert H. Wiebe, *Businessmen and Reform* (Cambridge, Mass., 1962), pp. 43 ff., 157 ff.

61. Wiebe, *Businessmen and Reform*, pp. 85 ff.; Keller, *Regulating a New Economy*, pp. 20 ff.; see below, chap. 8.

62. Gifford Pinchot, *Breaking New Ground* (New York, 1947); William Howard Taft, *Four Aspects of Civic Duty* (New York, 1906), pp. 8–12, 22–26; Walter Johnson, *Gifford Pinchot, Forester Politician* (New York, 1979), pp. 118–126; Nash, *Wilderness and the American Mind,* p. 358.

63. *Standard Oil* v. *United States,* 221 U.S. 59 ff. (1911); *Statutes at Large,* 26 (1888–91): 209 ff.; Taft, *Four Aspects of Civic Duty,* pp. 12–22, 111; Francis E. Leupp, "President Taft's Own Views," *Outlook* 99 (1911): 811 ff.; Henry Pringle, *Life and Times of William Howard Taft* (New York, 1939); Kenneth W. Heckler, *Insurgency* (New York, 1940).

64. Bellamy, *Looking Backward,* pp. 186 ff.; Elihu Root, *The Citizen's Part in Government* (New Haven, 1907), pp. 7–10; James Bryce, *Promoting Good Citizenship* (Boston, 1909); J. G. De Roulhac Hamilton and Edgar W. Knight, *The Making of Citizens* (Chicago, 1922), pp. 1–12.

65. Theodore Roosevelt, "The Trusts, the People, and the Square Deal," *Outlook,* 99 (1911): 653; John A. Garrity, *Right-Hand Man: The Life of George W. Perkins* (New York, 1960); Charles Forcey, *Crossroads of Liberalism* (New York, 1961).

66. Herbert Croly, *Progressive Democracy* (New York, 1914), pp. 15, 238–239.

67. Theodore Roosevelt, *Works,* 20 vols. (New York, 1926), 17: 254 ff.

68. *Social Democratic Vest Pocket Manual, 1912 Fall Campaign* (Milwaukee, Wis., 1912), pp. 10–11, 13; Emma Goldman, *Living My Life* (Salt Lake City, 1982), p. 221.

69. Croly, *Progressive Democracy,* pp. 16–17; Wiebe, *Businessmen and Reform,* pp. 127 ff.

70. Ward, *Psychic Factors in Civilization,* pp. 323 ff.; Lester F. Ward, *Glimpses of the Cosmos,* 6 vols. (New York, 1918), 6: 62; Croly, *Promise of American Life,* pp. 213–214.

71. Bernard M. Baruch, *American Industry in the War* (New York, 1941), pp. 4 ff.; Alton Ketchum, *Uncle Sam: The Man and the Legend* (New York, 1959), pp. 103–104.

72. F. Marion Crawford, *An American Politician* (New York, 1884), p. 349; Witherbee, *Spanish-American War Songs,* pp. 552–553; David Jayne Hill, *The People's Government* (New York, 1915), pp. 146–149, 162–163; Arthur Twining Hadley, *The Relations between Freedom and Responsibility in the Evolution of Democratic Government* (New Haven, Conn., 1903), pp. 26–27, 30–31, 42–43. See also McCormick, *From Realignment to Reform,* pp. 251–270; Richard M. Abrams, *Conservatism in a Progressive Era: Massachusetts Politics, 1900–1912* (Cambridge, Mass., 1964); Robert H. Wiebe, *The Search for Order, 1877–1920* (New York, 1967); David P. Thelen, *The New Citizenship: Origins of Progressivism in Wisconsin, 1885–1900* (Columbia, Mo., 1972); Paul Kleppner, "From Ethnoreligious Conflict to Social Harmony: Coalitional and Party Transformations in the 1890s," in *Emerging Coalitions in American Politics,* ed. Seymour Martin Lipset (San Francisco, 1978); Samuel P. Hayes, *The Response to Industrialism, 1885–1914* (Chicago, 1957).

VIII: ON LINE, IN STEP

1. Abraham Cahan, *Scribner's,* 26 (Dec. 1899); Jules Chametzky, *From the Ghetto: The Fiction of Abraham Cahan* (Amherst, Mass., 1977); p. 96; John Leng, *America in 1876: Pencillings during a Tour* (Dundee, Scotland, 1877), pp. 260–262; George R. Davis, *The World's Columbian Exposition: Chicago 1893* (Boston, 1893), pp. 12–13; Wayne Andrews, *The Vanderbilt Legend: The Story of the Vanderbilt Family, 1794–1940* (New York, 1941), p. 263.

2. Davis, *World's Columbian Exposition,* pp. 49–51, 443–455; *Final Report of Executive*

Committee of Awards, World's Columbian Commission (Washington, 1895), pp. 59–60; John Brisben Walker, *A World's Fair* (New York, 1893), pp. 520–522, 578–582, 602–605; H. B. Wandell, *Wandell's Annual Louisiana Purchase Exposition: In a Nutshell, the Story of a Great City* (St. Louis, 1904), pp. 20, 91, 111; Samuel W. Pennypacker, *Address upon Pennsylvania Day, August 20, 1904* (Harrisburg, Pa., 1904).

3. William L. Howarth, *Thoreau in the Mountains* (New York, 1982), pp. 160, 161; James McCague, *Moguls and Iron Men: The Story of the First Transcontinental Railroad* (New York, 1964), p. 41.

4. McCague, *Moguls and Iron Men,* pp. 30–34, 293–294, 328–333; F. E. Shearer, ed., *The Pacific Tourist: An Illustrated Guide* (New York, 1879), pp. 5–8; W. F. Rae, *Westward by Rail: The New Route to the Far East* (New York, 1871); Samuel Bowles, *The Pacific Railroad: Open, How to Go, What to See* (Boston, 1869); Richard C. Overton, *Burlington Route: A History of the Burlington Lines* (New York, 1965), pp. 39–175.

5. John Leng, *America in 1876,* pp. 311–313; Carl W. Condit, *American Building* (Chicago, 1968), pp. 93 ff.

6. Oscar O. Winther, *Transportation Frontier* (New York, 1964), pp. 67, 147 ff.; also Robert W. Fogel, *Railroads and American Economic Growth: Essays in Econometric History* (Baltimore, 1964), pp. 111–249.

7. Frank Norris, *The Octopus,* ed. Kenneth S. Lynn (Boston, 1958); Don Graham, ed., *Critical Essays on Frank Norris* (Boston, 1980), pp. 28–42, 138–151; Donald Pizer, ed., *The Literary Criticism of Frank Norris* (Austin, Tex., 1964), pp. 87–98.

8. Hamilton J. Eckenrode and Pocahontas Wight Edmunds, *E. H. Harriman: The Little Giant of Wall Street* (New York, 1981), pp. 93–100.

9. Edward C. Kirkland, *Industry Comes of Age* (Chicago, 1967); Edward C. Kirkland, *Men, Cities, and Transportation,* 2 vols. (Cambridge, Mass., 1948); Eugene V. Smalley, *History of the Northern Pacific Railroad* (New York, 1975), pp. 381–383.

10. Lee Benson, *Merchants, Farmers, and Railroads: Railroad Regulation and New York Politics, 1859–1887* (Cambridge, Mass., 1955), pp. 80–115.

11. John Brisben Walker, *Transportation Old and New* (n.p., n.d., originally published in *The Cosmopolitan,* 1893), pp. 584–590; Winther, *Transportation Frontier,* pp. 84, 85.

12. Martin Melosi, *Thomas A. Edison and the Modernization of America* (Boston, 1990); Daniel Calhoun, *The Intelligence of a People* (Princeton, N.J., 1973), pp. 298–304; David B. Steinman and Sarah Ruth Watson, *Bridges and their Builders,* rev. ed. (New York, 1957); Alan Trachtenberg, *Brooklyn Bridge: Fact and Symbol* (Chicago, 1979), pp. 57–64, 114–124; Clay McShane, *Technology and Reform: Street Railways and the Growth of Milwaukee, 1887–1900* (Madison, Wis., 1974), pp. 2–17, 19; Sam Bass Warner, Jr., *Streetcar Suburbs* (New York, 1968).

13. Stephen Kern, *The Culture of Time and Space, 1880–1918* (Cambridge, Mass., 1983), pp. 10–19; Sandford Fleming, *Time Reckoning for the Twentieth Century* (Washington, D.C., 1889); Harrison J. Cowan, *Time and Its Measurements* (Cleveland, 1958), p. 45; Henry Olerich, *A Cityless and Countryless World* (1893; reprint, New York, 1971), p. 173; George M. Beard, *American Nervousness* (New York, 1881), p. 103.

14. Oscar Handlin, *John Dewey's Challenge to Education* (New York, 1959), pp. 27 ff.; David B. Tyack, *The One Best System* (Cambridge, Mass., 1974), pp. 28, 126 ff.; Joseph F. Wall, *Andrew Carnegie* (New York, 1970), pp. 873 ff., 878 ff.

15. Herbert A. Miller, *The School and the Immigrant* (Cleveland, 1916), p. 92; Gerd Korman, *Industrialization, Immigrants, and Americanizers* (Madison, Wis., 1967), pp. 144, 145; Marvin Lazerson, *Origins of the Urban School* (Cambridge, Mass., 1971).

16. James H. Kyner, *End of Track,* ed. Hawthorne Daniel (Caldwell, Idaho, 1937), pp. 150 ff.; Condit, *American Building,* pp. 114 ff.

17. *Chicago Daily Tribune,* Jan. 17, 1857; Werner Sombart, *Warum gibt es in den Vereinigten Staaten keinen Sozialismus?* (Tübingen, 1906).
18. James Brough, *The Woolworths* (New York, 1982), pp. 4–7, 65–66; Lloyd Wendt and Herman Kogan, *Give the Lady What She Wants* (Chicago, 1952), pp. 85–89.
19. Gunther Barth, *City People: The Rise of Modern City Culture in Nineteenth-Century America* (Oxford, 1980), pp. 110–147; Alan Trachtenberg, *The Incorporation of America: Culture and Society in the Gilded Age* (New York, 1982), pp. 130–135; Susan Porter Benson, *Counter Cultures: Saleswomen, Managers, and Customers in American Department Stores* (Urbana, Ill., 1986), pp. 12–23; Wendt and Kogan, *Give the Lady What She Wants,* pp. 92–93; Ralph M. Hower, *History of Macy's of New York, 1858–1919* (Cambridge, Mass., 1943), pp. 118–121.
20. International Correspondence School, *The Advertiser's Handbook: A Book of Reference Dealing with Plans, Copy* (Scranton, Pa., 1910); Benson, *Counter Cultures,* pp. 17–18; Stuart Bruchey, *Enterprise: The Dynamic Economy of a Free People* (Cambridge, Mass., 1990), pp. 335–337.
21. Herman Melville, *The Confidence-Man* (New York, 1963), pp. 153 ff.; John K. Winkler, *Five and Ten: The Fabulous Life of F. W. Woolworth* (Freeport, N.Y., 1970), pp. 183–200.
22. Samuel L. Clemens, *Mark Twain's Mysterious Stranger Manuscripts,* ed. William M. Gibson (Berkeley, Calif., 1969), p. 154.
23. Kyner, *End of Track,* p. 170; K. Ross Toole, *The Rape of the Great Plains: Northwest America, Cattle and Coal* (Boston, 1976), pp. 28, 72; Charles M. Russell, *Trains Plowed Under* (Garden City, N.Y., 1927); Ernest S. Osgood, *The Day of the Cattleman* (Chicago, 1929).
24. Edwin R. A. Seligman, *Essays in Taxation* (New York, 1895), pp. 1–22; Charles Bullock, *A Classified Property Tax* (Columbus, Ohio, 1909), p. 95; Charles H. Ingersoll, *Boards of Trade* vs. *Boards of Assessors* (n.p., n.d., published originally in *The American City,* November 1915); Hartley Withers, *Our Money and the State* (New York, 1917), p. 73.
25. *Chicago Daily Tribune,* Nov. 13, 1857; Toole, *Rape of the Great Plains,* pp. 28, 159–160; Laurent Hodges, *Environmental Pollution: A Survey Emphasizing Physical and Chemical Principles* (New York, 1973), pp. 73–78.
26. Henry Foster Adams, *Advertising and Its Mental Laws* (New York, 1916), pp. 127–147; International Correspondence School, *The Advertiser's Handbook,* pp. 179, 241–242.
27. Bureau of the Census, *Historical Statistics of the United States* (Washington, 1949), pp. 179–187; Bruchey, *Enterprise,* pp. 310–311; Mira Wilkins, *The History of Foreign Investment in the United States* (Cambridge, Mass., 1989), pp. 141–189.
28. Hugh McCulloch, *Addresses, Speeches, Lectures, and Letters* (Washington, D.C., 1891), pp. 239 ff.
29. See above, chap. 6.
30. Morton Keller, *The Life Insurance Enterprise, 1885–1910: A Study in the Limits of Corporate Power* (Cambridge, Mass., 1963); Louis I. Dublin, *A Family of Thirty Million: The Story of the Metropolitan Life Insurance Company* (New York, 1943), pp. 25–76.
31. Andrew Sinclair, *Corsair: The Life of J. Pierpont Morgan* (Boston, 1981), p. 140.
32. Henrietta M. Larson, *Jay Cooke, Private Banker* (Cambridge, Mass., 1936), pp. 254–279; Herbert L. Satterlee, *J. Pierpont Morgan: An Intimate Portrait* (New York, 1939), p. 182.
33. *Historical Statistics of the United States,* pp. 263–267.
34. Robert Sobel, *Inside Wall Street* (New York, 1977), pp. 22–38.
35. Larson, *Jay Cooke,* pp. 152–175; George Francis Train, *Young America in Wall Street* (London, 1857), pp. v–vi.

36. Sobel, *Inside Wall Street,* pp. 38–39; James D. McCabe, Jr., *Light and Shadows of New York Life* (1872; New York, 1970), p. 280; see also above, chap. 5.

37. Robert Sobel, *Panic on Wall Street: A Classic History of America's Financial Disasters* (New York, 1988), pp. 154–156, 164–166; Madeleine B. Stern, ed., *The Victoria Woodhull Reader* (Weston, Mass., 1974), pp. 1–7; Andrews, *Vanderbilt Legend,* pp. 147–149; Emanie L. Sachs, *The Terrible Siren* (New York, 1928).

38. Eugene V. Debs, *Liberty* (Terre Haute, Ind., 1895), pp. 16–18.

39. William Dean Howells, *The Hazard of New Fortunes* (New York, 1890) treats the speculative mentality. See also William S. Porter, *Cabbages and Kings* (Garden City, 1904), *The Four Million* (New York, 1908), and *The Gentle Grafter* (New York, 1909); Thomas W. Lawson, *Frenzied Finance* (New York, 1905); Henry Clews, *Fifty Years in Wall Street* (New York, 1973), pp. 117–126, 436–446; John Tebbell, *The Marshall Fields* (New York, 1947), pp. 113–122.

40. *Chicago Daily Tribune,* May 4, 1858; *New York Times,* Jan. 24, 1879; *New York Herald,* Sept. 24, 1869; Theodore Dreiser, *The Financier* (New York, 1912); Kyner, *End of Track,* pp. 246 ff.; David A. Wells, *Recent Economic Changes* (New York, 1889), pp. 5 ff.; Sobel, *Panic on Wall Street,* pp. 184–196; Larson, *Jay Cooke,* pp. 408–410.

41. W. M. Thayer, *Marvels of the New West* (Norwich, Conn., 1887), pp. 628 ff.; 630 ff., 640 ff.; 710 ff.; W. A. Peffer, *The Farmer's Side* (New York, 1891), pp. 42, 56 ff., 121 ff.; Reynold M. Wik, *Steam Power on the American Farm* (Philadelphia, 1953); William H. Carwardine, *The Pullman Strike* (Chicago, 1894), pp. 23–25; Mark Schorer, *Sinclair Lewis* (New York, 1961); Edgar W. Howe, *Story of a Country Town* (Atchison, Kans., 1883); Herbert Quick, *One Man's Life* (Indianapolis, 1925), pp. 207 ff., 212 ff.; Hamlin Garland, *Main-Traveled Roads* (1891; New York, 1922), pp. 75 ff., 79 ff.; Clemens, *Mysterious Stranger,* p. 164.

42. *Nation,* Sept. 25, 1873; Wells, *Recent Economic Changes,* pp. 79 ff.; Mark Twain and Charles Dudley Warner, *The Gilded Age: A Tale of Today* (New York, 1901).

43. Thorstein Veblen, *The Theory of the Leisure Class* (New York, 1965); Roy Rosenzweig, *Eight Hours for What We Will* (Cambridge, Mass., 1983), p. 13; Burton Hersh, *The Mellon Family* (New York, 1978), pp. 107–108; Olivier Zunz, *Making America Corporate* (Chicago, 1990), p. 100.

44. Rachel S. Thorndike, ed., *The Sherman Letters* (New York, 1894), p. 258; Clews, *Fifty Years in Wall Street,* pp. 425–436, 604; Leon Stein, ed., *The Pullman Strike* (New York, 1969), p. 49; Frank A. Vanderlip, *From Farmboy to Financier* (New York, 1935), p. 101.

45. P. J. Hubert, Jr., "The Business of a Factory," *Scribner's Magazine,* 21 (1897): 307 ff.; Edith Ware, *Political Opinion in Massachusetts during the Civil War* (New York, 1916).

46. Clifton K. Yearley, Jr., *Enterprise and Anthracite: Economics and Democracy in Schuylkill County, 1820–1875* (Baltimore, 1961), pp. 195 ff.; Donald L. Miller and Richard E. Sharpless, *The Kingdom of Coal* (Philadelphia, 1985), pp. 52 ff.; Wall, *Carnegie,* pp. 478 ff.; John D. Rockefeller, "Testimony," in United States Industrial Commission *Report,* vol. 1 (Dec. 30, 1899), 796–797; David Freeman Hawke, *John D.: The Founding Father of the Rockefellers* (New York, 1980), pp. 126–131; Blewett, *Men, Women, and Work,* pp. 97 ff.; Vanderlip, *From Farmboy to Financier,* p. 161; Oscar Handlin, ed., *Readings in American History* (New York, 1962), p. 386.

47. Wall, *Carnegie,* pp. 797–884; Vanderlip, *From Farmboy to Financier,* pp. 223–224; Hersh, *Mellon Family,* pp. 271–278; Maury Klein, *The Life and Legend of Jay Gould* (Baltimore, 1986), pp. 218, 447–449; Edward N. Akin, *Flagler: Rockefeller Partner and Florida Baron* (Kent, Ohio, 1988), pp. 201–206.

48. Allan Nevins, *John D. Rockefeller* (New York, 1959); George W. Perkins, *The Modern Corporation* (New York, 1908), pp. 11–12; Alfred D. Chandler, *The Visible Hand: The Managerial Revolution in American Business* (Cambridge, Mass., 1977).

49. Carwardine, *Pullman Strike,* pp. 50–51; Alfred D. Chandler and Richard S. Tedlow, *The Coming of Managerial Capitalism: A Casebook on the History of American Economic Institutions* (Homewood, Ill., 1985), pp. 424–431; Zunz, *Making America Corporate,* pp. 41 ff.; Korman, *Industrialization, Immigrants, and Americanizers,* pp. 61 ff.

50. J. H. Bridge, *History of the Carnegie Steel Company* (New York, 1903), pp. 143, 144; David Brody, *Steel Workers in America* (New York, 1969); Count Peter Vay de Vaya, *Nach America* (Berlin, 1908), pp. 114 ff., 133 ff., 272 ff.; Giuseppe Giacosa, *Impressioni d'America* (Milano, 1908), pp. 85 ff.; Leon Stein, *The Pullman Strike* (New York, 1969), pp. 11–12; Debs, *Liberty,* p. 24.

51. Stanley Buder, *Pullman* (New York, 1967); Isaac J. Quillen, *Industrial City,* pp. 116 ff., 129 ff., 146; Joseph Husband, *America at Work* (Boston, 1915), pp. 20–31.

52. Henry Ford, *My Life and Work* (New York, 1922), pp. 16 ff., 105; Alma I. S. Hedin, *Arbetsglädje* (Stockholm, 1920), pp. 20 ff.; Bernard A. Weisberger, *The Dream Maker: William C. Durant, The Founder of General Motors* (Boston, 1979), p. 74.

53. Charles F. Beach, Jr., *The Problem of the Vanishing Profit* (n.p., 1891), pp. 1–16; F. Crouzet et al., eds., *Essays in European Economic History 1789–1914* (London, 1969), pp. 226 ff.; W. O. Henderson, *The Rise of German Industrial Power 1834–1914* (Berkeley, Calif., 1975), pp. 178 ff.

54. Woodrow Wilson, *The New Freedom* (New York, 1913), pp. 5, 8, 17, 30 ff.; Niels Aage Thorsen, *The Political Thought of Woodrow Wilson, 1875–1910* (Princeton, N.J., 1988), pp. 211–213.

55. "Owners of the United States," *Forum,* 8 (1889): 265 ff.; John Frost, *Self Made Men of America* (New York, 1848), pp. iii–iv; Stuart Bruchey, ed., *Memoirs of Three Railroad Pioneers* (New York, 1981), pp. 33–34; 39–43; Richard Henry Edwards, *Concentrated Wealth* (Madison, Wis., 1910), pp. 8–15.

56. William Graham Sumner, "The Absurd Attempt to Make the World Over," *Forum,* 17 (1894): 98–99, 100–102; Edwards, *Concentrated Wealth,* pp. 14–15; Arthur Jerome Eddy, *The New Competition* (New York, 1912), pp. 1–11; George Otis Draper, *More: A Study of Financial Conditions Now Prevalent* (Boston, 1908), pp. 1–3; Burton J. Hendrick, "The Story of Life Insurance," *McClure's,* 27 (1906): 36; 28 (1906): 61.

57. Charles G. Washburn, *Address on the Government Control of Corporations and Combinations of Capital* (Springfield, Mass., 1911), pp. 13–14; George W. Perkins, *A Constructive Suggestion,* pp. 6–7; Perkins, *Modern Corporation,* pp. 1–11.

58. Perkins, *Modern Corporation,* pp. 12, 13; William W. Cook, *Trusts: Recent Combinations in Trade* (New York, 1888), pp. 50–52, 66–68; "Problem of Monopolies," *Boston Transcript,* Mar. 22, 1899; David Loth, *Public Plunder: A History of Graft in America* (New York, 1938), p. 270.

59. E. D. Noyes, *Forty Years of American Finance* (New York, 1909), pp. 286 ff., 294 ff.; James B. Dill, *The College Man and the Corporate Proposition* (Williamstown, Mass., 1900), pp. 10–11; Loth, *Public Plunder,* p. 267.

60. Sinclair, *Corsair.*

61. Robert C. Brooks, *Corruption in American Politics and Life* (New York, 1910), pp. 16, 30, 31, 161, 164–165.

62. Dill, *College Man,* pp. 2–3.

63. Keller, *Life Insurance Enterprise.*

64. Weisberger, *The Dream Maker,* pp. 133–143.

65. Frederick Jackson Turner, *The Frontier in American History* (New York, 1920), pp. 293–310; "American Character Is Still Good," *Meadville Evening Republican,* March 16, 1901.

66. Charles Skinner, "Workers and Trusts in the Rolling Mills of South Chicago," *Boston Transcript,* Feb. 10, Mar. 10, 1900; Charles Skinner, "The Electric Trust and Its Employees," *Boston Transcript,* Feb. 3, 1900; Joseph Husband, *America at Work,* pp. 89–90; Oscar Handlin, *Truth in History* (Cambridge, Mass., 1979), pp. 316 ff.
67. Charles Skinner, "Workers and Trusts in the Tobacco Factories of Richmond," *Boston Transcript,* Mar. 10, 1900; Henry Ford, *My Life and Work* (Garden City, N.Y., 1922), pp. 112–113.
68. Henry Ford, *My Life and Work,* pp. 3–4; Edgar James Swift, *Psychology and the Day's Work* (New York, 1918), pp. 99, 119.
69. Henry Holt, *Talks on Civics* (New York, 1910), pp. v, 25–33, 39; Leon Stein, *Buying Brains* (New York, 1918), pp. 33–34.
70. John Dewey, *Democracy and Education* (1916; New York, 1924), pp. 108 ff.; Lawrence A. Cremin, *The Transformation of the School* (New York, 1961), pp. 90 ff., 179 ff.; Fremont Rider, *Melvil Dewey* (Chicago, 1944), pp. 27 ff.; Korman, *Industrialization, Immigrants, and Americanizers,* pp. 155, 158.
71. E. W. Howe, *The Blessings of Business* (Topeka, Kans., 1918), pp. 15, 30, 45; Dill, *College Man,* pp. 17–18; George W. Perkins, *A Constructive Suggestion* (Youngstown, Ohio, 1911), pp. 1–2; Lawrence A. Cremin, *American Education: The Metropolitan Experience* (New York, 1988), pp. 157 ff.

IX: BATTLEFIELDS

1. *Chicago Daily Tribune,* Nov. 24, 1859; Ednah D. Cheney, *Louisa May Alcott: Her Life, Letters, and Journals* (Boston, 1890), pp. 104, 127; Charles MacKay, *Life and Liberty in America: Sketches of a Tour in the United States* (New York, 1859), pp. 319–325; William Gilpin, *Mission of the North American People,* 2nd ed. (Philadelphia, 1874), pp. 99–104; John Smith Dye, *History of the Plots and Crimes of the Great Conspiracy to Overthrow Liberty in America* (New York, 1866), pp. 1–2; William G. Eggleston, "Our New National Hymn," in *Liberty Poems* (Boston, 1900), p. 27.
2. W. K. McNeil, "Popular Songs from New York Autograph Albums, 1820–1900," *Journal of Popular Culture,* 3 (1969): 49; James I. Robertson, *Soldiers Blue and Gray* (Columbia, S.C., 1988), p. 23.
3. Walt Whitman, "Specimen Days," in *Complete Prose Works* (New York, 1914), pp. 29, 30, 73, 74; James H. Kyner, *End of Track,* ed. Hawthorne Daniel (Caldwell, Idaho, 1937), pp. 61 ff.
4. Martin J. Wade, *Down with the Constitution, Soap Box Orator. Here, Don't Hit Him* (Iowa City, 1924), pp. 62–63; also James M. McPherson, *Battle Cry of Freedom* (New York, 1988), pp. 600 ff.
5. Oscar Handlin, ed., *Readings in American History* (New York, 1962), p. 363; Joel Porte, *Emerson in His Journals* (Cambridge, Mass., 1982), p. 528; James Elliot Cabot, *A Memoir of Ralph Waldo Emerson* (Boston, 1887), pp. 604 ff.; Virginia H. Harlow, *Thomas Sergeant Perry* (Durham, N.C., 1950), pp. 345, 384; Walt Whitman, "Poems of Joy," in *Poems* (New York, 1902), p. 212; Vachel Lindsay, "Abraham Lincoln Walks at Midnight," in *Collected Poems* (New York, 1923), pp. 53 ff.; Oscar Handlin, "The Civil War as Symbol and Actuality," *Massachusetts Review,* 3 (Fall, 1961): 133–143; Charles and Tess Hoffmann, "Henry James and the Civil War," *New England Quarterly,* 62 (1989): 551; Richard H. Ekman, "Northern Religion and the Civil War" (Harvard Doctoral diss., 1973); E. W. Reynolds, *The True Story of the Barons of the South* (Boston, 1862), pp. 1, 108, 239–240; Jack Lindeman, ed., *The Conflict of Convictions: American Writers Report the Civil War* (Philadelphia, 1962), pp. 112, 231, 282–285; George W. Smith and Charles Judah, *Life in the North during the Civil War: A Source History* (Al-

buqerque, N.Mex., 1966), pp. 345, 347; Earl J. Hess, *Liberty, Virtue, and Progress: Northerners and Their War for the Union* (New York, 1988), pp. 57, 104, 106, 114; George B. Lockwood, *Americanism* (Washington, D.C., 1921), pp. 168, 180; Harriet L. Matthews and Elizabeth E. Rule, eds., *Memorial Day: Hymns, Poems, and Patriotic Selections Compiled for Use in the Public Schools* (Lynn, Mass., 1893), p. 83.

6. From a lecture repeated more than 190 times, J. R. Farrar, *Johnny Reb, the Confederate and Rip Van Winkle, the Virginian That Slept Ten Years* (Richmond, 1869), p. 22; also Elizabeth Stuart Phelps, *The Gates Ajar*, ed. Helen S. Smith (Cambridge, Mass., 1964).

7. King C. Gillette, *The Human Drift*, ed. Kenneth Roemer (New York, 1976), pp. 73–75; Edmund Morris, *How to Get a Farm and Where to Find One, Showing That Homesteads May Be Had by Those Desirous of Securing Them* (New York, 1864), pp. 29–30, 340–342; Joe L. Dubbert, *A Man's Place: Masculinity in Transition* (Englewood Cliffs, N.J., 1979), pp. 148–153, 191–197; Hartley Burr Alexander, *Liberty and Democracy* (Boston, 1918), pp. 146–150; Randolph Bourne, *The History of a Literary Radical and Other Papers* (New York, 1956), pp. 242–249; Sheldon M. Norick, *Honorable Justice: The Life of Oliver Wendell Holmes* (Boston, 1989), pp. 176–177; George M. Frederickson, *The Inner Civil War* (New York, 1965), pp. 183–198, 218; Vincent F. Howard, *Liberty Poems Inspired by the Crisis of 1898–1900* (Boston, 1900), p. 56; Bernard Edward Brown, *American Conservatives: The Political Thought of Francis Lieber and John W. Burgess* (New York, 1951), pp. 61–92; Arnold Bennett Hall, *Dynamic Americanism* (Indianapolis, 1920), preface; George S. Wheat, *The Story of the American Legion* (New York, 1919), pp. 180–186.

8. John F. Aiken, *The History of Liberty: A Paper Read before the New York Historical Society, February 1866* (New York, 1877), pp. 11–13, 156–157; Howard, *Liberty Poems*, pp. 18–19; William Everett, *Patriotism: An Oration Delivered before the Phi Beta Kappa of Harvard College, 1900* (Boston, 1900), pp. 20–21.

9. Senator Henry Cabot Lodge: A Speech before the United States Senate, March 7, 1900, *Congressional Record*, 60th Cong., 1st sess., 1900, 33, 2618–2630; Frank A. Vanderlip, *From Farmboy to Financier* (New York, 1935), pp. 79–98; Jeremiah Whipple Jenks, *The Trust Problem* (New York, 1900), pp. 194–195; Frederickson, *Inner Civil War*, pp. 233–234; Howard, *Liberty Poems*, pp. 4–5, 11–12, 99; Brown, *American Conservatives*, pp. 134–135; George F. Hoar, *Autobiography of Seventy Years*, 2 vols. (New York, 1903), 2: 320; George F. Hoar, *The Lust of Empire: Speech on the Philippines* (New York, 1900), pp. 129–130, 139; Frederick Lawrence Knowles, ed., *Poems of American Patriotism* (Boston, 1918), p. 383; William Gilpin, *The Cosmopolitan Railway: Compacting and Fusing Together All the World's Continents* (San Francisco, 1890), pp. 298–300.

10. Marion S. Adams, *Alvin M. Owsley of Texas* (Waco, Tex., 1971), pp. 24–47; Raymond Moley, Jr., *The American Legion Story* (New York, 1966), pp. 97–108.

11. George Creel, *Rebel at Large* (New York, 1947), pp. 194 ff.; Frances A. Kellor, *Straight America* (New York, 1916), pp. 30 ff.; Dubbert, *A Man's Place*, pp. 165–166; *The Liberty Bell*, 3 (July 1917); William J. Breen, *Uncle Sam at Home: Civilian Mobilization, Wartime Federalism, and the Council of National Defense, 1917–1919* (Westport, Conn., 1984), pp. 3–4, 62–63, 69, 116–156, 171–175; J. Madison Gathany, *American Patriotism in Prose and Verse, 1775–1918* (New York, 1919), p. 122; also see above, chap. 1.

12. Edward Everett Hale, *Man without a Country* (Boston, 1889); Oscar Handlin, *The American People in the Twentieth Century* (Cambridge, Mass., 1954), pp. 67, 128, 129; Randolph Bourne, "Transnational America," in *The History of a Literary Radical* (New York, 1969), pp. 260–276; *The Liberty Bell*, 1 (March–June, 1915); Julian W. Mack, *Americanism and Zionism* (New York, 1919), pp. 3, 14–15; Gathany, *American Patriotism*, p. 255; George Whitfield Mead, *The Great Menace:*

Americanism or Bolshevism (New York, 1920), pp. 102, 108–111, 120, 126; Hermann Hagedorn, *You Are the Hope of the World: An Appeal to the Girls and Boys of America* (New York, 1917), pp. 87, 90; Paul Avrich, *An American Anarchist* (Princeton, N.J., 1978), p. 123.

13. George R. Lockwood, *Americanism* (Washington, D.C., 1921), pp. 64 ff.; Boston Committee for Americanism, *A Little Book for Immigrants* (Boston, 1921), pp. 60–61.

14. Kellor, *Straight America,* p. 23; Gillette, *The Human Drift,* pp. 4, 5, 8–9; Robert C. Brooks, *Corruption in American Politics and Life* (New York, 1910), pp. 277, 282–283, 296–297; A. Lawrence Lowell, *Public Opinion and Popular Government* (London, 1914), pp. 289–290, 303; Hartley Burr Alexander, *Liberty and Democracy and Other Essays in War Time* (Boston, 1918), pp. 28–47; Diomede Carito, *In the Land of Washington: My Impressions of the North American Psyche* (Naples, 1913), p. 83; Laurence Bergreen, *As Thousands Cheer: The Life of Irving Berlin* (New York, 1990), pp. 59–70, 89.

15. Harold Seymour, *Baseball,* 3 vols. (New York, 1960), 1: 169 ff.; Donald Gropman, *Say It Ain't So, Joe!* (Boston, 1979), pp. 158 ff.; Dubbert, *Man's Place,* pp. 164–172, 186; Phineas Thayer, *Casey at the Bat* (Chicago, 1912); Paul H. B. D'Estournelles De Constant, *America and Her Problems* (New York, 1915), pp. 205–206; Thorstein Veblen, *The Theory of the Leisure Class* (New York, 1899); Kenneth S. Lynn, *Hemingway* (New York, 1987), pp. 59–60; Donald Kagan, "George Will's Baseball—A Conservative Critique," *Public Interest,* 101 (Fall, 1990): 17; Miller Hageman, *Liberty, as delivered by the Goddess at her unveiling in the Harbor of New York, October 28, 1886* (New York, 1886), pp. 14, 37–38; Myron Lounsbury, "Flashes of Lightning: The Moving Pictures in the Progressive Era," *Journal of Popular Culture,* 3 (1970): 788; Stuart Chase, *Men and Machines* (New York, 1929), pp. 5–17; John G. Cawelti, *Apostles of the Self-Made Man* (Chicago, 1965), pp. 162–163; Earl J. Hess, *Liberty, Virtue, and Progress: Northerners and Their War for the Union* (New York, 1988), pp. 115–120; Brown, *American Conservatives: The Political Thought of Francis Lieber and John W. Burgess,* pp. 142, 155, 160–161; John W. Burgess, *The Foundations of Political Science* (1917; New York, 1933), pp. 97–102; Edouard Laboulaye, *Paris in America,* trans. Mary L. Booth (New York, 1863), pp. 93, 130, 353, 355.

16. Walt Whitman, "Democratic Vistas," in *Complete Prose Works,* 2: 50–53, 61–62, 143–145; John Dewey, *The Middle Works, 1899–1924,* ed. Jo Ann Boydston, 15 vols. (Carbondale, Ill., 1976–83) 11: ix–xx; Randolph Bourne, "War and the Intellectuals," in *The History of a Literary Radical,* pp. 206–222; Charles Mackay, *Life and Liberty in America; or, Sketches of a Tour in the United States* (New York, 1859), pp. 294–295; D'Estournelles De Constant, *America and Her Problems,* pp. 372–375; Carito, *In the Land of Washington,* pp. 112–116; Gillette, *Human Drift,* pp. 47–48; Edward J. Ward, *The Social Center* (New York, 1913), p. 101; Walt Whitman, "To a Foiled Revolter or Revoltress," in *Poems,* p. 295.

17. Fred A. Shannon, *Organization and Administration of the Union Army* (Cleveland, 1928), 1: 167–172; A. Howard Meneely, *The War Department, 1861* (New York, 1928), pp. 191 ff.

18. Kyner, *End of Track,* p. 65; Lockwood, *Americanism,* p. 149.

19. Edward Dudley and Maximilian Novak, eds., *The Wild Man Within* (Pittsburgh, 1972), pp. 275 ff.; Raymond F. Fancher, *The Intelligence Men* (New York, 1985), pp. 41 ff.

20. Gillette, *Human Drift,* pp. vii–viii; Bourne, *History of a Literary Radical,* pp. 228–240; Henry Ford, *My Life and Work* (Garden City, N.Y., 1922), pp. 240–247; Bergreen, *As Thousands Cheer,* pp. 100–113.

21. Annette Kuhn, *Cinema, Censorship, and Sexuality, 1909–1925* (London, 1988), pp.

52–53; Dubbert, *Man's Place,* pp. 191–199; T. J. Skeyhill, *Sergeant York: His Own Life Story and War Diary* (New York, 1928); Charles Thwing, *The American Colleges and Universities in the Great War* (New York, 1920).

22. David Glassberg, *American Historical Pageantry: The Uses of Tradition in the Early Twentieth Century* (Chapel Hill, N.C., 1990), pp. 203–227.

23. David M. Parry, *The Scarlet Empire* (New York, 1906), pp. 56, 60; Harold Stearns, *Liberalism in America* (New York, 1919); Hartley Burr Alexander, *Liberty and Democracy* (Boston, 1918), pp. 2, 4, 8–10, 24–27; M. F. Morris, *History of the Development of Constitutional and Civil Liberty* (Washington, D.C., 1898), pp. 257–261; Frank Johnson Goodnow, *The American Conception of Liberty* (Providence, R.I., 1916), pp. 29–30, 62–63; Glassberg, *American Historical Pageantry,* pp. 231–232, 234; John W. Burgess, *The Reconciliation of Government with Liberty* (New York, 1915), pp. 374–383; Wade, *Down with the Constitution,* pp. 17, 19, 31, 59; David Jayne Hill, *Americanism: What Is It?* (New York, 1917), pp. 36, 74, 77, 78; Tom Mann, *Americanism: A World Menace* (London, 1922), pp. 35–37; Gathany, *American Patriotism,* pp. 134–136; William Stull, *The Food Crisis and Americanism* (New York, 1919), p. 61; Ole Hanson, *Americanism versus Bolshevism* (Garden City, New York, 1920), pp. 240–241, 254–255, 277–278, 280, 282.

INDEX

415

ABOUT THE AUTHORS

OSCAR HANDLIN taught at Harvard University for almost fifty years; there his seminars helped train a whole generation of social historians and his lecture courses left a significant impression upon class after class of undergraduates. Addressing both students interested in professional careers as historians and those who turned to the subject as part of a liberal education, he learned the value of technical competence and also of clear expressive communication. The original scholarship that informed his instruction at every level also found expression in many books and articles, each grounded on careful research and each written in a style direct, eloquent, and accessible to every reader. The Pulitzer prize in history and numerous other awards and honorary degrees recognized his work.

Among his related activities were service as director of the Harvard University Library, as chairman of the United States Board of Foreign Scholarships, as editorial director of Channel 5-TV (Boston), and as author of a monthly column on books for *The Atlantic*.

LILIAN HANDLIN is a graduate of Queens College and Brown University, and received her Ph.D. at the Hebrew University of Jerusalem, where she was an associate professor in the Department of American Studies. She is author of *George Bancroft: The Intellectual as Democrat* (1984) and coauthor of *Abraham Lincoln and the Union* (Boston, 1980) and *A Restless People* (New York, 1982).